EUROPEAN UNION LAW
VOLUME II

European Union Law
Volume II

Towards a European Polity?

DAMIAN CHALMERS
and
ERIKA SZYSZCZAK

Ashgate

DARTMOUTH

Aldershot • Brookfield USA • Singapore • Sydney

Published by
Dartmouth Publishing Company Limited
Ashgate Publishing Limited
Gower House
Croft Road
Aldershot
Hants GU11 3HR
England

Ashgate Publishing Company
Old Post Road
Brookfield
Vermont 05036
USA

British Library Cataloguing in Publication Data
Chalmers, Damian
European Union law
Vol. 2: Towards a European Polity?
1.Law - European Union countries
I.Title II.Szyszczak, Erika, M.
341.2'422

Library of Congress Catalog Card Number: 98-73151

ISBN 1 84014 473 4 (Hbk)
ISBN 1 84014 479 3 (Pbk)

Printed and bound in Great Britain by
Biddles Ltd, Guildford and King's Lynn

Contents

Chapter 2
Citizenship and Culture

Chapter 3
Free Movement of Persons and Securitisation

Chapter 4
External Relations

Chapter 5
Economic and Monetary Union

Chapter 6
Free Movement of Goods

Chapter 7
Trade Restrictions and Public Goods

Chapter 8
The Service Economy

Chapter 9
Free Movement of Labour

Chapter 10
Social Policy

Chapter 11
Boundaries and Enforcement of EC Competition Law

Chapter 12
Cartels

Chapter 13
Abuse of Market Power

Chapter 14
Taxation

Table of Cases

Table of Treaties and Legislation

Treaty on European Union

Protocols to the Treaty on European Union

Declarations adopted by the IGC 1991

Treaty on European Union
(following ratification of the Treaty of Amsterdam)

Protocols to the Treaty on European Union

Declarations adopted by the IGC 1991

Declarations Adopted by the IGC at the Treaty of Amsterdam 1997

EC Treaty

EC Treaty
(following ratification of the Treaty of Amsterdam)

Protocols

Secondary Legislation

Regulations

Directives

Decisions

Merger Regulation Decisions

Declarations

Commission Notices

Conventions

Protocols

Note on Treaty Article Numbering and the Treaty of Amsterdam

The EC Treaty and the Treaty on European Union are to be renumbered upon the coming into force of the Treaty of Amsterdam. For existing provisions present numbering is used with the numbering anticipated by Amsterdam italicised and placed in square brackets after it, where appropriate. Where the Treaty of Amsterdam has introduced new Treaty provisions or ones that are substantially different from existing ones, only the anticipated numbering is used. All amendments introduced by the Treaty of Amsterdam have been italicised for the purposes of clarity.

Preface

How to categorise the European Union? Two words crop up most frequently in the debate - those of polity and process. The former implies that the European Union has moved towards being some discrete form of political organisation. The latter suggests that it is no more than an instrument through which other more powerful actors secure their interests. It is common place to suggest that certainly, since the Treaty on European Union, the European Union has moved to becoming a polity. How else can we explain the development of European citizenship and the Europeanisation of policies in fields such as culture, social policy and education? Yet, at the same time, the decision-making processes are used instrumentally, on a daily basis, by powerful actors, both public and private. For them the Union is simply one avenue among others through which to realise their preferences.

To admit that the European Union is both a polity and process takes us only so far. It is akin to calling the European Union *sui generis,* but it tells us nothing about its elements and the tools that should be used to examine it. We were both convinced, first, that the complex interaction between interests, discourses and values which takes place within the structures of the European Union could only be approached from an interdisciplinary perspective. Within that broad remit we choose five themes that have dominated debate within the European Union in the 1990s for our first five chapters - the single market, citizenship, free movement and security, the Community in the wider international arena and economic and monetary union. We felt that choosing such broad themes would better enable the complex interaction between structures, interests and values to be captured, and that each Chapter would emphasise in a distinct way the extent to which the European Union is both one battlefield and a series of battlefields between assimilative and counter-assimilative forces. A series of tensions and cleavages continually emerge. For example, why has the *Cassis de Dijon* approach not proved a 'quick fix' for the stagnation of conventional harmonisation? Why is the EU criticised for both being excessively regulatory and excessively deregulatory? Why is the EU interested in constitutional ideas, citizenship and culture, while at the same time securing its external frontiers and policing its denizens? Why, if foreign and defence policy goes to the heart of State sovereignty, has a common foreign and security policy emerged?

At the same time we believed that an understanding of these themes could not be achieved without examining from whence the Union came. The second half of the book addresses, albeit from an interdisciplinary perspective, the Community's older policies - notably the economic freedoms, social policy, tax and competition - policies which still constitute the bedrock of much of what the Union does.

It is impossible for any textbook to be comprehensive. Insofar as a book can only represent EU law and not mirror it, it will have distortive effects. We are well aware that many important areas have been omitted, but felt it was better to choose a few salient areas where the tensions and interactions were particularly apparent. We do so in the hope that the book comes out as a satisfying blend rather than an incoherent mish-mash.

In developing this book we are grateful to the milieu which has been offered to us by the London School of Economics and Political Science, particularly to our students for allowing their classes to be used as a 'laboratory' within which many of our ideas could be tried out and developed.

There are also a number of individual debts. We are grateful to John Irwin for his confidence in our venture. Ross Cranston, Marise Cremona, Pete Muchlinski and Steve Peers have read Chapters and proffered invaluable advice. Invaluable research assistance was provided by Stuart Brittenden, Julian Runnicles and Liz Start. Rhian Whitehead and Geraldine Gorham have shown tolerance, good humour and contributed to keeping the book on track. The final version, which was camera-ready copy, owes everything to the professional attention to detail and skill of Rhian Whitehead.

Finally, we extend our appreciation to our families, Flàvia, and Richard, Jamie, Larissa, and William, for their tolerance over our writing of this book, which prevented us from enjoying the pleasures of their company!

The law is as of 15 January 1998.

Acknowledgements

The authors and publishers wish to thank the following for permission to use copyright material.

Blackwell Publishers for the essays: P. Geroski & A. Jacquemin (1985) 'Industrial change, barriers to mobility and European industrial policy', *Economic Policy*, **1**, pp. 170, 182-183; I. Harden (1990), 'Sovereignty and the Eurofed', *Political Quarterly*, **61**, pp. 402, 413-414; J. Pelkmans, (1980), 'Economic Theories of Integration Revisited', *Journal of Common Market Studies* **18**, pp. 333, 333-335; M. Streit, & W. Musler (1995), 'The Economic Constitution of the European Community: From "Rome" to "Maastricht"', *European Law Journal*, **1**, pp. 5, 10-11; M. Poiares Maduro, (1997), 'Reforming the Market or the State? Article 30 and the European Constitution: Economic Freedom and Political Rights', *European Law Journal*, **3**, pp. 55, 60-61; B. Hindley and A. Smith (1984), 'Comparative Advantage and Trade in Services', *World Economy*, **7**, pp. 369, 370 & 375; R. Burdekin, Wihlborg & T. Willett (1992), 'A Monetary Constitution Case for an Independent European Central Bank', *World Economy*, **15**, pp. 231, 233; D. McBarnet & C. Whelan (1991), 'The Elusive Spirit of the Law: Formalism and the Struggle for Legal Control', *Modern Law Review*, **54**, pp. 848, 849-851; W. Bishop (1981), 'Price Discrimination under Article 86: Political Economy in the European Court', *Modern Law Review*, **44**, pp. 282, 289-290; J. Pelkmans (1987) 'The New Approach to Technical Harmonization and Standardization', *Journal of Common Market Studies*, **25**, pp. 257, 260; A. Jacquemin & K. George (1992), 'Dominant Firms and Mergers', *The Economic Journal*, **102** pp. 148,148-149 ; Christopher Hill, (1993), 'The Capability-Expectations Gap, or Conceptualizing Europe's International Role', *Journal of Common Market Studies*, **31** pp. 305,308-315; W Streeck (1995), 'Neo-Voluntarism: A New European Social Policy Regime?', *European Law Journal*, **1**, 1, pp. 31 & 32-38; Silvana Sciarra (1995), 'Social Values and the Multiple Sources of European Social Law' *European Law*

Journal, **1**, pp. 60, 73 & 76.

Butterworths for the extracts: R. Whish, *Competition Law* (3rd Edition, 1993, Butterworths) pp. 1-3, 469-470 & 725-726; J. Shaw (1995) 'Decentralization and Law Enforcement in EC Competition Law' *Legal Studies*, **15**, 128, 128-129 & 136-137

Cassell Plc for the essay: E. Szyszczak, (1993), 'Race Discrimination: The Limits of Market Equality?' in B. Hepple and E. Szyszczak (eds.) *Discrimination: The Limits of Law* (1993: London, Mansell) pp 127-129.

Center for Migration Studies for the essay: M. Ugur (1995), 'Freedom of Movement vs. Exclusion', *International Migration Review*, **25**, pp. 964, 972-973.

Comparative Politics for the essay: J. Goodman (1990), 'The Politics of Central Bank Independence', *Comparative Politics*, **23**, pp. 329, 330-331.

Dædalus for the essays: D. Schnapper (1997), 'The European Debate on Citizenship', *Dædalus*, **126**, pp. 199, 203-205. Reprinted by permission of Dædalus.

Frank Cass & Co Ltd for the essay: G. Majone (1994), 'The Rise of the Regulatory State in Europe', *West European Politics*, **17**, pp. 77, 85-87. Reprinted by permission from *West European Politics Vol. 17, No. 3* published by Frank Cass & Company, 900 Eastern Avenue, Illford, Essex, England. Copyright © Frank Cass & Co Ltd.

Elsevier Science for the extracts: R. Innam & D. Rubinfield (1994) 'The EMU and Fiscal Policy in the New European Community', *International Review of Law and Economics* **14**, pp. 147,150-151, with permission from Elsevier Science; N. Thygesen (1994) 'Why Is Economic and Monetary Union an Important Objective for Europe', *International Review of Law and Economics* **14**, pp. 133, 136-137, with permission from Elsevier Science.

Elsevier Science B.V. for the essay: C. Goodhart (1996), 'European monetary integration', *European Economic Review*, **40**, pp. 1083, 1089. Copyright © 1996 Elsevier Science.

Harvard University for the essays: R. M. Lastra (1992), 'The Independence of the European System of Central Banks', *Harvard Journal of International Law*, **33**, pp. 475, 479-480. Copyright © 1992 by the President and Fellows of Harvard College; D. Gerber (1994), 'The Transformation of European Community Competition Law' *Harvard International Law Journal*, **35**, pp. 97, 108-109. Copyright © 1994 by the President and Fellows of Harvard College.

Houghton Mifflin Company for the essay: F. Scherer and D. Ross (1990), 'Industrial Market Structure and Market Performance', (3rd Edition, Houghton, New York) pp. 53-54. Copyright © 1990 by Houghton Mifflin Company. Used with permission.

Kluwer Law International for the essay: S. O'Leary (1995), 'The Relationship Between Community Citizenship and the Protection of Fundamental Rights in Community Law', *Common Market Law Review*, **32**, pp. 519, 553-54; E. White (1989), 'In Search of the Limits to Article 30 of the EEC Treaty', *Common Market Law Review*, **26**, pp. 235, 245-247; E. Johnson and D. O'Keeffe (1994), 'From Discrimination To Obstacles To Free Movement: Recent Developments Concerning the Free Movement of Workers 1989-1994', *Common Market Law Review*, **31**, pp. 1313, 1329-130; W-H Roth , (1993), 'Note on *Säger*', *Common Market Law Review*, **30**, pp. 145, 152-153; V. Korah (1986), 'EEC Competition Policy-Legal Form or Economic Efficiency', *Current Legal Problems*, **39**, pp. 85, 87 & 93-94 & 103; K. Lenaerts (1994), 'Education in European Community Law After "Maastricht"', *Common Market Law Review*, **31**, pp. 7, 7 & 24-25; R. Lane (1993), 'New Community Competences Under The Maastricht Treaty', *Common Market Law Review*, **30**, pp. 939, 950-951 & 962-963; P. Vogelenzang 1976), 'Abuse of a Dominant Position in Article 86: The Problem of Causality and some Applications', *Common Market Law Review*, **13**, pp. 61, 64-66; B. Hawk and H. Huser (1993), 'A Bright Line Shareholding Test to End the Nightmare under the EEC Merger Regulation',

Common Market Law Review, **30**, pp. 1155, 1158-1161; I. Forrester I & C. Norrall (1984), 'The Laicization of Community Law: Self-Help and the Rule of Reason: How Competition Law Is and Could be Applied', *Common Market Law Review*, **21** pp. 11, 13-14 & 16-18; B. Terra (1989), 'VAT in the EEC: The Place of Supply', *Common Market Law Review*, **26**, pp. 449, 453-454; Wattel (1996), 'The EC Court's Attempts to Reconcile the Treaty Freedoms with International Tax Law' *Common Market Law Review*, **33**, pp. 223, 223-224; A. Easson (1981), 'Fiscal Discrimination: New Perspectives on Article 95 of the EEC Treaty', *Common Market Law Review*, **18**, pp. 521, 521; R. Barents (1986), 'Recent Case Law on the Prohibition of Fiscal Discrimination under Article 95', *Common Market Law Review*, **23**, pp. 641, 656-657; Weiler, (1983), 'The External Legal Relations of Non-Unitary Actors: Mixity and the Federal Principle', in O'Keefe & Schermers (eds.), *Mixed Agreements* (1983, Kluwer, Dordrecht) pp. 35, 75 & 80-81; E. Petersmann (1992), 'National Constitutions, Foreign Trade Policy and European Community Law', *European Journal of International Law*, **3, pp.** 1, 34, (Kluwer Law International); E. Regelsberger & W. Wessels (1996), 'The CFSP Institutions and Procedures: A Third Way for the Second Pillar', *European Foreign Affairs Review*, **1**, pp. 29, 31, (Kluwer Law International); M. Danusso and R. Denton (1990/1), 'Does the European Court of Justice Look for a Projectionist Motive under Article 95?', *Legal Issues of European Integration*, 67, 70-71; M. Schechter (1982/2)The Rule of Reason in European Competition Law', *Legal Issues of European Integration*, **1**, 17-19.

Lothian Foundation for the essay: M. Emerson (1995), 'Economic Rights within the European Union', in R. Bellamy, V. Buffacchi, & D. Castiglione (eds.) *Democracy and Constitutional Culture in the Union of Europe* (1995, Lothian Foundation, London) pp. 137, 138-140

The Michigan Law Review Association for the essay: H. Hovenkamp (1986), 'Antitrust Policy after Chicago', **84**, *Michigan Law Review*, pp. 213 at 226-228.

MIT Press Journals for the extract: S. Sosnick (1958) 'A Critique of Concepts of Workable Competition', *Quarterly Journal of Economics*,

72, pp. 380, 383-384. Copyright © 1958 by the President and Fellows of Harvard College.

Nomos Verlagsgesellschaft for the essay: R. Lauwaars (1988), 'The 'Model Directive' on Technical Harmonization' in R. Bieber, R.Dehousse, J. Pinder, & J. Weiler, *1992: One European Market* (1988, Nomos, Baden-Baden) pp.151, 152 & 167-168.

David O'Keeffe (1993), 'Union Citizenship', in D. O'Keeffe and P. Twomey (eds.) *Legal Issues of the Maastricht Treaty*, Chancery, London pp. 87 and 103. Copyright © 1993 David O'Keeffe.

David O'Keefe for the essay: C. Closa (1993), 'Citizenship of the Union and Nationality of the Member States' in D. O'Keeffe and P. Twomey (eds) *Legal Issues of the Maastricht Treaty* (Chancery, 1993, London) pp. 109, 111-112. Copyright © David O'Keefe.

Oxford University Press for the essays: N. Walker (1995) 'European Integration and Policing', **22**, pp. 35-37, in Anderson et al. (eds.) *Policing the European Union*, Clarendon, Oxford, by permission of Oxford University Press; J. Currall (1984) 'Some Aspects of the Relation between Articles 30-36 and Article 100 of the EEC Treaty with a Closer Look at Optional Harmonisation', *Yearbook of European Law*, **4**, pp 169, 185, by permission of Oxford University Press; P. Eeckhout (1994), 'The European Internal Market and International Trade: A Legal Analysis, *Clarendon Press, Oxford*, pp. 9-10, by permission of Oxford University Press; G. Marenco (1991), 'The Notion of Restriction on the Freedom of Establishment and Provision of Services in the Caselaw of the Court, *Yearbook of European Law* **11**, pp. 111, 113-114 & 128; M. Emerson, M. Aujean, M. Catinat, P. Goybet, A, Jacquemin (1988), 'The Economics of 1992, The EC Commission's Assessment of the Economic Effects of Completing the Internal Market, *Oxford University Press*, pp. 1-2, by permission of Oxford University Press; L. Tsoukalis (1997), 'The New European Economy Revisited', *Oxford University Press*, pp. 71-73 & 75-78, by permission of Oxford University Press; T. Tridimas and P. Eeckhout (1994), 'The External Competence of the Community and Case-Law of the Court of Justice: Principle versus Pragmatism' *Yearbook of European Law*, **14**, pp. 143, 174, by permission of Oxford

University Press; P. Farmer and R. Lyal, (1995), 'EC Tax Law', *Clarendon Press* pp. 85-86 & 136-137

Penguin UK for the extract: Stephen Weatherill & Paul Beaumont (1995) '*EC Law: The Essential Guide to the Legal Workings of the European Community*, Penguin Books, 2nd Edition, pp. 705. Copyright © Stephen Weatherill and Paul Beaumont 1993, 1995.

Routledge for the essay: B. Wynne (1994), 'Scientific Knowledge and the Global Environment', in M. Redclift & T. Benton (eds.) *Social Theory and the Global Environment* (Routledge, London) pp. 169, 175-176; J. Shaw (1994), 'Twin-Track Social Europe - The Inside Track' in D. O'Keeffe and P. Twomey (eds.), *Legal Issues of the Maastricht Treaty*, (London, Chancery, 1994) 295, 305.

Stanford Law School for the essay: R. Posner (1969) "Oligopoly and the Antitrust Laws: A Suggested Approach" 21 *Stanford Law Review* 1562, 1563-1564 (Stanford University, Stanford CA). Copyright © 1969 by the board of Trustees of the Leland Stanford Junior University.

Sweet & Maxwell Limited for the essays: Oliver, P. (1996), 'Free Movement of Goods in the EEC', (1996, 3rd Edn., Sweet & Maxwell, London) pp. 112; H-C von Heydebrand u.d. Lasa, (1991), 'Free Movement of Foodstuffs, Consumer Protection and Food Standards in the European Community: Has the Court of Justice Got It Wrong?', *European Law Review*, **16**, pp. 391, 408-409; D. O'Keeffe (1995), 'The Emergence of a European Immigration Policy', *European Law Review*, **20**, pp. 34-36; C. Baden Fuller (1979), 'Article 86 EEC: Economic Analysis of the Existence of a Dominant Position', **4**, *European Law Review*, pp. 423, 425-427 & 436-437; Ilona Cheyne (1994), 'International Agreements and the European Community Legal System', *European Law Review*, **19**, 581, 588-590;

Tulane Law Review for the essay: D. Gerber (1987), 'Law and the Abuse of Economic Power in Europe', *Tulane Law Review*, **62**, pp. 57, 69-70. Originally published in **62** *Tulane Law Review* 69-70 (1987), the Tulane Law Review Association. All rights reserved.

University of Chicago Press for the essay: N. Fligstein & I. Mara-Drita (1996), 'How to Make a Market: Reflections on the Attempt to Create a Single Market in the European Union', *American Journal of Sociology* **102**, pp. 1, 14-18

Every effort has been made to trace all the copyright holders, but if any have been inadvertently overlooked the publishers will be pleased to make the necessary arrangement at the first opportunity.

Abbreviations

AJCL	American Journal of Comparative Law
BYIL	British Yearbook of International Law
CAP	Common Agricultural Policy
CDE	Cahiers de Droit Européen
CFI	Court of First Instance
CFSP	Common Foreign and Security Policy
CLJ	Cambridge Law Journal
CMLR	Common Market Law Reports
CMLRev	Common Market Law Review
COREPER	Committee of Permanent Representatives
DG	Directorate General
ECB	European Central Banks
ECJ	European Court of Justice
ECHR	European Convention on Human Rights and Freedoms
ECLR	European Competition Law Review
ECSC	European Coal and Steel Community
EC	European Community
EC Bull	European Communities Bulletin
ECR	European Court Reports
EDC	European Defence Community
EEA	European Economic Area
EEC	European Economic Community
EFTA	European Free Trade Association
EIOP	European Integration Online Papers
EIPR	European Intellectual Property Review
EJIL	European Journal of International Law
ELJ	European Law Journal
ELRev	European Law Review
EMS	European Monetary System
EMU	Economic and Monetary Union

EPC	European Political Cooperation
ERM	Exchange Rate Mechanism
ERT	European Round Table of Industrialists
ESCB	European System of Central Banks
EU	European Union
EU Bull	European Union Bulletin
EuR	Europa Recht
Euratom	European Atomic Energy Community
GATT	General Agreement on Tariffs and Trade
GNP	Gross National Product
ICLQ	International and Comparative Law Quarterly
IGC	Inter-Governmental Conference
ILJ	Industrial Law Journal
JBL	Journal of Business Law
JCMS	Journal of Common Market Studies
JEL	Journal of Environmental Law
JEPP	Journal of European Public Policy
JHA	Justice and Home Affairs
LIEI	Legal Issues of European Integration
LQR	Law Quarterly Review
MLR	Modern Law Review
NATO	North Atlantic Treaty Organisation
NILQ	Northern Ireland Law Quarterly
OJ	Official Journal
OJLS	Oxford Journal of Legal Studies
PL	Public Law
QB	Queen's Bench Reports
RTDE	Revue Trimestrielle de Droit Européen
SEA	Single European Act
TEU	Treaty on European Union
WEP	West European Politics

1. The Single Market

I. Introduction

The establishment of the common market had been an objective of the EEC Treaty since its inception.[1] It had still not been realised by the time of the Single European Act (SEA). As a response to this, the Member States chose to introduce a new concept into the EC Treaty - that of the internal market.[2] There was no sense this marked the creation of a new European polity or suggested any shift in the identity of the European Communities. The SEA was famously described as a 'modest achievement' by Margaret Thatcher. It seemed to suggest merely the achievement of a limited set of objectives to be realised within a relatively short timetable.

Article 7a [*14*] EC. The Community shall adopt measures with the aim of progressively establishing the internal market over a period expiring on 31 December 1992, in accordance with the provisions of this Article and of Articles 7b [*repealed*], 7c [*15*], 28 [*26*], 57(2) [*47(2)*], 59 [*49*], 70(1) [*repealed*], 84 [*80*], 99 [*93*], 100a [*95*]and 100b [*repealed*] and without prejudice to the other provisions of this Treaty.

The internal market shall comprise an area without internal frontiers in which the free movement of goods, persons, services and capital is ensured in accordance with the provisions of this Treaty'.

To facilitate this, the Luxembourg Accords were abolished and provision was made for legislation completing the internal market to be adopted, in the main, by qualified majority voting.

---

1 Article 7 [*repealed*] EC.

2 On the background to the SEA see p 35 in Volume 1.

Article 100a [*95*](1) EC. By way of derogation from Article 100 [*94*] and save where otherwise provided for in the Treaty, the following provisions shall apply for the achievement of the objectives in Article 7a [*14*]. The Council shall, acting in accordance with the procedure referred to in Article 189b [*251*] and after consulting the Economic and Social Committee adopt the measures for the approximation of the provisions laid down by law, regulation or administrative action in Member States which have as their objective the establishment and functioning of the internal market.

2. Paragraph 1 shall not apply to fiscal provisions, to those relating to the movement of persons nor to those relating to the rights and interests of employed persons.

We now know that the impact of qualified majority voting resulted in the political metamorphosis of the integration process.[3] The unblocking of the legislative process resulted in a rush of legislation being adopted. By the end of 1993 265 of the measures proposed in the Commission White Paper had been adopted.[4] This increase in legislative output had knock-on effects. On the one hand, it provided the context and the impetus for the reform of the EC Treaty which took place at Maastricht. On the other, it had counterintegrative effects. Hitherto, the veto in the Council had been the instrument through which national governments had been able to ringfence their interests from EC intrusion. It was the removal of this veto which, more than any other measure, contributed to the legitimacy crisis which engulfed the European Union in the 1990s, as national clamour grew against the excessive interference which was perceived to come from Brussels.[5]

The Single Market Programme lies therefore at the roots of the European Union of the 1990s and even of the next millennium. It is, however, a peculiarly chameleon project which presents a number of different perspectives, dependent, in part, upon the prism through which it is analysed.

---

3 Weiler, J. 'The Transformation of Europe' (1990) 100 *Yale Law Journal* 2403, 2475.

4 EC Commission, *Community Internal Market - 1993* COM(94) 55, Report C.

5 Weiler, J. 'After Maastricht: Community Legitimacy in Post-1992 Europe' in Adams W. (ed.) *Singular Europe: Economy and Polity of the European Community after 1992* (1992, University of Michigan Press, Ann Arbor) 11, 23-24.

II. The Internal Market as a Legal Construct

The development of the internal market had a jurisdictional significance through the powers it granted to the EC Institutions to legislate under Article 100a [*95*] EC. Within this context it served not only to shape the formal capacities of the EC but also orientated expectations as to future legislative behaviour. With the benefit of hindsight, it is, thus, perhaps surprising to find that there were some integration-minded EC lawyers who considered the development of the internal market as a retrograde step.

Pescatore, in particular, considered realisation of the internal market to be a less ambitious objective than realisation of the common market. Whilst the latter was a 'well-balanced and complex notion' which covered not merely free movement of the factors of production, but also common rules on competition, general rules on non-discrimination, coordination of economic policy and a common commercial policy. The internal market, by contrast, was, a 'one sided' notion relating essentially only to the four freedoms to the exclusion of these other concepts.[6] Steindorff, conversely, noted that Article 7a [*14*] EC is stated to be 'without prejudice to the other provisions of the Treaty', and considered from this that its scope must extend beyond the common market.[7] The Court has taken a pragmatic view to this debate.

Case C-300/89 Commission v Council (Titanium Dioxide) [1991] ECR I-2867

In 1983 the Commission proposed a Directive to harmonise procedures for the reduction of waste from the titanium dioxide industry. The proposed legal bases for this Directive were Articles 100 [*94*] and 235[*308*] EC. Following the coming

---

6 Pescatore, P. 'Some critical remarks on the "Single European Act"' (1987) 24 *CMLRev* 11.

7 Steindorff, E. 'Gemeinsamer Markt als Binnenmarkt' (1986) 150 *Zeitschift für das Gesamte Handels - und Wirtschaftsrecht* (1986) 687, 700-702. For a summary of the various views see Barents, R. 'The Internal Market Unlimited: Some Observations on the Legal Basis of Community Legislation' (1993) 30 *CMLRev* 85, 102-104.

into force of the SEA the Commission changed this to Article 100a [*95*] EC. The Council adopted the Directive, but changed the legal base to Article 130s[*175*](1) EC, the legal base contained in the Title on the Environment. This allowed the measure to be adopted on the basis of the consultation procedure and by unanimity. The Commission, supported by the Parliament, challenged the measure. The Advocate General and the Court both found that the measure should have been based on Article 100a [*95*] EC.

Advocate-General Tesauro

... in determining whether measures like the Directive at issue here now fall within the scope of the new provision on harmonization of national laws, Article 100a, it must first be observed that the scope of that provision is not determined *ratione materiae* but rather by reference to a criterion of a functional nature, extending laterally to all measures designed to ensure attainment of the 'internal market'. Article 100a in fact concerns 'measures for the approximation of the provisions laid down by law, regulation or administrative action... which have as their object the establishment and functioning of the internal market'; in more general terms, it is confirmed that the purpose of that provision is the 'achievement of the objectives set out in Article 8a'. Article 8a defines the internal market as an 'area without internal frontiers, in which the free movement of goods, persons, services and capital is ensured in accordance with the provisions of this Treaty'.[[8]] It is clear, therefore, that definition of the term 'internal market' is an essential step in determining the scope of Article 100a, just as a definition of the term 'common market' is fundamental in establishing the limits within which Article 100 applies.

It seems to me to be fully consistent with the logic underlying the Single European Act to conclude that the 'area without internal frontiers' referred to in Article 8a is to be seen as a truly integrated area where the prevailing conditions are as close as possible to those of a single internal market: an area, therefore, in which there is harmonization not only of the rules concerning products but also of those which more generally affect the conditions of competition between undertakings. Indeed, I do not see how it is possible to achieve a genuinely single, integrated market without eliminating divergences between national legislation which, by having a differing impact on production costs, prevents the development of competition on the basis of real equality within the Community. That interpretation essentially bases the concept of 'internal market' on that of the 'common market', as defined by the Court both in its two judgments cited earlier in Cases 91 and 92/79 and, from a more general standpoint, in the judgment in *Schul* (Case 15/81 [1982] ECR 1409) in which is it stated that:

> 'the concept of a common market as defined by the Court in a consistent line of decisions involves the elimination of all obstacles to intra-Community trade in order to merge the national markets into a single market bringing about conditions as close as possible to those of a genuine internal market.'

---

[8] This Article became Article 7a [*14*] EC following the TEU.

Even if the substantive content of the internal market and the common market were identical, Article 7a [*14*] EC might still have had formal legal effects by virtue of the deadline it set of 31 December 1992. The legal effects of the deadline are, however, unclear. The Commission proposed initially that Article 7a [*14*] EC be directly effective. This proved too radical for the Member States,[9] who insisted upon the insertion of a Declaration to the SEA that the date of 31 December 1992 have no automatic legal effect. The effects of this Declaration are unclear, however. Some have argued that as it was not an integral part of the Treaty, as there was no requirement that it be ratified, it has no legal effect whatsoever.[10] Even if the Declaration were to have legal effects, however, it would, as a Declaration, only be of interpretative value and could not be invoked, *contra legem*, against the clear wording of Article 7a [*14*] EC. From this it has been argued that Article 7a [*14*] EC imposes a sufficiently precise obligation that failure to complete the internal market by 31 December 1992 could subject the EC Institutions both to an Article 175 [*232*] EC action requiring them to act and to an action in damages under Article 215 [*288*](2) EC unless it could be demonstrated that postponement was due to an overriding public interest.[11]

The arguments that the date 31 December 1992 generates legal effects are unconvincing for reasons which extend beyond the one that such a finding would contradict the will of the Member States as expressed at the time of the SEA. At a formal level the wording of the provision is no more prescriptive than that of Article 3[*3*] EC which sets out the objectives and activities of the Community. The latter has been held to be no more than programmatic in nature and to be fully dependent upon specific measures for its concretisation.[12] It would,

---

9 Ehlermann, C-D. 'The Internal Market following the Single European Act' (1987) 24 *CMLRev* 361, 370-371.

10 Toth, A. 'The legal status of the declarations attached to the Single European Act' (1987) 24 *CMLRev 803.*

11 Schermers, H. 'The Effect of the Date 31 December 1992' (1991) 28 *CMLRev* 275.

12 Joined Cases C-78-83/90 *Compagnie Commerciale de l'Ouest v Receveur Principal des Douanes de la Pallice Port* [1992] ECR I-847, [1994] 2 CMLR 425.

moreover, take a brave Court to hold that the deadline generates legal effects, given the litigation this would provoke.

The consequence of this is that, in formal terms, the internal market added nothing to the existing terminology. There is something deeply unsatisfactory about this. It reduces the 1992 project to a marketing device - a commitment in 1987 to establish in five years something which should have been established seventeen years previously. The wave of enthusiasm this created may have been only possible through a renaming of the project. Once this has died down, the internal market becomes merely tied to the raft of legislation it created. The resonance of this construct is thus likely to be a confined to a particular time and space, and is likely to diminish over time. At a micro-level, this will occur through the legislation slowly being amended and replaced. At a macrolevel it is likely to take place through new concepts emerging into which much of the legislation becomes subsumed.[13]

III. The Economics of 1992

The 1992 project was one of the 'few Community fields in which a consensus for more intensive Community actions was likely to emerge'.[14] It could be used instrumentally to secure a more politically integrated Europe, whilst enticing those who were opposed to greater political integration into the project by holding out tempting economic benefits. To garner consensus, the Commission thus chose to focus on the latter. In 1986 it commissioned a study to forecast the effects of 1992. The study was in part a public relations exercise, as its remit was to focus on the benefits of a single market rather than the 'Costs of non-Europe'. Nevertheless, as Lord Cockfield, the Commissioner responsible,

---

[13] A prime example is Article 8a [*18*] EC, which placed free movement of persons within the Citizenship provisions. At a formal level the provision added little to existing law. At a symbolic it suggested an identity for all provisions which touched on free movement of persons quite separate from that of the internal market.

[14] Dehousse, R. '1992 and Beyond: The Institutional Dimension of the Internal Market Programme' (1989/1) *LIEI* 109, 111.

remarked, it was one of the most ambitious market research exercises ever undertaken. In addition to the Commission, numerous universities, 15 firms of consultants and 11,000 enterprises cooperated in the exercise.[15] This study was divided into two - a detailed study, the principal conclusions of which are published below, and a separate summary.[16]

Emerson, M., Aujean, M., Catinat, M., Goybet, P. & Jacquemin, A. *The Economics of 1992, The EC Commission's Assessment of the Economic Effects of Completing the Internal Market* (1988, OUP, Oxford) 1-2

2. The Nature of the Community's Internal Market Barriers

Tariffs and quantitative restrictions on trade have largely been eliminated in the Community. The remaining barriers essentially consist of:
(i) differences in technical regulations between countries, which impose extra costs on intra-EC trade;
(ii) delays at frontiers for customs purposes, and related administrative burdens for companies and public administration, which impose further costs on trade;
(iii) restrictions on competition for public purchases through excluding bids from other Community suppliers, which often result in excessively high costs of purchase;
(iv) restrictions to engage in certain service transactions, or to become established in certain service activities in other Community countries. This concerns particularly financial and transport services, where the costs of market-entry barriers also appear to be substantial.

.....

3. The Nature of the Economic Gains to be Measured

The creation of the European internal market will, on the one hand, suppress a series of constraints that today prevent enterprises from being as efficient as they could be and from employing resources to the full, and on the other hand, establishing a more competitive environment which will incite them to exploit new opportunities. The removal of the constraints and the emergence of the new competitive incentives will lead to four principal types of effect:

---

15 Cockfield, *The European Union: Creating the Single Market* (1994, Chancery Press, London) 90.

16 Cecchini, P. *The European Challenge 1992, The Benefits of a Single Market* (1988, Gower, Aldershot).

(i) a significant reduction in costs due to a better exploitation of several kinds of economies of scale associated with the size of production units and enterprises;
(ii) an improved efficiency in enterprises, a rationalisation of industrial structures and a setting of prices closer to costs of production, all resulting from more competitive markets;
(iii) adjustments between industries on the basis of a fuller play of comparative advantages in an integrated market;
(iv) a flow of innovations, new processes and new products stimulated by the dynamics of the internal market.

These processes liberate resources for alternative productive uses, and when they are so used the total, sustainable level of consumption and investment in the economy will be increased. This is the fundamental criterion of economic gain.

These gains in economic welfare will also be reflected in macroeconomic indicators. It is implicit, in order to attain the highest sustainable level of consumption and investment, that productivity and employment be also of a high order. In particular, where rationalisation efforts cause labour to be made redundant, this resource has to be successfully re-employed. Also implicit is a high rate of growth in the economy. The sustainability condition, moreover, requires that the major macroeconomic equilibrium constraints are respected, notably as regards price stability, balance of payments and budget balances. It further implies a positive performance in terms of world-wide competitivity. These different objectives can, however, be achieved in different mixes; it is for macroeconomic policy to determine how to dispose of the potential gains made available by the microeconomic measures taken in order to complete the internal market.

Attempts were then made to give approximate quantifications to these gains. It was estimated that, in the medium-term, the increase in economic activity resulting from the single market would increase EC GDP by between 2.5% and 6.25%. Increased competition and prosperity in the single market would bring about a number of further beneficial consequences. Consumer prices would drop about 6% as a result of the increased competition. The increased economic activity would, it was estimated, create about 1.8 million new jobs, enabling unemployment rates to drop about 1.5%. Finally, budgetary balances would improve by an average of 2.2% of GDP, as a result of the uptake in economic activity and lower procurement costs.

The significance of this process of quantification probably lay in its presentation of the internal market as a series of practical benefits. There was little doubt that this rendered the concept more persuasive to policy-makers than the relatively abstract goal of the common market. Yet as a methodological exercise it was deeply flawed, both in its assumptions and in its failure to look at some of the potential consequences of realisation of the internal market.

Tsoukalis, L. *The New European Economy Revisited* (1997, 3rd Edition, OUP, Oxford) 71-73

With the notable exception of a study by Baldwin, who tried to incorporate the dynamic effects of the internal market on savings and investment,[[17]] most of the other attempts to measure ex ante the effects of the internal market produced significantly small net gains. In fact, the quantification part of all those studies was, arguably, of little value. In the Commission study, the direct benefits expected from the elimination of frontier controls were relatively small, while on the contrary big expectations were associated with the secondary, so-called dynamic effects, resulting from economies of scale, restructuring, and greater competition, for which it would be extremely difficult to produce anything more than educated guess.

Some years later, Helm wrote:

'These estimates have been extensively debated. The general conclusions which emerges is unsurprising: the margin of error is extremely large, and depends, sensitively, on the responses of European firms and consumers, as well as the trade effects compared with the counterfactual: what would have happened in the absence of policy. Since the latter is necessarily a theoretical construct, the lack of consensus reflects a more fundamental theoretical disagreement about the nature of microeconomic behaviour in general and models of oligopolistic competition in particular. The only generally accepted conclusion is that the net effects are likely to be positive for Europe as a whole.'[[18]]

In view of the very large degree of uncertainty and the multiplicity of factors involved, ex ante (and ex post) estimates of the internal market effects should therefore be treated at best as very rough indicators of the direction of those effects and the broad orders of magnitude.

One important question, which was left almost completely unanswered in the 'Costs of Non-Europe' study, was about the likely distribution of costs and benefits associated with the internal market programme. In this respect, the study has little to offer in terms of prediction, apart from acknowledging the problem and expressing the hope that EC redistributive policies would provide adequate means for compensating potential losers or, even better, for helping weaker economies and regions to face the strong winds of competition unleashed through the elimination of barriers.

Modern theories of international trade, with their emphasis on imperfect competition, economies of scale, and the dynamic effects of innovation suggest that a very

---

17 Baldwin, R. 'The Growth Effects of 1992' (1989) *Economic Policy* 9.

18 Helm, D. 'The Assessment: The European Internal Market: The Next Steps' (1993) *Oxford Review of Economic Policy* 4.

unequal distribution of gains from integration is a very concrete possibility. Comparative advantage is no longer seen as something determined by the particular factor endowments of a country. Instead, comparative advantage is created through deliberate policies directed at investment, education, and research and development. Countries pursue strategic trade policies in order to capture an ever-increasing share of dynamic sectors where demand is growing and where the benefits of scale economies, advantages of experience, and innovation can be reaped; in economic terms, sectors where there are good prospects for 'rent'. In such a world, which is thousand of kilometres apart from the assumptions made by traditional theories of international trade, a highly unequal distribution of gains and losses from integration can by no means be excluded. Krugman, for example, argues that trade based on economies of scale, which seems to be largely the case of intra-EC trade, 'probably involves less conflict of interest within countries and more conflict of interest between countries'.[19]

After the publication of the 'Costs of Non-Europe', the Commission tried to go further by identifying those industrial sectors which should be more affected by the elimination of remaining barriers.[20] Since the completion of the internal market is largely about Non-Tariff Barriers (discriminatory public procurement being one of the most important) it is not entirely surprising that many of the sectors found to be most affected were high technology sectors (telecommunications, computers) and more traditional, capital-intensive sectors (railway equipment, shipbuilding, electrical engineering). But the list of the sectors most sensitive to the 1992 programme also included certain mass-consumer products, such as textiles and clothing, where technical and other barriers continued to have a significant effect on intra-EC trade. While the former category of sectors is more associated with the developed, highly industrialised countries of the Union, textiles and clothing represent a disproportionately large share of industrial employment in the two least developed countries, namely Portugal and Greece.

Those studies also pointed to the inter-industry dimension of intra-EC trade which has grown significantly as a result of successive enlargements. There is a great deal of inter-industry trade between Germany on the one hand and Greece or Portugal on the other. Economic theory tells us that the adjustment costs from liberalisation are expected to be greater in the case of inter-industry trade, which means that adjustment in relation to the internal market should be more painful than what had been experienced in the years following the establishment of the EEC. The elimination of the remaining internal barriers could, for example, accentuate the tendency for geographical concentration of economic activity in high technology sectors for which the availability of skilled manpower and proximity to research, administrative, and financial centres can be extremely important; and this can be true of other sectors too. On the other hand, liberalisation and deregulation, applied for instance to financial services or

19 Krugman, P. 'Economic Integration in Europe: Some Conceptual Issues' in Pado-Schipoa, T. *Efficiency, Stability and Equity* (1987, OUP. Oxford).

20 EC Commission, 'The Impact of the Internal Market by Industrial Sector: The Challenge for the Member States' (1990) *European Economy Special Edition.*

telecommunications, should be expected to bring more sizeable benefits to the less developed countries of the periphery. The implicit assumption behind this argument would be that protection and heavy regulation in those countries has been the result of economically irrational policies and thus rationality imported from Brussels should have important beneficial effects: perhaps, not a totally implausible argument.

As mentioned earlier, the first years of the internal market programme coincided with an economic boom to which it did itself, arguably, contribute. The programme enjoyed strong support from the business community, and most notably the large firms represented in the European Round Table. Some important early decisions, such as the decision to liberalise capital movements, accompanied by a very active promotion strategy adopted in Brussels, helped to influence further business expectations which were in turn translated into investment decisions. The rapid increase in cross-frontier mergers and acquisitions and the spectacular growth of foreign direct investment (FDI) were also not unrelated to the prospect of a single European market. Early business surveys pointed to a '1992 effect', which, if true, would be a purely anticipatory effect.[21] Similarly, Malinvaud talked about the 'Schumpeterian' effect of 1992, this effect being generally identified with a boost to entrepreneurship producing in turn a shift in the behaviour of private economic agents; and economists find it difficult to analyse and forecast such an effect.[22]

If part of the secret of 1992 lay in the hype surrounding it, it is no surprise to find that subsequent studies have shown its anticipated positive and negative effects to have been both considerably overestimated.[23]

Tsoukalis, L. *The New European Economy Revisited* (1997, 3rd Edition, OUP, Oxford) 75-78

In an OECD study published in 1994, the authors concluded that 'it is difficult to find strong evidence that the single market programme has yet had sizeable effects on aggregate output'.[24] They estimated a cumulative gain of 1.5 per cent of GDP so far,

---

21 EC Commission, 'The Creation of a European Financial Area' (1989) 36 *European Economy*.

22 Malinvaud, E. *Macroeconomic Research and European Policy Formation* (1991, EUI, Florence).

23 The Commission study referred to in the next piece can be found in *European Economy* (March 1997). A more accessible summary for non-economists is in EC Commission, *The Impact and Effectiveness of the Single Market* COM(96) 520.

24 Hoeller, P. & Loupe, M. 'The EC's Internal Market: Implementation and Economic Effects' (1994) *OECD Economic Studies* 93.

although this numerical estimate had, arguably, as much validity as earlier ex ante predictions. The new studies commissioned for an ex post evaluation of the internal market programme have to deal with the notorious problem of the counterfactual, thus having to isolate the internal market effect from that of many other important developments which took place during the same period, such as globalisation trends, the unification of Germany, the Iberian enlargement, and the gradual opening of the economies of the Central and East European Countries; with inadequate data which usually do not correspond to the sophisticated techniques developed by economists; and with late implementation in many cases, which in turn means that the period for which the effects of the internal market can be measured is uncomfortably short while the time-lags during which an adequate response of economic agents can be expected in response to institutional changes may be rather long.

The studies commissioned on the internal market effects have produced some interesting results. It appears that there has been significant trade creation, leading to a further increase in intra-EU trade which is now estimated to reach 68 per cent of total trade for the Fifteen. Statistics on intra-EU trade have, however, become less reliable since the elimination of border controls. There is no evidence of substantial trade diversion. On the contrary, import penetration from the rest of the world has grown in most sectors, and this trend has been even more pronounced in the case of several sectors which are considered most sensitive to the internal market programme. Intra-industry trade is still large for Greece, Portugal, Ireland, and (interestingly enough) Denmark. Germany has a comparative advantage in high price quality product ranges, followed by France, while at the other end of the spectrum, Greece and Portugal seem to specialise only in low price products.

The evidence available points to a strong internal market effect on FDI flows, both intra-EU and from outside, which have been growing faster than trade. The EU share of the world FDI inflows has grown significantly in recent years, reaching 44 per cent in the early 1990s; but this may also have something to do with early fears about a 'Fortress Europe', which have, however, proved to be unfounded. The big bulk of FDI has gone to services sectors; not only because they have been growing fast, but also presumably because they are less tradable. FDI outflows from Germany and the UK have registered a particularly strong preference for the financial services sector.

The recent period has also been characterised by a very substantial industrial restructuring, although it is not always easy to separate the effect of the internal market from global trends. And this has been accompanied by a significant increase in concentration, especially in technologically intensive industries. Evidence has also been found of increasing concentration in industries which are closely related to public procurement, such as telecommunications and transport, and also in food industries and mass consumer goods. These are sectors which have been particularly affected by the internal market programme and its liberalising effects. There are still remarkable differences in the average size of firms even among the large economies. Thus, in Germany the average size of gross value added per firm is one third higher than in France or the UK. Despite the considerable increase in cross-border mergers and acquisitions, concentration has still been taking place mostly within domestic markets: national boundaries inside the EU are therefore still far from irrelevant.

On the other hand, there is little indication that Europe's industrial core has gained at the expense of the periphery. From the second half of the 1980's onwards, three among the least developed economies of the Union, namely Portugal, Spain, and even more so Ireland, have been growing faster than the average. Higher growth rates can be at least partly attributed to large inflows of foreign investment. It is also interesting that, according to business surveys, economic agents in peripheral countries have perceived a stronger effect of the internal market and, broadly speaking, this effect has been deemed to be positive.

The internal market programme was aiming at economies of scale combined with the strengthening of competition which should ensure that cost reductions are being passed on to the consumer. There are several cases of substantial price reductions in sectors which have been progressively opened to competition, such as telecommunications and also segments of air transport and banking; but nothing like the reduction in prices, for example in financial services, which had been expected (or hoped for) in the study on the 'Costs of Non-Europe'. There has also been some price convergence across the EU, which is, of course, an indication of a more integrated European market. It has been more pronounced in the case of consumer and equipment goods. On the contrary, price dispersion for energy, services, and construction remains significant, which in turn suggests that there are still important barriers in those sectors separating different national markets.

In its attempt to assess the effects of the internal market, the Commission has finally succumbed to the temptation of producing numerical estimates of the macroeconomic effects, although, apparently, fully aware of the serious limitations of such an exercise. Perhaps understandably, politicians feel the need for precise figures which they can in turn offer to their electorates, while the wide margins of error to which such figures are usually subject appear only in small footnotes that very few people read. It is often difficult to reconcile scientific rigour and political exigencies, and the European Commission, like other institutions, must have often been caught between the two. Whichever way it is calculated, the macroeconomic impact of the internal market seems to have been rather small; and certainly smaller than expected. According to estimates released by the Commission, the impact of the internal market on GDP has been between 1.1 and 1.5 per cent, with the impact on investment being close to 3 per cent. Between 300,000 and 900,000 jobs have been directly attributed to the internal market, and approximately 1 per cent reduction in prices.

The ex post estimates of the macroeconomic impact, for whatever they are worth, are significantly smaller than the ex ante estimates which had appeared in the study on the 'Costs of Non-Europe'. But expectation had been deliberately inflated, and the implementation of the internal market programme took place in the highly unfavourable economic climate of the early 1990s. A convenient way out of this problem might therefore be to argue that the effects of the internal market will be long-lasting; a convenient way out and perhaps also an argument which is not too far from the truth.

IV. The Internal Market as Regulatory Strategy

i. The Adoption of the 'New Approach'

Simple repackaging could not have sustained the change in the legislative culture of the EC brought about by '1992'. Nor can the change be put down to the qualified majority voting introduced by Article 100a [*95*] EC. Qualified majority voting had existed in other areas of EC law, notably agriculture and commercial policy, since the inception of the EC Treaty, yet had broken down with the introduction of the Luxembourg Accords. There was every reason to suppose that this might reoccur if legislation was passed which did not respect national autonomy or was insufficiently sensitive to local concerns. The dangers were particularly apparent in view of the 'traditional' approach that the Commission had adopted towards the approximation of laws. This had been set out in its General Programme on the Removal to Technical Obstacles to Trade in 1969.[25] The Programme consisted of three prongs:

- EC legislation harmonising national legislation in each industrial sector;
- mutual recognition of inspections; and
- a procedure for adapting Community legislation to technical progress.

It had proved to be extremely unsuccessful.

Lauwaars, R. 'The "Model Directive" on Technical Harmonization' in Bieber, R., Dehousse, R., Pinder, J. & Weiler, J. *1992: One European Market* (1988, Nomos, Baden-Baden) 151, 154-155

In accordance with the 'traditional' approach, ..., the Council had, by the end of 1984, established 177 directives, adapted by 56 directives of the Commission. ...
During the same period the following problems, however became apparent:-

- Time-consuming and laborious procedures: The preparation and adoption of a draft directive by the Commission, the establishment of the directive by the Council and its implementation by the Member States take years, sometimes

25 OJ 1969 C 76/1.

more than ten years, which is clearly incompatible with the requirements of the relevant sector;

- Excessive uniformity: The Community legislator strived for too many details (total harmonization) and did not leave enough room for alternative solutions;
- The unanimity rule: According to Article 100 of the EEC Treaty, directives on harmonization of legislation may only be adopted unanimously, which is an additional and important cause of delay of the decision-making process;
- Insufficient delegation of powers: According to Article 155, last indent, of the EEC Treaty the Council may delegate to the Commission the powers necessary for the implementation of the rules laid down by the former. However the Council has applied this provision in relatively few cases and, when it has delegated, has added a complicated decision-making procedure;
- The discrepancy between harmonization and European normalization: Apart from the directives in the field of electrical equipment, the Community legislator did not make sufficient use of existing or possible European 'normalization', i.e. the establishment of European standards by international standardization bodies.

The genius of the 1992 project was that it devised a new regulatory strategy which was sufficiently malleable both to facilitate Community legislation whilst appearing to accommodate Member State fears about loss of autonomy and lack of sensitivity to local interests. The 'new approach' was set out in the Commission's White Paper and was accepted by the Council in its Resolution of 7 May 1985 on a new approach to technical harmonisation and standards.[26]

White Paper from the Commission to the European Council (Milan, 28-29 June 1985) COM (85) 310 final

57. The elimination of border controls, important as it is, does not of itself create a genuine common market. Goods and people moving within the Community should not find obstacles inside the different Member States as opposed to meeting them at the border.

58. This does not mean that there should be the same rules everywhere, but that goods as well as citizens and companies should be able to move freely within the Community. Subject to certain important constraints (see paragraph 65 below), the general principle should be approved that, if a product is lawfully manufactured and marketed in one Member State, there is no reason why it should not be sold freely throughout the

---

26 OJ 1985 C 136/1.

Community. Indeed the objectives of national legislation, such as the protection of human health and life and of the environment, are more often than not identical. It follows that the rules and controls developed to achieve these objectives, although they may take different forms, essentially come down to the same thing, and so should normally be accorded recognition in all Member States, not forgetting the possibilities of cooperation between national authorities. What is true for goods, is also true for services and for people. If a Community citizen or company meets the requirements for its activity in one Member State, there should be no valid reason why those citizens or companies should not exercise their economic activities also in other parts of the Community.

59. The Commission is fully aware that this strategy implies a change in habits and in traditional ways of thinking. What is needed is a radical change of attitude which would lead to new and innovative solutions for problems - real or apparent - which may appear when border controls no longer exist.

.....

62. The new strategy must be coherent in that it will need not merely to take into account the objective of realizing a common market per se, but also to serve the further objectives of building an expanding market and a flexible market. It must aim not simply to remove technical barriers to trade, but to do so in a manner which will contribute to increasing industrial efficiency and competitiveness, leading to greater wealth and job creation.

63. In principle, therefore given the Council's recognition (Conclusions on Standardization, 16 July 1984) of the essential equivalence of the objectives of national legislation, mutual recognition could be an effective strategy for bringing about a common market in a trading sense. This strategy is supported in particular by Articles 30 to 36 of the EEC Treaty, which prohibit national measures which would have excessively and unjustifiably restrictive effects on free movement.

64. But while a strategy based purely on mutual recognition would remove barriers to trade and lead to the creation of a genuine common trading market, it might well prove inadequate for the purposes of building up of an expanded market based on the competitiveness which a continental-scale uniform market can generate. On the other hand experience has shown that the alternative of relying on a strategy based totally on harmonization would be over-regulatory, would take a long time to implement, would be inflexible and could stifle innovation. What is needed is a strategy that combines the best of both approaches but, above all, allows for progress to be made more quickly than in the past.

The chosen strategy

65. The Commission takes into account the underlying reasons for the existence of barriers to trade, and recognizes the essential equivalence of Member States' legislative objectives in the protection of health and safety, and of the environment. Its harmonization approach is based on the following principles:

- a clear distinction needs to be drawn in future internal market initiatives between what is essential to harmonize, and what may be left to mutual recognition of national regulations and standards; this implies that, on the occasion of each harmonization initiative, the Commission will determine whether national regulations are excessive in relation to the mandatory requirements pursued and, thus, constitute unjustified barriers to trade according to Article 30 to 36 of the EEC Treaty;
- legislative harmonization (Council Directives based on Article 100 EEC) will in future be restricted to laying down essential health and safety requirements which will be obligatory in all Member States. Conformity with this will entitle a product to free movement;
- harmonization of industrial standards by the elaboration of European standards will be promoted to the maximum extent, but the absence of European standards should not be allowed to be used as a barrier to free movement. During the waiting period while European standards are being developed, the mutual acceptance of national standards, with agreed procedures, should be the guiding principle.

.....

68. ... The task of defining the technical specifications of products which will be deemed to conform to legislated requirements, will be entrusted to European Standards issued by the Comité Européen de la Normalisation (CEN) or by sectoral European standards in the electrical and building sectors such as CENELEC, UEAtc or RILEM, acting on qualified majority votes.

69. The Commission is taking steps to strengthen the capacity of these European Standards bodies and also, in the telecommunications sector, of CEPT. This is seen not only as a necessary adjunct to the new approach, but as an essential ingredient in the gradual replacement of national standards by European standards in all areas.

70. The Council generally should off-load technical matters by making more use of its powers of delegation as recommended by the European Council. Article 155 of the EEC Treaty makes express provision for this possibility and opens the way to a simplified legislative procedure. This procedure has already been used successfully in customs matters and with the adaptation of existing directives to technological progress. The encouraging results suggest that this procedure should be extended.

Whilst they are interrelated, there are three principle strands to the 'new approach'. These are the principle of mutual recognition; harmonisation by the Council of only 'essential requirements' and the use of bodies other than the Council, in particular private bodies, to develop European standards.[27]

ii. The Principle of Mutual Recognition

a. The Development of Mutual Recognition

The principle of mutual recognition was developed as a result of tactical opportunism by the Commission in response to the *Cassis de Dijon* judgment of the Court of Justice.

Case 120/78 REWE-Zentral AG v Bundesmonopolverwaltung für Branntwein [1979] ECR 649, [1979] 3 CMLR 494

REWE-Zentral AG, a German trading company, requested authorization from the Bundesmonopolverwaltung (Federal Monopoly Administration for Spirits) to import a consignment of a French liqueur 'Cassis de Dijon' into Germany. The authorization was refused under a 1958 law which required that spirits, including liqueurs, have a minimum alcoholic content of 25%. The alcoholic content of 'Cassis de Dijon' ranged between 15 and 20%. The law in question applied to all spirits marketed in Germany, both imports and domestic products. It was, in other words, a straightforward technical standard. This case represented, however, the first time that such a measure was being challenged on the grounds that it was incompatible with Article 30 [*28*] EC, the provision on free movement of goods.

8. In the absence of common rules relating to the production and marketing of alcohol - a proposal for a regulation submitted to the Council by the Commission on 7 December

---

[27] On the 'new approach' see Pelkmans, J. 'The New Approach to Technical Harmonization and Standardization' (1987) 25 *JCMS* 249; Schmidt von Sydow, H. 'The Basic Strategies of the Commission's White Paper' and Pelkmans, J. 'A Grand Design by the Piece? An Appraisal of the Internal Market Strategy' in Bieber, R., Dehousse, R., Pinder, J. & Weiler, J. *1992: One European Market* (1988, Nomos, Baden-Baden); Burrows, N. 'Harmonisation of Technical Standards: Reculer pour Mieux Sauter' (1990) 53 *MLR* 711.

1976 (Official Journal C 309, p.2) not yet having received the Council's approval - it is for the Member States to regulate all matters relating to the production and marketing of alcohol and alcoholic beverages on their territory.

Obstacles to movement within the Community resulting from disparities between the national laws relating to the marketing of the products in question must be accepted in so far as those provisions may be recognized as being necessary in order to satisfy mandatory requirements relating in particular to the effectiveness of fiscal supervision, the protection of public health, the fairness of commercial transactions and the defence of the consumer.

.....

14. It is clear from the foregoing that the requirements relating to the minimum alcohol content of alcoholic beverages do not serve a purpose which is in the general interest and such as to take precedence over the requirements of the free movement of goods, which constitutes one of the fundamental rules of the Community.

In practice, the principle effect of requirements of this nature is to promote alcoholic beverages having a high alcohol content by excluding from the national market products of other Member States which do not answer that description.

It therefore appears that the unilateral requirement imposed by the rules of a Member State of a minimum alcohol content for the purposes of the sale of alcoholic beverages constitutes an obstacle to trade which is incompatible with the provisions of Article 30 of the Treaty.

There is therefore no valid reason why, provided that they have been lawfully produced and marketed in one of the Member States, alcoholic beverages should not be introduced into any other Member State; the sale of such products may not be subject to a legal prohibition on the marketing of beverages with an alcohol content lower than the limit set by the national rules.

15. Consequently, the first question should be answered to the effect that the concept of 'measures having equivalent effect to quantitative restrictions on imports' contained in Article 30 of the Treaty is to be understood to mean that the fixing of a minimum alcohol content for alcoholic beverages intended for human consumption by the legislation of a Member State also falls within the prohibition laid down in that provision where the importation of alcoholic beverages lawfully produced and marketed in another Member State is concerned.

On a formal basis the judgment is highly ambiguous. Its wording was sufficiently open-ended that some critics thought it suggested that Member States could only regulate imports if they could show the existence of a legitimate reason for the measure in question.[28] Within the context of the case, however, the judgment only stood for a narrower interpretation, namely that certain non-tariff barriers barring access to Member State markets were illegal. It was the Commission's willingness to bring the judgment into the wider political arena through publishing a Communication setting out the judgment as authority for the principle of mutual recognition.[29]

Commission Practice Note on Import Prohibitions: Communication from the Commission Concerning the Consequences of the Judgment given by the Court of Justice on 20 February 1979 in Case 120/78 ('Cassis de Dijon')[30]

Whereas Member States may, with respect to domestic products and in the absence of relevant Community provisions, regulate the terms on which such products are marketed, the case is different for products imported from other Member States.

Any product imported from another Member State must in principle be admitted to the territory of the importing Member State if it has been lawfully produced, that is, conforms to the rules and processes of manufacture that are customarily and traditionally accepted in the exporting country, and is marketed in the territory of the latter.

This principle implies that Member States, when drawing up commercial or technical rules liable to affect the free movement of goods, may not take an exclusively national viewpoint and take account only of requirements confined to domestic products. The proper functioning of the common market demands that each Member State also give consideration to the legitimate requirements of the other Member States.

.....

... a Member State may not in principle prohibit the sale in its territory of a product lawfully produced and marketed in another Member State even if the product is produced according to technical or quality requirements which differ from those imposed on its domestic products. Where a product 'suitably and satisfactorily' fulfils the legitimate objective of a Member State's own rules (public safety, protection of the consumer or the environment, etc.), the importing country cannot justify prohibiting its sale in its territory by claiming that the way it fulfils the objective is different from that imposed on domestic products.

---

28 Barents, R. 'New Developments in Measures Having Equivalent Effect' (1981) 18 *CMLRev* 271, 295.

29 On this see Alter, K. & Meunier-Aitsahalia, S. 'Judicial Politics in the European Community: European Integration and the Pathbreaking Cassis de Dijon Decision' (1994) 26 *Comparative Political Studies* 535.

30 OJ 1980 C 256/2.

It is tempting to speculate how much effect this Communication would have had, were it not for the unfolding of the wider backdrop which led to the signing of the SEA. As it was, the principle was placed at the heart of the 'new approach'. This was spelt out not just in the Commission's White Paper,[31] but was also carried forward into the EC Treaty by the SEA.

Article 100b EC. 1. During 1992 the Commission shall, together with each Member State, draw up an inventory of national laws, regulations and administrative provisions which fall under Article 100a and which have not been harmonised pursuant to that Article.

The Council acting in accordance with the provisions of Article 100a, may decide that the provisions in force in a Member State must be recognised as equivalent to those applied by another Member State.

2. The provisions of Article 100a(4) apply by analogy.

3. The Commission shall draw up the inventory referred to in the first subparagraph of paragraph 1 and shall submit appropriate proposals in good time to allow the Council to act before the end of 1992.

There were a number of reasons why this might have been the case. Ideologically, the keeping in place of the diverse regulatory traditions within the internal market enhanced inter-brand consumer choice. Brands would no longer need to conform to one Euro-standard to circulate around the internal market. Instead, not only would diverse regulatory regimes be kept in place but these regimes would be 'exported' throughout the Community with a corresponding expansion in consumer choice. The result would be that, as one commentator famously put it, German beer drinkers could now drink Newcastle Brown Ale rather than simply 'Euro-beer'.[32]

More cynically, the principle conformed with existing national government and industrial preferences by holding out a promise to act

---

31 See p 2 and p 18.

32 Welch, D. 'From "Euro Beer" to "Newcastle Brown", A Review of European Community Action to Dismantle Divergent "Food" Laws' (1983) 22 *JCMS* 47, 66.

as a bulwark against excessive, centralised EC intervention through generating a decentralised governance structure within which each Member State would retain considerable autonomy over its national market.

Fligstein, N. & Mara-Drita, I. 'How To Make a Market: Reflections on the Attempt to Create a Single Market in the European Union' (1996) 102 *American Journal of Sociology* 1, 14-18

In order to consider what kind of market was constructed, it is necessary to consider a sociology of market institutions. ... A market can be defined as a social situation where trade in an item occurs and a price mechanism that determines the value of the item exists. The price mechanism implies the existence of 'money' and the quantity of 'money' that one might pay for an item. It does not specify how the arena for trade or the price mechanisms themselves operate nor does it suggest a structure for the social relations that will come to exist among suppliers, producers, consumers, and the state.

In order for markets to exist, elaborate social relations must appear to structure the arena of trade. At a minimum, these relations consist of property rights, governance structures, and rules of exchange. Property rights concern legal definitions of ownership. Traditionally, property rights concerned control over objects, particularly land but as capitalism developed, the concept has come to include control over ideas, processes, and skills. Legal forms define the ability to own and dispose of property and include sole proprietorships, partnerships, and joint stock corporations. Patents and skill certification are also property rights because their holders are granted exclusive rights to practice and gain from the designations.

The constitution of property rights is a contested political process where states, employees, local communities, suppliers and customers can affect how owners can dispose of property. For instance, workers in some societies have votes on corporate boards on issues regarding investment. In all societies, local communities can confiscate property and prevent property owners from doing what they like with their property (ie environmental regulation and zoning laws). Professionals who injure their clients can be sanctioned by having their property rights (i.e. their license to practice) taken from them.

Governance structures refer to laws and informal practices that set the legal boundaries of competition and cooperation. Every advanced industrial society has laws that are referred to as antitrust, competition policy, and rules over what are legal and illegal forms of cooperation such as cartels, joint ventures, and mergers to control competition. These rules have been translated into understandings that at any given time constitute what are legal and illegal forms of cooperation and competition between firms.

Within a market, firms try to create stable social relations among themselves in order to avoid direct competition. These social relations produce 'local knowledge',[[33]]

---

[33] Geertz, C. *Local Knowledge* (1980, Princeton University Press).

or what has been called a 'conception of control',[34] which allows actors to interpret the behaviour or others in a market. A stable market refers to a small set of firms that share such a conception of control. This mutuality allows firms to anticipate, interpret, and respond to one another's actions in a way that promotes their own existence without compromising the other's, that is, in a way that avoids direct competition. Finally, competition can be legally controlled by state intervention and regulation. States must explicitly or implicitly ratify the local conception of control.

Rules of exchange facilitate trade by establishing the rules under which transactions are undertaken. They define who can trade with whom and guarantee that goods will be delivered in working order and will be paid for. Thus they promote the movement of goods by making rules simpler, clearer, and less costly. Rules of exchange establish project definitions and product safety. Like the social relations we call property rights and governance structures, rules of exchange have legal backing since they provide mechanisms by which firms can get relief if conditions of trade are not met. The importance of rules of exchange relating to shipping, billing, insurance, and the exchange of money are even more salient when trade is occurring across national borders or whole societies.

These conceptual categories are linked in a number of ways. For instance, forbidding foreign firms to own local firms might be construed as using property rights to control competition (ie governance structures). Similarly, banning products because they were thought to be unhealthy would be a way to control competition as well. We nonetheless separate these categories analytically because doing so gives us a language to understand how rules for markets are created.

... states are implicated in all features of markets because states claim to set the rules for economic activity in their geographic boundaries. While sovereignty usually refers to a general ability to make and enforce rules in a territory, states actually vary appreciably in their ability to intervene in their economies and civil societies more generally. Sovereignty varies in terms of the number of arenas in which states intervene, and in the amount of discretion states actually have in each arena. Thus sovereignty is both multidimensional and quantitative in nature. Organised groups can contest the extension of state power and structure these arenas. Sovereignty is a claim that is contested, not an absolute given attribute of states.

There are at least three dimensions to their claim in the context of markets. First, regulating property rights and competition is more central to states' claim on sovereignty than rules of exchange. These define the relation of states to their own economic elites. The elites who own and manage firms have created stable worlds in their markets, worlds dependent on current property rights and conceptions of control. Disrupting these arrangements means that states face opposition of their best politically organised firms.

Second, states have symbolic stakes in making their own rules. Since part of the claim of a modern state is to be a nation and to represent its people, states have an interest in actively organising life within their national borders. In negotiations with other

---

34 Fligstein, N. *The Transformation of Corporate Control* (1990, Harvard University Press, Cambridge).

states, states will prefer their own rules although the distinctions among choices may at times be materially inconsequential. States will resist another state's standards or rules, particularly in the sensitive areas of property rights and governance structures. Rules of exchange are less symbolically charged because they facilitate trade with others and do not undermine claims to make rules governing the organisation of property.

Finally, states have a great deal of interest in maintaining their regulatory capacities. The ability to take action and use legal sanctions is at the core of what sovereignty means, and states are loathe to relinquish this form of control. Bureaucracies, police forces, and armies are the organisations that represent the ability of state actors to act. Sovereignty is clearly diminished if these capacities are impaired.

Theoretically, a single market implies rules that (1) produce a well-defined system of property rights, (2) sanction certain forms of competition and co-operation, and, (3) minimise the cost of transactions between economic units. Some scholars might add that a single market also implies a single currency and a single regulatory structure.

The problems of creating a single market within a single country is formidable. The United States, for instance, contains many different laws and jurisdictions for property rights. These problems are even more complex across countries precisely because states and their economic elites will prefer their own rules. In the EU, the states have their own rules around property rights, governance structures, and rules of exchange. These rules involve long traditions of law. Moreover, these rules define the current relations between political and economic elites in each society. The legitimacy and sovereignty of national bureaucratic apparatuses are dependent on these traditions and keeping the allegiance of elites. There was natural resistance from many quarters including the states and firms towards the disruption of these social relations. Given that the EU had unanimous decision-making rules, it is amazing that negotiations for any kind of single market were underway.

The sociology of markets just presented can be used to consider how the SMP [Single Market Programme] was negotiated. The basic problem was that the European Commission would have to mobilise existing centres of power in the European economy and states and work to prevent the mobilisation of the opposition. The European Commission's ability to create a political coalition given the existing distribution of actors and institutions meant that the SMP had to cut cunningly across lines that had previously seemed unresolvable because of unanimous voting procedures.

So, what kind of single market did the Europe 1992 project create? The short answer is that it made exchange easier for firms that were already exporting, and it preserved the power of states to control property rights and governance as one might expect from the theory of market institutions just proposed. The SMP did not create new European-wide regulatory capacity, and it opened markets only in industries that could be argued to be connected to the completion of a single market: transportation, financial services, and professionals and business services.

It is useful to consider which owners and managers of firms came to support the SMP. Survey data showed that managers of firms who were already involved in exporting were the most favourable toward the SMP.[35] These managers felt that their costs of production would be less, their markets larger, and therefore that their firm and country would fare better under the SMP. Managers in firms in industries with a high degree of government ownership were less positive about the effects of the SMP.

This argument can be buttressed by examining two other features of the EU. First, the organisations that most frequently complained to the EU were large multinational corporations since they were most likely to have problems in interstate trade. Second, the groups that joined the pro-SMP coalition were representatives of the largest corporations.

The practical political implication is that very few managers or owners of exporting firms were interested in reforming governance structures or property rights and indeed, some (eg managers of state-owned firms) would be hostile to these reforms. On the other hand, managers of firms involved in exporting were very interested in reducing restrictions around problems of trade, what we have termed rules of exchange. States would also be reticent to reorganise their property rights and governance structures because they did not want to lose that power and because they feared alienating powerful economic elites.

b. The Requirement of Prior Notification of Technical Standards

The substantive obligation for a Member State to take account, in drawing up and applying its own technical standards, of the 'legitimate requirements of other Member States' was also proceduralised through the adoption of Directive 83/189/EEC.[36] This requires Member States to notify draft technical regulations to the Commission, who, in turn, notifies other Member States.[37] Member States are under a duty to

---

35 Fligstein, N. & Brantley, P. 'The 1992 Single Market Program and the Interests of Business' in Eichengreen, B. & Frieden, J. (eds.) *Politics and Institutions in an Integrated Europe* (1995, Springer, New York).

36 Directive 83/189/ EEC, OJ 1983, L 109/8, as amended by Directive 88/182 EEC, OJ 1988 L 81/75 and Directive 94/10 EC, OJ 1994 L 100/30. Weatherill, S. 'Compulsory Notification of Draft Technical Standards: the Contribution of Directive 83/189 to the Management of the Internal Market' (1996) 16 *YBEL* 129.

37 Ibid., Article 8. Other Member States frequently take up the opportunity to comment on the draft technical regulations with 34% and 31% being subject to comments in 1993 and 1994 respectively. EC Commission, *Report on Operation of Directive 83/189/I EEC in 1992, 1993 and 1994* COM (96) 286, 27. Out of the 523 measures notified in 1996 the Commission made

postpone adoption of a draft measure for three months from the date of receipt by the Commission of the notification. The purpose of this was, initially, to identify and prevent potential obstacles to the free movement of goods at an early stage.[38] Increasingly, particularly with later amendments, it has been recognised as having the additional value of fostering transparency in national-standard setting processes.

The early record of the Directive was patchy. There was a lack of clarity as to what should be notified, with the majority of standards considered by the Commission being found to fall outside the ambit of the Directive.[39] In 1994, the scope of the technical standards covered by the Directive was enlarged to include:

- laws, regulations or administrative practices which refer either to technical specifications, other requirements or codes of practice which in turn refer to technical specifications;

- voluntary agreements to which a public authority is a party and which refer to technical specifications; and

- fiscal and financial measures which are used to encourage adoption of particular technical standards.[40]

The system of prior notification was also extended by a separate instrument, Decision 3052/95/EC,[41] to cover more general measures which derogate from the principle of free movement of goods. A similar system of notification applies to that contained in Directive 83/189/EC wherever a Member State places prevents a good from being marketed

---

observations in 87 cases and the Member States in 110. EC Commission, *General Report on the Activities of the European Union 1996* (1997, OOPEC, Luxembourg) para 111.

38 Supra n.36, Article 9 (1). This obligation does not apply to measures which have to be adopted for urgent reasons, occasioned by serious and unforeseeable circumstances, relating to the protection of public health or safety, protection of animals or preservation of plants'. Ibid., Article 9 (7).

39 A Commission report discovered a total of 4340 national measures were adopted in 1993 and 1994, of which 30% fell outside the scope of the Directive, COM (96) 286.

40 Supra n.36, Article 1(9).

41 OJ 1995, L 321/1.

or requires that it be modified before it be placed on the market. The Commission is notified and in turn disseminates the information not just to national governments but on a Community-wide basis.

In the early years notification of draft measures which clearly fell within the Directive was also poor. In the first five years notifications amounted to about two hundred a year. Of these, one Member State alone, Germany, accounted for over a third of the notifications.[42] Matters have improved, with about five hundred draft standards being currently notified to the Commission each year.[43] The Commission still considers that the duty of prior notification is being insufficiently observed. Part of the problem has been the sheer volume of national standards drafted every year whose monitoring places a considerable strain upon Commission resources. In this respect the Court has provided an alternate sanction applicable through national courts, namely that any standard which a Member State has failed to notify can not be enforced against a trader.

Case C-194/94 CIA Security International SA v Signalson SA and Securitel SPRL [1996] ECR I-2201

CIA Security brought a libel action against Signalson and Securitel who had claimed it marketed an alarm system which had not received the required authorisation under Belgian law. The latter brought a counteraction restraining CIA Security from carrying on its business on the grounds that it was marketing an unauthorised alarm system. The Belgian requirement of prior authorisation had not been notified to the Commission under Directive 83/189. The national court asked, *inter alia*, what the effect of non-notification was upon the Belgian law.

40. The first point which must be made is that Directive 83/189 is designed to protect, by means of preventive control, freedom of movement for goods, which is one of the

---

42 *EC Commission Report on the Operation of Directive 83/189/EEC laying down a procedure for the provision of information in the field of technical standards and regulations,* COM (88) 722 final, esp. paras 107-125.

43 523 were notified in 1996 and 3,853 have been notified since the coming into force of the Directive. EC Commission, *General Report on the Activities of the European Union 1996* (1997, OOPEC, Luxembourg) para 111.

foundations of the Community. This control serves a useful purpose in that technical regulations covered by the directive may constitute obstacles to trade in goods between Member States, such obstacles being permissible only if they are necessary to satisfy compelling public interest requirements. The control is also effective in that all draft technical regulations covered by the directive must be notified and, except in the case of those regulations whose urgency justifies an exception, their adoption or entry into force must be suspended during the periods laid down by Article 9.

41. The notification and the period of suspension therefore afford the Commission and the other Member States an opportunity to examine whether the draft regulations in question create obstacles to trade contrary to the EC Treaty or obstacles which are to be avoided through the adoption of common or harmonized measures and also to propose amendments to the national measures envisaged. This procedure also enables the Commission to propose or adopt Community rules regulating the matter dealt with by the envisaged measure.

.....

48. ... As pointed out above, it is undisputed that the aim of the directive is to protect freedom of movement for goods by means of preventive control and that the obligation to notify is essential for achieving such Community control. The effectiveness of Community control will be that much greater if the directive is interpreted as meaning that breach of the obligation to notify constitutes a substantial procedural defect such as to render the technical regulations in question inapplicable to individuals.

49. That interpretation of the Directive is in accordance with the judgment given in Case 380/87 *Enichem Base and Others v Comune di Cinisello Balsamo* [1989] ECR 2491, paragraphs 19 to 24. In that judgment, in which the Court ruled on the obligation for Member States to communicate to the Commission national draft rules falling within the scope of an Article of Council Directive 75/442/EEC of 15 July 1975 on waste (OJ 1975 L 194, p. 39), the Court held that neither the wording nor the purpose of the provision in question provided any support for the view that failure by the Member States to observe their obligation to give notice in itself rendered unlawful the rules thus adopted. In this regard, the Court expressly considered that the provision in question was confined to imposing an obligation to give prior notice which did not make entry into force of the envisaged rules subject to the Commission's agreement or lack of opposition and which did not lay down the procedure for Community control of the drafts in question. The Court therefore concluded that the provision under examination concerned relations between the Member States and the Commission but that it did not afford individuals any right capable of being infringed in the event of breach by a Member State of its obligation to give prior notice of its draft regulations to the Commission.

50. In the present case, however, the aim of the directive is not simply to inform the Commission. As already found in paragraph 41 of this judgment, the directive has, precisely, a more general aim of eliminating or restricting obstacles to trade, to inform other States of technical regulations envisaged by a State, to give the Commission and the other Member States time to react and to propose amendments for lessening restrictions to the free movement of goods arising from the envisaged measure and to afford the Commission time to propose a harmonizing directive. Moreover, the wording of Articles 8 and 9 of Directive 83/189 is clear in that those Articles provide for a procedure for Community control of draft national regulations and the date of their entry into force is made subject to the Commission's agreement or lack of opposition.

51. Finally, it must be examined whether, as the United Kingdom in particular observes, there are reasons specific to Directive 83/189 which preclude it from being interpreted as rendering technical regulations adopted in breach of the directive inapplicable to third parties.

52. In this regard, it has already been observed that if such regulations were not enforceable against third parties, this would create a legislative vacuum in the national legal system in question and could therefore entail serious drawbacks, particularly where safety regulations were concerned.

53. This argument cannot be accepted. A Member State may use the urgent-case procedure provided for in Article 9(3) of Directive 83/189 where, for reasons defined by that provision, it considers it necessary to prepare technical regulations in a very short space of time which must be enacted and brought into force immediately without any consultations being possible.

54. In view of the foregoing considerations, it must be concluded that Directive 83/189 is to be interpreted as meaning that breach of the obligation to notify renders the technical regulations concerned inapplicable, so that they are unenforceable against individuals.

CIA is likely to lead to a better system of prior notification. It is not without its problems, however. In particular, it creates the danger of 'regulatory gaps'. The technical standards in question do not merely restrict trade. They serve other purposes such as the protection of the consumer, public health or the environment. If a standard is disapplied because of a Member State's failure to comply with its procedural obligations, the loser is not likely to be the Member State but the public interest that standard was intended to protect.

c. The Limits of Mutual Recognition

An early critique argued that mutual recognition suggested a false equivalence between products which might result in a reduction in consumer protection. If certain food stuffs are brought onto the market which lack even the essential characteristics of those in other Member States - i.e. ice cream which does not contain milk or sausages that do not contain meat - the consumer was likely to be increasingly confused or misled as to what he or she was buying.[44] In practice, this has not happened as a result of a far more devastating critique. This notes of the principle does no more than establish a weak presumption of equivalence which can be easily rebutted by the host Member State. In practice, the lack of trust or convergence between national administrations has resulted in mutual recognition being infrequently applied and being unable to act as a barrier against increasing centralisation.

Majone, G. *Mutual Trust, Credible Commitments and the Evolution of the Rules of the Single Market* EUI Working Paper RSC No. 95/1 (1995, European University Institutute, Florence) 16-17[45]

Advocates of mutual recognition often do not seem to realize how demanding the principle is. An American scholar has noted that the mutual recognition approach may require a higher degree of comity among Member States than the commerce clause of the U.S. Constitution requires among individual states. The commerce clause has been interpreted by the U.S. Supreme Court to allow each state to insist on its own product quality standards - unless the subject-matter has been preempted by federal legislation, or unless the state standards would unduly burden interstate commerce.

The crucial importance of trust between national administrations is demonstrated by the failure of earlier attempts to harmonize national regulations for the approval of new medical drugs. The old EC procedure included a set of harmonized criteria for testing new products, and the mutual recognition of toxicological and clinical

---

44 Brouwer, O. 'Free Movement of Foodstuffs and Quality Requirements: Has the Commission got it Wrong?' (1988) 25 *CMLRev* 237, 249.

45 For more detailed analysis on the case-study of pharmaceuticals see Kaufer, E. 'The Regulation of New Product Development in the Drug Industry' in Majone, G. (ed.) *Deregulation or Re-regulation* (1990, London, Pinter); Hancher, L. 'The European Pharmaceutical Market: Problems of Partial Harmonisation' (1990) 15 *ELRev* 9.

trials, provided they were conducted according to EC rules. In order to speed up the process of mutual recognition, a 'multi-state drug application procedure' (MSAP) was introduced in 1975. Under the MSAP, a company that had received a marketing authorization from the regulatory agency of a Member State could ask for mutual recognition of that approval by at least five other countries. The agencies of the countries nominated by the company had to approve or raise objections within 120 days. In case of objections, the Committee for Proprietary Medicinal Products (CPMP) - a group which includes experts from Member States and Commission representatives - had to be notified. The CPMP would express its opinion within 60 days, and could be overruled by the national agency that had raised objections.

The procedure did not work well. Actual decision times were much longer than those prescribed by the 1975 Directive, and national regulators did not appear to be bound either by decisions of other regulatory bodies, or by the opinions of the CPMP. Because of these disappointing results, the procedure was revised in 1983. Now only two countries had to be nominated in order to be able to apply for a multi-state approval. But even the new procedure did not succeed in streamlining the approval process since national regulators continued to raise objections against each other almost routinely. These difficulties finally induced the Commission to propose the establishment of a European Agency for the Evaluation of Medicinal Products and the creation of a new centralized Community procedure, compulsory for biotechnology products and certain types of veterinary medicines, and available on an optional basis for other products, leading to a Community authorization. Both the agency and the centralized procedure have been established by Council Regulation No 2309/93 of 22 July 1993.

The problems posed for the single market by a lack of trust were predicted at a relatively early stage by the Commission. It recognised there were three situations in which lack of trust might undermine mutual recognition. First, EC legislation could not require mutual recognition if the standards designated inspection bodies had to meet were not equivalent. Secondly, in areas where there was no EC legislation manufacturers could not benefit from mutual recognition if the authorities in the host State did not have full confidence in the credibility of the body that carried out tests in the home State. Finally, purchasers had to have faith in the certification procedures in exporting States if they were not to insist in a product being certified twice, once in the country of origin and once in the country of destination.[46]

---

46 The 'Global Approach to Conformity Assessment' was adopted by Council Resolution of December 21, 1989, OJ 1990 C 10/1.

EC Commission Communication, 'A Global Approach to Certification and Testing'[47]

The necessity for a global approach to certification, inspection and testing thus arise out of this basic need to create conditions that are conducive to confidence and, to that end, to bring the structures and procedures involved in those activities more closely into line.

III. Measures Necessary for the Global Approach

A. Action for Basic Structures

The basic structures for the evaluation of conformity are the bodies responsible for certification and inspection of the testing laboratories, and the manufacturers' quality systems. The aim is to make these structures as homogenous, transparent and credible as possible throughout the Community, since this is a precondition for the proper functioning of conformity assessment, both compulsory and voluntary.

To this end the Commission took steps, as it had announced in its White Paper on completing the internal market, to encourage the drafting of technical guidelines setting out the criteria to be used when evaluating the competence of operators in the field of conformity assessment. ...

B. Action on Regulations

The conformity assessment procedures in Community regulations must take account of the considerable progress made and the new mechanisms available (quality assurance, accreditation, standardized assessment criteria and so on).

A global approach which involves drawing up a set of modules for the various operations is designed to allow the Community legislator to lay down the most appropriate procedures in the harmonizing directives, using what has already been done in the field of European and international standardization as a basis. The fundamental principles of the modular approach are as follows:

- the directives must define the limits of the choice of procedures open to the manufacturer for ensuring compliance with the essential requirements;
- the affixing of the CE mark on the products is the tangible sign of their conformity to Community rules;
- the bodies involved in the conformity assessment procedures as designated by the Member States are notified to the Commission and the other Member States in accordance with the common assessment criteria.

---

47 OJ 1989 C 267/3.

C. The Need for a European Infrastructure for Certification and Testing

... the efforts to remove barriers to trade that arise from the existence of national voluntary certification arrangements will have to be accompanied by incentives for cooperation between organizations and laboratories at European level - as was the case in fact with standardization - with a view to the establishment of joint systems for certification and the recognition of test results.

Within this overall framework a twofold approach has been adopted. In areas where there is EC legislation a series of 'modular' procedures have been established to assess whether a product conforms to a particular standard.[48] A series of 'modules' are set out - each of which sets out broad criteria to be applied to a distinct phase of the production and design process. If these criteria are met, the product is entitled to carry the CE mark and to be marketed in all other Member States without further approval being required. In areas where there is no EC legislation in place, provision is made for mutual recognition agreements to be made between assessment bodies. These agreements have to be approved by a pan-European certification body - the European Organisation for Testing and Certification (EOTC).

The global approach has met only limited success. In surveys carried out for the Commission in 1996 it was found that the EOTC had been unsuccessful in developing mutual recognition arrangements. Furthermore, wherever serious health and safety issues arose mutual recognition worked poorly in the absence of formal arrangements.[49] In 1997 the Commission proposed to remedy this by suggesting more centralised mechanisms such as joint inspection schemes and more detailed inspection procedures.[50]

---

48 Directive 93/465/EC concerning the modules for the various phases of the conformity assessment procedures and the rules for the affixing and use of the CE conformity marking, OJ 1993, L 220/23. On adaptation of various Directives to the modular approach see Directive 93/68/EC, OJ 1993, L 220/1.

49 Atkins, W. *Technical Barriers to Trade* (1996, Single Market Review Series, OOPEC, Luxembourg).

50 EC Commission, *Action Plan for the Single Market* CSE (97) 1 final, 8.

iii. The Harmonisation of Only 'Essential Requirements'

The perceived advantages of limiting Council intervention to harmonising merely essential health and safety requirements over the 'old approach' are described below.

Pelkmans, J. 'Regulation and the Single Market: An Economic Perspective' in Siebert, H. (ed.) *The Completion of the Internal Market* (1989, Mohr, Tübingen) 91, 106

Procedures are less time-consuming and laborious, uniformity merely relates to the 'essential' requirements, unanimity is replaced by qualified majority voting, harmonization of technical regulations (at the public level) now benefits from - and is no longer inconsistent with - standardization (at the private level), European standards are currently promoted so that reference can actually be made to European standards, implementation in the laws of the member states is facilitated by the focus on essential requirements, and, finally, the lack of political interest at ministerial level is overcome by the concentration on health and safety objectives rather than the technicalities of product engineering as well as by the fact that the new approach can group many thousands of similar products together in terms of their health/safety/environmental properties (e.g. the Toys Directive, adopted in 1987, is estimated to apply to approximately 55,000 varieties of toys!).

In an earlier piece Pelkmans suggested these immediate advantages might in turn lead to more considerable long-term advantages.

Pelkmans. J. 'The New Approach to Technical Harmonization and Standardization' (1987) 25 *Journal of Common Market Studies* 257, 260

In the first place the new approach is linked to the issue of *improvement in the competitiveness of European industry*. Harmonization and standardization are still viewed in many branches of industry or in individual companies as a potential threat to the market position or a cause of unwanted adaption costs. Except for extremely specific conditions in a large market, however, protectionism leads in dues course to a worsening of international competitiveness.

If, on the other hand, standard quality is such that penetration into many foreign markets is possible, then standardization can be seen in quite another light. Because specialization is becoming ever more refined, and scale effects in many cases form an important determinant of the export position, the quality approach offers a much better perspective, not only for industry and the consumer but also for the economy as a whole. Seen in this way, emphasis will come to lie on quality and international acceptance of the standard, two matters which - except in the case of far-fetched protectionism - are closely connected. The new approach stimulates this because it aims at making market penetration easier and at the same time at pursuing a quality policy.

.....

Secondly, it can be expected that the workload on some Commission services will be considerably reduced by the new approach and that excessively detailed regulations will gradually become of lesser importance. The Commission has already withdrawn various draft directives which were laid before the Council in the context of the traditional approach. The reduction in the Commission's workload is welcome because attention can then be given to more urgent problems in the field of technical trade barriers which have a more direct and greater effect on the free intra-EC movement of goods. ...

.....

Reduction in the Commission's workload can also lead to more attention being given to implementation and enforcement questions in the Member States. For many years responses have only been made to complaints and the question is whether even these have been pursued adequately.

The principal difference between the 'new' strategy and the 'old' strategy was that EC legislation is granted only a residual role, merely providing minimum guarantees ensuring some measure of equivalence between the differing national legal regimes in the Member States. Like mutual recognition, the strategy is there also being a degree of mutual trust between administrations. This lack of trust has resulted in the 'new approach' being less widespread than was perhaps expected, with its covering only 17% of industrial input.[51] The passage of time, indeed, suggests the resilience of the 'old approach' which accounts for 30% of

---

51 EC Commission, *The Impact and Effectiveness of the Single Market* COM (96) 520 final, 17.

industrial output.[52] This has led in certain areas, notably product safety[53] and insurance,[54] to EC law having the re-regulatory effect of imposing more comprehensive requirements than existed in many Member States.[55]

iv. The Development of Technical Standards by Private Bodies

The delegation of standard-making powers to private standardisation bodies such as CEN or CENELEC was seen as having two advantages. Under the traditional approach there was the danger of a gap opening up between the harmonisation process and existing industrial standards, with the result that industry would be subjected to needless adjustment costs in order to comply with EC technical standards that did not necessarily offer an increased degree of protection. Secondly, as industry was more directly affected by technical standards, it had a greater expertise in this field than public servants. Delegating the process of preparing these standards to industry would not only lift the work burden from the Commission but also result in higher quality standards. The process has, however, also been criticised for its lack of checks and balances.

Lauwaars, R. 'The "Model Directive" on Technical Harmonization' in Bieber, R., Dehousse, R., Pinder, J. & Weiler, J. *1992: One European Market* (1988, Nomos, Baden-Baden) 151, 167-168

... The 'new approach' also raises some questions as to the delimitation of responsibilities.

---

52 Ibid., 16.

53 Joerges, C. 'European Economic Law, the Nation-State and the Maastricht Treaty' 29, 45 in Dehousse, R. (ed) *Europe After Maastricht: An Ever Closer Union?* (1994, Law Books in Europe, Munich).

54 Roth, W-H. 'Article 59 EEC Treaty and Its Implications for Conflicts Law in the Field of Insurance Contracts' in Facilides & d'Oliveira, H-J. (eds.) *International Insurance Contract Law in the European Community* (1994, Kluwer, Dordrecht).

55 See generally Ogus, A. 'Quality Control for European Regulation' (1995) 2 *Maastricht Journal of European & Comparative Law* 325.

In principle the Council is responsible for the establishment of the 'essential safety requirements' and the European standardization body for the adoption of 'technical specifications'. The application of the latter prescriptions is subjected to either EC verification or EC surveillance on an EC declaration of conformity (as appropriate). This 'mixture' of public and private rule-making gives rise to two kinds of problems, namely:
(I) the relationship between public authorities and industry (*problem of liability*);
(II) the relationship between the Community legislator and the European Parliament/national parliaments (*problem of political responsibility*).
(III) Liability for defective products is the subject of Council Directive 85/374/EEC of 25 July 1985 (O.J. 1985 L 210/29). According to Article 7(d) of the Directive the producer is liable unless he proves 'that the defect is due to compliance of the product with mandatory requirements issued by the public authorities'. The conformity with European or national standards will not prevent the Courts from establishing liability; apart from the standards being non-binding, a product which complies with these standards will only be 'presumed' to fulfil the essential safety requirements.
(II) Although the European Parliament in a resolution of 16 October 1980 urged the Commission and the Council substantially to increase cooperation between the Commission, CEN or CENELEC and the standards institutions of the Community Member States,' it has not, up to now, adopted a similar position as regards the 'new approach'. This approach, however, removes a part of Community law-making from European or national parliamentary control; the national parliaments of the Member States will also lose influence at the stage of implementation.

In general I would plead for a clear distinction of responsibilities between private industry and public authorities. A blurring of responsibilities should be avoided. If not, on the one hand, political institutions will be able to 'hide' behind private activities and, on the other hand, private associations - which are not responsible for the general interest, but only for their private interest - will be asked to undertake inappropriate tasks.

In terms of the creation of European standards, the system has only been a partial success. Whilst the output of CEN and CENELEC was six and a half times as great in 1989, compared to its output in 1982, the number of European standards created was still small in relation to the number of national standards existing. In 1989, for example, there were about 1250 European standards. In Germany alone, there were estimated to be about 20,000 national standards. The Commission found in its Green Paper on European Standardisation that the decision-making and consultative procedures of these organisations were often slow and that information on European standards was not made available in a clear and comprehensive manner to European industry. The result is that there is still no universal coverage, and industry is often unaware of the standards that do exist.[56]

V. Public Intervention and the Single Market

The 'new approach' addresses in quite a sophisticated manner the relationship between the EC and national legislatures. It fails to direct itself, however, to the more difficult question of the relationship between the State and the market.[57] The question of public intervention is one that the EC cannot avoid. Albeit in an often fragmented and ad hoc manner, the EC has, therefore, remodelled national regulatory cultures through introducing new influences, and, in so doing, has helped shape the contours of that relationship.[58]

i. The Single Market as Incipient Ordoliberal Economic Constitution

Freedom to trade and the provision of a system of undistorted competition are to be the heart of the single market. Attempts have therefore been drawn, notably in the German literature, to portray the single market as an incipient 'economic constitution' which can be used

---

56 EC Commission, *Green Paper on the Development of European Standardisation* COM (90) 456 final, 17-18. See also EC Commission, *Making the Most of the Internal Market: Strategic Programme* COM (93) 632 final. The average European standard currently takes five years to come into being. EC Commission, *The Impact and Effectiveness of the Single Market* COM (96) 520, 17.

57 Dehousse, R. 'Integration v Regulation? On the Dynamics of Regulation in the European Community' (1993) 30 *JCMS* 383.

58 In many areas, therefore, national governments have responded to this by trying to bring the EC legislature to adopt their style of regulation. Héritier, A., Knill, C. & Mingers, S. *Ringing the Changes in Europe: Regulatory Competition and Redefinition of the State. Britain, France and Germany* (1996, De Gruyter, Berlin).

to curb and rationalise State intervention in the market place.[59] This term owes its origins to the Ordoliberal School, which originated in Freiburg in the 1930s. The starting point of this School was that society had to be organised around certain constitutive principles, which should seek to preserve individual freedoms. Within this schema, economic freedoms, such as the right to transact or the right to own property, were as central as political freedoms. Just as civil and political rights were protected in a constitution, so too should economic freedoms. Failure to do so would leave either unprotected and subject to arbitrary action. For this purpose, certain regulatory principles should be introduced to curb the exercise of power by organs of the State.

Gerber, D. 'Constitutionalizing the Economy: German Neo-liberalism, Competition Law and the "New Europe"' (1994) 42 *American Journal of Comparative Law* 25, 45-48

According to the ordoliberals and here Franz Böhm's contributions were particularly influential, an economic constitution is 'a comprehensive decision (Gesamtentscheidung) concerning the nature (Art) and form of the process of socio-economic cooperation'. It represents a political decision about the kind of economy a community wants in the same way that the political community represents basic decisions about the kind of political system a community wants. According to Böhm, 'Only a focus on this idea makes it possible to achieve truly dependable and cogent principles for the interpretation of the parts of private and public law'.

This concept of an economic constitution intertwined legal and economic perspectives and discourses. It turned the core idea of classic liberalism - that the economy should be divorced from law and politics - on its head by arguing that the characteristics and the effectiveness of the economy *depended* on its relationship to the political and legal systems. The ordoliberals recognized that fundamental political choices created the basic structure of an economic system.

D. Ordnungspolitik: The Untranslatable Soul of Ordoliberalism

The choice of an economic constitution could be effective, the ordoliberals said, if the legal system were structured to implement that choice. When a political unit chose a

59 On the EC as an economic liberal constitution see Constantinesco, V. 'La Constitution Économique Européenne' (1977) *RTDE* 244; Streit, M. & Musler, W. 'The Economic Constitution of the European Community: From "Rome" to "Maastricht"' (1995) 1 *ELJ* 5.

transaction economy in its economic constitution, for example, that choice required the development of governmental policies designed to create and maintain that system. This the ordoliberals called 'Ordnungspolitik' (order based policy), and it was the soul of their programme.

1. Implementing the Constitutional Decision

According to the ordoliberal conception of Ordnungspolitik, individual government decisions should both flow from and be constrained by, the principles embodied in the economic constitution. The economic constitution is to set out a framework of principles and ideals, and governmental policy is to implement these principles and seek to attain these ideals. Where the economic constitution calls for a transaction economy, Ordnungspolitik demands that the legal system be configured so as to create and maintain the conditions of complete competition which would allow that type of economic system to function most effectively. In effect, law is to be used to implement the model of complete competition.

For the ordoliberals, this meant that economic knowledge had to be translated into normative language. In order to establish policy based on the economic constitution, Böhm wrote, 'the body of doctrine (Lehrgebäude) of classical economic philosophy had to be translated from the language of economics into the language of legal science'. The idea was that economic science would describe the conditions of complete competition, and this information would provide the standards for legal decision-making.

2. Law's Roles

In addition to this substantive dimension, Ordnungspolitik also had a process dimension. In order for a transaction economy to achieve its goals, governmental involvement must itself have certain characteristics and play certain roles. Above all, government could act only to implement the general norms or laws that derived from the economic constitution. Law would provide basic principles of economic conduct, and government officials would have no discretion to intervene in the economy except for the purpose of enforcing those principles.

This conception of the role of law is critical to the entire Ordoliberal programme. The ordoliberal emphasized that Ordnungspolitik did not permit discretionary governmental intervention in the economy; rather, it required the opposite - legal principles that directed but also constrained government conduct! ... Decisions about the legal environment of the market would thus be subject to the economic constitution in the same way that political decisions were subject to the political constitution. As such, they could not 'interfere' with the operations of the competitive system because they were, by definition, consistent with that system.

Ordnungspolitik represented an adaptation and transfer of ideas from liberal political theory to the economy. Its roots are in the German political theory of the *Rechtsstaat*, or 'law-based state'. Developed in the nineteenth century, this conception of the state focused on the dependability and certainty of the law as a bulwark against abuses of power. It was a means of establishing control over the discretionary power of the sovereign ('If we can't reduce the actual power of the sovereign, we can convince him that he is subject to law'). Central to this image of law is its neutrality and objectivity: the law must be outside the discretion of those wielding governmental power. The state has to provide a basic level of 'legal security' (*Rechtssicherheit*) by assuring that law is knowledgable, dependable and not subject to manipulation. The ordoliberals used these ideas as the basis for their concept of *Ordnungspolitik*.

3. The Principle of Indirect Regulation

The ordoliberals referred to Ordnungspolitik as 'indirect regulation'. Government did not direct the processes of the economy but merely established forms or structural conditions within which these processes could function effectively. For the ordoliberals, one of the benefits of this concept of regulation was that it avoided ad hoc governmental decision-making. If governmental activity relating to the economy was not subject to the ordering function of an economic constitution, they said, it would be beset by problems of inconsistency and contradiction. The consequences of any individual action were likely to be counteracted by some other actions, and the probable result would be inefficiency, confusion and ultimately, economic chaos. Ordnungspolitik confronted these problems by requiring the organization of governmental action around the principles of the economic constitution.

The concept of indirect regulation was supported by both 'constitutive' and 'regulative' principles. Constitutive principles were the fundamental principles of economic policy for a transaction economy. Their function was to establish the basic 'form' of the economy. For Eucken, they included the principles of monetary stability (the need to maintain a stable monetary unit), open markets, private property, contractual freedom, liability (legal responsibility for one's acts) and policy consistency (the need to avoid frequent changes in economic policy). Regulative principles flowed from constitutive principles and were bound by them, but were more specific and served to maintain the effectiveness of the constitutive principles. For example, the all-important principles of competition law were regulative principles that flowed primarily from the constitutive postulates of open markets and contractual freedom.

This conception of the roles of law in relation to the economy reflected the ordoliberals' deep distrust of the executive branch of government and their confidence in the legislative and judicial branches. In the ordoliberal system, the legislature would make the fundamental decisions about the content of the economic constitution and translate the economic model into normative language. The judiciary would then be responsible for assuring that specific governmental acts were consistent with these basic norms. The executive branch had little power in this scheme; administrators were to follow the dictates of the legislature, and, at least in principle, there was minimal room for discretion.

Implementing the ordoliberal program required a comprehensive view of a community's legal, political and economic systems. For the ordoliberals, all governmental decisions that might affect the economy should flow from the economic constitution. They repeatedly emphasized the need for an 'integrated policy perspective

(*Ganzheitsbetrachtung*)' in which each individual decision had to be understood as part of a greater whole from which it received its meaning and effect. Only thus could the program function effectively. Monetary, social, labour and trade policy, for example, all had to flow from the same basic principles and support each other.

The portrayal of the EC as an 'economic constitution' has increasingly come under fire for a number of reasons. As guardians of the economic freedoms, judges are placed at the epicentre of the political process. The vision shows a faith in the neutrality of the judicial process and the determinacy of norms that many academics in the late twentieth century would question. Secondly, the analogy it draws between economic freedoms and political freedoms is controversial. The language of individual freedoms marginalises collective interests such as environmental policy or economic and social cohesion.

Equally tellingly, within the EC context, it can be argued that the economic constitution analogy provides an inaccurate description of the development of the EC. It fails to explain why special regimes apply to agriculture, public undertakings, and trade relations with third States,[60] or why market freedoms are not applied with the same rigour to EC Institutions as Member States.[61] Finally, the language of economic rights is insufficiently differentiated to deal with complex questions such as risk allocation or multi-level governance. It suggests a series of inflexible, black and white answers with little suggestive value for the dilemma of mutual accommodation or for identifying the responsibilities of the different actors.

---

60 Ehlermann, C-D. 'Comment on Manfred Streit and Werner Mussler: 'The Economic Constitution of the European Community - From "Rome" to "Maastricht"' (1995) 1 *ELJ* 84.

61 Case C-63/89 *Les Assurances du Crédit and Compagnie Belge d'Assurance v Council and Commission* [1991] ECR I-1799; Case C-51/93 *Meyhui v Schott* [1994] ECR I-3879.

ii. The Single Market and Economic Law

Perhaps the most innovative analysis of recent years has come from Joerges. He argues that the single market has served to 'denationalize' the economy. It must therefore be treated as a form of economic law whose problems are no different from those faced within a purely national context.

Joerges, C. 'European Economic Law, the Nation-State and the Maastricht Treaty' in Dehousse, R. (ed), *Europe After Maastricht: An Ever Closer Union?* (1994, Law Books in Europe, Munich) 29,48

Economic law mediates between functional imperatives and normative claims, between the autonomy of societal actors and regulatory interventions. The generation of institutional structures capable of absorbing interest conflicts and ensuring the 'public responsibility' of economic systems does not follow from the transformation of economic rationality by some invisible hand or from legislative activities alone. Courts and administrative bodies, organized interests and all sorts of societal actors participate in the formation of institutions and interest arrangements. The legitimacy of economic law rests upon this very process of reconciling the autonomy of individuals with societal demands through constitutionally structured political processes. This dependency of economic law on the whole of legal and political culture is the core problem faced by the Europeanization process: European economic law faces the same type of choices as does any national legal system. The regulatory options it chooses are not distinctly European. It is not possible to shield it from 'political' debates by basing it upon preconceived economic or technocratic rationality criteria. Its true problem is the discrepancy between its 'political' substance and its 'immature' political infrastructure.

Joerges argues that two instruments have traditionally been used to legitimise EC economic law - the principle of unanimity and the limitation of EC powers. Joerges considers neither principle carries out an effective legitimising function. Unanimity in the Council presupposes that governmental officials effectively represent the national interest - a premise that is distinctly shaky. He considers, furthermore, that it is not possible to limit EC competencies to narrow economic objectives as this denies it its function of mediating between economic objectives and regulatory concerns. He thus suggests three ways in which the legitimacy gap could be lessened:

- differentiated integration between different societal subsystems. The EC might proceed at a faster pace in, say, competition law than, say, insurance law. By setting priorities, the EC might be more successful in providing comprehensive policies in those areas;

- 'juridification' of Community regulatory activities. In what amounts to a call for institutional innovation, Joerges suggests greater transparency, greater political accountability and judicial control, greater access for societal actors and more 'horizontal interaction' between national agencies;

- acceptance of imperfect legal integration. EC law should try to coordinate rather than override national law. Intervention would only take place where essential interests were at stake, and harmonisation would be less than detailed.

The questions Joerges raises are thus complex, problematic ones. Even within his piece, however, the genus of future problems and tensions begin to emerge. For example, is there not a tension between, on the one hand, suggesting the Community should prioritise in order to ensure comprehensive policies and, on the other, suggesting Community legislation should not be detailed and have only a coordinating function? Similarly, the idea that societal subsystems should integrate at different paces, whilst attractive, is at odds with the neo-functionalist concept that the interrelatedness of society and the economy results not only in spillover, but that the lack of integration in one area will create a dysfunction in other more integrated areas. The development of horizontal relationships between national courts, whilst having many advantages, threatens to marginalise the 'vertical' relationship between national courts and the Court of Justice.

VI. The European Union as a Regulatory State

The EU does not participate significantly in certain areas classically undertaken by States, such as crime control or redistribution. The brunt of its work is, instead, regulatory, involving 'sustained and focused control' over socially valued activities, in particular market activities. From this empirical evidence academics have suggested that it is a new form of 'regulatory State'.[62]

Majone, G. 'The Rise of the Regulatory State in Europe' (1994) 17 *West European Politics* 77, 85-87

Apart from competition rules and measures necessary to the integration of national markets, few regulatory policies or programmes are explicitly mentioned in the Treaty of Rome. Transport and energy policies which could have given rise to significant regulatory activities, have remained until lately largely undeveloped. On the other hand, agriculture, fisheries, regional development, social programmes and aid to developing countries, which together account for more than 80 per cent of the Community budget are mostly distributive or redistributive rather than regulatory in nature.

This budget of almost ECU 47 billion represents less than 1.3 per cent of the gross domestic product (GDP) of the Community and less than 4 per cent of the central government spending of member states. Given such limited resources, how can one explain the continuous growth of Community regulation, even in the absence of explicit legal mandates? Take the case of environmental protection, an area not even mentioned by the Treaty of Rome. In the two decades from 1967 to 1987, when the Single European Act finally recognised the authority of the Community to legislate in this area, almost 200 directives, regulations, and decisions were introduced by the Commission. Moreover, the rate of growth of environmental regulation appears to have been largely unaffected by the political vicissitudes, budgetary crises, and recurrent waves of Europessimism of the 1970s and early 1980s. From the single directive on preventing risks by testing of 1969

---

62 Majone, G. 'The European Community between Social Policy and Social Regulation' (1993) 31 *JCMS* 153; Majone, G. 'The European Community: An "Independent Fourth Branch of Government"' in Bruggemeyer, G. (ed) *Verfassungen für ein ziviles Europa* (1994, Nomos, Baden-Baden); Dehousse, R., Joerges, C., Majone, G., Snyder, F. & Everson, M. *Europe after 1992 - New Regulatory Strategies* (1992, EUI Working Paper No. 92/31, Florence); Wilks, S. 'Regulatory Compliance and Capitalist Diversity in Europe' (1996) 3 *JEPP* 536; McGowan, F. & Wallace, H. 'Towards a European Regulatory State' (1996) 3 *JEPP* 560; Majone, G. (ed.) *Regulating Europe* (1997, Routledge, London).

we pass to 10 directives/decisions in 1975, 13 in 1980, 20 in 1982, 23 in 1984, 24 in 1985 and 17 in the six months immediately preceding passage of the Single European Act.

The case of environmental regulation is particularly striking, partly because of the political salience of environmental issues, but it is by no means unique. The volume and depth of Community regulation in the areas of consumer product safety, medical drug testing, banking and financial services and, of course, competition law is hardly less impressive. In fact, the hundreds of regulatory measures proposed by the Commission's White Paper on the completion of the internal market represent only the acceleration of a trend set in motion decades ago. The continuous growth of supranational regulation is not easily explained by traditional theories of Community policy making. At most, such theories suggest that the serious implementation gap that exists in the European Community may make it easier for the member states, and their representatives in the Council, to accept Commission proposals which they have not serious intention of applying. The main limitation of this argument is that it fails to differentiate between areas where policy development has been slow and uncertain (for example, transport, energy or research) and areas such as environmental protection where significant policy development has taken place even in the absence of a clear legal basis.

Moreover, existing theories of Union policy making do not usually draw any clear distinction between regulatory and other types of policies. Now, an important characteristic of regulatory policy making is the limited influence of budgetary limitations on the activities of regulators. The size of non-regulatory, direct-expenditure programmes is constrained by budgetary appropriations and, ultimately, by the size of government tax revenues. In contrast, the real costs of most regulatory programmes are borne directly by the firms and individuals who have to comply with them. Compared with these costs, the resources needed to produce the regulations are trivial.

It is difficult to overstate the significance of this structural difference between regulatory policies and policies involving the direct expenditure of public funds. The distinction is particularly important for the analysis of Community policy making, since not only the economic, but also the political and administrative costs of enforcing EC regulations are borne by the member states. As already noted, the financial resources of the Community go, for the most part, to the Common Agricultural Policy and to a handful of distributive programmes. The remaining resources are insufficient to support large-scale initiatives in areas such as industrial policy, energy, research, or technological innovation. Given this constraint, the only way for the Commission to increase its role was to expand the scope of its regulatory activities.

Majone's strengths are that he seeks both to explain the integration process and to place it within an ideological setting. The integration process has thus arisen through a series of institutional incentives, whose context is the increase in risk brought about by industrialisation. This placed strains on traditional structures of government, as considerable expertise is needed to deal with risk, and legislative procedures are often too cumbersome to react swiftly enough to it. A need thus developed for new arms of government such as regulatory agencies and the EC.[63]

There is much about Majone's sophisticated analysis which is persuasive. It has been criticised on two fronts. The first is that its characterisation of the EU is essentially a technocratic one. Experience suggests, however, that technocratic efficiency alone is insufficient for any Institution to garner legitimacy.[64] The second criticism is that the use of institutional incentives is too narrow a base to explain the integration process, and pays insufficient attention to the role of social movements or 'belief systems'.[65]

Further Reading

Barents, R. 'The Community and the Unity of the Common Market' (1991) 30 *German Yearbook of International Law* 9

Bieber, R. 'On the Mutual Completion of Overlapping Legal Systems: The Case of the European Communities and the National Legal Orders' (1988) 13 *European Law Review* 147

Burrows, N. 'Harmonization of Technical Standards: Reculer Pour Mieux Sauter' (1990) 53 *Modern Law Review* 597

Dehousse, R. '1992 and Beyond: the Institutional Dimension of the Internal Market Programme' (1989/1) *Legal Issues of European Integration* 109

Everson, M. 'Independent Agencies: Hierarchy Beaters' (1995) 1 *European Law Journal* 204

63 See also Everson, M. 'Independent Agencies: Hierarchy Beaters' (1995) 1 *ELJ* 204.

64 Dehousse, R. 'Regulation by networks in the European Community: the role of European agencies' (1997) 4 *JEPP* 246, 258; Shapiro, M. 'The Problems of Independent Agencies in the United States and the European Union' (1997) 4 *JEPP* 276, 286-287.

65 Caporaso, J. 'The European Union and Forms of State: Westphalian, Regulatory or Post Modern' (1996) 34 *JCMS* 29, 43-44.

Forwood, N. & Clough, M. 'The Single European Act and Free Movement: Legal Implications of the Provisions for the Completion of the Internal Market' (1986) 11 *European Law Review* 383
Glaesner, H. 'The Single European Act: Attempt at an Appraisal' (1987) *Fordham Journal of International Law* 446
Gormley, L. 'Some Reflections on the Internal Market and Free Movement of Goods' *Legal Issues of European Integration* (1989/1) 9
Majone, G. (ed.) *Regulating Europe* (1996, Routledge, London)
McGee, A. & Weatherill, S. 'The Evolution of the Single Market-Harmonisation or Liberalisation' (1990) 53 *Modern Law Review* 578
Slot, P-J. & Van der Woude, M. *Exploiting the Internal Market* (1988, Kluwer)
Slot, P-J. 'Harmonisation' (1996) 21 *European Law Review* 378

2. Citizenship and Culture

Anderson has argued that the necessity for nation-states to have some idea of national identity and national culture is part of an *Imagined Community.*[1] The development of the European Union, undertaking tasks normally associated with national governance, has challenged the emergent national identities of the Member States and yet failed to replace those identities with either a concrete - or imagined - identity. The search for a replacement identity is shaped by two particular factors and handled by two particular fabrications. The first, by creating a notion of outsider/insiders. In the early stages of the development of the Common Market the common denominator mobilising economic union was to build a Western European fortress against the common enemy of Eastern European Communism. With the collapse of the Berlin Wall there has been a de-stabilisation of the image of Western Europe. This has intensified the search for a common identity within a set of geo-political boundaries which have yet to be finalised. The second fabrication was to build up a common identity of Europe through processes of common cultural heritage and the creating of notions of citizenship rights. The development of both ideas has been fragmentary and uneven. It is useful to separate out the two areas for individual discussion. We will begin by looking at Citizenship.

I. The Debate on Citizenship

Schnapper argues that national citizenship (or what she terms 'classical citizenship') is a historical construction which has been devalued over time, particularly because of the exclusionary nature of linking

---

1 Anderson, B. *Imagined Communities. Reflections on the Origin and Spread of Nationalism* (1983, Verso, London).

citizenship rights to nationality rights - and thereby excluding many non-nationals who are legally resident within the nation-state. She argues for an acknowledgment of the decline of political citizenship and replacing it with the 'new citizenship' which is essentially economic and social in nature.

Schnapper, D. 'The European Debate on Citizenship' (1997) 126 *Daedalus* 199, 203-205

Theorists of the 'new citizenship' strongly criticize the notion of citizenship in its classical definition on the basis of both fact and value. They note that it is devalued yet at the same time consider this a welcome evolution. In their view, its devaluation is both positive and desirable; classical citizenship should be replaced by a new conception of citizenship, of an economic and social nature, that will become the basis of a new democratic practice, defined as 'participatory'. After stating the facts, they go on to enunciate a political norm. These analyses are made from two different viewpoints, but they both lead to a redefined notion of citizenship; some theorists start with a reflection on the creation of a new legal code by EC institutions; others focus instead on the new opportunity created by the permanent presence of foreign-born populations who would like to be 'citizens in a different way'. Both groups concur in suggesting a new conception of citizenship that would be in the making at the European level. For them, citizenship can no longer only be defined by a set of liberty rights, the political definition; it must incorporate claim rights, or more specifically, economic and social rights - claim rights that have become the actual political rights.

The Multiple Citizenship of European Citizens. I will borrow the arguments for this position, essentially, from Elizabeth Meehan. In her view, the distinction between citizens and noncitizens is from now on socially less significant and less meaningful for the fate of individuals than the distinction separating citizens and, on the one hand, legally settled foreigners who enjoy the right to stay and work and benefit from social protection - those Tomas Hammar calls denizens - and, on the other hand, foreigners in a precarious or even illegal situation. What has become important in the life of the community is economic and social participation. True membership in the community is no longer defined by political participation but by economic activity.

The purely political nature of citizenship has been linked to the time when nationalism and nation-states were established. In the nineteenth century the national states' new citizens were freed from the bonds inherited from a feudal society that had become obsolete; likewise, the construction of Europe today is liberating economic actors from the restrictions imposed by national borders and from legislations dating back to the era of nations and nationalism. National citizenship no longer provides legal status and rights by itself; European institutions today are building a new citizenship. The link between nation-state and citizenship, despite its historical nature, is not necessary, and citizenship can be exercised at a different level.

To think that economic and social rights are simply the condition necessary to exercise political citizenship is to continue thinking in terms of the classical citizenship. In fact, these rights represent the basis of the 'new citizenship', in that their impact also affects the political status of the individuals. European institutions develop primarily social law: they define the status of the 'salaried employee' and the rights attached to it; they guarantee the right to work, the social rights of immigrants, and gender equality. Thus they give European citizens and foreigners legally settled in the European space a strictly political status, as rights, practices, and loyalties are expressed from now on at the European level politically. EC law is about to create a specific citizenship founded on a conception of solidarity and social justice that is common to all Europeans. The national state undoubtedly remains the only authority that con confer the status of European citizen through nationality law. But European citizens can take their case to the European citizens against their own national state. There is now a European as well as a national citizenship.

II. Background

The concept of a 'European Citizenship' emerged early in the development of the EC but there was little clarity as to the meaning of 'citizenship' rights. For some commentators the free movement provisions were regarded as 'an incipient form of European citizenship'.[2] Everson has argued that the impetus of the rights to free movement was the construction of the notion of a 'market citizen'.[3] However, the focus on purely economic rights as the means to, or even substitution for, citizenship rights has led to the perceived 'legitimacy' crisis in the European Union - particularly post-Maastricht. It has been questioned whether purely economic rights can be disentangled from other citizenship-type rights, including social and political rights and whether the various forms of rights which are perceived to make up the bundle of so-called citizenship rights and which are protected at the national level can also be disentangled and be guaranteed by different instances of control - at national, supranational or even regional levels. What has

2 *Bull. EC* 11-1968, 5-9; Plender, R. 'An Incipient Form of European Citizenship' in Jacobs, F. (ed.) *European Law and the Individual* (1976, North-Holland, Oxford).

3 Everson, M. 'The Legacy of the Market Citizen' in Shaw, J. & More, G. *New Legal Dynamics of European Union* (1995, Clarendon Press, Oxford).

happened in the development of the Community has been very much a conceptual isolation of economic rights - and this divorce from political and social rights - the classical view of citizenship rights as a comprehensive and interconnected series of social, political and economic rights is what makes the whole 'Citizenship' project troublesome for the EU.

Everson, M. 'Economic Rights Within The European Union' 137, 138-140 in Bellamy, R., Buffacchi, V. & Castiglione, D. (eds.) *Democracy and Constitutional Culture in the Union of Europe* (1995, Lothian Foundation Press, London)

A Typology of Economic Rights and the Economic Constitution

Entering straightaway into the core of controversy, the use of the very term economic *right* is calculated to elicit an extreme response: in which sense is the economic agent clothed with economic rights? Are such actors to be perceived of as being in possession of normative economic rights, bearing much the same qualities as civic rights, and being as a consequence all but unassailable from the viewpoint of state intervention? Alternatively, is the expression right to misnomer, such persons merely being endowed with the necessary functional economic competencies to enable them either to play their part within the market economy, or to fulfil their allotted role in some limited form of market, the latter to a greater or lesser degree being devised through political processes?

These questions point to the possibility of there being at least two, and possibly three, material forms of economic 'right'. The different characteristics possessed by each of these groups of right are clearly fundamental, both in determining exactly which variety of market exists or should exist and, following on from this, the manner in which such a market can or should be guaranteed by law, and accordingly the exact nature of the relationship between the market and other spheres within society. To engage in a closer analysis, the precise qualities of these forms of economic right, the types of market which flow from them, the role of law in securing them and the consequences which this has for relations between economic and further societal areas, may be detailed within the following typology of economic rights.

Intrinsic economic rights will be dealt with very briefly. In effect, all persons are afforded the right to enter into economic transactions purely by virtue of their existence, such transactions merely being one amongst many ways in which the self might be expressed. This obviously gives rise to a pre-political vision of the market which itself somewhat limits the analysis: the most constructive statement which might be made about such rights is that the law must find some way of securing them, not only as against state intervention, but also as regards any of their individual civil or social counterparts which may be in conflict with them.

To move to more fertile ground, however, the distinction drawn between the market as a construction and the market as a fact might be used to shed more light upon the notion of *economic competencies*. According to the latter view, the market economy is seen as simply the most efficient form of resource management, and is furthermore believed to allow for the generation of sufficient wealth upon which to build a modern state. This 'free' market, however, requires particular fixed structures before it can function properly. These structures must on the one hand infuse economic transactions with sufficient certainty that individuals be prepared to enter into them. On the other hand, such frameworks must also preserve the uncertainty of the market, and hence competition and economic advancement, not to be stifled. Here the notion of rights takes on an empowering aura. The individual is equipped with competencies to enable him or her to engage in market transactions. Vitally, such rights are guaranteed by the law. These *legal* rights firstly aim to preserve the certainty of the market, erecting established structures for the transacting of economic business. Secondly, those rights which might be read as restraining restrictive state intervention into the market, preserve the uncertainty upon which that same market thrives. Such enabling economic competences are them a double-edged sword both maintaining the internal security of the market, and safeguarding it against any external intrusions motivated by extra-market considerations. Here the notion of the economic constitution comes into its own. Once the market has been accepted as a fact, the law might legitimately be deployed not only to oversee the internal workings of that market, but also to police its boundaries, even as against the actions of democratic institutions whose proposed intervention is not based upon market considerations. This is clearly fundamental, logically determining that an individual might have an economic status, clearly distinguishable from his or her political functions.

Within the view of the market as a creation, the individual might be said to possess *instrumentalist economic competencies*. Thus, the particular characteristics of this form of market depend largely upon on-going political visions as to what it should encompass. The individual is therefore once again equipped with enabling economic rights to that he or she might aid in the creation of this market. The balance, however, is tipped in favour of instrumentalism. Uncertainty is no longer the subject of protection. In other words, this market is not secured against state intervention. In a democratic world this might mean that any encroachment into the economy, and hence into the sphere of economic competencies, for extra-market reasons themselves derived from a political decision, is legitimate. This form of economy, based on a fluid political process might therefore not be entrenched within an economic constitution. Accordingly, the law might claim no boundary policing role and might on the contrary be deployed to dictate to the market the exact manner in which it may or may not operate. Under this schema, the economic activities of the individual are clearly linked to his or her political functions: the citizen exercising his or her political rights to determine the exact nature and extent of his or her economic competencies.

The idea and notion of a 'People's Europe' beginning with the 'special rights' debate initiated at the Paris Summit Meeting of 1974[4] also embraced the idea of 'citizenship' rights.[5] In 1985, the Addonino Report, 'A People's Europe',[6] focused upon special rights of Community citizens in the areas of education, culture, communication exchanges and the image and identity of the Community. The Advocates General and the European Court of Justice also contributed to the development of citizenship ideas predominantly through cases involving the free movement principle.

Case 7/75 F v Belgian State [1975] ECR 679, [1975] 2 CMLR 442

The applicants who were Italian migrant workers in Belgium were refused a grant for their handicapped child on the grounds that he neither possessed Belgian nationality or satisfied the residence requirements for the receipt of such a grant. The Court was asked to rule on whether the issue fell within Article 12 of Regulation 1612/68/EEC and/or Regulation 1405/71/EEC.

Advocate General Trabucchi[7]

The migrant worker is not regarded by Community Law - nor is he by the internal legal systems - as a mere source of labour but is viewed as a human being. In this context the Community legislature is not concerned solely to guarantee him the right to equal pay and social benefits in connection with the employer-employee relationship; it also emphasised the need to eliminate obstacles to the mobility of the worker *inter alia* with regard to the 'conditions for the integration of his family into the host country' (Regulation 1612/68/EEC, Recital 5).

---

4 See Wiener, A. *Building Institutions: The Developing Practice of 'European' Citizenship* (1997, Westview, Boulder Col.).

5 'Towards a Citizens' Europe' *Bull. EC Supp.* 7-1975, 11. *A People's Europe* COM (84) 446.

6 Reports of the ad hoc Committee on a People's Europe to the European Council, *Bull EC Supp. 7/85.*

7 Ibid., 696.

Case 186/87 Cowan v Trésor Public [1989] ECR 195, [1990] 2 CMLR 613

Cowan, a British national, was attacked at the exit of a Paris Metro station. His attacker could not be identified and he applied for compensation from the Commission d'indemnisation des victimes d'infraction under Article 706-3 of the Code de procedure penale. It was argued by the Law Officer of the Treasury that Cowan could not claim compensation on the grounds that only persons who were of French nationality or foreign nationals who prove they are nationals of a State which has concluded a reciprocal agreement with France for the application of the said provisions and that they satisfy the conditions laid down in the agreement or that they are holders of a residence permit could make such a claim. Cowan claimed that such conditions were contrary to Article 7 (now Article 6 [*12*] EC).

10. By prohibiting 'any discrimination on grounds of nationality' Article 7 of the Treaty requires that persons in a situation governed by Community law be placed on a completely equal footing with nationals of the Member State. In so far as this principle is applicable it therefore precludes a Member State from making the grant of a right to such a person subject to the condition that he reside on the territory of that state - that condition is not imposed on the state's own nationals.

.....

16. At the hearing the French Government submitted that as Community law now stands a recipient of services may not rely on the prohibition of discrimination to the extent that the national law at issue does not create any barrier to freedom of movement. A provision such as that at issue in the main proceedings, it says, imposes no restrictions in that respect. Furthermore, it concerns a right which is a manifestation of the principle of national solidarity. Such a right presupposes a closer bond with the state than that of a recipient of services, and for that reason it may be restricted to persons who are either nationals of that state or foreign nationals resident on the territory of that state.

17. That reasoning cannot be accepted. When Community law guarantees a natural person the freedom to go to another Member State the protection of that person from harm in the Member State in question, on the same basis as that of nationals and persons residing there, is a corollary of that freedom of movement. It follows that the prohibition of discrimination is applicable to recipients of services within the meaning of the Treaty as regards protection against the risk of assault and the right to obtain financial compensation provided for by national law when that risk materialises. The fact that the compensation at issue is financed by the Public Treasury cannot alter the rules regarding the protection of the rights guaranteed by the Treaty.

.....

19 ... legislative provisions may not discriminate against persons to whom Community law gives the right to equal treatment or restrict the fundamental freedoms guaranteed by Community law.

Weatherill argues that '... the decision constitutes a step towards the creation of a *de facto* Community citizenship, developed through a broad interpretation of the individual's economic activity ...'.[8] Although the notion of citizenship rights here is very one-sided, a different version of the free movement rights as *civil rights* is demonstrated by Advocate General Jacobs - ideas which are not taken up by the Court.[9]

Case C-168/91 Konstantinidis [1993] ECR I-1191

This was a challenge to a German law which required Greek names to be transliterated into Roman characters which resulted in Konstantindis' name being phonetically inaccurate.

Advocate General Jacobs[10]

In view of the above considerations I do not think that it would be right to say that the German authorities' treatment of Mr Konstantinidis is necessarily consistent with the European Convention on Human Rights simply because the Convention does not contain express provisions recognising the individual's right to his name or protecting his moral integrity. On the contrary, I consider that it ought to be possible, by means of a broad interpretation of Article 8 of the Convention, to arrive at the view that the Convention does indeed protect the individual's right to oppose unjustified interference with his name.

The more difficult question is to determine whether a person who exercises his right of free movement under Articles 48, 52 or 59 of the Treaty is entitled, as a matter of Community law, to object to treatment which constitutes a breach of his fundamental rights. On that point the court's case law has developed considerably in recent years. The most complete statement of the present position is contained in the judgment in Case C-260/89 ERT [1991] ECR I-2925.

.....

---

8 (1989) 26 *CML Rev* 563.

9 See also, in a similar vein, the Opinion of Advocate General Léger in Case C-214/94 *Boukhalfa v Federal Republic of Germany* [1996] ECR I-2253, [1996] 3 CMLR 22.

10 Ibid., para 41.

But let us suppose that the view is taken that the German authorities' treatment of Mr Konstantinidis is *not* discriminatory. Does that mean that it cannot be contrary to Article 52, even though it infringes Mr Konstantinidis' fundamental rights? The implications of that question are perhaps easier to see if a more drastic example is considered. Suppose that a Member State introduces a draconian penal code under which theft is punishable by amputation of the right hand. A national of another Member State goes to that country in exercise of the rights of free movement conferred on him by Article 48 et seq. of the Treaty, steals a loaf of bread and is sentenced to have his right hand cut off. Such a penalty would undoubtedly constitute inhuman and degrading punishment contrary to Article 3 of the European Convention on Human Rights. But would it be a breach of the individual's rights under Community law, even though it were applied in a non-discriminatory manner? I believe that it would.

In my opinion, a Community national who goes to another Member State as a worker or self-employed person under Articles 48, 52 or 59 of the Treaty is entitled not just to pursue his trade or profession and to enjoy the same living and working conditions as nationals of the host state; he is in addition entitled to assume that, wherever he goes to earn his living in the European Community, he will be treated in accordance with a common code of fundamental values, in particular those laid down in the European Convention on Human Rights. In other words, he is entitled to say '*civis europeus sum*' and to invoke that status in order to oppose any violation of his fundamental rights.

III. Citizenship Rights After the Treaty on European Union

At the Rome Summit in December 1990 the European Council[11] decided that the concept of Citizenship should be included in formalising plans for the EU but the provisions which were eventually included in the TEU were neither novel nor radical. The question arises as to why the operation of the Internal Market requires Citizenship rights to be enacted. In particular, do rights to Citizenship enhance the operation of 'free markets - or impede them'? Turner[12] argues that divergent national history, traditions and choices about the formation of the state, constitution and individual participation determine the role and significance of citizenship historically and geographically. This may help us to explain why it was that the TEU was seen as the most convenient

---

11 The Spanish government pressed for the inclusion of a concept of Citizenship in a Memorandum presented to the 1990 IGC: 'Towards A European Citizenship' *Europe Documents*, No. 1653 2 October 1990.

12 Turner, B. 'Outline of a Theory of Citizenship' (1990) 24 *Sociology* 187.

time to introduce a set of constitutional citizenship rights.

A number of reasons can be put forward to explain why Citizenship has become part of a political agenda. A purely evolutionary explanation relates to the relative success story of the Single Market project. As Shaw[13] points out, a supra-national legal order has developed creating a system in which individuals have been constructed as 'subjects' of EC law with a panaply of socio-economic, procedural and remedial rights. The constitutional nature of the EC has been raised in the political, legal and academic sphere since the Court's ruling in *Van Gend en Loos*.[14] A question which has been raised is the role of the 'people'. What is the constituent 'membership' of the new form of polity created by the EU and what is the membership's relationship with the polity? The idea of post-national identity has emerged in a number of academic writings as a way of explaining the disillusion felt with the European integration programme, both pre-and-post Maastricht. Laffan[15] argues that the politics of identity - that the EU needs to offer an identity to individuals beyond pure economic rights - has hit a critical period now that the 'Monnet' method of integration has reached its limits.

Other commentators offer analysis of why support for the integration project subsided. According to Weiler's[16] analysis a crisis in the *telos* of European integration increased after the decision of the German Constitutional Court in *Brunner*.[17] Here, while the German Constitutional Court found no constitutional barrier to the German ratification of the TEU, the Court argued that there was no European *demos* and, therefore, because citizenship and nationality are conflated in the German constitution with a notion of people/*Volk* and lineage there can be no democracy at the European level. Any legitimacy ascribed to the EU is given (or indeed borrowed) only through

---

13 'Citizenship of the Union: Towards Post National Membership' Collected Courses of the Academy of European Law 1995, Vol. VI. No 1, (1998, Kluwer Law International, The Hague).

14 Case 26/62 [1963] ECR 1; [1963] CMLR 105.

15 Laffan, B. The Politics of Identity and Political Order in Europe (1996) 34 *JCMS* 81.

16 Weiler, J. 'Does Europe Need A Constitution? Reflections on Demos, Telos and the German Maastricht Decision' (1995) 1 *ELJ* 219.

17 22 Bverf GE 293.

democratic institutions at the national level. Thus, Weiler argues that it is the need to provide a foundation for the EU which can bring together 'shared values, a shared understanding of rights and societal duties and shared rational, intellectual culture which transcend organic - national differences'. The EU response had been along such lines when we look at the statements found in the Treaties. For example, one of the objectives of the Union, laid down in Article B [*2*] TEU is

> ... to strengthen the protection of the rights and interests of the nationals of its Member States through the introduction of a citizenship of the Union.

But as a legal concept, Citizenship is defined as a set of seven positive rights which are generally regarded to be of limited value in terms of creating a coherent pattern of Citizenship ideas.[18] The Edinburgh European Council stated:[19]

1. Citizenship of the Union is a political and legal concept which is entirely different from the concept of citizenship within the meaning of the Constitution of the kingdom of Denmark and of the Danish legal system. ...

2. Citizenship of the Union in no way in itself gives a national of another Member State the right to obtain Danish citizenship or any of the rights, duties, privileges or advantages that are inherent in Danish citizenship ... Denmark will fully respect all specific rights expressly provided for in the Treaty and applying to the nationals of the Member States.

---

18 See the penetrating critique of Weiler that the provisions of Article 8 [*17-22*] EC trivialise the concept of Citizenship to the point of embarassment, in Winter, J., Curtin, D., Kellermann, A. & de Witte, B. (eds.) *Reforming the Treaty on European Union. The Legal Debate* (1996, Kluwer Law International/TMC Asser Instituut, The Hague) 65. See also Lyons, C. *'Citizenship in the Constitution of the EU: Rhetoric or Reality?'* in Bellamy, R. (ed.) *Constitutionalism, Democracy and Sovereignty: American and European Perspectives* (1996, Avebury, Aldershot).

19 EC Bulletin 12-1992, Part B, Annex 3, 57-59.

The Edinburgh European Council also declared:[20]

The provisions of part Two of the Treaty establishing the European Community relating to citizenship of the Union give nationals of the Member States additional rights and protection as specified in that Part. They do not in any way take the place of national citizenship. The question whether an individual possesses the nationality of a Member State will be settled solely by reference to the national law of the Member State concerned.

This failure of the Maastricht Treaty to establish sufficiently clear that Citizenship of the Union is a *supplement* to and not a *substitute for* national citizenship was rectified in the Treaty of Amsterdam.

i. Citizenship of the Union

Article 8 (1) EC [*17(1)*]. Citizenship of Union is hereby established.

Every person holding the nationality of a Member State shall be a citizen of the Union. *Citizenship of the Union shall complement and not replace national citizenship.*[21]

2. Citizens of the Union shall enjoy the rights conferred by this Treaty and shall be subject to the duties imposed thereby.

There are quite clear symbolic implications of calling the concept 'Citizenship of the *Union*' rather than the Community and yet, in terms of general notions of citizenship rights - social, economic and political - by embracing the whole of the three pillar structure into the concept serves to highlight even more poignantly the *lack* of protection of citizenship rights in the current second and third pillars of the Union

---

20 This Declaration does not demarcate clearly the boundaries between national and Union Citizenship and its legal status, in terms of Community law principles may be questioned. Cf Toth, A. 'The Legal Status of Declarations annexed to the Single European Act 1986' (1986) 23 *CMLRev* 803.

21 Note also Article F *[6] TEU. (1) [3] The Union shall respect the identities of its Member States...*

structure. The catalogue of citizenship rights is brief and is in no way comparable with national concepts of citizenship. One of the key concessions made to Denmark after the first Danish referendum which narrowly rejected the TEU was the Declaration from the Edinburgh Summit that nothing in the TEU displaces national citizenship. A Declaration attached to the TEU at Maastricht also states:

> The Conference declares that, wherever in the Treaty establishing the European Community reference is made to nationals of the Member States, the question whether an individual possesses the nationality of a Member State shall be settled solely by reference to the national law of the Member State concerned. Member States may declare, for information, who are to be considered their nationals for Community purposes by way of a Declaration lodged with the Presidency and may amend any such Declaration when necessary.

Under the EC Treaty and rulings of the Court of Justice it is assumed that the nationality law of a Member State for EC law purposes may not necessarily be identical to its nationality law for other purposes. In *Micheletti*[22] the Spanish authorities refused to give Michelleti, a dual Argentinian and Italian national, a card identifying him as an EC national for the purposes of working in Spain as an odontologist. The refusal was based upon Article 9 of the Spanish Civil Code, under which, in cases of dual nationality neither of which was Spanish, precedence had to be accorded to the nationality corresponding to the habitual residence of the person prior to their entry into Spain. In this instance the Argentinean nationality took precedence. The Court held that although the definition of conditions governing the acquisition and loss of nationality were, according to international law, matters which fell within the competence of each Member State, that competence had to be exercised in compliance with EC law. A Member State was not entitled to restrict the effects of the attribution of nationality of another Member State by imposing an additional condition on recognition of that nationality for the purpose of exercising the fundamental freedoms of the EC Treaty. Thus it was held that provided a person was able to produce

---

22 Case C-369/90 *Micheletti and others v Delegación del Gobierno Cantabria* [1992] ECR I-4239.

one of the documents referred to in Directive 73/148/EEC in order to show that they were nationals of a Member State, other Member States were not entitled to dispute that status on the ground that the persons concerned were also nationals of a non-Member State, the nationality of which took precedence under the host State's law.

The question as to whether 'nationality' should be an EC law concept is vexed.[23] The Member States are adamant that they should retain this sovereign right. The Edinburgh European Council thus concluded:

> The question whether an individual possesses the nationality of a Member State will be settled solely by reference to the national law of the Member State concerned.[24]

This exclusionary personal scope of Union Citizenship is described by Kostakopoulou as resulting from the imposition of nationalist trappings onto supra-national ideals and institutions which may have repercussions for future ideas for 'community-building' in the EU.[25] The exclusion of third country nationals from the definition of 'Citizenship of the Union' in Article 8 [*17*] EC immediately creates boundaries of exclusion and inclusion. As d'Oliveira[26] has argued '... if a category of persons, endowed with certain rights (and duties) is created or defined, then, by the same token, other persons are excluded. The inclusion of certain groups implies the exclusion of others'. Thus we see a definitive boundary being drawn whereby the common enemy of Communism is replaced by a generic group of 'foreigners' or non-Europeans. Part of the creation of the European identity has been a resort to negative coherence - to confirm what Europe is not. That

---

23 See Evans, A. 'European Citizenship' (1982) 45 *MLR* 497; 'European Citizenship: A Novel Concept in EEC Law' (1984) 32 *AJCL* 679; 'Nationality Law and European Integration' (1991) 16 *ELRev* 190.

24 EC Bulletin 12-1992, I.42.

25 Kostakopoulou, T. 'Why a "Community of Europeans" Could Be A Community of Exclusion: A Reply To Howe' (1997) 35 *JCMS* 301.

26 d' Oliveira, H-J. 'European Citizenship: Its Meaning, Its Potential' in Dehousse, R. (ed.) *Europe After Maastricht* (1994, Law Books in Europe, Munich) .

which is 'non-European' is being defined with increasing precision - in terms of citizenship rights and cultural rights. Shore argues that in the official definition of Europe which is being constructed '... new European order ... is coming to mean a sharper boundary between 'European' and 'non-European'.[27] The resulting emergent citizenship is thus conceived and operative in nationalist terms. It moves beyond 'market citizenship' and is also a true form of citizenship in terms of its potent exclusion of non-citizens.

In the first Report From the Commission on Citizenship of the Union[28] the constitutional significance of Citizenship is emphasised:

> The introduction of these new provisions underscores the fact that the Treaty of Rome is not concerned solely with economic matters, as is also plainly demonstrated by the change of name from the EEC to the EC. For the first time, the Treaty has created a direct political link between the citizens of the member States and the European Union such as never existed within the Community, with the aim of fostering a sense of identity with the Union. As testimony to their importance, the Intergovernmental Conference placed them immediately after the introductory provisions of the Treaty of Rome, such as Article 6 [*13*]EC ... which prohibits discrimination on the grounds of nationality, and Article 7A [*14*] EC ..., which provides for the establishment of the internal market *inter alia* for persons. Thus citizenship of the Union appears in the Treaty even before the four freedoms which together make up the internal market.

Marias[29] argues that the ruling in *Van Gend en Loos*[30] paved the way for the creation of a genuine civil society. But arguably it was not until Union Citizenship created a set of particular rights, severed from specific socio-economic goals, that coherence was granted to such a concept.

---

27 Shore, C. 'Inventing the "Peoples Europe"? Critical Approaches to European "Cultural Policy"' (1993) 28 *Man*.

28 COM (93) 702 final.

29 Marias, E. 'From Market Citizen to Union Citizen' in Marias, E. (ed.) *European Citizenship* (1994, EIPA, Maastricht).

30 Case 26/62 *Van Gend en Loos* [1963] ECR 1, [1963] CMLR 105.

ii. Free Movement

Article 8a(1) [*18(1)*] EC. Every citizen of the Union shall have the right to move and reside freely within the territory of the Member States, subject to the limitations and conditions laid down in this Treaty and by the measures adopted to give it effect.

2. The Council may adopt provisions with a view to facilitating the exercise of the rights referred to in paragraph 1; save as otherwise provided in this Treaty, the Council shall act unanimously on a proposal from the Commission and after obtaining the assent of the European Parliament. [*The Council shall act in accordance with the procedure referred to in Article 251.The Council shall act unanimously throughout this procedure.*]

Article 8a [*18*] EC appears to have created more problems than it has solved. It turns the right to free movement into a political right without clarifying how far it improves upon the existing economic rights to free movement. For example it does not spell out what limitations there are to this right. It does not address the right of third country nationals to accompany EU family members to another Member State. It does not address its relationship with Article 7a [*14*] EC. The division of legal powers between the EC Treaty and JHA has resulted in divisions between the Member States and the Institutions as to both the objective to be sought and the means of achieving the aims of Article 7a [*14*] EC. One of the concerns of the Treaty of Amsterdam was to integrate the goal of achieving a high level of security in the internal area without frontiers with the finalisation of an external frontier. The Commission had made proposals to widen the ambit of the free movement provisions in 1980.[31] In 1990 three Directives granting rights of residence to students[32]; employed and self-employed persons who had ceased to work[33] and persons who did not enjoy a right of residence under EC law.[34] More recently the Commission has put forward a package of measures formally ending all controls on persons crossing the border

---

31 COM (80) 358.

32 Council Directive 90/366, replaced by Council Directive 93/96 OJ 1993 L 317/59.

33 Council Directive 90/365, OJ 1990 L 180/28.

34 Council Directive 90/364, OJ 1990 L 180/26.

between one Member State and another.[35]

Amendments were made by the TEU to Articles 49 [*40*], 54 [*44*], 56 [*46*] and 57 [*47*] EC allowing for the use of the new Article 189b [*251*] EC procedure for the issue of new Directives or Regulations to bring about freedom of movement of workers, establishment, to take up and pursue activities as self-employed persons. The Treaty of Amsterdam introduced the co-decision procedure for the free movement provisions - although unanimity still applies to Council voting procedures. The same - somewhat anomalous - procedure will also apply for social security measures for migrant workers (Article 51 [*42*] EC) and the recognition of professional qualifications (Article 57(2) [*47(2)*] EC).

It has been argued that the evolution of Citizenship rights, derived from employment status and mobility, may institutionalise a dependent and inferior status for women,[36] and also, for other groups, for example, for people with disabilities, the right to free movement may be illusory. While academic attention has focused upon the gender implications of the free movement provisions disabled people may also not be able to trigger the free movement easily particularly where the coordination of disability benefits between the Member States is lacking. In *Snares*[37] a British worker with severely impaired mobility after an accident at work was in receipt of a disability living allowance in Britain. He decided to settle in Tenerife (Spain) where his mother lived in order that she could look after him. The United Kingdom authorities decided to set aside his disability living allowance because he was no longer

---

35 COM(95) 347 final; COM(95) 348 final. Note the Commission Communication to the Council of Ministers and the European Parliament on the Abolition of Border Controls, 8th May 1992. *Agence Europe* No 5724, 7 May 1992; No 5726, 9 May 1992.

36 See, *inter alia*, Everson, M. 'Women and Citizenship of the European Union' in Hervey, T. & O'Keeffe, D. (eds.) *Sex Equality Law in the European Union* (1996, Wiley, London); Ackers, L. 'Women, Citizenship and European Community Law: The Gender Implications of the Free Movement Provisions' (1994) *JSWFL* 391 and 'Citizenship, Gender and Dependency in the European Union: Women and Internal Migration' in Hervey, T. & O'Keeffe, D. (eds.) *op. cit;* Vogel, U. 'Is Citizenship Gender-Specific?' in Vogel, U. & Moran, M. (eds.) *The Frontiers of Citizenship* (1991, Macmillan, Basingstoke).

37 Case C-20/96 *Snares v Adjudication Officer*, Judgment of 4 November 1997.

resident in the UK. The Court of Justice ruled that this was not contrary to Community law since the provisions of Regulation 1408/71 provided that certain kinds of social security benefit cannot be exported. In the absence of harmonisation in social security matters the Member States remained competent to define the conditions for granting social security benefits, even if this results in a more strict application in their own State. The only proviso was that the conditions for eligibility must not involve overt or disguised discrimination between Community workers. This ruling is in marked contrast to the wider approach taken in the sphere of the economic rights to free movement where the Court has moved beyond a non-discrimination approach to tackle and barriers and disincentives which might face an economic migrant.

In the *Second Report from the Commission on Citizenship of the Union*[38] the concept of free movement is described as a right conferred on every citizen of the Union. It is now regarded as a fundamental and personal right, within the European Community, which may be exercised outside the context of an economic activity. The Second Report highlights areas where free movement is not a reality for many people. For example the right to reside in another Member State is still subject to different provisions applicable to different categories of citizens, the transposal of the secondary legislation, particularly the rights of residence Directives, has not always been carried out satisfactorily,[39] EC law is ill-adapted to certain particular situations such as trainees and voluntary workers.[40] It is recognised that Article 8a [*18*] EC does not constitute a comprehensive legal base from which all rights relating to the free movement of citizens derive. It cannot take the place of other existing legal bases dealing with the distinctions and limitations of the various categories of persons granted free movement rights under

---

38 COM (97) 230 final.

39 See the 12th, 13th, and 14th, Annual Reports by the Commission on monitoring the application of Community law, respectively OJ 1994 C 254/1; OJ 1995 C 303/1.

40 See The Green Paper on Education-Training-Research: The Obstacles to transnational mobility, COM (96) 462 final. On 24 January 1996 the Commission appointed a High Level Panel on the Free Movement of Persons to examine the remaining obstacles to free movement. The Panel's Report was presented to the Commission on 18 March 1997 and is currently being examined by the Institutions.

Community law.[41] Thus the Commission proposed a revision of Article 8a [*18*] EC:

> From a supplementary legal basis it could be upgraded to a specific legal basis apt to revise the complex body of secondary legislation. This would certainly increase the transparency of Community law, ease implementation measures and increase the citizens' understanding of the rights effectively conferred.[42]

The Court of Justice has ruled that the right to free movement in Article 8a [*18*] is residual and not the basis, or starting point, for an analysis of the constitutional nature of the right to free movement under EC law. In *Skanavi*[43] the Court was asked whether, prior to the implementation of Directive 91/439, Articles 6 [*12*], 8a [*18*] and 52 [*43*] EC precluded a Member State from requiring the holder of a driving licence issued by another Member State to exchange that licence for a licence of the host Member State within one year of taking up normal residence in that Member State in order to remain entitled to drive a motor vehicle there. The Court ruled that while Article 8a [*18*] EC sets out generally the right of every Citizen of the Union to move and reside freely within the territory of the Member States it finds specific expression in Article 52 [*43*] EC and that since the applicants had established themselves in the host State in order to carry out an economic activity the case fell within the scope of Article 52 [*43*] EC and it was not necessary to rule on the implementation of Article 8a [*18*]

41 For example, in relation to the right to entry and residence alone there are two Regulations (Council Regulation 1612/68 and Commission Regulation 1251/70) and nine Directives (Council Directive 68/360/EEC, Council Directive 73/148/EEC, Council Directive 75/34/EEC, Council Directive 90/364/EEC, Council Directive 90/365, Council Directive 93/96/EEC, Council Directive 64/221/EEC, Council Directive 72/194/EEC, Council Directive 75/35/EEC). Other measures such as the co-ordination of social security also have an effect upon residence rights.

42 Second Report from the Commission on Citizenship of the Union COM (97) 230 final, 4.

43 Case C-193/94 *Skanavi and Chryssanthakopoulos* [1996] ECR I-929, [1996] 2 CMLR 372.

EC. A more direct question was put to the Court in *Adams*[44] when the Court was asked whether Article 8a [*18*] EC conferred rights of free movement *additional* to those which existed under the EC Treaty prior to the adoption of the TEU. The reference was withdrawn[45] when the legal situation changed in the United Kingdom (here an exclusion order was withdrawn. In *Kremzow*[46] the applicant sought to rely upon Article 8a [*18*] EC when arguing that a Member State had infringed his right to free movement and residence by illegally imprisoning him and that the Member State should be obliged, in accordance with Community law, to provide compensation. The Court ruled that the issue did not fall within the scope and application of Community law.

In his Opinion in *Stober and Pereira*[47] Advocate General La Pergola emphasised that the ultimate objective of the Treaty provisions on Citizenship is to found a growing assimilation between the Citizens of the Union regardless of their nationality. He argued that German legislation requiring the children of self-employed people to reside in Germany in order to qualify for a children's allowance was in conflict with the right to free movement and residence in Article 8a [*18*] EC since this condition would deny such persons (and their families) the possibility of fully exercising their rights as Union Citizens within the meaning of Article 8a [*18*] EC. The Court chose not to address this issue but addressed the questions referred to it on the grounds of Article 48 [*39*] EC and Regulation 1408/71. We see Advocate General La Pergola urging the Court to address the relationship between Article 8a [*18*] EC and the economic free movement rights. The Commission points out in its submissions that the central question being posed here is whether the fact that one of the conditions imposed by the rights to residence Directives (i.e. the fact that the applicant receives a welfare benefit) is not satisfied results in the right not existing *at all.* The Advocate General La Pergola in his Opinion has accepted that Article 8a [*18*] EC confers a right of free movement and residence flowing *directly from the Treaty* and the limitations and weaknesses which it entails concern only the

---

44 Case C-229/94, OJ 1994 C 275.

45 1995 OJ C 159/20.

46 Case C-299/95 *Kremzow v Republic Österreich*, Judgment of 25 May 1997.

47 Joined Cases C-65/95 & C-111/95 *Stober and Pereira v Bundesanstalt für Arbeit* [1997] ECR I- 511.

exercise of this right. In La Pergola's view the right of free movement and residence is inseparable from Union Citizenship. He has urged the Court to move a step forward and, in the light of the *Cowan* ruling, to rule that Member State nationals in the same position as Cowan can rely not only on their situation as economic actors (i.e. potential recipients of services) but also on the nationality of one of the Member States and, by implication, their Citizenship of the Union, in order to invoke the principle of non-discrimination in the field of application of Community law.

Advocate General Ruiz-Jarabo Colomer has described Article 8a [*18*] EC in the following expansive terms:

> The creation of citizenship of the Union, with the corollary described above of freedom of movement for citizens throughout the territory of the Member States, represents a considerable qualitative step forward in that, as the Commission rightly points out, it separates that freedom from its functional or instrumental elements (the link with an economic activity or attainment of the internal market) and raises it to the level of a genuinely independent right inherent in the political status of the citizens of the Union.[48]

Thus, to date, there is no ruling from the Court indicating that Article 8a [*18*] EC grants broader rights to individuals than those already found within the EC Treaty and secondary legislation.[49] In fact to date the only substantive contribution by the Court has been a negative one. This is seen in cases involving reverse discrimination where the third country national (Russian and Norwegian) spouses of two German citizens who were resident and working in Germany challenged the discriminatory provisions of their employment contract. The Court ruled that there was no Community law element but added a note on Article 8a [*18*]EC.

---

48 Joined Cases C-65 & C-111/95 *R v Secretary of State for the Home Department ex parte Shingara* [1997] ECR I- 3343, [1997] CMLR 703, para 34.

49 See also the Court of First Instance in Case T-66/95 *Kuchlenz-Winter* [1997] ECR II-637.

Joined Cases C-64/96 and C-65/96 Land Nordrhein-Westfalen v Uecker and Jacquet v Land Nordrhein [1997] ECR I-3171

22. Finally, the national court asks whether the fundamental principles of a Community moving towards European Union still permit a rule of national law which is incompatible with Community law because it is in breach of Article 48(2) of the Treaty to continue to be applied by a member state against its own nationals and their spouse from non-member countries.

23. In that regard, it must be noted that citizenship of the Union, established by Article 8 of the EC Treaty, is not intended to extend the scope of *ratione materiae* of the Treaty also to internal situations which have no link with Community law. Furthermore, Article M of the Treaty on European Union provides that nothing in that Treaty is to affect the Treaties establishing the European Communities, subject to the provisions expressly amending those treaties. Any discrimination which nationals of a member state may suffer under the law of that state fall within the scope of that law and must therefore be dealt with within the framework of the internal system of that state.

24. The answer to be given must therefore be that a national of a non-member country married to a worker having the nationality of a member state cannot rely on the right conferred by Article 11 of Regulation 1612/68 when that worker has never exercised the right to freedom of movement within the Community.

The right to free movement may conflict with some duties relating to the development of national identity. The interpretation of free movement may be considered as outweighing the fulfilment of national duties which are regarded as part of national identity, for example, the fulfilment of military service. In *Giagounidis v Stadt Reutlingen*[50] a Greek national living in Germany was deprived of his passport because of his failure to fulfil his military obligations. The Court ruled that the German authorities were bound to grant him a residence permit since he held a national identity card which was only valid within the home State but which provided sufficient proof of his status and entitlement to EC law rights.

---

50 Case C-376/89 *Giagounidis v Stadt Reutlingen* [1991] ECR I-1069.

iii. The Right to Vote and Stand in Municipal Elections and Elections to the European Parliament

Article 8b(1) [*19(1)*] EC. Every citizen of the Union residing in a Member State of which he is not a national shall have the right to vote and to stand as a candidate at municipal elections in the Member State in which he resides, under the same conditions as nationals of that State. This right shall be exercised subject to detailed arrangements to be adopted before 31 December 1994 by the Council, acting unanimously on a proposal from the Commission and after consulting the European Parliament; these arrangements may provide for derogations where warranted by problems specific to a Member State.

2. Without prejudice to Article 138(3) [*190(3)*] and to the provisions adopted for its implementation, every citizen of the Union residing in a Member State of which he is not a national shall have the right to vote and to stand as a candidate in elections to the European Parliament in the Member State in which he resides, under the same conditions as nationals of that State. This right shall be exercised subject to detailed arrangements to be adopted before 31 December 1993 by the Council, acting unanimously on a proposal from the Commission and after consulting the European Parliament; these arrangements may provide for derogations where warranted by problems specific to a Member State.

European Parliament elections are regulated by Directive 93/109/EC laying down detailed arrangements for the exercise of the right to vote and stand as a candidate in elections to the European Parliament for Citizens of the European Union residing in a Member State of which they are not nationals.[51] The earlier deadline was chosen so that arrangements could be in place for the European Parliament elections of June 1994. In fact only one Union Citizen was successful in a Member State other than the Member State of origin in the 1994 European Parliament elections and statistics compiled by the Commission showed that there was a huge disparity between the number of EU Citizens entitled to vote on the basis of Article 8b(2) [*19(2)*] and those who actually enrolled for the election.[52] Oliver states that the provisions relating to the elections to the European Parliament gave rise

---

51 OJ 1993 L 329/34.

52 Annex to the Commission's Report on the Functioning of the TEU With A View To The 1996 IGC.

to few constitutional or political difficulties whereas, in contrast, in some Member States granting to nationals of other Member States the right to vote and stand in municipal elections raised acute constitutional and political difficulties.[53] Somewhat paradoxically it was the Member States who are very pro-European integration (Belgium, France, Germany and Luxembourg) where the problems were the greatest. In contrast Denmark, Ireland and the United Kingdom had already granted some electoral rights to foreigners and perhaps tended to focus on other problematic issues. The principal features of Directive 93/109/EC are that it is intended to interfere as little as possible with national electoral laws and is designed to confer new electoral rights, not to remove existing ones.[54] Community voters have a right, not an obligation, to vote in their country of residence[55] (although the concept of residence is not defined).

Article 14 of the Directive establishes the possibility of reserving voting rights with a qualifying period of residence in the host Member State for those Member States in which the share of non-national citizens of the Union is more than 20%. In reality this refers only to Luxembourg where nationals of other Member States represent some 29% of the electorate.

Article 8b(1) [*19(1)*] EC has been implemented by Directive 94/80/EC laying down detailed arrangements for the exercise of the right to vote and stand as a candidate in municipal elections by Citizens of the Union residing in a Member State of which they are not nationals.[56] Yet the goals of achieving a common procedure for the elections to the European Parliament remain unrealised. The crucial question is whether the link between democracy and Citizenship established in Article 8b [*19*] be influential in reducing the EU's democratic deficit.[57] Weiler

---

53 'Electoral Rights Under Article 8B of the Treaty of Rome' (1996) 33 *CMLRev* 473.

54 Articles 1(2) and 14(2).

55 Articles 4(1) and 8.

56 OJ 1994, L 368/38.

57 Boyce, B. 'The Democratic Deficit of the European Community' (1993) 46 *Parliamentary Affairs* 458; Raworth, P. 'A Timid Step Forwards: Maastricht and the Democratisation of the European Community' (1994) 19 *ELRev* 33; Neunreither, K. 'The Democratic Deficit of the EU: Towards Closer Cooperation Between the European Parliament and National Parliaments'

argues that by establishing Union Citizenship the Member States recognised that given the increase in EC powers the linkages between citizens and the exercise of public authority had to be reinforced, otherwise public authority loses its legitimacy.[58]

iv. The Right to Diplomatic Protection

Article 8c [*20*] EC. Every citizen of the Union shall, in the territory of a third country in which the Member State of which he is a national is not represented, be entitled to protection by the diplomatic or consular authorities of any Member State, on the same conditions as the nationals of that State. Before 31 December 1993, Member States shall establish the necessary rules among themselves and start the international negotiations required to secure this protection.

This entitlement is granted only at the level of the Member State *not at that of* Community or Union. It has been argued by Kovar and Simon,[59] that this right is merely the extension of normal practice in that Article 6 of the Vienna Convention of 18 April 1961 on Diplomatic Relations foresaw the possibility of common diplomatic representation. In contrast O'Leary[60] argues that this is a novel extension of the principle of equal treatment to the external dimension of EC law, reflecting a certain State-like behaviour on the part of the EU. But there are a number of limitations. The modalities of consular protection were defined in EPC Directives issued in 1993 and approved by the Ministers of Foreign Affairs within the EPC framework. There is thus no mechanism for converting these instruments into EC law and allowing them to create direct effect.

There is also no homogeneous interpretation of this right. In

---

(1994) 29 *Government and Opposition* 299.

58 Weiler, J. 'European Citizenship and Human Rights' in *The TEU - Suggestions For Revision* (1995, TMC Asser Instituut, The Hague). On the disempowerment of European Citizens, see Weiler, J. 'The European Union Belongs To Its Citizens: Three Immodest Proposals' (1997) 22 *ELRev* 150.

59 Kovar, R. & Simon, D. 'La citoyenneté européenne' (1994) *CDE* 299.

60 'Leary, S. 'Nationality Law and Community Citizenship: A Tale of Two Uneasy Bedfellows' (1992) 12 *YEL* 375, 383.

some Member States it is construed as a constitutional obligation; in others it is discretionary State competence. The right of protection has only a subsidiary nature. Thus the provisions do not grant an enforceable right of protection. Thirdly the Directives refer to EC nationals and not to Union citizens. Thus the reliance on the right on nationality is a requirement that may be invoked by a third party to prevent its application as a right of Union Citizenship.

In the Second Report the Commission notes that the practical impact of this right is not negligible since there only five non-EU States (Russian Federation, Japan, USA, China and Switzerland) where all the Member States are represented and seventeen non-EU States where only two Member States are represented.[61] In May 1993 a first set of guidelines for the protection of unrepresented Union citizens by Member States' missions in third countries was adopted and on 19 December 1995 the Representatives of the Governments of the Member States meeting within the Council adopted two Decisions, the first[62] regarding protection for citizens of the Union by diplomatic and consular representations and the second on the implementing measures to be adopted by consular officials.[63] On 25 June 1996 the Representatives of the Governments of the Member States meeting within the Council laid down the rules for the deliverance of an emergency travel document.[64] However none of these provisions will take effect until all the Member States have adopted the necessary procedures for their application. Steps have been taken to bring these arrangements to the attention of Citizens of the Union by the Member States and the Commission agreeing the text of a leaflet.[65]

---

61 COM (97) 230 final, 11.

62 Decision 95/553/EC OJ 1995 L 314/73.

63 Not published.

64 Decision 96/409/CFSP OJ 1996 L 168/4.

65 *Consular Protection for Citizens of the European Union* DOC SN 3230/96 of 17 June 1996.

v. The Right to Address the European Parliament, to Petition the EP and to Apply to a Community Ombudsman

Article 8d [*21*] EC. Every citizen of the Union shall have the right to petition the European Parliament in accordance with Article 138d [*194*].

Every citizen of the Union may apply to the Ombudsman established in accordance with Article 138e [*195*].

Every citizen of the Union may write to any of the institutions or bodies referred to in this Article or in Article 7 in one of the languages mentioned in Article 314 and have an answer in the same language.

In establishing Citizenship of the Union non-judicial mechanisms are also employed to protect Citizens' rights. The right to petition the European Parliament already existed under the Rules of the European Parliament. The remit - as with that of the Ombudsman - only deals with *Community* not *Union* activities. This is one of the rights of Union Citizenship where it is not necessary to hold the nationality of one of the Member States.[66] Detailed rules on the regulations governing the Ombudsman's duties were adopted by the European Parliament on 9 March 1994[67] and Jacob Soderman, a former Finnish Ombudsman, was appointed to the post of European Union Ombudsman on 12 July 1995.[68] Not surprisingly the Ombudsman's first annual report revealed a large rush of complaints to the new office but nearly 80 per cent of applications made to the Ombudsman in his first year of office were declared inadmissible.[69] In 1996 the Ombudsman initiated three

---

66 Marias, E. 'The Right To Petition the European Parliament After Maastricht' (1994) 19 *ELRev* 169; Magliveras, K. 'Best Intentions But Empty Words: The European Ombudsman' (1995) 20 *EL Rev* 401.

67 Statute of the Ombudsman, European Parliament Decision 94/262/ECSC/EC/Euratom of 9 March 1994 on the regulations and general conditions governing the performance of the Ombudsman's duties OJ 1994 L 113/15.

68 He took up office in Strasbourg on 27 September 1995 after having been sworn in before the Court of Justice.

69 See the first report OJ 1996 C 234/1. Cf the European Parliament's reaction to the report, Doc PE 217.098. The second report is at OJ 1997 C 272/1. Available also at: http://www.euro-ombudsman.eu.int.

investigations on his own initiative.[70] However the office is lacking in independent enforcement powers and is therefore dependent to a large degree upon placing trust in both complainants and administrators and the need to publicise the activities of the office. Both Tierney [71]and Hedemann-Robinson[72] stress the importance of the role of the Ombudsman in terms of the symbolic value - that the Community is accountable to its constituent individuals - but equally the lack of enforcement powers and the inability of the Ombudsman to advocate law reform are major limitations on the rights granted to Citizens of the Union. In the *Second Report From the Commission on Citizenship of the Union* the Commission declares:

> '... it should be kept in mind that the function of the Ombudsman is to make the institutions more open and democratically accountable, and his action is an incentive for the institutions under scrutiny to remedy inappropriate administrative practices.'[73]

In the Second Report the Commission notes that the number of inadmissible petitions and complaints that have emerged reveals a lack of understanding of these rights. From the end of the legislative 1993/94 to the first half of 1996/97 parliamentary year a total of 4,131 petitions were addressed to the European Parliament. Of these 2,239 petitions were declared admissible. These concerned citizens rights in the area of social affairs (health insurance and pension rights), freedom of movement (residence permits) taxation and mutual recognition of

---

70 These related to information and transparency in relation to rules of access to documents followed by Community institutions other than the Commission and Council (where a code of conduct already operates: 93/730/EC OJ 1993 L 340/41), information and recruitment procedure and, finally, information given to citizens who complain to the Commission alleging a breach of Community law.

71 Tierney, S. 'European Citizenship in Practice? The First Annual Report of the European Ombudsman' (1996) 2 *European Public Law* 517.

72 Hedemann-Robinson, M. 'The Individual and the EC Ombudsman' (1994) *New Law Journal* 609.

73 COM (197) 230.

diplomas. Consumer protection and environmental concerns were also raised.[74]

The addition to Article 8d [*21*] EC was at the instigation of Belgium, in order to achieve recognition of the use of the twelve official languages of the EU. Belgium was also behind an amendment to Article 128(4) [*151(4)*] EC which now provides that:

> *The Community shall take cultural aspects into account in its action under other provisions of this Treaty, in particular in order to respect and to promote the diversity of its cultures.*

IV. The Future Direction of Citizenship of the Union

Article 8e [*22*] EC. The Commission shall report to the European Parliament, to the Council and to the Economic and Social Committee before 31 December 1993 and then every three years on the application of the provisions of this Part. This report shall take account of the development of the Union. On this basis, and without prejudice to the other provisions of this Treaty, the Council, acting unanimously on a proposal from the Commission and after consulting the European Parliament, may adopt provisions to strengthen or to add to the rights laid down in this Part, which it shall recommend to the Member States for adoption in accordance with their respective constitutional requirements.

Closa[75] terms this Article as the 'dynamic' character of citizenship, perhaps paving the way for the progressive development of new, social rights.[76] There are a number of rights pertaining to citizenship scattered about in the TEU and the EC Treaty. For example, Article B[*2*] TEU, the human rights clause, Article F(2) [*6(2)*] TEU which attempts to consolidate the Court's case law. Other provisions

---

74 *Second Report From The Commission on Citizenship of the Union,* COM (197) 230, 12. For details see the annual reports of the Committee on petitions (Docs PE 218.896, PE 217.615; PE 212.500; PE 208.029).

75 'The creation of the concept of citizenship during the 1991 IGC on Political Union' (1991, University of Hull ECRU Research Papers).

76 See further, Closa, C. 'Citizenship of the Union and Nationality of Member States' (1995) 32 *CMLRev* 487.

might include Article 138a [*191*] EC which provides that political parties are an important factor for integration in that they contribute to the forming of a European awareness and express the political will of the citizens of Europe. Equally it is arguable that other areas which have developed as flanking or horizontal policies to the Internal Market programme could be perceived of, and interpreted as, citizenship rights.[77]

V. Criticisms of the Citizenship Provisions

i. Citizenship of the Union and Exclusion of Non-Union Nationals

The Treaties establishing the European Union do allow non-Member State nationals to bring complaints or actions where their rights are affected by Community law. One of the problems of linking the privileges of Citizenship to nationality of one of the Member States serves to reinforce the growing tendency of exclusion that the Internal Market - or 'Fortress Europe' - programme has created. In Article 1 of the Convention for the Protection of Human Rights and Fundamental Freedoms 1950 a precedent has been set allowing for non-Member State nationals to use its provisions within the jurisdiction of the Convention. Yet Citizenship of the Union has been reserved as an exclusive membership of a club for persons holding nationality of one of the Member States.

Habermas[78] has argued that the marginalisation of groups for various, spurious, reasons, is the characteristic of modernism and of the modern polity. Ward[79] has pointed out that the margins of the 'new' Europe are most acutely observed in the exclusion of those groups of

---

77 For example, Title VIII EC (social policy, education, vocational training); Title IX EC (culture) (Title XII) ;Title XI EC (consumer protection) XIV; Title XVI XIX EC (environment).

78 Habermas, J. 'Citizenship and Nationality Identity: Some Reflections on the Future of Europe' (1992) *Praxis International* 1.

79 Ward, I. 'Law and the Other Europeans' (1997) 35 *JCMS* 79.

people who are defined as 'non-European'. He argues that law plays a critical role in marginalising certain groups from the full benefits of European integration. In Chapter Three we discuss how the EU has, incrementally, since 1986, addressed TCN issues as security issues rather than immigration or human rights or citizenship issues. The securitisation of the external frontiers of the EU with the attempts to 'integrate' existing third country migrants into the fabric of EU society is one example where the positive image of 'Europe' is achieved. This is explained by Miles[80] in the categorisation of 'problem' TCN migrants sharing common characteristics:

> They originate from nation states beyond the European definition of the boundary of Europe and from nation states which are included in the diffuse notion of the 'Third World' ... This spatial and material origin is over determined by a set of signified cultural (e.g. Muslim) and somatic (e.g. 'Black skin') characteristics which constitute further signs of difference, if not inferiority'.

ii. Human Rights

One of the major initial criticisms of the Citizenship provisions was that they did not include any reference to human rights. Equating Citizenship with protection of human rights standards had appeared in a number of the previous attempts to draw up a concept of European Citizenship. For some commentators human rights are a necessary component of Citizenship rights.

O'Keeffe, D. 'Union Citizenship' in O'Keeffe, D. & Twomey, P. (eds.) *Legal Issues of the Maastricht Treaty* (1993, Chancery, London) 103

It is to be regretted that the citizenship provisions do not have a human rights component. As Rosy Bindi pointed out in her report to the European Parliament, 'it is inconceivable to base citizenship on anything other than the expansion of fundamental rights and

---

80 Miles, R. *Racism after 'Race Relations'* (1993, Routledge, London) 207.

freedoms in addition to their recognition and protection'.[81]

The TEU citizenship provisions may be compared with the Council of Europe Convention of 5 February 1992 on the Participation of Foreigners in Public Life at Local Level which guarantees to all foreign residents certain basic rights such as the freedoms of expression, assembly and association, as well as active and passive voting rights at local elections. The combination of fundamental rights and political rights in the one package is, it is submitted, a useful precedent.

Closa, C. 'Citizenship of the Union and Nationality of the Member States' in O'Keeffe, D. and Twomey, P. (eds.) *Legal Issues of the Maastricht Treaty* (1993, Chancery, London) 111-112

In contrast to the universalization of the enjoyment of human rights enshrined by constitutional orders, states still consider that there are certain privileges exclusively attached to the notion of citizen or national. The legitimacy of the sovereign entity's discretionary power to grant different rights to different individuals has not been challenged, although Western European states reserve nowadays only few rights, with a high socio-economic or political content, of which the criterion for their enjoyment is that of being a national. Given this agreement on certain essential rights, differences are caused not only by divergent conceptions of the relationship of the individual with the state, but also by the stage of socio-economic development achieved by a society.

The construction of the concept of citizenship in the TEU has not mirrored this constitutional model, since citizenship has been effectively dissociated from human rights. The catalogue of rights comprised by the citizenship of the union does not include human rights, although mention of these is made in the common provisions of the TEU, where the Union is commanded to respect human rights as a general principle of Community law. The belief commonly shared was, though, that the concept of citizenship of the Union *should* be the natural channel for the explicit and positive incorporation of human rights into the Community legal order. Prior to the TEU, human rights featured permanently as one of the constitutive elements in the proposals on citizens' rights or a people's Europe, and the claim was further repeated by most of the submissions to the 1991 intergovernmental conference.

The severing of this link, first postulated by the Spanish contribution to the intergovernmental conference, may be explained by doctrinal as well as practical reasons. Union citizenship has been created and defined as being additional to nationality, which implies that the substantive rights granted are additional to the ones recognized in the respective constitutional orders for nationals. Since human rights are a basic component of the constitutional orders of the 12 Member States, either in a positive sense or as interpretative criteria of the basic rights, it may, therefore be argued that the legitimating function which inspired the creation of citizenship of the Union might be brought into

---

81 Union Citizenship. Contributions by the Commission to the Intergovernmental Conference, Supplement 2/91 Bull EC. PE Doc. A 3-0139/91, 23 May 1991.

question because of the absence of human rights from the catalogue of rights. However, it is difficult to accept that the inclusion of a positive catalogue of rights within the concept of Union citizenship would have afforded a greater protection of human rights for *nationals of Member States* than that guaranteed by national constitutional orders. In fact, there have been cases where constitutional courts have blocked the passage of EC legislation by invoking the defence of constitutionally guaranteed human rights.

O'Leary, S. 'The Relationship Between Community Citizenship and the Protection of Fundamental Rights in Community Law' (1995) 32 *Common Market Law Review* 519, 553-554

... the protection and furtherance of individual rights should be the central objective of both Community citizenship and the adherence to fundamental rights in Community law. Both categories of rights have been weakened by the failure to recognize this essential purpose of the protection of individual rights in and against the national and supranational legal orders. Community citizenship should be relied on in future to establish a more direct legal and political relationship between the Community and its citizens and as a vehicle to represent their interests. Fundamental rights should also be enforced in conformity with the Court's powerful principle of effective judicial protection. Otherwise, both categories of rights will merely be a means to pay lip service to the involvement of Community citizens in European integration and will be used to cover up for the lack of accountability and legitimacy in the Community's political and legislative processes.

Fundamental rights and citizenship could be a means to redefine a European polity and, on that basis, to assert greater social legitimacy as Community integration proceeds. However, if the protection of the individual within the categories of rights outlined above is not increasingly identified as the fundamental element of the Community's social contract with Member States and their nationals, it is difficult to see how its social legitimacy can be enhanced. The process of integration to date has opted for market efficiency and competition, ideologies which at the national level have been fiercely debated and which have had marked social, political and even historical consequences. To proceed, even at this stage of integration, without deepening the social legitimacy of the Community would be a grave error. To ignore the essential role which individual Member State nationals should play in defining the content and limits of this new European polity on which the future of the Communities and Union so much depends would be even graver. The construction of a relationship between the protection of fundamental rights in Community law and Community citizenship could provide some solutions.

VI. Citizenship: The Way Forward?

The description of Union Citizenship as a 'futures market' by d'Oliveira[82] has cast the question of what the character of what Union Citizenship *might* become as one which Everson[83] describes as a 'normative' one. Everson argues that rather than following a narrative approach of detailing the *existing* nature of Citizenship we need to concentrate upon the future status of what citizenship could become. The underlying theme of exclusion and inclusion of individuals within the Community has provided the focus or lynchpin around which constructive accounts of how the shape of European Citizenship might evolve. For many commentators merely 'adding on' human rights protection will not solve the problem of exclusion which the TEU concept of Citizenship has created. Weiler[84] argues that the use of nationality in Article 8 [*17*] EC has transferred the previous intra-Community forms of alienation to a new form of inter-Community alienation. This has led some authors to look at alternative models of Citizenship.

One obvious, practical and immediate solution would be to dilute the nationality-citizenship nexus. A number of commentators,[85] have argued for a model of 'social citizenship'. Habermas[86] has emphasised the need for 'solidarity' as the basis for a new non-nationality citizenship. This would involve an acceptance of pluralism as well as constitutional guarantees. The shift in emphasis is a focus upon individuals being

---

82 D'Oliveira, H. 'European Citizenship: Its Meaning, Its Potential' in Dehousse, R. *et al.* (eds.) *Europe After Maastricht. An Ever Closer Union?* (1994, Law Books in Europe, Munich).

83 Everson, M. 'The Legacy of the Market Citizen' in Shaw, J. & More, G. *New Legal Dynamics of European Union* (1995, Clarendon Press, Oxford).

84 Weiler, J. 'Thou Shalt Not Oppress A Stranger: On the Judicial Protection of the Human Rights of Non-EC Nationals - A Critique' (1992) 3 *EJIL* 65.

85 See the discussion in Shaw, J. 'The Many Pasts and Futures of Citizenship in the European Union' (1997) 22 *ELRev* 554. Cf. Bercusson, B. *et al.* 'A Manifesto for Social Europe' (1997) 3 *ELJ* 189.

86 Habermas, J. 'The European National State. Its Achievements and Its Limitations. On the Past and Future of Sovereignty and Citizenship' (1996) *Ratio Juris* 125.

respected as 'people' rather than economic/political components. Weiler[87] has suggested an idea of supra-nationalism. This form of 'citizenship' is seen as a sense of 'coming home' as a civic, rational construct rather than relying on the EU's current baggage of nationality and forms of cultural nationalism. But this idea of *demos* would not be exclusive; would operate alongside other forms of identity (for example, national, regional, religious identities). As Weiler notes, the greatest challenge would be how to accommodate and settle conflicting loyalties within these multiple identities.

Preuß[88] argues that the most progressive aspect for European Citizenship is the creation of *opportunities* for citizens to 'engage in manifold economic, social, cultural, scholarly and even political activities irrespective of the traditional territorial boundaries of the European nation-states...'. In Preuß's analysis the idea of European citizenship is to be seen as an amplified bundle to options within a physically broadened and functionally more differentiated space than a definitive legal status. Like Weiler, he believes this helps to abolish hierarchies between different loyalties and allow individuals a multiplicity of associative relations without tying them to a specific nationality.

While the new concept of Citizenship of the Union can be described as post-national since it has evolved in ways which are different from, and do not replicate, the experience of State-based national citizenship model, the result is a list of bare statements contained within Articles 8a-e [*17-22*] EC. Shaw,[89] using the terminology of Walzer,[90] describes these as 'thin' minimal statements which require contextualisation within a 'thicker' and 'maximal' vision of what it is to be a 'member' of the EU under the legal, political and socio-economic orders of the EU. Shaw argues that the process of constitution-building and polity-formation through the enhancement of

---

87 Weiler, J. 'Does Europe Need A Constitution? Reflections On Demos, Telos and the German Maastricht Decision' (1995) 1 *ELJ* 219.

88 Preuß, U. 'Problems of a Concept of European Citizenship' (1995) 1 *ELJ* 267, 280.

89 Shaw, J. 'European Union Citizenship: The IGC and Beyond' (1997) 3 *Public Law* 413.

90 Walzer, M. *Thick and Thin: Moral Argument at Home and Abroad* (1994, University of Notre Dame Press, Notre Dame).

citizenship rights may be part of a set of political processes whereby EU citizens themselves, through their practices as citizens build the type of Community of which they wish to be members, creating a form of 'thick' citizenship instantiating principles of communitarian principles to rights and morality.

Extending legal rights at a constitutional level has been another avenue explored, but not developed at the Amsterdam IGC. The suggestion of incorporating a general non-discrimination clause (modelled on Article 6[*12*] EC) was put before the agenda of the 1997 IGC and presented in the drafts for amendment of the Treaties and supported by the Commission and the European Parliament. The Court of Justice indicated that it would want to be involved in considering that implications for judicial review if the idea of constitutional review on human rights issues was incorporated into the text of the Treaty. In contrast the Comité des Sages recommended the need for a participatory process to formulate a modern list of civic and social rights and duties:

> ... citizenship is not merely a collection of rights: it is also a way of living, of recognizing one's obligations to others, of participating in society through a multiplicity of relationships with its members. A simple list of rights does not properly reflect this dimension of citizenship, whereas a sufficiently lengthy process of collective formulation of rights, would make it possible to give expression to citizenship and to arrive at a more balanced view of rights and duties.[91]

These ideas found only a limited expression in the Treaty of Amsterdam, with the addition of a new legal base to develop a wider plank of anti-discrimination legislation. The original draft proposed by the Irish Presidency included a long 'wish-list' of forms of discrimination which would receive protection: sex, racial, ethnic or social origin, religious belief, disability, age or sexual orientation. The final version of the non-discrimination clause was watered down considerably. The new Article 13 EC became a legal base clause of further Community action in a restricted number of areas.

---

91 (1996, OOPEC, Luxembourg) & (1996) 6 *JESP* 241, 242.

Another theme has been that of transparency and open government. D'Oliveira[92] makes the point that the political dimension of Citizenship of the Union is underdeveloped. Armstrong[93] argues that the wide-ranging exclusion of the Citizen from EU decision-making processes results in a paradox at the heart of the concept of Citizenship of the Union. He argues that the concept of Citizenship has been involved as a counter balance to the seemingly remote Institutions of the EU in order to attach political legitimacy to EU governance.

VII. Culture

It has been argued in this Chapter that the process of creating a European identity has been a resort to negative coherence - to confirm what Europe is not. When faced with the question of what then is Europe, a notion of cultural identity has appeared only recently on the political agenda. There is even less precision than with the 'thin' set of citizenship rights so widely criticised above when we look at the creation of a European cultural policy. The original Treaty of Rome 1957 contained few references to the protection of culture. For example, Article 36 [*30*] EC allows for the restriction of the free movement of goods based on the need to protect 'national treasures possessing artistic, historic or archeological value'. As we shall discover the inclusion of cultural interests by this means has in fact resulted in the suppression of national culture in favour of the economic pursuits of a common market internal market.

The starting point for the emergence of an EC policy on culture was the recognition in 1969 by the Heads of State or Government of the Member States of the need to preserve Europe as 'an exceptional seat of development, culture and progress'.[94] But no action was taken by the

---

92 d' Oliveira, H-J. 'European Citizenship: Its Meaning, Its Potential' in Dehousse, R. *et al* (eds.) *Europe After Maastricht. An Ever Closer Union*? (1994, Law Books in Europe, Munich).

93 Armstrong, K. 'Citizenship of the Union? Lessons From *Carvel and The Guardian*' (1996) 59 *MLR* 582, 586.

94 Point 4 of the Communiqué, *EC Bulletin* 1-1970 Part One, Ch.1.

Commission until 1977 in a document *Community Action in the Cultural Sector.*[95] Recognition of the need for action in the cultural sector to realise the completion of the Internal Market was made in the Commission document, *A Fresh Boost For Culture in the European Community.*[96] It was recognised that with the abolition of controls on the free movement of goods at the end of 1992 trade in cultural goods would increase. Thus Regulation 3911/92/EEC on the export of cultural goods[97] and Directive 93/7/EEC [98] were enacted to protect cultural objects within the Internal Market. Other areas of priority action were identified by the Council (differing from the Commission's list) as the audio-visual sector, books and the training of cultural workers. The amendments made to the EC Treaty as a result of the TEU extend the scope for EC action in the fields of culture. Article 3(p)(*q*) EC provides that the Community shall contribute to the 'flowering of the cultures of the Member States'.[99] An amendment to Article 92 [*87*] EC allows for the granting of State aid 'To promote culture and heritage conservation'. But the major change was to be found in Article 128 [*151*] EC.

Article 3(p) [*3(q)*] EC. [For the purposes set out in Article 2 [*2*], the activities of the Community shall include, as provided by this Treaty and in accordance with the timetable set out therein] .... a contribution to education and training of quality and to the flowering of the cultures of the Member States.

TITLE IX [*XII*] CULTURE

Article 128(1) [*151(1)*]EC. The Community shall contribute to the flowering of the cultures of the Member States, while respecting their national and regional diversity and at the same time bringing the common cultural heritage to the fore.

2. Action by the Community shall be aimed at encouraging cooperation between Member States and, if necessary, supporting and supplementing their action in the following areas:

- improvement of the knowledge and dissemination of the culture and history of the European peoples;

---

95 *EC Bulletin Supp* 6/77.

96 *EC Bulletin Supp* 4/87, 5.

97 OJ 1992 L 395/1.

98 OJ 1993 L 74/1.

99 Note also Article 3(b)[*5*] EC which introduces the principle of subsidiarity.

- conservation and safeguarding of cultural heritage of European significance;
- non-commercial cultural exchanges;
- artistic and literary creation, including the audiovisual sector.

3. The Community and the Member States shall foster cooperation with third countries and the competent international organizations in the sphere of culture, in particular the Council of Europe.

4. The Community shall take cultural aspects into account in its action under other provisions of this Treaty. [In particular in order to respect and to promote the diversity of its cultures.]

5. In order to contribute to the achievement of the objectives referred to in this Article, the Council:

- acting in accordance with the procedure referred to in Article 189b and after consulting the Committee of the regions, shall adopt incentive measures, excluding any harmonization of the laws and regulations of the Member States. The Council shall act unanimously throughout the procedure referred to in Article 189b;
- acting unanimously on a proposal from the Commission, shall adopt recommendations.

Lane, R. 'New Community Competences Under The Maastricht Treaty' (1993) 30 *Common Market Law Review* 939, 951-958

Even more so than education, culture is a radically new and controversial field of Community competence. The constitutional difficulties and those affecting the application of the 'subsidiarity plus' rule discussed above for education apply equally - and perhaps even more so ....The Maastricht approach to culture is therefore at least as circumspect as that of education, providing safeguards for national autonomy and only minimal and supplementary Community authority to act.

In its context, Article 128 cannot be said to be an example of the draughtsman's finer arts. Culture is not defined, its 'flowering' more botanical than justiciable, and the Member States' common cultural heritage is at least as amorphous as the European dimension in education. (Oddly, the Community is to promote *Community* cultural heritage but *European* education.) Is the Notting Hill carnival in London an aspect of common Community culture? Is it to include only commonly accepted manifestations of culture, or can it stretch to political culture; to language; to moral and spiritual culture; and in any medium? Equally oddly, the Community is bound to take notice of the Member States' cultural and linguistic diversity when acting in the field of education, [Art. 126(1) EC] but is not specifically so bound in the field of culture. And it is not bound by Article 128 to be mindful of a high level of protection in cultural matters, as it is for education ('quality' education), public health, the consumer and the environment.

The basic problem remains: culture is, and ought to be, nation and sub-nation specific. Protecting a common Community cultural heritage ... is well and good, but the true threat to culture, felt especially keenly by the smaller Member States and nations within Member States, comes not from outside the Community but from within, from the 'Europeanization' or homogenization that is a necessary product of the Treaty and the internal market. And to those concerned to ensure cultural diversity *within* the Community *against* the Community, the entrails are not good.

The Court of Justice has addressed issues relating to culture raised by Member States wishing to take protectionist measures in all of the four freedoms.[100] For example, under Article 36 [*30*] EC there is protection for national treasures possessing artistic, historic or archaeological value. The Court has also recognised cultural protection as a mandatory requirement under the *Cassis de Dijon* formula. However to date the Court has not yet accepted any of the cultural policy reasons advanced by the Member States as objectively justified.

In the following case the Court accepts that certain provisions which hinder the free movement of goods may be objectively justified provided the measures taken are proportionate. Thus the protection or enhancement of artistic work may be added to the *Cassis de Dijion* list of mandatory requirements.

Cases 6 & 61/84, Cinéthèque v Fédération National des Cinémas Français [1985] ECR 2605, [1986] 1 CMLR 365

A French law banning the sale or hire of videos during the first year in which a film was released was challenged as being contrary to Article 30 [*28*] EC. The law was justified to protect cinematographic production.

15. ... What was at issue was the protection of the cinema as a means of cultural expression, which protection was necessary in view of the rapid development of other modes of film distribution.

.....

---

100 But the Court has not ruled on the impact of cultural policy on competition law: see Joined Cases 43/82 *VBVB &VBBB v Commission* [1984] ECR 19, [1985] 1 CMLR 27.

18. The Commission states that the national legislation in question, by prohibiting the marketing of video-cassettes of cinematographic works shown in cinemas, undeniably has the effect of hindering imports of video- recordings lawfully produced and marketed in another Member State and in free circulation there ... The Commission maintains, however, that cultural aims may justify certain restrictions on the free movement of goods provided that those restrictions apply to national and imported products without distinction, that they are appropriate to the cultural aim which is being pursued and that they constitute the means of achieving them which affects intra-Community trade the least.

.....

22. ... the application of such a system may create barriers to intra-Community trade in video-cassettes because of the disparities between the system operated in the different Member States and between the conditions for the release of cinematographic works in the cinemas of those states. In those circumstances a prohibition of exploitation laid down by such a system is not compatible with the principle of the free movement of goods provided for in the Treaty unless any obstacle to intra-Community trade thereby created does not exceed that which is necessary in order to ensure the attainment of the objective in view and unless that objective is justified with regard to Community law.

23. It must be conceded that a national system which, in order to encourage the creation of cinematographic works irrespective of their origin, gives priority, for a limited period, to the distribution of such works through the cinema, is so justified. The question of the compatibility of the national measures with Article 10 of the European Convention for the Protection of Human Rights and Fundamental Freedoms was also raised by the plaintiffs.

National rules requiring linguistic competence have been raised by the Member States as barriers to the principle of free movement of persons.

Case 379/87 Groener v Minister for Education [1989] ECR 3967, [1990] 1 CMLR 401

Groener, a Dutch national, challenged a rule making appointment to a permanent, full time post in a state college conditional on proficiency in the Irish language. It was not necessary for teachers to teach in the Irish language once appointed. The Irish government justified the rule as part of a policy to promote the use of Irish as a means of expressing national identity and culture. Groener argued that the rule was contrary to Article 48 [*39*] EC and Article 3 of Regulation 1612/68.

19. The EEC Treaty does not prohibit the adoption of a policy for the protection and promotion of a language of a Member State which is both the national language and the first official language. However, the implementation of such a policy must not encroach upon a fundamental freedom such as that of the free movement of workers. Therefore, the requirements deriving from measures intended to implement such a policy must not in any circumstances be disproportionate in relation to the aim pursued and the manner in which they are applied must not bring about discrimination against nationals of other Member States.

20. The importance of education for the implementation of such a policy must be recognised. Teachers have an essential role to play, not only through the teaching which they provide but also by their participation in the daily life of the school and the privileged relationship which they have with their pupils. In those circumstances, it is not unreasonable to require them to have some knowledge of the first national language.

21. It follows that the requirement imposed on teachers to have an adequate knowledge of such a language must, provided that the level of knowledge required is not disproportionate in relation to the objective pursued, be regarded as a condition corresponding to the knowledge required by reason of the nature of the post to be filled within the meaning of [Article 3(1) of Regulation 1612/68].

22. It must also be pointed out that where the national provisions provide for the possibility of exemption from that linguistic requirement where no other fully qualified candidate has applied for the post to be filled, Community law requires that power to grant exemptions to be exercised by the minister in a non-discriminatory manner.

23. Moreover, the principle of non-discrimination precludes the imposition of any requirement that the linguistic knowledge in question must have been acquired within the national territory. It also implies that the nationals of other Member States should have an opportunity to retake the oral examination, in the event of their having previously failed it, when they again apply for a post of assistant lecturer or lecturer.

24. Accordingly, the reply to [the] question must be that a permanent full-time post of a lecturer in public vocational education institutions is a post of such a nature as to justify the requirement of linguistic knowledge, within the meaning of [Article 3(1) of Regulation 1612/68], provided that the linguistic requirement in question is imposed as part of a policy for the promotion of the national language which is, at the same time, the first official language and provided that requirement is applied in a proportionate and non-discriminatory manner.

In *Groener* the Court seems aware of the importance of cultural diversity and the protection of minority languages as well as taking cognisance of the role of teachers in the educational process. Under Article 59 [*49*] EC the Court has recognised that cultural protection may constitute an imperative reason of general interest protected by Article 10 ECHR 1951 which may justify restrictions of the provision of services.

Case C-288/89 Stichting Collective Antennevoorziening Gouda v Commissariaat voor de media [1991] ECR I-4007

Ten operators of cable networks in the Netherlands were fined for transmitting programmes with advertisements in Dutch. A Dutch law which forbade advertising to the Dutch public had the objective of the law being to maintain a pluralistic and non-commercial broadcasting system.

23. A cultural policy understood in that sense may indeed constitute an overriding requirement relating to the general interest which justifies a restriction on the freedom to provide services. The maintenance of the pluralism which that Dutch policy seeks to safeguard is connected with freedom of expression, as protected by Article 10 of the European Convention on Human Rights and Fundamental Freedoms which is one of the fundamental rights guaranteed by the Community legal order (Case 4/73 *Nold v Commission* [1974] ECR 491, paragraph 13).

24. However, it should be observed that there is no necessary connection between such a cultural policy and the conditions relating to the structure of foreign broadcasting bodies. In order to ensure pluralism in the audio-visual sector it is not indispensable for the national legislation to require broadcasting bodies established in other Member States to align themselves to the Dutch model should they intend to broadcast programmes containing advertisements intended for the Dutch public. In order to secure the pluralism which it wishes to maintain the Netherlands Government may very well confine itself to formulating the statutes of its own bodies in an appropriate manner.

25. Conditions affecting the structure of foreign broadcasting bodies cannot therefore be regarded as being objectively necessary in order to safeguard the general interest in maintaining a national radio and television system which secures pluralism.

.....

27. ... restrictions on the broadcasting of advertisements, such as a prohibition on advertising particular products or on certain days, a limitation of the duration or frequency of advertisements or restrictions designed to enable listeners or viewers not to confuse advertising with other parts of the programme, may be justified by overriding reasons relating to the general interest. Such restrictions may be imposed in order to protect consumers against excessive advertising or, as an objective of cultural policy, in order to maintain a level of programme quality.

.....

29. ... the provisions of the Mediawet at issue in this case no longer reserve to STER all the revenue from advertising intended specifically for the Dutch public. However by laying down rules on the broadcasting of such advertisements, they restrict the competition to which the STER may be exposed in that market from foreign broadcasting bodies. Accordingly the result is that they protect the revenue of STER ... and therefore pursue the same objective as the previous legislation.

30. ... restrictions of the kind at issue are not justified by overriding requirements relating to the general interest.

Case C-369/89 Piageme v BVBA Peeters [1991] ECR I-2971, [1993] 3 CMLR 725

Peeters was established in Belgium, in the Flemish speaking region. It marketed mineral water with labels printed in French and German. Piageme and other companies importing mineral water argued that this was contrary to Belgian legislation on labelling. This legislation required the particulars on labels to be in the language of the region where the foodstuffs were being sold. The defendant argued that the Belgian laws were contrary to Article 30 [*28*] EC and Directive 79/112/EEC.[101] Article 14 of the Directive provided that the relevant particulars as regards the labelling of foodstuffs must be 'in a language easily understood by purchasers, unless other measures have been taken to ensure that the purchaser is informed'. In interpreting the Directive's provisions the Court held:

---

101 OJ 1979 L 33/1.

13. The only obligation is therefore to prohibit the sale of products whose labelling is not easily understood by the purchaser rather than to require the use of a particular language.

14. It is true that, according to a literal interpretation, Article 14 does not preclude a national law which allows for the information of the consumer, only the use of the language or languages of the region where the products are sold, in so far as such a law would allow purchasers to understand easily the particulars appearing on the products. The language of the linguistic region is the language which seems to be the most 'easily understood'.

15. Such an interpretation of Article 14 fails, however, to take account of the aims of the Directive. It follows from the first three recitals in the preamble that Directive 79/112 seeks in particular to eliminate the differences which exist between national provisions and which hinder the free movement of goods. It is because of that aim that Article 14 is limited to the requirement of a language easily understood by the purchaser and proves that the entry of the foodstuffs into the territory of a Member State may be authorised where the relevant particulars do not appear in a language easily understood 'if other measures have been taken to ensure that the purchaser is informed'.

16. It follows from the foregoing that, on the one hand imposing a stricter obligation than the use of a language easily understood, that is to say for example the exclusive use of the language of a linguistic region and, on the other hand, failing to acknowledge the possibility of ensuring that the purchaser is informed by other measures, goes beyond the requirements of the Directive. The obligation exclusively to use the language of the linguistic region constitutes a measure having an equivalent effect to a quantitative restriction on imports prohibited by Article 30 of the Treaty.

17. Consequently, the reply to the question referred by the national court should be that Article 30 of the EEC Treaty and Article 14 of Directive 79/112/EEC preclude a national law from requiring the exclusive use of a specific language for the labelling of foodstuffs without allowing for the possibility of using another language easily understood by persons or of ensuring that the purchaser is informed by other measures.

In the context of the provision of services in the 'tourist guide' infringement actions the Court has stated that '... the general interest in consumer protection and in the conservation of the national historic and artistic heritage can constitute an overriding reason justifying a restriction on the freedom to provide services ...'.[102]

---

102 Case C-180/89 *Commission v Italy* [1991] ECR I-709. Note the slight difference in Case C-154/89 *Commission v France* [1991] ECR I-659, para 4 '... The general interest in the proper appreciation of places and things of

Lane, R. 'New Community Competences Under the Maastricht Treaty' (1993) 30 *Common Market Law Review* 939, 956-958

... the political institutions, ... will have to be very careful in deploying their (limited) powers under Articles 126 and 128, not only because of the most stringent of procedural requirements (co-decision, consultation with the Committee of the Regions and, for culture, unanimity within the Council) and the hurdles they must clear in order to justify Community action, but also because, having done so, they will be venturing into extraordinarily sensitive areas of which the Community has no experience. Alongside the activities of the European Union, they are a function of the Community's contribution to a 'People's Europe', and are likely to acquire a higher profile and greater public notice than a reading of the texts would suggest. The Community will require a deftness of touch lest it be, or be seen to be, impartial, clumsy and/or heavy-handed. And the deftness will have to be surer still with the recent rise, real or apprehended, of racism and xenophobia in the Community.

Cultural concerns, more so than education, are also likely to trench upon other areas of Community activity. The political institutions must therefore be mindful of the requirements of the integration clause of Article 128(4), which gives rise to four interconnected and complex questions: (a) is the meaning of 'cultural aspects' as used in Article 128(4) synonymous with the meaning of culture as used in Article 128 generally, whatever they mean, or does it mean something else, and if so what?; (b) is it intended to constitute merely policy guidelines for the due consideration of the political institutions, and/or (c) a normative rule and/or a rule of interpretation for measures adopted, and if so, (d) is it justiciable? Experience to date of the one equivalent provision existing in the present Treaty, in the field of the environment, suggests that the requirement to take notice of Article 128(4) will not be overly burdensome [Article 130r(2)].

The Court too will have to be on its mettle, both in defining the meaning and breadth of Community education and cultural competences and the subsidiarity and integration provisions, but also for another reason: much of its intrusion hitherto into sensitive national domains has been, and has been

---

historical interest and the widest possible dissemination of knowledge of the artistic cultural heritage can constitute an overriding reason justifying a restriction on the freedom to provide services.' The exception is stated in a different way in Case C-198/89 *Commission v Greece* [1991] ECR I-727, para 4, '... The general interest in the proper appreciation of the artistic and archaeological heritage of a country and in consumer protection can constitute an overriding reason justifying a restriction on the freedom to provide services...'

accepted as being, justified by the economic interests of the common/internal markets. Education and culture however are sensitive non-economic spheres, of which the Court has had little experience. Its reasoning may therefore be coloured by, and subject to attack on grounds of, not economic analysis but ideology. And this may put to the test the consistent, if not entirely unwavering, loyalty to the Court which has hitherto been shown by the Member States and by their courts.[103]

The negative affirmation of what Europe is not has clouded over the fact that the differences between the Member States - as well as within the Member States - linked to the desire not to suppress the Member States out of existence has led to a process or sense of creating Europe which replicates the nation-state but which in fact has led to few positive images of what a common European heritage is. Pietrse,[104] quoting the Netherlands Ambassador for International Cultural Co-operation argues the following is the standard definition put out by European elites:

> What determines and characterises European culture?... Europe is formed by the .... community of nations which are largely characterised by the inherited civilisation whose most important sources are: the Judaeo-Christian religion, the Greek-Hellenistic ideas in the fields of government, philosophy, arts and science, and finally, the Roman views concerning law.

A more proactive development of a European cultural policy is being developed by the Commission. The Commission's Communication to the European Parliament and the Council of the European Union *European Community Action To Promote Culture*[105] served as a framework for the adoption of three Action Programmes: *Kaleidoscope,* relating to artistic and cultural activities; *Ariane*, relating to books and reading; *Raphael*, cultural heritage. In the *First Report on the*

---

103 COM (92) 149 final.

104 Pietrse, J. 'Fictions of Europe' (1991) 32 *Race and Class* 3.

105 COM (94) 356.

Consideration of Cultural Aspects in European Community Action[106] the Commission recognises the potential for conflict between the demands of the Internal Market and the need of the Member States to protect cultural works. The Community is given the responsibility for reconciling these tensions:

> ... cultural policy must make a contribution to strengthening and to expanding the influence of the 'European model of society built upon a set of values common to European societies' (Opinion of the Commission on the convening of the 1996 Intergovernmental Conference).[107]

To this end two priority areas are identified to ensure and increase convergence of a European cultural policy:

- enhancement of cultural roots and currents which are common to Europeans
- cultural action to develop permanent networks between cultural operators in the Member States

The issue of a 'Fortress Europe' also emerges:

> Finally outside the European Union, Community cultural policy must provide an expansion in the cultural influence of European people and of the European model of society. If it constitutes an integration factor within the Union, for the outside it represents an instrument of co-operation which must be used to promote dialogue between cultures.[108]

Thus cultural policy, like citizenship, is being used as a mediator for integration and as a metaphor for building a concept of Europe - as well as defining its boundaries. 'Europe' is being used as a signifier not only from a linguistic point of view in terms of European integration but also in terms of attempting a cultural identity. What is being developed

---

106 COM (96) 160 final.

107 Conclusion 2, Pt V p.2.

108 Pt V, p.3.

is a notion of what Kymlicka[109] describes as *societal* culture.[110] The creation and growth of 'societal cultures' is linked with the process of modernisation. Modernisation involves the diffusion throughout a given society of a common culture through the use of a standardised language ('euro-speak') which is embedded in common economic, political and educational institutions. Kymlicka, drawing upon Gellner's work, argues that the reasons for this development of a societal culture are both functional - a modern European economy needs a mobile, educated, literate labour-force - and political - there is a high need for solidarity within modern democratic states so that citizens will have a strong sense of common identity and common membership and will make sacrifices for each other. Such messages are brought over in the Commission's White Paper on the Internal Market with the stark facts of the re-structuring necessary to modernise the Common Market and in messages relating to the fact that fiscal discipline in some Member States is the necessary medicine to achieve EMU. Kymlica's third explanation for the development of societal cultures is that the diffusion of a common culture is required by the modern commitment to equal opportunity - seen in the EU in the use not only of the non-discrimination principle in Article 6 [*12*] EC but also in the moves to tackle barriers to integration for economic actors throughout the EU.

The economic rights to free movement and the idea of a 'citizenship' right to free movement signal the cultural closeness and similarity between the Member States and invent a constructed communality not only in securing the external borders but also in securitising the internal area of free movement. More so than in the development of a concept of Citizenship, we are left with a clear impression of what a European culture is not - but with an unfocused picture of what it is. The EU has attempted to present itself, not as transcending itself into a *different* sovereign power or supra-national body but rather by containing the image of the Member States by a *replication* of their own ideas of citizenship and culture. In the early stages of the development of a European citizenship and culture Schepel

---

109 Kymlicka, W. *Multicultural Citizenship* (1995, OUP, Oxford), 76.

110 See the use of this term by Gellner, E. *Nations and Nationalism* (1983, Blackwell, Oxford).

and Wesseling[111] observe the use of a malign set of attributes associated with the nation-state and national sovereignty - war, economic decline, nationalism - these images were arraigned against what was portrayed a benign 'common market' inherently able to deliver more positive goods - a raised standard of living, peace, prosperity, integration cosmopolitanism - and law.[112] The subsequent creation of an identity for Europe has been described as calculating and tawdry as those used by national elites - in the creation of rituals, traditions, public symbols and ancestor figures.[113] The recent creation of Jean Monnet and Jacques Delors Chairs within European universities continues the theme of European passports, a European flag and the adoption of Beethoven's 'Ode to Joy' as the anthem of the EU. The weakness of this approach is that the Member States - and their peoples - are disappointed at the failure of 'Europe' to replicate the more advanced and sophisticated imagined communities that they have felt secure with at the national level.[114] Yet that failure is attributable to a reluctance of the Member States to let go of the imagined communities they have fought hard to create.

---

111 Schepel, H. and Wessling, R. 'La Communità giudici, avvocati, funzionaire e *clerks* nella scrittura dell'Europa' (1996) *Sociologia del Diritto* 223.

112 Although as Anderson observes, was it really necessary to have the full panoply of an executive authority, a legislature, a supreme court to run a mere customs union? Anderson, P. 'Under the Sign of the Interim' (1996) *London Review of Books*, 4 January.

113 Shore, C. and Black, A. 'Citizens, Europe and the Construction of European Identity' in Goddard, V. *et al.* (eds.) *The Anthropology of Europe: Identity and Boundaries in Conflict* (1994, Berg, Oxford); Shore, C. 'Inventing the "People's Europe"? Critical Approaches to European Community "Cultural Policy"' (1993) 28 *Man*; Shore, C. 'Imagining the New Europe: Identity, Heritage in European Community Discourse' in Graves-Brown, P. *et al.* (eds.) Cultural Identity and Archeology: *The Construction of European Communities* (1996, Routledge, London).

114 A new view of what is seen to be part of the common cultural heritage of Europe is seen in the preludes to membership of the EU found in the *Agenda 2000* (COM (97) 2000) programme for a select few of the central and eastern European states. Equally in the Treaty of Amsterdam Article F [*6*] TEU is revised. Instead of the first sub-clause referring to the national identities of the Member States, it now speaks of liberty, democracy, human rights and the rule of law.

Further Reading

Ackers, L. 'Citizenship, Gender and Dependency in the European Union: The Position of Migrant Women' (1996) *Social Politics*

Closa, C. 'Citizenship of the Union and Nationality of the Member States' in O'Keeffe, D. & Twomey, P. (eds.) *Legal Issues of the Maastricht Treaty* (1993, Chancery, London)

----- 'The Concept of Citizenship in the Treaty on European Union' (1992) 29 *Common Market Law Review* 1137

d'Oliveira, H. 'Expanding External and Shrinking Internal Borders: Europe's Defense Mechanisms in the Areas of Free Movement, Immigration and Asylum' in O'Keeffe & Twomey (eds.) *op. cit.*

Habermas, J. 'Citizenship and National Identity: Some Reflections on the Future of Europe' (1992-1993) 12 *Praxis International* 1

Hall, S. 'Loss of Union Citizenship in Breach of Fundamental Rights' (1996) 21 *European Law Review 129*

Koslowski, R. 'Intra-E.U. Migration, Citizenship and Political Union' (1994) 32 *Journal of Common Market Studies* 369

La Torre, M. 'Citizenship: a European Wager' (1995) 8 *Ratio Juris* 113

Lardy, H. 'The Political Rights of Union Citizenship' (1996) 2 *European Public Law* 611

Marias, E. (ed.) European Citizenship (1994, European Institute of Public Administration, Maastricht)

McMahon, J. *Education and Culture in European Community Law* (1995, The Athlone Press, London)

Meehan, E. 'Citizenship of the European Community' (1993) 64 *Political Quarterly* 185

----- *Citizenship and the European Community* (1993, Sage, London)

O'Keeffe, D. 'The Free Movement of Persons and the Single Market' (1992) 17 *European Law Review* 3

O'Leary, S. *The Evolving Concept of Community Citizenship* (1995, Martinus Nijhoff, Dordrecht)

Ross, M. 'Cultural Protection: a Matter of Union Citizenship or Human Rights?' in Neuwahl, N. & Rosas, a. (eds.) *The European Union and Human Rights* (1995, Martinus Nijhoff, The Hague)

Szyszczak, E. 'Race Discrimination: The Limits of Market Equality' in

Hepple, B. & Szyszczak, E. (eds.) *Discrimination: The Limits of Law* (1992, Mansell, London)
Taschner, H. 'Free Movement of Students, Retired Persons and other European Citizens in H. Schermers *et al.* (eds.) *Free Movement of Persons in Europe* (1991, Martinus Nijhoff, Dordrecht)
Twomey, P. 'The European Union: Three Pillars Without a Human Rights Foundation' in O'Keeffe & Twomey (eds.) *op. cit.*
Von Plehwe, T. 'European Union and The Free Movement of Cultural Goods' (1995) 20 *European Law Review* 431

3. Free Movement of Persons and Securitisation

I. The Development of Free Movement

Since its inception, free movement of persons has been one of the fundamental objectives of the EC Treaty.[1] It was a right which was initially reserved only for the economically active. One only had the right to enter another Member State if one was going to work there (Article 48 [*39*] EC); seeking to establish oneself (Article 52 [*43*] EC) or was going to provide or receive a service (Article 59 [*49*] EC). Secondary legislation has extended this right to enter and reside in another Member State to the 'economically independent'. Rights of entry and residence have therefore been granted specifically to students, employees and the self-employed who have ceased their occupational activity, and to people generally provided that they have sufficient funds and social security insurance to avoid becoming a burden on the social assistance system of the host State.[2]

These rights were limited in a number of ways. They applied only to those who enjoyed a certain economic status. Since 1968 it has been assumed that they are not directly extended to third country nationals (TCNs).[3] More generally, these rights have been contingent rights.

---

1 Article 3(c) [*3(c)*] EC.

2 Directive 90/364/EEC on the right of residence, OJ 1990 L 180/26; Directive 90/365/EEC on the right of residence for employees and self-employed persons who have ceased their occupational activity, OJ 1990 L 180/28; Directive 93/96/EEC on the right of residence for students, OJ 1993 L 317/59.

3 Article 6 [*12*] EC gives no suggestion as to who can enjoy the protection of the principle of non-discrimination. Article 48(2) [*39(2)*] and EC secondary legislation suggests that it is confined to EC nationals and members of their families, Directive 68/360/EEC, OJ Spec Ed. 1968, L 257/13, Article 1. See the debates in Böhning, W. *The Migration of Workers in Britain and the EC*

Member States have always been permitted to deny entry to an immigrant on grounds of public policy, public security and public health.[4] Whilst the Court has reserved the right to review these measures,[5] free movement rights were subordinated and ultimately limited by national security concerns.[6] This did not simply result in access being denied to individuals who posed a threat to public security, public health or public policy, it also provided a rationale for more general limitations on free movement in the form of border controls.[7]

Case C- 68/89 Commission v Netherlands [1991] ECR 2637

The Commission brought an Article 169 [*226*] EC action against the Netherlands challenging the Dutch practice of immigration officials asking nationals of another Member State to answer questions concerning the purpose and duration of their stay and the financial means at their disposal before being permitted to enter its territory, arguing that such a practice was in breach of the obligations under Articles 3(c)[*3(c)*], 48 [*39*], 52 [*43*] and 59 [*49*] EC and Directives 68/360/EEC and 73/148/EEC which provide, respectively, for the abolition of restrictions on free movement for workers, and with regard to establishment and provision of services.[8] Both Directives allow entry to another Member State's territory on production of a passport or identity card.

10. It must be stated in the first place that, as the Commission has rightly emphasized, nationals of the Member States of the Community generally have the right to enter the territory of the other Member States in the exercise of the various freedoms recognized by the Treaty and in particular the freedom to provide services which, according to now settled case-law, is enjoyed both by providers and by recipients of services (see most recently the judgment in Case 186/87 *Cowan* [1989] ECR 195).

(1972, OUP/Institute for Race Relations, Oxford); Oliver, P. 'Non-Community Nationals and the Treaty of Rome' (1985) *YBEL* 57.

4 Article 48(3) [*39(3)*] EC; Article 56 [*46*] EC & Article 66 [*55*] EC. On these see pp. 446 ff.

5 See pp. 452ff.

6 Peers, S. 'National Security and European Law' (1996) 16 *YBEL* 363.

7 Case 321/87 *Commission v Belgium* [1989] ECR 997, [1990] 2 CMLR 492.

8 OJ Spec Ed. (1968) II, 485; OJ 1973 L 172/14.

11. Secondly, as the Court held in its judgment in Case 321/87 *Commission* v *Belgium* [1989] ECR 997, the only precondition which Member States may impose on the right of entry into their territory of the persons covered by the abovementioned directives is the production of a valid identity document or passport.

12. That condition, which is the only one laid down by Article 3 of the two directives, cannot be supplemented by the requirement of proving inclusion in one of the classes of persons mentioned in those directives. It is apparent from the system established by those directives, and in particular from Article 4 of Directive 68/360 and Article 6 of Directive 73/148, that it is only upon the issue of a residence card or permit that the authorities of a Member State may ask the persons concerned, under the conditions laid down in those Articles, to furnish evidence of their right of residence.

13. More generally, the obligation to answer questions put by frontier officials cannot be a precondition for the entry of a national of one Member State into the territory of another.

14. The United Kingdom, however, insists that it is necessary to ask questions in order to verify the validity of the identity documents produced.

15. In that connection, it need merely be observed that the lawfulness of controls as to the validity of the document produced derives from the requirement laid down in Article 3 of both Directives that the identity card or passport should be 'valid'.

16. It follows from the foregoing that, by maintaining in force and by applying legislation by virtue of which citizens of a Member State may be required to answer questions put by border officials regarding the purpose and duration of their journey and the financial means at their disposal for it before they are permitted to enter Netherlands territory, the Kingdom of the Netherlands has failed to fulfil the obligations imposed on it by Directives 68/360 and 73/148.

The Single European Act hinted at a new balance between free movement rights and security concerns. In its White Paper the Commission sought 'not merely to simplify existing procedures, but to do away with internal frontier controls in their entirety'.[9] The Treaty amendments were more ambiguous. Article 7a [*14*] EC establishes 'an area without internal frontiers in which the free movement of ... persons ... is ensured in accordance with the provisions of the Treaty'. Both the

---

9 EC Commission, *Completing the Internal Market* COM (85) 310 final, para 27.

Commission and the Parliament take the view that this requires the abolition of all border controls. The Commission has also argued that it is directly effective.[10] The Parliament, meanwhile, has taken a number of steps to pressurise the Commission into proposing legislation for that purpose.[11]

The United Kingdom and, to a lesser extent, Denmark have contested this and argue that Article 7a [*14*] EC allows Member States to retain the right to check the nationality of foreigners attempting to enter their territory. This dispute raged on, at times very acrimoniously, during the 1980s and 1990s.[12] It was not resolved at Maastricht. Whilst the right to move and reside freely within the territory of the Member States was granted to *all EU citizens*, it was stated to be subject to the limitations and conditions laid down in the Treaty and secondary legislation.[13]

Not all of the Member States have experienced difficulty with creating a frontier-free Europe and a smaller group were prepared to create a fast-track for the free movement of persons outside EC

---

10 SEC (92) 877 final, 8 May 1992. A Working Group under the Chair of Mme Weil has been established to investigate and make proposals to counteract the remaining barriers to free movement of persons, http://europa.eu.int/comm/dg15/enpeople/hlp/summ.htm. The latest proposal to come from this was for a Directive on safeguarding the supplementary pension rights of employed and self-employed persons moving within the EU, COM(97) 457.

11 It did this by bringing an Article 175 [232] EC action Case C-445/93 *Parliament v Commission.* The President of the Court issued an order withdrawing the case on 11 July 1996 following measures brought forward by the Commission. See Commission proposals for a Directive on the elimination of controls on persons crossing internal frontiers COM(95) 347; amendment of Directive 68/360/EEC on the abolition of restrictions on movement and residence within the Community for workers of Member States and their families, as well as the corresponding Directive 73/148 with regard to establishment and the provision of services COM(95) 348 final; See Editorial, (1996) 33 *CMLRev* 1. These have now been amended by COM (97) 106.

12 The most recent account can be found in House of Lords Select Committee on the European Communities, *Elimination of Controls on Persons at Internal Frontiers* (Session 1997-98, 2nd Report, HMSO, London).

13 Article 8a [*18*] EC.

structures. The Schengen Agreement of 14 June 1985[14] entered into force, as from its signature, between France, Germany and the Benelux states.[15] The 1985 Agreement merely provided for the facilitation of free movement between States. Border checks were to be confined to visual checks wherever possible. It did not abolish frontier controls. More wide ranging was the Implementing Convention of 19 June 1990 which entered into force on 26 March 1995.[16]

1990 Convention Applying the Schengen Agreement of 14 June 1985

Article 2(1). Internal borders may be crossed at any point without any checks on persons being carried out.

2. Where public policy or national security so require, however, a Contracting Party may, after consulting the other Contracting Parties, decide that for a limited period national border checks appropriate to the situation will be carried out at internal borders. If public policy or national security require immediate action, the Contracting Party concerned shall take the necessary measures and shall inform the other Contracting Parties thereof at the earliest opportunity.

After a trial period of three months France refused to abolish border controls completely arguing that the relaxation of such controls had led to an increase in drugs trafficking. Although the Schengen Agreements were concluded outside the framework of the European Union they have, in principle, created an area within which there is free

---

14 (1991) ILM 73. For critical comment on Schengen see Schutte, J. 'Schengen: Its meaning for the free movement of persons in Europe' (1991) 28 CMLRev 549; Meijers, H. *et al.* (ed.) *Schengen: internationalisation of central chapters of the law of aliens, refugees, privacy, security and police* (1992, 2nd Rev Ed., Stichting NJM-Boekerij, Leiden); O'Keeffe, D. 'The Schengen Convention: A Suitable Model for European Integration?' (1992) 12 *YBEL* 185.

15 All EU States are party to Schengen with the exception of the United Kingdom and Ireland. The other members are Iceland and Norway. For the purposes of applying the common immigration policy, British, Irish and Danish nationals are treated as 'Schengen nationals' since Article 6 [*12*] EC prohibits any discrimination based on nationality.

16 (1991) ILM 84.

movement of persons, irrespective of their origin. At Amsterdam an attempt was made to integrated free movement more firmly within EC structures through the establishment of an area of 'freedom, security and justice'.

Article 62 EC*. The Council, acting in accordance with the procedure referred to in Article 67, shall, within a period of five years after the entry into force of the Treaty of Amsterdam, adopt:*
(1) measures with a view to ensuring, in compliance with Article 14, the absence of any controls on persons, be they citizens of the Union or nationals of third countries, when crossing internal borders...

A price has been exacted for this abolition of border controls. The United Kingdom made it very clear that it was unwilling to give up its border controls.

Protocol on the application of certain aspects of Article 14 of the EC Treaty to the United Kingdom and to Ireland

Article 1*.The United Kingdom shall be entitled, notwithstanding Article 14 of the Treaty establishing the European Community, any other provision of that Treaty or of the Treaty on European Union, any measure adopted under those Treaties, or any international agreement concluded by the Community or by the Community and its Member States with one or more third States, to exercise at its frontiers with other Member States such controls on persons seeking to enter the United Kingdom as it may consider necessary for the purpose:*

(a) of verifying the right to enter the United Kingdom of citizens of States which are Contracting Parties to the Agreement on the European Economic Area and of their dependants exercising rights conferred by Community law, as well as citizens of other States on whom such rights have been conferred by an agreement by which the United Kingdom is bound; and
(b) of determining whether or not to grant other persons permission to enter the United Kingdom.

Nothing in Article 14 of the Treaty establishing the European Community or in any other provision of that Treaty or of the Treaty on European Union or in any measure adopted under them shall prejudice the right of the United Kingdom to adopt or exercise any such controls. References to the United Kingdom in this Article shall include territories for whose external relations the United Kingdom is responsible.

The problem was complicated by the United Kingdom's forming a common travel area with Ireland. If Ireland were to relax its border controls on persons coming from other parts of the EU, these would be able to enter the United Kingdom free of control via Ireland. Ireland was placed in a quandary. If it were to relax its border controls with other Member States, it would have to forego its common travel area with the United Kingdom. It was unwilling to do this. The Protocol applies therefore to both the United Kingdom and Ireland. Ireland issued a Declaration, however, stating that it would relax its border controls to the maximum extent compatible with the common travel area. The other Member States exacted a revenge for this. Article 2 of the Protocol states they may impose border checks on persons coming from the United Kingdom and Ireland.

The position is further complicated by the position of Denmark. Denmark has signed no Protocol allowing it to maintain border checks following the entry into force of the new area of freedom, security and justice. A Protocol was agreed, however, which states, *inter alia*, that it will not be bound by or participate in the adoption of measures under *Article 62(1) EC*.[17] It is thus bound by Article 7a [*14*] EC which posits the abolition of internal frontiers, albeit within the context of the internal market, but *not* by the main legislative procedure intended to secure it. Whether it is required to abolish its border controls is thus uncertain and will have to await interpretation of Article 7a [*14*] EC by the Court of Justice.

There is a paradox in all this. The abolition of frontiers has a totemic significance for all sides as being central to the forging of a 'European identity'. The relaxation of border controls envisaged at Amsterdam is bought at the price of fragmenting this identity. It is likely that the increased ease in moving between some Member States will be balanced by increased difficulties in moving between others.

It is not this which is so controversial about Amsterdam. Free movement raised the 'spectre' of national loss of control over migration and many forms of criminal activity. The debate on the removal of checks at frontiers has been accompanied by a complimentary one on the need for *compensatory measures*. This has taken two forms. The first is

---

17 *Protocol on Denmark, Article 1.*

the need for a strong external frontier to compensate for the absence of internal measures. The second is increased cooperation in the field of internal security. Many commentators have noted that as part of this process a 'security continuum' had to be created which linked a number of activities under a broad umbrella and which provided a linkage between internal and external security 'threats'.[18]

Anderson, M., ***et al. Policing The European Union*** **(1995, Clarendon Press, Oxford) 164-166**

The linkage between security fields lies at the core of the redefinition of the West European security situation. Integration of the tasks and functions of police services, immigration services, customs and intelligence services, is supported within high policing discourse by the gradual shaping of an 'internal security continuum', connecting terrorism, crime, immigration and asylum-seeking. Indeed, a crucial factor behind the merging of internal and external security has been the definition of immigration and asylum-seeking as problems for the internal security of West European states. This linking process operates at the level of cultural meaning and is associated with a variety of discursive techniques. The image of migratory flows jeopardizing internal security is often integrated into the vocabulary of law and order. There is an increasing tendency to view immigrants as presumptively deviant: this builds on an existing tendency to link indigenous coloured minorities with crime. Other discursive features are the association between immigration and unlawful social benefit claims, the fear, nurtured by xenophobes, of a connection between mass immigration and social instability, the blurring of the distinction between refugees and immigrants, and the insertion of provocative terms like 'manifestly unfounded' into official discourse on asylum.

There are three modes in which internal security concerns have become amalgamated with immigration and asylum. The first of these is ideological merging: law enforcement agencies in Europe started to redefine internal security threats. The old external threat of communism was replaced by an external threat established by mass immigration, organized crime, and imported terrorism, the penetration of which would, like the old threat, lead to the destabilisation of 'well-balanced' western societies. The second component - instrumental merging - is to be found in the range of instruments which are employed against illegal immigration. There is an increase in the use of intelligence, of 'high tec' detection equipment, and of concerted proactive investigation generally by all agencies involved in immigration control. The EU Ministers of Justice

---

18 Bigo, D. 'The European Internal Security Field: Stakes and Rivalries in a Newly Developing Area of Police Intervention' in Anderson, M. & Den Boer, M. (eds.) *Policing Across National Boundaries* (1994, Pinter, London). See also Waever, O. 'European Security Identities' (1996) 34 *JCMS* 103.

and Interior have negotiated the introduction of joint compensatory measures and instruments of control. Striking examples are international information systems (such as the SIS, and in the future, the EIS), fingerprint systems, carrier sanctions and visa requirements. Law enforcement officials will have on-line access to these international information systems. These instruments used for migration and asylum controls will simultaneously be used for crime control. The third component is institutional merging: institutions engaged in international police co-operation and immigration, such as Trevi and the Ad Hoc Group on Immigration are - as a consequence of the Treaty on European Union - reconstituted and merged into the K4 Co-ordinating Committee.

Indeed, the third pillar of TEU may be seen as the culmination of the integration between international law enforcement concerns and concerns about migratory movements and asylum seekers.

The creation of the security continuum is also apparent in a narrower organisational sense. The association between organised crime and ethnic groups encourages a linking of law enforcement agencies: co-operation between ordinary police forces, immigration services, customs and intelligence agencies, therefore, is based on and reinforces the continuum which runs from terrorism to immigration, and from ordinary crime to political and subversive crime. In most European countries, immigration control is a shared responsibility of a variety of law enforcement agencies. Although this does not result in a merging of institutions, close relationships must be maintained on a daily basis. Immigration services, customs services and border control agencies, and regular police forces are all involved in certain stages of immigration control. Police services have assumed an expanding role in this field. In addition to enforcing the criminal law against illegal and clandestine immigrants, police officers also tend to perform the administrative function of registration, and to play a co-operative role alongside the immigration service in the enforcement of immigration law in areas such as housing and employment. But even where the police are entrusted with administrative functions, they often retain a level of discretion normally associated with the policing function.

II. The External Frontier

i. Explaining EU Approaches to TCN Migration

Initially, labour shortages and the expanding economics of the original Member States resulted in a laissez-faire approach to third country migration. The shift from a toleration of the management of TCNs at the national level to the construction of them as a security issue for Europe began to emerge during the 1980s.[19] Increasingly, the right to control admission of TCNs was becoming wound up with questions of national sovereignty and cultural identity.[20] Member States were reluctant to cede the matter to EC Institutions precisely because TCN immigration was perceived as a matter of national security. A General Declaration was attached to the SEA which stated:

> Nothing in these provisions shall affect the right of Member States to take such measures as they consider necessary for the purposes of controlling immigration from third countries and to combat terrorism, crime, the traffic in drugs and illicit trading in works of art and antiques.

Non-statal pressures have had a countervailing tendency, however. Immigration is a societal issue which is affected by internal societal developments and ideological shifts.[21] There is also an umbilical link between migratory flows and a State's labour market. In times of full employment migration is central both to preventing labour shortage and control of labour costs.[22] Restrictive practices will not just lead to inflation and labour shortages, but, in time, capital flight, as investors look for more competitive labour markets. In times of high unemployment, however, migratory flows exacerbate the competition for scarce jobs. These structural forces increasingly provide incentives

---

19 See Hammar, T. (ed.) *European Immigration Policy: A Comparative Study* (1985, CUP, Cambridge); Baldwin-Edwards, M. & Schain, M. (eds.) *The Politics of Immigration in Europe* (1994) 17/2 *West European Politics*.

20 Pieterse, P. 'Fictions of Europe' (1991) 32 *Race and Class* 3.

21 Heisler, M. 'Migration, International Relations and the New Europe: Theoretical Perspectives from Institutional Political Sociology' (1992) 26 *International Migration Review* 596.

22 Some Member States had an interest in tolerating illegal immigration for economic reasons, see Claude-Valentin, M. 'Entre economie et politique: le "clandestin", une figure sociale à géométrie variable' (1988) 47 *Pouvoirs* 75: Castles, S. & Kosack, G. *Immigrant Workers and Class Structure in Western Europe* (1973, OUP/Institute for Race Relations, Oxford).

for States to cooperate not just with sending States but also with other receiving States.[23]

The Member States did therefore commit themselves towards co-operation outside the formal EC Treaty structure in a Political Declaration on the SEA:

> In order to promote the free movement of persons, the Member States shall co-operate without prejudice to the powers of the Community, in particular as regards the entry, movement and residence of nationals of third countries. They shall also co-operate in the combatting of terrorism, crime, the traffic in drugs and illicit trading in works of art and antiques.

Ugur argues that any explanation must take account of both those accounts which he labels as state-centric, which tie migration to questions of national sovereignty, and those 'society-centric' accounts which push for convergence of migration policies. Whilst the latter has resulted in a degree of coordination, migration is currently a matter, he argues, which is non-divisible and non-transparent. That is to say the link that has been established between it and more organic concepts of identity and sovereignty make it ill-suited in the current climate to being the subject-matter of package deals and bargains.

Ugur, M. 'Freedom of Movement v Exclusion' (1995) 25 *International Migration Review* 964, 972-973

Having explained the typology of international regulatory frameworks for policy coordination, it is now necessary to identify the nature of the immigration policy issue. We argue here that immigration is a nontransparent/nondivisible policy issue because of the link established between the immigration issues on the one hand and nationality and societal security on the other. This is especially the case in Europe. Hollifield observes that in Europe the debate on immigration has focused on citizenship.[[24]] The implication of this has been the politicization of the immigration issue - a situation that contrasts with

---

23 Straubhaar, T. & Zimmermann, K. 'Towards a European Migration Policy' (1993) 12 *Population Research and Policy Review* 225.

24 Hollifield, J. 'Migration and International Relations: Control and Cooperation in the European Community' (1992) 26 *International Migration Review* 568, 585.

the twist that the debate has taken in the United States, where it is '... couched more in terms of interest group politics'. The implication of this tradition has been to make the immigration issue in Europe nondivisible - a feature that makes it possible to present parochial claims as national interest. On the other hand, Heisler and Layton-Henry indicate that immigration in Europe is perceived by societal forces as a threat to established visions of identity and societal integrity.[25] Such perceptions make the immigration issue nontransparent and therefore the policy debate is forced to move away from transparent cost-benefit analysis towards nontransparent claims and counterclaims involving nonquantifiable symbolic/cultural values.

The irony resulting from this situation is that both governments and constituents place themselves in a suboptimal predicament of their own making. The government, as the executive arm of the state, is under pressure to be responsive to the demands of its own nationals who emerge as a veto group. Therefore, its autonomy in policy making and its capacity to undertake commitments in an integrated framework are highly reduced. On the other hand, nationals may be able to act as veto groups, but this ability is associated with a cost. The cost here is the suboptimal provision of privileges associated with nationality. The government, under pressure from the veto group, will have to devote a substantial amount of resources for ensuring exclusion of foreigners - border controls, internal checks, visa processing centres in countries of potential emigration etc. These activities will have to be financed through either increased taxation or lower welfare spending. The nationals will intensify their demands for exclusion either when the possibility of entry is high or when the provision of club good declines as a result of high levels of unemployment or curtailed welfare state provision. This situation is similar to the suboptimal situation of an exclusive club.

Based on this analysis, there are two hypotheses that can be proposed with respect to EU policy on migration. The first one concerns intra-EU migration and can be stated as follows: policy making in this area will proceed within integrative frameworks and the stance of the policy will be inclusive as the non transparency/nondivisibility of the policy issue is reduced by delinking intra-EU migration from a narrowly defined concept of nationality. The second hypothesis is that EU policy making on third country immigration will tend to be characterized by intergovernmental procedures and exclusionisms because of the maintenance of the linkage between non-EU immigration and nationality. These hypotheses are in contrast to the neo-functionalist 'spillover' hypothesis that envisages a quasi automatic process of integration because of interpolicy linkages that render the completion of the initial integrative step (intra-EU migration) impossible without integration of further policy areas (such as third country immigration, asylum policies, etc).

One implication of these hypotheses is that the Commission's emphasis on linkages between intra-EU freedom of movement and third country immigration is not likely to bear fruit in terms of enabling it to derive implied competence. Indeed, as it will

---

25 Heisler, M. & Layton-Henry, Z. 'Migration and the Links between Social and Societal Security' in Waever, O. (ed.) *Identity, Migration and the New Security Agenda* (1993, Pinter, London).

be demonstrated below, the success of the Commission has been highly limited, and when any agreement was reached between the Member States it had been a result of essentially intergovernmental bargaining and tended to be exclusionist. That is due to the fact that intra-EU migration is made transparent/divisible by creating an 'insider group' of EU nationals who are entitled to privileges within a European social space that exclude an 'outsider group' of third country nationals. Looked at from this perspective, it can be then seen that the intergovernmental/exclusionist stance against third country immigrants is then both a necessary condition for and a result of free movement on the basis of nationality. In this sense, the much abused concept of 'fortress Europe' should neither be associated with the advent of the Single Market nor should it be seen as a conspiracy of an essentially xenophobic political elite. 'Fortress Europe' has been with us since 1968 when intra-EU freedom of movement was established by Regulation 1612/68. The recent surge of exclusionist policies must be seen in the context of an ongoing interaction between the tendency of the European political elites to resort to blame avoidance in the face of rising unemployment and a faltering welfare state, as well as the rising constituent assertiveness reclaiming the privileges associated with nationality.

The other implication of the proposed hypotheses is that they enable us to predict the likely direction that EU immigration policy might take if changes occur in the degree of centrifugal societal tendencies and/or the level of transparency/divisibility associated with the issue of third country immigration. If we are to observe an increase in centrifugal societal tendencies - revealed, for example, as higher claims for privileges associated with nationality - then it is possible to expect a drive towards higher levels of immigration policy approximation. This drive, however, will tend to be characterized by intergovernmentalism and exclusionisms unless some ways of inputting transparency/divisibility on the issue of third country immigration can be devised. There may be, however some scope for partial policy integration and inclusion with respect to existing third country immigrants as a result of legitimation concerns at both national and Union levels. This positive development, however, will be conditional on the consolidation of exclusionist measures - determined mostly within intergovernmental frameworks - against potential immigrants.

A further variable has to be thrown into the equation, and that is the role of the EC Institutions in 'Europeanising' the question of migration. These have pushed for immigration to be brought fully within the EC Treaty framework. Unilateral controls by Member States on TCNs has disruptive consequences for the single market, as, in the absence of common external controls, it entitles Member States to vet the entry of all persons entering their territory. The Commission, therefore, in its White Paper on Completing the Internal Market suggested that non-EC migrants who are lawfully resident in the EC should be given rights to live and work in all Member States.[26] In the late 1980s in *Germany v Commission* the Court ruled that the EC had few general powers in the field of external migration policy.[27] As a consequence the Commission pushed repeatedly for measures to be taken predominantly through intergovernmental cooperation.[28] It has returned repeatedly to the logic of the Single Market which it considers implies the elimination of the condition of nationality for the exercise of certain rights[29] and that TCNs should be able to move around the EC freely on the basis of a residence permit which would replace any existing visa requirements.[30]

ii. The Quilting of European Immigration Policy in the 1990s

Regulation of TCNs by EU States in the 1990s has been a curious patchwork of measures, both intergovernmental and communautaire, within and outside EU structures. Broadly, it has followed the pattern laid out by Ugur. Matters which could be discretely separated from issues of national security and identity have been dealt with under the EC aegis. Broader questions of TCN migration have been handled on an intergovernmental basis.

---

26 COM (85) 310 final, paras 15-16.

27 Joined Cases 281, 283-85, 287/85 *Germany v Commission* [1987] ECR 3203, [1988] 1 CMLR 11. See Plender, R. 'Competence, EC Law and Nationals of Non Member States' (1990) 39 *ICLQ* 599.

28 For an account by a Commission official see Callovi, G. 'Regulation of Immigration in 1993: Pieces of the European Community Jig-Saw Puzzle' (1992) 26 *International Migration Review* 353.

29 SEC (91) 1855 final.

30 COM (94) 23, 34.

a. Intergovernmental Cooperation Prior to the TEU

A patchwork of intergovernmental responses to TCN migration developed around the time of the SEA.[31] The coordination which took place during this period developed against a backdrop which was dominated by two images. The first was that the removal of border checks between Member States led to pressure for stronger checks at the 'external frontiers' on persons arriving from third countries. There were also external pressures for increased coordination. The collapse of the COMECON and advances in international transport raised the prospects of large numbers of both refugees and economic migrants seeking to enter the EC from Central and Eastern Europe. How to react to this became one of the central issues in the negotiations on Political Union which led up to the TEU.[32] Asylum had become increasingly problematic for Europe in the postwar period because of the conflicting tensions found between the global regime, which contained respect for the sanctity of human life and a liberal understanding of the freedom of movement for individuals,[33] and the principle of state sovereignty, that is States ultimately decide who may cross borders. Joly describes the 1970s and early 1980s as a period of 'uncoordinated liberalism', the late 1980s and 1990s, by contrast, have been years of 'harmonized restrictionism'.[34]

In 1986 the TREVI Group, a group set up in 1975 initially to discuss terrorism and organised crime, set up an *Ad Hoc* group to consider migration.[35] In 1988 a group of national coordinators was set

---

31 On these see Butt Phillip, A. 'European Union Immigration Policy: Phantom, Fantasy or Fact?' (1994) 17 WEP 168; Weber-Panarello, P. *The Integration of Matters of Justice and Home Affairs into Title VI of the TEU: A Step Towards More Democracy?* (RSC 95/32, EUI, Florence).

32 Middlemas, K. *Orchestrating Europe: The Informal Politics of European Union 1973-1995* (1995, Fontana, London) 184-186.

33 Skran, C. *Refugees in Inter-war Europe: the Emergence of a Regime* (1995, Clarendon Press, Oxford).

34 Joly, D. 'The porous dam: European harmonization on asylum in the nineties' (1994) 6 *International Journal of Refugee Law* 159.

35 Benyon, J. *et al. Police Cooperation in Europe: An Investigation* (1993, Centre for Study of Public Order, Leicester) 162.

up to consider questions of free movement. This group produced the 'Palma Document' in 1989. This Document which was only made public by order of the House of Lords set out 80 measures which needed to be taken.[36] Most, it considered, should be taken within the framework of the TREVI Group. Only a few matters, notably goods carried by travellers, were to be taken within the aegis of the EC.

Throughout the late 1980s and early 1990s cooperation took place within the TREVI framework. Two conventions emerged out of this framework. The first was the Dublin Asylum Convention of 1990. This sought to prevent multiple asylum applications by individual applicants, and provided that it should be the Member State where the applicant first entered the Union which should be responsible for considering the application.[37] The other was the draft Convention on External Frontiers.[38] This has not yet been adopted because of a dispute between the United Kingdom and Spain over its application to Gibraltar.

Considerable intergovernmental cooperation also occurred between those Member States party to the Schengen Convention following the signing of the 1990 Implementing Convention (SIA).[39] An extensive range of 'compensatory' measures were included in the Implementing Convention to compensate for the removal of the 'filter' function carried out by border controls. These included implementation of unified, stricter external border controls,[40] the unification of entry and visa requirements,[41] common rules on the responsibilities of carriers to ensure TCNs possess correct travel documents;[42] the establishment of

---

36 House of Lords Select Committee on the European Communities, *1992: Border Control of People* (Session 1988-1989, 22nd Report, HMSO, London) 55.

37 The text is set out in OJ 1997, C 254/1. Müller-Graf, P. 'The Dublin Convention: Pioneer and lesson for Third Pillar Conventions' in Bieber, R. & Monar, J. (eds.) *Justice and Home Affairs in the European Union: the development of the third pillar* (1995, European Interuniversity, Brussels).

38 OJ 1994 C 11/15.

39 (1991) ILM 73.

40 Articles 3-8 SIA.

41 Articles 9-25 SIA.

42 Articles 26-27 SIA.

unified criteria to establish responsibility for asylum applications and the exchange of information on asylum related matters.[43]

The 1990 Agreement also set up a system of institutional machinery to implement this security apparatus. This took two forms. The first was the creation of a 'Schengen Information System, which is a databank of people and objects who may pose a threat to security.[44] The second was the setting up of an Executive Committee to implement the Convention.[45] Justice Ministers from each State sit on this Committee and take measures by a unanimous vote. Its meetings are surrounded by great secrecy. What is known is that it has been extremely active, developing a plethora of measures that have come to be known as the *Schengen Acquis*.

This series of agreement has led to a network of contacts which Huysmans has described as the 'quilting' of migration policy.[46]

> This quilting is best understood as a retroactive constitution of a formation given coherence and unity to a diversity of past practices which at the stage of their conception were not united into a particular formation of practices. Once quilted the chaotic practices of the past receive a certain post-facto unity.

The beginning of the 1990s saw a frenzied pace of intergovernmental activity and the 'magnitude of time, effort, and resources poured into the clarification of the regional

---

43 Articles 28-38 SIA. Meijers, H. 'Refugees in Western Europe: "Schengen" affects the entire refugee law' (1990) 2 *International Journal of Refugee Law* 433. The Dublin Convention has identical provisions to the SIA and the Schengen Executive Committee passed a Resolution on 26 April 1994 which led to a Protocol declaring that once the Dublin Convention came into force the asylum provisions of the SIA would cease to be applicable, Conference of the Representatives of the Governments of the Member States, Dublin II, Brussels, 5 December 1996, CONF 2500/96.

44 Articles 92-119 SIA.

45 Articles 131-133 SIA.

46 Huysmans, J. 'Securitising Europe, Europeanising Security, The Construction of Migration in the EU' Paper presented at a Conference *Defining and Projecting Europe's Identity: Issues and Trade Offs', The Graduate Institute of International Studies,* Geneva, 21-22 March 1996.

immigration/asylum regime reflected perceived salience of the issue for the parties involved'.[47] In 1991 there were some 100 'official' meetings of the officials from Member States and eight ministerial conferences on immigration/asylum issues. As Uçarer points out the drive towards regionalisation was a marked departure from most of the Western European States' earlier positions.[48]

This quilting resulted in the 'Europeanisation' of migration policy where 'Europe' increasingly became the signifier for the discussion and organisation of migration policy not only of the Member States individually but also in more concrete terms of defining the outer boundaries of Europe.[49]

As a consequence, a majority of Member States, the Parliament and the Commission wished to bring control of TCNs within the EC Treaty at Maastricht. A number of Member States, however - notably the British, the Irish, the Greeks and the Danes - were unwilling to see an abolition of the national veto in this area. The result was the creation of the third pillar of the TEU, that of Justice and Home Affairs. Whilst this pillar is predominantly intergovernmental in nature, it is principally distinguished from the second pillar on Common Foreign and Security Policy, in that some provision is made for the Council, acting unanimously, to transfer matters from this pillar to the EC Treaty.[50]

---

47 Uçarer, E. 'Europe's search for policy: the harmonization of asylum policy and European integration' in Uçarer, E. & Puchala, D. (eds.) *Immigration Into Western Societies Problems and Policies* (1997, Pinter, London) 291.

48 Ibid.

49 See also Tuitt, P. *False Images: Law's Construction of the Refugee* (1996, Pluto, London).

50 Article K.9 TEU. Unsurprisingly, no measure has yet been transferred.

b. Justice and Home Affairs

The ambit of JHA is set out in Article K.1 TEU.[51]

Article K.1 TEU. For the purposes of achieving the objectives of the Union, in particular the free movement of persons, and without prejudice to the powers of the European Community, Member States shall regard the following areas as matters of common interest:

1. asylum policy;
2. rules governing the crossing by persons of the external borders of the Member States and the exercise of controls thereon;
3. immigration policy and policy regarding nationals of third countries:
(a) conditions of entry and movement by nationals of third countries on the territory of Member States;
(b) conditions of residence by nationals of third countries on the territory of Member States, including family reunion and access to employment;
(c) combatting unauthorized immigration, residence and work by nationals of third countries on the territory of Member States;
4. combatting drug addiction in so far as this is not covered by 7 to 9;
5. combatting fraud on an international scale in so far as this is not covered by 7 to 9;
6. judicial cooperation in civil matters;
7. judicial cooperation in criminal matters;
8. customs cooperation;
9. police cooperation for the purposes of preventing and combatting terrorism, unlawful drug trafficking and other serious forms of international crime, including if necessary certain aspects of customs cooperation, in connection with the organization of a Union-wide system for exchanging information within a European Police Office (Europol).

---

51 The literature on the third pillar is considerable. See Monar, J. & Morgan, R. (eds.) *The Third Pillar of the European Union* (1994, European Interuniversity Press, Brussels); Müller-Graf, P. 'The legal bases of the third pillar and its position in the framework of the Union Treaty' (1994) 31 *CMLRev* 494; McMahon, R. 'Maastricht's Third Pillar - Load Bearing or Purely Decorative?' (1995/1) *LIEI* 59; O'Keeffe, D. 'Recasting the Third Pillar' (1995) 32 *CMLRev* 893; Bieber, R. & Monar, J. (eds.) *Justice and Home Affairs in the European Union: the development of the third pillar* (1995, European Interuniversity, Brussels).

It is the Council which sits at the fulcrum of JHA, and which adopts the measures necessary to meet these objectives.

Article K.3(1) TEU. In the areas referred to in Article K.1, Member States shall inform and consult one another within the Council with a view to coordinating their action. To that end, they shall establish collaboration between the relevant departments of their administrations.

2. The Council may:
- on the initiative of any Member State or of the Commission, in the areas referred to in Article K.1(1) to (6);
- on the initiative of any Member State, in the areas referred to in Article K1(7) to (9):

(a) adopt joint positions and promote, using the appropriate form and procedures, any cooperation contributing to the pursuit of the objectives of the Union;
(b) adopt joint action in so far as the objectives of the Union can be attained better by joint action than by the Member States acting individually on account of the scale or effects of the action envisaged; it may decide that measures implementing joint action are to be adopted by a qualified majority;
(c) without prejudice to Article 220 of the Treaty establishing the European Community, draw up conventions which it shall recommend to the Member States for adoption in accordance with their respective constitutional requirements.

Unless otherwise provided by such conventions, measures implementing them shall be adopted within the Council by a majority of two-thirds of the High Contracting Parties.

Such conventions may stipulate that the Court of Justice shall have jurisdiction to interpret their provisions and to rule on any disputes regarding their application, in accordance with such arrangements as they may lay down.

The other EC Institutions are marginalised within JHA. Parliament's powers are very limited under the pillar. It is to be informed of discussions which occur within JHA. It may also ask questions of the Council or make recommendations to it, and each year it must hold a debate on the progress made in implementing JHA. Its central power is, however the right to be consulted by the Presidency of the Council on the principal aspects of activities carried out in JHA. In this regard the Presidency is under a duty to ensure that its views are taken into consideration.[52] Given the lack of transparency of policy-making in this area, it is difficult to know how seriously this duty is observed.

The Court of Justice is almost fully excluded from reviewing JHA. It cannot review any of the Treaty Articles. It is also excluded from interpreting or reviewing the validity of joint actions or joint positions adopted within JHA. There is one exception to this general exclusion. Conventions adopted under JHA may confer jurisdiction upon the Court to interpret their provisions and to rule on disputes concerning their application. To this end the Court can interpret Article K.3(2)(c) TEU, the provision which provides for such Conventions to be drawn up.[53]

Provision is made for the Commission to be fully associated with the work in JHA. The bulk of the administration and preparation for Council meetings is carried out by national civil services acting within the aegis of the 'K-4' Committee.

Article K.4 (1) TEU. A Coordinating Committee shall be set up consisting of senior officials. In addition to its coordinating role, it shall be the task of the Committee to:

- give opinions for the attention of the Council, either at the Council's request or on its own initiative;
- contribute, without prejudice to Article 151 of the Treaty establishing the European Community, to the preparation of the Council's discussions in the areas referred to in Article K.1 and, in accordance with the conditions laid down in Article 100d of the Treaty establishing the European Community, in the areas referred to in Article 100c of that Treaty.

2. The Commission shall be fully associated with the work in the areas referred to in this Title.

3. The Council shall act unanimously, except on matters of procedure and in cases where Article K.3 expressly provides for other voting rules.

Where the Council is required to act by a qualified majority, the votes of its members shall be weighted as laid down in Article 148(2) of the Treaty establishing the European Community, and for their adoption, acts of the Council shall require at least fifty-four votes in favour, cast by at least eight members.

---

52 The powers of the Parliament are set out in Article K.6 TEU.

53 The Court's powers are set out in Article L TEU.

This Committee acts as a filter between the Council and a large number of steering groups. Composed of national civil servants, separate groups exist for migration, asylum, external frontiers and forged documents. Certainly, it is within these Steering Groups that much of the operational activity of JHA takes place.

Much of the activity in the field has taken the form of Recommendations or Resolutions. There has been a Resolution on the admission of TCNs to Member States for employment. This suggests a TCN should only be admitted if it can be shown that the vacancy cannot be filled by an EC national. Prior authorisation for the employment must be given before the TCN enters the territory of the Member State concerned.[54] In a similar Resolution concerning admission of TCNs for the purpose of pursuing activities as self-employed persons, Member States are only to admit TCNs if it can be shown that the activity is of economic benefit to the Member State concerned.[55] There is finally a Resolution on the admission of TCNs for study purposes. In principle, the right to reside should only be given for the purpose of study and a student should not be allowed to seek employment in the Member State concerned following study.[56]

A Recommendation was also adopted harmonising the means of combatting illegal immigration. Member States are encouraged to ensure that TCNs always have appropriate documentation evidencing their right to reside in the Member State concerned. Attention is drawn to the 'risk' of marriages of convenience and employers are to be encouraged to verify the residence and employment situations of any foreign national they employ.[57]

In the field of asylum a Resolution was adopted in 1995 setting minimum guarantees for asylum procedures. This give asylum seekers a right to be heard and imposes positive duties upon the part of the Member States to provide specialised staff who can provide translating services, legal advice and who have knowledge in the field of asylum and refugee matters and an understanding of the applicant's particular situation. In principle, the asylum seeker must also be given the right to

---

54 OJ 1996 C 274/3.

55 OJ 1996 C 274/7.

56 OJ 1996 C 274/10.

57 OJ 1996 C 5/1.

appeal against any adverse decision and sufficient time to prepare that appeal. This right may be denied, however, in the case of 'manifestly unfounded' applications.

The number of joint actions taken is limited compared to the number of Resolutions and Recommendations adopted.[58] Other than Decisions providing for exchange of information,[59] few Joint Actions of note have been taken. These provide for easing of travel facilities for TCN school pupils who are resident in the EU;[60] the development of a system of transit visas in all Member States;[61] a uniform format for residence permits,[62] and burden sharing with regard to the admission and residence of displaced persons.[63]

The resort to so much soft law suggests an unwillingness by Member States to be bound even by joint actions or joint positions in this area.[64] The cohesion of JHA has been further undermined by a number of issues being dealt with under the other two pillars of the TEU.

c. CFSP and TCNs

The Edinburgh European Council adopted a Declaration in 1992[65] on principles governing external aspects of migration policy. These embrace, *inter alia:*

- the preservation and restoration of peace, and the full respect for human rights and the rule of law, which would diminish migratory movements resulting from war and oppressive regimes;

---

58 Resolutions have also been adopted on travel of unaccompanied TCN minors, OJ 1997 C 221/23, and the status of TCNs residing on a long-term basis in the territory of the Member States, OJ 1996 C 80/2.

59 See, most recently, Decision 97/420/JHA, OJ 1997 L 178/6.

60 Decision 94/795/JHA, OJ 1994 L 327/1.

61 Decision 96/197/JHA, OJ 1996 L 63/8.

62 Decision 97/11/JHA, OJ 1997 L 7/1.

63 Decision 96/198/JHA, OJ 1996 L 63/10.

64 EC Commission, *Report for the Reflection Group* (1995, OOPEC, Brussels) para 119.

65 EC Bulletin 12-1992, I.31.

- the protection and assistance of displaced people in the nearest safe area to their homes;
- the promotion of liberal trade and economic co-operation with countries of emigration, which would reduce economic motives for migration;
- targeting development aid and job creation, and the alleviation of poverty;
- combating illegal immigration;
- the conclusion of bilateral or multilateral agreements with countries of origin or transit, to ensure that illegal immigrants were returned to their home countries;
- the assessment of home countries' practices in readmitting their nationals after they are expelled from the territories of the Member States;
- the increase in co-operation in responding to the particular challenge of persons fleeing from armed conflict and persecution in former Yugoslavia.

This has been followed up within the context of the Euro-Mediterranean partnership by the Barcelona Declaration and Programme of Action which refers to the need to address root causes of forced migration such as violence, poverty, illegal immigration and the fight against racial discrimination.[66]

iii. The EC Pillar

Prior to the TEU certain issues concerning TCNs were dealt with by the EC Treaty. In a more liberal age Association Agreements, notably that with Turkey, have been signed which granted long-term residents a number of rights.[67] EC migrants were also granted family rights which

---

66 *Barcelona Declaration and Work Programme* (1995, Brussels). On the second pillar and TCNs see Hix, S. & Niessen, J. *Reconsidering European Migration Policies: The 1996 Intergovernmental Conference and the Reform of the Maastricht Treaty* (1996, Migration Policy Group, Brussels) 20-22.

67 OJ 1973 C 113/2 and 1970 Protocol OJ 1972 L 293/1.

protected certain TCN family members.[68] Both of these were discrete subjects. They did not suffer from the problem of indivisibility which has bedevilled migration more generally. At Maastricht one area of migration policy was brought within the remit of the EC Treaty and that was visa policy.

Article 100c(1) EC. The Council, acting unanimously on a proposal from the Commission and after consulting the European Parliament, shall determine the third countries whose nationals must be in possession of a visa when crossing the external borders of the Member States.

2. However, in the event of an emergency situation in a third country posing a threat of a sudden inflow of nationals from that country into the Community, the Council, acting by a qualified majority on a recommendation from the Commission, may introduce, for a period not exceeding six months, a visa requirement for nationals from the country in question. The visa requirement established under this paragraph may be extended in accordance with the procedure referred to in paragraph 1.

3. From 1 January 1996, the Council shall adopt the decisions referred to in paragraph 1 by a qualified majority. The Council shall, before that date, acting by a qualified majority on a proposal from the Commission and after consulting the European Parliament, adopt measures relating to a uniform format for visas.

4. In the areas referred to in this Article, the Commission shall examine any request made by a Member State that it submit a proposal to the Council.

Despite its formal communautarisation the common visa policy has been bedevilled by intergovernmentalism. A Regulation was adopted which determined the third countries whose nationals must be in possession of a visa when crossing the external frontiers of the Member States.[69] The Regulation did not prevent Member States from imposing visa requirements on nationals from other third States. The States which were placed on the list were also the subject of controversy. Most were from Africa and the Caribbean resulting in the list having more than a racist hint. The measure has been declared illegal by the Court as the

---

68 See pp. 439 ff.

69 Regulation 2317/95/EC OJ 1995 L 234/1. See Peers, S. 'The Visa Regulation: Free Movement Blocked Indefinitely' (1996) 21 *ELRev* 150.

Council failed to reconsult the Parliament after introducing substantial alterations to the Regulation.[70] An identical measure has been re-issued.[71]

More generally, the Commission has also sought to communatarise policy on TCNs through linking a policy on the latter to completion of the single market. In 1995 it proposed lifting family members' visas requirements, a Directive abolishing internal frontier checks on any individuals and a Directive on the travel rights of third country nationals.[72] In particular the right to travel Directive would grant third country nationals substantial new rights. All non-EU citizens legally resident in a Member State would be allowed to travel visa-free throughout the Member States for three months, regardless of whether they are family members of a EU citizen or whether they would be otherwise obliged to obtain a visa. TCNs not resident in a Member State would be entitled to circulate visa-free in any Member State which did not impose a visa requirement on them. Both rights would be limited only by the obligation to hold a travel document and a residence permit where relevant and the usual Member States' discretion to impose the 'public order' restrictions on foreigners.[73]

In other areas the Commission has sought to bring TCNs incrementally within EC competence. Its Communication on Immigration and Asylum Policies[74] and White Paper on European Social Policy[75] envisaged several new measures to benefit permanently resident third country nationals including coverage for health care when travelling in the EU, the right to go abroad to obtain medical treatment, a right to enter other Member States without a visa and priority for job openings in other Member States where no EC national or local third

---

70 Case C-392/95 *Parliament v Council* [1997] ECR I-3213, [1997] 3 CMLR 896.

71 OJ 1997 C 180/18. The laying down of a uniform format for visas has proved less problematic, Regulation 1683/95/EC, OJ 1995 L 164/1.

72 COM (95) 346, 347 & 348.

73 The Member States retain the right to require TCN to report their presence to the host authorities as well as allowing the Member States to expel TCNs on the ground that the TCN represents a threat to its international relations: COM (95) 346, Article 4(5).

74 COM (94) 23.

75 COM (94) 333.

country national was available. The Commission proposed that full free movement of third country nationals should be granted later. It was also proposed that equal treatment in access to employment and social benefits should be granted.

Member States have been unwilling, however, to see any expansion of EC competence. A measure on transit visas was only accepted under JHA.[76] The proposal by the Commission to base a measure which would allow TCN school children resident within the EU visa-free travel within the EU met with such fierce opposition that it became a matter of discussion for the IGC.[77] Once again the measure was adopted finally under JHA.[78]

iv. Dissatisfaction with EU Immigration Policy

Criticisms of the EU's treatment of TCNs have emerged upon a number of fronts. By its own terms it had enjoyed only limited effect. The requirement of unanimity has brought measures down to the lowest common denominator. Little resort has been made to the instruments set out in Article K.3 TEU. Even when they were used, their effectiveness was limited. It is not this which has generated the most severe criticism. The tightening up of the rules on asylum have been criticised.[79] The regime has also attracted strong condemnation for its oppressive and

---

76 Decision 96/197/JHA, OJ 1996 L 63/8. This is notwithstanding that the visa format Regulation specifically applies to them, Regulation 1683/95, supra n.71, Article 5. As Peers, S. argues 'Surely no Community institution or Member State can credibly argue that transit visas fall under Article 100c(3) EC but not Article 100c(1)!' (1996) 21 *ELRev* 150, 154.

77 EC Commission, *Report for the Reflection Group* (1995, OOPEC, Brussels) para 126.

78 Decision 94/795/JHA, OJ 1994 L 327/1.

79 O'Keeffe, D. 'The Schengen Conventions: a suitable model for European integration?' (1991) 11 *YBEL* 185; Bolten, J. 'From Schengen to Dublin: the new frontiers of refugee law' in Meijers, H. *et al.* (eds.) *Schengen, Internalisation of Central Chapters of the Law of Aliens, Refugees, Privacy, Security and the Police* (1991, Kluwer, Antwerp).

exclusionary treatment of TCNs, and the stark dichotomy it draws between them and EU nationals.[80] As Miles points out

> ... within Europe, there is now a widely held view of cultural closeness and similarity between all the 'nations' of Western Europe, a commonality which is constructed and legitimated by means of signifying and naturalising difference in relation to the population of the peripheries of the world economy who 'for their own good' are requested to remain where they naturally belong.[81]

The procedures have also been condemned on grounds of their opaque nature and the lack of judicial and parliamentary control.[82] The secrecy and workings of the Executive Committee of the Schengen Agreement have attracted particular opprobrium in this respect. The Belgian Council of State expressed serious reservations about the lack of democratic controls at the time of Belgium's ratification of Schengen.[83] The lack of transparency has been criticised by European Parliament.[84] More generally, there was dissatisfaction at the creation of a regime outside EU structures.

---

80 e.g. Geddes, A. 'Immigrant and Ethnic Minorities and the EU's Democratic Deficit' (1995) 33 *JCMS* 197; Hedemann-Robinson, M. 'Third-Country Nationals, European Union Citizenship, and Free Movement of Persons: a Time for Bridges rather than Divisions' (1996) 16 *YBEL* 321, 356-361; Ward, I. 'Law and Other Europeans' (1997) 35 *JCMS* 79.

81 Thrändardt, D. & Miles, R. 'Introduction: European Integration, Migration and Processes of Inclusion and Exclusion', in Thrändardt, D. and Miles, R. *Migration and European Integration. The Dynamics of Inclusion and Exclusion* (1995, Pinter, London).

82 Curtin, D. & Meijers, H. 'The principle of open government in Schengen and the European Union: Democratic Regression?' (1995) 32 *CMLRev* 391.

83 Benyon, J. *et al. Police Cooperation in Europe: An Investigation* (1993, University of Leicester Centre for the Study of Public Order) 138.

84 See OJ 1989 C 323/98.

O'Keeffe, D. 'The Emergence of a European Immigration Policy
***European Law Review* 20, 34-36**

The price of abolishing internal frontier controls as required by Article 7a appear to be the establishment of compensatory controls which provide for jud police co-operation, the exchange of information on persons, the possibility o intrusions in private life by spot checks on the territory of a Member State to control identity and legal residence, and increased controls at the external frontiers. The Schengen Convention has (with various differences) largely become a model for the initiatives at the level of the Twelve: the Dublin Convention; the draft decision establishing the External Frontiers Convention; the draft Visa Regulation; and a computerised information system. As a result of this process, the position of asylum seekers has become more difficult...

In developing policies to deal with immigration and free movement, the Community/Union must respect international human rights standards and the Conventions to which the Member States are party. The Court of Justice has declared that the Community is based on the rule of law. The Member States and the Community itself practice a high respect for human rights standards. To be sure, the issue of immigration is one of the greatest problems facing the Community/Union, but in meeting this challenge, the Community/Union should respond in a way which respects fundamental rights and reflects the way in which we view ourselves as a society.

It would seem that a genuine European immigration policy will not materialise until the Community takes over responsibility for the areas listed in Article K1(1) to (6). At that point, the involvement of the Community institutions, including the Commission, European parliament and Court of Justice could remedy the defects of the intergovernmental response noted above. In particular, the involvement of the European Parliament would be a powerful lobby for the rights of third country nationals, and the involvement of the Court of Justice would be a guarantee that human rights standards were observed. Such a step, however, would mean the transfer of sovereignty in these fields to the community, which the intergovernmental pillar structure designed at Maastricht was precisely designed to avoid, given the Member States' concern to retain sovereignty in these areas which they regard as being of critical importance.

v. The Treaty of Amsterdam

a. The Communitarisation of Third Country National Immigration

Some of these difficulties have been addressed by the transfer into EC law of the areas of immigration, asylum, external borders and judicial co-

ͅeration in civil matters with the creation of a new Title IV in the EC Treaty.[85]

Article 61 EC. *In order to establish progressively an area of freedom, security and justice, the Council shall adopt:*

(a) within a period of five years after the entry into force of the Treaty of Amsterdam, measures aimed at ensuring the free movement of persons in accordance with Article 14, in conjunction with directly related flanking measures with respect to external border controls, asylum and immigration, in accordance with the provisions of Article 62(2) and (3) and Article 63(1)(a) and (2)(a), and measures to prevent and combat crime in accordance with the provisions of Article 31(e) of the Treaty on European Union;
(b) other measures in the fields of asylum, immigration and safeguarding the rights of nationals of third countries, in accordance with the provisions of Article 63;
(c) measures in the field of judicial cooperation in civil matters as provided for in Article 65;
(d) appropriate measures to encourage and strengthen administrative cooperation, as provided for in Article 66...

EC competence over these areas of policy is set out in more detail in the following Articles. *Article 62 EC* provides for EC legislation in the following areas:

- standards and procedures to be followed by Member States in carrying out checks on persons at external borders;
- rules on visas for intended stays of no more than three months;
- measures setting out the conditions under which nationals of third countries shall have the freedom to travel within the territory of the Member States during a period of no more than three months.

The area which is dealt with in most extensive detail is that of asylum policy.

---

85 The latter is dealt with in *Article 65 EC*.

Article 63 EC. *The Council, acting in accordance with the procedure referred to in Article 67, shall, within a period of five years after the entry into force of the Treaty of Amsterdam, adopt:*

(1) *measures on asylum, in accordance with the Geneva Convention of 28 July 1951 and the Protocol of 31 January 1967 relating to the status of refugees and other relevant treaties, within the following areas:*
(a) criteria and mechanisms for determining which Member State is responsible for considering an application for asylum submitted by a national of a third country in one of the Member States,
(b) minimum standards on the reception of asylum seekers in Member States,
(c) minimum standards with respect to the qualification of nationals of third countries as refugees,
(d) minimum standards on procedures in Member States for granting or withdrawing refugee status;

(2) *measures on refugees and displaced persons within the following areas:*
(a) minimum standards for giving temporary protection to displaced persons from third countries who cannot return to their country of origin and for persons who otherwise need international protection,
(b) promoting a balance of effort between Member States in receiving and bearing the consequences of receiving refugees and displaced persons;

(3) *measures on immigration policy within the following areas:*
(a) conditions of entry and residence, and standards on procedures for the issue by Member States of long term visas and residence permits, including those for the purpose of family reunion,
(b) illegal immigration and illegal residence, including repatriation of illegal residents;

(4) *measures defining the rights and conditions under which nationals of third countries who are legally resident in a Member State may reside in other Member States.*

Measures adopted by the Council pursuant to points 3 and 4 shall not prevent any Member State from maintaining or introducing in the areas concerned national provisions which are compatible with this Treaty and with international agreements.

Measures to be adopted pursuant to points 2(b), 3(a) and 4 shall not be subject to the five year period referred to above.

The Treaty of Amsterdam goes further than the Schengen/Dublin arrangements by attempting to coordinate Member States' asylum policies. *Article 63(2) EC* places an obligation on the Council to enact measures on refugees and displaced persons to see minimum standards for giving temporary protection to displaced persons from third countries who cannot return to their country of origin and for persons who otherwise need international protection. There is also an obligation in *Article 63(2)(b) EC* to promote a balance of effort between the Member States in receiving and bearing the consequences of receiving refugees and displaced persons. This provision was introduced to appease Germany which has borne the brunt of asylum seekers from the crisis in the former Yugoslavia. It must be placed next to *Article 64(2) EC* which provides that, in the case of emergency influx of refugees, the Council may, acting on a qualified majority on a proposal from the Commission, adopt provisional measures for up to six months.

Bringing these matters within EC procedures will undoubtedly make decision-making more transparent. Yet intergovernmentalism still permeates this area.[86]

Article 67(1) EC. *During a transitional period of five years following the entry into force of the Treaty of Amsterdam, the Council shall act unanimously on a proposal from the Commission or on the initiative of a Member State and after consulting the European Parliament.*

The one exception to this requirement of unanimity is in the field of visa policy. Rules on the list of countries whose nationals must be in possession of visas and on a uniform format for visas can be adopted by qualified majority following ratification of Amsterdam. Five years after ratification rules on the remainder of visa policy will automatically be adopted by qualified majority.[87]

Aware that the existence of the national veto might impede effective decision-making provision is made to review the matter five years after ratification of the Treaty.

---

86 e.g. A Protocol was attached which retains Member States' rights to conclude agreements with third countries on the crossing of external borders so long as they respect EC law and other relevant international agreements, *Protocol to the EC Treaty on External Relations of the Member States with Regard to the Crossing of External Borders.*

87 *Article 67(3) EC.*

Article 67(2) EC. *After this period of five years:*
- the Council shall act on proposals from the Commission; the Commission shall examine any request made by a Member State that it submit a proposal to the Council;
- the Council, acting unanimously after consulting the European Parliament, shall take a decision with a view to providing for all or parts of the areas covered by this Title to be governed by the procedure referred to in Article 251 and adapting the provisions relating to the powers of the Court of Justice.

From a civil liberties perspective immigration and asylum issues are now brought within the jurisdiction of the Court of Justice. The Court's powers are more limited in this area, however, than in other areas of the EC Treaty.

Article 68(1) EC. Article 234 shall apply to this Title under the following circumstances and conditions: where a question on the interpretation of this Title or on the validity or interpretation of acts of the institutions of the Community based on this Title is raised in a case pending before a court or a tribunal of a Member State against whose decisions there is no judicial remedy under national law, that court or tribunal shall, if it considers that a decision on the question is necessary to enable it to give judgment, request the Court of Justice to give a ruling thereon.

2. In any event, the Court of Justice shall not have jurisdiction to rule on any measure or decision taken pursuant to Article 62(1) relating to the maintenance of law and order and the safeguarding of internal security.

3. The Council, the Commission or a Member State may request the Court of Justice to give a ruling on a question of interpretation of this Title or of acts of the institutions of the Community based on this Title. The ruling given by the Court of Justice in response to such a request shall not apply to judgments of courts or tribunals of the Member States which have become res judicata.

The ability of only a court against whose decisions there is no judicial remedy in national law to refer could prove, in practice, to be a big barrier for TCNs. Rare will be the migrant who, in the absence of external support, will have enough resources to exhaust national appeal processes before seeking a reference.

b. The Incorporation of the Schengen Agreement into the New Treaty

The Amsterdam Treaty attempted to secure some institutional coherence by integrating the *Schengen Acquis* into the TEU by means of a Protocol.

Protocol integrating the Schengen Acquis into the framework of the European Union

Article 2(1). *From the date of entry into force of the Treaty of Amsterdam, the Schengen Acquis, including the decisions of the Executive Committee established by the Schengen agreements which have been adopted before this date, shall immediately apply to the thirteen Member States referred to in Article 1, without prejudice to the provisions of paragraph 2 of this Article. From the same date, the Council will substitute itself for the said Executive Committee.*

The Council, acting by the unanimity of its Members referred to in Article 1, shall take any measure necessary for the implementation of this paragraph. The Council, acting unanimously, shall determine, in conformity with the relevant provisions of the Treaties, the legal basis for each of the provisions or decisions which constitute the Schengen Acquis.

With regard to such provisions and decisions and in accordance with that determination, the Court of Justice of the European Communities shall exercise the powers conferred upon it by the relevant applicable provisions of the Treaties. In any event, the Court of Justice shall have no jurisdiction on measures or decisions relating to the maintenance of law and order and the safeguarding of internal security.

Under the leadership of the Dutch Presidency the Amsterdam Summit invited the Council to take appropriate measures as soon as possible so that when the Treaty of Amsterdam enters into force implementing measures will be adopted to incorporate the *Schengen Acquis* into the Treaty. This would include the integration of the Schengen Secretariat into the Council's General Secretariat.[88] It is

---

[88] *Protocol to the TEU integrating the Schengen Acquis into the European Union, Article 7.*

predicted by den Boer[89] that it is most likely that a special Committee[90] will be created to deal with the institutional and legal aspects of the incorporation of Schengen into the new Treaty.

Whilst the Protocol brings institutional coherence and should eliminate the lack of transparency which characterises Schengen, it brings with it worrying overtones. Den Boer notes that the *Schengen Acquis* may have a negative or contaminatory effect on EC legislation since it is largely negotiated in secrecy in the absence of any system of checks or balances.[91] These fears seem to be confirmed by a Declaration[92] on the Schengen Protocol, which states that the level of protection and security within the new area should remain the same as under Schengen.

c. The British and Danish 'Opt-Outs'

The communitarisation of JHA and the *Schengen Acquis* has been achieved at the cost of creating a multi-speed Europe. The simplicity of this structure is lost with the use of Protocols and Declarations that 'clarify' the position of the various Member States. These give a number of Member States a wide margin of discretion as to when, and, if, they will opt-in or opt-out of integration/partial integration in the future.

In line with the Protocol on the Application of Article 14 EC, a second Protocol was adopted, the *Protocol on the Position of the United Kingdom and Ireland,* which states that they will not participate in the new Title, and that no measures adopted under the Title or Court

---

89 Den Boer, M. 'Step by Step Progress: An Update on the Free Movement of Persons and Internal Security' (1997/2) *EIPA SCOPE* 8.

90 Composed of Members of the Schengen Secretariat, the Secretariat of the Council and the European Commission 'but individual lawyers (public officials of national ministries) who have been actively involved in masterminding this operation may also get a seat on the Committee'. Den Boer, M. Ibid.,10.

91 Ibid.

92 Insisted upon by the French who have retained border controls with Belgium and Luxembourg.

Decision interpreting the Title shall bind them.[93] The effect of this is a repatriation of visa policy for these two Member States.

Possibility is made for ad hoc participation by them in the new Title. Under Article 3(1) of the *Protocol,* Britain and Ireland may, within three months of the Commission's publication of a proposal, 'opt-in' and participate in the adoption and application of any proposed measures. Yet the bargaining strength of each is reduced by Article 3(2) as the Council may adopt the measure without either's participation if 'after a reasonable period of time a measure ... cannot be adopted with the United Kingdom or Ireland taking part'. Each may also subsequently adopt a measure by notifying the Council and Commission of its intention to do so.[94] The Commission shall give its opinion to the Council on such a notification within three months and what arrangements it deems necessary.

The ability of the United Kingdom and Ireland to 'opt-in' to any measure is complicated by their not being parties to the Schengen Convention. Spain realised that the inclusion of the United Kingdom in a measure could have implications for the status of the frontiers in Gibraltar. Whilst provision is made in the *Protocol Integrating the Schengen Acquis into the Framework of the European Union* for the United Kingdom and Ireland to request to participate in any of the provisions of this *Acquis*, the request will only be acceded to by a unanimity vote in the Council.[95] As if this were not complicated enough, the veto will not apply to measures which build upon the *Acquis*, and in which the United Kingdom and Ireland may participate should they so wish.[96] It will therefore not only be very difficult for the United Kingdom and Ireland to participate in a lot of measures adopted under this Title, but there are likely to be considerable disputes as to when a measure forms part of the *Acquis* and when it does not.

The position is further complicated by the position of Denmark. The Danes also secured an opt-out from the new Title IV of the EC

---

93 *Protocol on the Position of the United Kingdom and Ireland, Articles 1 & 2.*

94 Ibid., Article 4.

95 *Protocol Integrating the Schengen Acquis into the Framework of the European Union, Article 4.*

96 Ibid., *Article 5.*

Treaty.[97] In one sense its 'opt-out' is stronger as it provides no possibility for adoption or application of measures agreed under the Title.[98] Denmark was unwilling to repatriate visa policy, however, so will participate on measures relating to a uniform format for visas and determining the third countries whose nationals must be in possession of a visa when crossing the external border of the Member States.[99]

More problematically, Denmark is also party to the Schengen Convention which commits it, in international law, to adopt many of the measures which will be agreed under Title IV. In Article 5(1) of the *Protocol on the Position of Denmark* it is agreed that if the Council decides to build upon the *Schengen Acquis*, Denmark has 6 months to decide whether it will implement the decision in international law. If it decides to do so, this decision will create an obligation under international law between Denmark and those Member States who participated in the measure. If Denmark decides not to implement the measure, under Article 5(2) of the Protocol these Member States are to consider what appropriate measures should be taken. This is likely to create its own problems, as, given the weakness of international law sanctions, it is unclear what will happen if Denmark implements a measure but does not apply it wholeheartedly.

III. Internal Security

i. Police Cooperation and Cooperation in the Criminal Sphere Prior to the Treaty of Amsterdam

The starting point, in recent times, for police cooperation among the EU Member States was the establishment of the TREVI Group in 1975. Set up between the Council of Ministers in the context of European Political

97 *Protocol on the Position of Denmark, Articles 1 & 2.*

98 Although, the Danes may, in accordance with their constitutional requirements, decide that they no longer wish to avail themselves of all or part of the Protocol, Ibid., *Article 7.*

99 Ibid., *Article 5.*

Cooperation, it provided initially for regular meetings between Justice Ministers. From 1977 onwards a series of Working Groups were set up. The first two were initially upon anti-terrorism and police cooperation in police training and public order. From 1985 onwards the activities of TREVI expanded. In that year a Working Group was set up on Serious International Organised Crime, and in 1988 a further Working Group was set up to consider the consequences for policing of completion of the internal market.[100]

The SEA acted as a stimulus for increased cooperation. The removal of internal frontiers raised the 'spectre of loss of control over terrorists, drug traffickers, money launderers, fraudsters...'.[101] As Walker has observed, the insecurities generated by the hypothetical possibilities this offered for crime made it easy to mobilise public opinion.[102] This enabled a variety of discrete subjects, such as terrorism and drugs, to be brought together under a general banner of 'European internal security'.[103]

The 1990 Schengen Implementing Convention contained a number of provisions on police cooperation and judicial cooperation in the criminal field. These included intensification of cooperation between national police forces, particularly in the fields of hot pursuit and observation,[104] mutual assistance in criminal matters,[105] extradition,[106] transfer of the execution of criminal judgments,[107] cooperation in the

---

100 On TREVI see Benyon, J. *et al. Police Cooperation in Europe: An Investigation* (1993, Centre for Study of Public Order, University of Leicester) 152-168.

101 Anderson, M. *et al. Policing the European Union* (1995, OUP, Oxford)132.

102 Walker, N. 'European Integration and European Policing' 22, 35 in Anderson, M. *et al.* (ed.) *Policing Across National Boundaries* (1994, Pinter, London).

103 On the emergence of a European criminal space see Den Boer, M. & Walker, N. 'European Policing after 1992' (1993) 31 *JCMS* 3; Fijnaut, C. 'International Policing in Europe: Present and Future' (1994) 19 ELRev 599; Dorn, N. & White, S. 'Beyond "Pillars" and "Passerelle" Debates: The European Union's Emerging Crime Prevention Space (1996/1) *LIEI* 79.

104 Articles 39-47 SIA.

105 Articles 48-53 SIA.

106 Articles 59-66 SIA.

107 Articles 67-69 SIA.

fight against drugs,[108] and coordination of firearms legislation.[109] Provision was also made for the Schengen Information System to include data on persons wanted for arrest for extradition purposes; TCNs who are reported for the purpose of being refused entry to the Contracting Parties; persons who have disappeared or need to be placed in safehouses; witnesses and persons summoned to appear before judicial authorities, and objects sought for the purpose of seizure or as evidence for criminal proceedings.[110]

Judicial cooperation in criminal matters and police cooperation for the purposes of preventing and combating terrorism, unlawful drug trafficking and other serious forms of international crime were brought within JHA.[111] The same institutional apparatus applied to these matters as to other areas of JHA. With the coming into force of the TEU it replaced the cooperation that had been taking place under TREVI. The structure of TREVI was maintained with Steering Groups operating under the aegis of the 'K4' Committee on terrorism, police cooperation, drugs and serious organised crime. In addition a series of Steering Groups were set up in the field of Judicial Cooperation. In the criminal field these exist for extradition, international organised crime, penal law, withdrawal of driving licences and exchange of trial documents.[112]

This structure has generated a considerable amount of activity. The Cannes European Council in 1995 agreed upon an action plan to combat drugs.[113] Measures adopted under this programme include Joint Actions on approximating laws and practices to combat drug addiction

---

108 Articles 70-76 SIA.

109 Articles 77-91 SIA.

110 Articles 92-101 SIA.

111 Article K.1(1)- K.1(7) TEU.

112 On this aspect of JHA see Den Boer, M. 'Police Cooperation in the TEU: Tiger in a Trojan Horse?' (1995) 32 *CMLRev* 555; Guyomarch, A. 'Problems and Prospects for European Police Cooperation after Maastricht' (1995) 5 *Policing & Society* 249; Schutte, J. 'Judicial Cooperation under the Union Treaty'; Swart, A. 'Cooperation in the Field of Criminal Law: Some Comments'; Ravillard, P. 'Customs Cooperation in the Context of Title VI of the Treaty on European Union' in Monar, J. & Morgan, R. (eds.) *The Third Pillar of the European Union* (1994, European Interuniversity Press, Brussels).

113 EU Bulletin 6-1995, I.24.

and to prevent and combat illegal drug trafficking;[114] cooperation between customs authorities and business organisations;[115] information exchange, risk assessment and control of new synthetic drugs,[116] and the refining of target criteria and collection of customs and police information.[117]

Likewise an Action to combat Organised Crime has been adopted.[118] Only one Joint Action has been adopted under it providing for peer evaluation by the Member States of implementation of international commitments by each to combat organised crime.[119]

The other main area of activity is combating terrorism. On 23 November 1995 the Council made a Declaration noting that terrorism constituted a threat to democracy, had stepped up its activity and was operating on a transnational scale. The Council declared that as a result of this there needed to be an increase in exchange of operational information between Member States about terrorist groups, improvement of coordination between judicial authorities and, having regard to international agreements, the handing over to judicial authorities of those responsible for terrorist acts.[120] Other assorted measures which have been taken include Joint Actions on the combatting of trafficking in human beings and exploitation of children[121] and on large groups of people who pose a threat to law and order,[122] and a not yet ratified Convention on Simplifying Extradition Procedures between the Member States.[123]

The most significant development, however, was the setting up of a European Police Office (EUROPOL). This was agreed in December 1991 and provision is made for its establishment in Article K.1(9) TEU. Due to disagreements over the role of the Court of Justice, the

---

114 Decision 96/750/JHA, OJ 1996 L 342/6.

115 Decision 96/698/JHA, OJ 1996 L 322/

116 Decision 97/396/JHA, OJ 1997 L 167/1.

117 Decision 97/372/JHA, OJ 1997 L 159/1.

118 OJ 1997 C 251/1.

119 Decision 97/827/JHA, OJ 1997 L 344/7.

120 EU Bulletin 11-1995, I.5.10.

121 Decision 97/154/JHA, OJ 1997 L 63/2.

122 Decision 97/339/JHA, OJ 1997 L 147/1.

123 OJ 1995 C 78/2; OJ 1996 C 313/11.

Convention was not signed until July 1995.[124] A precursor, the European Drugs Unit, was set up and has been operational since 1 January 1994.[125] It is seen as to all intents and purposes a provisional EUROPOL.

The objectives of EUROPOL are to improve the effectiveness and cooperation of the competent authorities in combating certain forms of crime - namely terrorism, drug trafficking and other serious forms of international crime - where an organised criminal structure is involved, and two or more Member States are affected by the form of crime in question in such a way as to require a common approach owing to the scale, significance and consequences of the offences concerned.[126] To achieve these aims the tasks of EUROPOL are to:

- facilitate the exchange of information between the Member States;
- obtain, collate and analyse information and intelligence;
- notify the competent authorities of the Member States of information concerning them and of any connections identified between criminal offences;
- aid investigations in the Member States by forwarding all relevant information to the national units;
- maintain a computerised system of collected information.[127]

A Protocol was attached to the Convention giving the Court of Justice jurisdiction to interpret it. Article 2 of the Protocol allows Member States to make a Declaration entitling either courts of last resort or all courts may refer questions under the Convention to the Court. All Member States other than the United Kingdom have already made Declarations to the effect that they will allow courts against whose decisions there is no judicial remedy in national law to refer questions about the Convention to the Court.[128] As of December 1997 four Member States have yet to ratify the Convention. On present evidence

---

124 OJ 1995 C 316/1. See Monaco, R. 'EUROPOL: The Culmination of the European Union's International Police Cooperation Efforts' (1995) 19 *Fordham International Law Journal* 247.

125 The Unit's status was formalised in Decision 95/73/JHA OJ 1995 L 62/1.

126 Supra n.124, Article 2.

127 Ibid., Article 3(1).

128 OJ 1996 C 299/1.

it appears that EUROPOL will be busy. In 1995 the European Drug Unit received 1474 requests for criminal intelligence.[129]

ii. Police Cooperation following the Treaty of Amsterdam

Despite all this activity the strong centrifugal tensions which pull against further integration in this area should not be underestimated. Article K.2(2) TEU stated that nothing in JHA should affect the exercise of Member States' responsibilities with regard to the maintenance of law and order and the safeguarding of internal security. Likewise only a few discrete measures affecting criminal activities have been adopted within the EC pillar.[130] Whilst the Court has stated that Member States are under a duty to ensure that EC law is applied and to police EC law, subject to that caveat, it also has recognised the exclusive responsibilities of Member States for law and order and internal security upon their territories.[131]

Member States were unwilling to communitarise police cooperation and judicial cooperation in criminal matters at Amsterdam. These constitute what remains of the third pillar. That said, the remit of cooperation under the third pillar has been extended in the remaining fields.

This is done, first by integrating that part of the *Schengen Acquis* which is not integrated into the EC pillar into the new JHA. This partitioning of the *Acquis* will create controversy as to which pillar it should fall under. Article 2(1) of the *Protocol integrating the Schengen Acquis into the framework of the European Union* makes provision for this to be decided by the Council, acting unanimously. Until a decision is taken by the Council any measure forming part of the *Acquis* will

---

129 Foreign & Commonwealth Office, *A Partnership of Nations* (1996, HMSO, London) para 48.

130 Directive 91/308/EEC, on prevention of the use of the financial system for the purpose of money laundering, OJ 1991 L 166/77. Directive 91/477/EEC, on control of the acquisition and possession of weapons, OJ 1991 L 256/51.

131 Case C-265/95 *Commission v France*, Judgment of 9 December 1997.

remain within JHA. Secondly, the ambit of cooperation in these fields has been widened.

Article 29 TEU. *Without prejudice to the powers of the European Community, the Union's objective shall be to provide citizens with a high level of safety within an area of freedom, security and justice by developing common action among the Member States in the fields of police and judicial cooperation in criminal matters and by preventing and combatting racism and xenophobia.*

That objective shall be achieved by preventing and combatting crime, organised or otherwise, in particular terrorism, trafficking in persons and offences against children, illicit drug trafficking and illicit arms trafficking, corruption and fraud, through:

- closer cooperation between police forces, customs authorities and other competent authorities in the Member States, both directly and through the European Police Office (Europol), in accordance with the provisions of Articles 30 and 32;
- closer cooperation between judicial and other competent authorities of the Member States in accordance with the provisions of Articles 31(a) to (d) and 32;
- approximation, where necessary, of rules on criminal matters in the Member States, in accordance with the provisions of Article 31(e).

In police cooperation the main change is to be an increase in EUROPOL's powers. It is to move from being a vessel for the processing of information to having a more operational role.

Article 30(2) TEU. *The Council shall promote cooperation through Europol and shall in particular, within a period of five years after the date of entry into force of the Treaty of Amsterdam:*

(a) enable Europol to facilitate and support the preparation, and to encourage the coordination and carrying out, of specific investigative actions by the competent authorities of the Member States, including operational actions of joint teams comprising representatives of Europol in a support capacity;
(b) adopt measures allowing Europol to ask the competent authorities of the Member States to conduct and coordinate their investigations in specific cases and to develop specific expertise which may be put at the disposal of Member States to assist them in investigating cases of organised crime;
(c) promote liaison arrangements between prosecuting/investigating officials specialising in the fight against organised crime in close cooperation with Europol;

(d) establish a research, documentation and statistical network on cross-border crime.

In the judicial sphere the most significant advance is in *Article 31(e) TEU* which provides for some convergence of criminal legislation.

Article 31 TEU. *Common action on judicial cooperation in criminal matters shall include:*

.....

(e) progressively adopting measures establishing minimum rules relating to the constituent elements of criminal acts and to penalties in the fields of organised crime, terrorism and illicit drug trafficking.

To cope with the extended EU remit in the field, the number of instruments available to the Council has been expanded. The Joint Action has been replaced by two new instruments - decisions and framework decisions. The distinction between the two is that framework decisions are quasi-normative, applying, as they do, to measures providing for the approximation of laws.

Article 34(2) TEU. *The Council shall take measures and promote cooperation, using the appropriate form and procedures as set out in this Title, contributing to the pursuit of the objectives of the Union. To that end, acting unanimously on the initiative of any Member State or of the Commission, the Council may:*

(a) adopt common positions defining the approach of the Union to a particular matter;

(b) adopt framework decisions for the purpose of approximation of the laws and regulations of the Member States. Framework decisions shall be binding upon the Member States as to the result to be achieved but shall leave to the national authorities the choice of form and methods. They shall not entail direct effect;

(c) adopt decisions for any other purpose consistent with the objectives of this Title, excluding any approximation of the laws and regulations of the Member States. These decisions shall be binding and shall not entail direct effect; the Council, acting by a qualified majority, shall adopt measures necessary to implement those decisions at the level of the Union;

(d) establish conventions which it shall recommend to the Member States for adoption in accordance with their respective constitutional requirements. Member States shall begin the procedures applicable within a time limit to be set by the Council.

Unless they provide otherwise, conventions shall, once adopted by at least half of the Member States, enter into force for those Member States. Measures implementing conventions shall be adopted within the Council by a majority of two-thirds of the Contracting Parties.

Transparency has been increased through the addition of a Declaration which states that all initiatives and acts adopted under this provision will be published in the Official Journal. Unsurprisingly, the Council still retains its central role, however. The 'K-4' Committee is also retained.[132] The Parliament's powers are expanded, however. It must now be consulted before *any* decision, framework decision or convention is adopted.[133] It is doubtful, though, whether this will satisfy the criticisms about the absence of parliamentary control which are a feature of JHA, pre-ratification of Amsterdam.

The most significant institutional innovation is the granting of jurisdiction to the Court of Justice over JHA.[134] Its jurisdiction is tempered by its having no power to review the validity or proportionality of operations carried out by the police or other law enforcement services of a Member State. It also is to have no power to review the exercise of responsibilities incumbent upon Member States with regard to the maintenance of law and order and the safeguarding of internal security.[135] That does not mean that these areas will not be subject to judicial controls. A Declaration was attached which states that action in the field of police cooperation, including activities of EUROPOL, shall be subject to appropriate judicial review by the competent national authorities in accordance with the rules applicable in each Member State.

Subject to that, the Court shall have jurisdiction in four circumstances. First, it may review the legality of framework decisions

---

132 *Article 36 TEU.* The new Article means that the Committee will probably need a new title!

133 *Article 39(1) TEU.*

134 *Article 35(1) TEU.*

135 *Article 35(5) TEU.*

and decisions in actions brought by a Member State or the Commission on grounds of lack of competence, infringement of an essential procedural requirement, infringement of the Treaty or of any rule of law relating to its application, or misuse of powers.[136] Secondly, it can rule on any dispute between Member States regarding the interpretation or the application of acts adopted under JHA whenever such dispute cannot be settled by the Council within six months of its being referred to the Council by one of its members.[137] Thirdly the Court shall also have jurisdiction to rule on any dispute between Member States and the Commission regarding the interpretation or the application of conventions established under *Article 34(2)(d) TEU.*[138]

It is the fourth circumstance in which the Court has jurisdiction which is likely to prove the most controversial. Following the model of certain conventions agreed under JHA,[139] *Article 35(2) TEU* allows Member States to accept the jurisdiction of the Court to give preliminary rulings.[140] Any Member State making such a declaration whether only courts against whose decisions there is no judicial remedy under national law may make a ruling or whether all courts may make a ruling.[141] The provision is a strange one. For any ruling of the Court is likely to be binding on all courts within the Union, whether they have the power to make references or not. There would seem to be little incentive for Member States not to allow their courts to refer.

Even within JHA Amsterdam would have seemed to bring about a certain pull, establishing, as it does, quasi-legislative, administrative and judicial apparatuses - all of which could contribute towards creating

---

136 *Article 35(6) TEU.*

137 *Article 35(7) TEU.*

138 *Article 35(7) TEU.*

139 Protocol on the interpretation by the Court of Justice of the European Communities on the Convention on the establishment of a European Police Office, OJ 1996 C 299/1; Protocol on the interpretation by the Court of Justice of the European Communities of the Convention on the protection of the European Communities' financial interests, OJ 1997 C 151/1; Protocol on the interpretation by the Court of Justice of the European Communities of the Convention on the use of information technology for customs purposes, OJ 1997 C 151/15.

140 *Article 35(2) TEU.*

141 *Article 35(3) TEU.*

a common European criminal law. Provision is made for even closer integration in two ways. The passarelle between JHA and the EC pillar is retained so that any measure may be transferred by the Council, acting unanimously, to the EC pillar.[142] Provision is also made for Member States to establish closer cooperation between themselves.[143] There are very strong counter-assimilative tendencies still present within the pillar, however. In particular, *Article 33 TEU* states:

> *This Title shall not affect the exercise of the responsibilities incumbent upon Member States with regard to the maintenance of law and order and the safeguarding of internal security.*[144]

It is noticeable also that many of the Court's powers are powers to review the Institutions. They allow Member States who have unwillingly accepted an act in the field a form of double veto by then challenging the matter before the Court. Limits are also placed upon the degree of convergence which can be attained in the criminal field by a Declaration which states that no State whose legal system does not provide for minimum sentences should be obliged to adopt them.

More generally, it is notable how much of the cooperation under JHA actually reinforces Member State control over their populations. Cooperation on extradition thus allows a Member State to reassert control over an offence committed in its jurisdiction even though the perpetrator has fled. The most severe example of this reinforced control is the *Protocol on Asylum for Nationals of the EU Member States*. The background to the Protocol was a dispute between Belgium and Spain as a result of a Belgian court refusing to accede to a Spanish request to extradite a suspected ETA terrorist. Its basic premise is that all Member

---

142 *Article 42 TEU*. It will almost certainly never be used. A Declaration by Denmark states that, in accordance its constitutional requirements, if the transfer involves any transfer of sovereignty it will need approval by a majority of five sixths of members of the Danish Parliament, or by a majority of the Parliament and a majority of voters in a referendum.

143 *Article 40 TEU*. On the conditions which apply see pp 262-264 in Volume I.

144 For an identical provision in relation to the EC Treaty see *Article 64(1) EC*.

States are safe countries for the purposes of asylum and that the national should be returned to the country of origin and the request refused. An application may be admissible if the State of origin has suspended the European Convention on Human Rights and Freedoms or measures have been initiated or taken under *Article 7 TEU* for serious and persistent breaches by a Member State of the rule of law or fundamental rights. In other circumstances a Member State may find an asylum request admissible but must immediately inform the Council.

The presumption against asylum sits uneasily with the 1951 Geneva Convention relating to the Status of Refugees which provides for due process to be given to every asylum seeker. At Amsterdam the Dutch Presidency proposed adding a Declaration stipulating that the Protocol should be interpreted in accordance with the 1951 Geneva Convention but only Belgium has made a Declaration to this effect.

Further Reading

Anderson, M. *et al. Policing Across National Boundaries* (1994, Pinter, London)

Barrett, G. *Justice Cooperation in the European Union. The Creation of a European Legal Space* (1997, European Interuniversity Press, Brussels)

Bieber, R. & Monar, J. (eds.) *Justice and Home Affairs in the European Union: The Development of the Third Pillar* (1995, European Interuniversity, Brussels)

Collinson, S. *Beyond Borders: West European Migration Policy Towards the 21st Century* (1993, RIIA, London)

----- *Europe and International Migration* (1993, Pinter, London)

Fulbrook, M. & Cesarani, D. (eds.) *Citizenship, Nationality and Migration in Europe* (1996, Routledge, London)

Guild, E. & Nielsen, J. *The Emerging Immigration and Asylum Policies of the European Union* (1996, Kluwer, Dordrecht)

Handoll, J. *Free Movement of Persons in the European Union* (1995, Wiley, Chichester)

Hedemann-Robinson, M. 'Third Country Nationals, European Citizenship and Free Movement of Persons: A Time for Bridges Rather than Divisions' (1996) 16 *Yearbook of European Law* 321

Koslowski, R. 'Intra-European Union Migration, Citizenship and Political Union' (1994) 32 *Journal of Common Market Studies* 371

Kovella, G. & Twomey, P. (eds.) *Towards a European Immigration Policy* (1993, European Interuniversity Press, Brussels)

Meijers, H. *et al.* (ed.) *Schengen: internationalisation of central chapters of the law of aliens, refugees, privacy, security and police* (1992, 2nd Rev Ed., Stichting NJM-Boekerij, Leiden)

Monar, J. & Morgan, R. (eds.) *The Third Pillar of the European Union* (1994, European Interuniversity Press, Brussels)

Peers, S. 'National Security and European Law' (1996) 16 *Yearbook of European Law* 363

Schermers, H. *Free Movement of Persons in Europe: legal problems and experiences* (1993, Martijnus Nijhoff, Dordrecht)

4. External Relations

I. Introduction

EU policies affect other States, their nationals and their enterprises in a variety of ways. Every time a third State national enters the European Union that national has to comply with European Union laws. Activities instigated by parties outside the European Union are subject to the jurisdiction of Community law if 'implemented' within the European Union.[1] Finally, the extraterritorial effects of activities occurring within the European Union, and for which the European Union is responsible, either exclusively or partially, may also affect third States and their nationals.

If all this were to be considered external relations, there is little in this book which would not fall within this Chapter. For our purposes external relations has been given a narrower definition. It concerns those EC powers which allow it to establish relations specifically with third parties.[2] This requires, first, that the European Union has to have an *international* capacity separate from its *domestic* capacity. For the EC this is provided by Article 210 [*281*] EC.

Article 210 [*281*] EC. The Community shall have legal personality.

The legal personality of the Union was only formally addressed for the first time at Amsterdam. There was not consensus on where it should have legal personality. Provision was made for international

---

1 Joined Cases 89, 104, 114, 116-117, 125-9/85 *Ahlström et al. v Commission* [1988] ECR 5193, [1988] 4 CMLR 901.

2 Any partitioning is inevitably somewhat stilted. The definition above would include immigration policy and third country nationals. For the sake of convenience this has been dealt with in the Chapter on Free Movement of Persons.

agreements to be concluded by EU Institutions when implementing CFSP.

Article 24 TEU. *When it is necessary to conclude an agreement with one or more States or international organisations in implementation of this Title, the Council, acting unanimously, may authorise the Presidency, assisted by the Commission as appropriate, to open negotiations to that effect. Such agreements shall be concluded by the Council acting unanimously on a recommendation from the Presidency. No agreement shall be binding on a Member State whose representative in the Council states that it has to comply with the requirements of its own constitutional procedure; the other members of the Council may agree that the agreement shall apply provisionally to them.*

Whilst any agreement concluded by the Council binds Member States, it would be wrong to infer from this that the provision confers legal autonomy on the Union. A Declaration was attached to the Treaty of Amsterdam making quite clear that the provision implies no transfer of competence from Member States to the Union. A better interpretation is that the Council acts as a proxy for and on behalf of the Member States when concluding an agreement under the Article.[3]

Legal autonomy alone is in any case insufficient to give either the EC or the EU more generally an international capability.[4]

Hill, C. 'The Capability-Expectations Gap, or Conceptualizing Europe's International Role' (1993) 31 *Journal of Common Market Studies* 305, 308-309

The two indispensable concepts which do not derive neatly from any of the major schools of thought about integration are *actorness* and *presence*. 'Actorness' in the world is something which most non-theoretical observers automatically assume that the European Community possesses, but which on closer examination might be seriously doubted, on the grounds that the EC in foreign policy is solely intergovernmental, and is therefore no more than the sum of what the Member States severally decide. The truth, as those

---

3 We are indebted to Marise Cremona for this point.

4 See also Smith, M. 'The European Union, foreign economic policy and the changing world arena' (1994) 1 *JEPP* 283.

writers who have addressed the problem have pointed out, is that the Community is a genuine international actor in some respects but not all, and that what is fascinating about the history of the last 20 years is to assess the various effects which have been made to increase the scope of actorness, as well as the consequences in this respect of the more organic changes in the relations between the EC and the rest of the world. 'Actorness' provides us with a theoretical perspective which can incorporate both the internal dynamics of institutional development (in this case CFSP [common foreign and security policy]) and the changing nature of the international environment in which it has to operate. In other words, if the EC is less than a state, but more than a conventional intergovernmental organization (IGO), in what ways can it be termed a genuinely independent actor in international relations? This approach enables us to chart the EC's changing role in the world without becoming distracted by the 'is it or isn't it a superpower' red herring. ... Following Sjöstedt, an international actor can be said to be an entity which is (1) *delimited* from others, and from its environment; which is (2) *autonomous*, in the sense of making its own laws and decisions ('sovereignty' could be used here were it not for the spectre of statehood which the term raises); and which (3) possesses certain *structural prerequisites* for action on the international level, such as legal personality, a set of diplomatic agents and the capability to conduct negotiations with third parties [[5]].

The second concept, taken from Allen and Smith, is that of western Europe's 'variable and multidimensional presence' in international affairs, which accepts the reality of a cohesive European impact on international relations despite the messy way in which it is produced.[[6]] In other words, it gets us off the hook of analysing EPC [European Political Cooperation] in terms of sovereignty and supranationalism, which might lead us to suppose that there was in fact no European foreign policy when common sense and the experience of other states tell us precisely the opposite. It is a consequentialist notion which emphasises outside perceptions of the Community and the significant effects it has on both the psychological and the operational environments of third parties.

The potential benefits such a European foreign policy might offer are considerable.

---

5 Sjöstedt, G. *The External Role of the European Community* (1977, Saxon House, Farnborough).

6 Allen, D. & Smith, M. 'Western Europe's Presence in the Contemporary International Arena' (1990) 16 *Review of International Studies* 20.

Hill C. 'The Capability-Expectations Gap, or Conceptualizing Europe's International Role' (1993) 31 *Journal of Common Market Studies* 305, 310-315

EC Functions in the International System up to the Present

(1) The stabilizing of western Europe. The EC has not, of course, been the only cause of the peace which has become institutionalized in the region since 1945 (the Cold War paradoxically also takes some credit, together with economic growth), but without the Community such key elements as Franco-German entente and the democratic transitions of Greece, Portugal and Spain would have been much less likely.
(2) *Managing world trade.* World trade is not very effectively 'managed' even through the GATT, but to the extent that it is, the EC is the single most important actor in the negotiating process which produces the various trade regimes. At around 16 per cent (excluding intra-EC trade) it has the biggest share of any state or trading group in world trade, and its weight has become steadily more apparent over the 35 years since 1958, culminating in the dramatic external impact of the Single Market programme after 1985. ... Although the Twelve conduct the major part of their trade with each other, a trend which enlargement would accentuate, there is no chance of the Community ceasing to be, with the USA and Japan, one of the crucial players in world trade politics for the foreseeable future.
(3) *Principal voice of the developed world in relations with the South.* In the 1970's the EC constructed an unusual and imaginative development policy with the first two Lomé Conventions, to the effect that not only did the EC and its Members become easily the most important source of aid in the developed world, but also the rich countries most likely to win trust and exert influence in the South, particularly in Africa, where American, Japanese and Soviet policies were either absent or ineffective. Since then it is arguable that this position has atrophied, partly because of the structural limits on co-operation between very poor and relatively rich states, and partly because of ideological shifts in the 1980's. Nonetheless, the EC remains the principal interlocutor with the poor majority in the UN. With the inclusion of the Lomé system, the Mediterranean preferences, and its agreements with ASEAN and the Contradora countries, the EC enjoys institutionalized relations with at least 90 of the world's poorer countries, who in turn constitute around 80 per cent of the membership of the United Nations.
(4) *Providing a second western voice in international diplomacy.* It may or may not be true that multipolarity provides more stability in the international system than bipolarity in which case the development of a collective European diplomacy has served wider needs than its own, but EPC [European Political Cooperation] has certainly evolved because of a perceived need to provide an alternative view to that of the United States, both within the western world and on behalf of it. US leadership has served European interests well in many respects, but the gradual changes of historical context during the 1960s and 1970s have highlighted the problems. Accordingly, and channelled largely through EPC, a second and interestingly distinctive western voice has emerged, particularly where there seem to be possibilities of mediating dangerous conflicts between third states. We have now reached the point where even the United States

looked first to the EC to manage the reconstruction of eastern Europe after 1989, and to stabilize ex-Yugoslavia. That it has not been able to do so does not invalidate the point that the EC has achieved a salience in the international political system which was simply absent in the 1960s.

Conceivable Future Functions for the EC in the Current Flux

Given that the international system is in a condition of transition, without anyone having much idea of the end point, that the Soviet Union has disappeared, and that the United States is in no position to exert worldwide leadership, it is not surprising that a more self-confident and maturing EC should seem capable of extending its global activity. There are six main ways in which it might do so. The EC is potentially:

(i) *A replacement for the USSR in the global balance of power*. If we assume, with traditional accounts of international relations, that there always exists either a balance of power or a tendency towards balancing preponderant power, then we are drawn to the conclusion that there is now a power vacuum in the international system. One of its two major forces, locked together in an antagonistic equilibrium, has suddenly been removed from the scene, with destabilizing consequences which are becoming ever more apparent. On the further assumption that, at least in the short term, the nature of international relations cannot be transformed into a post-power politics, we shall need to think of the EC as a candidate to fill the vacuum. There is certainly no alternative in terms of balancing American strength globally. It would be a mistake to think that this means ineluctable military rivalry. Fortunately grand strategy between similar social systems is more likely to revolve around economics and diplomacy than armed might. But there can be no doubt that even if the EC takes over only some of the roles left vacant by the Soviet Union, then competition and conflict with the USA will increase in proportion.

(ii) *Regional pacifier*. The withdrawal of the Soviet Union's iron fist from central and eastern Europe has created the possibility of serious disputes breaking out between and within the newly liberated states of the region. Since the United States is currently looking to reduce rather than to increase its commitments in Europe, while the EC is becoming ever more ambitious, it falls to the latter to act as mediator/coercive arbiter when the peace of the whole region seems under threat. This has clearly been the general expectation (so far unmet) in the case of Yugoslavia. In institutional terms, it means the Community acting as the motor for the CSCE and for the Council of Europe, taking its legitimacy from the broader constituency of states and citizens represented in these fora, but itself providing the dynamism and capacity to mobilize resources for action that purely parliamentary bodies are unlikely to achieve. The EC also has the capacity to act as a magnet and a model for the countries of eastern Europe. If all persist in wanting to join the Community, then the latter will by definition dominate the international politics of Europe, although it will risk destabilization itself. If, on the other hand, it can achieve a structure in which most countries to the east remain outside but closely tied to the EC, then there is the chance of being able to promote similar forms of international co-operation among the non-member countries.

(iii) *Global intervenor*. Growing out of the previous two potential functions is the possibility of the EC intervening in crises on a global basis. If it becomes a hegemon in

Europe, however benign, then the pressures and opportunities which already exist for action further afield are bound to multiply. If relations with the United States deteriorate, then Europe may end up competing with American interventions; if they stay sound, then the Europeans may have to face substituting for a less outwardly-oriented USA. What this means - and it should not be hidden in euphemisms - is that the EC would interfere, on occasions by military force but more often with economic and political instruments, in states or regions where instability seemed likely to threaten European interests and/or the peaceful evolution of the international community of states. At present it seems likely that this second criterion would be judged by the Security Council of the United Nations (where the Europeans have at least a quarter of the votes and two-fifths of the vetoes), but such a legitimization might resemble the limited humanitarian operation of the USA in Somalia in late 1992 and early 1993. In maximalist terms, it might mean the Europeans choosing to take major responsibility for a 'Desert Storm' style campaign, instead of just making up the American numbers.

(iv) *Mediator of conflicts*. The line between forceful intervention and the provision of services to enable third parties to resolve their conflicts is a fine one. But it is easier and more natural at present for the EC to act diplomatically than to exert coercion, even economically. Thus we saw considerable diplomatic effort and creativity in the early stages of the Yugoslavian imbroglio, continued thereafter in harness with the United Nations. Over a much longer period, EPC has made it a major priority to work at narrowing the gap between Israel and the Palestine Liberation Organisation (PLO), and eventually it might well be judged to have had some success. If any state or group of states is to achieve much in the area of mediation, then the EC has more claims than most. Between them, its Member States can claim considerable experience in relations with most parts of the globe, they have come through the period of decolonization without incurring too much long-term odium, and thus far they possess the singular advantage of not being perceived as a superpower and potential hegemon. Individual European states carry historical baggage which makes them distrusted in states such as Iran and Iraq; collectively, they represent more of a new beginning, and their claim to neutrality carries more weight.

(v) *Bridge between rich and poor*. As we have seen, the 'privileged' relationship between the EC and the poor majority in the international system have deteriorated in recent years, while still leaving the Europeans pre-eminent among developed states in their concern for the south. The Community now faces an important choice in this respect: whether to accept the impossibility of a special relationship with a very large number of countries at a much lower level of wealth and power, thus allowing the Lomé system to peter out, or whether to make renewed efforts (political and financial) to assist with the relief of poverty and to prevent North-South relations degenerating into mutual hostility or disregard. Nor is this an academic choice. European decisions on central questions like agriculture, immigration, the budget and the environment, to say nothing of trade, will automatically have profound repercussions for the poor states who look to Brussels for help. It follows that unless the Community is now to be indifferent to the Third World, it should factor these considerations into its overall policy-making process. Concrete and short-term interests certainly must be protected, but internal and external policies are now umbilically connected, and the EC should at least be aware of the trade-offs at stake, not least on such a significant issue for the long-term future of its own external environment.

(vi) *Joint supervisor of the world economy.* The recent dominance of laissez-faire thinking notwithstanding, it is more and more evident that the notion of 'a world economy' with attendant management needs is taking hold in the minds of public and private decision-makers. Accordingly, it is increasingly important for governments to find mechanisms whereby such influence as they can exert over the vicissitudes of the market is efficiently co-ordinated. In practice, this means the most powerful economies of the western world joining together in the yearly G-7 summits, in the IMF ministerial meetings and in the Group of Ten meetings of central bankers. The EC states are already powerfully represented in this process, and the opportunity lies before them to increase their weight of influence. With even limited progress towards a single currency, the Europeans will be more likely to make international monetary decisions the preserve of themselves, Japan and the United States. On the trade front, the history of the Uruguay Round has shown how the GATT has become a forum for trials of strength between the EC (strengthened by the Single Market programme) and the USA, while the G-7 will become a G-3, with Canada in the observers' gallery, if the major European states can hold together and develop a common sense of identity. This would mean developing an actorness it does not currently possess in the IMF, World Bank, International Atomic Energy Agency et al., but in terms of institutional recognition and the capacity to act coherently and consistently. If this happens a further issue opens up, that of whether a 'G-3 world' (and such modish simplifications should always be suspect) would mean the EC working in harness with Japan and the US, or whether it would produced tripolar conflict and instability.

External relations goes, however, to the heart of the institutional identity of the European Union. For it is seen, traditionally, as a prerequisite for the establishment of a federal State.[7]

Weiler, J. 'The External Legal Relations of Non-Unitary Actors: Mixity and the Federal Principle' in O'Keeffe, D. & Schermers, H. (eds.) *Mixed Agreements* (1983, Kluwer, Dordrecht) 35, 80-81.

1. Our analysis so far has revealed two possible constructions for the application of the federal principle to the international legal relations of non-unitary actors. According to one view external relations in general and treaty-making in particular are *instruments* and as such must be subordinate to the internal division of competences between the central authority and the constituent members.

---

7 Wheare, K. *Federal Government* (1963, 4th Edition, OUP, London) 169.

2. A second view is that external capacity and power have a *substantive* quality and are themselves not mere instruments to further other policies. In earlier times it could perhaps be maintained that the issues of foreign policy and external legal relations fell naturally within the central authority domain. But when it became clear that matters which were reserved to the constituent units rather than the central authority could have international implications, this second view was reconstructed. Now it is suggested that as regards any matter with an international dimension, even in non-unitary states, the exercise of international legal relations by the central authority maximizes in the international environment the power of the federal entity as a whole which is consequently also beneficial to the constituent member states. Under this view the concentration of external power and capacity in the central authority is in itself part of the federal allocation of competences within the non-unitary entity, and the interests of the constituent units could at best be vindicated by the internal processes of foreign policy formation.

It is this second view which has characterized the constitutional doctrine and practice of federal states. The other instrumental view, if taken to its logical conclusion, seemed an unacceptable option to the federations. It raised the spectre not only of a multiplicity of different foreign policies but also of a multiplicity of international legal relations which would, because of their internal effects, over-accentuate diversity rather than unity within the body politic and call into question the very *raison d'etre* of the federal state in which the one and the many, the uniform and the diverse, must find a workable equilibrium. In one sense the federal state experience might allay fears regarding respect for the internal autonomy of member states. All writers speak of a federal reluctance to exploit the wide external capacity, power and implementing competence to the detriment of the authority of constituent units. The respect for the member state is manifested either by refraining from treaty conclusion or by developing structures for co-operative federalism. It is clearly however a *centralist model* and one which historically has seen the effective elimination of member states as serious international actors.

If the development of an EU foreign policy raises the fear of empire-building, it also arouses fears, real or not, about the suppression of the nation-state. It appears to remove, or at least considerably restrict, individual national capacity to participate in international society and, more importantly, to be recognised as part of international society - a feature essential to traditional perceptions of a State's survival or existence.[8]

---

[8] Waever, O. 'European Security Identities' (1996) 34 *JCMS* 103, 115-120.

Regelsberger, E. & Wessels, W. 'The CFSP Institutions and Procedures: A Third Way for the Second Pillar' (1996) 1 *European Foreign Affairs Review* 29, 31

Experiences show that foreign policy cooperation has always been one of the most difficult areas in which to operate in common. Indeed, a DDS (discreet, discretionary, sovereignty) syndrome is at work: cooperation in the foreign and security areas raises immediately, and most visibly, issues of national sovereignty. Common efforts have to accommodate different historical traditions, to consider specific sensitivities and prejudices in public opinion. In the peoples' collective consciousness foreign policy, defence and currency are basic ingredients of the national state in a way in which coal, steel and the economy, however important, are not. Decisions on the physical and territorial survival of a nation might have to be taken. Foreign policy is also supposed to be discreet: confidentiality within small circles is perceived as vital; transparent procedures are not liked. Normal ways of doing business in Brussels are thought to be too open. Unlike internal market legislation foreign policy is also discretionary: action has to be decided on quickly according to specific situations, not by a long deliberation for systematic cases.

These characteristics do not, however, automatically imply the intergovernmental fallacy that institutions do not matter. The fundamental assumption of presenting reform proposals is that major CFSP shortcomings can be located in institutional and procedural deficiencies of mobilising and shaping the political will and of running/implementing the machinery, ie we are not partisans of the view that the positions and the vital national interests of EU countries are so different and that they are even diverging more rapidly after history has been taken out of the 'refrigerator' in '1989'. Though we observe centrifugal trends towards a renationalisation we consider that centripetal forces towards some kind of Europeanisation are and will be stronger. Governments and diplomats of Member States do want to make decisions which are 'shaping' international events and not just object of decisions taken somewhere else. What is thus needed are the institutional and procedural 'means necessary to attain its objectives and carry through its policies' (Article F.3 TEU).

II. The Competencies of the European Community

i. The External Instruments of the European Community

The first form of external power the European Community has are *autonomous* powers. These are powers whose exercise does not require the assent of a third State. The instruments used are therefore the same as those used purely for domestic matters, be they Regulations, Directives, Decisions etc. Examples might include, in the field of environmental law, the Regulation banning the import of animals caught in leghold traps,[9] or, in the field of commercial policy, the safeguard Regulation which establishes procedures for the adoption of safeguard measures in respect of third country imports.[10] The legal bases and procedures used are identical to those used for purely internal measures.

The other form of power is *treaty-making* powers. Treaties are taken to be any undertaking which is binding in international law.[11] Whatever the subject-matter, the procedure for concluding treaties is contained in Article 228 [*300*] EC.

Article 228(2) [*300(2)*] EC. Subject to the powers vested in the Commission in this field, the agreements shall be concluded by the Council, acting by a qualified majority on a proposal from the Commission. The Council shall act unanimously when the agreement covers a field for which unanimity is required for the adoption of internal rules, and for the agreements referred to in Article 238 [*310*].

3. The Council shall conclude agreements after consulting the European Parliament, except for the agreements referred to Article 113(3)[*133(3)*], including cases where the agreement covers a field for which the procedure referred to Article 189b [*251*] or that referred to Article 189c [*252*] is required for the adoption of internal rules. The European Parliament shall deliver its opinion within a time limit which the Council may lay down according to the urgency of the matter. In the absence of an opinion within that time limit, the Council may act.

By way of derogation from the previous subparagraph, agreements referred to in Article 238 [*310*], other agreements establishing a specific institutional framework by organising cooperation procedures, agreements having important budgetary implications for the Community and agreements entailing amendment of an act adopted under the procedure referred to in Article 189b [*251*] shall be concluded after the assent of the European Parliament has been obtained.

---

9 Regulation 3254/91/EEC, OJ 1991 L 308/1.

10 Regulation 3285/94/EC, OJ 1994 L 349/53.

11 Case C-327/91 *France v Commission* [1994] ECR I-3641, [1994] 5 CMLR 517. A 1991 'administrative agreement' between the Commission and the United States authorities on the application of competition law was therefore found to be illegal because it did not conform to the procedure set out in Article 228 [*300*] EC.

4. When concluding an agreement, the Council, by way of derogation from paragraph 2, empower the Commission to approve modifications on behalf of the Community where the agreement provides for them to be adopted by a simplified procedure or by a body set up by the agreement; it may attach specific conditions ro such empowerment.

The most striking feature is the asymmetry between the Parliament's treaty-making powers and its other powers. The simple trichotomy in its treaty-making powers between areas requiring its assent, its consultation and agreements where, formally at least, it need not even be consulted is far less nuanced than the procedures for autonomous legislation.[12] This is almost certainly because there is less of a tradition of parliaments participating in the field of external relations. Nevertheless, this does raise questions about the 'democratic deficit' in this area, particularly as treaties can have internal legislative effects.[13]

ii. The Express Powers of the European Community

The EC has express powers in a limited number of areas. It has autonomous powers to establish a common external tariff (Article 28 [*26*] EC) and a common commercial policy (Article 113(1) [*133(1)*] EC). It has express treaty-making powers in the following areas:-

- monetary and foreign exchange regimes (Article 109(3) [*111(3)*] EC);
- common commercial policy (Article 113(3) [*133(3)*] EC);
- participation in research and development within the context of existing multiannual framework programmes (Article 130l [*169*] EC);
- environment (Article 130r(4) [*174(4)*]EC);
- development cooperation (Article 130y [*181*]EC);

---

12 Under the Luns-Westerthorp Procedure, developed in 1977, Parliament is consulted by the Council on all 'significant' agreements in advance, and is notified of the other agreements, OJ 1982 C 66/68.

13 Gosalbo Bono, R. 'The International Powers of the European Parliament, the Democratic Deficit and the Treaty of Maastricht' (1992) 12 *YBEL* 85. On the internal legislative effects of treaties see pp. 189-197.

- association agreements (Article 238 [*310*] EC).

In addition, the EC is competent to foster international cooperation with a number of international organisations, in particular the United Nationals and its specialised agencies, the Council of Europe and the Organisation for Economic Cooperation and Development,[14] and in a number of areas, notably education,[15] vocational training,[16] culture,[17] public health[18] and trans-European networks.[19]

iii. The Implied Powers of the European Community

Many of the competencies listed above are recent ones, granted either by the SEA or the TEU. This lack of express competencies might initially have posed problems for the EC. In some areas it is impossible to run an internal policy without an external one. The EC could not, for example, regulate the quality of the Mediterranean if other maritime States were to continue to emit pollution, or, in the field of transport, regulate haulage capacity if third States separating Member States refused to recognise such limits. To counter this, the doctrine of implied powers has been developed in the field of external relations.

Case 22/70 Commission v Council (ERTA) [1971] ECR 263, [1971] CMLR 335

An international agreement regulating the work of crews engaged in international transport (ERTA) was signed in 1970 within the auspices of the United Nations Economic Commission for Europe. The Member States passed a Resolution within the Council stating that they would conclude it. The Commission brought

---

14 Articles 229-231 [*302-304*] EC.
15 Article 126(3) [*149(3)*]EC.
16 Article 127(3) [*150(3)*] EC.
17 Article 128(3) [*151(3)*] EC.
18 Article 129(3) [*152(3)*] EC.
19 Article 129c(3) [*155(3)*] EC.

an action against the Council claiming that it was the Community which should conclude the agreement rather than the Member States as competence had now passed in the field of transport to the Community.

12. In the absence of specific provisions of the Treaty relating to the negotiation and conclusion of international agreements in the sphere of transport policy - a category into which, essentially, the AETR falls - one must turn to the general system of Community law in the sphere of relations with third countries.

13. Article 210 provides that 'The Community shall have legal personality'.

14. This provision, placed at the head of Part Six of the Treaty, devoted to 'General and Final Provisions', means that in its external relations the Community enjoys the capacity to establish contractual links with third countries over the whole field of objectives defined in Part One of the Treaty, which Part Six supplements.

15. To determine in a particular case the Community's authority to enter into international agreements, regard must be had to the whole scheme of the Treaty no less than to its substantive provisions.

16. Such authority arises not only from an express conferment by the Treaty - as is the case with Articles 113 and 114 for tariff and trade agreements and with Article 238 for association agreements - but may equally flow from other provisions of the Treaty and from measures adopted, within the framework of those provisions, by the Community institutions.

17. In particular, each time the Community, with a view to implementing a common policy envisaged by the Treaty, adopts provisions laying down common rules, whatever form these may take, the Member States no longer have the right, acting individually or even collectively, to undertake obligations with third countries which affect those rules.

18. As and when such common rules come into being, the Community alone is in a position to assume and carry out contractual obligations towards third countries affecting the whole sphere of application of the Community legal system.

19. With regard to the implementation of the provisions of the Treaty the system of internal Community measures may not therefore be separated from that of external relations.

20. Under Article 3(e), the adoption of a common policy in the sphere of transport is specially mentioned amongst the objectives of the Community.

21. Under Article 5, the Member States are required on the one hand to take all appropriate measures to ensure fulfilment of the obligations arising out of the Treaty or resulting from action taken by the institutions and, on the other hand, to abstain from any measure which might jeopardize the attainment of the objectives of the Treaty.

22. If these two provisions are read in conjunction, it follows that to the extent to which Community rules are promulgated for the attainment of the objectives of the Treaty, the Member States cannot, outside the framework of the Community institutions, assume obligations which might affect those rules or alter their scope.

23. According to Article 74, the objectives of the Treaty in matters of transport are to be pursued within the framework of a common policy.

24. With this in view, Article 75 (1) directs the Council to lay down common rules and, in addition, 'any other appropriate provisions'.

25. By the terms of subparagraph (a) of the same provision, those common rules are applicable 'to international transport to or from the territory of a Member State or passing across the territory of one or more Member States'.

26. This provision is equally concerned with transport from or to third countries, as regards that part of the journey which takes place on Community territory.

27. It thus assumes that the powers of the Community extend to relationships arising from international law, and hence involve the need in the sphere in question for agreements with the third countries concerned.

28. Although it is true that Articles 74 and 75 do not expressly confer on the Community authority to enter into international agreements, nevertheless the bringing into force, on 25 March 1969, of Regulation No 543/69 of the Council on the harmonization of certain social legislation relating to road transport (OJ L 77, p.49) necessarily vested in the Community power to enter into any agreements with third countries relating to the subject-matter governed by that Regulation.

29. This grant of power is moreover expressly recognized by Article 3 of the said Regulation which prescribes that: 'The Community shall enter into any negotiations with third countries which may prove necessary for the purpose of implementing this Regulation'.

30. Since the subject-matter of the AETR falls within the scope of Regulation No 543/69, the Community has been empowered to negotiate and conclude the agreement in question since the entry into force of the said Regulation.

31. These Community powers exclude the possibility of concurrent powers on the part of Member States, since any steps taken outside the framework of the Community institutions would be incompatible with the unity of the common market and the uniform application of Community law.

The *ERTA* judgment concerned a matter where there was already internal EC legislation in place. Subsequent developments established that the EC has implied treaty-making powers even where there is no internal legislation.[20] The *ERTA* judgment also suggests that the EC only has those implied powers which are necessary to the securing of its internal objectives. The Court has, however, shown great reticence in determining whether a measure is 'necessary' or not.[21] A doctrine of parallelism has been adopted, whereby the EC has corresponding external competencies in any field within which it has internal competencies. This effectively removes the distinction between express and implied powers.

Opinion 2/91 Re ILO Convention 170 on Chemicals at Work [1993] ECR I-1061, [1993] 3 CMLR 800

A Convention was signed in 1990 under the auspices of the International Labour Organisation (ILO) on safety on the use of chemicals at work. The Commission sought an Opinion from the Court stating, first, that the Community was competent to conclude the agreement on the basis of its internal competence in health and safety in Article 118a [*137(2)*] EC.

7. ... The Court must point out that as it stated in particular [in paragraph 3 of *Opinion 1/76* [1977] ECR 741] authority to enter into international agreements may not only arise from an express attribution by the Treaty, but may also flow implicitly from its provisions. The Court concluded, in particular, that whenever Community law created for the institutions of the Community powers within its internal system for the purpose of attaining a specific objective the Community had authority to enter the international commitments necessary for the attainment of that objective even in the absence of an express provision in that connection. At paragraph 20 in its judgment in Joined Cases 3,4 and 6/76 *Kramer* [1976] ECR 1279 the Court had already pointed out that such authority could flow by implication from other measures adopted by the Community institutions within the framework of the Treaty provisions or the acts of accession.

---

20 Opinion 1/76 *Re: European Laying Up Fund for Inland Waterway Vessels* [1977] ECR 754, [1977] CMLR 279.

21 Hartley, T. 'The Commission as Legislator Under the EEC Treaty' (1988) 14 *ELRev* 122; Dehousse, R. 'Community Competences: Are there Limits to Growth?' 103, 115-117 in Dehousse, R. (ed.) *Europe after Maastricht: An Ever Closer Union?* (1994, Law Books in Europe, Munich).

.....

13. It is necessary to bear in mind the foregoing when examining the question whether Convention 170 comes within the Community's sphere of competence and, if so, whether that competence is exclusive in nature.

14. Convention 170 concerns safety in the use of chemicals at work. According to the Preamble, its essential objective is to prevent or reduce the incidence of chemicals induced illnesses and injuries at work by ensuring that all chemicals are evaluated to determine their hazards, by providing employers and workers with the information necessary for their protection and, finally, by establishing principles for protective programmes.

15. The field covered by Convention 170 falls within the 'social provisions' of the EEC Treaty which constitute Chapter 1 of Title III on social policy.

16. Under Article 118a EEC, Member States are required to pay particular attention to encouraging improvements, especially in the working environment, as regards the health and safety of workers, and to set as their objective the harmonization of conditions in this area, while maintaining the improvements made. In order to help achieve this objective, the Council has the power to adopt minimum requirements by means of Directives. If follows from Article 118a (3) EEC that the provisions adopted pursuant to that Article are not to prevent any Member State from maintaining or introducing more stringent measures for the protection of working conditions compatible with the Treaty.

17. The Community thus enjoys an internal legislative competence in the area of social policy. Consequently, Convention 170, whose subject-matter coincides, moreover, with that of several directives adopted under Article 118a EEC, falls within the Community's area of competence.

III. The External Economic Relations of the European Community

i. The Customs Union

The establishment of the customs union in Article 9 [*23*] EC entails the adoption of a common customs tariff (CCT) in Member States' relations with third countries. Article 28 EC [*26*] states:

> Any autonomous alteration or suspension of duties in the common customs tariff shall be decided by the Council, acting by a qualified majority on a proposal from the Commission.

It was initially unclear whether the CCT covered merely customs duties or whether it parallelled Article 12 [*25*] EC and extended to charges having equivalent effect to a customs duty. In *Indiamex* the Court ruled on the legality of a Belgian charge of 0.33% on the import of diamonds from third countries which went towards the establishment of a social fund for Belgian workers in the industry.[22] It stated:

> [The purpose of the common custom tariff] is the equalization of customs charges levied at the frontier of the Community on products imported from third countries, in order to avoid any deflection of trade in relation with those countries and any distortion of internal circulation or of competitive conditions.

As the CCT and the common commercial policy required uniform external protection the Court considered that Member States were prevented from establishing their own customs duties or supplementary charges following the setting up of the CCT.[23]

The CCT is in one sense the Community's most successful external policy. The customs union does give rise to difficult questions concerning the classification, valuation and origin of goods.[24] It was, however, established two years ahead of time in 1968.[25] Duties on products are contained in a nomenclature which the Commission has

---

22 Joined Cases 37-38/73 *Sociaal Fonds voor de Diamantarbeiders v NV Indiamex et al.* [1973] ECR 1609, [1976] 2 CMLR 222.

23 Case C-125/94 *Aprile en liquidation v Amministrazione delle Finanze dello Stato* [1995] ECR I-2919. There is one small exception to this. Charges having equivalent effect to a customs duty on third country goods which were in place prior to 1968 may be retained, Case C-126/94 *Société Cadi Surgélé v Ministre des Finances* [1996] ECR I-5647.

24 For a summary of the issues see Usher, J. 'The Consequences of the Customs Union' in Emiliou, N. & O'Keeffe, D. (eds.) *The European Union and World Trade Law after the GATT Uruguay Round* (1996, John Wiley, Chichester).

25 Regulation 950/68/EEC [1968] I OJ Spec Ed. 275.

been delegated powers to review.[26] This success is due, in part, to the declining role tariffs play in international trade. The level of tariffs for industrial goods entering OECD countries is very low, and the principal obstructions to international trade in goods are not tariffs but technical 'Cassis de Dijon' style measures and so-called 'administered trade', where the exporting State agrees to limit its exports 'voluntarily' at the behest of the importing State.[27]

Within the EC, tariffs are therefore increasingly seen as just one small part of the common commercial policy. This view was facilitated by the Court's ruling in its *Harmonised System* decision.[28] In considering the legal base of the Community nomenclature, it stated that any measure which altered tariffs should be based not just upon Article 28 EC [*26*] but also upon Article 113[*133*] EC, the common commercial policy provision.

ii. The Common Commercial Policy

The common commercial policy (CCP) is contained in Article 113 [*133*] EC:

1. The common commercial policy shall be based on uniform principles, particularly in regard to changes in tariff rates, the conclusion of tariff and trade agreements, the achievement of uniformity in measures of liberalisation, export policy, and measures to protect trade such as those to be taken in case of dumping or subsidies.
2. The Commission shall submit proposals to the Council for implementing the common commercial policy.
3. Where agreements with one or more States or international organizations need to be negotiated, the Commission shall make recommendations to the Council, which shall authorize the Commission to open the necessary negotiations.

---

26 Most significantly, recently, see Commission Regulation 3009/95/EC, OJ 1995, L 319/1.

27 For an introduction to these measures see Jones, K. 'The Political Economy of Voluntary Export Restraint Arrangements' (1984) 10 *Kyklos* 82; Kostecki, M. 'Export Restraint Arrangements and Trade Liberalisation' (1987) 10 *World Economy* 425.

28 Case 165/87 *Commission v Council* [1988] ECR 5545, [1990] 1 CMLR 457.

The Commission shall conduct these negotiations in consultation with a special committee appointed by the Council to assist the Commission in this task and within the framework of such directives as the Council may issue to it.

The relevant provisions of Article 228 [*300*] shall apply.

4. In exercising the powers conferred upon it by this Article, the Council shall act by a qualified majority.

The CCP is seen by some commentators as *the* external face of the single market.[29] Eeckhout stated that if the '[common market] were a building, the CCP would be its facade'.[30] On such a view, Article 113 [*133*] EC should be extended to cover the external dimension of all those matters which fall within the single market. Areas such as technical barriers, government procurement, services, professional qualifications would all fall within the ambit of Article 113 [*133*] EC.

The CCP can be seen as having a narrower function, however, namely that of establishing EC *preference*. The EC, as a regional system of integration, is a select club which confers mutual benefits upon its members. The role of the CCP is therefore merely concerned with those rules which apply a different regime for non-members.

> If no preference is provided for, if, in other words, EC regulation in areas such as services, technical regulations and public procurement, genuinely applies across-the-board, without making any distinction between domestic and imported products, or Community-base and foreign economic actors, then there is little scope for a commercial policy in those areas: there is no specific regulation of third country access to the internal market. If, on the other hand, it is decided that there ought to be elements of discrimination, introducing a degree of internal preference, then there *is* scope for a commercial policy.[31]

---

29 Ehlermann, C-D. 'The Scope of Article 113 of the EEC Treaty' in *Mélanges Offerts à Pierre-Henri Teitgen* (1984, Pedone, Paris); Everling, U. 'The Law of the External Economic Relations of the European Community' in Hilf, M., Jacobs, F. & Petersmann E-U. (eds.) *The European Community and the GATT* (1989, 2nd Edition, Kluwer, Deventer).

30 Eeckhout, P. *The European Internal Market and International Trade* (1994, Clarendon Press, Oxford) 344.

31 Eeckhout, P. 'The External Dimension of the Internal Market and the Scope and Content of a Modern Commercial Policy' 79, 92 in Maresceau, M. (ed.) *The European Community's Commercial Policy after 1992: The Legal Dimension* (1993, Kluwer, Deventer).

Such an approach takes a narrower view of Article 113 [*133*] EC, holding that only those activities which *specifically regulate* third country goods or nationals fall within the scope of the common commercial policy. Other measures, although they might affect third country imports or traders, would not establish an EC preference and would thus be linked instead to the 'internal' Community policy. Elements of both approaches can be found in the recent case law on the subject.

Opinion 1/94 Re World Trade Organisation [1994] ECR I-5267, [1995] 1 CMLR 205

In December 1993, following seven years of negotiations, the World Trade Organisation (WTO) Agreement was signed. The Agreement created the WTO which was to replace the GATT and the substantive agreements reached were contained in four Annexes to the Agreement. The Agreement could however be divided into three. There were a number of agreements which were labelled the Multilateral Trade in Goods Agreements (MTA); there was the General Agreement in Trade in Services (GATS), and there was the Agreement on Trade-Related Aspects of Intellectual Property Rights (TRIPs). The Court was asked to rule by the Commission upon whether the Community had exclusive competence to conclude the Agreement in these three fields.

VI. The Multilateral Agreements on Trade in Goods

22. The Commission and the parties which have submitted observations agree that the Multilateral Agreements on Trade in Goods are for the most part covered by the exclusive competence conferred on the Community in matters concerning the common commercial policy by Article 113 of the EC Treaty. The differences between them relate only to specific points.

.....

32. According to the Netherlands Government, the joint participation of the Community and the Member States in the WTO Agreement is justified, since the Member States have their own competence in relation to technical barriers to trade by reason of the optional nature of certain Community directives in that area, and because complete harmonization has not been achieved and is not envisaged in that field.

33. That argument cannot be accepted. The Agreement on Technical Barriers to Trade, the provisions of which are designed merely to ensure that technical regulations and standards and procedures for assessment of conformity with technical regulations and standards do not create unnecessary obstacles to international trade (see the preamble and Articles 2.2 and 5.1.2 of the Agreement), falls within the ambit of the common commercial policy.

.....

VII. Article 113 EC of the EC Treaty, GATS and TRIPs

.....

38. As regards the first category, it should be recalled at the outset that in *Opinion 1/75* the Court, which had been asked to rule on the scope of Community competence as to the arrangements relating to a local cost standard, held that 'the field of the common commercial policy, and more particularly that of export policy, necessarily covers systems of aid for exports and more particularly measures concerning credits for the financing of local costs linked to export operations' ([1975] ECR 1362). The local costs in question concerned expenses incurred for the supply of both goods and services. Nevertheless, the Court recognized the exclusive competence of the Community, without drawing a distinction between goods and services.

39. In its *Opinion 1/78*, cited above (paragraph 44) [1978 (ECR) ECR 2909], the Court rejected an interpretation of Article 113 'the effect of which would be to restrict the common commercial policy to the use of instruments intended to have an effect only on the traditional aspects of external trade'. On the contrary, it considered that 'the question of external trade must be governed form a wide point of view', as is confirmed by 'the fact that the enumeration in Article 113 of the subjects covered by commercial policy ... is conceived as a non-exhaustive enumeration' (*Opinion 1/78*, cited above, paragraph 45).

40. The Commission points out in its request for an opinion that in certain developed countries the services sector has become the dominant sector of the economy and that the global economy has been undergoing fundamental structural changes. The trend is for basic industry to be transferred to developing countries, whilst the developed economies have tended to become, in the main, exporters of services and of goods with a high value-added content. The Court notes that this trend is borne out by the WTO Agreement and its annexes, which were the subject of a single process of negotiation covering both goods and services.

41. Having regard to this trend in international trade, it follows from the open nature of the common commercial policy, within the meaning of the Treaty, that trade in services cannot immediately, and as a matter of principle, be excluded from the scope of Article 113, as some of the Governments which have submitted observations contend.

42. In order to make that conclusion more specific, however, one must take into account definition of trade in services given in GATS in order to see whether the overall scheme of the Treaty is not such as to limit the extent to which trade in services can be included within Article 113.

43. Under Article 1(2) of GATS, trade in services is defined, for the purposes of that agreement, as comprising four modes of supply of services: (1) cross-frontier supplies not involving any movement of persons; (2) consumption abroad, which entails the movement of the consumer into the territory of the WTO member country in which the supplier is established; (3) commercial presence, ie the presence of a subsidiary or branch in the territory of the WTO member country in which the service is to be rendered; (4) the presence of natural persons from a WTO member country, enabling a supplier from one member country to supply services within the territory of any other member country.

44. As regards cross-frontier supplies, the service is rendered by a supplier established in one country to a consumer residing in another. The supplier does not move to the consumer's country; nor, conversely, does the consumer move to the supplier's country. That situation is, therefore, not unlike trade in goods, which is unquestionably covered by the common commercial policy within the meaning of the Treaty. There is thus no particular reason why such a supply should not fall within the concept of the common commercial policy.

45. The same cannot be said of the other three modes of supply of services covered by GATS, namely, consumption abroad, commercial presence and the presence of natural persons.

46. As regards natural persons, it is clear from Article 3 of the Treaty, which distinguishes between 'a common commercial policy' in paragraph (b) and 'measures concerning the entry and movement of persons' in paragraph (d), that the treatment of nationals of non-member countries on crossing the external frontiers of Member States cannot be regarded as falling within the common commercial policy. More generally, the existence in the Treaty of specific chapters on the free movement of natural and legal persons shows that those matters do not fall within the common commercial policy.

47. It follows that the modes of supply of services referred to by GATS as 'consumption abroad', 'commercial presence' and the 'presence of natural persons' are not covered by the common commercial policy.

.....

54. The Commission's argument in support of its contention that the Community has exclusive competence under Article 113 is essentially that the rules concerning intellectual property rights are closely linked to trade in the products are services to which they apply.

55. It should be noted, first, that Section 4 of Part III of TRIPs which concerns the means of enforcement of intellectual property rights, contains specific rules as to measures to be applied at border crossing points. As the United Kingdom has pointed out, that section has its counterpart in the provisions of Council Regulation (EEC) No 3842/86 of 1 December 1986 laying down measures to prohibit the release for free circulation of counterfeit goods (OJ 1986 L 357, p.1). Inasmuch as that regulation concerns the prohibition of the release into free circulation of counterfeit goods, it was rightly based on Article 113 of the Treaty: it relates to measures to be taken by the customs authorities at the external frontiers of the Community. Since measures of that type can be adopted autonomously by the Community institutions on the basis of Article 113 of the EC Treaty, it is for the Community alone to conclude international agreements on such matters.

56. However, as regards matters other than the provisions of TRIPs on the release into free circulation of counterfeit goods, the Commission's arguments cannot be accepted.

57. Admittedly, there is a connection between intellectual property and trade in goods. Intellectual property rights enable those holding them to prevent third parties from carrying out certain acts. The power to prohibit the use of a trade mark, the manufacture of a product, the copying of a design or the reproduction of a book, a disc or a videocassette inevitably has effects on trade. Intellectual property rights are moreover specifically designed to produce such effects. That is not enough to bring them within the scope of Article 113. Intellectual property rights do not relate specifically to international trade: they affect internal trade just as much as, if not more than, international trade.

58. As the French Government has rightly observed, the primary objectives of TRIPs is to strengthen and harmonize the protection of intellectual property on a worldwide scale. The Commission has itself conceded that, since TRIPs lays down rules in fields in which there are no Community harmonization measures, its conclusion would make it possible at the same time to achieve harmonization within the Community and thereby to contribute to the establishment and functioning of the common market.

59. It should be noted here that, at the level of internal legislation, the Community is competent, in the field of intellectual property, to harmonize national laws pursuant to Articles 100 and 100a and may use Article 235 as the basis for creating new rights superimposed on national rights, as it did in Council Regulation (EC) No 40/94 of 20 December 1993 on the Community trade mark (OJ 1994 L 11, p.1). Those measures are subject to voting rules (unanimity in the case of Article 100 and 235) or rules of procedure (consultation of the Parliament in the case of Articles 100 and 235, the joint decision-making procedure in the case of Article 100a) which are different from those applicable under Article 113.

60. If the Community were to be recognized as having exclusive competence to enter into agreements with non-member countries to harmonize the protection of intellectual property and, at the same time, to achieve harmonization at Community level, the

Community institutions would be able to escape the internal constraints to which they are subject in relation to procedures and to rules as to voting.

.....

71. In the light of the foregoing, it must be held that apart from those of its provisions which concern the prohibition of the release into free circulation of counterfeit goods, TRIPS does not fall within the scope of the common commercial policy.

The Opinion was criticised on a number of grounds. The first was that the division of competences it established between the EC and the Member States in the TRIPs and GATS Agreements was a very fuzzy one. In some parts of the Agreements Member States and EC Institutions enjoyed parallel competences. In other parts, the EC had exclusive competence. This was felt to be administratively unworkable.[32] The Member States responded to this at Amsterdam by providing for extension of Article 113 [*133*] EC.

Article 133 (5) EC. *The Council acting unanimously on a proposal from the Commission and after consulting the European Parliament, may extend the application of paragraphs 1 to 4 to international negotiations and agreements on services and intellectual property insofar as they are not covered by these paragraphs.*

The second criticism of *Opinion 1/94* was the inconsistent reasoning, in particular the differing treatment of technical barriers and TRIPs. If the ground on which TRIPs were found to fall outside Article 113 [*133*] EC was that intellectual property rights did not specifically relate to international trade, then the Agreement on Technical Barriers to Trade would seem equally to fall outside Article 113 [*133*] EC on the

---

32 Bourgeois, M. 'The EC in the WTO and Advisory Opinion 1/94: An Echternach Procession' (1995) 32 *CMLRev* 763, 786; Hilf, M. 'The ECJ's Opinion 1/94 on the WTO - No Surprise but Wise' (1995) 6 *EJIL* 245, 258; Emiliou, N. 'The Death of Exclusive Competence?' (1996) 21 *ELRev* 294, 310-311.

same basis. Yet the former was held to fall outside Article 113 [*133*] EC, whilst the latter was considered to fall within Article 113 [*133*] EC.[33]

The final difficulty is the relationship between trade and investment. These are often interchangeable. An American producer may export its goods from the United States to Europe, or it may locate a factory there. Regulation of one will automatically affect the other. If the trader cannot send its goods to the European Union because of trade barriers, for example, there is a possibility it may invest there as an alternative. It would seem artificial therefore to make a rigid distinction between the two. In the Uruguay Round therefore an Agreement on Trade-Related Investment Measures (TRIMs) was signed which required Member States not to apply any investment measure related to trade in goods which discriminated against third country nationals.

In *Opinion 1/94* the Agreement on TRIMs, insofar as it related to trade in goods, was found to be one of the Agreements which could be concluded on the basis of Article 113 [*133*] EC. Following a subsequent Opinion exclusive EC competence in the field of TRIMs is not so clear.[34]

---

33 Bourgeois, J. 'The EC in the WTO and Advisory Opinion 1/94: An Echternach Procession' (1995) 32 *CMLRev* 763, 776-777; Chalmers, D. 'Legal Base and the External Relations of the European Community' 46, 59-60 in Emiliou, N. & O'Keeffe, D. (ed.) *The European Union and World Trade Law after the GATT Uruguay Round* (1996, John Wiley, Chichester). On the Opinion see also Hilf, M. 'The ECJ's Opinion 1/94 on the WTO - No Surprise, but Wise?' (1995) 6 *EJIL* 245.

34 Analogous reasoning was also adopted in relation to a 1993 Agreement between the European Community and the United States to afford each other's nationals equal treatment in the area of government procurement in the Utilities sector. The Court found that the agreement covered services, yet as it applied predominantly to the supply of services by persons who already had a commercial presence within the European Union, there was no transfrontier supply of services, and Article 113 [*133*] EC was therefore inappropriate. This decision was less controversial than *Opinion 2/92*, however, as the Court had already made it clear in *Opinion 1/94* that services supplied by somebody who had a commercial presence within the European Union fell outside Article 113 [*133*] EC, Case C-360/93 *Parliament v Council* [1996] ECR I-1195.

Opinion 2/92 Re Third Revised Decision of the OECD on National Treatment [1995] ECR I-521, [1996] 2 CMLR 325

The Belgian Government requested an Opinion from the Court upon whether the Community was exclusively competent regarding a 1991 Decision of the OECD which expanded upon the latter's 1976 Declaration on International Investment and Multi-national Enterprises. In this Decision OECD States expressed an intention to give undertakings which were owned or controlled, directly or indirectly, by another Member State's nationals - the same treatment as those owned or controlled by their own nationals in five areas. These were government procurement; official aids and subsidies; access to local finance; tax obligations, and the rules applicable to certain forms of investment.

24. Although it is apparent from the foregoing that the national treatment rule concerns mainly the conditions for the participation of foreign-controlled undertakings in the internal economic life of the Member States in which they operate, the fact remains that it also applies to the conditions for their participation in trade between the Member States and non-member countries, conditions which are the subject of the common commercial policy of the Community.

25. So far as the participation of foreign-controlled undertakings in intra-Community trade is concerned, such trade is governed by the Community's internal market rules and not by the rules of its common commercial policy.

26. Accordingly, the national treatment rule relates only partially to international trade with non-member countries; it affects internal trade to the same extent as international trade, if not more so.

.....

28. It follows from the foregoing that Article 113 does not confer exclusive competence on the Commission to participate in the Third Decision.

IV. Legal Base and the External Economic Relations of the European Union

The refusal of the Court to allow Article 113 [*133*] EC to be used as a catch-all for the Community's external economic relations has resulted in increased resort to other legal bases. The choice of legal base is complicated in the field of external relations, as the legal base determines not merely the appropriate legislative procedure but also whether the Community has exclusive competence or whether it is to be shared with the Member States.

Nevertheless, the same reasoning governs the choice of legal base in the field of external relations as elsewhere.[35] As is the case of internal legislation, it is not always easy to discern which is the appropriate legal base.

Case C-62/88 Greece v Council [1991] ECR I-1527, [1991] 2 CMLR 649

Greece challenged the legal base of Regulation 3955/87/EEC, which fixed maximum radiation levels for agricultural imports into the Community from third countries. It had been based upon Article 113 [*133*] EC. Greece claimed the Regulation should have been based upon Article 31 EURATOM, which dealt with the setting of standards protecting the general public against the dangers of radiation. Unlike Article 113 [*133*] EC, this latter base required that the Parliament and Economic and Social Committee be consulted. On its face it looked as if Greece might have a strong case, as according to the Regulation's Preamble, one of its purposes was to set up common arrangements to safeguard the health of consumers.

13. The Court held in its judgment of 26 March 1987 in Case 45/86 *Commission v Council* [1987] ECR 1493, paragraph 11, that in the context of the organization of the powers of the Community the choice of the legal basis for a measure must be based on objective factors which are amenable to judicial review.

14. As far as the objective pursued is concerned, the preamble to Regulation No 3955/87 indicates that 'the Community must continue to ensure that agricultural products and processed agricultural products intended for human consumption and likely to be contaminated are introduced into the Community only according to common arrangements' and that those 'common arrangements should safeguard the health of consumers, maintain, without having unduly adverse effects on trade between the

---

35 On legal base in the field of external relations see Close, G. 'External Relations in the Air Transport Sector: Air Transport Policy or the Common Commercial Policy' (1990) 27 *CMLRev* 107; Chalmers, D. 'Legal Base and the External Relations of the European Community' in Emiliou, N. & O'Keeffe, D. (eds.) *The European Union and World Trade Law after the GATT Uruguay Round* (1996, John Wiley, Chichester).

Community and third countries, the unified nature of the market and prevent deflections of trade'.

15. Regulation No 3955/87 establishes uniform rules regarding the conditions under which agricultural products likely to be contaminated may be imported into the Community from non-member countries.

16. It follows that, according to its objective and its content, as they appear from the very terms of the Regulation, the Regulation is intended to regulate trade between the Community and non-member countries; accordingly it comes within the common commercial policy within the meaning of Article 113 of the EEC Treaty.

17. Recourse to Article 113 as the legal basis for the contested Regulation cannot be excluded on the ground that Article 30 *et seq.* of the EAEC Treaty lay down specific rules governing the basic standards for protection of the health of the general public against the dangers arising from ionizing radiation. Those provisions, which appear in a chapter entitled 'health and safety', which forms part of the second title of the EAEC Treaty entitled 'provisions for the encouragement of progress in the field of nuclear energy', are intended to provide for the protection of public health in the nuclear sector. They are not intended to regulate trade between the Community and non-member countries.

18. The fact that maximum permitted levels of radioactive contamination are fixed in response to a concern to protect public health and that the protection of public health is also one of the objectives of Community action in environmental matters, in accordance with the Article 130r(1), likewise cannot remove Regulation No 3955/87 from the sphere of the common commercial policy.

In external relations there is a further complication. There is considerable overlap between the external reach of Article 100a [*95*] EC, the internal market provision, and Article 113 [*133*] EC, as both seem to be concerned with securing the external aspect of the single market. The borderline seems to be dependent upon the reach of Article 113 [*133*] EC. If a measure falls within its scope, then resort to Article 100a [*95*] EC is excluded. Otherwise, use must be made of Article 100a [*95*] EC.

V. Community Law and the International Capacity of Member States

In his seminal article on external legal relations and non-unitary actors, Weiler stated that tensions between central and local actors arose on three fronts. The first has been considered and is the external competence, in particular the treaty-making power of the central authority. The second relates to the international capacity of the central authority and its constituent members - i.e. will Member States lose their right to engage in international relations in those areas where the Community has competence?[36] The third is the division of internal implementing competence between the central and local authorities. For Member States it is the second aspect which is usually the most problematic, as it is this which most directly affects their autonomy and results in their being increasingly dependent upon EC Institutions to further their national interests. From an EC perspective, however, exclusive competencies have many benefits. They result in an increased autonomy for the EC by forcing third States to deal exclusively with the Community; contribute to a Community identity by making the EC the external representative of internal interests, and strengthen the EC Institutions' negotiating position vis-à-vis Member States on internal matters by giving the former an additional source of power which they can wield.

i. Exclusive Competences of the Community

There are a limited number of areas in which the EC enjoys exclusive competence. The mere existence of EC competence in principle prohibits Member States from acting in these areas. The most notable of these is

---

36 Weiler, J. 'The External Legal Relations of Non-Unitary Actors: Mixity and the Federal Principle' 35, 38 in O'Keeffe, D. & Schermers, H. (eds.), *Mixed Agreements* (1983, Kluwer, Dordrecht).

Article 113 [*133*] EC, the common commercial policy.[37] Member States are particularly reluctant to agree to the extension of Community competences, signalling, as this does, the loss of their own capacity in that field. A resolution has been sought through the phenomenon of mixed agreements.[38]

Opinion 1/78 Re International Agreement on Natural Rubber [1979] ECR 2909, [1979] 3 CMLR 639

The Court was asked to consider whether the Community had exclusive competence under Article 113 [*133*] EC to be a party to the International Agreement on Natural Rubber, a commodity agreement signed within the auspices of the United Nations Conference on Trade and Development (UNCTAD). The purpose was to ensure both reliable supplies for the importing States and stable prices for the exporting States. This was done through the setting up of a buffer stock of rubber. Rubber would be sold from this stock when prices became too high and would be bought for the buffer stock if prices became too low. This buffer stock was financed by the parties to the Agreement. Amongst these were the Member States of the European Community who had already paid in contributions.

57. With regard to the system of financing it should be borne in mind in the first place that, in its recommendation to the Council on 5 October 1978 under Article 113, the Commission had proposed that the application of the financial clauses of the agreement on natural rubber should be effected by the Community itself with a direct contribution from the Community budget. Whilst accepting that this method of financing would be possible having regard to the financial provisions of the EEC Treaty, the Council expressed its preference for financing by the Member States. However, no formal

---

37 There are two other areas where the Community has been found to have exclusive powers. These are the common customs tariff, Joined Cases 2 & 3/69 *Sociaal Fonds voor de Diamantarbeiders v Brachfield* [1969] ECR 211, [1969] CMLR 335, and fisheries, Case 804/79 *Commission v United Kingdom* [1981] ECR 1045, [1982] CMLR 543.

38 On this see, in addition, O'Keeffe, D. & Schermers, H. *Mixed Agreements* (1983, Kluwer, Deventer); Nollkaemper, A.'The European Community and international environmental agreements - legal aspects of external Community powers' (1987/2) *LIEI* 55; Neuwahl, N. 'Joint participation in international treaties and the exercise of power by the EEC and its Member States' (1991) 27 *CMLRev* 717.

decision has yet been taken on this question. Moreover, there is no certainty as regards the attitude of the various Member States on this particular question and its implications for the apportionment of the financial burdens.

58. Having regard to the uncertainty which exists as regards the final solution to be adopted for this problem, the Court feels bound to have regard to two possible situations: one in which the financial burdens envisaged by the agreement would be entered in the Community budget and one in which the burdens would be directly charged to the budgets of the Member States. The Court itself is in no position, within the limits of the present proceedings, to make any choice between the two alternatives.

59. In the first case no problem would arise as regards the exclusive powers of the Community to conclude the agreement in question. As has been indicated above, the mechanism of the buffer stock has the purpose of regulating trade and from this point of view constitutes an instrument of the common commercial policy. It follows that Community financing of the charges arising would have to be regarded as a solution in conformity with the Treaty.

60. The facts of the problem would be different if the second alternative were to be preferred. It cannot in fact be denied that the financing of the buffer stock constitutes an essential feature of the scheme for regulating the market which it is proposed to set up. The extent of and the detailed arrangements for the financial undertakings which the Member States will be required to satisfy will directly condition the possibilities and the degree of efficiency of intervention by the buffer mechanism whilst the decisions to be taken as regards the level of the central reference price and the margins of fluctuation to be permitted either upwards or downwards will have immediate repercussions on the use of the financial means put at the disposal of the International Rubber Council which is to be set up and on the extent of the financial means to be put at its disposal. Furthermore sight must not be lost of the fact that the financial structure which it is proposed to set up will make necessary, as is mentioned in the documents submitted to the Court and reflecting the most recent stage of negotiations, co-ordination between the use of the specific financial means put at the disposal of the future International Rubber Council and those which it might find in the Common Fund which is to be set up. If the financing of the agreement is a matter for the Community the necessary decisions will be taken according to the appropriate Community procedures. If on the other hand the financing is to be by the Member States that will imply the participation of those States in the decision-making machinery or, at least, their agreement with regard to the arrangements for financing envisaged and consequently their participation in the agreement together with the Community. The exclusive competence of the Community could not be envisaged in such a case.

Opinion 1/78 would seem to be at odds with the doctrine of exclusivity, as it allows Member States to participate within an agreement, notwithstanding that it falls within the scope of Article 113 [*133*] EC. Given that the exclusive nature of Article 113 [*133*] EC has been repeatedly reaffirmed,[39] *Opinion 1/78* might therefore seem an aberration.[40] Mixed agreements do, however diffuse some of the difficulties posed by exclusivity.

Weiler, J. 'The External Legal Relations of Non-Unitary Actors: Mixity and the Federal Principle' in O'Keeffe, D. & Schermers, H. (eds.), *Mixed Agreements* (1983, Kluwer, Dordrecht) 35, 75

Mixed agreements, especially when they do not specify the demarcation line between Community and Member States, diffuse at a stroke the explosive issues of the scope of Community competences (and treaty making power) and the parameters of the preemptive effect. It may thus be employed, illegally, ... even in those cases where the Community should act alone. From the legal point of view this particular practice must be condemned since it is a breach of the principle of preemption-exclusivity. ... But preemption does not operate in a legal vacuum. One purpose of the doctrine of preemption in general is to induce, even force, the Member States to act in a Community framework. Preemption is designed for situations where there is an objective necessity for action. By precluding unilateral Member State activity (or joint non-Community action) it is hoped that the objective necessity will force the Member States into joint *Community* action. In some cases the reluctance of Member States to allow exclusive Community action might be so great - especially if this could mean, say, a *de facto* confirmation of the ever-growing scope of the Common Commercial Policy - that they would prefer not to act at all. It may be that mixity is the best compromise between Community exclusivity and no action at all. Since most mixed agreements do not specify the demarcation between Community and Member State competences, this issue is left murky though it can surface again in the implementation of the mixed agreement, its amendment, termination and/or breach. Mixity may also have advantages, even in this 'false' situation, from the international point of view in terms of voting or other rights in multilateral contexts. In conclusion, one can say that this type of mixity is a symptom of the cleavage between legal doctrine and political power which at present seems unavoidable.

---

39 e.g. most recently see Opinion 2/92 *Re: Third Revised Decision of the OECD on National Treatment* [1995] ECR I-521, [1996] 2 CMLR 325; Case C-83/94 *Leifer et al.* [1995] ECR I-3231.

40 Cremona, M. 'The Doctrine of Exclusivity and the Position of Mixed Agreements in the External Relations of the European Community' (1982) 2 *OJLS* 393, 414-418.

The autonomy granted to Member States by mixed agreements is limited. EC accession to a treaty binds Member States on the international plane and, as shall be seen, international treaties concluded by the EC may have direct effect with the consequence that they have internal legal effects within Member States. This has led some commentators to take a less tolerant view of mixed agreements.

Tridimas, T. & Eeckhout, P. 'The External Competence of the Community and Case-Law of the Court of Justice: Principle versus Pragmatism' (1994) 14 *Yearbook of European Law* 143, 174

... There may be good reason for excluding recourse to the form of mixed agreement where the agreement comes entirely within the Community's competence. Where that is the case, in principle, the participation by the Member States in the conclusion of the agreement appears to serve no purpose. The effects of an agreement in the legal order of the Community and of the Member States are the same, whether the agreement is only concluded by the Community or by the Community and the Member States acting jointly. The agreement is an integral part of Community law and therefore also of the law of the Member States. In the case of a mixed agreement, the Court does not appear to distinguish between those parts of an agreement 'concluded' by the Community and those parts 'concluded' by the Member States: the agreement requires a uniform interpretation.[[41]] Participation by the Member States may in effect substitute supranational decision-making with intergovernmental decision-making, in some cases even substituting qualified majority voting with unanimity. That is inconsistent with Article 5 of the Treaty, according to which the Member States must facilitate the achievement of the Community's tasks and must abstain from any measure which could jeopardize the attainment of the objectives of the Treaty.

It might be argued that the approach submitted above ushers in exclusivity by the back door and characterizes all external competences of the Community as exclusive in character. That is not the case. There is no *a priori* exclusivity. The Community is free to decide whether it wishes to negotiate and conclude an agreement. If it decides not to do so (in practice if there is no sufficient majority in the Council), the Member States are free to conclude the agreement. That is different in the case of exclusive Community competence where the Member States are barred, as a matter of principle, from committing themselves internationally.

---

41 Case C-192/89 *Sevince* [1990] ECR I-3461, [1992] 2 CMLR 57.

Exclusive competence also leads to the very real danger of the development of a regulatory gap, namely that the Court would prevent Member States from acting whilst the Member States, acting in the Council, would prevent the EC from acting. Although the Community commercial policy was supposed to have been developed on uniform principles by 1970, the necessary legislation was (and is) only partially in place.[42]

Case 41/76 Donckerwolcke & Schou v Procureur de la République [1976] ECR 1921, [1977] 2 CMLR 535.

Donckerwolcke and Schou were fined and given suspended terms of imprisonment for falsely representing that synthetic yarn which they had imported into France from Belgium came from Belgium rather than from Syria and Lebanon. They appealed and when the matter was referred to the Court of Justice, it had to consider whether the French restrictions on synthetic yarn from those countries violated Article 113 [*133*] EC.

25. The assimilation to products originating within the Member States of goods in 'free circulation' may only take full effect if these goods are subject to the same conditions of importation both with regard to customs and commercial considerations, irrespective of the State in which they were put in free circulation.

26. Under Article 113 of the Treaty this unification should have been achieved by the expiry of the transitional period and supplanted by the establishment of a common commercial policy based on uniform principles.

27. The fact that at the expiry of the transitional period the Community commercial policy was not fully achieved is one of a number of circumstances calculated to maintain in being between the Member States differences in commercial policy capable of bringing about deflections of trade or of causing economic difficulties in certain Member States.

.....

---

42 The principal regime on common rules for imports is currently contained in Regulation 3285/94/EC, OJ 1994 L 349/53. On the difficulties posed see Cremona, M. 'The Completion of the Internal Market and the Incomplete Commercial Policy of the European Community' (1990) 15 *ELRev* 283; O'Cléareacáin, S. 'Europe 1992 and Gaps in the EC's Common Commercial Policy' (1990) 28 *JCMS* 298.

32. As full responsibility in the matter of commercial policy was transferred to the Community by means of Article 113 (1) measures of commercial policy of a national character are only permissible after the end of the transitional period by virtue of specific authorization by the Community.

Advocate General Verloren Van Themaat subsequently stated that, in *Donckerwolcke,* the Court:

> 'recognised that the fact that the common commercial policy was not fully achieved at the end of the transitional period is a reality which may have legal consequences.'[43]

The consequence was an institutional compromise. Member States are allowed to maintain existing national policies. This is subject to EC Institutions being given a new power to authorise and vet national policies. The compromise has aroused the fear of renationalisation of EC policies, whereby, through a series of wide authorisations, EC institutions effectively hand back control of certain policies to the Member States. It has therefore been suggested that EC Institutions should only be able to grant authorisations which are narrow in scope and which are subject to strict judicial control.[44]

Notwithstanding this, the Court has been reluctant to review authorisations of national policies granted by EC Institutions. In *Bulk Oil*[45] a contractual dispute arose over the delivery of some North Sea crude oil, as it was to be delivered to Israel, a State to which, at that time, the British Government prohibited the export of petroleum. Regulation 2603/69[46] authorised the British Government to apply export restrictions on petroleum, as well as authorising all existing national restrictions on imports or exports to third countries. It was argued that such an authorisation was too wideranging, yet the Court considered

---

43 Case 59/84 *Tezi Textiel v Commission* [1986] ECR 887, 903.

44 Temple Lang, J. 'The ERTA judgment and the Court's case-law on competence and conflict' (1986) 6 *YBEL* 183, 207.

45 Case 174/84 *Bulk Oil v Sun International* [1986] ECR 559, [1986] 2 CMLR 732.

46 OJ, English Special Edition, (1969 (II) p.590), Article 10.

such a measure fell within the margin of discretion enjoyed by Community Institutions.

A still wider margin of discretion was given in *Werner* which concerned the refusal of the German Government to grant a licence for the export of a smelting oven to Libya on the ground it could be used for military purposes.[47] Article 11 of Regulation 2603/69 allows Member States to apply unilateral export restrictions for public policy reasons. The Court did not consider such a wideranging authorisation which inevitably leaves a considerable margin of discretion to Member States to be incompatible with Article 113 [*133*] EC, rather stressing that Member States should enjoy, at the very least, the same margin of discretion vis-à-vis imports from third States as they enjoy in respect of imports from other Member States.

ii. The Field Is Covered by Autonomous EC Secondary Legislation

The second area where the EC will have exclusive competence is where EC legislation pre-empts Member States from adopting domestic legislation in the field. The doctrine of preemption operates in a similar manner in the field of external relations as elsewhere. If a field is occupied by EC harmonising measures, Member States will be preempted from acting in that field.

Opinion 1/94 Re World Trade Organisation [1994] ECR I-5267[48]

88. ... It is undeniable that where harmonizing powers have been exercised, the harmonization measures may limit, or even remove, the freedom of the Member States to negotiate with non-member countries. However, an internal power to harmonize which

---

47 Case C-70/94 *Werner Industrie-Ausrüstungen v Federal Republic of Germany* [1995] ECR I-3189. Identical issues were raised in the prosecution of a number of businesses by the German authorities for the sale of dual-use goods to Iraq without having first obtained an export licence, Case C-83/94 *Leifer et al.* [1995] ECR I-3231.

48 For the facts see p. 169.

has not been exercised in a specific field cannot confer exclusive external competence in that field on the Community.

.....

95. Whenever the Community has included in its internal legislative acts provisions relating to the treatment of nationals of non member countries or expressly conferred on its institutions powers to negotiate with non-member countries, it acquires exclusive external competence in the spheres covered by those acts.

96. The same applies in any event, even in the absence of any express provision authorizing its institutions to negotiate with non-member countries, where the Community has achieved complete harmonization of the rules governing access to a self-employed activity, because the common rules thus adopted could be affected within the meaning of the *AETR* judgment if the Member States retained freedom to negotiate with non-member countries.

97. That is not the case in all service sectors, however, as the Commission has itself acknowledged.

98. It follows that competence to conclude GATS is shared between the Community and the Member States.

The same uncertainties and limits concerning preemption apply in this field as elsewhere. Whether a Member State is preempted from acting in a particular field will depend upon the scope of the Community instrument. This, in turn, is dependent upon the vagaries of the interpretation process. As importantly, it must be remembered that the doctrine will not apply in those areas governed by minimum harmonisation provisions.[49]

---

49 i.e. Article 118a(3) [*137(5)*] EC (health and safety); Article 129a(3) [*153(3)*] EC (consumer protection); Article 130t [*176*] EC (environment). It appears also that EC competence in the field of development aid cannot be exclusive. See Case C-316/91 *Parliament v Council* [1994] ECR I-625.

iii. Internal Community Objectives are Inextricably Linked to the Conclusion of an International Agreement

There is one situation in which Member States are pre-empted from acting which is peculiar to the field of external relations. This is where the EC has been given powers to realise an objective, but this objective can only be realised through an international agreement and not through other instruments. Interpreted widely, this power could be extremely divisive. Not only does it extend exclusive EC jurisdiction into virgin areas where there is no other EC legislation, but, in so doing, it alters the internal balance of powers between Member States and the EC. For any international agreement concluded in this way by the EC is also EC secondary legislation, which in turn will preempt the Member States from regulating that matter at a purely domestic level. For this reason recent practice has been to confine this doctrine to a narrow set of circumstances.

Opinion 1/94 Re World Trade Organisation [1994] ECR I-5267, [1995] 1 CMLR 205[50]

85. Opinion 1/76 related to an issue different from that arising from GATS. It concerned rationalisation of the economic situation in the inland waterways sector in the Rhine and Moselle basins and throughout all the Netherlands inland waterways and the German inland waterways linked to the Rhine basin, by elimination of short-term overcapacity. It was not possible to achieve objective by the establishment of autonomous common rules, because of the traditional participation of vessels from Switzerland in navigation on the waterways in question. It was necessary, therefore, to bring Switzerland into the scheme envisaged by means of an international agreement (see Opinion 1/76, paragraph 2). Similarly, in the context of conservation of resources of the seas, the restrictions, by means of internal legislative measures, of fishing on the high seas of vessels flying the flag of a Member State would hardly be effective if the same restrictions were not to apply to vessels flying the flag of a non-member country bordering on the same seas. It is understand therefore that external powers may be exercised, and thus become exclusive, without any internal legislation having first been adopted.

---

50 For the facts see p. 169.

86. That is not the situation in the sphere of services: attainment of freedom of establishment and freedom to provide services for nationals of the Member States is not inextricably linked to the treatment to be afforded in the Community to nationals of non-member countries or in non-member countries to nationals of Member States of the Community.

iv. Concurrent Competence and the Duty of Cooperation

Even in the case of mixed agreements which fall partially outside EC competencies Member States cannot pursue fully autonomous policies in the international arena. They are bound by the duty of cooperation which requires them not to frustrate Community objectives. For a period this duty seemed vague and unenforceable.

Case C-25/94 Commission v Council [1996] ECR I-1469

In 1991 the European Community was admitted to the United Nations Food and Agricultural Organisation (FAO). Under the rules of the FAO, before any meeting, to prevent duplication, the Community or the Member States had to indicate who was voting. An arrangement was made between the Commission and the Council whereby, under paragraph 2.3, if matters fell within both Community and Member State competence, attempts would be made to reach a common position by consensus. Where the thrust of the matter fell within Member State competence, the President of the Council would represent the common position and Member States would vote in accordance with that position. Where it fell within EC competence the Commission would represent the common position and the Commission would vote in accordance with that position.

A draft agreement was drawn up within FAO on the flagging of vessels on the high seas to promote compliance with internationally agreed conservation and management measures, an agreement which fell within EC and Member State competence. The COREPER, subsequently confirmed by the Council, stated that the bulk of the agreement fell within Member State competence and that it should therefore be Member States who had the right to vote. This was communicated to the FAO. The Commission brought an action that it should have been the Commission which had the right to vote. The Court agreed with the Commission that the thrust of the FAO agreement fell within Community competence.

48. It must be remembered that where it is apparent that the subject-matter of an agreement or convention falls partly within the competence of the Community and partly within that of its Member States, it is essential to ensure close cooperation between the Member States and the Community Institutions, both in the process of negotiation and conclusion and in the fulfilment of the commitments entered into. That obligation to cooperate flows from the requirement of unity in the international representation of the Community (*Ruling 1/78* [1978] ECR 2151, paragraphs 34 to 36, *Opinion 2/91* [1993] ECR I-1061, paragraph 36, and *Opinion 1/94* [1994] ECR I-5267, paragraph 108). The Community institutions and the Member States must take all necessary steps to ensure the best possible cooperation in that regard (*Opinion 2/91*, paragraph 38).

49. In the present case, section 2.3 of the Arrangement between the Council and the Commission represents fulfilment of that duty of cooperation between the Community and its Member States within the FAO. It is clear, moreover, from the terms of the arrangement, that the two institutions intended to enter into a binding commitment towards each other. Nor has the Council contested its effect at any moment in the proceedings.

50. Consequently, by concluding that the draft agreement concerned an issue whose thrust did not lie in an area within the exclusive competence of the Community and accordingly giving the Member States the right to vote for the adoption of that draft, the Council acted in breach of section 2.3 of the arrangement which it was required to observe.

VI. The Internal Implementation of External Acts

Autonomous EC acts in the field of external relations have the same internal legal effects as EC acts in other fields. A Regulation, the most common instrument in this field, is thus directly applicable and capable of direct effect in this area as in other areas. There is one instrument, the international agreement, which, by its nature, however, only occurs in external relations. This instrument poses a quandary. Some Member States are monist in nature, whereby international agreements enter automatically into the domestic order and can be directly invoked before national courts. Other States are dualist in nature. In such States treaties cannot be directly invoked before national courts but require internal implementing legislation. The dualist nature of some States compounded by the limited institutional framework in Article 228 [*300*] EC might have caused the Court to consider that international agreements should not be capable of direct effect.

Case 21-24/72 International Fruit Company v Produktschap voor Groenten en Fruit [1972] ECR 1219, [1975] 2 CMLR 1

The plaintiffs sought to challenge the refusal of import licences for apples from third countries. The decision to reject the application was based upon EC Regulations, which, the applicant maintained, were incompatible with certain provisions of the GATT.

7. Before the incompatibility of a Community measure with a provision of international law can affect the validity of that measure, the Community must first of all be bound by that provision.

8. Before invalidity can be relied upon before a national court, that provision of international law must also be capable of conferring rights on citizens of the Community which they can invoke before the courts. ...

.....

18. It therefore appears that, in so far as under the EEC Treaty the Community has assumed powers previously exercised by the Member States in the area governed by the General Agreement, the provisions of that agreement have the effect of binding the Community.

19. It is also necessary to examine whether the provisions of the General Agreement confer rights on citizens of the Community on which they can rely before the courts in contesting the validity of the Community measure.

20. For this purpose, the spirit, the general scheme and the terms of the General Agreement must be considered.

21. This agreement which, according to its preamble, is based on the principle of negotiations undertaken on the basis of 'reciprocal and mutually advantageous arrangements' is characterized by the great flexibility of its provisions, in particular those conferring the possibility of derogation, the measures to be taken when confronted with exceptional difficulties and the settlement of conflicts between the Contracting Parties.

22. Consequently, according to the first paragraph of Article XXII 'Each Contracting Party shall accord sympathetic considerations to, and shall afford adequate opportunity for consultation regarding, such representations as may be made by any other Contracting Party with respect to ... all matters affecting the operation of this Agreement'.

23. According to the second paragraph of the same Article, 'the Contracting Parties' - this name designates 'the Contracting Parties acting jointly' as stated in the first paragraph of Article XXV - 'may consult with one of more Contracting Parties on any question to which a satisfactory solution cannot be found through the consultations provided under paragraph (1)'.

24. If any Contracting Party should consider 'that any benefit accruing to it directly or indirectly under this Agreement is being nullified or impaired or that the attainment of any objective of the Agreement is being impeded as a result of', inter alia, 'the failure of another Contracting Party to carry out its obligations under this Agreement', Article XXIII lays down in detail the measures which the parties concerned or the contracting parties acting jointly, may or must take in regard to such a situation.

25. Those measures include, for the settlement of conflicts, written recommendations or proposals which are to be 'given sympathetic consideration', investigations possibly followed by recommendations, consultations between or decisions of the Contracting Parties, including that of authorising certain contracting parties to suspend the application to any others of any obligations or concessions under the General Agreement and, finally, in the event of such suspension, the power of the Party concerned to withdraw from that agreement.

26. Finally, where by reason of an obligation assumed under the General Agreement or of a concession relating to a benefit, some producers suffer or are threatened with serious damage, Article XIX gives a Contracting Party power unilaterally to suspend the obligation and to withdraw or modify the concession, either after consulting the contracting parties concerned, or even, if the matter is urgent and on a temporary basis, without prior consultation.

27. Those factors are sufficient to show that, when examined in such a context, Article XI of the General Agreement is not capable of conferring on citizens of the Community rights which they can invoke before the courts.

International Fruit Company is a classic give-and-take judgment where the Court establishes the principle but rules against the party invoking it. Every agreement other than the GATT on which the Court has ruled, it has found to be capable of direct effect. Its expansionist approach towards the direct effect of international agreements is highlighted by two further developments.

In *Demirel*[51] a Turkish woman entered Germany to join her husband on a tourist visa rather than a family reunification visa. When required to leave Germany on the expiry of her visa, she invoked the EEC-Turkey Association Agreement, claiming that it gave her a right to family reunion. The Court held that it did not but stated that in deciding whether a provision of an international agreement is directly effective regard must be had to whether the provision is sufficiently clear and precise in the light of the purpose and nature of the agreement. This test is less restrictive than the two-tier one suggested by *International Fruit* under which one first examines whether the agreement is capable of direct effect and then whether the provision is sufficiently precise.

Secondly, many Association Agreements set up Councils consisting of EC representatives and representatives of the third country. These Councils often have decision-making powers. The Court has held in a series of decisions that as these Decisions are directly connected to the Agreement itself, they are capable of direct effect, thereby enhancing the legislative powers of these bodies.[52]

Cheyne, I. 'International Agreements and the European Community Legal System' (1994) 19 *European Law Review* 581, 588-590

... the strict question of whether an international agreement is directly applicable is relevant only where there is a question as to whether further internal implementation is required. In many cases, the facts do not give rise to any difficulty. The issue of direct effect, however, is rather more problematic. While it may be argued that direct effect can be assumed for any Treaty Article or Community legislation which satisfies the test of direct applicability, a more cautious approach is called for with regard to international agreements. The intentions of the parties and the implications of finding direct effect require separate and careful consideration. It must be both a finding of direct applicability and the satisfying of a narrower test of whether individuals are entitled to rely upon its provisions.

---

51 Case 12/86 *Demirel v Stadt Schwäbisch Gmünd* [1987] ECR 3719, [1989] 1 CMLR 421.

52 Case C-192/89 *Sevince v Staatsecretaris van Justitie* [1990] ECR I-3461, [1992] 2 CMLR 57; Case C-355/93 *Eroglu v Land Baden Württemberg* [1994] ECR I-5113; Case C-434/93 *Bozkurt v Staatsecretaris van Justitie* [1995] ECR I-1475.

The practical consequences of finding direct effect for international agreements are clearly important. The direct effect doctrine in Community law has had the result of allowing private individuals, untrammelled by the political and economic hesitations of the Member States and institutions, to raise issues with which the Court could promote the integration of the Community. One commentator has argued that, if the Court had not taken its position allowing individual reliance on the Treaty, 'Community law would have remained an abstract skeleton and a great variety and number of Treaty violations would have remained undisclosed and unredressed'.[53] The same argument can be made with respect to international agreements and the reluctance of institutions to enforce them. Ehlermann, for example, suggests that one reason that the Community does not use Article 169 is because 'it dislikes the idea of using specifically Community provisions to do non-member countries' business for them'.[54] In the light of repeated accusations of Community trade protectionism in particular, and in the absence of Member State legal actions in this field, the issue of whether concerned individuals can bring actions reliant upon the provisions of the GATT has become of considerable importance. In practice, greater direct effect would mean that increased judicial attention would be paid to the protection of those individuals who would particularly benefit from the implementation of GATT freedoms, such as consumers.

The Court's approach is tempered by its taking a less expansionist approach to interpretation of the substantive obligations imposed by these agreements. As these agreements aim for a lower level of integration than the EC Treaty it is unwilling to hold that institutions are bound to the same degree, even where there is a remarkable parallelism between the wording of a provision of an international agreement and that of the EC Treaty.

---

53 Stein, E. 'Lawyers, Judges, and the Making of a Transnational Constitution' (1981) 75 *AJIL* 1, 6. See also Schermers, H. 'The Direct Application of Treaties with Third States: Note Concerning the *Polydor* and *Pabst* Cases' (1982) 19 *CMLRev* 563, 564-566, 567; Petersmann, E-U. 'The EEC as a GATT Member - Legal Conflicts Between GATT Law and European Community Law' in Hilf, M., Jacobs, F. and Petersmann, E-U. *The European Community and GATT* 54-55.

54 'Application of GATT Rules in the European Community' in Hilf, M., Jacobs, F. & Petersmann, E-U. ibid. 138-139.

Case 270/80 Polydor & RSO Records v Harlequin Record Shops Ltd. & Simon Records Ltd. [1982] ECR 329, [1982] 1 CMLR 677

Polydor and RSO Records brought an action against Harlequin claiming it had infringed their copyright by marketing a number of Bee Gees records in the United Kingdom. Harlequin had purchased the recordings from two Portuguese companies who had been licensed by RSO to market the recordings in Portugal. If Portugal had been a Member State of the EC at that time the plaintiffs would have been precluded from bringing an action by virtue of Article 30 [*28*] EC. Harlequin invoked Articles 14(2) and 23(2) of the EEC-Portugal Association Agreement which were identically worded to Articles 30 [*28*] and 36 [*30*] EC, claiming that the exhaustion of rights doctrine therefore applied here.

18. The considerations which led to that interpretation of Articles 30 and 36 of the Treaty do not apply in the context of the relations between the Community and Portugal as defined by the Agreement. It is apparent from an examination of the Agreement that although it makes provision for the unconditional abolition of certain restrictions on trade between the Community and Portugal, such as quantitative restrictions and measures having equivalent effect, it does not have the same purpose as the EEC Treaty, inasmuch as the latter, as has been stated above, seeks to create a single market reproducing as closely as possible the conditions of a domestic market.

19. It follows that in the context of the Agreement restrictions on trade in goods may be considered to be justified on the ground of the protection of industrial and commercial property in a situation in which their justification would not be possible within the Community.

20. In the present case such a distinction is all the more necessary inasmuch as the instruments which the Community has at its disposal in order to achieve the uniform application of Community law and the progressive abolition of legislative disparities within the common market have no equivalent in the context of the relations between the Community and Portugal.

21. It follows from the foregoing that a prohibition on the importation into the Community of a product originating in Portugal based on the protection of copyright is justified in the framework of the free-trade arrangements established by the agreement by virtue of the first sentence of Article 23. The findings of the national court do not disclose any factor which would permit the conclusion that the enforcement of copyright in a case such as the present constitutes a means of arbitrary discrimination or a disguised restriction on trade within the meaning of the second sentence of that Article.

Within the context of its subsequent treatment of other international agreements it might be thought that the Court would alter its initial decision in *International Fruit Company* and find the GATT to be directly effective. For if treatment of the GATT represents an anomaly, it represents a rather big anomaly, as it is the GATT, and its successor the WTO, which is the central instrument governing the EC's external economic relations with the rest of the world. Yet the Court has repeatedly reaffirmed that the GATT is not directly effective.[55] Indeed in the *German Bananas* judgment, where the German Government claimed that the Community banana import regime violated the GATT, the Court went further and stated that even where a Member State brought an Article 173 [*230*] EC action claiming that the GATT had been breached, it would be unable to invoke GATT provisions.[56] This refusal by the Court to allow GATT provisions to be invoked directly before it has been heavily criticised. For the GATT and the WTO contain a number of principles, namely non-discrimination, transparency, due process and voluntary trade liberalisation, which, it has been argued, it would be desirable to entrench more firmly into the external economic relations law of the Community.

Petersmann, E. 'National Constitutions, Foreign Trade Policy and European Community Law' (1992) 3 *European Journal of International Law* 1, 34

From the perspective of constitutionally limited democracies, such as those of the major trading countries, liberalism and internationalism must therefore begin at home. Problems in the implementation of international trade rules arise mostly at the level of domestic trade law and policy-making. International legal prohibitions of mutually harmful trade

---

55 Case 266/81 *SIOT v Ministero delle Finanze* [1983] ECR 731, [1984] 2 CMLR 231; Joined Cases 267-269/81 *Amministrazione delle Finanze v Societa Petrolifera Italiana* [1983] ECR 801, [1984] 1 CMLR 354; Case C-469/93 *Amministrazione dello Finanze v Chiquita Italia SpA* [1995] ECR I-4533.

56 Case C-280/93 *Germany v Council* [1994] ECR I-4973. For a fierce denunciation of this judgment see Petersmann, E-U. 'Proposals for a New Constitution for the European Union: Building Blocks for a Constitutional Theory and Constitutional Law of the EU' (1995) 32 *CMLRev* 1123, 1164-1170.

restrictions and trade discrimination are necessary not only for the external relations of states but even more so for protecting the equal liberties and property rights of domestic citizens participating in and benefitting from the international division of labour. The effectiveness of international GATT obligations depends upon the more effective incorporation of the international rules into a domestic 'trade policy constitution' so that the rules are binding and protected under domestic laws.

Such a 'constitutional' approach would require a number of important policy changes. Rather than leaving the domestic implementation of liberal international trade rules to the discretion of each government, international trade agreements should regulate their 'domestic law effects' in a manner enabling producers, traders and consumers to invoke and defend their 'freedoms of foreign trade' against government restrictions and against non-transparent interest group politics. International trade agreements should also provide for domestic judicial review, for it is the courts which ultimately have to protect the transnational exercise of individual rights by domestic citizens. Likewise, the effectiveness of individual rights and their judicial protection depend upon *procedural* guarantees of due process and access to justice as well as on the interpretation of international and domestic foreign trade law as mutually complementary rules designed to enhance the individual rights and welfare of domestic citizens.

Others have suggested that there may be more pragmatic reasons why the GATT should be denied direct effect.

Cheyne, I. 'International Agreements and the European Community Legal System' (1994) 19 *European Law Review* 581, 590

Both the Commission and the Court of Justice itself have been reluctant to allow direct effect for international agreements such as the GATT for practical reasons. However, there are also legal difficulties in allowing individual reliance upon, and judicial interpretation of, broadly worded provisions. Fundamentally, it may be asked whether it is desirable for the Court of Justice to become frequently involved in adjudicating upon the Community's actions under an agreement such as the GATT. First, it makes it more likely that the Court of Justice will be called upon to make a binding decision which interferes with the freedom of the other Community institutions to act in external affairs. Secondly, The Court of Justice would be in danger of making a decision, albeit within Community law, that was at variance with findings of other domestic tribunals or the Contracting Parties of GATT. These problems would apply less forcefully to actions brought by Member States who, it can be argued, would have greater appreciation of the international implications involved.

Institutional motivations probably provide the best explanations for the Court's behaviour. It has not therefore questioned the justiciability of GATT provisions where they have been introduced into EC secondary legislation, and has indeed used them as an aid to interpretation of such legislation.[57] These norms are clearly therefore sufficiently precise to be capable of being adjudicated. Yet in such circumstances those norms have been introduced into the EC legal order by secondary legislation, the Court is not therefore taking the process of incorporation upon itself in the way it would by holding GATT provisions to be directly effective.

The Court has been given a clear hint by the other Institutions that they would not take kindly to the GATT being found to be directly effective. At the conclusion of the Uruguay Round it was considered that the successor to the GATT, the World Trade Organisation, might be sufficiently different that the Court would find it to be directly effective.[58] To guard against this, in its Decision concluding the Agreement the Council stated, unusually, in the Preamble that the Agreement was not to have direct effect.[59]

---

57 Case 70/87 *Fediol v Commission* [1989] ECR 1781, [1991] 2 CMLR 489; Case C-69/89 *Nakijima v Council* [1991] ECR I-2069; Case T-162/94 *NMB France SARL & Others v Commission* [1996] ECR II-427.

58 Castillo de la Torre, F. 'The Status of GATT in EC Law Revisited' (1995) 29 *JWTL* 53; Scott, J. 'The GATT and Community Law: Rethinking the "Regulatory Gap"' in Shaw, J. & More, G. (eds.) *New Legal Dynamics of the European Union* (1995, Clarendon Press, Oxford).

59 Decision 94/800 EC, OJ 1994 L 336/1. On this see Kuijper, P. 'The Conclusion and Implementation of the Uruguay Round' (1995) 6 *EJIL* 220; Mengozzi, P. 'The Marrakesh DSU and Its Implications on the International and European Level' in Bourgeois, J. (ed.) *'The Uruguay Round Results - A European Lawyers' Perspective* (1995, European Interuniversity Press, Brussels).

VII. The Common Foreign and Security Policy

i. The Development of a European Union Foreign and Security Policy

Plans for a common defence policy predate those for the European Economic Community. One of the motivations behind the establishment of the European Coal and Steel Community was to take the means of producing the weapons of war out of the hands of the Member States. Similarly, the failed Treaty establishing the European Defence Community, dreamt up in the Pléven Plan of 1950 and signed in 1952, would have set up a European army with a similar quadripartite institutional structure similar to that of the EEC, with a Board of Commissioners, an Assembly, a Council and a Court of Justice.

Following the establishment of the EEC Treaty, it was, paradoxically, De Gaulle who first suggested that there should be a European foreign policy. Anxious to assert European independence from the United States and to create a structure which would control the supranational Community institutions, he proposed in 1960 that there should be organised cooperation between Member States in a number of fields, including defence. This proposal led to the Fouchet Plan of 1961 which proposed a treaty establishing a common foreign and defence policy along intergovernmental lines. This would have consisted of a Council of Heads of Government, which would meet three times a year, meetings of Foreign Ministers four times a year and a Political Committee of Foreign Office officials. This plan eventually collapsed because of disagreements between the Member States about its relations with the Community Institutions and with NATO.[60]

A more substantial step was taken at The Hague in 1969 where the Heads of Government instructed their Foreign Ministers to study the 'best way for achieving progress in the matter of political unification'. The result was the Luxembourg (Davignon) Report of 1970 which

---

[60] Gerbet, P. 'In Search of Political Union: The Fouchet Plan Negotiations' in Pryce, R. (ed.) *The Dynamics of European Union* (1989, Routledge, London).

considered that political union should be established in successive stages and that the initial phase should be one 'harmonising views regarding international affairs'. A commitment was given to the setting up of common positions in foreign policy, and a system, finessed in Copenhagen three years later, was set up for the exchange of information and for regular meetings between Foreign Ministers' officials.

Whilst the level of consultation and exchange of information intensified through the 1970s and 1980s, European Political Cooperation was criticised during this period for substituting procedure for policy.[61] It was noticeable that whilst Member States had procedures for coordinating their activity within the United Nations, there was no increase in the percentage of General Assembly Resolutions in which the Member States all voted in a similar way.[62] The Dooge Committee thus recommended in 1985 that the 'common political will of the Member States ... must be expressed by the formulation of a genuine political entity among European States'.[63] It was for the Member States to decide how this was to be done, although the Dooge Committee recommended that whilst European Political Cooperation and the European Community should be kept separate, they could be brought more closely together. These recommendations were largely adopted in the SEA. This established a new Title in the EEC Treaty on European Political Cooperation in Foreign Policy which formalised existing practice. In addition, it provided for closer association of the Parliament and the Commission with EPC than previously, and for the establishment of a permanent secretariat.

The new Title did not last long. The perceived failure of the

---

61 For good analyses of European Political Cooperation see Nuttall, S. *European Political Cooperation* (1992, Clarendon Press, Oxford); Regelsberger, E. 'EPC in the 1980s: Reaching Another Plateau' in Pijpers, A., Regelsberger, E. & Wessels, W. (eds.) *European Political Cooperation in the 1980's: A Common Foreign Policy for Western Europe?* (1988, Martijnus Nijhoff, Dordrecht).

62 Pijpers, A. 'The Twelve Out-of-Area: A Civilian Power in an Uncivil World?' in Pijpers, A., Regelsberger, E. & Wessels, W. (eds.) *European Political Cooperation in the 1980's: A Common Foreign Policy for Western Europe?* (1988, Martijnus Nijhoff, Dordrecht).

63 EC Bulletin 3-1985, 3.5.1.

Member States to respond in a collective manner to the Gulf crisis and the Franco-German commitment 'to obtain the best content and institutional formulas for the implementation of a common foreign and security policy that will allow Europe to act effectively in the world's important affairs'[64] led to its replacement at Maastricht with the Common Foreign and Security Policy in the Second Pillar of the Treaty on European Union. That said, foreign and defence policy was one of the most contentious issues at Maastricht with the United Kingdom, Denmark and Portugal all wishing to retain national control over foreign policy. The result was that the second pillar represents only a limited advance on what previously existed.

The 1990s represented a change in expectations of the European Union. Increasingly, it was seen as being required to be in a position where it could respond effectively to events occurring in Central and Eastern Europe following the collapse of Communism.[65] Within this context CFSP is not perceived to have operated effectively.[66] At Amsterdam, whilst there was recognition of a need for change, there was not universal enthusiasm for deep-rooted reform. The result was considerable tinkering which one Commission official described as 'without fundamentally altering the approach that resulted from Maastricht, it probably endows the common foreign policy with much-needed new powers'.[67]

---

64 This communiqué is taken from Agence Europe, 23 March 1991 in Holland, M. *European Integration: From Community to Union* (1994, Pinter, London) 124.

65 The Reflection Group Report talks therefore about the EU having 'increased responsibilities' in this context to face 'new challenges'. SN 520/95 December 1995, para 146.

66 Ibid., para 148.

67 Pettite, M. 'The Treaty of Amsterdam' (Harvard Jean Monnet Working Paper 98/2).

ii. The Remit of CFSP

The ambit of EPC before and after the SEA had been rather vague, talking merely of cooperation in foreign policy. The TEU extends this cooperation not just to all aspects of foreign policy but also to all aspects of security policy.[68]

Article J.1.1 TEU. The Union and its Member States shall define and implement a common foreign and security policy, governed by the provisions of this Title and covering all areas of foreign and security policy.

2. The objectives of the common foreign and security policy shall be:

- to safeguard the common values, fundamental interests and independence of the Union;
- to strengthen the security of the Union and its Member States in all ways;
- to preserve peace and strengthen international security, in accordance with the principles of the United Nations Charter as well as the principles of the Helsinki Final Act and the objectives of the Paris Charter;
- to promote international co-operation;
- to develop and consolidate democracy and the rule of law, and respect for human rights and fundamental freedoms.

There was support among some Member States for transforming the Western European Union (WEU), a European defence organisation established by the Treaty of London in 1954, into the military arm of the

68 Hooijer, F. 'The Common Foreign and Security Policy of the European Union' (1994) 5 *EJIL* 173. For an excellent discussion of CFSP see McGoldrick, D. *International Relations Law of the European Union* (1997, Longmans, Harlow) 138-173.

EU and giving the EU an autonomous defence identity. This was problematic because of Member States' different relationships with NATO. The United Kingdom, supported by the Dutch, Portuguese and Danes, are wary about absorbing defence too firmly into EU structures, fearing that this might weaken NATO. The British were prepared to consider, however, enhancing on a pragmatic basis relations between the WEU and the EU.[69] A further difficulty, however, was that five EU Member States are not full members of the WEU.[70] At the Edinburgh European Council 1992, it was stated that nothing in the TEU committed Denmark to full membership of the WEU.[71] These difficulties were postponed at Maastricht by a distinction being made between defence policy and other areas of policy. Article J.4(1) TEU merely states that CFSP might include the eventual framing of a common defence policy, which might in time lead to a common defence.[72] Most of the Member States at Amsterdam felt that these provisions needed to be strengthened to grant the EU a more autonomous foreign and security policy.

Article 11(1) TEU. *The Union shall define and implement a common foreign and security policy, covering all areas of foreign and security policy, the objectives of the common foreign and security policy shall be:*
- to safeguard the common values, fundamental interests and independence of the Union in conformity with the principles of the United Nations Charter;
- to strengthen the security of the Union in all ways;
- to preserve peace and strengthen international security, in accordance with the principles of the United Nations Charter as well as the principles of the Helsinki Final

---

69 A Partnership of Nations: The British Approach to the European Union Intergovernmental Conference 1996 (1996, Cm 3181, HMSO, London) paragraphs 43-47. On the debate see Wyn Rees, G. 'Constructing a European Defence Identity: The Perspectives of Britain, France and Germany' (1996) 1 *European Foreign Affairs Review* 231.

70 These are Austria, Ireland, Finland, Sweden and Denmark.

71 Edinburgh European Council EC Bull 12-1992, Section C.

72 Declaration No. 30 on West European Union was attached to the TEU by those Member States who are members of the Western European Union stating that the latter should be developed as 'the defence component of the European Union and as a means to strengthen the European pillar of the Atlantic Alliance'.

Act and the objectives of the Paris Charter, including those on external borders;
- to promote international co-operation;
- to develop and consolidate democracy and the rule of law, and respect for human rights and fundamental freedoms.

Secondly, the role of CFSP in the field of defence was eased by the Danish opt-out from matters with defence implications being formalised in a Protocol.[73] This allowed the EU to enhance its relationship with the WEU. Formally, a delicate balance is trod between, on the one hand, establishing closer relations between the EU and the WEU, whilst, on the other, allowing Member States to maintain the specific character of their defence policies.

Article 17 (1) TEU. *The common foreign and security policy shall include all questions relating to the security of the Union, including the progressive framing of a common defence policy, in accordance with the second subparagraph, which might lead to a common defence, should the European Council so decide. It shall in that case recommend to the Member States the adoption of such a decision in accordance with their respective constitutional requirements.*

The Western European Union (WEU) is an integral part of the development of the Union providing the Union with access to an operational capability notably in the context of paragraph 2. It supports the Union in framing the defence aspects of the common foreign and security policy as set out in this Article. The Union shall accordingly foster closer institutional relations with the WEU with a view to the possibility of the integration of the WEU into the Union, should the European Council so decide. It shall in that case recommend to the Member States the adoption of such a decision in accordance with their respective constitutional requirements.

The policy of the Union in accordance with this Article shall not prejudice the specific character of the security and defence policy of certain Member States and shall respect the obligations of certain Member States, which see their common defence realised in the North Atlantic Treaty Organisation (NATO), under the North Atlantic Treaty and be compatible with the common security and defence policy established within that framework.

The progressive framing of common defence policy will be supported, as Member States consider appropriate, by cooperation between them in the field of armaments.

---

73 Protocol on the position of Denmark, Article 6.

2. Questions referred to in this Article shall include humanitarian and rescue tasks, peacekeeping tasks and tasks of combat forces in crisis management, including peacemaking.

3. The Union will avail itself of the WEU to elaborate and implement decisions and actions of the Union which have defence implications.

The competence of the European Council to establish guidelines in accordance with Article 13 shall also obtain in respect of the WEU for those matters for which the Union avails itself of the WEU.

When the Union avails itself of the WEU to elaborate and implement decisions of the Union on the tasks referred to in paragraph 2 all Member States of the Union shall be entitled to participate fully the tasks in question. The Council, in agreement with the institutions of the WEU, shall adopt the necessary practical arrangements to allow all Member States contributing to the tasks in question to participate fully and on an equal footing in planning and decision-taking in the WEU.

Decisions having defence implications dealt with under this paragraph shall be taken without prejudice to the policies and obligations referred to in paragraph 1, third subparagraph.

Amsterdam marked a substantial shift towards making the WEU the defence component of the EU. This is evidenced by a Declaration of 22 July 1997 of the WEU Council of Ministers of which the Amsterdam Treaty takes note.[74] This Declaration establishes:

- the EU may avail itself of the WEU and that the WEU will act within guidelines provided by the EU European Council;

- coordination and enhanced administrative cooperation between the WEU and the EU in all fields, including those of armaments. It also allows for the EU to draw on the resources of the WEU;

- when the WEU implements an EU decision, all EU States, irrespective of WEU membership, may participate fully and on an equal footing in planning and decision-making within the EU;

- enhanced cooperation between the EU and NATO.

---

74 *Declaration Relating to Western European Union.*

iii. The Instruments of Common Foreign and Security Policy

CFSP continued the process of consultation between Member States formalised by the SEA.

Article J.2.1 [*16*] TEU. Member States shall inform and consult one another within the Council on any matter of foreign and security policy of general interest in order to ensure that their combined influence is exerted as effectively as possible by means of concerted and convergent action.

.....

3. [*19(1)*]. Member States shall co-ordinate their action in international organisations and at international conferences. They shall uphold the common positions in such fora. In international organisations and at international conferences where not all the Member States participate, those which do take part shall uphold the common positions.

Maastricht also marked the development of instruments which could be adopted in this field. Provision had been made by the SEA for the adoption of common positions. These did no more than act as reference points for the policies of the Member States.[75] CFSP expanded their effects.[76]

Article J.2.2 TEU. Whenever it deems it necessary, the Council shall define a common position. Member States shall ensure that their national policies conform to the common positions.

CFSP also introduced a new instrument, that of the joint action. These were clearly anticipated to be discrete from the common position.

---

75 Article 30(2) SEA.

76 In addition, diplomatic and consular missions of Member States and Commission Delegations are under a duty to comply with and implement these common positions, Article J.6 [*20*] TEU.

They were not to apply to issues having defence implications.[77] They were only to apply in areas where Member States had 'important interests in common'.[78] Furthermore, a separate procedure was established for their adoption.

Article J.3 TEU. The procedure for adopting joint action in matters covered by the foreign and the security policy shall be the following:

1. The Council shall decide, on the basis of general guidelines from the European Council, that a matter should be the subject of joint action. Whenever the Council decides on the principle of joint action, it shall lay down the specific scope, the Union's general and specific objectives in carrying out such action, if necessary its duration, and the means, procedures and conditions for its implementation.

.....

3. [*14(2)*]. If there is a change in circumstances having a substantial effect on a question subject to joint action, the Council shall review the principles and objectives of that action and take the necessary decisions. As long as the Council has not acted, the joint action shall stand.

4. [*14(3)*]. Joint actions shall commit the Member States in the positions they adopt and in the conduct of their activity.

[14(4). The Council may request the Commission to submit to it any appropriate proposals relating to the common foreign and security policy to ensure the implementation of a joint action.]

5. [*14(5)*]. Whenever there is any plan to adopt a national position or take national action pursuant to a joint action, information shall be provided in time to allow, if necessary, for prior consultations within the Council. The obligation to provide prior information shall not apply to measures which are merely a national transposition of Council decisions.

---

77 Article J.4.3 TEU.

78 Article J.1.3 TEU. At the 1992 Lisbon European Council it was agreed that a number of factors would be used to determine when this was the case. This included geographical proximity of the region or country; important interests in the political and economic stability of a region or country, and the existence of a threat to the security interests of the Union. EC Bulletin 6-1992, 19. McGoldrick, D. *International Relations Law of the European Union* (1997, Longman, Harlow) 153-156.

6. [*14(6)*]. In cases of imperative need arising from changes in the situation and failing a Council decision, Member States may take the necessary measures as a matter of urgency having regard to the general objectives of the joint action. The Member State concerned shall inform the Council immediately of any such measures.

7. [*14(7)*]. Should there be any major difficulties in implementing a joint action, a Member State shall refer them to the Council which shall discuss them and seek appropriate solutions. Such solutions shall not run counter to the objectives of the joint action or impair its effectiveness.

In practice common actions and joint positions have been used interchangeably.[79] Attempts were made to distinguish between the two at Amsterdam. Joint actions are operational in nature.

Article 14(1) TEU. *The Council shall adopt joint actions. Joint actions shall address specific situations where operational action by the Union is deemed to be required. They shall lay down their objectives, scope, the means to be made available to the Union, if necessary their duration, and the conditions for their implementation.*

Common positions, meanwhile, relate to less concrete situations.

Article 15 TEU. *The Council shall adopt common positions. Common positions shall define the approach of the Union to a particular matter of a geographical or thematic nature. Member States shall ensure that their positions conform to the common positions.*

---

79 EC Commission, *Report for the Reflection Group: Intergovernmental Conference 1996* (1995, OOPEC, Luxembourg) paragraph 152.

iv. The Institutional Framework of CFSP

a. The European Council and the Council of Ministers

CFSP is the EU pillar within which the European Council enjoys most power. The latter sits at its apex orientating the direction of the EU's foreign and security policy.

Article J.8 [*13*] 1. TEU. The European Council shall define the principles of and general guidelines for the common foreign and security policy, [*including for matters with defence implications*].

2. [13(*3*)]. The Council shall take the decisions necessary for defining and implementing the common foreign and security policy on the basis of the general guidelines adopted [*defined*] by the European Council.

It is the Council, however, which adopts the instruments of CFSP - be they joint actions or common positions. Formally, the autonomy left to the Council depends upon the instrument in question. The Council is given considerable leeway to adopt common positions. These can be developed even if no general guidelines have been developed by the European Council.[80] A precondition for the adoption of joint actions, by contrast, are the existence of general guidelines provided by the European Council.[81] Given the interchangeability of joint actions and common positions, this precondition has not amounted to much and was dropped at Amsterdam.

Provision was made for some measures to be taken by qualified majority in CFSP.

---

80 Article J.2(2) TEU.

81 Article J.3(1) TEU.

Article J.3.2 TEU. The Council shall, when adopting the joint action and at any stage during its development, define those matters on which decisions are to be taken by a qualified majority.

Where the Council is required to act by a qualified majority pursuant to the preceding subparagraph, the votes of its members shall be weighted in accordance with Article 148(2) of the Treaty establishing the European Community, and for their adoption, acts of the Council shall require at least 62 votes in favour, cast by at least 10 members.

In addition, there was a more general hope that even where unanimity requirements were imposed, Member States would attempt to reach agreement by qualified majority.

Declaration No 27 TEU. The Conference agrees that, with regard to Council decisions requiring unanimity, Member States will, to the extent possible, avoid preventing a unanimous decision where a qualified majority exists in favour of that decision.

In practice all decisions within CFSP have been taken by unanimity. The Commission has been critical of this[82] and the Parliament considers that humanitarian, diplomatic or military action should be possible on a qualified majority vote.[83] Yet the European Parliament has itself acknowledged that if actions were taken by qualified majority, then no Member State should be forced to take part if it did not so wish.[84]

The difficulties of achieving a common policy which goes against the wishes of one Member State were brought home by the crisis generated by the Former Yugoslav Republic of Macedonia. Most Member States wished to recognise this former Republic as a State. For historical and territorial reasons Greece was unwilling to do so, and imposed a trade embargo on the Republic. The Commission considered this embargo was a violation of Article 113 [*133*] EC, and sought an

---

82 EC Commission, *Report for the Reflection Group: Intergovernmental Conference 1996* (1995, OOPEC, Luxembourg) paragraph 154.

83 Resolution on the functioning of the Treaty on European Union with a view to the 1996 Intergovernmental Conference (A4-0102/95) paragraph 3.

84 Ibid.

interim order from the Court to have it suspended.[85] Whilst finding that the Commission had a *prima facie* case in law, the Court refused to give an order as it could find no proof of damage to Community interests from the Greek action. Yet even if there had been a ruling against Greece, it is difficult to imagine how this judgment would have been enforced, given the passions that this affair aroused in Greece.

The question of voting was addressed at some length at Amsterdam. The first reform to be made was to allow decisions to be adopted where Member States abstained. The quid pro quo for this were two-fold. The first was that if Member States representing more than one third of the votes abstained, the measure could not be adopted. The second was that Member States abstaining were provided with the safeguard whereby they would not be bound by the Decision if they made a formal declaration at the time.

Article 23(1) TEU. *Decisions under this Title shall be taken by the Council acting unanimously. Abstentions by members present in person or represented shall not prevent the adoption of such decisions.*

When abstaining in a vote, any member of the Council may qualify its abstention by making a formal declaration under the present subparagraph. In that case, it shall not be obliged to apply the decision, but shall accept that the decision commits the Union. In a spirit of mutual solidarity, the Member State concerned shall refrain from any action likely to conflict with or impede Union action based on that decision and the other Member States shall respect its position. If the members of the Council qualifying their absentation in this way represent more than one third of the votes weighted in accordance with Article 205(2) of the Treaty establishing the European Community, the decision shall not be adopted.

The second reform was for votes to be taken by qualified majority in the case of certain implementing measures. The first kind of measure to which qualified majority voting shall apply are decisions implementing joint actions or common positions. More significantly, joint actions and common actions may be taken by qualified majority voting when adopted on the basis of a *common strategy*. This is a new instrument developed at Amsterdam.

---

85 Case C-120/94R *Commission v Greece* [1994] ECR I-3037.

Article 13(2) TEU. *The European Council shall decide on common strategies to be implemented by the Union in areas where the Member States have important interests in common.*

Common strategies shall set out their objectives, duration and the means to be made available by the Union and the Member States.

The ghost of the Luxembourg Accords has been resurrected here, however, as no vote shall be taken if a Member State opposes the decision for important and stated reasons of national policy.

Article 23(2) TEU. *By derogation from the provision of paragraph 1, the Council shall act by qualified majority:*

- *when adopting joint actions, common position or taking any other decision on the basis of a common strategy;*
- *when adopting any decision implementing a joint action or a common position.*

If a member of the Council declares that, for important and stated reasons of national policy, it does not intend to oppose the adoption of a decision to be taken by qualified majority, a vote shall not be taken. The Council may, acting by a qualified majority, request that the matter be referred to the European Council for decision by unanimity.

The votes of the members of the Council shall be weighted in accordance with Article 205 (2) of the Treaty establishing the European Community. For their adoption, decisions shall require at least 62 votes in favour, cast by at least 10 members.

This paragraph shall not apply to decisions having military or defence implications.

b. The Commission and the Parliament

The role of the Commission and Parliament in CFSP are auxiliary. The Commission had enjoyed some influence in EPC through having a coordinating role between EPC and the Council and through being able to secure continuity between Presidencies.[86] CFSP not only retains this role,[87] but has also given the Commission the power to submit proposals to the Council and to refer to the latter any question relating to the common foreign policy.[88]

CFSP also increased Parliament's powers. The most important power it enjoys is the one to ask questions of the Council and to make recommendations to the latter.[89] It is also to be consulted by the Presidency on the main aspects and the basic choices of the CFSP. The Presidency is also under a duty to ensure that its views are taken into consideration. It is also to be regularly informed by the Presidency and the Commission of the development of the Union's foreign and security policy. The Parliament is required to hold an annual debate on progress in implementing the common foreign and security policy. The Parliament proposal at the IGC that it should be consulted on all joint actions was not accepted at Amsterdam.[90] Given the experience of the consultation procedure elsewhere, it is doubtful whether this would provide a sufficient democratic control over CFSP even if one were to believe that the 'democratic deficit' could be resolved simply through an increase in the powers of the European Parliament. Others have noted that any institutional centralisation is problematic given the lack of convergence of national public opinions on foreign affairs.[91]

---

86 Neuwahl, N. 'Foreign and Security Policy and the Implementation of the Requirement of "Consistency" under the Treaty on European Union' 227, 241 in O'Keeffe, D. & Twomey, P. (eds.) *Legal Issues of the Maastricht Treaty* (1994, Chancery Press, Chichester).

87 Article J.9 [*27*] TEU.

88 This power is one shared with the Member States, Article J.8.3 [*22*] TEU.

89 The Parliament's powers are contained in Article J.7 [*21*] TEU.

90 Resolution on the functioning of the Treaty on European Union with a view to the 1996 Intergovernmental Conference (A4-0102/95) paragraph 3 (iii).

91 The position of the EU institutions on the FYROM caused great offence within Greece, for example. Stavridis, S. 'The Democratic Control of the CFSP' in Holland, M. (ed.) *Common Foreign and Security Policy: The Record and Reforms* (1997, Cassell, London).

c. The Court of Justice

The Court of Justice is formally excluded from the CFSP.[92] This is unsurprising as there is no tradition of judicial review of foreign policy in many Member States. The Court has limited powers to review foreign policy in two circumstances. The first is through the policing of the frontiers of Article 113 [*133*] EC. There was a danger of the EC's Institutions, procedures and norms being subverted by the Member States acting through CFSP.[93] The Court has thus repeatedly stated that a measure's having foreign and security objectives will not prevent its falling within the ambit of Article 113 [*133*] EC.[94] The other is the case of sanctions, where no clear-cut division between CFSP and the EC Treaty exists as EC measures are required to implement decisions taken within the framework of CFSP.[95]

Article 228a [*301*] EC. Where it is provided, in a common position or in a joint action adopted according to the provisions of the Treaty on European Union relating to the common foreign and security policy, for an action by the Community to interrupt or reduce, in part or completely, economic relations with one or more third countries, the Council shall take the necessary urgent measures. The Council shall act by a qualified majority on a proposal from the Commission.

---

92 Article L [*46*] TEU.

93 Cremona, M. 'The Common Foreign and Security Policy of the European Union and the External Relations Powers of the European Community' 247, 256-257 in O'Keeffe, D. & Twomey, P. *Legal Issues of the Maastricht Treaty* (1994, Chancery Press, West Chichester).

94 Case C-70/94 *Werner v Germany* [1995] ECR I-3189; Case C-124/95 *R, ex parte Centro-Com v HM Treasury & Bank of England* [1997] ECR I-81.

95 Article 228a [*301*] EC formalised existing practice, where, in the light of a dispute between the Commission and the Council over whether sanctions fell within Article 113 [*133*] EC, sanctions were always adopted on the basis of Article 113 [*133*] EC following a decision taken within the framework of European Political Cooperation. See Kuijper, P. 'Trade Sanctions, Security and Human Rights and Commercial Policy' in Maresceau, M. (ed.) *The European Community's Commercial Policy after 1992: The Legal Dimension* (1993, Kluwer, Deventer).

It seems at the very least arguable that, to interpret Article 228a [*301*] EC, the Court will have to consider whether a common position or joint action has been correctly adopted.[96] Yet if the effects of Article 228a [*301*] EC are that the Court may be able to adjudicate upon certain parts of CFSP, the converse is that it has allowed EC decision-making procedures to be subverted by CFSP.[97] There was therefore an instance in 1994 where there was a qualified majority in favour of full sanctions being applied against Haiti in protest at the regime then in power, but because these were dependent first upon the taking of a common position within CFSP, which required unanimity, a compromise had to be made, which allowed only selective sanctions to be made, so that the wishes of one Member State could be accommodated.[98]

d. The Presidency of CFSP

The Member State holding the Presidency enjoys particular importance in CFSP. It is the Presidency, first, which sets the agenda. This power was further enhanced at Amsterdam which provides for the Presidency to convene an extraordinary Council meeting within 48 hours or, in an emergency, in a shorter period, in cases requiring a rapid decision.[99] This agenda-setting power allows matters of particular concern to the Member State holding the Presidency to be brought to the fore. In this respect this power is perceived as being important to smaller State interests, as it prevents CFSP becoming an instrument through which the policies of the larger Member States can be imposed.[100]

---

96 Bohr, S. 'Sanctions by the UN Security Council and the European Community' (1993) 4 *EJIL* 256.

97 EC Commission, *Report for the Reflection Group: Intergovernmental Conference 1996* (1995, OOPEC, Luxembourg) paragraph 132.

98 Regulation 1263/94/EC, OJ 1994 L 139/1.

99 *Article 22(2) TEU.*

100 Allen, D. 'The European Rescue of National Foreign Policy?' 288, 294 in Hill, C. (ed.) *The Actors in Europe's Foreign Policy* (1996, Routledge, London).

Secondly, the President represents the EU in matters coming within CFSP.[101] As it is also the Presidency which is responsible for implementing common measures, it must also express the position of the Union in international organisations and international conferences.[102] These powers of representation and agenda-setting could allow one Member State to hijack the CFSP were it not for the troika system. Begun in 1981, this was formalised by the TEU, and allows the Presidency, 'if needs be', to be assisted by the previous and subsequent Member States to hold the Presidency.[103] The purpose of the troika is in part to ensure continuity. A convention has developed, however, where the EU is represented on all significant matters by the troika rather than just the President alone.

The rotating door nature of the Presidency was seen by the Westerdorp Committee as undermining the stability and continuity of the CFSP.[104] Proposals were put forward to have a single figurehead, a 'Mr or Mrs CFSP', who would represent the Union externally.[105] In the end the value of the Presidency to individual Member States resulted in its being supplemented rather than replaced.

Article 18(3) TEU. *The Presidency shall be assisted by the Secretary-General of the Council who shall exercise the function of High Representative for the common foreign and security policy.*

The subsidiary role of the Secretary-General to the Presidency suggests the post of High Representative is there to ensure continuity rather than to enhance the profile of CFSP. There is a danger that even this continuity may be sacrificed in cases where Member States seek to assert agendas of strictly national concern during their Presidencies. It is possible that the EU's profile may be enhanced in relation to specific

---

101 Article J.5.1 [*18(1)*] TEU.
102 Article J.5.2 [*18(2)*] TEU.
103 Article J.5.3. TEU.
104 Supra n.63, para 157.
105 Ibid., paras 157-162.

issues, as it was agreed that the Council could appoint special representatives with a mandate in relation to particular policy issues.[106]

e. The Administration of CFSP

It would be foolish to blame CFSP's limitations purely on its intergovernmental nature. The EU has very few of the resources necessary to conduct a fully-fledged foreign policy. It has, *inter alia*, no Defence or Foreign Ministry, intelligence services, armed services.[107] If one puts aside military matters, on the grounds that defence falls almost entirely outside CFSP, and highly emotive questions for particular Member States, then the record of joint actions looks considerably better. They have led to a common regime on dual use goods[108] and convergence of national regimes on the export of anti-personnel mines.[109] In addition, it was following joint action within CFSP that the 1994 Pact on Stability on Europe was signed,[110] and joint action has, *inter alia*, led to Community action in the South African,[111] Middle Eastern[112] and Bosnia-Herzegovina[113] peace processes.

Notwithstanding this, CFSP has been perceived to be suffering from an administrative deficit. The Commission is to be fully associated with CFSP and, to this end, a new Directorate General, DG IA, on external political relations was created in 1994. Yet possibly fearing

---

106 *Article 18(5) TEU.*

107 Hill, C. 'The Capability-Expectations Gap, or Conceptualizing Europe's International Role' (1993) 31 *JCMS* 305, 317.

108 Regulation 3381/94/EC, OJ 1994 L 367/1, as amended by Regulation 837/95/EC, OJ 1995 L 90/1.

109 Decision 95/170/CFSP, OJ 1995 L 115/1; Decision 95/251/CFSP, OJ 1995 L 87/3; Decision 96/588/CFSP, OJ 1996 L 260/1.

110 Decision 93/728/CFSP, OJ 1993 L 339/1; Decision 94/367/CFSP, OJ 1994 L 165/2.

111 Decision 93/678/CFSP, OJ 1993 L 316/45.

112 Decision 94/276/CFSP, OJ 1994 L 119/1; Decision 95/205/CFSP, OJ 1995 L 130/1.

113 Decision 95/545/CFSP, OJ 1995 L 309/2; Decision 96/745/CFSP, OJ 1996 L 340/3; Decision 97/476/CFSP, OJ 1997 L 205/2.

creeping intergovernmentalisation and a diversion of resources from those granted for the EC pillar, it has played only a limited role.[114] Predominant responsibility for administration of CFSP lies with the Political Committee. Set up by the SEA, it consists of Political Directors from each Member State and has the duty of monitoring the international situation and implementation of agreed policies, and delivering opinions to the Council.[115] It is considered to have had difficulties discharging its role. There was an insufficiently clear demarcation of responsibilities between it and COREPER, and the overall responsibility of Political Directors at a national level for foreign policy did not allow them sufficient time for CFSP.[116] The Westerdorp Committee agreed therefore that there was a need for an 'analysis, forecasting, early warning and planning unit' to be set up.[117] This has once again been turned over to the Secretariat General.

Article 26 TEU. *The Secretary-General of the Council, High Representative for the common foreign and security policy, shall assist the Council in matters coming within the scope of the common foreign and security policy, in particular through contributing to the formulation, preparation and implementation of policy decisions, and, when appropriate acting on behalf of the Council at the request of the Presidency, through conducting political dialogue with third parties.*

The organisation and tasks of the Unit are set out in a Declaration attached to the TEU at Amsterdam.[118] It shall consist of personnel from the General Secretariat, the Member States, the Commission and the WEU. Its tasks include monitoring developments; providing assessments of the Union's foreign and security policy interests

---

114 Ginsberg, R. 'The EU's CFSP: the Politics of Procedure' in Holland, M. (ed.) *Common Foreign and Security Policy* (1997, Cassell, London) 12, 26.

115 Article J.8.5 [*25*] TEU.

116 Regelsberger, E. & Wessels, W. 'The CFSP Institutions and Procedures: A Third Way for the Second Pillar' (1996) 1 *European Foreign Affairs Review* 29,36.

117 Supra n.65, para 153.

118 *Declaration on the Establishment of a Policy Planning and Early Warning Unit.*

and identifying areas where the CFSP could focus in future; providing timely assessments and early warnings of events or situations which may have significant repercussions for the Union's foreign and security policy, and producing policy options papers. These tasks are wideranging. If well-resourced, the exercise of these tasks could transform the Unit into an extremely powerful body. The reason for this is that because it has a predictive and anticipatory role, it will be well-placed to set the agenda in the event of some sudden foreign policy shock.

Further Reading

Eeckhout, P. *The European Internal Market and International Trade* (1994, Clarendon Press, Oxford)

Emiliou, N. & O'Keeffe, D. (eds.), *The European Union and World Trade Law* (1996, John Wiley, Chichester)

Hill, C. (ed.) *The Actors in Europe's Foreign Policy* (1996, Routledge, London)

Holland, M. (ed.) *Common Foreign and Security Policy: The Record and Reforms* (1997, Cassell, London)

Macleod, I., Hendry, T. & Hyett, S. *The External Relations of the European Communities* (1996, Clarendon, Oxford)

Maresceau, M. (ed.), *The European Community's Commercial Policy after 1992: The Legal Dimension* (1993, Kluwer, Deventer)

McGoldrick, D. *International Relations Law of the European Union* (1997, Longman, Harlow)

Neuwahl, N. 'Shared Powers or Combined Incompetence? More on Mixity' (1996) 33 *Common Market Law Review* 667

Völker, E. *Barriers to Internal and External Trade* (1993, Kluwer, Deventer)

5. Economic and Monetary Union

I. International Money

The concept of money pervades modern economic life. Without money we would live in a barter economy where any vendor of a good or service would have to find a purchaser who could offer the vendor something of equivalent value. There are clearly huge transaction costs in finding such a person. Money avoids this by providing a common means of payment. Secondly, money acts as a store of value by enabling individuals to accumulate purchasing power. Finally, money is also often used as a unit of account. Planning is only possible through knowledge of the value of one's existing stock. Translating goods into monetary terms is therefore often necessary for accounting purposes.[1]

The concept of international money, whereby one State allows its currency to be bought by persons outside its jurisdiction and exchanged for other currencies, is more complicated still. The first reason why a State might want its currency to be convertible is that it facilitates payments for imports. Exporters will not be inclined to sell their goods to another Member State unless they are able to convert the payment into a currency which is of use to them. 'Free movement of payments' is therefore necessary within a single market if there is to be movement of the other factors of production - goods, services and labour.

Increasingly, other reasons have developed why a State might want its currency to be traded on the international market. The principal one is that it can facilitate public borrowing. Like all debtors, the terms on which States can borrow money on the capital markets improves as

---

1 For analysis of the functions of money see Goodhart, C. *Money, Information and Uncertainty* (1989, 2nd Edition, Macmillan, Basingstoke).

their assets expand. A State's central asset is its money. Allowing a currency to be converted on the international capital market is that the value of this asset grows as demand for it grows. Consequently, as demand for money increases, the State has to pay people less, in the form of lower interest rates, to invest in its debt issues.[2]

Yet if allowing one's currency to be traded for other currencies on the world's capital markets has benefits, it also has many risks. Whilst, within a purely domestic context, a State can force those subject to its jurisdiction to use the money, it has no such instruments available to it in the case of international markets. The value of its money thus becomes one of confidence - a problem which increases as a greater share of its money is traded upon international markets.[3] It is powerless to stop people selling its money with the consequent deterioration this might bring in its terms of trade, public sector finances and interest rates.

Pelkmans, J. 'The Institutional Economics of European Integration' in Cappelletti, M., Seccombe, M. & Weiler, J. *Integration Through Law: Volume 1, Methods, Tools and Institutions* (1986, De Gruyter, Berlin) 341-342

Although the pure common market may be theoretically envisaged, it would constrain the operation of domestic stabilization and redistribution policies so much that its realization seems to be entirely dependent on developments in macro-economic integration. ...

Autonomous money supply or interest rate policies would be impossible as money and short-term financial assets would flow in or out as soon as the interest differential with neighbouring economies becomes smaller or larger than the risk premium for expected exchange rate changes. If exchange rates are assumed (by private economic agents) to be stable over a given period intra-union nominal interest rates could hardly differ. Autonomous budgetary deficits are possible but will lead immediately (perhaps even anticipatorily, after the announcement of budget outlines) to exchange rate or interest rate reactions, more or less neutralizing the desired expansionary effects. If the deficits are financed by money creation, this is likely to be offset by financial capital

2 On 'international money' see De Grauwe, P. *International Money* (1996, 2nd Edition, OUP, Oxford) 7-15.

3 In October 1994 the value of notes in circulation in the United Kingdom was estimated to be just over £18 billion. The average daily turnover on the London foreign exchange is $400 billion, Lipsey, R. & Chrystal, K. *An Introduction to Positive Economics* (1995, 8th Edition, OUP, Oxford) 679-691.

outflows, set in motion by a fear for later exchange rate losses. If the deficits are financed by public borrowing in the (union) capital market this will cause a rise in the (chain of interdependent) interest rates, making it more difficult for domestic firms to borrow *and* making borrowing more costly in other union countries (both for public and private purposes).

Exchange rate policy becomes next to impossible. If it is attempted via interest rate policies, it might temporarily succeed but at the risk of great volatility of the exchange rate whenever short term capital moves out again, for whatever reason. If it is attempted by interventions on the foreign exchange market, they would be swamped if underlying conditions would not justify the initial rate.

II. The Development of Free Movement of Capital

The institutional structure of the Treaty of Rome, whilst imposing a duty of coordination upon Member States, placed economic policy firmly within the national domain.[4] It therefore required the EC institutions not to do anything which might prejudice the internal and external financial stability of the Member States.[5] The destabilising effects of capital movements threatened this institutional balance. Stability was therefore achieved by placing certain limitations on the movement of capital.

A distinction was made, following the one made in the articles of association of the International Monetary Fund between payments and movements of other forms of capital.[6] Payments - those transfers of capital connected with the movement of goods, persons and services[7] were to be liberalised to the same extent as that factor of production with whose transfer they were connected was liberalised.[8] Subject to safeguards which could be introduced for balance of payments reasons,[9] the right to free movement of payments was therefore as wide-ranging

4 Article 6(1) EEC.

5 Article 6(2) EEC.

6 Article VIII(2), Articles of Association of International Monetary Fund 1944.

7 Case 203/80 *Casati* [1981] ECR 2595, [1982] 1 CMLR 365.

8 Article 106 EEC.

9 Articles 108 & 109 EEC.

as the other economic freedoms. It was, moreover, a directly effective right.[10]

Other movements of capital were subject to a more limited regime.[11] The most extreme limitation was that there was a right to such movements only to 'the extent necessary to ensure the proper functioning of the common market'.[12] The right was therefore considered insufficiently unconditional to be directly effective,[13] and was exclusively dependent upon the harmonisation process for its development. Furthermore wide-ranging safeguards could be introduced by a Member State, albeit after having obtained authorisation from the Commission, whenever movements led to disturbances in its capital market.[14] The result was that for the greater part of the history of the Community, movement of capital was, by some way, the most undeveloped economic freedom of all.

Secondary legislation initially classified capital movements, other than payments, under four headings. Each of these was subject to a different degree of liberalisation.[15] In the mid-1980s these categories were tinkered around with to allow greater liberalisation.[16] Yet substantial liberalisation was only brought about by Directive 88/361/EEC.[17] Whilst Ireland, Greece, Spain and Portugal [18] were permitted to keep in place certain temporary restrictions, for all the other

---

10 Joined Cases 286/82 & 26/83 *Luisi & Carbone v Ministero del Tesoro* [1984] ECR 377, [1985] 3 CMLR 52.

11 Articles 67-73 EEC.

12 Article 67(1) EEC.

13 Case 203/80 *Casati* [1981] ECR 2595, [1982] 1 CMLR 365. On this see Louis, J-V. 'Free Movement of Capital in the Community: The Casati Judgment' (1982) 19 *CMLRev* 443; Petersen, M. 'Capital Movements and Payments under the EEC Treaty after Casati' (1982) 7 *ELRev* 167.

14 Article 73(1) EEC.

15 Directive 63/21/EEC OJ English Special Edition 1963-1964, 5 amending the First Capital Directive of 11 May 1960, OJ English Special Edition 1959-1962, 49.

16 Directive 86/566/EEC, OJ 1986 L 332/22.

17 OJ 1988 L 178/5. For analysis see Oliver, P. & Baché, J-P. 'Free Movement of Capital between the Member States: Recent Developments' (1989) 26 *CMLRev* 61.

18 Ibid., Article 6(2).

Member States restrictions on capital movements were to be abolished.[19] There were certain exceptions to this principle, but these were of a comparatively limited nature.[20]

III. Capital Movements Following the Treaty on European Union

i. The Right to Trade in Foreign Capital

Directive 88/361/EEC abolished the distinction between payments and capital. This was 'constitutionalised' by the TEU.

Article 73b(1) [*56(1)*] EC. Within the framework of the provisions set out in this Chapter, all restrictions on the movement of capital between Member States and between Member States and third countries shall be prohibited.

2. Within the framework of the provisions set out in this Chapter, all restrictions on payments between Member States and between Member States and third countries shall be prohibited.

The provision has already been held to be directly effective.[21] It thus appears that free movement of capital is being brought into line with the other freedoms with the same possibilities and uncertainties which that entails. The first question concerns the ambit of the provision. It appears that it prohibits, at the very least, discriminatory measures which make foreign capital either more difficult to obtain than domestic

---

19 Ibid., Article 1(1).

20 Restrictions could be imposed in cases where short-term capital movements were leading to serious disturbances in a State's monetary or exchange rate policies, Ibid., Article 3(1). Furthermore, the freedom did not affect a Member State's freedom to prevent infringement of its laws in the fields of taxation and prudential supervision of financial institutions or its freedom to lay down procedures for the declaration of capital movements for purposes of administrative or statistical information, Ibid., Article 4.

21 Joined Cases C-163/94, C-165/94 & C-250/94 *Sanz de Lera & Others* [1995] ECR I-4821, [1996] 1 CMLR 631.

capital or which discriminate between the terms under which a State's own nationals and other EU citizens can obtain capital.

Case C-484/93 Svensson & Gustavsson v Ministre du Logement et de l'Urbanisme [1995] ECR I-3955

Svensson and Gustavsson, a Luxembourgeoise couple, took out a loan for a house from a financial institution based in Liège. They applied for an interest rate subsidy from the Luxembourgeoise Housing Ministry on the grounds that dependent children were living there. They were refused on the grounds that the loan had not been taken out with a Luxembourgeoise institution. The national court asked whether this was compatible with Article 1 of Directive 88/361/EEC, a provision which was identical to Article 73b [*56*] EC.

8. It is accordingly necessary to ascertain whether rules such as that at issue in this case constitute an obstacle to the movements of capital thus liberalized.

9. It should be noted that according to Article 1 of the Grand-Ducal Regulation the interest rate subsidy may only be granted if the persons meeting certain conditions are also able to show 'that they have obtained from a credit institution approved in the grand duchy of Luxembourg, or from social security pension agencies, a loan intended for the construction, acquisition or improvement of a dwelling situated on the territory of the Grand Duchy of Luxembourg and effectively and permanently occupied by the applicant'. The reply given by the Luxembourg Government to a question put by the court indicates that in order to obtain such approval the bank must have been constituted or established in Luxembourg, whether as an agency or as a branch.

10. Provisions implying that a bank must be established in a Member State in order for recipients of loans residing in its territory to obtain an interest rate subsidy from the state out of public funds are liable to dissuade those concerned from approaching banks established in another Member State and therefore constitute an obstacle to movements of capital such as bank loans.

The position is less clear in respect of non-discriminatory restrictions on capital movements. *Svennson* uses the same effects-based style of reasoning used to such effect in the fields of services, persons and goods. One set of authors have therefore suggested that any measure which discourages inward investment from other Member States or outward investments to other Member States might breach the provision.[22] On this basis, restrictions on the use of certain financial instruments, such as certain derivatives, could be challenged before the national courts. Yet whilst restricting the use of such financial instruments may prevent expansion of capital markets, there is a danger that intervention by courts in such complicated and unstable markets could have unpredictable and not necessarily desirable consequences.

ii. Permissible Restrictions on the Movement of Capital

Restrictions which may be imposed on movements of capital for reasons other than balance of payments are contained in Article 73d [*58*] EC.

Article 73d(1) [*58(1)*] EC. The provisions of Article 73b [*56*] EC shall be without prejudice to the right of Member States:
(a) to apply the relevant provisions of their tax law which distinguish between tax-payers who are not in the same situation with regard to their place of residence or with regard to where their capital is invested;
(b) to take all requisite measures to prevent infringements of national law and regulations, in particular in the field of taxation and the prudential supervision of financial institutions, or to lay down procedures for the declaration of capital movements for purposes of administrative or statistical information, or to take measures which are justified on grounds of public policy or public security.

2. The provisions of this Chapter shall be without prejudice to the applicability of restrictions on the right of establishment which are compatible with this Treaty.

3. The measures and procedures referred to in paragraphs 1 and 2 shall not constitute a means of arbitrary discrimination or a disguised restriction on the free movement of capital and payments as defined in Article 73b [*56*].

All the restrictions permitted in Articles 73d(1) and (2) are subject to the constraint that they be neither a disguised restriction on the movement of capital nor constitute an arbitrary form of discrimination. The Court has interpreted this to subject them to a

---

22 Farmer, P. & Lyal, R. *EC Tax Law* (1994, OUP, Oxford) 334.

proportionality requirement. They will only be justified insofar as they are necessary to achieve a legitimate objective.

Joined Cases C-163/94, C-165/94 & C-250/94 Sanz de Lera & Others [1995] ECR I-4821, [1996] 1 CMLR 631[23]

A number of cases had been brought against people who had taken Spanish pesetas out of the country without authorisation. Under Spanish law persons taking more than 5 million pesetas out of the country in coins, bank notes or cheques required such authorisation.

19. Article 73b(1) of the Treaty gave effect to the liberalization of capital movements between Member States and between Member States and non-member countries. To that end, it provides that, within the framework of the provisions of Chapter 4 of the Treaty, entitled 'capital and payments', all restrictions on the movement of capital between Member States and non-member countries are to be prohibited.

20. By virtue of Article 73d(1)(b) of the Treaty, Article 73b(1) is to be without prejudice to the right of the Member States 'to take all requisite measures to prevent infringement of national law and regulations, in particular in the field of taxation and the prudential supervision of financial institutions, or to lay down procedures for the declaration of capital movements for purposes of administrative or statistical information or to take measures which are justified on grounds of public policy or public security'.

21. Pursuant to Article 73d(3) of the Treaty, those measures and procedures 'shall not constitute a means of arbitrary discrimination or a disguised restriction on the free movement of capital ... as defined in Article 73b'.

.....

23. It is therefore necessary to consider whether the requirement of an authorization or a prior declaration for the export of coins, banknotes or bearer cheques is necessary in order to uphold the objectives pursued and whether those objectives might be attained by measures less restrictive of the free movement of capital.

24. As the Court held in [paragraph 24 of *Bordessa*], authorization has the effect of suspending currency exports and makes them conditional in each case upon the consent of the administrative authorities, which must be sought by means of a special application.

---

23 Analogous reasoning had been used earlier in a similar case in relation to Directive 88/361/EEC, Joined Cases C-358/93 & 416/93 *Ministerio Fiscal v Bordessa* [1995] ECR I-361, [1996] 2 CMLR 13.

25. The effect of such a requirement is to cause the exercise of the free movement of capital to be subject to the discretion of the administrative authorities and thus be such as to render that freedom illusory (see Bordessa, paragraph 25, and Joined Cases 286/82 and 26/83 *Luisi and Carbone v Ministero del Tesoro* [1984] ECR 377, paragraph 34).

26. However, the restriction on the free movement of capital resulting from that requirement could be eliminated without thereby detracting from the effective pursuit of the aims of those rules.

27. As the Commission has rightly pointed out, it would be sufficient to set up an adequate system of declarations indicating the nature of the planned operation and the identity of the declarant, which would require the competent authorities to proceed with a rapid examination of the declaration and enable them, if necessary, to carry out in due time the investigations found to be necessary to determine whether capital was being unlawfully transferred and to impose the requisite penalties if national legislation was being contravened.

28. Thus, unlike prior authorization, such a system of declarations would not suspend the operation concerned but would nevertheless enable the national authorities to carry out, in order to uphold public policy, effective supervision to prevent infringements of national law and regulations.

29. As regards the Spanish Government's argument that only a system of authorization makes it possible to establish that a criminal offence has been committed and impose penalties under criminal law, such considerations cannot justify the maintenance of measures which are incompatible with Community law.

a. Protection of National Fiscal Regimes

Restrictions on movements of capital may be imposed to protect national fiscal regimes for two reasons. The first, contained in Article 73d(1)(b) [*58(1)(b)*] EC, is to prevent tax evasion. The second, contained in Article 73d(1)(a) [*58(1)(a)*] EC, allows Member States to distinguish between tax-payers who are not in the same situation with regard either to their place of residence or to where their capital is invested.[24] There

[24] They may not discriminate in an arbitrary manner, however. See p. 742 ff.

are constraints on this freedom.[25] Article 73d[*58*] EC was accompanied by a Declaration at the TEU:-

> The Conference affirms that the right of Member States to apply the relevant provisions of their tax law as referred in Article 73d(1)(a) of this Treaty will apply only with respect to the relevant provisions which exist at the end of 1993. However, this Declaration shall apply only to capital movements between Member States and to payments effected between Member States.

Declarations only having interpretative value, it is extremely doubtful whether a Declaration could impose a temporal limitation on substantive provisions of the Treaty, as this would result in its overriding the EC Treaty provision from the end of 1993. A greater constraint is that any distinction drawn should not constitute a form of 'arbitrary discrimination' under Article 73d(3) [*58(3)*] EC. A differentiation will only be allowed therefore if it is required by the nature and object of the system of taxation and if an external rationale can be found for the distinction, such as the facilitation of the collection of revenue.[26]

b. Restrictions Compatible with the Right of Establishment

There was a danger that Article 73b [*56*] EC might undermine the balance contained within Article 52 [*43*] EC. Article 52 [*43*] EC, it will be remembered, does not give undertakings the right to move their registered office, central administration or place of administration to another Member State.[27] It also allowed Member States to distinguish

---

25 This exception does not cover physical transfers of capital. Joined Cases C-163/94, C-165/94 & C-250/94 *Sanz de Lera & Others* [1995] ECR I-4821, [1996] 1 CMLR 631.

26 See Case C-300/90 *Commission v Belgium* [1992] ECR I-305, [1993] 1 CMLR 785. More generally on the difficulties of the non-discrimination principle see Green, R. 'The Troubled Rule of Non-Discrimination in Taxing Foreign Direct Investment' (1994) 26 *Law & Policy in International Business* 113.

27 Case 81/87 *R v HM Treasury ex parte Daily Mail* [1988] ECR 5483, [1988] 3 CMLR 713.

between residents and non-residents where the latter were earning the majority of their income in another Member State.[28] Potentially, both these forms of restriction would have contravened Article 73b [*56*] EC.

Article 73d(2) [*58(2)*] EC seeks to remedy this by stating Article 73b [*56*] EC shall not constrain those restrictions on freedom of establishment which are compatible with the Treaty. This exception does raise the more general question of Article 73b [*56*] EC's relationship with the other economic freedoms, such as Article 48 [*39*] EC or 59 [*49*] EC.[29] Whilst the question has not been raised since the coming into force of the TEU, it had been raised earlier.

Case C-204/90 Bachmann v Belgian State [1992] ECR I-249, [1993] 1 CMLR 785

Bachmann was a German who worked in Belgium. Unlike Belgian nationals, he was refused tax exemptions from the contributions he made to a life assurance scheme. The reason for this, the authorities claimed, was that Belgians were taxed on the receipts from the scheme, and they could not ensure that he would be so taxed if he was living abroad. Bachmann claimed that this differential treatment violated, *inter alia*, Article 67 EEC, the provision then regulating movement of capital.

34. Provisions such as those contained in Article 54 of the CIR are not incompatible with Articles 67 and 106 of the Treaty. It need merely be observed in that regard, first, that Article 67 does not prohibit restrictions which do not relate to the movement of capital but which result indirectly from restrictions on other fundamental freedoms, and, secondly, that provisions such as those at issue before the national court preclude neither the payment of insurance contributions to insurers established in another Member State nor their payment in the currency of the Member State in which the insurer is established.

---

28 Case C-270/93 *Finanzamt-Köln Altstadt v Schumacker* [1995] ECR I-225, [1996] 2 CMLR 450; Case C-107/94 *Asscher v Staatsecretaris van Financiën*, [1996] ECR I-3089, [1996] 3 CMLR 61.

29 See also Case C-148/91 *Vereniging Veronica Omroep Organisatie v Commissariaat voor de Media* [1993] ECR I-487; Case C-484/93 *Svensson & Gustavsson v Ministre du Logement et de l'Urbanisme* [1995] ECR I-3955, Opinion of Advocate-General Elmer, paragraphs 9 & 10.

The rule that the EC Treaty provisions on capital will not protect movements of capital provisions will not apply where the restriction on the movement of capital occurs as a result of restrictions on the movement of other factors of production bears strong parallels with the case of 'mixed' provision of goods and services. The governing provision will depend upon whether it is the supply of the good or the supply of service which is perceived as constituting the heart of the transaction.[30] In the case of capital this will require considering whether the transfer of capital is instrumental to the free movement of a good or service, or vice versa. This position is not only very hard to apply in industries such as banking, but would also create a paradox. It would reintroduce the distinction between payments and capital, as payments are transfers of capital instrumental to the exercise of the other freedoms. These would now fall outside the ambit of Article 73b [*56*] EC and be considered under the other economic freedoms.

c. Restrictions Imposed in the Public Interest

Article 73d(1)(b) [*58(1)(b)*] EC also allows restrictions to be imposed for a hotchpotch of other reasons justified in the public interest. Member States can require declarations of capital movements to be made for statistical or administrative reasons. Restrictions can also be imposed for public policy or public security reasons. Such restrictions must not constitute a means of arbitrary discrimination or a disguised restriction on trade. The public policy and public security exceptions are analogous to those contained in relation to free movement of goods in Article 36 [*30*] EC, and it is to be expected that they will be developed in an identical manner.

In *Thompson* the Court held that Member States could place limits on the amount of coins taken out of their jurisdiction under the public policy exception. This was because, in the Court's view, every State retained the exclusive right to mint its own coins.[31] Whether the

---

30 Case C-275/92 *Schindler et al. v Her Majesty's Customs & Excise* [1994] ECR I-1039, [1995] 1 CMLR 4; Case C-55/93 *Van Schaik* [1994] ECR I-4837.

31 Case 7/78 *R v Thompson* [1978] ECR 2247, [1979] 1 CMLR 47.

Court would rule in this manner following the TEU is open to question. A right to free movement of capital now exists which did not exist previously. Furthermore, the proviso that nothing should be done to destabilise States' monetary or economic policies, which then existed in Article 6 EEC, has now been removed.

d. Restrictions Imposed for Balance of Payments Reasons

Restrictions may be imposed where Member States encounter balance of payments difficulties. The present provisions, whilst being rearranged, almost exactly reproduce in content Articles 108 and 109 EEC. They reflect the view expressed by the Court in *Luisi and Carbone* that safeguard measures may be needed for balance of payments reasons even after free movement of capital had been achieved.[32]

Article 109h(1) [*119(1)*] EC. Where a Member State is in difficulties or seriously threatened with difficulties as regards its balance of payments either as a result of an overall disequilibrium in its balance of payments, or as a result of the type of currency at its disposal, and where such difficulties are liable in particular to jeopardise the functioning of the common market or the progressive implementation of the common commercial policy, the Commission shall immediately investigate the position of the State in question and the action which, making use of all the means at its disposal, that State has taken or may take in accordance with the provisions of this Treaty. The Commission shall state what measures it recommends the State concerned to take.

If the action taken by a Member State and the measures suggested by the Commission do not prove sufficient to overcome the difficulties which have arisen or threaten, the Commission shall after consulting the Committee referred to in Article 109c [*114*],[33] recommend to the Council the granting of mutual assistance and appropriate methods therefor.

The Commission shall keep the Council regularly informed of the situation and how it is developing.

2. The Council, acting by a qualified majority, shall grant such mutual assistance; it shall adopt directives or decisions laying down the conditions and details of such assistance,

---

32 Joined Cases 286/82 & 26/83 *Luisi & Carbone v Ministero del Tesoro* [1984] ECR 377, [1985] 3 CMLR 52.

33 This is the Monetary Committee. See p. 242.

which may take such forms as:
(a) a concerted approach to or within any other international organisations to which Member States may have recourse;
(b) measures needed to avoid deflection of trade where the State which is in difficulties maintains or reintroduces quantitative restrictions against third countries;
(c) the granting of limited credits by other Member States, subject to their agreement.

3. If the mutual assistance recommended by the Commission is not granted by the Council or if the mutual assistance granted and the measures taken are insufficient, the Commission shall authorise the State which is in difficulties to take protective measures, the conditions and details of which the Commission shall determine.

Such authorisation may be revoked and such conditions and details may be changed by the Council acting by a qualified majority.

4. Subject to Article 109k(6) [*122(6)*], this Article shall cease to apply from the beginning of the third stage.

Article 109i(1) [*120(1)*] EC. Where a sudden crisis in the balance of payments occurs and a decision within the meaning of Article 109h(2) [*119(2)*] is not immediately taken, the Member State concerned may, as a precaution, take the necessary protective measures. Such measures must cause the least possible disturbance in the functioning of the common market and must not be wider in scope than is strictly necessary to remedy the sudden difficulties which have arisen.

2. The Commission and the other Member States shall be informed of such protective measures not later than when they enter into force. The Commission may recommend to the Council the granting of mutual assistance under Article 109h [*119*].

3. After the Commission has delivered an opinion and the Committee referred to in Article 109c [*114*] has been consulted, the Council may, acting by a qualified majority, decide that the State concerned shall amend, suspend or abolish the protective measures referred to above.

4. Subject to Article 109k(6) [*122(6)*], this Article shall cease to apply from the beginning of the third stage.

Article 109k(6) [*122(6)*] EC. Articles 109h [*119*] and 109i [*120*] shall continue to apply to a Member State with a derogation.[34]

---

34 Member States not meeting the convergence criteria when the decision is taken to go to the third stage of monetary union can be given a derogation exempting them from the principal requirements, Article 109k(1) [*122(1)*] EC. They are

The experience of their predecessors suggests that the core provision will be Article 109h(3) [*119(3)*] EC, which allows the Commission to authorise protective measures.[35] The difficulties with this provision have been that the Court has been willing to allow the Commission to authorise safeguards over extensive periods.[36] In such circumstances there appeared a danger at the time of the entry into force of the TEU that the economic freedom in Article 73b [*56*] EC could be undermined through an inter-institutional cabal between the Commission and the Member State involved under which the Commission would allow the Member State to suspend free movement of capital indefinitely. The provisions are to be contrasted with the provision which allows safeguard measures to be taken for the euro following the entry into force of stage three of EMU, which imposes a series of strict time limits.

Article 73f [*59*] EC. Where in exceptional circumstances, movements of capital to or from third countries cause or threaten to cause, serious difficulties for the operation of economic and monetary union, the Council acting by a qualified majority on a proposal from the Commission and after consulting the ECB, may take safeguard measures with regard to third countries for a period not exceeding six months if such measures are strictly necessary.

In practice these controls have been of little utility to Member States in the 1990s. The reasons for this arise out of the approach to the third stage of monetary union. Entry is contingent, as we shall see, upon a Member States's currency being sufficiently stable and limits being imposed upon the size of their national debt. Imposing balance of payments restrictions is likely to undermine both these objectives. It weakens the currency in the long-term, as investors will perceive that there is a risk that they will be unable to convert it. This, in turn, exacerbates difficulties in servicing the national debt as the Member

---

still constrained by Articles 109h [*119*] and 109i [*120*] EC.

35 Usher, J. 'Capital Movements and the Treaty on European Union' (1992) 12 *YBEL* 35, 49.

36 Case 157/85 *Brugnoni & Ruffinengo v Cassa di Risparmio di Genovia e Imperia* [1986] ECR 2013. In that instance the Commission authorised in 1985 the continuation of safeguards which had begun in 1974.

State will have to pay an increased rate in order to obtain finance, as lenders will be less secure of a Member State's ability to pay.

IV. Monetary Union

i. The Costs and Benefits of Monetary Union

Monetary union can take two forms. It can either constitute an area within which there are several currencies, but which are set at irrevocably fixed exchange rates, or, more usually, it is an area within which there is a single currency controlled by a single central bank. Whilst monetary union raises questions about national identity and sovereignty and about the control of public power,[37] the arguments most invoked to justify it are those of economic welfare. In 1990, therefore, the Commission prepared a study in 1990 which attempted to evaluate the costs and benefits of economic and monetary union in the same manner that the Cecchini Report attempted to do so for the Internal Market.[38] This concluded that economic and monetary union was beneficial. The principal non-institutional benefits are described below by one of the advisers to the Report.

Thygesen, N. 'Why Is Economic and Monetary Union an Important Objective for Europe' (1994) 14 *International Review of Law and Economics* 133, 136-137

Progressing from the stable EMS of the late 1980s to a single currency would on the basis of an extrapolation of past experience, only yield marginally more trade inside

---

37 Harden, I. 'Sovereignty and the Eurofed' (1990) 61 *Political Quarterly* 402, 406.

38 EC Commission, 'One Market, One Money' (1990) *European Economy* 44. Everson, M., Gros, D., Italianer, A., Pisani-Ferry, J. & Reichenbach, H. *One Market, One Money: An Evaluation of the Costs and Benefits of Forming an Economic and Monetary Union* (1992, OUP, Oxford). A summary of this study can be read in Emerson, M. & Huhne, C. *The ECU Report* (1991, Pan Books, London).

Europe. Surely, it was argued by critics of going all the way to a common currency, the growing sophistication of financial markets could be expected to provide hedging opportunities for the residual risk at moderate cost. Furthermore, the elimination of transaction costs of currency exchange, the other important benefit seen by business enterprises, seemed to many economists to be of almost trivial significance. Yet the business view may be closer to the truth than that of the economists.

The potential savings in transaction costs were estimated to be small but not trivial; the major empirical study of the EC Commission[39] suggested them to be in the order of 0.3-0.4% of Community GDP, assuming - as seems realistic - that an efficient EC-wide payments and clearing system is developed. ...

But this is only the tip of the iceberg. The continuing existence of national currencies would entail substantial indirect microeconomic costs. Firms can more easily engage in price discrimination between national markets when separate currencies allow them to charge higher prices in markets where demand is relatively insensitive. For consumers, used to evaluating prices in their own national currency, it is inconvenient to compare prices in different currencies, even if exchange rates are fixed. Transparency in the Internal Market, and hence competition, would be greatly increased with the more uniform price structure inherent in the transition to a common currency. This is presumably why the latter has won favour also with the consumer organisations in the EC - although not as yet with the consumers they represent. The potential for indirect benefits from a single currency are very much larger than the studies of the most visible gains - larger trade flows from reduced exchange rate volatility and elimination of transaction costs would suggest. Only a common currency can assure that all the benefits from goods market integration will be attained. It is not easy to put a figure on these benefits, but it would appear that some of the very substantial expected gains from creating the Internal Market estimated in the late 1980s could only materialise within a common currency area.

Even these indirect gains are likely to underestimate the total benefits, because they look only at once-and-for-all, or so called, static, effects. The common currency should bring efficiency gains also by raising the rate of growth of output, i.e., in a dynamic sense. The marginal productivity of capital can be expected to increase as a result of a more efficient financial environment. The higher capital stock means more output with the same labour force; hence the output effects of the initial increase in efficiency may be approximately doubled according to one major study by Baldwin.[40] The welfare effects will be smaller, since the increase in the capital stock has to be paid for by a reduction in consumption.

Finally, one may argue that the dynamic effects of a common currency are still understated to the extent that the risk premium attached to investment is reduced in a more predictable environment for exchange rates and monetary policy. This effect may well be small, as is the impact of reduced exchange-rate volatility on trade flows, but

---

39 Ibid.

40 Baldwin, R. 'On the microeconomics of the European Monetary Union' (1991) *European Economy* Special Edition No.1.

even a very modest increase in the growth rate has a cumulatively significant, exponentially increasing effect on the level of income over time. Even a minute increase in the growth rate would be more important than the direct gains in terms of saved transaction costs.

The rather dismissive attitude by many economists, notably in the United States, to the potential microeconomic benefits of a single currency is open to serious criticism. Without overstating the case, it is therefore possible to share the perception of business enterprises that a common currency is a highly desirable complement to the Internal Market. This becomes more obvious if it is kept in mind that the benchmark to which comparisons are made is no longer the stable EMS, as it existed up to September 1992, but rather a system with more exchange-rate flexibility and uncertainty. The potential microeconomic benefits of a common currency stand out more clearly now than in the heyday of confidence in a stable EMS in which many of these benefits could be claimed to have already been largely achieved.

Whilst critics diverge considerably as to their weight, the potential economic welfare costs derived from Member States' loss of the exchange rate as a tool of economic policy are generally considered to be three-fold.[41]

The first relates to public choice and is that monetary union prevents Member States having different policy preferences. If State A, which prefers policies allowing for higher inflation but lower unemployment, forms a monetary union with State B, which prefers policies resulting in lower inflation but higher unemployment, the result is likely to be a policy mix which neither State will regard as optimal. For monetary policy can not be conducted in a way which accommodates both States' preferences. The assumption behind this argument, however, is that Member States have considerable autonomy in deciding the economic policy they pursue. In a world of mobile capital it is doubtful whether this is so.[42] De Grauwe has observed therefore that where inflation develops, this in turn generates inflationary expectations for the future which reduces authorities' choice.[43]

---

41 An excellent analysis can be found in De Grauwe, P. *The Economics of Monetary Integration* (1997, 3rd Edition, OUP, Oxford) Chapter1. See also Corden, M. *Economic Policy, Exchange Rates and the International System* (1994, OUP, Oxford) 127-135.

42 On this see also Scharpf, F. 'Democratic Policy in Europe' (1996) 2 *ELJ* 136, 139-141.

43 Supra n.41, 15.

The second potential cost is that of 'asymmetric shocks'. Monetary policy must be conducted with regard to the state of the economy in the currency as a whole. It may be, however, that an economic shock hits one part of the currency area (an asymmetric shock) without affecting other parts nearly so severely. In such circumstances, the monetary policy will necessarily be insensitive to the needs of part of the area - be it the part in boom or the part in recession. There was therefore much debate as to whether Texas, the major oil producing state in the USA, would have benefited from having its own currency during the turbulence in the oil markets in the 1970s and 1980s. Since the 1960s the theory of 'optimum currency areas' has therefore seen convergence in economic performance as a *sine qua non* for monetary union.[44] There is general consensus that the European Union is not an optimal currency area, although some parts of it taken together might be.[45]

Yet this argument must be taken with a pinch of salt. The 'optimum currency area' is a model. Very few national currency areas meet up to this ideal. The test must therefore be a relative one, namely whether the European Union is more 'optimal' than various national currency areas. The answer to this is likely to vary.[46] This argument also presupposes that the exchange rate is an effective instrument of economic policy. Some economists see the primary cause of lack of competitiveness as structural - lack of investment, poor management etc. Changing the exchange rate does not unravel these structural

---

44 Mundell, R. 'A Theory of Optimal Currency Areas' (1961) 51 *American Economic Review* 657; McKinnon, R. 'Optimum Currency Areas' (1963) 53 *American Economic Review* 717.

45 For a brief summary see Tavlas, G. 'The "New" Theory of Optimum Currency Areas' (1993) 16 *World Economy* 663.

46 Recent research found that over the four year period 1989-1993 83% of unemployment in the different Member States was due to pan-European shocks rather than domestic forces. This was a higher figure than the United States, and suggested not only that unemployment within the European Union has increasingly common economic roots but that there is considerable convergence, Viñals, J. & Jimeno, J. 'Monetary Union and European Unemployment' (1996, CEPR Discussion Paper No 1485, London). See also Viñals, J. 'European Monetary Integration: A Narrow or Wide EMU?' (1996) 40 *European Economic Review* 1103.

disadvantages and can even buttress them.[47] Others consider that even if this were so in the long-term, economic life is made principally of these short-term glitches and therefore manipulation of the exchange-rate can be a valuable short-term mechanism.

The final potential cost deriving from monetary union arises from labour market inflexibilities. A supposed benefit from monetary union is increased competitiveness. Simultaneously, Member States are robbed of one instrument, the exchange rate, which can allow them to buttress the competitiveness of their industry. A flexible labour market is seen as a *sine qua non* for monetary union if mass unemployment is to be unavoided. For the latter can only be avoided by uncompetitive firms reducing labour costs or individuals moving from areas of labour surplus to areas of labour shortage. Yet this is also the language of 'sweatshop economics'. In social terms, its logic leads to people having to accept levels of wages and a degree of mobility and social dislocation which many would regard as unacceptable. It is doubtful whether such a scenario is socially acceptable or politically feasible. Federations deal with this problem through a system of inter-regional transfers of wealth from rich regions to poor regions, yet no comparable mechanism on such a scale exists within the Union. A rise in unemployment in some regions of the European Union is therefore highly likely as a result of economic and monetary union. Once again, however, this argument needs qualification. Such a development is also likely to happen from one State pegging its currency to another's. This has already happened within the context of the Exchange Rate Mechanism for a number of years. Monetary union may, in this respect expand employment in the outer regions. For the central authority will no longer be the central bank of the base currency - in Europe's case the Deutschmark - but a European body which will be able to adopt a wider perspective and adopt a policy geared to European rather than to national interests.

---

47 On this see Thygesen, N. 'Why Is Economic and Monetary Union an Important Objective for Europe?' (1994) 14 *International Review of Law and Economics* 133.

ii. The Route to Monetary Union

The TEU sets out a phased approach to economic and monetary union. In this it follows the structure of the earlier Delors Report which suggested a three stage approach to economic and monetary union.[48] The first stage finished on 31 December 1993. By that date each Member State had to ensure free movement of capital unless granted a derogation by the Council.[49] Member States also were required to adopt multiannual programmes intended to ensure the lasting convergence necessary for the achievement of economic and monetary union. These had to have regard to price stability and sound public finances. These reports also had to enable the Council to make an assessment on the progress made with regard to economic and monetary union and the progress on implementation of the internal market.[50]

The second stage began on 1 January 1994. During that stage Member States are to regard their exchange rate policy as a matter of common interest.[51] In the wake of the weakening of the exchange rate mechanism in Autumn 1992, this can be seen as at most a very loose commitment. The key to understanding to the second stage is, however, that it is a 'fitness test' for the third stage of monetary union. Entry for the third stage will be considered by the Council on the basis of whether Member States meet certain financial targets, more commonly known as convergence criteria. The targets are the following:

- a high degree of price stability. This is taken to mean an average rate of inflation, taken over the year before examination, which is not more than 1.5% higher than the average of the three best performing States;[52]

---

48 Committee for the Study of Economic and Monetary Union, *Report on economic and monetary union in the European Community* (1989, OOPEC, Luxembourg). See Louis, J-V. 'A Monetary Union for Tomorrow' (1989) 26 *CMLRev* 301.

49 Article 109e(2)(a) [*116(2)(a)*] EC. Such derogations existed for Greece and Portugal. They ended on 31 December 1995, Article 73e [*repealed*] EC.

50 Article 109e(2)(b) [*116(2)(b)*] EC.

51 Article 109m(1) [*124(1)*] EC.

52 Protocol on the Convergence Criteria referred to in Article 109j [*121*], Article 1.

- the avoidance of an excessive budgetary deficit. A deficit will be considered excessive if either the planned or actual deficit exceeds 3% of GDP or total government debt exceeds 60% of GDP.[53]

- the Member State's currency has remained within the narrow margins of the Exchange Rate Mechanism for two years without devaluation or severe tensions;[54]

- the long-term interest rates of a Member State do not exceed by more than 2% the average of the three Member States with the lowest rates of inflation.[55]

These convergence criteria are odd. The economic logic behind them has been criticised as being inflexible and insufficiently sensitive to the economic backdrop.[56] They can, in any case, be replaced by the Council acting unanimously.[57] There are no checks as to how Member States implement them, and indeed, some of the devices used, such as the use of French pension funds to reduce the size of the French national debt, look to be little more than questionable accounting methods. Furthermore, it does not appear they are binding on the EC Institutions when they come to make their decision but form merely a basis for decision.[58] Indeed, there is tacit acknowledgment that one of the criteria, namely that a currency be within the narrow bands of the Exchange Rate Mechanism for two years without devaluation or severe tensions, has been dropped for a requirement merely that the currency be sufficiently stable.[59] Yet Member State economic policy is increasingly being guided by these criteria and the ability of the Member States to meet these

---

53 Protocol on the Excessive Deficit Procedure, Article 1.

54 Protocol on the Convergence Criteria referred to in Article 109j [*121*], Article 3.

55 Ibid., Article 4.

56 For a summary of the literature see De Grauwe, P. 'The Political Economy of Monetary Union in Europe' (1993) 16 *World Economy* 653, 657-660; De Grauwe, P. 'Monetary Union and Convergence Economics' (1996) 40 *European Economic Review* 1091.

57 Protocol on the Convergence Criteria, Article 6.

58 Article 109j(2) [*121(2)*] EC.

59 See evidence of the Rt. Honourable Kenneth Clarke QC in House of Lords Select Committee on the European Communities, *An EMU of 'Ins' and 'Outs'* (Session 1995-1996, 11th Report, HMSO) 276.

criteria, or to come close to meeting these criteria, is central to the success of the whole enterprise. The reasons are twofold. The first is the need to convince the capital markets of the credibility of the euro.[60] The second is for institutional reasons. The most influential financial institution in Europe, the German Bundesbank, has made it clear that it would be unwilling to see Germany relinquish a stable mark for an unstable euro. The convergence criteria are therefore seen as the price the Bundesbank has exacted for German entry into the third stage of monetary union.[61]

The beginning of the second stage also marked the beginning of a number of institutional developments. The principal one is the establishment of the predecessor of the European Central Bank, the European Monetary Institute (EMI).[62] The Institute is managed by a Council which consists of the governors of the national central banks and a president,[63] who are appointed by common accord among the Governments of the Member States.[64]

The EMI has a variety of coordinatory and advisory tasks. Its first is to ensure the smooth functioning of the existing monetary order within the European Union.[65] The second consists of technical preparations for the transition to and the operation of the third stage of monetary union.[66] Thirdly, the EMI issues recommendations and opinions on the overall orientation of monetary policy and exchange

---

60 This name was given to the future currency at the Madrid European Council in 1995, Conclusions of the Presidency, EU Bulletin 12-1995, pt. I.3.2.

61 See evidence of Lord Lawson in House of Lords Select Committee on the European Communities, *An EMU of 'Ins' and 'Outs'* (Session 1995-1996, 11th Report, HMSO) 147 *et seq.*

62 Article 109f(1) [*117(1)*] EC.

63 The Belgian, Professor Lamfalussy, was installed as the first President. He has now been replaced by the Dutchman, Wim Duisenberg.

64 Article 109f(2) [*117(2)*] EC.

65 Article 109f(2) [*117(2)*] EC; Protocol on the Statute of the EMI, Article 4.1.These include facilitating use of the ECU and certain operational and technical functions in respect of the Exchange Rate Mechanism such as receiving monetary reserves from the national central banks for the purpose of implementing the EMS, administering the short-term financing and monetary support mechanisms of the EMS and holding reserves as an agent of national central banks.

66 Article 109f(3) [*117(3)*] EC; Protocol on the Statute of the EMI, Article 4.2.

rate, on policies which might affect the internal and external monetary situation in the Community and the functioning of the EMS and on national monetary policy.[67] Finally, it must be consulted by the Council regarding any action which falls within its competence.[68]

The EMI's authority is diminished by its recommendations not normally being published, as they can only be published if the Council of the EMI agrees to it unanimously.[69] It is also marginalised by the establishment of the Monetary Committee.[70] This is a Committee, two of whose members are appointed by each Member State and two of whom are appointed by the Commission, which has a number of advisory tasks, including review of the monetary and financial situations of the Member States and contributing to the preparation of the work of the Council in the fields of movement of capital and economic and monetary policy. This Committee is less autonomous from the Council of Ministers than the EMI, and to the extent that its work overlaps with the EMI it could be seen to balkanise decision-making and marginalise the EMI.[71]

The powers of the EMI are considerably less than those envisaged for the equivalent institution by the Delors Report which envisaged a pooling of monetary sovereignty between national and EC Institutions, with powers gradually accruing to the latter during the second stage. The TEU rejected this in favour of the principle of the *indivisibility of monetary sovereignty*, whereby, at any one time, monetary sovereignty is clearly seen to lie with one particular authority.[72] The advantages of this approach are that it encourages monetary stability, as the markets are not confused by conflicting signals coming from different authorities. The disadvantage is that when, or if,

---

67 Article 109f(4) [*117(4)*] EC ; Protocol of the Statute of the EMI, Article 5.

68 Article 109f(6) [*117(6)*] EC.

69 Article 109f(5) [*117(5)*] EC.

70 Article 109c(1) [*114(1)*] EC.

71 The Economic and Financial Committee replaces the Monetary Committee at the beginning of the third stage of economic and monetary union. It is also an advisory body and its duties are to deliver opinions, keep under review the financial situation of the Community and the Member States, and to carry out any advisory or preparatory tasks in the monetary field assigned to it by the Council, Article 109c(2) [*114(2)*] EC.

72 Artis, M. 'The Maastricht Road to Monetary Union' (1992) 30 *JCMS* 299.

monetary union comes, it will require a bigger adjustment of perceptions in seeing the ECB rather than national banks as the preeminent source of authority.

Critics have consequently suggested that the EMI's role is at best marginal to the process of monetary integration.[73] Yet the role of the EMI must be placed within the shift in power to national central banks during stage two, as Member States must start the process leading to the independence of their central bank during that stage.[74] The EMI provides a forum within which these increasingly powerful institutions can meet and develop ideas, policies and alliances on a multilateral basis. One commentator has suggested that this process is facilitating a convergence of views among national central banks and an increased assertiveness on the part of national central banks against other government institutions within their respective Member States.[75]

iii. Arriving at Monetary Union

The date for the start of the third stage is 1 January 1999.[76] Before 1 July 1998 the Commission and EMI are required to report on the progress Member States are making towards economic and monetary union. These reports, in particular, have to examine whether Member States are meeting the convergence criteria and their national banking legislation complies with the requirements of the third stage.[77] On the basis of these reports, the Council, acting by a qualified majority on a

---

73 Andenas, M. 'Economic and Monetary Union: Stage Two' (1993) 14 *Company Lawyer* 233.

74 Article 109e(5) [*116(5)*] EC. See Duprat, J-P. 'The Independence of the Banque de France: Constitutional and European Aspects' (1995) *PL* 133; McGuire, K. 'Banking Beyond the Single Market: Monetary Policy and the European Central Bank' in Cranston, R. (ed.) *The Single Market and the Law of Banking* (1995, 2nd Edition, Lloyds Press, London).

75 Kapstein, E. 'Between Power and Purpose: Central Banks and the Politics of Regulating Converged' (1992) 46 *International Organisation* 265.

76 Article 109j(4) [*121(4)*] EC. The date could have been set earlier, Article 109j(3) [*121(3)*] EC. At the Cannes European Council in 1995 the Member States decided it should be 1 January 1999, Conclusions of the Presidency, EU Bulletin 6-1995, pt. I.11.

77 Article 109j(1) [*121(1)*] EC.

recommendation from the Commission after consulting the Parliament, has to assess which Member States meet these targets by 1 July 1998.[78] Member States may be excluded against their will from participating in economic and monetary union on the grounds that their economy or national legislation is not ready for the third stage. Such States, referred to as 'Member States with a derogation',[79] are to be considered by the Council once every two years as to whether they fulfil the necessary conditions to participate in the third stage.[80]

The fixed nature of 1 January 1999 suggests an irreversibility to the process. The monetary instability precipitating and following the undermining of the Exchange Rate Mechanism in August 1992 and the economic stagnation across Europe in the 1990s led for a considerable period to doubt as to whether this would be the case. By the end of 1997, there was considerable doubt as to how many Member States would meet the convergence criteria. According to Commission figures in September 1997, only five Member States out of fifteen - Denmark, Finland, Ireland, Luxembourg and the Netherlands - satisfied all the criteria.[81] It seems highly unlikely, in particular, that Belgium, Italy and Greece, all of whom have total debts twice, or nearly twice, the size allowed by the criteria can reduce them sufficiently in the time available. Yet a monetary union of 'ins' and 'outs' is politically divisive and may cause considerable economic instability for those economies which are excluded.

Dwarfing the problems of economic convergence are those of political will.[82] The process, being an act of *positive integration*, is dependent upon a decision by the Council under Article 109j(4) [*121(4)*] EC. The legal consequences of the Council failing to take that decision are unclear. More fundamentally, it is difficult to see how EMU can be sustainable in the long-term without sufficient belief in it either by the governments or the populations of the European Union. Yet public

---

78 Article 109j(2) [*121(2)*] EC.

79 Article 109k(1) [*122(1)*] EC.

80 Article 109k(2) [*122(2)*] EC.

81 EC Commission, *EC Economic Data Pocket Book No 8-9/97* (1997, OOPEC, Luxembourg) 10.

82 Cohen, B. 'Beyond EMU: The Problem of Sustainability' (1993) 5 *Economics and Politics* 187.

opinion is heavily divided over monetary union across Europe.[83] The United Kingdom and Denmark celebratedly negotiated opt-outs which allowed them to notify the other Member States that they will not be going to the third stage.[84] Denmark notified the other Member States at the Edinburgh European Council that it will not be going to the third stage.[85] The United Kingdom has also notified the other Member States in Autumn 1997 that it will not participate in the third stage on 1 January 1997. Even in those Member States which have not negotiated opt-outs, there are doubts. The Swedish government has already indicated that it will only enter following a referendum. President Chirac has indicated that this might also be required in France. Following the *Brunner* judgment, even Germany can only enter the third stage following a positive vote in the Bundestag.[86]

As it has become clear that some Member States will not participate in the third stage of economic and monetary union, either because they do not wish to or because they are not considered to meet the convergence criteria, attention has increasingly been paid to the relationship between participants and non-participants.[87] There was, in particular, concern that non-participants might be subjected to turbulent treatment on international capital markets either because of the perceived instability of their currencies vis-à-vis the euro or because of

---

83 In June 1997 47% of EU citizens were in favour of a single currency with 40% opposed. The remainder were undecided. There were majorities against introduction of a single currency in six Member States. EC Commission, *Eurobarometer: Report No. 47* (1997, OOPEC, Luxembourg).

84 Protocol to the Treaty on European Union on Certain Provisions Relating to the United Kingdom of Great Britain and Northern Ireland; Protocol to the Treaty on European Union on Certain Provisions Relating to Denmark. The United Kingdom must notify the other Member States whether it will go to the third stage before 1 January 1998. Ibid., Article 1. The United Kingdom, unlike Denmark, has the possibility of participating in monetary union at a later date provided that it fulfils the necessary conditions, Ibid., Article 10. All three main political parties within the United Kingdom are committed to a referendum on the matter should the British government decide to enter the third stage.

85 Conclusions of the Presidency, EC Bulletin 12-1992, pt. I.36.

86 *Brunner v European Union Treaty* [1994] 1 CMLR 57.

87 See, in particular, House of Lords Select Committee on the European Communities, *An EMU of 'Ins' and 'Outs'* (HMSO, Session 1995-96, 11th Report).

policies adopted by the ECB which do not accommodate their interests. At the Dublin European Council in December 1996 it was agreed that the way to resolve this would be to create a new fortified Exchange Rate Mechanism based around the euro, participation in which will be voluntary.[88] The details of this Mechanism were fleshed out in June 1997 at Amsterdam.[89] It will be based on central-rates against the euro with a relatively wide fluctuation band of plus or minus 15%. The width of this band is to prevent the inflexibilities which led to the demise of the old ERM in Autumn 1992. That said, provision is made for narrower bands to be agreed on a case-by-case basis. All bands will be supported by intervention from central banks.

iv. The European Central Bank and the European System of Central Banks: Their Composition and Functions

Immediately after a decision has been taken to go to the third stage of Economic and Monetary Union, the President, Vice-President and Executive Council of the European Central Bank (ECB) will be appointed by common accord of those Heads of Government participating in the third stage who do not have a derogation, after they have consulted the European Parliament and the EMI.[90] With the appointment of its Executive Board the ECB is established. It initially takes over the tasks of the EMI, which is then liquidated,[91] and only fully exercises the powers conferred upon it from the beginning of the third stage. The central power of the ECB is the exclusive power to authorise the issue of money, and, with that, to set short-term interest rates.

---

88 EU Bulletin 12-1996, 22.

89 Resolution of the European Council on the establishment of an exchange-rate mechanism in the third stage of economic and monetary union, OJ 1997 C 236/5.

90 Article 109l(1) [*123(1)*] EC; Protocol on the Statute of the European System of Central Banks and of the European Central Bank (hereinafter known as the Statute), Article 50.

91 Article 109l(2) [*123(2)*] EC.

Article 105a(1) [*106(1)*] EC. The ECB shall have the exclusive right to authorise the issue of bank notes within the Community. The ECB and the national central banks may issue such notes. The bank notes issued by the ECB shall be the only such notes to have the status of legal tender within the Community.

The ECB has its own independent legal personality,[92] and has two decision-making bodies. The first is the Executive Board. This consists of the President and Vice-President of the ECB and four other members.[93] Its method of appointment has been outlined above. Its members should be persons of recognised standing and professional experience in monetary or banking matters.[94] The other body is the Governing Council. This consists of members of the Executive Board plus governors of those national central banks whose States are participating without a derogation in the third stage of monetary union.[95] The President of the Council and a member of the Commission may participate in its meetings but do not have the right to vote.[96] In general, each body votes by a simple majority.[97]

The ECB must be placed alongside the European System of Central Banks (ESCB). The ESCB is composed of the ECB and the national central banks.[98] Its membership is wider than the Governing Council of the ECB in that it includes the Executive Board and national central banks of those Member States who are not fully participating in the third stage of economic and monetary union. Unlike the ECB, the ESCB has no legal personality and has been described as 'a set of rules

---

92 Article 106(2) [*107(2)*] EC.

93 Article 109a(2)(a) [*112(2)(a)*] EC; Statute, Article 11(1).

94 Article 109a(2)(b) [*112(2)(b)*] EC; Statute, Article 11(2).

95 Article 109a(1) [*112(1)*] EC; Statute, Articles 10(1) & 43(4).

96 Article 109b [*113*] EC.

97 Statute, Articles 10.2 and 11.5. The biggest exception to this rule concerns decisions relating to the income of national central banks; the capital of the ECB and subscription to that capital; the transfer of foreign reserves and the allocation of ECB profits. In all these areas members of the Executive Board have no vote and a decision will require votes cast in favour to represent at least two thirds of the subscribed capital of the ECB and to represent at least half of the shareholders, Statute, Article 10.3.

98 Article 106(1) [*107(1)*] EC.

and an institutional framework, rather than an institution in itself'.[99] It provides therefore no more than a structure through which the ECB and national central banks can conduct the monetary policy of the European Union. Its functions are described below.

Article 105(1) [*105(1)*] EC. The primary objective of the ESCB shall be to maintain price stability. Without prejudice to the objective of price stability, the ESCB shall support the general economic policies of the Community with a view to contributing to the achievement of the objectives of the Community as laid down in Article 2 [*2*]. The ESCB shall act in accordance with the principle of an open market economy with free competition, favouring an efficient allocation of resources, and in compliance with the principles set out in Article 3a [*4*].

2. The basic tasks to be carried out through the ESCB shall be:
- to define and implement the monetary policy of the Community;
- to conduct foreign exchange operations consistent with the provisions of Article 109 [*111*];
- to hold and manage the official foreign reserves of the Member States;
- to promote the smooth operation of payment systems.

3. The third indent of paragraph 2 shall be without prejudice to the holding and management by the governments of Member States of foreign exchange working balances.

4. The ECB shall be consulted:
- on any proposed Community act in its field of competence;
- by national authorities regarding any draft legislative provision in its fields of competence, but within the limits and under the conditions set out by the Council in accordance with the procedure laid down in Article 106(6) [*107(6)*].

The ECB may submit opinions to the appropriate Community institutions or bodies or to national authorities on matters in its field of competence.

5. The ESCB shall contribute to the smooth conduct of policies pursued by the competent authorities relating to the prudential supervision of credit institutions and the stability of the financial system.

6. The Council, acting unanimously on a proposal from the Commission and after consulting the ECB and after receiving the assent of the European Parliament, confer

---

99 Snyder, F. 'EMU-Metaphor for European Union? Institutions, Rules and Types of Regulation' 63, 80 in Dehousse, R. *Europe After Maastricht: An Ever Closer Union?* (1994, Law Books in Europe, Munich).

upon the ECB specific tasks concerning policies relating to the prudential supervision of credit institutions and other financial institutions with the exception of insurance undertakings.

The ESCB is governed by the decision-making bodies of the ECB.[100] To carry out the tasks entrusted to the ESCB the ECB can adopt regulations, decisions and recommendations.[101] Within limits to be set by the Council, it also has the power to impose fines and penalty payments on undertakings which do not comply with these regulations or decisions.[102] It can also bring national central banks before the Court of Justice who are not fulfilling their obligations under either the Treaty or ESCB Statute.[103]

Within this broad framework the Governing Council of the ECB is responsible for adopting the guidelines and taking the decisions necessary for the performance of the tasks entrusted to the ESCB. It therefore formulates the monetary policy of the Community including decisions relating to intermediary monetary objectives, key interest rates and supply of reserves in the ESCB. The Executive Board is responsible for implementing these guidelines and giving the necessary instructions to national central banks.[104]

v. The Independence and Accountability of the ECB and the ESCB

The most vaunted feature of the ECB is its independence.

Article 107 [*108*] EC. When exercising the powers and carrying out the tasks and duties conferred upon them by this Treaty and the Statute of the ESCB, neither the ECB nor a national central bank, nor any member of their decision-making bodies shall seek or take instructions from Community institutions or bodies, from any government of a Member State or from any other body. The Community Institutions and bodies and the

---

100 Article 106(3) [*107(3)*] EC.
101 Article 108a(1) [*110(1)*] EC.
102 Article 108a(3) [*110(3)*] EC.
103 Article 180(d) [*237(d)*] EC.
104 The respective powers of the bodies are contained in the Statute, Article 12.

governments of the Member States undertake to respect this principle and not to seek to influence the members of the decision-making bodies of the ECB or of the national central banks in the performance of their tasks.

The question of independence should not be seen in black and white terms. There are a number of ways in which control can be exercised and independence undermined.

Goodman, J. 'The Politics of Central Bank Independence' (1990) 23 *Comparative Politics* 329, 330-331

Independence is a continuous, not dichotomous variable. In other words, there are degrees of central bank independence. Defining and measuring the degree of independence is not a simple task, because independence can be enhanced or undermined in a variety of ways. There are two general ways to measure independence, one behavioural, the other formal. Woolley, for example, uses a behavioural definition. 'A central bank,' he argues 'is independent if it can set policy instruments without prior approval from other actors and if for some minimal time period (say a calender quarter), the instrument settings clearly differ from those preferred by other actors.'[[105]] One therefore looks to autonomous behaviour as a sign of independence. But I prefer to define independence formally, in terms of the law governing the organization and operations of a central bank, because changes in laws and statutes provide a means to specify more precisely when an actual shift in central bank independence occurs.

Seeking to specify independence formally, Bade and Parkin identified three dimensions; the assignment of responsibility for monetary policy, the sources of appointment of the governors and their terms of office - as being critical in measuring the degree of central bank independence.[[106]] In general, they argue, central banks enjoy greater independence when they are assigned the legal authority to both set and implement monetary policy. Independence is also enhanced in countries where a majority of bank directors is not directly appointed by the central government and where the directors enjoy lengthy tenure in office. Of course, a central bank which appears to be formally independent might still face significant pressures to adopt policies favourable to the government, especially regarding the financing of its deficits. For this reason, I incorporate two other dimensions - limits on direct central bank financing of government deficits (through a current account) and limits on central bank purchases of government bills. Explicit limits on the extent to which a central bank can or must monetize government deficits through either facility bolster its ability to resist government demands

---

105 Wooley, J. *Monetary Politics: The Federal Reserve and the Politics of Monetary Policy* (1984, CUP, Cambridge) 16.

106 Bade, R. & Parkin, N. 'Central Bank Laws and Monetary Policy' (1978, mimeo, Western Ontario, Department of Economics).

to stimulate the economy.

a. Personal Independence

For the ECB and ESCB to be independent, it is necessary not merely that members of the Executive Board be independent but also governors of national central banks. For the latter both sit on the Governing Council of the ECB and form part of the ESCB. Snyder has therefore pointedly observed that if one takes procedure of appointment as an index, the ECB is only partially supra-national, as national central bank governors are obviously appointed by national authorities.[107]

Article 11.1 Statute. In accordance with Article 109a(2) [*112(2)*] of this Treaty, the Executive Board shall comprise the President, the Vice-President and four other members.

The members shall perform their duties on a full-time basis. No member shall engage in any occupation, whether gainful or not, unless exemption is exceptionally granted by the Governing Council.

2. In accordance with Article 109a(2)(b) [*112(2)(b)*] of this Treaty, the President, the Vice-President and the other Members of the Executive Board shall be appointed from among persons of recognised standing and professional experience in monetary or banking matters by common accord of the governments of the Member States at the level of the Heads of State or of Government, on a recommendation from the Council after it has consulted the European Parliament and the Governing Council.

Their term of office shall be 8 years and shall not be renewable.[108] Only nationals of Member States may be members of the Executive Board. ...

4 If a member of the Executive Board no longer fulfils the conditions required for the performance of his duties or if he has been guilty of serious misconduct, the Court of Justice may, on application by the Governing Council or the Executive Board compulsorily retire him.

---

107 Snyder, F. 'EMU-Metaphor for European Union? Institutions, Rules and Types of Regulation' 63, 78 in Dehousse, R. *Europe after Maastricht: An Ever Closer Union?* (1994, Law Books in Europe, Munich)

108 There is an exception in relation to the initial establishment of the Executive Board, whose members may be appointed for terms of office between five and eight years. Statute, Article 50.

Article 14.2 Statute. The statutes of the national central banks shall, in particular provide that the term of office of a Governor of a national central bank shall be no less than five years.

A Governor may be relieved from office only if he no longer fulfils the conditions required for the performance of his duties or he has been guilty of serious misconduct. A decision to this effect may be referred to the Court of Justice by the governor concerned or the Governing Council on grounds of infringement of this Treaty or of any rule of law relating to its application. Such proceedings shall be instituted within two months of the publication of the decision or of its notification to the plaintiff or, in the absence thereof, of the day on which it came to the knowledge of the latter, as the case may be.

The length of the term of office is important, first, because it relieves the holder of pressures concerning reappointment, and, secondly, because, if it is longer than the electoral cycle, the holder cannot be sure that bowing to government pressures at the beginning of his term of office will not be counterproductive if another political party enters office. In this respect, it is strange that different rules should apply both about renewability and length of term to members of the Executive Board on the one hand and national central bank governors on the other. The implication is that the latter may be more sensitive to national pressures than the former. There is a more general lacuna, however. Personal independence can be compromised as much by private actors as by governments. In this respect, it is regrettable that no constraints are placed on what office-holders might do after their period of office.

b. The Operational Independence of the ECB and the ESCB

The area in which the independence of the ECB and ESCB is most central is in their operational independence. Independence can be compromised either if they do not have sufficient powers to conduct an independent monetary policy, or if institutions possess powers which could seriously undermine the pursuit of that policy. Concern has been expressed in two areas in this respect.

The first is in the interrelated fields of external monetary relations and exchange rate policy. It is the Council which has the predominant role in these fields with the ECB being limited to a consultative capacity or issuing recommendations. For it is the Council which decides on the position of the Community at international level on issues of particular relevance to economic and monetary union,[109] and which formulates general orientations for exchange rate policy in relation to other currencies.[110] In both these two instances, despite the need for consultation with the ECB, there is a very real risk of dysfunction with the Council adopting an external position that the ECB is unwilling to support internally.

The Council can also conclude agreements either committing the ECU to entry into an exchange rate system with other currencies[111] or to more general monetary or foreign exchange rate regimes.[112] International agreements being part of the Community legal order bind the ECB.[113] These powers pose a real threat to the ECB's independence, particularly in cases where the euro is committed to an exchange rate system. The purpose of such systems is to prevent sharp currency movements. This can often only be done by alignment of Contracting States' interest rates, in other words alignment of their money supply policies. The result is a threat to the ECB's exclusive right to authorise issue of tender, as it will be constrained in how much it can issue by the modalities of the exchange rate system to which the Council has committed it.[114]

The other area in which concern has been expressed is that of prudential supervision of banks. The ECB merely contributes to these policies with the possibility of additional powers being conferred upon it by the Council.[115] It has been argued that as the credibility of a currency is partly dependent upon the soundness of its banking system,

---

109 Article 109(4) [*111(4)*] EC.

110 Article 109f(2) [*117(2)*] EC.

111 Article 109f(1) [*117(1)*] EC.

112 Article 109f(3) [*117(3)*] EC.

113 Joined Cases 21-24/72 *International Fruit Co. v Produktschap voor Groenten en Fruit* [1972] ECR 1226, [1975] 2 CMLR 1.

114 See Slot, P-J. 'The Institutional Provisions of the EMU' in Curtin, D. & Heukels, T. (eds.) *Institutional Dynamics of European Integration: Liber Amicorum Henry Schermers* (1994, Martijnus Nijhoff, Dordrecht) 229, 248.

115 Articles 105(5) & (6) EC.

this division of powers could have disruptive consequences in the case of failures of supervision by the Council.[116] Others critics are more sanguine about this point, arguing that the credibility of the banking system only affects currency stability where the banking institutions are very fragile indeed. As this is not the case in any of the Member States, they consider that the problem of systemic risk is unlikely to arise.[117]

vi. The Politics of Central Bank Independence

The reasons for allowing independent central banks to control money supply are that independent central banks are seen as more likely to generate lower inflation at less costs to the economy, thereby providing a stable environment for long-term growth and investment.

Burdekin, R., Wihlborg, C. & Willett, T. 'A Monetary Constitution Case for an Independent European Central Bank' (1992) 15 *World Economy* 231, 233

The case for creation of an independent ESCB comes from the considerable evidence showing that the more institutionally independent central banks across the industrial countries have been associated with substantially lower rates of inflation. Moreover, these gains appear to have been realised at little or no cost in terms of average rates of unemployment or real output growth. For the few industrialised countries whose central banks have substantial degrees of formal institutional independence, differences in inflationary performance correlate rather well with differences in the respective degrees of institutional independence. Thus, whilst we cannot prove that the variations in performance are not due exclusively to differences in the underlying social, economic and political milieux that have generated both the institutional structures and the inflation records, we suspect that variations in institutional structures have made nontrivial contributions to the variation in inflation records.

---

116 Lastra, R-M. 'The Independence of the European System of Central Banks' (1992) 33 *Harvard Journal of International Law* 475, 513-514.

117 Andenas, M. & Hadjiemannuil, C. 'Banking Supervision, The Internal Market and European Monetary Union' 374, 389 in Andenas, M., Gormley, L., Hadjiemannuil, C. & Harden, I. (eds.) *European Economic and Monetary Union: The Institutional Framework* (1998, Kluwer Law International, Deventer).

The potential benefits of having an independent central bank have recently been detailed by Masciandaro, who points to the dangers arising from government incentives for inflation as a means of generating seigniorage, or of boosting the economy for political business cycle or partisan purposes.[118]

The setting of monetary policy is a considerable power, however, as it is central to the running of economic policy. It cannot be divorced from questions of accountability and public participation. Others therefore see an independent central bank as a potential Frankenstein in the power that it holds and its lack of accountability.

Harden, I. 'Sovereignty and the Eurofed' (1990) 61 *Political Quarterly* 402, 413-414

Central banks can exercise a great deal of control over both real and nominal interest rates (particularly short-term ones) and over the creation of credit money by commercial banks. In turn, the amount and cost of money have important macro-economic effects on the level of economic activity and the general price level. Movements in the price level and in real interest rates also have important distributional consequences; most clearly and directly, for example, as between creditors and borrowers. These distributional effects, and predictions of future effects, alter the pattern of incentives to engage in different types of economic activity and so have a dynamic impact.

One response to this is to say that such questions are all obviously 'political' and that central banks should therefore be constitutionally subordinated to democratic governments as in Britain. Another is to say that inflation is so great an evil that governments should be constitutionally required to prevent it. In practice, this would mean having an 'independent' central bank, charged with ensuring price stability as its overriding and paramount objective, something which does not exist anywhere in the world.

Neither of these responses is convincing. They both ignore the fact that central banks are at the heart of the political compromises underpinning the relationship between democracy, Executive government and financial capital ... Furthermore, legal duties and constitutional status are not the only factors which influence the behaviour of central banks or which determine the degree of autonomy they have in deciding the policies that they will pursue. Their role necessarily means that they are political actors and that the policies they pursue are political compromises. ...

---

118 Masciandaro, D. 'Central Bank Independence, Macroeconomic Models and Monetary Regimes' (1991, Centre for Monetary and Financial Economics, Universita Commerciale Luigi Bocconi, Milan).

The job of a constitution is to structure processes of political compromise and to set limits, procedural and substantive on what may be done. A constitution should also ensure that, so far as may be possible, public power is visible and its exercise transparent and accountable. Accountability requires explanation and justification, but not necessarily control by elected politicians. Even in a democracy, perhaps especially in a democracy. there is no reason for all public power to be concentrated in the hands of Executive government.

A number of institutional controls are placed on the ECB. The first form of control is judicial. The ECB is subject to the rule of law and can be brought before the Court of Justice like all the other Community Institutions.[119] All regulations and decisions of the ECB must be published in the *Official Journal*, and there is a duty on it to state reasons for the measure in question.[120] There are in addition certain non-judicial controls.

Article 15.1 Statute. The ECB shall draw up and publish reports on the activities of the ESCB at least quarterly.

2. A consolidated financial statement of the ESCB shall be published each week.

3. In accordance with Article 109b(3) [*113(3)*] of this Treaty, the ECB shall address an annual report on the activities of both the previous and the current year to the European Parliament, the Council and the Commission, and also to the European Council.

4. The report and statements referred to in this Article shall be made available to interested parties free of charge.

Article 109b(3) [*113(3)*] EC. The ECB shall address an annual report on the activities of the ESCB and on the monetary policy of both the previous and current year to the European Parliament, the Council and the Commission, and also to the European Council. The President of the ECB shall present this report to the Council and to the European Parliament, which may hold a general debate on that basis.

The President of the ECB and the other members of the Executive Board may,

---

119 Article 173(1) [*230(1)*] EC. In this respect it is similar to the European Parliament as it can bring other Community Institutions before the Court in order to protect its prerogatives, Article 173(3) [*230(3)*] EC.

120 Article 108a(2) [*110(2)*] EC.

at the request of the European Parliament or on their own initiative, be heard by the competent Committees of the European Parliament.

These are perceived by some as not being sufficient and two other alternatives, the Dutch model and the New Zealand model have been suggested.[121] Both the Dutch Central Bank and the New Zealand Reserve Bank are independent but their autonomy is curtailed. In the case of the Netherlands this is done primarily through the Dutch Minister of Finance being able to issue an instruction to the Bank on monetary policy. The Bank can object but the Minister has the last word. In addition the Bank is monitored by a Royal Commissioner who is responsible to the Minister. Accountability is preserved through the Minister's accountability to Parliament. Under the New Zealand model an inflation target is agreed between the Reserve Bank Governor and the government. If the Governor fails to meet this target, he can be dismissed. Public participation is established through the government setting the broad monetary targets.

A third model has been put forward by Daintith. He is sceptical of any form of parliamentary control, believing it inevitably compromises the behaviour of the Central Bank and therefore the goal of price stability, which was the rationale for handing over control of the money supply to the central bank in the first place. He claims instead that resort should be had to the 'federal' principle, whereby the governing bodies of the ECB are dominated by representatives of local interests.[122] To some extent this will be the case with the Governing Council of the ECB and with the ESCB, as national central bank governors will be present. Yet democracy extends beyond merely having regional representatives, and it is not clear how such a proposal would make the ECB any more accountable or any more transparent.

---

121 Busch, A. 'Central Bank Independence and the Westminster Model' (1994) 17 *WEP* 53; Gormley L. & de Haan, J. 'The democratic deficit of the European Central Bank' (1996) 21 *ELRev* 95.

122 Daintith, T. 'Between Domestic Democracy and an Alien Rule of Law? Some Thoughts on the "Independence" of the Bank of England' (1995) *PL* 118.

V. Economic Union

Economic union is something of a misnomer. With the exception of budgetary policy, other elements of economic policy are not subject to the three stage process which applies to monetary union. Nor is control of these transferred to supranational institutions in the same manner as monetary policy. The emphasis in the provisions on general economic policy is, instead, on coordination with economic sovereignty formally resting with the Member States.

Article 102a [*98*] EC. Member States shall conduct their economic policies with a view to contributing to the achievement of the objectives of the Community, as defined in Article 2, and in the context of the broad guidelines referred to in Article 103(2) [*99*]. The Member States and the Community shall act in accordance with the principle of an open market economy with free competition, favouring an efficient allocation of resources, and in compliance with the principles set out in Article 3a [*4*].

The danger with this is that a dysfunction might arise between the economic policies being pursued by any or all of the Member States and the monetary policy pursued by the ECB.

Lastra, R-M.'The Independence of the European System of Central Banks' (1992) 33 *Harvard Journal of International Law* 475, 479-480

... [a] major objection posed to the independence of Central Banks is that it hinders the maintenance of a consistent economic policy. Some economists fear that 'friction losses' would result from uncoordinated monetary and fiscal policy. Consequently, they argue that the Central Bank should be subordinated to the government.

These economists might oppose, for example, the inclusion in the EC Treaty of a formal commitment to control inflation because the current policy given by most governments and public opinion to price stability over other economic goals might not endure. The Statute of the European System of Central Banks and of the European Central Bank explicitly states that '(w)ithout prejudice to the objective of price stability, it {the ESCB} shall support the general economic policies in the Community'. Therefore, monetary policy at an EC level cannot be conducted in isolation, ignoring other objectives of economic policy.

In addition to responding to changing economic policy objectives, a consistent economic policy at the EC level should aim at diminishing regional disparities. Yet the coordination between a single monetary policy and twelve (or more, if other European

States become EC members) different fiscal policies will not be easy either. Under the Maastricht Treaty, the determination of fiscal policies largely remains the domain of national fiscal authorities. The required coordination might be disruptive, as Professor Goodhart has pointed out: '{A} single federal monetary system i.e. EMU, will require the support of a much more centralised fiscal system, involving automatic regional transfers, than is presently envisaged.'[[123]]

The principal instrument to reduce these 'friction losses' is contained in Article 103 [*99*]EC.

Article 103(1) [*99(1)*] EC. Member States shall regard their economic policies as a matter of common concern and shall coordinate them within the Council, in accordance with the provisions of Article 102a [*98*].

2. The Council shall, acting by a qualified majority on a recommendation from the Commission, formulate a draft for the broad guidelines of the economic policies of the Member States, and shall report its findings to the European Council.

The European Council shall, acting on the basis of the report from the Council, discuss a conclusion on the broad guidelines of the economic policies of the Member States and of the Community.

On the basis of this conclusion, the Council shall, acting by a qualified majority, adopt a recommendation setting out these broad guidelines. The Council shall inform the European Parliament of its recommendations.

There are two further controls. The first is that the Council is required to monitor national economic performance on the basis of reports prepared by the Commission.[124] Where it considers that a Member State's economic policies either are not consistent with Council guidelines or risk jeopardising the proper functioning of economic and monetary union it can make, acting by qualified majority on a recommendation from the Commission, recommendations to the Member State concerned. These recommendations can also be made public.[125] If the possibility of public reprimand is the stick for bringing about economic coordination, the carrot is that Community financial

---

123 Goodhart, C. 'Fiscal Policy and EMU' at 94, Paper Presented at CEP/FMG Conference at the London School of Economics (Nov 9 1990).

124 Article 103(3) [*99(3)*] EC.

125 Article 103(4) [*99(4)*] EC.

assistance may, from the third stage,[126] be granted by the Council to Member States in difficulties which were caused by exceptional occurrences beyond their control.[127] It is unclear how significant this provision will be. Except in the case of natural disasters, any award must be done unanimously. It stretches credulity to believe that other Member States will willingly grant financial assistance to a Member State outside the framework of the regional funds. In any case, the Community budget being limited, it is unlikely that the size of the assistance will be significant.

The second point raised by Lastra is the use of economic policy to reduce any regional disparities which might result from EMU. It has been argued by some that the development of some minimum common fiscal policy is a *sine qua non* for this and for a successful economic and monetary union.[128] Yet Member States have jealously preserved their fiscal sovereignty.

Innam, R. & Rubinfield, D. 'The EMU and Fiscal Policy in the New European Community: An Issue for Economic Federalism' (1994) 14 *International Review of Law and Economics* 147, 150-151

For the larger EC countries, the potential benefits of the EMU come at a price, however, the loss of effective monetary policy to manage country-specific recessions. This cost could be reduced if the use of fiscal policy were an effective alternative policy, as it might well be in the larger EC countries.

The aggressive use of local fiscal policy to control local unemployment has its own risks, however. First, as Canzoneri and Diba argue, when capital is mobile, an expansionary fiscal policy in one country may lead to higher interest rates in that country and elsewhere if that country's demand for funds is large relative to the relevant capital market.[[129]] As a consequence, interest rates may increase throughout the EC as one member adopts an expansionary fiscal policy. Inefficiencies will then be created to the extent that other, non-expansionary governments are forced to raise distortionary taxes to finance the interest charges on their own debt.

---

126 Article 109e(3) [*116(3)*] EC.

127 Article 103a(2) [*100(2)*] EC.

128 Masson, P. & Taylor, M. 'Fiscal Policy within Common Currency Areas' (1993) 31 *JCMS* 29.

129 Canzoneri, M. & Diba, B. 'Fiscal Deficits, Financial Integration and a Central Bank for Europe' (1991) 5 *Journal of the Japanese and International Economies* 381.

Second, if capital markets anticipate a central government 'bailout' of large local government debts, then there are moral hazard reasons to expect excessive local government borrowing. ... Such bailouts are most likely when the country is large and its debt becomes an important part of other member country portfolios. Both arguments suggest that there may be important negative spillovers from the use of decentralized deficit policies for managing unemployment risk.

There is an alternative fiscal policy strategy that will reduce the costs of the EMU to large country members and provide an added benefit to small country members. This is a central government policy of cross-country fiscal assistance in times of country-specific recessions. Such assistance can be paid as grants to the ailing country or directly as assistance to families in unemployment. Transfers would be paid from a centrally managed fund into which all EC-member countries make contributions. To the extent possible, contributions should be experience rated based on each country's cyclical history of employment. In effect, such policies are insurance policies among Member States in which the Member States pool their risks of country-specific, asymmetric unemployment shocks. Here is an example of a positive spillover among all EC countries - risk pooling - that central government fiscal policy can internalize.

The United States uses such insurance programmes extensively. They include unemployment insurance (mandated by the central government, but financed primarily by the individual states), progressive federal taxation (primarily the personal income tax), progressive government grants (allocated by the federal government in part on the basis of state income), and federal income redistribution programmes (including Aid to Families with Dependent Children and Medicare). Sachs and Sala-i-Martin estimate that the US system of coinsurance offsets about 35% of any income loss that an individual state suffers.[130] While this effect may be overstated, since it includes insurance of permanent as well as cyclical shocks, it is clearly significant.

Currently, the EC does not have the fiscal capability to effect substantial intergovernmental transfers, however. The EC budget is only about 1% of EC gross domestic product and 5% of the government spending of individual EC members. If the EC is to engage in the provision of substantial intergovernmental transfers, a number of important options must be considered. First, the EC must decide whether transfers are to be person specific or region specific. Region- (or state-) specific transfers are less desirable since they run the risk of perpetuating permanently depressed regions and consequently discouraging the efficient location of economic resources. Structural funds that are aimed at regions such as southern Italy are unlikely to be effective in the long run. Person-specific transfers are to be encouraged.

Second, the EC should consider the introduction of a system of EC unemployment insurance. There are risks, of course, since insurance creates moral hazard, as, for example, when domestic labour unions push for higher wages, knowing

---

130 Sachs, J. & Sala-I-Martin, X. 'Federal Fiscal Policy and Optimum Currency Areas: Evidence for Europe from the United States' in Canzoneri, M., Grilli, G. & Masson, P. (eds.) *Establishing a Central Bank: Issues in Europe and Lessons from the US* (1992, Cambridge University Press, Cambridge).

that the costs (unemployment) will be borne by the central government. But, we believe that the programme can be worthwhile. Mimicking the US structure could resolve the moral hazard problem; in the United States individual states manage their own unemployment trust fund.

VI. Budgetary Policy

There is one area of economic policy which receives special attention in the EC Treaty because of the particular problems it can cause for monetary policy, and that is budgetary policy.

During the second stage Member States are to endeavour to avoid excessive government deficits.[131] The Commission is to monitor national deficits and debts,[132] and if a Member State does not meet the criteria set out in the Protocol on the Excessive Deficit Procedure, the Commission must prepare a Report.[133] It may then recommend to the Council that an excessive deficit exists in a particular Member State. Acting by a qualified majority, and after having consulted the Monetary Committee and listened to the Member State in question's observations, the Council may decide that this is the case,[134] and make recommendations to the Member State to bring the situation to an end.[135]

The enforcement of these recommendations is problematic. The procedure is essentially non-justiciable. No action may be brought under either Article 169 [*226*] or 170 [*227*] EC for breach of these provisions.[136] Even if the matter came up before the Court, it is difficult to believe that it would adjudge on the question of whether a Member State had incurred an excessive budgetary deficit. The sanction available is that of market pressure, as the Council can, if the Member State takes no effective action, publish its recommendation.[137] The effect of such a

---

131 Article 109e(4) [*116(4)*] EC.
132 Article 104c(2) [*104(2)*] EC.
133 Article 104c(3) [*104(3)*] EC.
134 Article 104c(6) [*104(6)*] EC.
135 Article 104c(7) [*104(7)*] EC.
136 Article 104c(10) [*104(10)*] EC.
137 Article 104c(8) [*104(8)*] EC.

vote of no-confidence would be to place the State's currency in considerable difficulty on the capital markets. It is however a blunt weapon that is unlikely to be used. Many Member States have large debts. They are unlikely to turn upon one of their own. Secondly, the undermining of a State's currency provokes greater monetary instability, making monetary union yet more remote. It is therefore something of a counterproductive weapon. It is thus noticeable that the budgetary provisions are honoured more in their breach than their observance.

The other means of ensuring budgetary discipline has been to foreclose certain avenues of credit. It is prohibited for either national central banks, or the ECB when it comes into existence, to offer overdraft facilities to any public authority - be it EC, national or local - any public undertaking, or to any body governed by public law.[138] In addition, public authorities, both Community and national, are denied privileged access to financial institutions where that access is not based on prudential considerations.[139] Finally neither the Community nor other Member States are to assume the commitments of other central governments, public authorities or public undertakings.[140]

With the arrival of the third stage, a more tightly worded obligation is imposed on Member States to avoid excessive budgetary deficit, reflected the increased spillover effects of excessive deficits in monetary unions. Member States must no longer endeavour to avoid excessive deficits, they must simply avoid them.[141] Paradoxically, however, the instruments of control available to the Council during the second stage are, because of Member States' increased interdependence, of even less value during the third stage. A public statement denouncing the deficit in one Member State will reflect badly on the single currency and pattern of governance of the Community as a whole, and thus any market reaction is likely to affect all Member States adversely. To that

---

138 Article 104 (1) [*101(1)*] EC. See also Regulation 3603/93/EC, specifying definitions for the application of the prohibitions referred to in Articles 104 and 104b(1) EC, OJ 1993 L 332/1.

139 Article 104a [*102*] EC.

140 Article 104b [*103*] EC.

141 Article 104c(1) [*104(1)*] EC.

end a particular procedure is put in place from the beginning of the third stage to combat this.[142]

Article 104c(9) [*104(9)*] EC. If a Member State persists in failing to put into practice the recommendations of the Council, the Council may decide to give notice to the Member State to take, within a specified time limit, measures for the deficit reduction which is judged necessary by the Council in order to remedy the situation.

In such case, the Council may request the Member State concerned to submit reports in accordance with a specific timetable in order to examine the adjustment efforts of that Member State...

.....

11. As long as a Member State fails to comply with a decision taken in accordance with paragraph 9, the Council may decide to apply or, as the case may be, intensify one or more of the following measures:
- to require the Member State concerned to publish additional information to be specified by the Council, before issuing bonds and securities;
- to invite the European Investment Bank to reconsider its lending policy towards the Member State concerned;
- to require the Member State concerned to make a non-interest-bearing deposit of an appropriate size with the Community until the excessive deficit has, in the view of the Council been corrected;
- to impose fines of an appropriate size.

The President of the Council shall inform the European Parliament of the decisions taken.

The procedure was considered to be loose and unsatisfactory, with dissatisfaction rising to a head at the Dublin European Council in December 1996. At the European Council it was agreed that budgetary discipline needed to be reinforced through a 'Stability and Growth Pact'.[143] The Pact is a tripartite one.

It was agreed, first, that there should be a strong commitment to budgetary discipline from each Member State. To this end each Member State should commit itself to a balanced budget over the medium-term. To facilitate this a system of multilateral surveillance of national

---

142 On the application of the excessive deficit procedure see Regulation 3605/93/EC, OJ 1993 L 332/7.

143 On this see EU Bulletin 12-1996, 23.

budgetary positions and economic positions were put in place.[144] Each Member State participating in the third stage of economic and monetary union is committed to submitting a stability programme before 1 March 1999, and thereafter on an annual basis, describing how it is going to achieve a budget which is either balanced or in surplus over the medium-term.[145] The Council will give an opinion on these, having obtained an assessment from the Commission and after having consulted the Monetary Committee. In particular, it will assess whether the economic assumptions of the stability programme are realistic, whether it provides a safety margin to ensure the avoidance of an excessive deficit, and whether it is sufficient to achieve the medium-term budgetary objective.[146]

The British Government objected that Member States which did not participate in the third stage of economic and monetary union should not be required to submit 'stability programmes'. It was agreed, however, that non-participating States' budgetary positions should be subject to multilateral surveillance. To this end, an amazingly arcane compromise was agreed whereby non-participating States are subject to the same procedure as participating States except that they must subject 'convergence programmes' not 'stability programmes'. The two are to have the same content, however.[147]

If the first part of the Pact was to put in place a system of surveillance which provided for budgetary discipline over the medium-term, the second part was to put in place a mechanism which would give an early warning of an impending excessive deficit. The Council is required to monitor the implementation of the stability/convergence programmes of the Member States with a view to identifying actual or expected significant divergence from the medium-term budgetary objective. If it identifies such a divergence, it is entitled to make a recommendation to the Member State concerned to take the necessary adjustment measures. In the event that the problem persists or worsens,

---

144 This part of the Pact is contained in Regulation 1466/97/EC, OJ 1997 L 209/1.

145 Ibid., Articles 3-4.

146 Ibid., Article 5.

147 Ibid., Articles 7-10. Not unsurprisingly, the German Government considered the distinction to be totally unnecessary.

it can issue a further recommendation, this time publishing the contents of the recommendation.[148]

It was however the third part of the Pact that proved most problematic. The German Government, in particular, considered that the procedure for imposing sanctions granted too much discretion to the Council. As the latter was composed of politicians with incentives to increase public expenditure in their own States, it was doubtful how frequently it would punish offending Member States, particularly in view of the acrimony this would cause between Member States. The German Government proposed that a procedure be installed which would take effect, quasi-automatically, whenever a Member State ran an excessive budget deficit. This was opposed by the French Government which considered such a procedure to be too inflexible. The compromise agreed was a complicated one.[149] Its principal components are the following:

- As a quid pro quo for making the procedure for applying sanctions more formalistic, some flexibility is granted in deciding when a deficit exists. The Commission, in preparing its report, is not to consider a Member State's budget deficit excessive, whatever its amount, if the Member State is undergoing an exceptionally severe economic downturn. This will normally be considered to be at least an annual fall in real GDP of 2%. This figure is so high, however, that Member States could provide supporting evidence in cases where the fall was less than 2% to show that the downturn was still exceptionally severe.[150]

- Council discretion in the application of the sanctions is nominally reduced. In principle, the Council is required to apply sanctions wherever the conditions to apply Article 104c(11) [*104(11)*] EC are met. The Council, however, still has discretion to decide whether these criteria are met.[151]

- The sanctions for running an excessive deficit are spelt out. For the first two years of running a deficit, the Member State is required to leave a deposit with the Council. The size of the deposit is large, amounting to a sum which is 0.2% of GDP and one tenth of the size of the excessive deficit for each year the State

---

148 The early warning system is contained in Regulation 1466/97/EC supra n.144, Article 6 (for participating States) and Article 10 (for non-participating States).

149 It is now contained in Regulation 1467/97/EC, OJ 1997 L 209/6.

150 Ibid., Article 2.

151 Ibid., Article 6.

runs an excess deficit.[152] In principle, if the deficit is not brought under control within two years, this deposit is to be converted into a fine.[153] One is talking fantastic sums here, with Member States potentially being fined billions of euros. It is difficult to believe this will take place, and flexibility is built into the process by these sums only being spelt out 'as the rule'.

The Stability and Growth Pact undoubtedly subjects national budgetary policies to a more rigorous regime. It is unclear, however, whether this will be sufficient, as the difficulties go deeper to the heart of popular support for economic and monetary union. The trimming of budget deficits involves the cutting of public spending and therefore reduction in spending on matters such as public health or social security. It will be easy for national politicians to argue that any such cuts were forced upon them by 'Europe'. The success of economic and monetary union will depend upon the response of EU citizens to such claims.

Goodhart, C. 'European Monetary Integration' (1996) 40 *European Economic Review* 1083, 1089

If the European Union is unable to point to the overt provision of any financial support to a country, or region, in particular difficulties, how can it expect to counter the siren cries of politicians seeking to blame depression on EMU, and advocating revoking the irrevocable? Almost inevitably, EMU will be perceived in due course as seriously damaging the economic interests of some large part of some member country. When that does happen, just what do you think will keep that country willing to remain within EMU? The costs of withdrawing from a single currency, and re-establishing a separate currency, are not in reality so great. When the central political cement disintegrates, as in USSR, Yugoslavia or Czechoslovakia recently, the costs of moving from a single, to multiple currencies, are of second-order importance.

One must ask the larger question whether countries which do not feel sufficient cohesion to agree a larger transfer of fiscal competences to the federal centre are sufficiently cohesive to maintain a single currency. It is, however, partly a chicken and egg problem. Once we do have a single currency, and no balance of payments data, it will, happily, become considerably harder to estimate the net costs, or benefits, to any constituent nation of any fiscal measure. If each county in the UK had its separate

---

152 Ibid., Article 12.

153 Ibid., Article 13.

currency, could assess the effect on itself of every UK fiscal proposal, and veto those adversely affecting itself, nothing would ever get done at Westminster.

While some may, indeed, see merits in that, (and the whole subject of fiscal federalism, or subsidiarity, is intellectually fascinating), my point is only that the very existence of a single currency could help to erode national selfishness in a manner that would facilitate the subsequent transfer of suitable fiscal competences to the federal centre. Such a transfer could then further serve to support the single currency. But how can we get through the early years when a single currency is in place without either overwhelming political support or the mutual benefit of a sizeable or well designed federal budget? It will be an extremely dangerous corner to turn.

Further Reading

On the economics of monetary integration see:

Connolly, B. *The Rotten Heart of Europe: the dirty war for Europe's money* (1995, Faber & Faber, London)

De Grauwe P. *The Economics of Monetary Integration* (1997, 3rd Edition, OUP, Oxford)

Dornbusch, R. 'Euro-Fantasies' (1996) 75 *Foreign Affairs* 110

Emerson, M. *et al.*, *One Market, One Money: An Evaluation of the Potential Benefits and Costs of Forming an Economic and Monetary Union* (1992, OUP, Oxford)

Feldstein, M. 'The Political Economy of the European Economic and Monetary Union: Political Sources of an Economic Liability' (1997) 11 *Journal of Economic Perspectives* 23

Giovanni, M. *The Debate on Money in Europe* (1995, MIT Press, Cambridge)

Goodhart, C. *The Central Bank and the Financial System* (1995, Macmillan, Basingstoke)

Gros, D. & Thygesen, N. *European Monetary Integration: From the European Monetary System to European Monetary Union* (1992, Longman, London)

House of Lords Select Committee on the European Communities, An EMU of 'Ins' and 'Outs' (HMSO, Session 1995-96, 11th Report)

Johnson, C. *In with the Euro, Out with the Pound* (1996, Penguin, Harmondsworth)

Wyplosz, C. 'EMU: Why and How It Might Happen (1997) 11 *Journal of Economic Perspectives* 3

For non-economic literature see:

Busch, A. 'Central Bank Independence and the Westminster Model' (1994) 17 *West European Politics* 53
Campanella, M. 'Getting the Core: Neo-Institutionalism and the EMU' (1995) 30 *Government and Opposition* 347
Daintith, T. 'Between Domestic Democracy and an Alien Rule of Law? Some Thoughts on the "Independence" of the Bank of England' (1995) *Public Law* 118
Gormley L. & de Haan, J. 'The democratic deficit of the European Central Bank' (1996) 21 *European Law Review* 95.
Hahn, H. 'The European Central Bank: Key to European Monetary Union or Targets' (1991) 28 *Common Market Law Review* 783
Pipkorn, J. 'Legal Arrangements in the Treaty of Maastricht for the Effectiveness of the Economic and Monetary Union' (1994) 31 *Common Market Law Review* 263
Slot, P. 'The Institutional Provisions of the EMU' in Curtin, D. & Heukels, T. (eds.) *Institutional Dynamics of European Integration: Liber Amicorum Henry Schermers* (1994, Martijnus Nijhoff, Dordrecht)
Snyder, F. 'EMU-Metaphor for European Union? Institutions, Rules and Types of Regulation' in Dehousse, R. (ed) *Europe after Maastricht: An Ever Closer Union?* (1994, Law Books in Europe, Munich)
Usher, J. *The Law of Money and Financial Services in the European Community* (1994, Clarendon Press, Oxford)

6. Free Movement of Goods

I. Introduction

The model of integration initially adopted by the EC Treaty, a common market, is a form of market integration. The core of the common market is a series of 'individual economic freedoms' which limit Member State's ability to intervene in, and thus impede, this transaction economy. Streit and Musler have therefore stated that the route adopted was 'integration from below' whereby integration would occur through economic actors transacting across national frontiers.[1] Within such a view the role of free movement of goods is central, for the bulk of transnational trade still involves trade in goods.[2] Member States' ability to restrict free movement of goods is limited by a number of provisions.

Fiscal impediments to free movement are controlled by Article 12 [*25*] EC, which outlaws those taxes, customs duties and charges having equivalent effect, which are levied as a result of a good crossing a frontier, and Article 95 [*90*] EC which prohibits Member States from levying internal taxation which discriminates against imports or exports.[3]

The provisions on State aids, Articles 92-94 [*87-89*] EC, and public undertakings, Article 90 EC [*86*], further limit the extent to which Member States can adopt protectionist measures. In addition, there are

---

1 Streit, M. & Mussler, E. 'The Economic Constitution of the European Community: From "Rome" to "Maastricht"' (1995) 1 *ELJ* 5, 13. See, however the Comment by Ehlermann, C-D. (1995) 1 *ELJ* 84 who notes that through its transport, agricultural and commercial policies the EEC Treaty provided for 'integration by intervention'.

2 Internal Community trade accounted for 13.3% of Community GDP in 1992, the last year on which statistics are available, *Basic Statistics of the European Community* (1994, 31st Edition, OOPEC, Luxembourg) 299.

3 See pp. 708 ff.

general duties imposed upon Member States not to adopt any measures which will facilitate anti-competitive practices by undertakings.[4]

The most wideranging restriction, however, is that contained in Article 30 [*28*] EC.[5]

Article 30 [*28*] EC. Quantitative restrictions on imports and all measures having equivalent effect shall, without prejudice to the following provisions, be prohibited between Member States.

The restriction on quantitative restrictions and measures having equivalent (MEE) on imports contained in Article 30 [*28*] EC is mirrored by an identically worded prohibition in relation to exports in Article 34 [*29*] EC.

Article 34 [*29*] EC. Quantitative restrictions on exports, and all measures having equivalent effect, shall be prohibited between Member States.

This separation of market integration from other forms of integration is artificial. Markets do not exist in a vacuum but are embedded in and forged by surrounding social relations.[6] Normatively, it is difficult within a mixed economy therefore to detach the market from other areas of policy or social life without disruptive side-effects.

---

4 e.g. Case C-2/91 *Meng* [1993] ECR I-5751. Gyselen, L. 'Anti-competitive State Measures under the EC Treaty: Towards a Substantive Test of Illegality' (1994) 19 *European Law Review Competition Checklist* 55.

5 A consequence of the general nature of Article 30 [*28*] EC is that where a measure may fall within both the ambit of it and another provision of the EC Treaty which regulates free movement of goods it will be regulated by the latter provision, Case 74/76 *Ianelli et al. v Meroni* [1977] ECR 557. The one exception to this is State aids. See Joined Cases C-78-83/90 *Compagnie Commerciale de l'Ouest v Receveur principal des Douanes de la Pallice Port* [1992] ECR I-1847, [1994] 2 CMLR 425. For criticism see Fernandez Martin, J-M. & Stehmann, O. 'Product Market Integration versus Regional Cohesion in the Community' (1991) 16 *ELRev* 216.

6 Granovetter, M. 'Economic Action, Social Structure and Embeddedness' (1985) 91 *American Journal of Sociology* 481.

Excessive concentration on the 'market' may thus obscure other areas of social concern, in particular collective goods such as protection of the environment or protection of public health, or even undermine the very social relations that led to the establishment of the market in the first place.

Pelkmans, J. 'Economic Theories of Integration Revisited' (1980) 18 *Journal of Common Market Studies* 333, 333-335

The European Communities attempt to integrate developed economies of a mixed, capitalist variety. Such economies are characterised by a predominance of private ownership of the means of production over public ownership and by the allocation of considerable economic decision-making power to the government complementing or superseding that of private economic agents. How predominant private ownership is, how considerable the decision-making power of the government is and what means parliament and social pressures will permit the government to use are questions that indicate the wide range of actual manifestations of the mixed economic order to be expected...

Though there is surely merit in distinguishing the concepts of market and policy integration, the sharp separation of the two is inconsistent with the nature of the mixed economic order. I label the separation of market and policy integration the '*dichotomy of economic integration theory*'.

The dichotomy finds its origin in the discussion about economic integration during the 1950s. Whilst the 'liberalists' and 'dirigists' agreed about the desirability of removing governmental border intervention, they differed sharply about the necessity of creating common policies. In the constitutional negotiations about the European Communities, therefore the understandable tendency has been to emphasize the points of agreement and seek for vague, common denominators on elements of potential policy conflict or leave them out altogether. As Pinder has forcefully argued, the Rome Treaty and the process of economic integration in the Western European practice are predominantly concerned with market integration and the negative policy integration it requires.[7] Positive policy integration is typically avoided, except in agriculture, and in matters of competition which once again refers to market integration. The dichotomy of economic integration theory is the counterpart of the separation of negative and positive integration in practice.

Notwithstanding this, only limited provision was made for protection of public goods in Article 36 [*30*] EC.

---

7 Pinder, R. 'Positive and negative integration: some problems of economic union in the EEC' (1968) *The World Today* 88.

Article 36 [*30*] EC. The provisions of Articles 30 to 34 shall not preclude prohibitions or restrictions on imports, exports or goods in transit justified on grounds of public morality, public policy or public security; the protection of health and life of humans, animals or plants; the protection of national treasures possessing artistic, historic or archaeological value or the protection of industrial or commercial property. Such prohibitions or restrictions shall not, however, constitute a means of arbitrary discrimination or a disguised restriction on trade between Member States.

II. The Expansion of Article 30 [*28*] EC

The reason for the limited nature of Article 36 [*30*] EC was that Article 30 [*28*] EC was only intended to have a limited remit. The Spaak Report suggests that it was only intended to outlaw measures which had an obvious protectionist intent and effect[8] and it bore a strong resemblance to trade provisions in other treaties, such as Article XI in the General Agreement on Tariffs and Trade, which had only that role.[9] Any suggestion that Article 30 [*28*] EC should be interpreted in a similar manner was swept away in the *Dassonville* judgment.

Case 8/74 Procureur du Roi v Dassonville [1974] ECR 837, [1974] 2 CMLR 436

Under Belgian law products, such as Scotch whisky, which bore a designation of origin could be sold if accompanied by a certificate of origin. Benoit and Dassonville, two Brussels traders, were prosecuted for selling Scotch whisky, 'VAT 69' and 'Johnny Walker', without this certificate of origin. They had imported this whisky not directly from the United Kingdom, which was impossible as competitors had exclusive dealing agreements with the British producers, but via France. In France, however, there was no requirement as to

---

8 For discussion see Marenco, G. 'Pour Une Interpretation Traditionelle de la Notion de Mesure d'Effet Equivalent à une Restriction Quantitative' (1984) *CDE* 291, 316-317.

9 Jackson, J. *World Trade and the Law of GATT (A Legal Analysis of the General Agreement on Tariffs and Trade)* (1969, Michie, Charlottesville, VA) 314-315.

certificate of origin, and it was thus very difficult to obtain a certificate of origin for products purchased there.

4. It emerges from the file and from the oral proceedings that a trader wishing to import into Belgium Scotch whisky which is already in free circulation in France, can obtain such a certificate only with great difficulty, unlike the importer who imports directly from the producer country.

5. All trading rules enacted by Member States which are capable of hindering, directly or indirectly, actually or potentially intra-Community trade are to be considered as measures having an effect equivalent to quantitative restrictions.

6. In the absence of a Community system guaranteeing for consumers the authenticity of a producer's designation of origin, if a Member State takes measures to prevent unfair practices in this connexion, it is however subject to the condition that these measures should be reasonable and that the means of proof required should not act as a hindrance to trade between Member States and should, in consequence, be accessible to all Community nationals.

7. Even without having to examine whether or not such measures are covered by Article 36, they must not in any case, by virtue of the principle expressed in the second sentence of that Article, constitute a means of arbitrary discrimination or a disguised restriction on trade between Member States.

8. That may be the case with formalities, required by a Member State for the purpose of proving the origin of a product, which only direct importers are really in a position to satisfy without facing serious difficulties.

9. Consequently, the requirement by a Member State of a certificate of authenticity which is less easily obtainable by importers of an authentic product which has been put into free circulation in a regular manner in another Member State than by importers of the same product coming directly from the country of origin constitutes a measure having equivalent effect to a quantitative restriction as prohibited by the Treaty.

It is therefore the *effects* of the measure rather than its *intent* which determines whether there has been a breach of Article 30 [*28*] EC. Beyond that, the precise ambit of *Dassonville* is uncertain. It is not subject to any *de minimis* threshold or to any requirement that the restrictive effects of the measure be demonstrated empirically.[10] Yet, interpreted literally, any State measure which affects conditions of supply or demand would fall foul of Article 30 [*28*] EC and have to be justified before the Court. Law restricting pub opening times or newspaper rounds; age limits on who can buy alcohol; a statutory minimum wage, all potentially fall within the definition.

Traditionally, many authors have believed that this formula accurately states the law. Any measure that affects, or potentially affects, trade therefore falls within the ambit of Article 30 [*28*] EC.[11] The advantages of this approach are perceived to be that it widens the scope of judicial review, and that it provides a broad tableau against which national measures can be rationalised, whereby they will only be deemed to be legal if they are in the public interest, do not arbitrarily discriminate and are proportionate. On such a basis the test renders Article 30 [*28*] EC into the catalyst for the transformation of the EC Treaty into an 'economic constitution',[12] whereby any measure affecting economic activity is subject to judicial review.

The sheer breadth of such an approach has provoked scepticism amongst other commentators. Some have argued that it should not be applied mechanically.[13] Others reject its normative basis outright on the grounds that it is impossible to apply consistently, and indeed has not been applied consistently and that it places disputes before the Court

---

10 e.g. Cases 177 & 178/82 *Van de Haar* [1984] ECR 1797, [1985] 2 CMLR 566; Case C-126/91 *Schutzverband gegen Unwesen in der Wirtschaft v Yves Rocher GmbH* [1993] ECR I-2361.

11 Gormley, L. 'Recent Case Law on the Free Movement of Goods: Some Hot Potatoes' (1990) 27 *CMLRev* 825; Gormley, L. '"Actually or Potentially, Directly or Indirectly"? Obstacles to the Free Movement of Goods' (1989) 9 *YEL* 197; Arnull, A. 'What shall we do on Sunday?' (1991) 16 *ELRev* 112; Verloren Van Themaat, P. 'The Contribution to the Establishment of the Internal Market by the Case-Law of the Court of Justice of the European Communities' in Bieber, R., Dehousse, R. & Weiler J. (eds.) *1992: One European Market* (1988, Baden Baden, Nomos).

12 See Chapter 17.

13 Advocate-General Van Gerven in Case 145/88 *Torfaen BC v B & Q* [1989] ECR 765, [1990] 1 CMLR 337; Advocate-General Tesauro in Case C-292/92 *Hünermund v Landesapotheker Baden-Würtemburg* [1993] ECR I-6787; Steiner, J. 'Drawing the Line: Uses and Abuses of Article 30 EEC' (1992) 29 *CMLRev.* 749, 758-759.

which the latter is ill-equipped to resolve.[14] It has also been argued that the test misconstrues the EC Treaty, which is only a system of partial integration, and which must therefore tread a careful path between the needs of the single market and the regulatory concerns of Member States.[15]

The debate will no doubt continue. The Court's continued reference to *Dassonville* has resulted in critics being unable to ignore it. The uncertainty of the subsequent case law has meant, however, that the supporters of the *Dassonville* formula are unable to resort to it without further ado and that the other strands in Article 30 [*28*] EC must also be examined.

III. The Prohibition on Discrimination

i. Discrimination and the Political Economy of the Market

Within EC law a link has been established between the non-discrimination principle and notions of fairness. The principle has thus been declared to be a fundamental right.[16] One observer has thus stated that 'all attempts to comprehend the content of the equality principle ... concentrate on the concept of arbitrary action which, as the contrary correlate of justice, means nothing less than the "radical, absolute negation" of justice and consequently covers every equal and unequal treatment which is simply irreconcilable with a sense of what is right and wrong.'[17]

---

14 Chalmers, D. 'Free Movement of Goods within the European Community: An Unhealthy Addiction to Scotch Whisky?' (1993) 42 *ICLQ* 269, 274-278.

15 Wils, W. 'The Search for the Rule in Article 30 EEC: much ado about nothing' (1993) 19 *ELRev* 475, 482.

16 e.g. Case C-44/89 *Von Deetzen v Hauptzollamt Oldenburg* [1991] ECR I-5119.

17 Schwarze, J. *European Administrative Law* (1992, OOPEC, Sweet & Maxwell, London) 553-554.

Its operation within the market economy, whereby it requires that Member States treat competing imports and domestic products in an identical manner, suggests a narrower function, namely to ensure the terms of competition are not distorted[18]:-

> exclusive discriminatory arrangements tend to establish favoured markets in favour of the signatories from whom the goods of other countries are excluded and in doing so deny the opportunity to producers outside the country to sell their goods on a competitive basis. Instead of the trade flowing in accordance with relative price considerations and other market conditions, it is securely directed in channels leading to an assured market with no fear of outside competition and thereby, in many instances, affording protection to high cost industries.[19]

Such a concept takes a narrow view of fairness. It rewards only those who are competitive and well-equipped to take advantage of the market. A wider concept of non-discrimination which aimed at 'substantive fairness' would not take as its comparators whether goods were competing or not. It would take into account other social concerns. For example, it might look at whether goods had an equivalent impact on the environment. In terms of regional or social cohesion it might examine whether the goods had a different impact upon the region. The Court has traditionally rejected such an approach.

Case C-21/88 Du Pont de Nemours Italiana SpA v Unità sanitaria locale No 2 di Carrara [1990] ECR I-889, [1991] 3 CMLR 25.

All Italian public authorities were required to purchase at least 30% of their supplies from undertakings based in Mezzogiorno region of Southern Italy, one of the poorest regions of that State. The local health authority of Carrara issued a tender procedure for supply of radiological films and liquids. The procedure was divided into two lots, one for undertakings from the Mezzogiorno, the other

---

18 See also, in this respect, Joined Cases 32-33/58 *SNUPAT v High Authority* [1959] ECR 127.

19 Hyder, K. *Equality of Treatment and Trade Discrimination in International Law* (1968, Martijnus Nijhoff, The Hague) 5-6.

for all other undertakings. Du Pont de Nemours Italiana SpA claimed that this division breached, *inter alia*, Article 30 [*28*] EC.

7. In its first question the national court seeks to ascertain whether national rules reserving to undertakings established in certain regions of the national territory a proportion of public supply contracts are contrary to Article 30, which prohibits quantitative restrictions on imports and all measures having equivalent effect.

.....

11. It must be pointed out in that regard that such a system, which favours goods processed in a particular region of a Member State, prevents the authorities and public bodies concerned from procuring some of the supplies they need from undertakings situated in other Member States. Accordingly, it must be held that products originating in other Member States suffer discrimination in comparison with products manufactured in the Member State in question, with the result that the normal course of intra-Community trade is hindered.

12. That conclusion is not affected by the fact that the restrictive effects of a preferential system of the kind at issue are borne in the same measure both by products manufactured by undertakings from the Member State in question which are not situated in the region covered by the preferential system and by products manufactured by undertakings established in other Member States.

13. It must be emphasised in the first place that, although not all the products of the Member State in question benefit by comparison with products abroad, the fact remains that all the products benefiting by the preferential system are domestic products; secondly, the fact that the restrictive effect exercised by a State measure on imports does not benefit all domestic products but only some cannot exempt the measure in question from the prohibition set out in Article 30.

The defence of such a position is normally grounded on the basis that discriminatory trade measures has a cost through its stymieing of individual choice and imposition of a 'tax' on local consumers by preventing them from purchasing the cheapest product at the cheapest price. The benefits of such action are, meanwhile, rarely apparent as unforeseen consequences and risks are an inherent part of State intervention and often frustrate the objects of that intervention.[20]

Streit, M. & Musler, W. 'The Economic Constitution of the European Community: From "Rome" to "Maastricht"' (1995) 1 *European Law Journal* 5, 10-11

Modern economic constitutions, however, are heavily influenced by political attempts to pursue material objectives as opposed to the 'formal rationality'. As a consequence of political efforts to assign particular economic results to specific groups, formal law becomes 'materialised'. 'Ethical imperatives or utilitarian rules of expediency or political maxims' are used to pursue specific material objectives. The ethical imperative which is predominantly employed to justify material legislation and to acquiesce in activities of interest groups is the maxim of social justice.

To legislate in accordance with this maxim requires the setting of concrete purposes to a self-organising system, although such a system has no purpose of its own. Conceptualisations of social justice always imply the presence of an external observer of the economic system who compares and judges in particular perceived individual possibilities to earn a market income as well as achieved income positions. Furthermore, it is assumed that (1) the system lends itself to an effective end-dependent rule-setting and (2) that sufficient steering-knowledge is available to achieve ends related to what is considered as social justice.

It can be countered that because the State will never have sufficient steering-knowledge to predict all the consequences of intervention, it does not follow that all those consequences will necessarily be undesirable. The existence of the European Social Fund (Articles 123 - 125 [*146-148*] EC), and the Titles on Industry (Article 130 [*157*] EC) and Economic and Social Cohesion (Articles 130a - 130e [*158-162*] EC) allow for the adoption of such an approach, and this has been reinforced by TEU moving the Community away from being a predominantly economic community towards being a political community.

---

20 An extensive discussion of 'the mirage of social justice' can be found in Hayek, F. *Law, Legislation and Liberty*, Vol.2, 'The Mirage of Social Justice' (1976, The University of Chicago Press).

Case C-2/90 Commission v Belgium [1992] ECR I-4431, [1993] 1 CMLR 365

In 1987 the Belgian region of Wallonia amended a Decree prohibiting, with a small number of exceptions, the storage, tipping, dumping of waste produced outside Wallonia. The Commission brought an Article 169 [*226*] EC action, claiming that such a law violated, *inter alia*, Article 30 [*28*] EC. The Court considered that such a ban was a restriction on free movement of goods. The ban could only be justified on environment grounds, however, if it was found not to discriminate against imported waste.

33. However, the Commission contends that these mandatory requirements cannot be invoked in the present case because the measure in question discriminates against waste from other Member States which is no more harmful than the waste produced in Wallonia.

34. It is true that the mandatory requirements are to be taken into account only with regard to measures which apply to national and imported products without distinction: see Case C-1/90, *Aragonesa de Publicidad* [1991] ECR I-4151. However, in order to determine whether the obstacle in question is discriminatory, the particular type of waste must be taken into account. The principle that environmental damage should as a priority be rectified at source - a principle laid down by Article 130r(2) EEC for action by the Community relating to the environment - means that it is for each region, commune or other local entity to take appropriate measures to receive, process and dispose of its own waste. Consequently, waste should be disposed of as close as possible to the place where it is produced in order to keep the transport of waste to the minimum practicable.

35. Furthermore this principle accords with the principles of self-sufficiency and proximity set out in the Basle Convention of 22 March 1989 on the control of transborder movements of hazardous waste and the disposal thereof, to which the Community is a party.

36. It follows that, having regard to the differences between waste produced in one place and that in another and its connection with the place where it is produced, the contested measures cannot be considered to be discriminatory.

This analysis can be applied to areas beyond the environment. Local authority grants to museums to enable them to purchase works of local cultural interest fall within Article 30 [*28*] EC, yet could similarly be argued to be non-discriminatory. The reason for this is that certain policies, environmental and cultural protection being the most prominent, have a spatial element in the sense that they envisage a local culture or a local environment which needs protecting. This will often justify a more favourable treatment of home production. This contradicts the notion of comparative advantage, as it suggests the development of a policy whereby particular operators will be placed at a competitive advantage because of their location or nationality.[21]

ii. The Non-Discrimination Principle and Local Autonomy

Overt discrimination, which uses criteria which make explicit reference to either nationality or origin is prohibited by Article 30 [*28*] EC. In addition covert discrimination, the use of criteria which on their face are neutral but which in fact also prejudice imports more than domestic products, is also prohibited.

Case 207/83 Commission v United Kingdom [1985] ECR 1201, [1985] 2 CMLR 259

A British statutory instrument required that four categories of goods - textiles, domestic electrical appliances, cutlery and footwear - must be marked with an indication of origin unless they were second-hand goods or supplied in certain special circumstances. The Commission brought an action under Article 169 [*226*] EC, claiming that, notwithstanding that it also applied to British goods, the requirement of an indication of origin also breached Article 30 [*28*] EC.

15. As regards the possible effect of the contested Order on trade, the United Kingdom points out that the requirements laid down in Article 2 of the Order concern the retail sale of all goods covered by the Order, whether imported or not. Some of these goods, for example woollen knitwear and cutlery, are produced in the United Kingdom in substantial quantities.

16. It should first be observed, with regard to that argument, that in order to escape the obligations imposed on him by the legislation in question, the retailer will tend, as the

---

21 Chalmers, D. 'The Single Market: From Prima Donna to Journeyman' in Shaw, J. & More, G. (eds.) *New Legal Dynamics of the European Union* (1995, Clarendon, Oxford).

Commission has rightly pointed out, to ask his wholesalers to supply him with goods which are already origin marked. That tendency has been confirmed by complaints received by the Commission. Thus, it emerges from the documents before the Court that the Groupement des industries françaises des appareils d'équipement ménager [French Domestic Appliance Manufacturers' Association] informed the Commission that French manufacturers of domestic appliances who wish to sell their products on the United Kingdom market have had to mark such products systematically in response to pressure brought to bear on them by their distributors. The effects of the contested provisions are therefore liable to spread to the wholesale trade and even to manufacturers.

17. Secondly, it has to be recognized that the purpose of indications of origin or origin-marking is to enable consumers to distinguish between domestic and imported products and that this enables them to assert any prejudices which they may have had against foreign products. As the Court has had occasion to emphasize in various contexts, the Treaty, by establishing a common market and progressively approximating the economic policies of the Member States seeks to unite national markets in a single market having the characteristics of a domestic market. Within such a market, the origin-marking requirement not only makes the marketing in a Member State of goods produced in other Member States in the sector in question more difficult; it also has the effect of slowing down economic interpenetration in the Community by handicapping the sale of goods produced as a result of the division of labour between Member States.

A broad interpretation of covert discrimination poses considerable difficulties for national regulatory regimes. Most regimes contain two features - they impose regulatory burdens on those they seek to regulate and, insofar as they seek to guide behaviour in a particular manner, those costs will require different levels of adjustment from individual operators, many of whom will be competing. At one very broad level all regulatory regimes are, therefore, discriminatory. The solution to this dilemma is described below.

Joined Cases C-401/92 & C-402/92 Criminal Proceedings against Tankstation 't Heukske vof and J.B.E. Boermans [1994] ECR I-2199, [1995] 3 CMLR 501

Advocate-General Van Gerven

23. ..., the question arises as to when measures affect in the same manner in law, 'in law' and 'in fact', the marketing of domestic and imported goods.

In my view, a measure affects the marketing of products in the same manner where, depending on its aim and its wording, it applies in the same manner to domestic and imported products - by this I mean essentially that it is applicable 'without distinction' - and this continues to be the case where the measure is considered to be in conjunction with other legal rules.

Through the requirement that the measure 'should affect in the same manner, in fact, the marketing of domestic products', the Court doubtless means that in fact, that is to say, *in point of its effects*, the measure may not give rise to unequal access to the market on the part of domestic and imported products. However, the question is how those effects are to be examined. Does it turn on the effects of a national measure in individual situations ('is a situation involved in which the national measure gives rise to unequal treatment of domestic or imported products, or is such a situation conceivable') or, on the contrary following the Court's case-law on equal treatment of men and women - does it turn on the overall effect of the measure ('on an overall view, is the national measure liable to restrict the access to the market of imported products more than that of domestic products')?

In *Keck* and *Mithouard*,[22] the Court seems to me to have opted for an overall assessment and therefore not for an assessment of individual situations (which should, moreover, for the most part be left to the national court). Whereas in my two Opinions in those cases I argued that the French prohibition of resale at a loss could, in some cases, impede imported products' access to the French market more than that of domestic products, in its judgment of the Court simply held that Article 30 of the EC Treaty 'is to be interpreted as not applying to legislation of a Member State imposing a general prohibition of resale at a loss'. The Court was manifestly convinced that, on an overall view, national legislation such as that at issue did not impede the access to the market of imported products more than that of domestic products.

Even allowing for such constraints, the width of the non-discrimination principle is considerable. It could be argued, for example, that a requirement that one drive on the left-hand side of the road is discriminatory, as it is imported left-hand side drive cars which are most prejudiced by this. The principle also engenders considerable uncertainty. The discriminatory nature of the measure will depend on shifts in comparative advantage between imports and domestic products. A measure which might not be discriminatory one year could be discriminatory the following year. Equally, analysis of whether a measure acts disproportionately to the detriment of imports would require the collection and analysis of a considerable amount of data. Few

22 Joined Cases C-267 & C-268/91 *Criminal Proceedings against Keck and Mithouard* [1993] ECR-I 6097, [1995] 1 CMLR 101.

litigants would have the means to carry out such a task, and it is arguable whether the Court is ill-equipped to carry out such a task.

It can be argued that the question of whether a measure is discriminatory should not simply be dependent on the collection of economic data, but regard should also be had to other factors. In other areas of EC law, this has been done by stating where a measure is *prima facie* indirectly discriminatory it will not be illegal where it can be objectively justified.[23] The danger with such an approach is that many local measures, the British left hand drive one being a prime example, have no justification other than the assertion of local choice. These would still be threatened by such an analysis.

A third approach might be the one suggested more generally for Article 30 [*28*] EC by Wils.[24] He has suggested that the ambit of Article 30 [*28*] EC should be determined by balancing in each case the degree of obstruction created by the measure against its valued regulatory effect and its effectiveness in pursuing its objectives. The value of such an approach is that it squarely addresses the problems posed for local autonomy posed by a wide interpretation of Article 30 [*28*] EC. The disadvantages are that there would be little legal certainty with each case having little predictive value for subsequent cases. There is also a danger in giving such a large amount of discretion to national judges. Different judges might take account of very different influences with the risk that not only the application of the non-discrimination principle would oscillate wildly in different jurisdictions but that some would interpret it in such a minimalist manner as to negate its effect.

iii. The Operation of the Non-Discrimination Principle

The non-discrimination principle prohibits not only national measures which discriminate in favour of domestic products and against imports, but also those which discriminate between imports.

---

23 See pp. 725-728.

24 Wils, W. 'The Search for the Rule in Article 30 EEC: much ado about nothing' (1993) 18 *ELRev* 475.

Case 104/75 Officier van Justitie te Rotterdam v De Peiper [1976] ECR 613, [1976] 2 CMLR 271

Dutch legislation required that a 'file' on any pharmaceutical, containing details of its packaging, composition and method of preparation, must be presented to the competent authorities in the Netherlands for certification. The details in the file had to be signed and endorsed by 'the person who is responsible for the manufacture abroad'. Centrafarm was engaged in parallel imports of Valium from the United Kingdom, whereby rather than purchasing the drug from the manufacturer, Hoffman La Roche, it bought them from a wholesaler in the United Kingdom, and then shipped them into the Netherlands. Hoffman La Roche refused to give the documents to Centrafarm necessary for preparation of the latter's file. De Peiper, the manager director of Centrafarm, was then prosecuted under Dutch law when it marketed Valium in the Netherlands under its own trademark, 'Diazepam', without having had the file endorsed by the authorities.

10. The first question envisages a factual situation which the Kantonrechter describes as follows:
- a pharmaceutical product prepared in accordance with a uniform method of preparation and qualitative and quantitative composition is lawfully in circulation in several Member States, in the sense that, in pursuance of the national systems of legislation of these States, the requisite authorizations have been granted in relation to that product to the manufacturer 'or the person responsible for putting the product on the market' in the Member State in question.
- the fact that such authorizations have been granted in each of the Member States is made known by general notice given by official publication or in some other way; and
- this product is in every respect similar to a product in respect of which the public health authorities of the Member State into which the first product has been imported already possess the documents relating to the method of preparation and also to the quantitative and qualitative composition, since these documents were produced to them previously by the manufacturer or his duly appointed importer in support of an application for authorization to place them on the market.

11. The Court is asked to rule whether national authorities faced with such a situation adopt a measure equivalent to a quantitative restriction and prohibited by the Treaty when they make the authorization to place a product on the market, for which a parallel importer has applied, conditional upon the production of documents identical with those which the manufacturer or his duly appointed importer has already lodged with them.

12. National measures of the kind in question have an effect equivalent to a quantitative restriction and are prohibited under Article 30 of the Treaty if they are likely to constitute an obstacle, directly or indirectly, actually or potentially, to imports between Member States.

13. Rules or practices which result in imports being channelled in such a way that only certain traders can effect these imports, whereas others are prevented from doing so, constitute such an obstacle to imports.

In view of the difficulties in ascertaining when a measure indirectly discriminates against imports, the circumstances in which the Court will find a measure to discriminate indirectly between imports are likely to be rare.

The principle of non-discrimination in EC law does not apply uniformly, however. Whilst it acts to protect imports, it does not reach so far as to prevent Member States according national products worse treatment than imports. This situation is known as reverse discrimination.

Case 98/86 Ministère Public v Mathot [1987] ECR 809, [1988] 1 CMLR 411

Mathot was prosecuted under a Belgian law which required Belgian processors of butter to indicate their name and address on the packaging of the butter. Imports of butter were exempt from this requirement. Mathot pleaded that this breached Article 30 [*28*] EC as it placed Belgian producers of butter at a competitive disadvantage vis-à-vis other producers.

7. With regard to Article 30 EEC, it must be emphasised that the purpose of that provision is to eliminate obstacles to the importation of goods and not to ensure that goods of national origin always enjoy the same treatment as imported goods. A difference of treatment as between goods which is not capable of restricting imports or of prejudicing the marketing of imported goods does not fall within the prohibition contained in that Article (judgment of 23 October 1986 in Case 355/85, *Driancourt v Cognet* [1986] ECR 323).

8. However, in a case such as that described in the order for reference, and even if there is discrimination against domestically-produced butter, such a difference of treatment can in no circumstances restrict the importation of butter or prejudice the marketing of imported butter. Article 30 EEC is not therefore infringed by such rules.

9. With regard to the question whether the difference of treatment mentioned above is of such a nature as to infringe the general principle of non-discrimination, it should be remembered that, according to the case law of the Court, treatment which works to the detriment of national products as compared with imported products and which is put into effect by a member-State in a sector which is not subject to Community rules or in relation to which there has been no harmonisation of national laws does not come within the scope of Community law (judgment of 23 October 1986 in *Driancourt v Cognet* cited above).

It has been argued that the notion of reverse discrimination flies in the face of Article 6 [*12*] EC, the non-discrimination provision, which, on its face, applies to all Community operators or goods.[25] Reverse discrimination can be distinguished, however, on the grounds that it arises out of the limits on the reach of Community law. As the matter falls outside Community law, Article 6 [*12*] EC does not apply as the matter does not fall within the Treaty.

In this respect two situations must be distinguished. The first is where the Member State discriminates against domestic products for reasons that do not stem out of EC law. A provision which allows higher taxes to be imposed upon domestic products is an example. The second situation is where imports enjoy certain EC law rights, but a Member State refuses to extend these rights to domestic products. It is in this latter situation that abolition of reverse discrimination might prove problematic. Reverse discrimination results here from imports being granted privileges by EC law, which go beyond merely being accorded equal treatment on the market of the importing Member State.

The distinction is important as a result of the *Cassis de Dijon* judgment.[26] Whilst restraints were placed on Member States' freedom to regulate imports, they were free to regulate the conditions of production of domestic products. This doctrine would be undermined by the abolition of reverse discrimination. For domestic production could argue that a restriction which was illegal in respect of imports, which had to

---

25 Kon, S. 'Aspects of Reverse Discrimination in Community Law' (1981) 6 *ELRev* 75.

26 Case 120/78 *REWE Zentral v Bundesmonopolverwaltung für Branntwein* [1979] ECR 649, [1979] 3 CMLR 494.

comply with their own domestic regime, would be discriminatory if it was applied to it.

Creating a dual regime in this manner, with one law for imports and another for domestic products, provides incentives for operators to cheat by passing off domestic products as imports and creates the danger of trade distortion.

Case 229/83 Association des Centres Distributeurs Leclerc & Others v Sarl 'Au blé vert' & Others [1985] ECR 1, [1985] 2 CMLR 286

French law required retailers, subject to a few exceptions, to sell books at between 95-100% of a price fixed for them by the publisher in the case of books produced in France, and by the importer in the case of imports. In the case of reimports books could not be sold at below 95% of that initially fixed by the French publisher. A number of booksellers brought an action to stop Thouars Distribution, a member of the 'Centre Leclerc' supermarket chain, from selling books at below these fixed prices. It was argued that this regime constituted a breach of Article 30 [*28*] EC. The Court considered that, in general, the French scheme discriminated against imports, as the importer was at a different stage in the commercial process from the publisher.

26. ... in so far as the legislation applies to books published in the Member State concerned and re-imported following exportation to another Member State, a provision requiring such books to be sold at the retail price fixed by the publisher does not make a distinction between domestic and imported books. Nevertheless, such a provision discourages the marketing of re-imported books by preventing the importer from passing on in the retail price an advantage resulting from a lower price obtained in the exporting Member State. Accordingly, it constitutes a measure equivalent in effect to a quantitative restriction on imports, contrary to Article 30.

27. However, the above finding is not applicable where it is established that the books in question were exported for the sole purpose of re-importation in order to circumvent legislation of the type at issue.

Wyatt and Dashwood perceive *Leclerc* to be no different from *Matthot*. They consider the measure to be in commercial reality a purely 'internal measure', and therefore indistinguishable from the other reverse discrimination cases.[27] Others suggest an alternate rationale, namely that the judgment developed an 'abuse of rights' doctrine, whereby the Court would not allow a trader to create an artificial situation merely to bring a national regime down.[28] The distinction is important as it affects the burden of proof, something which will often be difficult to establish in this area. If the question is, in essence, one of reverse discrimination it is for the trader to establish that the purpose of the trade was not to circumvent the national legislation in order to bring it within Article 30 [*28*] EC. The abuse of rights doctrine provides a defence for a Member State to do a measure that falls within Article 30 [*28*] EC. As an exception to the general prohibition contained in that provision, the burden of proof falls upon the Member State.[29]

IV. Non-Discriminatory Restrictions on Imports

i. Cassis de Dijon and Market Integration

If Article 30 [*28*] EC were merely confined to outlawing discriminatory measures, it would only liberalise trade to a limited extent. The principal barriers to trade in the late twentieth century arise not from protectionist 'frontier' measures but from the technical regulations with which all goods must comply. The number for each Member State runs into the thousands. In 1989 alone the Commission estimated that France, Germany and the United Kingdom published 350, 650 and 400 new standards each.[30] Traditionally, these regulations differed from one country to another and even where they were similar they were not

---

27 Wyatt, D. & Dashwood, A. *European Community Law* (1993, 3rd Edition, Sweet & Maxwell, London) 232.

28 Oliver, P. 'A Review of the Case Law of the Court of Justice on Articles 30 to 36 EEC in 1985' (1986) 23 *CMLRev* 325, 327.

29 Case C-131/93 *Commission v Germany* [1994] ECR I-3303, [1995] 2 CMLR 278.

30 EC Commission, *Green Paper on the Development of European Standardisation*, COM (90) 456 final, 9 n.3.

necessarily recognised as such by the different Member States. The consequence was that goods had to be adapted for each national market.

In *Cassis de Dijon* the Court extended Article 30 [*28*] EC to cover any measure, albeit a non-discriminatory one, which restricted an import entering a Member State's market unless it was necessary to satisfy a public interest requirement.[31] A good lawfully marketed or manufactured in one Member State had, in the absence of good reason, to be admitted to another Member State. At its simplest the judgment had three strands.

It widened the scope of Article 30 [*28*] EC considerably. The focus of the provision was shifted from whether a measure had a discriminatory effect to whether it had a *restrictive* effect upon trade. This prevented Member States from insulating national markets within a thicket of national regulations, and allowed for increased competition and consumer choice. The British consumer could expect to find in British supermarkets not just beer made according to traditional British methods of production but also German, Belgian and Italian each made according to their own traditional methods of products.

The philosophy underlying Article 30 [*28*] EC is also altered. The non-discrimination principle does not affect the regulatory model chosen by a Member State provided that model is applied equally to everyone. By contrast, *Cassis de Dijon* is deregulatory in nature. It implies that some models of regulation insofar as they affect imports will never be justified, and thus have no place within the single market. It asserts a freedom to trade, albeit a heavily conditioned one, which can be asserted in a unitary manner throughout the single market, no matter what regime the Member State has chosen.[32]

The second is, if not the establishment, then at least the development of the 'mandatory requirements' doctrine.[33] The expansion of the market norms in *Cassis de Dijon* posed a threat to national

---

31 Case 120/78 *REWE-Zentral AG v Bundesmonopolverwaltung für Branntwein* [1979] ECR 649, [1979] 3 CMLR 494. This case has already been set out at p. 18.

32 Chalmers, D. 'Repackaging the Internal Market - The Ramifications of the *Keck* Judgment (1994) 19 *ELRev* 385, 392-396.

33 This was arguably established in Case 8/74 *Procureur du Roi v Dassonville* [1974] ECR 837, [1974] 2 CMLR 436.

measures protecting interests such as protection of the consumer and protection of the environment, which are not included in Article 36 [*30*] EC. The mandatory requirements doctrine accommodates this by allowing Member States to restrict trade for reasons other than those contained in Article 36 [*30*] EC. Yet it can be queried whether it does this satisfactorily. It will be the European Court, not any legislature, which will decide which interests are sufficiently valuable to merit protection. Furthermore, it is courts, not necessarily the best institutions to make difficult social choices, who are given the task of reconciling conflicts between the market norms contained in Article 30 [*28*] EC and other social policies.

The third strand is the development of the doctrine of equivalence or mutual recognition. In applying restrictions Member States are required to take into account the requirements that imports have had to satisfy in other Member States. The implication from this is that where imports have had to satisfy equivalent requirements in other Member States, Member States should not be able to regulate them anew. On its face, this seems very sensible as it cuts out duplicatory regulation. As shall be seen, however, it has become increasingly difficult to assess when equivalence exists.[34]

ii. The Reach of Cassis de Dijon

The extent of the shift in the interpretation of Article 30 [*28*] EC generated by *Cassis de Dijon* was unclear. Barents argued that if goods had been lawfully marketed and produced in one Member State, then any regulation by the importing Member State would amount to a form of double taxation. Any regulation of imports, be it direct or indirect, by a Member State therefore fell within Article 30 [*28*] EC, and was only permissible if it fell within either Article 36 [*30*] EC or the mandatory requirements doctrine.[35]

---

34 See p. 319.

35 Barents, R. 'New Developments in Measures Having Equivalent Effect' (1981) 18 *CMLRev* 271, 291-296.

Conversely, Marenco has argued that laws such as the one at issue in *Cassis de Dijon* were merely an example of hidden discrimination, as they entailed extra costs for imports by forcing them to comply with compositional requirements in Germany when they had already been submitted to compositional requirements in Article 30 [*28*] EC. Cassis de Dijon did not therefore mark a huge shift from earlier case law. Furthermore, it did not extend to cover all regulation which affected imports. A law, such as one limiting retail opening hours, on the other hand would fall outside Article 30 [*28*] EC as its burden fell equally upon both imports and domestic products.[36] A third view is the one stated below:

Chalmers, D. 'Free Movement of Goods within the European Community: An Unhealthy Addiction to Scotch Whisky?' (1993) 42 *International and Comparative Law Quarterly* 269, 280-282

An alternative interpretation of *Cassis de Dijon* is that it only prohibits regulation of the entry of goods to the national market. The penultimate paragraph, in which it is stated once a product has been lawfully marketed and produced in another Member State there is considered to be no valid reason why it should not be *introduced* into the importing member State, clearly introduces a doctrine of mutual recognition. Member States should acknowledge, namely, in applying their laws to imports from other member States, that account will already have been taken of the interests that Community law considers as justifiable for the formulation of those laws. A link subsequently arises between this proviso and the doctrine of 'mandatory requirements', as it is only where the other member States fail to regulate effectively the production or marketing of goods that a member State may plead the 'mandatory requirements' doctrine.

If that is the function of the doctrine of mutual recognition, then *Cassis de Dijon* also sets possible limits on the ambit of Article 30. For the prohibition in Article 30 can only be extended to those areas where the exporting member State, when legislating for its home market, is capable of protecting those interests in the importing member State which are justified under Community law. It does not extend to requiring that once goods

---

36 Marenco, G.'Pour une Interprétation Traditionelle de la Notion de Mesure d'Effet Equivalent à une Restriction Quantitative' (1984) *CDE* 291. See also Defalque, L. 'Le concept de discrimination en matière de Libre Circulation des Marchandises' (1987) *CDE* 471. A summary of this argument in English can be found in Marenco, G. & Banks, K. 'Intellectual Property and the Community Rules on Free Movement: Discrimination Unearthed' (1990) 14 *ELRev* 224, 238-241.

have been submitted to the laws of one member State they can not be submitted to any of the laws of another. The doctrine cannot thus extend to those regulations which set no precondition for entry to the home market. No precondition being set, none can be satisfied by the exporting member State's legislation. These laws are strictly territorial in nature and the exporting State is incapable of acting to protect those interests which lead to their formulation through the legislation it prepares for the marketing or production of goods on its own market.

The case law in the fifteen years following *Cassis de Dijon* followed a number of conflicting paths, which in turn spawned a cottage industry in articles on how Article 30 [*28*] EC should be delimited. The different strands of reasoning are well summarised in the piece below.

Case C-292/92 Hünermund v Landesapotheker Baden-Würtemburg [1993] ECR I-6787

Advocate General Tesauro

12. The first group consists of those decisions in which the Court has considered that the rules in question had no connection whatever with imports and in any case were not capable of hindering trade between Member States.[37] The Court came to that conclusion by stressing the fact that the measures concerned were not designed to control trade, did not concern other forms of marketing the same product or, in any event, left open the possibility of sales through other channels. In *Oebel*, for example, in which the issue was a rule prohibiting the production and distribution of bread at certain specified hours, the Court held that the provision had no connection with imports since 'trade within the Community remains possible at all times, subject to the single exception that delivery to consumers and retailers is restricted to the same extent for all producers, wherever they are established'. Then, in *Blesgen*, the Court held that a prohibition on the sale for consumption on the premises of certain alcoholic beverages in certain commercial premises did not fall within the scope of Article 30 in so far as it did not concern 'other forms of marketing' the same product.

The reasoning is more or less similar in the judgments in which the Court ruled on provisions prohibiting the sale of sex articles in unlicensed establishments. It pointed out that those provisions 'have no connection with intra-Community trade, since the products covered by the act may be marketed through licensed establishments and other

37 Case 155/80 *Oebel* [1981] ECR 1993, [1983] 1 CMLR 390; Case 75/81 *Blesgen* [1982] ECR 1211, [1983] 1 CMLR 431; Case C-23/89 *Quietlynn and Richards* [1990] ECR I-3059, [1990] 3 CMLR 55 and Case C-350/89 *Sheptonhurst* [1991] ECR I-2387, [1991] 3 CMLR 463.

channels' and 'are therefore not of such a nature as to impede trade between Member States'.[38]

13. In the cases just referred to, the Court therefore regarded as immaterial, for the purposes of the applicability of Article 30, a possible reduction in imports as a result of a reduction in sales opportunities affecting domestic and imported products to the same extent. It goes without saying that the prohibition on consumption on the premises of beverages with a high alcoholic strength (Blesgen) or on the sale of sex articles in unlicensed establishments (Quietlynn) are undoubtedly such as to be capable of having an adverse effect on demand and thus of affecting the volume of imports, it being (from that point of view) quite irrelevant that the prohibition in question does not concern other forms of marketing of the same product or that sales are possible in licensed establishments.

Such an approach is not, however, confined to rules concerning the marketing arrangements for products. A closer look reveals that many are the other cases in which the Court has not mechanically applied the *Dassonville* principle, to begin with those concerning price-control systems,[39] and also those concerning measures of various kinds but all sharing the common feature of displaying no connection, other than indirectly and vaguely, with imports and of affecting domestic and imported goods in the same way.[40]

14. A second group comprises those judgments in which the Court has recognized that the prohibition under Article 30 applies in principle also to measures of the kind at issue in this case, confining itself however to a rather 'atypical' examination of their proportionality.

I refer in particular to the judgments on 'Sunday trading',[41] in which the Court stated that provisions prohibiting employment of workers (or commercial activity) on

---

38 Case C-23/89 *Quietlynn and Richards* [1990] ECR I-3059, [1990] 3 CMLR 55 paragraph 11; to the same effect, see Case C-350/89 *Sheptonhurst* [1991] ECR I-2387, [1991] 3 CMLR 463.

39 Case 188/86 *Lefevre* [1987] ECR 2963; Case C-347/88 *Commission v Greece* [1990] ECR I-4747; Joined Cases 80/85 and 159/85 *Nederlandse Bakkerij Stichting and Others v Edah* [1986] ECR 3359; and Case C-287/89 *Commission v Belgium* [1991] ECR I-2233, [1993] 2 CMLR 142.

40 Case 148/85 *Direction Generale des Impots v Forest* [1986] ECR 3449, [1988] 2 CMLR 577; Case C-69/88 *Krantz v Ontvanger der Directe Belastingen* [1990] ECR I-583; Case C-93/92 *CMC Motorradcenter* [1993] ECR I-5009.

41 Case C-145/88 *Torfaen Borough Council v B & Q* [1989] ECR I-3851, [1990] I CMLR 337; Case C-312/89 *Conforama and Others* [1991] ECR I-997, [1993] 3 CMLR 746; Case C-332/89 *Marchandise and Others* [1991] ECR I-1027, [1993] 3 CMLR 746; Case C-169/91 *Council of the City of Stoke-on-Trent v B & Q* [1992] ECR I-6635, [1993] 1 CMLR 426.

Sundays, while not being designed to control trade and although 'it is improbable that the closure (...) on Sundays will cause consumers to refrain altogether from purchasing products which are available on week-days', may none the less 'have negative repercussions on the volume of sales and hence on the volume of imports'.[42] Those restrictive effects on trade, even though hypothetical and unsubstantiated, have accordingly been held to be sufficient for the relevant measures to be covered by Article 30. The Court seems thus to have recognized that the principle set out in *Dassonville* applies (mechanically) to national provisions of the kind in question, from which it follows that there is a twofold condition to be satisfied if they are to be compatible with Article 30: (a) the rule in question must pursue an objective which is legitimate with respect to Community law and (b) it must not exceed what is necessary in order to attain that objective, which is the case where the resulting obstacles to trade do not 'exceed the limit of the effects intrinsic to commercial regulation'.

15. Given that the intention of ensuring that working and non-working hours are so arranged as to accord with national or regional socio-cultural characteristics is legitimate, with respect to Community law, the Court confined itself however in those judgments to stating that 'the restrictive effects on trade which may stem from such rules do not seem disproportionate to the aim pursued', and in its most recent judgment in the matter, went on to make it clear that, in order to verify that the restrictive effects of such rules do not exceed what is necessary to achieve the aim in view, it must be considered whether those effects 'are direct, indirect or purely speculative and whether those effects do not impede the marketing of imported products more than the marketing of national products'.[43]

Such an approach would therefore seem to imply an only marginal review of the rules concerned, a review directed to the question whether the measure in point is reasonable, and more precisely whether it is appropriate with regard to (any) restrictive effects. In other words, instead of undertaking a 'classical' examination designed to ascertain whether the relevant rules satisfy imperative requirements and whether the measures selected are proportionate to the aim in view, the Court appears to look for the existence of a justifying cause, having regard to the effects on intra-Community trade which might result from the rules under consideration. That said, there can be no disguising the fact that such an approach, even though characterized by a far gentler, or at least more superficial, appraisal than that usually carried out in the context of Articles 30 and 36, is at variance with the approach inaugurated in the *Oebel* judgment.

16. Finally, there is a third group comprising those decisions in which the Court, because it considered that the provisions concerning sales, while not directly affecting imports, were nevertheless capable of hindering intra-Community trade, in so far as they were liable to affect possibilities for distributing (also) imported goods and hence to lead to a

---

42 Case C-312/89 *Conforama* [1991] ECR I-997, [1993] 3 CMLR 746, paragraph 8.

43 Case C-169/91 *Council of the City of Stoke-on-Trent* [1992] ECR I-6635, [1993] 1 CMLR 426, paragraph 15.

reduction in the volume of imports, undertook the classical examination designed to ascertain, first, whether the measures in question pursued public-interest objectives recognized by the Community legal order (consumer protection, health protection etc., according to the circumstances) and, secondly, whether the measures adopted were proportionate to the (legitimate) objective pursued.[44]

Not, as will be seen, by chance, most of the measures to which that approach has been applied relate to selling or sales promotion methods. As regards that class of measures, the Court has held that 'the possibility cannot be ruled out that to compel a producer either to adopt advertising or sales promotion schemes which differ from one Member State to another or to discontinue a scheme which he considers to be particularly effective may constitute an obstacle to imports even if the legislation in question applies to domestic products and imported products without distinction'.[45]

In other words, national legislation, without operating directly and specifically to the detriment of imported goods, may constitute a measure having equivalent effect where, by prohibiting the use of a certain method of selling lawfully used in the Member State of origin, it is such as to make access to the market more difficult and/or less profitable for traders in that sector: and this is so, *a fortiori*, as the Court has explained, when the trader realizes almost all his sales by the marketing method in question. The possible reduction in the volume of imports is therefore closely connected, in cases like *Oosthoek* (sales with free gifts), *Buet* (door-to-door sales), *Delattre* (mail-order sales) and *Boscher* (sale by public auction), with the obstacles caused by the legislation in question for a (single) trader in that area.

17. In the same way, certain rules restricting opportunities to advertise certain products have been held to fall within the ambit of Article 30 in so far as it cannot be ruled out, as the court has stressed, that to modify the form or the content of an advertising campaign depending on the Member States in which it is carried out may constitute an obstacle to imports, even if the legislation in question applies to domestic products and imported products without distinction.

In the same way the following have been held to be incompatible with Article 30: the prohibition of a certain form of advertising, in so far as it affected (also) a chain of supermarkets operating in another (bordering) Member State in which, on the

---

44 Case 286/81 *Oosthoek's Uitgeversmaatschappij* [1982] ECR 4575, [1983] 3 CMLR 428; Case 382/87 *Buet and Another v Ministere Public* [1989] ECR 1235, [1993] 3 CMLR 659; Case C-369/88 *Delattre* [1991] ECR I-1487, [1993] 2 CMLR 445; Case C-60/89 *Monteil and Samanni* [1991] ECR I-1547, [1992] 3 CMLR 425; Case C-239/90 *Boscher* [1991] ECR I-2023; Case C-271/92 *Société Laboratoire des Prothèses Oculaires* [1993] ECR I-2899; Case C-362/88 *GB-INNO-BM* [1990] ECR I-667, [1991] 2 CMLR 801; Case C-241/89 *SARPP* [1990] ECR I-4695; Joined Cases C-1/90 *Aragonesa de Publicidad* [1991] ECR I-4151; Case 126/91 *Schutzverband gegen Unwesen in der Wirtschaft v Yves Rocher* [1993] ECR I-2361.

45 Case 286/81 *Oosthoek* [1982] ECR 4575, [1983] 3 CMLR 428, paragraph 15.

contrary, that type of advertising was entirely lawful;[46] the prohibition of all statements alluding to the word 'sugar' in advertising a certain product, which forced the trader concerned, in view of the disparity between national laws on that point, to alter the actual content of advertisements used in the Member State in which the product at issue was marketed (*SARPP*); and lastly, the prohibition on advertisements showing the old price crossed out and the new one in red next to it, in so far as that form of advertising was lawful in the Member State from which the goods in question came (*Yves Rocher*).

18. To sum up, then, the Court has subjected to verification of their compatibility with Articles 30 and 36 those measures relating to marketing which, because they prohibit a certain method of selling or advertising, are (or can be) such as to make access to the market more difficult for the traders concerned, who are obliged to discontinue a method which they lawfully use in the Member State of origin.

In such cases, the Court has, therefore, emphasized the disparity between national laws, in so far as such disparity constitutes an 'obstacle' for the trader concerned and thus, in the final analysis, for the product marketed. The difference in approach as compared with the case of the rules considered in sections 12 to 15 is, therefore, a result, in situations of this kind, of the role played by disparity between national laws, in conformity with the line of reasoning, let it be understood, adopted in the 'Cassis de Dijon' case-law.

19. The Court arrived, however, at the same result (incompatibility in principle, subject to verifying whether there is justification under Article 36 or whether there are imperative requirements) in the case of rules in relation to which any disparity between laws is irrelevant, both for the product as such and for the trader marketing it.

That is above all the case with regard to those rules which reserve to a single class of traders (pharmacists, opticians) the right to sell certain categories of goods (medicinal products, contact lenses), making it impossible to market such goods except through the channels prescribed by law and thus involving a formal channelling of sales.[47] That is also the case where there is a prohibition, applicable in one part of a Member State and in certain circumstances, on advertising beverages having an alcoholic strength of more than 23 degrees:[48] the only effect on imports might be the result of a more general fall in sales, arising in its turn from the effect of the prohibition in question on demand for the products concerned.

---

46 Case C-362/88 *GB-INNO* [1990] ECR I-667, [1991] 2 CMLR 801.

47 Case C-60/89 *Monteil and Samanni* [1991] ECR I-1547, [1992] 3 CMLR 425; Case C-369/88 *Delattre* [1991] ECR I-1487, [1993] 2 CMLR 445; Case C-271/92 *Société Laboratoire des Prothèses Oculaires* [1993] ECR I-2899.

48 Case C-176/90 *Aragonesa de Publicidad* [1991] ECR I-4151, [1994] 1 CMLR 85.

iii. The 'November Revolution' of 1993

The normative chaos surrounding Article 30 [*28*] EC was further complicated by the institutional backdrop against which it took place. The deepening of Article 30 [*28*] EC resulted simultaneously both in an expansion of the judicial role and in an increasing diminution of autonomy for national authorities.

Maduro, M. 'Reforming the Market or the State? Article 30 and the European Constitution: Economic Freedom and Political Rights' (1997) 3 *European Law Journal* 55, 60-61

In the case law on Article 30 a deepening and broadening occurred simultaneously. As a result, almost any state measure could be submitted to judicial review under the Dassonville test. With few exceptions, commentators have long stressed the inability of restrictive tests (such as discrimination) to control state activities which affect the free movement of goods, and have argued in favour of greater judicial control over national regulations. In so doing, they have often neglected the institutional choice inherent in that view. They underline the need to balance free movement with regulatory aims, and examine the problems involved in leaving it to States to define that balance; they do not, however, analyse the problems involved in allowing the Court to define the balance. To have the Court balance the costs and benefits of a certain provision under a test of proportionality means, to a great extent, making it responsible for defining the appropriate regulatory policy. The institutional choice involved should compare the merits and demerits of both the States and the Court. As Komesar puts it: 'an institution is inefficient only when it functions less perfectly than an alternative available institution.'[[49]] The capacity of the courts is limited by their structure (measures brought to court are supposed to be exceptional events and not part of an everyday participation in the regulatory process). Moreover, they often lack expertise and have high administrative costs, are subject to information problems (information is closely dependent on those who are sufficiently organised to participate in the judicial process), and may decide issues without hearing some of the affected interests (some interested parties are unable to participate for lack of standing). Above all, they face questions of legitimacy, which has consequences for the acceptance of their decisions and their authority.

---

49 Komesar, N.'In Search of a General Approach to Legal Analysis: A Comparative Institutional Alternative' (1981) 79 *Michigan Law Review* 1350, 1359.

The decision of when the Court should balance the costs and benefits of a measure and when this should be left to the Member States depends largely on the position one takes regarding the European Economic Constitution and its relation to the rules of free movement. There are basically two general alternative concepts behind the control of the application of the rules of free movement, and especially behind the control of the application of Article 30. They reflect different conceptions of the economic constitution of the Community or the European Union. Commentators, however, have often neglected the conflict between these two conceptions. They have also ignored the dilemma, reflecting them, which faces the case-law of the Court. In Hünermund, Advocate-General Tesauro finally took up this constitutional dilemma: 'Is Article 30 of the Treaty a provision intended to liberalise intra-Community trade or is it intended more generally to encourage the unhindered pursuit of commerce in individual Member States?' The first concept can be summed up with the idea that the aim of Article 30 is to prevent state protectionism. Such protectionism assumes subtle forms which require constant refinement of the criteria used to review national measures. The second concept leads to the transformation of Article 30 into a kind of 'economic due process' clause. It is based on a conception of the economic constitution of the Community built on the free market, open competition, and a particular view of the kinds of regulation that are acceptable. According to this concept, judicial review of national rules under Article 30 should assess state intervention in the market.

The conflicting path of the Court's case law following Cassis de Dijon suggested that it had not been able to resolve this question. In *Keck* it implied it was definitively taking a step away from viewing Article 30 [*28*] EC as the basis for some form of incipient economic constitution.

Joined Cases C-267 and C-268/91 Criminal Proceedings against Keck and Mithouard [1993] ECR-I 6097, [1995] 1 CMLR 101

French law prohibited the retail of products for a price below that for which they had been purchased. Two supermarket owners were charged with having sold some 'Picon' beer and 'Sati Rouge' coffee at below the price for which they had actually been purchased. They pleaded that the law breached Article 30 [*28*] EC.

11. By virtue of Article 30, quantitative restrictions on imports and all measures having equivalent effect are prohibited between Member States. The Court has consistently held that any measure which is capable of directly or indirectly, actually or potentially, hindering intra-Community trade constitutes a measure having equivalent effect to a quantitative restriction.

12. It is not the purpose of national legislation imposing a general prohibition on resale at a loss to regulate trade in goods between Member States.

13. Such legislation may, admittedly, restrict the volume of sales, and hence the volume of sales of products from other Member States, in so far as it deprives traders of a method of sales promotion. But the question remains whether such a possibility is sufficient to characterize the legislation in question as a measure having equivalent effect to a quantitative restriction on imports.

14. In view of the increasing tendency of traders to invoke Article 30 of the Treaty as a means of challenging any rules whose effect is to limit their commercial freedom even where such rules are not aimed at products from other Member States, the Court considers it necessary to re-examine and clarify its case-law on this matter.

15. In 'Cassis de Dijon' (Case 120/78 *Rewe-Zentral v Bundesmonopolverwaltung für Branntwein* [1979] ECR 649) it was held that, in the absence of harmonization of legislation, measures of equivalent effect prohibited by Article 30 include obstacles to the free movement of goods where they are the consequence of applying rules that lay down requirements to be met by such goods (such as requirements as to designation, form, size, weight, composition, presentation, labelling, packaging) to goods from other Member States where they are lawfully manufactured and marketed, even if those rules apply without distinction to all products unless their application can be justified by a public-interest objective taking precedence over the free movement of goods.

16. However, contrary to what has previously been decided, the application to other products from other Member States of national provisions restricting or prohibiting certain selling arrangements is not such as to hinder directly or indirectly, actually or potentially, trade between Member States within the meaning of the Dassonville judgment (Case 8/74 [1974] ECR 837), provided that those provisions apply to all affected traders operating within the national territory and provided that they affect in the same manner, in law and in fact, the marketing of domestic products and of those from other Member States.

17. Where those conditions are fulfilled, the application of such rules to the sale of products from another Member State meeting the requirements laid down by that State is not by nature such as to prevent their access to the market or to impede access any more than it impedes the access of domestic products. Such rules therefore fall outside the scope of Article 30 of the Treaty.

18. Accordingly the reply to be given to the national court is that Article 30 of the EEC Treaty is to be interpreted as not applying to legislation of a Member State imposing a general prohibition on resale at a loss.

A distinction is drawn between measures imposing 'product requirements', which fall within Article 30 [*28*] EC, and laws regulating 'marketing circumstances', which in the absence of discrimination, fall outside Article 30 [*28*] EC. These two concepts can be distinguished in that the former (size, composition, shape etc.) relate directly to each *individual* product, and must therefore be satisfied by each product before it can be placed on the market in question. Laws regulating market circumstances restrict trade more indirectly, as, formally at least, they do not prevent a product being placed on the market, but prevent sales by restricting the circumstances in which it may be marketed or used.[50]

The Court has thus subsequently found presentational requirements;[51] packaging requirements;[52] laws requiring products to be labelled in a particular manner;[53] precious metals to carry a hallmark;[54] bread to have a maximum salt or ash content,[55] and the contents of magazines[56] to fall within Article 30 [*28*] EC. In contrast, non-discriminatory laws establishing State monopolies[57] and regulating

---

50 Chalmers, D. 'Repackaging the Internal Market - The Ramifications of the *Keck* Judgment' (1994) 19 *E.L.Rev.* 385. On possible uncertainties see Reich, N. 'The "November Revolution" of the Court of Justice: *Keck*, *Meng* and *Audi* Revisited' (1994) 31 *CMLRev* 459, 486-487.

51 Case C-51/93 *Meyhui v Schott* [1994] ECR I-3879; Case C-470/93 *Verein gegen Unwesen in Handel und Gewerbe Köln v Mars GmbH* [1995] ECR I-1923, [1995] 3 CMLR 1.

52 Case C-317/92 *Commission v Germany* [1994] ECR I-2039.

53 Case C-315/92 *Verband Sozialer Wettbewerb v Clinique Laboratories and Others* [1994] ECR I-317; Case C-85/94 *Piageme v Peeters* [1995] ECR I-2955.

54 Case C-293/93 *Houtwipper* [1994] ECR I-4249.

55 Case C-17/93 *Van der Veldt* [1994] ECR I-3537, [1995] 1 CMLR 621; Case C-358/95 *Morellatto v Unità Sanitaria Locale n.11 di Pordenone* [1997] ECR I-1431.

56 Case C-368/95 *Vereinigte Familiapress Zeitungsverlags- und vertriebs v Bauer Verlag* [1997] ECR I-3689.

57 Case C-96/94 *Centro Servizi Spediparto srl v Spezioni Marittima del Golfo srl* [1995] ECR I-2883; Case C-387/93 *Banchero* [1995] ECR I-4663, [1996] 1 CMLR 829.

advertising,[58] Sunday trading,[59] petrol station opening hours,[60] the outlets which may sell baby milk powder[61] and minimum profit margins on transactions[62] all to fall outside Article 30 [*28*] EC.

The distinction is generally accepted to have been first drawn by Eric White acting as Legal Counsel for the Commission in Torfaen, a case on the then British Sunday trading laws.[63] He subsequently expounded on the rationale in the following article:

White, E. 'In Search of the Limits to Article 30 of the EEC Treaty' (1989) 26 *Common Market Law Review* 235, 245-247.

The logic of the Court appears to be that Article 30 be interpreted in the light of its objective which is the creation of a unified market. ...

Accordingly, goods should be manufactured wherever the conditions are most favourable. These conditions need not only relate to the economic environment, they should also include the legal environment. If the legal situation in one Member State is particularly favourable for the manufacture of a particular product, then production should be centred there in the same way as producers should be free to seek out the most favourable economic climate.

National rules are inconsistent with this principle if they hinder the free circulation of such goods for reasons relating or arising out of the different legal and economic environment in which they were produced. This, it is submitted, is the explanation of the Court's reference to 'disparities between national rules'.

---

58 Case C-292/92 *Hünermund v Landesapotheker Baden-Würtemburg* [1993] ECR I-6787; Case C-412/93 *Leclerc-Siplec v TF1 Publicité and Others* [1995] ECR I-179, [1995] 3 CMLR 422; Joined Cases C-34-C-36/95 *Konsumentombudsmannen (KO) v Di Agostini (Svenska) Forlag*, Judgment of 9 July 1997.

59 Joined Cases C-69/93 & C-258/93 *Punto Casa SpA v Sindaco del Comune di Capena and Others* [1994] ECR I-2355; Joined Cases C-418-421/93, C-460-464/93, C-9-11/94, C-14-15/94, C-23-24/94 & C-332/94 *Semarano Casa Uno Srl v Sindaco del Comuni di Erbusco* [1996] ECR I-2975.

60 Joined Cases C-401-402/92 *Criminal Proceedings against Tankstation 't Heukske vof and J.B.E. Boermans* [1994] ECR I-2199, [1995] 3 CMLR 501.

61 Case C-391/92 *Commission v Greece* [1995] ECR I-1621, [1996] 1 CMLR 359.

62 Case C-63/94 *Groupement Nationale des negociants en pommes de terre de Belgique v ITM Belgium & Vocamex* [1995] ECR I-2467.

63 Case 145/88 *Torfaen v B & Q* [1989] ECR 765, [1990] 1 CMLR 337.

The different legal and economic environment of the Member State of origin finds its expression in the different *characteristics* of an imported product compared with the national product. Consequently, as the judgment of the Court in *Cassis de Dijon* clearly shows, Member States are not entitled to require that imported products have the same *characteristics* as are required of, or are traditional in, domestic products unless this is strictly necessary for the protection of some legitimate interest. There is not, however, the same need to require the rules relating to the *circumstances* in which certain goods may be sold or used in the importing Member State to be overridden for the purpose as long as imported products enjoy *equal access* to the market of the importing Member State compared with national goods. In such a case the imported product is not deprived of any advantage it derives from the different legal and economic environment prevailing in the place of production. In fact, any reduction of total sales (and therefore of imports) which may result from restrictions on the circumstances in which they may be sold does not arise out of disparities between national rules but rather out of the existence of the rules in the importing Member State.

White's argument is that such rules impose an extra burden on individuals. The argument can be recast in terms of regulatory autonomy, namely that a Member State should be free to regulate a part of the good's life cycle which has not already been regulated by another Member State.

Case C-292/92 Hünermund v Landesapotheker Baden-Würtemburg [1993] ECR I-6787

Advocate-General Tesauro

25. ... As for me, I am of the opinion that the *Dassonville* test cannot be construed as meaning that a potential reduction in imports caused solely and exclusively by a more general (and hypothetical) contraction of sales, can constitute a measure having equivalent effect to a quantitative restriction on imports.

I consider that measures, whose subject is the manner in which trading activity is carried on, are in principle to be regarded as falling outside the scope of Article 30, inasmuch as they are not designed to regulate trade itself, and have no connection with the parity or disparity of the national laws in point and, moreover, are not liable to make access to the market less profitable for the operators concerned and thus, indirectly, to make access more difficult for the products in question. Such a solution, therefore, based on the principle of mutual recognition, reflects the reasoning underlying the 'Cassis de Dijon' approach and does not in any way undermine the truly integrationist inspiration of that approach.

.....

27. Article 30 would otherwise come to be relied on and used, not for its proper purposes but in order to enable certain traders to avoid the application of national provisions which, in regulating a given activity, restrict freedom to trade, whether by imposing opening hours on shops, or by requiring prior authorization in order to carry on a given activity (why not, even a simple trading licence), or else by imposing professional requirements (sometimes technical as well) on those intending to sell certain classes of goods.

In that context, I cannot refrain from pointing out that such a use of Article 30 would ultimately render nugatory the Treaty provisions on the free movement of goods and on establishment, or in any event devalue them.

Let me explain: a shop-keeper wishing to trade on Sundays too, or a pharmacist seeking to advertise the sale of quasi-pharmaceutical products, are invoking nothing more or less than the right to the unhindered pursuit of their commercial activity: and it is therefore only in order to escape certain obligations that they allege that these are incompatible with the provisions on the movement of goods. On closer examination, however, it will be found that the obligations attach rather to services and establishment, that is to say provisions on which those operators cannot rely, simply because the situation in which they find themselves is purely internal.

Viewed in terms of the preservation of the regulatory autonomy of Member States, the *Keck* judgment follows a certain logic. It implies that a good should be regulated once throughout its life cycle without that regulation being subject to judicial scrutiny on the grounds of its restrictive effects on trade. The State of production is thus free to impose any requirements it considers necessary on goods produced within its territory. Conversely, the importing State is free to impose any requirements it considers necessary on the marketing, distribution and consumption of goods within its territory. The one exception to this is that the logic of mutual recognition entails that the importing State cannot impose any product requirements on imports in the absence of a good reason ('the mandatory requirements doctrine'). The reason for this is that those product requirements *could* have been regulated in the State of production, as these requirements attach to the good and 'travel' with it. There is therefore a presumption under the principle of mutual recognition that the importing State should accept the adequacy of the former's regime. In *Mars* the Court adopted the earlier rationale, however.

Case C-470/93 Verein gegen Unwesen in Handel und Gewerbe Köln v Mars GmbH [1995] ECR I-1923, [1995] 3 CMLR 1

A consumer association brought an action against Mars claiming that the marking of its ice cream bar wrappers with the logo '+10%' violated the German Unfair Competition Law. The association claimed in particular that it obscured the fact that the price may been increased by 10% and that the consumer may have thought that he was getting the extra ice cream covered by the logo, which took up more than 10% of the surface area of the wrapper.

12. According to the case-law of the Court, Article 30 is designed to prohibit any trading rules of member states which are capable of hindering, directly or indirectly, actually or potentially, intra-Community trade (see the judgment in Case 8/74 *Procureur du Roi v Dassonville* [1974] ECR 837, paragraph 5). The Court has held that, in the absence of harmonization of legislation, obstacles to the free movement of goods that are the consequence of applying, to goods coming from other Member States where they are lawfully manufactured and marketed, rules that lay down requirements to be met by such goods, such as those relating, for example, to their presentation, labelling and packaging, are prohibited by Article 30, even if those rules apply without distinction to national products and to imported products (judgment in Joined Cases C-267/91 and C-268/91 *Keck and Mithouard* [1993] ECR I-6097, paragraph 15).

13. Although it applies to all products without distinction, a prohibition such as that in question in the main proceedings, which relates to the marketing in a Member State of products bearing the same publicity markings as those lawfully used in other Member States, is by nature such to hinder intra-Community trade. It may compel the importer to adjust the presentation of his products according to the place where they are to be marketed and consequently to incur additional packaging and advertising costs

14. Such a prohibition therefore falls within the scope of Article 30 of the Treaty.

The problem with such a rationale is that it is simply not true to assert that product requirements are more restrictive of trade than other forms of restriction. To take the old chestnut of British driving laws. A law requiring cars driven in Britain to have the steering wheel on the right-hand side of the car clearly falls within Article 30 [*28*] EC, post *Keck*, as a product requirement. A law requiring people to drive cars on the left-hand side of the road would fall outside Article 30 [*28*] EC. Yet nobody could sensibly assert that these two measures do not have almost identical effects on trade.

The *Keck* judgment has been subjected to considerable criticism on two fronts.[64] The first is simply that it is too narrow. In *Leclerc-Siplec*,[65] Advocate General Jacobs, whilst considering French restrictions on advertising, suggested that the Keck test was too narrow:

41. The question then is what test should be applied in order to determine whether a measure falls within the scope of Article 30. There is one guiding principle which seems to provide an appropriate test; that principle is that all undertakings which engage in a legitimate economic activity in a Member State should have unfettered access to the whole of the Community market, unless there is a valid reason for denying them full access to a part of that market. In spite of occasional inconsistencies in the reasoning of certain judgments, that seems to be the underlying principle which has inspired the Court's approach from *Dassonville* through 'Cassis de Dijon' to *Keck*. Virtually all of these cases are, in their result, consistent with the principle, even though some of them appear to be based on different reasoning.

42. If the principle is that all undertakings should have unfettered access to the whole of the Community market, then the appropriate test in my view is whether there is a substantial restriction on that access. That would of course amount to introducing a *de minimis* test in Article 30. Once it is recognized that there is no need to limit the scope of Article 30 in order to prevent excessive interference in the regulatory powers of the Member States, a test based on the extent to which a measure hinders trade between Member States by restricting market access seems the most obvious solution. Indeed it is perhaps surprising that, in view of the avowed aim of preventing excessive resource to Article 30, the Court did not opt for such a solution in *Keck*. The reason may be that the Court was concerned lest a *de minimis* test, if applied to all measures affecting trade in goods, might induce national courts, who have primary responsibility for applying Article 30, to exclude too many measures from the scope of the prohibition laid down by that provision. Caution must therefore be exercised and if a *de minimis* test is to be

---

64 See also Moore, S. 'Re-visiting the limits of Article 30 EC' (1994) 19 *ELRev* 195; Gormley, L. 'Reasoning Renounced? The remarkable judgment in *Keck*.....' (1994) *European Business Law Review* 63; Reich, N. 'The "November Revolution" of the European Court of Justice: *Keck*, *Meng* and *Audi* Revisited' (1994) 31 *CMLRev* 459; Roth, W. *Casenote on Keck and Hünermund* (1994) 31 *CMLRev* 845; Ross, M. 'Keck - Grasping the Wrong Nettle' in Caiger & Floudas *1996 Onwards* (1996, John Wiley, Chancery); Stadlmeier, S. '"Contrary to What Has Previously been Decided...." The Search for the Rule Goes On' (1995/2) *LIEI* 9; Weatherill, S. 'After *Keck*: Some Thoughts on How to Clarify the Clarification' (1996) 33 *CMLRev* 885.

65 Case C-412/93 *Leclerc-Siplec v TF1 Publicité and M6 Publicité* [1995] ECR-179, [1995] 3 CMLR 422.

introduced it will be necessary to define carefully the circumstances in which it should apply.

.....

45. Where, on the other hand, a measure applicable without restriction simply restricts selling arrangements, by stipulating when, where, how, by whom or at what price goods may be sold, its impact will depend on a number of factors, such as whether it applies to certain goods ... or to most goods ..., or to all goods (as in *Keck*), on the extent to which other selling arrangements remain available, and on whether the effect of the measure is direct or indirect, immediate or remote, or purely speculative ... Accordingly, the magnitude of the barrier to market access may vary enormously: it may range from the insignificant to a quasi-prohibition. Clearly this is where a *de minimis* test could perform a useful function. The distinction recognized in *Keck* between a prohibition of the kind in issue in 'Cassis de Dijon' and a mere restriction on certain selling arrangements is therefore valuable: the former inevitably creates a substantial barrier to trade between Member States, whereas the latter may create such a barrier. But it cannot be maintained that the latter type of measure is not capable of hindering trade contrary to Article 30 in the absence of discrimination. It should therefore be recognized that such measures, unless overtly discriminatory, are not automatically caught by Article 30, as are measures of the type at issue in 'Cassis de Dijon', but may be caught if the restriction which they cause on access is substantial.

The Advocate General's *de minimis* approach was not adopted by the Court, and is not without its problems.

Gormley, L. 'Two Years after Keck' (1996) *Fordham International Law Journal* 866, 882-883.

A significant hindrance of access to the market would, in Mr Jacob's view, serve as the criterion for equally applicable measures which did not relate to the specific characteristics of the product. The purpose of the measure would, of course, play a part in the evaluation once that threshold were crossed. Advocate General Jacobs was entirely right to emphasise that if the Court wished to go down the de minimis route it would have to lay down clear criteria. But what would those criteria be? It is were 5% of the relevant product and geographical market Article 30 analysis would turn into economic analysis, something the Court has always avoided. A *de minimis* criterion in Article 30 is unworkable and the Court should continue to avoid it.

When arguments were presented years ago that the British local authorities adopting the London conditions of fitness for hackney carriages (taxis) were merely small local incidents and that if (which the United Kingdom Government did not accept) a restriction on trade resulted it was of minimal importance, some argued that such small matters should be left alone. Yet, within a few years an ever-increasing number of local authorities have adopted the conditions of fitness, spreading the London-style cabs of which there are now a small number of models made by different British manufacturers, further throughout the land, rather like an infection. The moment that the Court accepts a *de minimis* argument in Article 30, the descent along a very slippery slope will have commenced, and as sure as night follows day, it will lead to backdoor market fragmentation.

The second feature of *Keck* is its formalism. The advantages of formalism are a greater parameter of certainty. Its disadvantages are a selectiveness which can result in situations which are to all practical intents and purposes comparable being treated differently. The example has already been given of a distinction that would be drawn between the requirement of a right-hand drive car and a requirement to drive on the left-hand side of the road. These could possibly be distinguished on the grounds that the latter would be perceived as more intrusive on national autonomy than the latter. Increasingly, however, the formalism of *Keck* is pushing the Court towards making quite arbitrary distinctions.

Case C-368/95 Vereinigte Familiapresse Zeitungsverlags- und Vertriebs v Heinrich Bauer Verlag, [1997] ECR I-3689

Heinrich Bauer, a German publisher, sold a magazine in Austria, 'Laura', which offered crossword competitions with cash prizes for the winner. Austrian competition law prohibited the offering, advertising and distribution of free gifts to the purchasers of periodicals. A competitor sought an order restraining the sale of Laura on the grounds that the crossword competition breached this law. The Austrian Government argued that there was no violation of Article 30 [*28*] EC as restrictions on sales promotions techniques such as advertising had been found to fall outside the ambit of the provision.

10. The Austrian Government maintains that the prohibition at issue falls outside Article 30 of the Treaty. In its view, the possibility of offering readers of a periodical the chance to take part in prize competitions is merely a method of promoting sales and hence a selling arrangement within the meaning of the judgment in *Keck and Mithouard.*

11. The Court finds that, even though the relevant national legislation is directed against a method of sales promotion, in this case it bears on the actual content of the products, in so far as the competitions in question form an integral part of the magazine in which they appear. As a result, the national legislation in question as applied to the facts of the case is not a selling arrangement within the meaning of the judgment in *Keck and Mithouard.*

12. Moreover, since it requires traders established in other Member States to alter the contents of the periodical, the prohibition at issue impairs access of the product concerned to the market of the Member State of importation and consequently hinders free movement of goods. It therefore constitutes in principle a measure having equivalent effect within the meaning of Article 30 of the Treaty.

Pressure has mounted for a more adaptive approach. Weatherill has argued, for example, that a new test should be formulated whereby a measure breaches Article 30 [*28*] EC if it directly or substantially hinders imports.[66] Such a test would have the advantage that it would concentrate on the content rather than the form of the measure. There are signs, moreover, that the Court is beginning to abandon a rigid adherence to *Keck.*

Case C-189/95 Franzén [1997] ECR I-2471

In Sweden a State company, the Systembolaget, holds a monopoly over the retail of alcholic beverages. Operators require a 'production licence' or a 'wholesale licence' to engage in the manufacture or wholesale of alcohol. Importation is conditional upon holding one of these licences. The licence is issued by the Alcohol Inspectorate who charge SKR 25,000 per licence application, irrespective of whether the application is successful. Any licence must also show sufficient storage capacity to engage in the activity, and pay for the monitoring of the premises at rates set by the State. These varied from SKR 10,000 to SKR 323, 750. Franzén was prosecuted for selling without a licence wine imported from Denmark.

69. According to the established case-law of the Court, all trading rules which are capable of hindering, directly or indirectly, actually or potentially, intra-Community trade constitute measures having an effect equivalent to quantitative restrictions (judgment in Case 8/74 *Procureur du Roi v Dassonville* [1974] ECR 837, paragraph 5).

---

66 Weatherill, S. 'After *Keck*: Some Thoughts on How to Clarify the Clarification' (1996) 33 *CMLRev* 885, 898.

70. In a national system such as that in question in the main proceedings, only holders of production licences or wholesale licences are allowed to import alcoholic beverages, that is to say traders who fulfil the restrictive conditions to which issue of those licences is subject. According to the information provided to the Court during the proceedings, the traders in question must provide sufficient personal and financial guarantees to carry on the activities in question, concerning in particular their professional knowledge, their financial capacity and possession of storage capacity sufficient to meet the needs of their activities. Furthermore, the submission of an application is subject to payment of a high fixed charge (SKR 25,000), which is not reimbursed if the application is rejected. Finally, in order to keep his licence, a trader must pay an annual supervision fee, which is also high (between SKR 10,000 and SKR 323,750 for the basic amounts, depending on the kinds of beverage and the quantities produced or marketed).

71. The licensing system constitutes an obstacle to the importation of alcoholic beverages from other Member States in that it imposes additional costs on such beverages, such as intermediary costs, payment of charges and fees for the grant of a licence, and costs arising from the obligation to maintain storage capacity in Sweden.

72. According to the Swedish Government's own evidence, the number of licences issued is low (223 in October 1996) and almost all of these licences have been issued to traders established in Sweden.

73. Domestic legislation such as that in question in the main proceedings is therefore contrary to Article 30 of the Treaty.

It is the reasoning of *Franzén* rather than the result which is interesting. The restriction at issue was a direct one. Imports could not be carried out without the permission of a State agency. It would not required such a reworking of *Keck* for the licence, *per se*, to be found illegal. This was not the route taken by the Court, however. For it, it was the costs of the measure which were egregious. On such a basis, it is moving towards the test proposed by Advocate General Jacobs in *Leclerc-Siplec* whereby any measure which significantly restricts trade falls within Article 30 [*28*] EC.

V. Restrictions on Exports

Whilst Article 34 [*29*] EC prohibits discriminatory measures against exports, it does not catch restrictions on exports which apply equally to goods intended for the domestic market.

Case 15/79 Groenveld BV v Produktschap voor Vee en Vlees [1979] ECR 3409, [1981] 1 CMLR 207

It is impossible to detect the presence of horsemeat in processed meats. In the Netherlands, whilst unprocessed horsemeat could be traded, it was therefore prohibited to stock processed horsemeat. Groenveld imported horsemeat and wished to extend his activities to the manufacture of horsemeat sausages. He applied for, but was refused exemption from this Dutch law. It was claimed that the law infringed Article 34 [*29*] EC.

6. Article 34 of the EEC Treaty provides that 'quantitative restrictions on exports, and all measures having equivalent effect, shall be prohibited between Member States'.

7. That provision concerns national measures which have as their specific object or effect the restriction of patterns of exports and thereby the establishment of a difference in treatment between the domestic trade of a Member State and its export trade in such a way as to provide a particular advantage for national production or for the domestic market of the state in question at the expense of the production or of the trade of other Member States. This is not so in the case of a prohibition like that in question which is applied objectively to the production of goods of a certain kind without drawing a distinction depending on whether such goods are intended for the national market or for export.

8. The foregoing appreciation is not affected by the circumstance that the regulation in question has as its objective, inter alia, the safeguarding of the reputation of the national production of meat products in certain export markets within the Community and in non-member countries where there are obstacles of a psychological or legislative nature to the consumption of horsemeat when the same prohibition is applied identically to the product in the domestic market of the state in question. The objective nature of that prohibition is not modified by the fact that the regulation in force in the Netherlands permits the retail sale of horsemeat by butchers. In fact that concession at the level of local trade does not have the effect of bringing about a prohibition at the level of industrial manufacture of the same product regardless of its destination.

On its face, it is strange that Article 30 [*28*] EC and Article 34 [*29*] EC are interpreted differently, given their almost identical wording. The reason for this may lie in the principle of home State control. If Article 34 [*29*] EC were extended to cover non-discriminatory restrictions, the freedom States would enjoy over how goods were produced on their territory would be substantially diminished. Any production requirement could be challenged at source on the grounds that it increased costs and therefore diminished export opportunities.

There are therefore strong arguments on grounds of regulatory autonomy why Article 34 [*29*] EC should not be extended to cover non-discriminatory restrictions. Such an argument has been undermined by recent developments in the fields of services and workers where non-discriminatory restrictions on movement by the host State, the equivalent of the exporting State, have been found to be covered by the Treaty.[67] It has been argued that in the light of this Article 30 [*28*] EC and Article 34 [*29*] EC should be treated identically.[68] Such an argument is compelling provided one accepts that strong parallels should be drawn between the regulation of persons, services and goods. This question is returned to in the Chapter on Provision of Services.

Further Reading

Armstrong, K. 'Regulating the free movement of goods: institutions and institutional change' in Shaw, J. & More, G. *New Legal Dynamics of the European Union* (1995, Clarendon, Oxford)

Chalmers, D. 'Repackaging the Internal Market - The Ramifications of the Keck Judgment' (1994) 19 *European Law Review* 385

Dashwood, A. 'The *Cassis de Dijon* line of authority' in Bates, T. *In Memoriam J.D.B. Mitchell* (1983, Sweet & Maxwell, London)

67 Case C-384/93 *Alpine Investments v Minister van Financiën* [1995] ECR I-1141; Case C-415/93 *Union Royal Belge des Sociétés de Football Association ASBL v Bosman* [1995] ECR4921, [1996] 1 CMLR 645.

68 Weatherill, S. 'After *Keck*: Some Thoughts on How to Clarify the Clarification' (1996) 33 *CMLRev* 885, 902-903.

Friedbacher, T. 'Motive Unmasked: The European Court of Justice, the Free Movement of Goods and the Search for Legitimacy' (1996) 2 *European Law Journal* 226
Gormley, L. *Prohibiting Restrictions on Trade within the EEC* (1985, Elsevier/North Holland, Amsterdam)
----- 'Actually or Potentially, Directly or Indirectly? Obstacles to the Free Movement of Goods' (1989) 9 *Yearbook of European Law* 197
----- 'Some Reflections on the Internal Market and Free Movement of Goods'(1989/1) *Legal Issues of European Integration* 9
Maduro, M. 'Keck: The end? The beginning of the end? Or just the end of the beginning?' (1994) 3 *Irish Journal of European Law* 30
Mortelmans, K. 'Article 30 of the EEC Treaty and Legislation Relating to Marketing Circumstances: Time to Consider a New Definition' (1991) 28 *Common Market Law Review* 115
Oliver, P. Free Movement of Goods (1996, 3rd Edition, Sweet & Maxwell, London)
Reich, N. 'The "November Revolution" of the European Court of Justice: *Keck*, *Meng* and *Audi* Revisited' (1994) 31 *Common Market Law Review* 459
Ross, M. 'Keck - Grasping the Wrong Nettle' in Caiger & Floudas *1996 Onwards* (1996, John Wiley, Chichester)
Stadlmeier, S. '"Contrary to what has previously been decided..." The Search for the Rule Goes On' (1995/2) *Legal Issues of European Integration* 9
Steiner, J. 'Drawing the Line: Uses and Abuses of Article 30 EEC' (1992) 29 *Common Market Law Review* 749
Weatherill, S. 'After *Keck*: Some Thoughts on How to Clarify the Clarification' (1996) 33 *Common Market Law Review* 885
Wils, W. 'The Search for the Rule in Article 30 EEC: much ado about nothing' (1993) 18 *European Law Review* 475

7. Trade Restrictions and Public Goods

I. Introduction

Measures falling within Articles 30 [*28*] EC and 34 [*29*] EC could initially only be justified on the grounds provided by Article 36 [*30*] EC.[1] As the provision was considered to be an exception to a fundamental freedom, the Court was unwilling to extend the grounds protected by that Article.[2] This posed problems. The list of headings was narrowly drafted within the context of the concerns of the 1950's. Additions could only be made to Article 36 [*30*] EC through the cumbersome process of amending the Treaty, yet societal attitudes had evolved so that public goods such as protection of the consumer or the environment were increasingly being recognised. There was thus a danger of the free movement of goods provisions being seen as excessively deregulatory and insufficiently sensitive to local concerns. These concerns were addressed through the 'mandatory requirements' doctrine, established first in *Dassonville*,[3] and further developed in *Cassis de Dijon*[4] and its subsequent case law. This open-ended judge-made doctrine allows restrictions to be placed upon the importation of goods where the measure in question pursues an objective which is in the public interest.

---

1 See p. 272.

2 Case 46/76 *Bauhuis* [1977] ECR 5.

3 Case 8/74 *Procureur du Roi v Dassonville* [1974] ECR 837, [1974] 2 CMLR 436.

4 Case 120/78 *Rewe-Zentrale v Bundesmonopolverwaltung für Branntwein* [1979] ECR 649, [1979] 3 CMLR 494.

II. General Principles Mediating the Tension between Free Movement and Protection of Public Goods

i. The Principle of Proportionality

Both measures falling under Article 36 [*30*] EC and those falling under the mandatory requirements doctrine will only be compatible with the EC Treaty if they comply with the proportionality principle.

Case 104/75 Officier van Justitie v De Peiper [1976] ECR 613, [1976] 2 CMLR 271[5]

16. Nevertheless it emerges from Article 36 that national rules or practices which do restrict imports of pharmaceutical products or are capable of doing so are only compatible with the Treaty to the extent to which they are necessary for the effective protection of health and life of humans.

17. National rules or practices do not fall within the exception specified in Article 36 if the health and life of humans can be as effectively protected by measures which do not restrict intra-Community trade so much.

18. In particular Article 36 cannot be relied on to justify rules or practices which, even though they are beneficial, contain restrictions which are explained primarily by a concern to lighten the administration's burden or reduce public expenditure, unless, in the absence of the said rules or practices, this burden or expenditure clearly would exceed the limits of what can reasonably be required.

19. The situation described by the national court must be examined in the light of these considerations.

20. For this purpose a distinction must be drawn between on the one hand the documents relating to a medicinal preparation in general, in this case the 'file' prescribed by the Netherlands legislation, and, on the other hand, those relating to a specific batch of this medicinal preparation imported by a particular trader, in this case the 'records' which have to be kept under the said legislation.

21. (a) With regard to the documents relating to the medicinal preparation in general, if the public health authorities of the importing Member State already have in their

---

5 For the facts see p. 285.

possession, as a result of importation on a previous occasion, all the pharmaceutical particulars relating to the medicinal preparation in question and considered to be absolutely necessary for the purpose of checking that the medicinal preparation is effective and not harmful, it is clearly unnecessary, in order to protect the health and life of humans, for the said authorities to require a second trader who has imported a medicinal preparation which is in every respect the same, to produce the above-mentioned particulars to them again.

22. Therefore national rules or practices which lay down such a requirement are not justified on grounds of the protection of health and life of humans within the meaning of Article 36 of the Treaty.

23. (b) With regard to the documents relating to a specific batch of a medicinal preparation imported at a time when the public health authorities of the Member State of importation already have in their possession a file relating to this medicinal preparation, these authorities have a legitimate interest in being able at any time to carry out a thorough check to make certain that the said batch complies with the particulars on the file.

24. Nevertheless, having regard to the nature of the market for the pharmaceutical product in question, it is necessary to ask whether this objective cannot be equally well achieved if the national administrations, instead of waiting passively for the desired evidence to be produced to them - and in a form calculated to give the manufacturer of the product and his duly appointed representatives an advantage - were to admit, where appropriate, similar evidence and, in particular, to adopt a more active policy which could enable every trader to obtain the necessary evidence.

25. This question is all the more important because parallel importers are very often in a position to offer the goods at a price lower than the one applied by the duly appointed importer for the same product, a fact which, where medicinal preparations are concerned, should, where appropriate, encourage the public health authorities not to place parallel imports at a disadvantage, since the effective protection of health and like of humans also demands that medicinal preparations should be sold at reasonable prices.

26. National authorities possess legislative and administrative methods capable of compelling the manufacturer or his duly appointed representative to supply particulars making it possible to ascertain that the medicinal preparation which is in fact the subject of parallel importation is identical with the medicinal preparation in respect of which they are already informed.

27. Moreover, simple co-operation between the authorities of the Member States would enable them to obtain on a reciprocal basis the documents necessary for checking certain largely standardized and widely distributed products.

28. Taking into account all these possible ways of obtaining information the national public health authorities must consider whether the effective protection of health and life of humans' justifies a presumption of the non-conformity of an imported batch with the description of the medicinal preparation, or whether on the contrary it would not be sufficient to lay down a presumption of conformity with the result that, in appropriate cases, it would be for the administration to rebut this presumption.

29. Finally, even if it were absolutely necessary to require the parallel importer to prove this conformity, there would in any case be no justification under Article 36 for compelling him to do so with the help of documents to which he does not have access, when the administration, or as the case may be, the Court, finds that the evidence can be produced by other.

The proportionality principle is not a simple judicial balancing of the requirements of free trade against those of the public good. Instead, it involves a three-fold analysis.

It is for the Member State to decide upon the degree of protection in say the field of public health. In principle, therefore, if a Member State wishes to have a policy which safeguards a very high level of public health, it is free to do so, notwithstanding that this may severely curtail trade.

This discretion is constrained by there being an onus upon the Member State to demonstrate that the measure *effectively* protects the interest in question. In *De Peiper* the first measure fell precisely because the Court did not think public health was furthered by a Member State requesting information which it already had at its disposal.

In addition, the measure must be the least restrictive of trade necessary to secure the objective it pursues. The second restriction in *De Peiper* fell on this ground as the Court felt that cooperation between national authorities or acceptance of other forms of evidence as to the composition of the pharmaceutical would equally well protect public health, whilst allowing greater leeway for trade in parallel imports. Theoretically at least, this places the greatest restraint on Member State autonomy, for it implies that having chosen its objective, there exists only *one* set of instruments, those which are the least restrictive of trade.[6]

---

6 For a critique of proportionality see p 230 and p 519 in Volume I.

ii. The Principle of Equivalence

Linked to the proportionality principle is the principle of equivalence. This prevents the importing State duplicating measures which have already been taken by the exporting State. Duplication will only be found to exist, however, where the protection offered by the exporting State measure is equivalent to that demanded by the importing State.[7]

Case 272/80 Frans-Nederlandse Maatschappij voor Biologische Producten [1981] ECR 3277, [1982] 2 CMLR 497

Frans-Nederlandse Maatschaapij was prosecuted by the Dutch authorities for marketing a toxic plant protection product without having obtained prior authorisation from the Dutch authorities. It was argued that this requirement violated Article 30 [*28*] EC, as it entailed a series of laboratory analyses which the products had already undergone when placed on the French market.

13. It is not disputed that the national rules in question are intended to protect public health and that they therefore come within the exception provided for by Article 36. The measures of control applied by the Netherlands authorities, in particular as regards the approval of the product, may not therefore be challenged in principle. However, that leaves open the question whether the detailed procedures governing approvals, as indicated by the national court, may constitute a disguised restriction within the meaning of the last sentence of Article 36 EC, on trade between Member States, in view, on the one hand, of the dangerous nature of the product and, on the other hand, of the fact that it has been the subject of a procedure for approval in the Member State where it has been lawfully marketed.

14. Whilst a Member State is free to require a product of the type in question, which has already received approval in another Member State, to undergo a fresh procedure of examination and approval, the authorities of the Member States are nevertheless required to assist in bringing about a relaxation of the controls existing in intra-Community trade. It follows that they are not entitled unnecessarily to require technical or chemical analyses or laboratory tests where those analyses and tests have already been carried out in another Member State and their results are available to those authorities, or may at their request be placed at their disposal.

---

[7] See also Case C-293/94 *Brandsma* [1996] ECR I-3159.

15. For the same reasons, a Member State operating an approval procedure must ensure that no unnecessary control expenses are incurred if the practical effects of the control carried out in the Member State of origin satisfy the requirements of the protection of public health in the importing Member State. On the other hand, the mere fact that those expenses weigh more heavily on a trader marketing small quantities of an approved product than on his competitor who markets much greater quantities, does not justify the conclusion that such expenses constitute arbitrary discrimination or a disguised restriction within the meaning of Article 36.

The principle of equivalence places an exacting burden upon the judge. The procedures used by different Member States will rarely be identical. It has been therefore doubted whether it is possible in many cases to draw out a certain level of protection from one procedure which can be freely applied to another.

Currall, J. 'Some Aspects of the Relation between Articles 30-36 and Article 100 of the EEC Treaty with a Closer Look at Optional Harmonisation' (1984) 4 *Yearbook of European Law* 169, 185

... to judge correctly the equivalence of technical standards, which are frequently immensely complex, is a task before which courts will rightly quail: much will turn on the quality of expert evidence, and the litigation could be lengthy. There exists also a very substantial risk that courts will differ from State to State in the rigour with which they apply the test of equivalence, so that a product from A may be allowed in B but not in C, even if B has simply adopted C's standard, as frequently happens. Worse, in those Member States in which the doctrine of binding precedent is not known, it is perfectly possible that the same product may be permitted one day and forbidden the next, with no intervening change in the law either of the exporting State or of the importing State. The result is a potential fragmentation of the market; moreover, on a purely practical level, manufacturers will not wish to expand into other Member State's markets in conditions of such extreme uncertainty. Only specific rules provide that certainty - which means directives under Article 100. The real importance of the Rewe case may be, not that it provided a short cut to the unified market, as the Commission claimed (save perhaps for the very simplest trading rules, such as the rule in that very case), but that it provided a glimpse of such potential chaos that the fundamental necessity for speeding up harmonisation would be appreciated.

iii. Unequal Treatment

The range of interests covered by the mandatory requirements doctrine is open-ended and is capable of being continuously extended.[8] As the doctrine covers all the interests protected by Article 36 [*30*] EC and more, it therefore has the potential to subsume Article 36 [*30*] EC. This has traditionally been prevented by the mandatory requirements doctrine applying to a narrower class of instrument than Article 36 [30] EC. It has only been allowed to justify those restrictions which fell within Article 30 [*28*] EC as a result of the *Cassis de Dijon* judgment. On this view it cannot apply to restrictions caught by Article 34 [*29*] EC or discriminatory import restrictions.

Case 113/80 Commission v Ireland [1981] ECR 1625, [1982] 1 CMLR 706

An Irish statutory instrument forbade the sale of imported pieces of jewellery with characteristics, such as the depiction of a shamrock, which might suggest that they were Irish souvenirs unless they bore an indication of their country of origin or the word 'foreign'. The Irish Government sought to argue that this was necessary to protect the consumer from being misled.

10. ... The Court has repeatedly affirmed (in the judgments of 20 February 1979 in Case 120/78 *REWE* [1979] ECR 649, 26 June 1980 in Case 788/79 *Gilli & Andres* [1980] ECR 2071, 19 February 1981 in Case 130/80 *Kelderman* [1981] ECR 527) that 'in the absence of common rules relating to the production and marketing of the product in question it is for Member States to regulate all matters relating to its production, distribution and consumption on their own territory subject, however, to the condition that those rules do not present an obstacle ... to intra-Community trade' and that 'it is only where national rules, which apply without discrimination as to both domestic and imported products, may be justified as being necessary in order to satisfy imperative requirements relating in particular to ... the fairness of commercial transactions and the defence of the consumer that they may constitute an exception to the requirements arising under Article 30'.

11. The Orders concerned in the present case are not measures which are applicable to domestic products and to imported products without distinction but rather a set of rules

---

8 Case 302/86 *Commission v Denmark* [1988] ECR 4607, [1989] 1 CMLR 619.

which apply only to imported products and are therefore discriminatory in nature, with the result that the measures in issue are not covered by the decisions cited above which relate exclusively to provisions that regulate in a uniform manner the marketing of domestic products and imported products.

The burden measures falling under Article 36 [*30*] EC must satisfy would appear to be less demanding. They are simply required not to *arbitrarily discriminate* against imports. In other words, imports can be treated differently provided there is a good reason which justifies such treatment.

Case 4/75 Rewe-Zentralfinanz GmbH v Landwirtschaftskammer [1975] ECR 843, [1977] 1 CMLR 599

Apples imported into Germany were required to undergo phytosanitary inspections. This was to check for the existence of San José Scale, an extremely contagious disease. There was no similar requirement imposed on German apples. The apple trees, instead, were examined, and, if the disease was found, the area was isolated. Rewe, a German trading company, refused to submit a batch of French apples for phytosanitary inspection, claiming that the German regime breached Article 30 [*28*] EC, as it arbitrarily discriminated against imports by imposing checks on imported apples but not on German apples. At the proceedings the German Government argued that checks on German apple trees rather than on the apples themselves enabled any source of infection to be more easily identified.

6. Under the first sentence of Article 36 of the Treaty, the provisions of Articles 30 to 34 are not to preclude restrictions on imports and, therefore, measures having equivalent effect, which are justified for reasons of protection of the health of plants. In the light of the current community rules in this matter, a phytosanitary inspection carried out by a Member State on the importation of plant products constitutes, in principle, one of the restrictions on imports which are justified under the first sentence of Article 36 of the Treaty.

.....

8. However, the restrictions on imports referred to in the first sentence of Article 36 cannot be accepted under the second sentence of that Article if they constitute a means of arbitrary discrimination. The fact that plant products imported from another member state are subject to a phytosanitary inspection although domestic products are not subject to an equivalent examination when they are despatched within the Member State might constitute arbitrary discrimination within the meaning of the above-mentioned provision. ... The different treatment of imported and domestic products, based on the need to prevent the spread of the harmful organism could not, however, be regarded as arbitrary discrimination if effective measures are taken in order to prevent the distribution of contaminated domestic products and if there is reason to believe, in particular on the basis of previous experience, that there is a risk of the harmful organism's spreading if no inspection is held on importation.

The difference in treatment was permitted because imports and domestic products posed differing threats to public health. They were not truly comparable from a public health perspective. This test is clearly far more generous to the national regulatory regime than that set out in *Commission v Ireland.* It was difficult to understand why such a distinction should exist and why a less protective regime should apply to one public good than another. Oliver has thus consistently argued for a formal abandoning of the distinction.

Oliver, P. *Free Movement of Goods in the European Community* (1996, 3rd Edn., Sweet & Maxwell, London) 112

(a) This theory avoids the undue harshness resulting from the first theory with respect to 'distinctly applicable' measures *necessary* on, for instance, consumer protection grounds. According to the first theory, even though they are necessary, such measures are contrary to Article 30. According to the second theory, such measures are considered to fall under Article 30, but they may be justified under Article 36.
(b) It is submitted that the 'mandatory requirements' have the same properties as the grounds of justification in Article 36. Thus, for instance, the Member State bears the burden of proof that its measure is justified as with Article 36. Also,..., a measure will only be justified by a 'mandatory requirement' if it is necessary to attain that end - just as with Article 36. Again, it is submitted that the 'mandatory requirements' cannot justify a national measure where Community legislation containing sufficient guarantees with respect to those requirements has come into force, just as with Article 36.

Perhaps attracted by the logic behind these arguments, the Court has recently moved to abandoning the distinction.

Joined Cases C-34-36/95 Konsumentombudsmannen v De Agostini (Svenska) Förlag *et al.*, Judgment of 9 July 1997

Swedish law prohibited television advertising designed to attract the attention of children under the age of 12 years old. The Swedish Consumer Ombudsman brought an action under this law against De Agostini requiring it to alter the way it was advertising a magazine, 'Everything about Dinosaurs' on Swedish advertising. De Agostini claimed the law infringed both Article 30 [*28*] EC and Article 59 [*49*] EC, the provision on free movement of services. The Swedish authorities argued that the law was necessary to protect consumers and ensure fair trading.

44. ... an outright ban on advertising aimed at children less than 12 years of age and of misleading advertising, as provided for by the Swedish legislation, is not covered by Article 30 of the Treaty, unless it is shown that the ban does not affect in the same way, in fact and in law, the marketing of national products and of products from other Member States.

45. In the latter case, it is for the national court to determine whether the ban is necessary to satisfy overriding requirements of general public importance or one of the aims listed in Article 36 of the EC Treaty if it is proportionate to that purpose and if those aims or requirements could not have been attained or fulfilled by measures less restrictive of intra-Community trade.

The result of this has been a subsuming of Article 36 [*30*] EC within the mandatory requirements doctrine so that any measure is lawful if it is enacted to protect a public interest recognised by the Court of Justice, is proportionate and does not arbitrarily discriminate between domestic products and imports.

III. Public Goods Protected against Free Movement

i. Consumer Protection

Restrictions on free movement of goods will be permitted to protect where they enable the consumer to be informed about their purchase.

Case 27/80 Fietje [1980] ECR 3839, [1981] 3 CMLR 722

Fietje, a Dutch trader, was prosecuted under a 1953 Dutch law prohibiting alcoholic spirits from being marketed unless they were labelled with the word 'likeur'. The spirit in question was a German apple and wheat spirit, which, although it did not bear the word 'likeur', contained details about its composition and alcoholic strength on the label. Fietje argued that this allowed the consumer to be far better informed than the mere appendage of the word 'likeur'.

10. Although the extension to imported products of an obligation to use a certain name on the label does not wholly preclude the importation into the Member State concerned of products originating in other Member States or in free circulation in those States it may none the less make their marketing more difficult, especially in the case of parallel imports. As the Netherlands Government itself admits in its observations, such an extension of that obligation is thus capable of impeding, at least indirectly, trade between Member States. It is therefore necessary to consider whether it may be justified on the ground of the public interest in consumer protection...

11. If national rules relating to a given product include the obligation to use a description that is sufficiently precise to inform the purchaser of the nature of the product and to enable it to be distinguished from products with which it might be confused, it may well be necessary, in order to give consumers effective protection, to extend this obligation to imported products also, even in such a way as to make necessary the alteration of the original labels of some of these products. At the level of Community legislation, this possibility is recognized in several directives on the approximation of the laws of the Member States relating to certain foodstuffs as well as by Council Directive 79/112/EEC of 18 December 1978 on the approximation of the laws of the Member States relating to the labelling, presentation and advertising of foodstuffs for sale to the ultimate consumer (Official Journal 1979, L 33, p.1).

12. However, there is no longer any need for such protection if the details given on the original label of the imported product have as their content information on the nature of the product and that content includes at least the same information, and is just as capable of being understood by consumers in the importing State, as the description prescribed by the rules of that State. In the context of Article 177 of the EEC Treaty, the making of the findings of fact necessary in order to establish whether there is such equivalence is a matter for the national court.

The so-called *Fietje* doctrine provides that the consumer will normally be sufficiently informed by adequate labelling requirements. Requirements that products be packaged in a particular manner - such as a Belgian requirement that margarine be sold in cubes[9] or the German requirement that only certain German wine could be sold in the Bocksbeutel bottle[10] - have therefore been held to be illegal on the grounds of being excessively restrictive of trade. More controversially, the Court has also been unsympathetic to recipe standards. These are laws that establish minimum compositional requirements, such as the one in *Cassis de Dijon* that alcoholic spirits must have a minimum alcohol content.

Case 286/86 Ministère Public v Deserbais [1988] ECR 4907, [1989] 1 CMLR 516

In accordance with international norms France prohibited the marketing of 'Edam' cheese which had a fat content lower than 40%. Deserbais imported into France a consignment of cheese, using the name 'Edam', which only had a fat content of 34.3%. The cheese had been lawfully marketed as such in Germany.

10. In that connection, the national court starts from the premise that the cheese in question, containing 34% fat, has been lawfully and traditionally produced in the Federal Republic of Germany under the name 'Edam' in accordance with the laws and regulations applicable to it there, and that consumers' attention is adequately drawn to that fact by the labelling.

11. It must also be stated that at the present stage of development of Community law there are no common rules governing the names of the various types of cheeses in the Community. Accordingly, it cannot be stated in principle that a Member State may not

---

9 Case 261/81 *Rau v De Schmedt* [1982] ECR 3961, [1983] 2 CMLR 496.

10 Case 16/83 *Prantl* [1984] ECR 1299, [1985] 2 CMLR 238.

lay down rules making the use by national producers of a name for a cheese subject to the observance of a traditional minimum fat content.

12. However, it would be incompatible with Article 30 of the Treaty and the objectives of a common market to apply such rules to imported cheeses of the same type where those cheeses have been lawfully produced and marketed in another Member State under the same generic name but with a different minimum fat content. The Member State into which they are imported cannot prevent the importation and marketing of such cheeses where adequate information for the consumer is ensured.

13. The question may arise whether the same rule must be applied where a product presented under a particular name is so different, as regards its composition or production, from the products generally known by that name in the Community that it cannot be regarded as falling within the same category. However, no situation of that kind arises in the circumstances described by the national court in this case.

The reliance on labelling as the principal instrument of consumer information which this case law requires has been strongly criticised.[11]

von Heydebrand u.d. Lasa, H-C. 'Free Movement of Foodstuffs, Consumer Protection and Food Standards in the European Community: Has the Court of Justice Got It Wrong?' (1991) 16 *European Law Review* 391, 408-409.

First of all, the Court might simply not always be right in its judgment that consumers are adequately informed through labels. After all, the majority of consumers apparently do not pay much attention to the information given on the label.[[12]] How does the Court know that for example German consumers will not be misled by the traditional

---

11 See also Brouwer, O. 'Free Movement of Foodstuffs and Quality Requirements: Has the Commission Got It Wrong?' (1988) 25 *CMLRev* 237. For analysis of subsequent Community policy in this area see Lister, C. 'The naming of foods: the European Community's rules for non-brand product names' (1993) 18 *ELRev* 179.

12 It has been asserted that on average only approximately 20 per cent of the purchasers who are asked whether they read the list of ingredients when comparing two or more packages of the same type of food, say that they would do so. The higher the level of education, the higher the chance that the list will be used in making the choice: see *Walter Woods, Consumer Behaviour* (1981) at p.107, citing a study undertaken by Hoffman-LaRoche.

champagne-type bottles with a wired stopper which a French importer used for the marketing of partially fermented grape juice having an alcoholic strength below three per cent?[[13]] It was evident that the bottle shape and the wired stopper triggered the association with champagne. The German government had presented a survey which showed that about 75 per cent of the people who were shown a photograph of the bottle believed it contained sparkling wine or champagne. If the label stated in addition in German 'partially fermented grape must' still about 50 per cent of the people interviewed were subject to the same confusion.[[14]] Whether the findings of the survey are correct is not a question of law but of fact.[[15]] One would therefore expect in the judgment a weighing of the evidence which has been introduced. The Court however simply substituted its judgment for the conclusion reached by the German regulator when it held without much further reasoning that the label was sufficiently clear to offset the risk of a confusion caused by the shape of the bottle and the wired stopper.

Secondly, the Court's approach can confer an unfair competitive advantage on the importer ... the similarity of the squat and bulbous wine bottle from Italy with the traditional German 'Bocksbeutel' bottle[[16]] amount(s) to a marketing advantage for which the importer does not pay. The consumer associates with the name or presentation of the product a familiar domestic product of a certain quality which is not met by the imported product and will therefore perhaps be misled.

These criticisms cannot be easily directly countered on grounds relating to consumer protection. Yet those who argue that compositional requirements should be the principal instrument of consumer information fail to counter the disintegrative effect of such measures on the single market. Compositional requirements provide not only considerable barriers to market entry for importers but also, as the Court has itself stated, act to fragment the single market more indirectly by crystallising consumer habits and behaviour and discouraging consumers to experiment.[17]

Moreover, harmonisation of the compositional requirements of each good would have been a difficult and costly process which

---

13 Case 179/85 *Commission v Germany* [1986] ECR 3879, [1988] 1 CMLR 135.

14 See Opinion of the Advocate General, [1986] ECR 3889, 3991.

15 Christop Hauschka, 'Lauterkeitsrecht und Verbraucherschutz zwischen nationalem Regelungsanspruch und der Rechtsprechung der Europäischen Gerichtshofs' [1990] *Zeitschrift für Vergleichende Rechtswissenschaft* 166, 183.

16 Case 16/83 *Prantl* [1984] ECR 1299, [1985] 2 CMLR 238.

17 Case 178/84 *Commission v Germany* [1987] ECR 1227, [1988] 1 CMLR 780.

ultimately would have been impossible to achieve, given the number of goods present in the single market. It is doubtful, furthermore, whether it would have been a desirable objective, as the standardisation required - there would be one type of Euro-beer and one type of Euro-bread - would have resulted in an extremely rigid regime which curtailed consumer choice and competition.[18]

Given the limitations of labelling, however, if there is not to be a substantial erosion of consumer rights it is important that the Court be vigilant in those cases where labelling is inappropriate. Von Heydebrand u.d. Lasa noted with concern its dismissive attitude in the *German Sparkling Wine* judgment. Another example is provided below.

Case C-315/92 Verband Sozialer Wettbewerb v Clinique Laboratories [1994] ECR I-317

Estée Lauder marketed its cosmetic products under the name 'Clinique' in all Member States except Germany, where it marketed these products under the name 'Linique' because of an Unfair Competition Law, which forbade products to imply they contained medical properties that they did not possess. Estée Lauder decided to bring its practice in Germany into line with its practice elsewhere, and to market the products under the name 'Clinique'. Verband Sozialer Wettbewerb, a trade association, promptly brought an action against Estée Lauder's French and German subsidiaries, claiming a breach of the German law.

19. The prohibition ... of distribution within the Federal Republic of Germany of cosmetic products under the same name as that under which they are marketed in the other Member States constitutes in principle ... an obstacle to intra-Community trade. The fact that by reason of that prohibition the undertaking in question is obliged in that Member State alone to market its products under a different name and to bear additional packaging and advertising costs demonstrates that this measure does affect free trade.

20. In order to determine whether, in preventing a product being attributed with characteristics which it does not have, the prohibition of the use of the name 'Clinique' for the marketing of cosmetic products in the Federal Republic of Germany can be

---

18 Welsh, D. 'From "Euro Beer" to "Newcastle Brown", A Review of European Community Action to Dismantle Divergent "Food" Laws' (1983) 22 *JCMS* 47.

justified by the objective of protecting consumers or the health of humans, it is necessary to take into account the information set out in the order of reference.

21. In particular, it is apparent from that information that the range of cosmetic products manufactured by the Estée Lauder company is sold in the Federal Republic of Germany exclusively in perfumeries and cosmetic departments of large stores, and therefore none of those products is available in pharmacies. It is not disputed that those products are presented as cosmetic products and not as medicinal products. It is not suggested that, apart from the name of the products, this presentation does not comply with the rules applicable to cosmetic products. Finally, according to the very wording of the question referred, those products are ordinarily marketed in other countries under the name 'Clinique' and the use of that name apparently does not mislead consumers.

22. In the light of these facts, the prohibition of the use of that name in the Federal Republic of Germany does not appear necessary to satisfy the requirements of consumer protection and the health of humans.

Weatherill has observed that a common European notion of the consumer is emerging, which envisages a certain capability which is not in need of protection.[19] It is possible in this respect that consumer rights are being sacrificed on the altar of European integration. In *Clinique* the Court took into account other, arguably lower, national practices in evaluating German law. Yet this goes against the principle that it is for each Member State to determine its own level of protection. There are also national particularities which make it difficult to generalise about a European consumer capability. In this instance, the word 'Klinik' means hospital in German. This provides a basis for confusion which exists only in Germany and Austria.

The Court went even further in the *Mars* judgment.[20] One of the grounds on which the German law prevented Mars ice cream bars from bearing a '+10%' logo was that the logo covered more than 10% of the wrapper, and the consumer might consequently be mistaken as to the size of the increase in the ice cream. The Court rejected this argument,

---

19 Weatherill, S. 'The Evolution of European Consumer Law and Policy: From Well Informed Consumer to Confident Consumer' 424, 439-440 in Micklitz, H. *Rechtseinheit order Rechtsvielfalt in Europa?* (1996, Nomos, Baden-Baden).

20 Case C-470/93 *Verein gegen Unwesen in Handel und Gewerbe Köln v Mars GmbH* [1995] ECR I-1923, [1995] 3 CMLR 1.

stating that any 'reasonably circumspect consumer' would be aware that there would not necessarily be a correlation between the size of the logo and the increase. By definition, however, not all consumers, but probably only the literate and the well-informed who are reasonably circumspect. For the rest, it is a case of taking it as you find it. In such circumstances, the rhetoric of consumer choice is a shallow one. For it can mean little, if there is insufficient framework to guide that choice.

ii. Unfair Competition

Unfair competition is often linked to consumer protection, as the same set of circumstances often gives rise to issues of both. The rationale behind unfair competition laws, however, is protection of competing producers rather than of the consumer, as a comparison of these two cases illustrates.

Case 6/81 Industrie Diensten Groep v Beele [1982] ECR 707, [1982] 3 CMLR 102.

Beele had been marketing cable ducts in the Netherlands since 1963. The patent on these ducts expired in 1975. Following this, a German company, Industrie Diensten Groep, began marketing their own ducts which were practically identical to those marketed by Beele. Beele sought an injunction, claiming that this represented unfair competition under Dutch law.

9. National case-law prohibiting the precise imitation of someone else's product which is likely to cause confusion may indeed protect consumers and promote fair trading; these are general interests which ... may justify the existence of obstacles to movement within the community resulting from disparities between national laws relating to the marketing of products. That such a rule does meet mandatory requirements is moreover borne out by the fact that it accords with the principle underlying Article 10bis of the Paris Convention for the protection of Industrial Property, as last revised on 14 July 1967 at Stockholm, which prohibits *inter alia* all acts of such a nature as to create confusion with the goods of a competitor, and by the fact that this rule is recognized in principle in the case-law of most Member States.

10. In order to answer the question whether case-law such as that described in the judgment of the Gerechtshof is necessary to achieve the aforesaid objectives, or whether it goes beyond the limit which they may justify, the manner in which that case-law is applied, as described in the judgment, should be scrutinized.

11. As to that, the very wording of the question submitted shows first that in the provisional view of the national court the products which it intends to prohibit from being marketed are for no compelling reason practically identical to the products imitated and that the appellant in the main action thereby needlessly causes confusion. Furthermore, the judgment of the national court shows that the question whether or not such imitation is necessary was considered not only from the technical point of view, but also from the economic and commercial point of view.

12. Secondly, it is apparent from the wording of the question submitted and from the case-file that there is no indication of an agreement or of dependence between the Swedish manufacturer of the original product and the German manufacturer of the product which is supposed to be an imitation thereof and the marketing of which in the Netherlands is in dispute.

13. Where the circumstances mentioned by the national court are met a body of case-law prohibiting precise imitation of someone else's product may not be regarded as exceeding the scope of the mandatory requirements which the protection of consumers and the fairness of commercial transactions constitute.

If labels, as the implication from the case law earlier on suggests, allow consumers to distinguish goods individually, a less restrictive manner of preventing competition would have been simply to insist on the goods being adequately labelled. Patents have a limited life so that others can benefit from the technology after a particular period. If a product is sufficiently distinct, the effect of this judgment is to allow Member States to extend the lives of patents covertly, by allowing producers to bring passing off actions.

The judgment also sits ill at ease with the Court's constant encouragement of parallel imports. An enterprise is likely to be equally as uncomfortable with a competitor retailing its brand products at a price below its retail price as by a competitor producing a similar product.

Whilst the former are encouraged,[21] it is strange therefore that so strong a line is taken against the latter.

Case 16/83 Prantl [1984] ECR 1299, [1985] 2 CMLR 238

In Germany only wines from the region of Franconia, were permitted to be sold in a bulbous shaped bottle, known as the Bocksbeutel. Prantl was charged with stocking Italian red wine which was bottled in similar shaped bottles. Wine from certain regions of Italy had been traditionally stored in such bottles for more than one hundred years.

25. ... It is true, as the Court has held many times, that in the absence of comprehensive Community legislation on the bottling of the products in question, obstacles to free trade within the Community owing to disparities between national rules must be accepted in so far as such rules, applicable to domestic and imported products alike, may be justified on the ground that it is necessary to satisfy mandatory requirement relating in particular to consumer protection and fair trading.

26. In principle, the justification for adopting legislation designed to prevent customers from confusing wines of different quality and origin cannot be denied. That concern is particularly worthy in the case of wines, for traditions and peculiarities play an important role in this field. Moreover, the second recital in the preamble to Regulation No 355/79 states in this regard that: '... The purpose of any description and presentation should be to supply potential buyers and public bodies responsible for organizing and supervising the marketing of the products concerned with information which is sufficiently clear and accurate to enable them to form an opinion of the products; ... Rules should therefore be drawn up to ensure that this purpose is served.' The third recital in the preamble to the Regulation then states that: '... Steps should be taken to ensure that the information provided is as complete as possible and that it takes account of the different customs and traditional practices in the Member States and in third countries and complies with Community law.'

27. Where, however, it is a matter of determining whether the legislation of a Member State may, in order to protect an indirect designation of geographical origin in the interests of consumers, prohibit the marketing of wines imported in a certain type of bottle, it must be observed that in the system of the common market consumer protection and fair trading as regards the presentation of wines must be guaranteed with regard on all sides for the fair and traditional practices observed in the various Member States.

---

21 e.g. Case 104/75 *Officier van Justitie te Rotterdam v De Peiper* [1976] ECR 613, [1976] 2 CMLR 271.

28. In this regard the arguments advanced before the Court have revealed that bottles which are identical in shape to the *Bocksbeutel* bottle or differ from it only in ways imperceptible to the consumer are traditionally used to market wines originating in certain regions of Italy. An exclusive right to use a certain type of bottle granted by national legislation in a Member State may not therefore be used as a bar to imports of wines originating in another Member State put up in bottles of the same or similar shape in accordance with a fair and traditional practice observed in that Member State.

It is easy to have more sympathy with the motives of Prantl than those of Industrien Diensten Groep in Beele, yet if the purpose of unfair competition laws is to prevent imports benefiting from associations that consumers in the importing State have traditionally made with domestic products, the fact that a product has been traditionally marketed in another Member State appears to be hardly relevant. Not only this, but a new difficult concept, that of 'traditional usage' has been introduced which will be difficult to apply - would it have made any difference if the Italian wine had only been marketed in those bottles for the previous six months? - and which discriminates very firmly in favour of established producers and against market entrants.

iii. Environmental Protection

Case 302/86 Commission v Denmark [1988] ECR 4607, [1989] 1 CMLR 619

The Commission brought an action against a 1981 Danish law which required that all beer and soft drinks containers be reusable. As such a deposit-and-return system could only operate using a limiting number of types of container, the law also required that all containers must be approved by the National Agency for the Protection of the Environment, who could refuse permission if the container was either not reusable or was technically unsuitable for the system.

8. The Court has already held in its judgment of 7 February 1985 in Case 240/83 *Procureur de la République v Association de Défense des Brûleurs d'Huiles Usagées* [1985] ECR 531 that the protection of the environment is 'one of the Community's essential objectives', which may as such justify certain limitations of the principle of the free movement of goods. That view is moreover confirmed by the Single European Act.

9. In view of the foregoing, it must therefore be stated that the protection of the environment is a mandatory requirement which may limit the application of Article 30 of the Treaty.

.....

12. It is therefore necessary to examine whether all the restrictions which the contested rules impose on the free movement of goods are necessary to achieve the objectives pursued by those rules.

13. First of all, as regards the obligation to establish a deposit-and-return system for empty containers, it must be observed that this requirement is an indispensable element of a system intended to ensure the re-use of containers and therefore appears necessary to achieve the aims pursued by the contested rules. That being so, the restrictions which it imposes on the free movement of goods cannot be regarded as disproportionate.

14. Next, it is necessary to consider the requirement that producers and importers must use only containers approved by the National Agency for the Protection of the Environment.

15. The Danish Government stated in the proceedings before the Court that the present deposit-and-return system would not work if the number of approved containers were to exceed 30 or so, since the retailers taking part in the system would not be prepared to accept too many types of bottles owing to the higher handling costs and the need for more storage space. For that reason the agency has hitherto followed the practice of ensuring that fresh approvals are normally accompanied by the withdrawal of existing approvals.

16. Even though there is some force in that argument, it must nevertheless be observed that under the system at present in force in Denmark the Danish authorities may refuse approval to a foreign producer even if he is prepared to ensure that returned containers are re-used.

17. In those circumstances, a foreign producer who still wished to sell his products in Denmark would be obliged to manufacture or purchase containers of a type already approved, which would involve substantial additional costs for that producer and therefore make the importation of his products into Denmark very difficult.

18. To overcome that obstacle the Danish Government altered its rules by the aforementioned Order No 95 of 16 March 1984, which allows a producer to market up to 3,000 hectolitres of beer and soft drinks a year in non-approved containers, provided that a deposit-and-return system is established.

19. The provision in Order No 95 restricting the quantity of beer and soft drinks which may be marketed by a producer in non-approved containers to 3,000 hectolitres a year is challenged by the Commission on the ground that it is unnecessary to achieve the objectives pursued by the system.

20. It is undoubtedly true that the existing system for returning approved containers ensures a maximum rate of re-use and therefore a very considerable degree of protection of the environment since empty containers can be returned to any retailer of beverages. Non-approved containers, on the other hand, can be returned only to the retailer who sold the beverages, since it is impossible to set up such a comprehensive system for those containers as well.

21. Nevertheless, the system for returning non-approved containers is capable of protecting the environment and, as far as imports are concerned, affects only limited quantities of beverages compared with the quantity of beverages consumed in Denmark owing to the restrictive effect which the requirement that containers should be returnable has on imports. In those circumstances, a restriction of the quantity of products which may be marketed by importers is disproportionate to the objective pursued.

This judgment has been criticised as a classic example of how not to apply the proportionality principle. The Court acknowledged that the Danish system aimed at a high level of environmental protect, but, instead of examining whether the authorisation scheme was the optimal system to achieve that level of protection, it engaged in an arbitrary balancing exercise under which it held the trade interest outweighed the environmental interest.[22] The problem of 'misapplication' is particularly acute in cases involving protection of the environment. The ecological impact of individual transactions will often be slight and uncertain. It is the cumulative impact of transactions which is likely to be deleterious. In individual cases, therefore, whilst the impact on trade will be evident, it will be often difficult for courts to gauge both the effectiveness and need for environmental legislation.

As if to illustrate the fine tightrope the Court walks in these cases, the Court was criticised for leaning too much the other way in its

---

22 Jadot, B. 'Environnement et libre circulation' (1990) *CDE* 403, 426-427; Krämer, L. 'Environmental Protection and Article 30 EEC Treaty' (1993) 30 *CMLRev* 111, 120-127; Demiray, D. 'The Movement of Goods in a Green Market' (1994/1) *LIEI* 73, 88-91; Gerardin, D. & Stewardson, A. 'Trade and Environment: Some Lessons from Castlemaine Tooheys (Australia) and Danish Bottles (European Community)' (1995) 44 *ICLQ* 41, 66-70.

other major judgment in this area, *Belgian Waste.*[23] The Court found the Wallonian ban on the dumping, storage and tipping of non-Wallonian waste to justified on the basis of the proximity principle, namely there should be disposal of waste as close to the place of production as possible. The reach of the proximity principle is unclear. *Belgian Waste* covered a regional restriction, but it is far harder to justify a similar national restriction, as that would permit waste to be transported over long distances. More fundamentally, the principle is unsatisfactory as an instrument for allocating environmental costs.[24] The inevitable duplication of facilities associated with such a principle, in addition, increases the risk of facilities being placed in locations, which, in ecological terms, are far from ideal and deprives operators of the most suitable sites for waste disposal. The principle is also arguably unjust. Most industrial waste is produced in locations far away from where the good is consumed. In an integrated European economy, is it really fair to expect the people who live close to the factory to bear the full cost of disposal?

iv. Public Health

Case 178/84 Commission v Germany [1987] ECR 1227, [1988] 1 CMLR 780

The Commission brought an action against a German law, which had its origins in the Bavarian Reinheitsgebot (Purity Law) of 1516 which only allowed beer to be marketed in Germany and to have the designation 'Bier' if it was manufactured from barley, hops, yeast and water. All other additives, with the exception of certain processing aids and enzymes, were outlawed.

---

[23] Case C-2/90 *Commission v Belgium* [1992] ECR I-4431, [1993] 1 CMLR 365.

[24] Von Wilmowsky, P. 'Waste Disposal in the Internal Market: The State of Play after the ECJ's Ruling on the Wallon Import Ban' (1993) 30 *CMLRev* 541, 547-557; Chalmers, D. 'Community Policy on Waste Management - Managing Environmental Decline Gently' (1994) 14 *YBEL* 257, 280-284.

40. It is not contested that the prohibition on the marketing of beers containing additives constitutes a barrier to the importation from other Member States of beers containing additives authorized in those States, and is to that extent covered by Article 30 of the EEC Treaty. However, it must be ascertained whether it is possible to justify that prohibition under Article 36 of the Treaty on grounds of the protection of human health.

41. The Court has consistently held (in particular in the judgment of 14 July 1983 in Case 174/82 *Sandoz BV* [1983] ECR 2445) that 'in so far as there are uncertainties at the present state of scientific research it is for the Member States, in the absence of harmonization, to decide what degree of protection of the health and life of humans they intend to assure, having regard however to the requirements of the free movement of goods within the Community'.

42. As may also be seen from the decisions of the Court (and especially the judgment of 14 July 1983 in the *Sandoz* case, cited above, the judgment of 10 December 1985 in Case 247/84 *Motte* [1985] ECR 3887, and the judgment of 6 May 1986 in Case 304/84 *Ministère public v Muller and Others* [1986] ECR 1511), in such circumstances Community law does not preclude the adoption by the Member States of legislation whereby the use of additives is subjected to prior authorization granted by a measure of general application for specific additives, in respect of all products, for certain products only or for certain uses. Such legislation meets a genuine need of health policy, namely that of restricting the uncontrolled consumption of food additives.

43. However, the application to imported products of prohibitions on marketing products containing additives which are authorized in the Member State of production but prohibited in the Member State of importation is permissible only in so far as it complies with the requirements of Article 36 of the Treaty as it has been interpreted by the Court.

44. It must be borne in mind, in the first place, that in its judgments in the *Sandoz*, *Motte* and *Muller* cases, cited above, the Court inferred from the principle of proportionality underlying the last sentence of Article 36 of the Treaty that prohibitions on the marketing of products containing additives authorized in the Member State of production but prohibited in the Member State of importation must be restricted to what is actually necessary to secure the protection of public health. The Court also concluded that the use of a specific additive which is authorized in another Member State must be authorized in the case of a product imported from that Member State where, in view on the one hand of the findings of international scientific research, and in particular of the work of the Community's scientific committee for food, the Codex Alimentarius Committee of the Food and Agriculture Organization of the United Nations (FAO) and the World Health Organization, and, on the other hand, of the eating habits prevailing in the importing Member State, the additive in question does not present a risk to public health and meets a real need, especially a technical one.

45. Secondly, it should be remembered that, as the Court held in its judgment of 6 May 1986 in the *Muller* case, cited above, by virtue of the principle of proportionality, traders must also be able to apply, under a procedure which is easily accessible to them and can be concluded within a reasonable time, for the use of specific additives to be authorized by a measure of general application.

46. It should be pointed out that it must be open to traders to challenge before the courts an unjustified failure to grant authorization. Without prejudice to the right of the competent national authorities of the importing Member State to ask traders to produce the information in their possession which may be useful for the purpose of assessing the facts, it is for those authorities to demonstrate, as the Court held in its judgment of 6 May 1986 in the *Muller* case, cited above, that the prohibition is justified on grounds relating to the protection of the health of its population.

47. It must be observed that the German rules on additives applicable to beer result in the exclusion of all the additives authorized in the other Member States and not the exclusion of just some of them for which there is concrete justification by reason of the risks which they involve in view of the eating habits of the German population; moreover those rules do not lay down any procedure whereby traders can obtain authorization for the use of a specific additive in the manufacture of beer by means of a measure of general application.

48. As regards more specifically the harmfulness of additives, the German Government, citing experts' reports, has referred to the risks inherent in the ingestion of additives in general. It maintains that it is important, for reasons of general preventive health protection, to minimize the quantity of additives ingested, and that it is particularly advisable to prohibit altogether their use in the manufacture of beer, a foodstuff consumed in considerable quantities by the German population.

49. However, it appears from the tables of additives authorized for use in the various foodstuffs submitted by the German Government itself that some of the additives authorized in other Member States for use in the manufacture of beer are also authorized under the German rules, in particular the regulation on additives, for use in the manufacture of all, or virtually all, beverages. Mere reference to the potential risks of the ingestion of additives in general and to the fact that beer is a foodstuff consumed in large quantities does not suffice to justify the imposition of stricter rules in the case of beer.

50. As regards the need, and in particular the technological need, for additives, the German Government argues that there is no need for additives if beer is manufactured in accordance with the requirements of Article 9 of the Biersteuergesetz.

51. It must be emphasized that mere reference to the fact that beer can be manufactured without additives if it is made from only the raw materials prescribed in the Federal Republic of Germany does not suffice to preclude the possibility that some additives may meet a technological need. Such an interpretation of the concept of technological need, which results in favouring national production methods, constitutes a disguised means of restricting trade between Member States.

52. The concept of technological need must be assessed in the light of the raw materials utilized and bearing in mind the assessment made by the authorities of the Member State where the product was lawfully manufactured and marketed. Account must also be taken of the findings of international scientific research and in particular the work of the Community's scientific committee for food, the Codex Alimentarius Committee of the FAO and the World Health Organization.

53. Consequently, in so far as the German rules on additives in beer entail a general ban on additives, their application to beers imported from other Member States is contrary to the requirements of Community law as laid down in the case-law of the Court, since that prohibition is contrary to the principle of proportionality and is therefore not covered by the exception provided for in Article 36 of the EEC Treaty.

The Court is sufficiently reticent about its abilities that it will not evaluate the merits of conflicting scientific evidence. There need only be scientific uncertainty about the health effects of a product. There is an assumption here that science can provide reasonably certain answers which are capable of being gauged as such. Sociologists perceive uncertainty as endemic to policy driven science, that science which is used to facilitate the adoption of certain policies. This arises both from the technical limits of science[25] and from the social framework within which it must be conducted.

Wynne, B. 'Scientific Knowledge and the Global Environment' in Redclift, M. & Benton T. (eds.) *Social Theory and the Global Environment* (1994, Routledge, London) 169, 175-176.

Although the reflex reaction is still to understate and, where possible conceal scientific uncertainties in public policy issues, it is now commonplace to fine the inevitable limitations of scientific knowledge recognized as a fact of life which policy-makers and publics should learn to accept. Thus scientific uncertainty is widely discussed as the cross which policy-makers have to bear, and the main obstacle to better and more consensual or authoritative policies. Yet much of this debate still assumes that if only scientific knowledge could develop enough to reduce the technical uncertainty, then basic social consensus would follow, assuming that people could be educated into the truth as revealed by science.

---

25 Jasonoff, S. *The Fifth Branch: Science Advisers as Policy Makers* (1990, Cambridge, Mass.).

There are two main sociological strands of criticism of this dominant conventional perspective. The interests-oriented strand would note that even within the constraints of an accepted natural knowledge consensus, legitimate social interests - and hence favoured policies - can be in conflict. A perspective from the sociology of knowledge would go further, to argue that dominant interests control expertise and hence shape the available knowledge to reinforce their interests.

A more radical strand would suggest that beneath the level of conflicting explicit preferences or interests lies a deeper sense in which scientific knowledge tacitly reflects and reproduces normative models of social relations, cultural and moral identities, as if these are natural. Thus, for example, the level of intellectual aggregation of environmental data and variables such as radio caesium in the environment, when used to establish and justify restrictions on farmers operating in that environment, is effectively prescribing that degree of social or administrative standardization of the farmers.

In other words, at a deeper level than explicit interests the form in which scientific knowledge is practically articulated prescribes important aspects of their social relations and identities. In research on the interactions of scientists and farmers after Chernobyl, this point came out as the farmers' detailed and differentiated local knowledge of the environment and what it meant for optimal farming methods, even in the same valley, were denied by scientific knowledge whose 'natural' form aggregated and deleted them into single, uniform data categories combining and homogenising several different valleys and many farmers. As one farmer caught by the Chernobyl restrictions lamented in this respect: 'this is what they can't understand; they think a farm is a farm and a ewe is a ewe. They think we just stamp them off a production line or something.'

The Court has considered not only the substantive requirements of particular laws but also how they are administered. Whilst sampling of imports will often be permitted on grounds of public health, the Court has shown itself to be unsympathetic to systematic analysis. It was held disproportionate, in the absence of fraud or irregularities, for the French authorities to inspect three out of four consignments of Italian wine, and the Court ordered the French, in its interim measures, to inspect no more than 15% of the consignments.[26] Conversely, the Court considered a Directive authorising national authorities to check one in three consignments was not considered to be disproportionate.[27] This is an area, however, where there can clearly be very little certainty, as the

---

26 Case 42/82 *Commission v France* [1983] ECR 1013, [1984] 1 CMLR 160.

27 Case 37/83 *REWE-Zentrale v Landwirtschaftskammer Rheinland* [1984] ECR 1229, [1985] 2 CMLR 586.

number of inspections that may be permissible will depend upon the nature of the goods and other circumstances, such as whether there has been a recent outbreak of a particular disease.

v. Public Morality

Case 121/85 Conegate v Customs & Excise Commissioners [1986] ECR 1007, [1986] 1 CMLR 739

A batch of pornographic rubber dolls imported from Germany by Conegate Ltd., a British company, were seized under section 42 of the Customs Consolidation Act 1976, which prohibited the importation of obscene or indecent articles. The law in the United Kingdom on domestic products varied. In the Isle of Man and Scotland, at one extreme, the manufacture, sale and distribution of such articles was prohibited. In England and Wales, however, neither the manufacture nor sale was prohibited. The only controls were that such items could not be sold through the post, could not be displayed in a public place and had to be sold from licenced premises.

13. The Court would observe that the first question raises, in the first place, the general problem of whether a prohibition on the importation of certain goods may be justified on grounds of public morality where the legislation of the Member State concerned contains no prohibition on the manufacture or marketing of the same products within the national territory.

14. So far as that problem is concerned, it must be borne in mind that according to Article 36 of the EEC Treaty the provisions relating to the free movement of goods within the community do not preclude prohibitions on imports justified 'on grounds of public morality'. ... In principle it is for each Member State to determine in accordance with its own scale of values and in the form selected by it the requirements of public morality in its territory.

15. However, although Community law leaves the Member States free to make their own assessments of the indecent or obscene character of certain articles, it must be pointed out that the fact that goods cause offence cannot be regarded as sufficiently serious to justify restrictions on the free movement of goods where the Member State concerned does not adopt, with respect to the same goods manufactured or marketed within its territory, penal measures or other serious and effective measures intended to prevent the distribution of such goods in its territory.

16. It follows that a Member State may not rely on grounds of public morality in order to prohibit the importation of goods from other Member States when its legislation contains no prohibition on the manufacture or marketing of the same goods on its territory.

17. It is not for the Court, within the framework of the powers conferred upon it by Article 177 of the EEC Treaty, to consider whether, and to what extent, the United Kingdom legislation contains such a prohibition. However, the question whether or not such a prohibition exists in a state comprised of different constituent parts which have their own internal legislation, can be resolved only by taking into consideration all the relevant legislation. Although it is not necessary, for the purposes of the application of the above-mentioned rule, that the manufacture and marketing of the products whose importation has been prohibited should be prohibited in the territory of all the constituent parts, it must at least be possible to conclude from the applicable rules, taken as a whole, that their purpose is, in substance, to prohibit the manufacture and marketing of those products.

18. In this instance, in the actual wording of its first question the High Court took care to define the substance of the national legislation the compatibility of which with Community law is a question which it proposes to determine. Thus it refers to rules in the importing Member State under which the goods in question may be manufactured freely and marketed subject only to certain restrictions, which it sets out explicitly, namely an absolute prohibition on the transmission of such goods by post, a restriction on their public display and, in certain areas of the Member State concerned, a system of licencing of premises for the sale of those goods to customers aged 18 years and over. Such restrictions cannot however be regarded as equivalent in substance to a prohibition on manufacture and marketing.

The points of tension in this context are when situations are sufficiently comparable that differential treatment of imports amounts to arbitrary discrimination. What conclusion would the Court have reached if equivalent restrictions to those imposed on *Conegate* had been imposed upon pornographic dolls manufactured in the United Kingdom, but other items of 'hard' pornography were manufactured relatively freely in the United Kingdom?

The situation of Member States which do not have unitary regimes is particularly problematic. The Court states that an overall view should be taken of the national regime. Yet there is a danger that, with this, the preferences of smaller regions will be overridden. It is possible to imagine a situation where a pornographic item arrives at a Scottish airport whose manufacture and marketing is prohibited in Scotland but permitted in England. On a literal reading of *Conegate* such an item would have to be admitted, yet that would make a mockery of Scotland's ability to have separate laws from England.

vi. Public Policy

The public policy exception was potentially the most wideranging exception contained in Article 36 [*30*] EC, as it could be stretched to cover almost everything. The Court has been swift to narrow it down. The exception can only be used to protect the 'fundamental interests of society'.[28] This latter term is interpreted far more narrowly in relation to goods than it is in relation to workers.[29] Criminalisation of a particular product or a particular activity will be insufficient for a Member State to invoke the derogation,[30] and the derogation cannot be used to protect economic interests.[31]

The only instance of where a Member State has successfully invoked the public policy exception was in *Thompson*[32] where the United Kingdom was permitted to restrict the export of old silver coins, which were no longer legal tender, on the grounds that every Member State must be able to protect its exclusive right to mint coinage. In a similar vein it has also been accepted by the Court, although never applied, that a Member State could invoke the public policy proviso if there were otherwise a danger that civil disorder would develop which it would be unable to control.[33]

Other than that, the provision is undeveloped. The reasons for this are twofold. First the exception is so narrow that it has, in effect, become subsumed either within the public security exception in Article 36 [*30*] EC or within the exception in Article 224 [*297*] EC, which

---

28 Case 7/78 *R v Thompson* [1978] ECR 2247, [1979] 1 CMLR 47.

29 See Chapter 11.

30 Case 16/83 *Prantl* [1984] ECR 1299, [1985] 2 CMLR 238.

31 Case 72/83 *Campus Oil v Minister for Industry and Energy* [1984] ECR 2727, [1984] 3 CMLR 544.

32 Case 7/78 *R v Thompson* [1978] ECR 2247, [1979] 1 CMLR 47.

33 Case 231/83 *Cullet v Leclerc* [1985] ECR 305, [1985] 2 CMLR 524.

allows Member States to derogate from Treaty norms in the event of serious internal disturbances. Secondly, the open-ended nature of the mandatory requirements doctrine has resulted in Member States pleading their case under that heading rather than attempt to stretch the public policy exception.

vii. Public Security

This exception applies to both a Member State's internal security and to its external security.[34] In many systems the role of courts in vetting legislative or administrative activity in this area is marginal. In the United States, for example, one has the doctrine of the 'political question', which allows the President to declare war free from the fetters of the Supreme Court. In the United Kingdom court intervention is limited, as most of it falls within the Crown Prerogative. In the case of the European Community, the position is rendered more complicated not simply by the evocative nature of the subject-matter, but also by national administrations resenting their actions being fettered by some external force to which they owe less allegiance than the interests under scrutiny.

Case 72/83 Campus Oil v Minister for Industry and Energy [1984] ECR 2727, [1984] 3 CMLR 544

The Irish Government issued an Order in 1982 that all importers of petroleum obtain a minimum of 35% of their needs from the sole Irish refinery in Whitegate, County Cork. This refinery was owned by the Irish National Petroleum Company Ltd., a company which had been set up to ensure an orderly supply of petrol onto the Irish market. Campus Oil and a number of other traders contested the compatibility of this purchasing requirement with Article 30 [*28*] EC. The Irish Government claimed the measure was justified on grounds of public policy.

---

[34] Case C-367/89 *Ministre des Finances v Richardt* [1991] ECR I-4621, [1992] 1 CMLR 61.

34. It should be stated in this connection that petroleum products, because of their exceptional importance as an energy source in the modern economy, are of fundamental importance for a country's existence since not only its economy but above all its institutions, its essential public services and even the survival of its inhabitants depend upon them. An interruption of supplies of petroleum products, with the resultant dangers for the country's existence, could therefore seriously affect the public security that Article 36 allows States to protect.

35. It is true that ... Article 36 refers to matters of a non-economic nature. A Member State cannot be allowed to avoid the effects of measures provided for in the Treaty by pleading the economic difficulties caused by the elimination of barriers to intra-Community trade. However, in the light of the seriousness of the consequences that an interruption in supplies of petroleum products may have for a country's existence, the aim of ensuring a minimum supply of petroleum products at all times is to be regarded as transcending purely economic considerations and thus as capable of constituting an objective covered by the concept of public security.

36. It should be added that to come within the ambit of Article 36, the rules in question must be justified by objective circumstances corresponding to the needs of public security. Once that justification has been established, the fact that the rules are of such a nature as to make it possible to achieve, in addition to the objectives covered by the concept of public security, other objectives of an economic nature which the Member State may also seek to achieve, does not exclude the application of Article 36. The question is whether the measures are capable of ensuring supplies and the principle of proportionality.

.....

38. In that connection, the plaintiffs in the main action and the Commission cast doubt, in the first place, on whether the installation of a refinery can ensure supplies of petroleum products in the event of a crisis, since a crisis gives rise above all to a shortage of crude oil, so that the refinery would be unable to operate in such circumstances.

39. It is true that as the world oil market now stands, the immediate effect of a crisis would probably be an interruption or a severe reduction in deliveries of crude oil. It should, however, be pointed out that the fact of having refining capacity on its territory enables the State concerned to enter into long-term contracts with the oil-producing countries for the supply of crude oil to its refinery which offer a better guarantee of supplies in the event of a crisis. It is thus less at risk than a State which has no refining capacity of its own and which has no means of covering its needs other than by purchases on the free market.

.....

41. Furthermore, the existence of a national refinery constitutes a guarantee against the additional risk of an interruption in deliveries of refined products to which a State with no refining capacity of its own is exposed. Such a State would be dependent on the major oil companies which control refineries in other countries and on those companies' commercial policy. It may, therefore, be concluded that the presence of a refinery on the national territory, by reducing both of those types of risks, can effectively contribute to improving the security of supply of petroleum products to a State which does not have crude oil resources of its own.

42. The plaintiffs in the main action and the Commission consider, however, that even if the operation of a refinery is justified in the interest of public security, it is not necessary in order to achieve that objective, and, in any event, it is disproportionate in relation to that objective, to oblige importers to satisfy a certain proportion of their requirements by purchase from the national refinery at a price fixed by the competent Minister.

.....

45. In the present case, therefore, it is necessary to consider whether the obligation placed on importers of petroleum products to purchase at prices determined on the basis of the costs incurred by the refinery in question is necessary, albeit only temporarily, for the purpose of ensuring that enough of the refinery's production can be marketed so as to guarantee, in the interest of public security, a minimum supply of petroleum products to the state concerned in the event of a supply crisis.

46. That obligation could be necessary if the distributors that hold the major share of the market concerned refuse, as the Irish government contends, to purchase supplies from the refinery in question. It is on the assumption that the refinery charges prices which are competitive on the market concerned that it must be determined whether the refinery's products could be freely marketed. If it is not possible by means of industrial and commercial measures to avoid any financial losses resulting from such prices, those losses must be borne by the Member State concerned, subject to the application of Articles 92 and 93 of the Treaty.

47. As regards, in the next place, the quantities of petroleum products which may, as the case may be, be covered by such a system of purchasing obligations, it should be stressed that they must in no case exceed the minimum supply requirements of the State concerned without which its public security, as defined above, and in particular the operation of its essential public services and the survival of its inhabitants, would be affected.

48. Furthermore, the quantities of petroleum products whose marketing can be ensured under such a system must not exceed the quantities which are necessary, so far as production is concerned, on the one hand, for technical reasons in order that the refinery may operate currently at a sufficient level of its production capacity to ensure that its plant will be available in the event of a crisis and, on the other hand, in order that it may continue to refine at all times the crude oil covered by the long-term contracts which the State concerned has entered into so that it may be assured of regular supplies.

49. The proportion of the total needs of importers of petroleum products that may be made subject to a purchasing obligation must not, therefore, exceed the proportion which the quantities set out above represent of the current total consumption of petroleum products in the Member State concerned.

50. It is for the national court to decide whether the system established by the 1982 Order complies with those limits.

Although the Court stated that Article 36 [*30*] EC cannot be invoked to protect economic interests, the judgment does just that through developing a defence of economic security. The task of deciding what measures are the least restrictive necessary to secure economic security is fraught with difficulty, as it is trying to reconcile two diametrically opposed tensions, that of protectionism and free trade. The reasoning is thus less than convincing. The Court has to admit that the existence of the refinery will not secure oil supplies in all circumstances. A less onerous system of supporting the refinery, moreover, than through a purchasing commitment, might have been for the Irish Government to subsidise the refinery directly, where it, rather than the importers, would have borne the costs of keeping the refinery going.

In a more recent judgment, the Court took a much more severe line.[35] The Greek Government had reserved the exclusive right to import about 65% of the needs of the Greek domestic market for petrol to two State-owned refineries. Distributors were required to purchase a percentage of their supplies from these refineries. In addition distributors were required to provide supply programmes indicating, *inter alia*, their expected level of sales and the origin of their supplies for approval by the Greek authorities. Finally, distributors were allocated an individual quota with which to acquire petrol on the free market.

All these features of the scheme were found to fall within Article 30[*28*] EC. Whilst the Court accepted the notion of economic security as a derogation by accepting that Greece has a right to ensure a

[35] Case 347/88 *Commission v Greece* [1990] ECR I-4747.

minimum supply of petrol, it scrutinised the measure much more closely than in *Campus Oil*. It found that an obligation to purchase could only be justified if the refinery's production could not be disposed of at market prices, something that the Greek government had failed to prove. The Court was equally dismissive of the system of supply programmes and marketing quotas. It acknowledged that the information contained in procurement programmes enabled authorities to plan their requirements more effectively but this could not justify their having the power to authorise these plans.

Further Reading

Brouwer, O. 'Free Movement of Foodstuffs and Quality Requirements: Has the Commission got it Wrong?' (1988) 25 *Common Market Law Review* 237

Demiray, D. 'The Movement of Goods in a Green Market' (1994/1) *Legal Issues of European Integration* 73

Gerardin, D. & Stewardson, A. 'Trade and Environment: Some Lessons from Castlemaine Tooheys (Australia) and Danish Bottles (European Community)' (1995) 44 *International and Comparative Law Quarterly* 41

Gormley, L. 'Recent case law on the Free Movement of Goods: Some Hot Potatoes' (1990) 27 *Common Market Law Review* 835

Green, N., Hartley, T. & Usher, J. *The Legal Foundations of the Single European Market* (1991, Oxford University Press, Oxford) Chapter 7

Krämer, L. 'Environmental Protection and Article 30 EEC Treaty' (1993) 30 *Common Market Law Review* 111

Oliver, P. 'A Review of the case law of the Court of Justice on Articles 30 to 36 EEC in 1985' (1986) 23 *Common Market Law Review* 325

Van Rijn, T. 'A Review of the case law of the Court of Justice on Articles 30-36 in 1986 and 1987' (1988) 25 *Common Market Law Review* 593

Weatherill, S. 'The Evolution of European Consumer Law and Policy: From Well Informed Consumer to Confident Consumer' in Micklitz, H. *Rechtseinheit order Rechtsvielfalt in Europa?* (1996, Nomos, Baden-Baden)
Ziegler, A. *Trade and Environmental Law in the European Community* (1996, Clarendon, Oxford)

8. The Service Economy

I. Introduction

When juxtaposed next to the extensive amount of case law and academic literature on free movement of goods, the relatively recent nature of much of the case law and limited amount of literature on free movement of services can give the impression that services are no more than a handmaiden to goods. Such an impression is a false one. Service transactions now account for over 64% of Community GDP.[1] Whilst the bulk of these transactions are purely local, the inclusion of an Agreement on Services within the new World Trade Organisation (WTO) illustrates recognition of the importance and growth in international trade in services.

The position is further complicated by services moving in a variety of ways.[2]

Eeckhout, P. *The European Internal Market and International Trade: A Legal Analysis* (1994, Clarendon Press, Oxford) 9-10

Services are extremely diverse. They range from so-called 'smokestack services' such as banking and air transport to much more uncomplicated activities such as hairdressing and taxi driving. This diversity is also reflected in the way international trade in services takes place. Some examples may illustrate this. In tourism, it is the tourist who travels and consumes services abroad. In banking, it is possible to have financial transactions across the border, without the bank or the client moving towards one another. Or the foreign bank may wish to have some commercial presence in the client's country, in order to provide its services. Television allows the same programme to be broadcast at the same

---

1 In 1993 service transactions accounted for 64.3% of the GDP of the Twelve. Eurostat, *Basic Statistics of the Community* (1995, 32nd Edition, OOPEC, Luxembourg) 45.

2 See also Sampson, G. & Snape, R. 'Identifying the Issues in Trade in Services' (1985) 8 *World Economy* 171, 172-173.

time in different countries, with sometimes up to billions of viewers watching it in their respective homes. In hairdressing, by contrast, there is very little international exchange.

As a result it is difficult to define international trade in services. Nevertheless, it has been attempted to categorise international service transactions, and most of these attempts concentrate on the mobility of the 'actors' in the transaction, namely the producer and consumer of services, even though, however, there is no unanimity as to which categories should be distinguished. In the author's view, one can perceive four main categories:

1. The consumer moves towards the producer of the service, for example a Belgian tourist booking a room in an Austrian hotel.
2. The producer of the service moves to the consumer, as is the case when an orchestra performs abroad.
3. Consumer and producer of the service both move, the most important example being human transport.
4. Neither the producer nor the consumer moves, but it is the service itself which 'travels': television signals or a phone call.

The fact that trade in services can involve the international movement of the producer and/or consumer of services has important implications, which do not exist with respect to trade in goods. The latter does not require movement of people, except for the transporter (who performs a service!). The first implication is that one has to draw a line between international movement of people as such - in other words migration, which is a very sensitive issue - and service transactions involving people moving across borders. Often it is not easy to draw this line. Secondly, international service transactions may require the mobility of companies. For a number of these transactions, in the financial sector for example, it is necessary that the service provider has a form of (more or less permanent) commercial presence in the consumer's country. In other words, one cannot fully address international trade in services without also addressing investment and establishment issues.

The heterogeneous manner in which services move requires that one look at a number of provisions. The most general is that of Article 59 [*49*] EC.

Article 59 [*49*] EC. Within the framework of the provisions set out below, restrictions on freedom to provide services within the Community shall be progressively abolished during the transitional period in respect of nationals of Member States who are established in a State of the Community other than that of the person for whom the services are intended.

It must be placed alongside Article 52 [*43*] EC which deals with the situation where a service provider sets up in another Member State.

Article 52 [*43*] EC. Within the framework of the provisions set out below, restrictions on the freedom of establishment of nationals of a Member State in the territory of another Member State shall be abolished by progressive stages in the course of the transitional period. Such progressive abolition shall also apply to restrictions on the setting up of agencies, branches or subsidiaries by nationals of any Member State established in the territory of any Member State.

The notion of a service is like the dark. Everyone intuitively knows what it is, but it is very difficult to define. Economic analysis of this area has thus been bedeviled by definitional difficulties.[3] A definition of sorts is provided in Article 60 [*50*] EC.

Article 60 [*50*] EC. Services shall be considered to be 'services' within the meaning of this Treaty where they are normally provided for remuneration, in so far as they are not governed by the provisions relating to freedom of movement for goods, capital and persons.

'Services' shall in particular include:

(a) activities of an industrial character;

(b) activities of a commercial character;

(c) activities of craftsmen;

(d) activities of the professions.

This definition followed early economic analysis which simply contrasted services as being different from goods. Goods were storable whereas services were intangible, and were consumed simultaneously with production. This distinction proved to be unsuccessful as a consequence of the sheer variety of services. Many services are tangible, a haircut is an example, and have an element of permanence. Similarly, with many services, pension management being an example, consumption and provision are not done simultaneously. Recent

---

[3] For a discussion of the literature see Nicholaides, P. *Liberalizing Service Trade: Strategies for Success* (1989, RIIA, London) 6-12.

attempts have therefore focused upon services as a particular form of transaction. Nicholaides claims that a service is an explicit transaction involving the execution of, or the promise to execute, one or more specified tasks.[4] The difficulty with this is virtually anything can be transacted. Prostitution, fencing and drugdealing are as much based upon transactions as insurance or catering. All would be entitled to the protection of the economic freedoms in the EC Treaty.

Case C-159/90 Society for the Protection of the Unborn Child (SPUC) v Grogan [1991] ECR I-4685, [1991] 3 CMLR 849

In 1986 the Irish Supreme Court ruled that it was against Article 40.3.3 of the Irish Constitution for people to help Irish women to have abortions by informing them of the identity and location of abortion clinics abroad. A number of Irish student unions subsequently published literature giving details of the addresses of abortion clinics in the United Kingdom. The Society for the Protection of the Unborn Child (SPUC) wrote to the officers of these unions seeking an undertaking that the latter would not continue to publish this literature during the forthcoming academic year. When SPUC received no reply, it sought an injunction to prevent publication. The question arose whether the provision of information about abortion clinics in these circumstances constituted a service under Article 59 [*49*] EC.

17. According to the first paragraph of that provision [Article 60 EC], services are to be considered to be 'services' within the meaning of the Treaty where they are normally provided for remuneration, in so far as they are not governed by the provisions relating to freedom of movement for goods, capital or persons. Indent (d) of the second paragraph of Article 60 expressly states that activities of the professions fall within the definition of services.

18. It must be held that termination of pregnancy, as lawfully practised in several Member States, is a medical activity which is normally provided for remuneration and may be carried out as part of a professional activity. In any event, the Court has already held in the judgment in *Luisi and Carbone* (Joined Cases 286/82 and 26/83 *Luisi and Carbone v Ministero del Tesoro* [1984] ECR 377, paragraph 16) that medical activities fall within the scope of Article 60 of the Treaty.

---

4 Ibid., 11.

19. SPUC, however, maintains that the provision of abortion cannot be regarded as being a service, on the grounds that it is grossly immoral and involves the destruction of the life of a human being, namely the unborn child.

20. Whatever the merits of those arguments on the moral plane, they cannot influence the answer to the national court's first question. It is not for the Court to substitute its assessment for that of the legislature in those Member States where the activities in question are practised legally.

21. Consequently, the answer to the national court's first question must be that medical termination of pregnancy, performed in accordance with the law of the State in which it is carried out, constitutes a service within the meaning of Article 60 of the Treaty.

22. Having regard to the facts of the case, it must be considered that, in its second and third questions, the national court seeks essentially to establish whether it is contrary to Community law for a Member State in which medical termination of pregnancy is forbidden to prohibit students' associations from distributing information about the identity and location of clinics in another Member State where medical termination of pregnancy is lawfully carried out and the means of communicating with those clinics, where the clinics in question have no involvement in the distribution of the said information.

.....

24. As regards, first, the provisions of Article 59 of the Treaty, which prohibit any restriction on the freedom to supply services, it is apparent from the facts of the case that the link between the activity of the students' associations of which Mr Grogan and the other defendants are officers and medical terminations of pregnancies carried out in clinics in another Member State is too tenuous for the prohibition on the distribution of information to be capable of being regarded as a restriction within the meaning of Article 59 of the Treaty.

25. The situation in which students' associations distributing the information at issue in the main proceedings are not in cooperation with the clinics whose addresses they publish can be distinguished from the situation which gave rise to the judgment in *GB-INNO-BM* (Case C-362/88 *GB-INNO-BM v Confédération du Commerce Luxembourgeois* [1990] ECR I-667), in which the Court held that a prohibition on the distribution of advertising was capable of constituting a barrier to the free movement of goods and therefore had to be examined in the light of Articles 30, 31 and 36 of the EEC Treaty.

26. The information to which the national court's questions refer is not distributed on behalf of an economic operator established in another Member State. On the contrary, the information constitutes a manifestation of freedom of expression and of the freedom to impart and receive information which is independent of the economic activity carried on by clinics established in another Member State.

27. It follows that, in any event, a prohibition on the distribution of information in circumstances such as those which are the subject of the main proceedings cannot be regarded as a restriction within the meaning of Article 59 of the Treaty.

The Court has therefore taken a hybrid approach. Services are to be distinguished from goods,[5] but, subject to this proviso, it is rather the quality of *exchange*, expressed in Article 60(1) [*50(1)*] EC in the need for remuneration, which characterises the services provisions. There must be consideration provided from the recipient of the service to the provider, although this can be in kind.[6] The requirement of exchange seems to be a formality rather than having any substantive content. Article 2 of the Sixth VAT Directive is similarly phrased to Article 60 [*50*] EC. It states that services provided by a taxable person must, in principle, be taxed if they made for payment or consideration.[7] In *Coöperative Aardappelenbewaarplaats*[8] the Court considered that whilst the consideration must be capable of being expressed in money, no other constraints were placed on the adequacy of the consideration.

The other limit to Article 59 [*49*] EC is that public services provided at below cost price fall outside it. In *Humbel* provision of education within the public sector was held not to constitute economic activity, and therefore not to be subject to the rigours of the economic freedoms, notwithstanding that fees were being charged for the

---

5 Article 60(1) [*50(1)*]EC. On the borderline between Article 30 [*28*] EC and Article 59 [*49*] EC see Case C-275/92 *Her Majesty's Customs and Excise v Schindler Brothers* [1994] ECR I-1039, [1995] 1 CMLR 4; Case C-55/93 *Van Schaik* [1994] ECR I-4837.

6 Case 196/87 *Steymann v Staatssecretaris van Justitie* [1988] ECR 6159, [1989] 1 CMLR 449.

7 Directive 77/388/EEC, OJ 1977 L 145/1.

8 Case 154/80 *Staatsecretaris van Financiëen v Coöperative Aardappelenbewaarplaats* [1981] ECR 445. See also Case 324/82 *Commission v Belgium* [1984] ECR 1861; Case C-288/94 *Argos Distributors Ltd v Commissioners of Customs & Excise,* Judgment of 24 October 1996; Case C-317/94 *Gibbs v Commissioners of Customs & Excise,* Judgment of 24 October 1996.

provision of education.[9] The reason was that, in setting up an education system, the State was not intending to engage in economic activities but to achieve objectives in the social, cultural and education fields, which were to be financed principally out of the public purse. The rationale adopted, therefore, seems to be that public services, such as education, health and transport, are, in the jargon of public sector economists, 'mixed goods', namely they are goods or services provided free or sold at below their cost of production. Without controls there are strong incentives for 'free riders' to consume these goods irrespective of the economic costs involved. In the absence of a common transport, education or health policy which is funded by a common exchequer it would seem unjust that taxpayers who fund a particularly high level of service in one Member State should also bear the cost of 'free riders' from other Member States.

Notwithstanding this, it has been argued that the same principles underlying free movement of goods should apply to services.

Hindley, B. and Smith, A. 'Comparative Advantage and Trade in Services' (1984) 7 *World Economy* 369, 370 & 375

The theory of comparative cost comes in two parts. The first is a positive or descriptive theory; the second, a normative or prescriptive one. It is of central importance to keep the distinction between the two clear.

Positive theory attempts to explain why production of particular goods is cheaper (relative to other goods) in one location than in another and, therefore, why some classes of goods are exported from, and others imported to, a particular location.

Normative theory asks whether the pattern of production and specialisation which results from international cost differences is economically efficient and socially desirable and investigates what are the optimal government policies towards international trade.

.....

From the observation that trade and foreign direct investment may be close substitutes in the case of some services (such as insurance) and that trade and mobility of labour may be close substitutes in other cases (such as management services), some

9 Case 263/86 *Humbel v Belgium* [1988] ECR 5365, [1989] 1 CMLR 393. See also Case C-109/92 *Wirth v Landeshauptstadt Hannover* [1993] ECR I-6447.

people have drawn the conclusion that there are problems in the application of standard trade theory, as developed for trade in goods, to the services sector. It is not all clear why this should be so. Certainly, there is a particular problem for the positive theory, in that it may be hard to predict whether a comparative advantage will manifest itself as a trade flow, an investment flow or a labour flow. But from the viewpoint of the normative theory there is less of a problem. A country gains from importing services *or* allowing immigration of labour *or* receiving foreign direct investment if the terms on which these transactions take place are more favourable than the terms available on domestic transactions. The basic reasoning is the same in each case. To the extent that the three modes of commerce are close substitutes, the welfare effect of the three should almost be the same.

Parallels must also be drawn with Article 48 [*39*] EC, the provision on workers. Whilst EC law does not consider that a person can simultaneously be working and providing a service for the same person,[10] in many situations the economic activities carried out will also be economically substitutable. Furthermore, a self-employed person is likely to be as integrated into the society of a Member State as an employed person. It would seem to run contrary to the notion of European Citizenship if one were treated more favourably than the other. These provisions have therefore been interpreted identically on a number of matters.

First, Articles 48 [*39*], 52 [*43*], and 59 [*49*] have all been found to be directly effective.[11] The direct effect of these provisions, however, falls into a unique category which straddles the traditional distinctions drawn between vertical and horizontal direct effect.[12]

---

10 On the distinction between a worker and a service provider see Case 66/85 *Lawrie Blum v Land Baden Wurttemberg* [1986] ECR 2121, [1987] 3 CMLR 389.

11 On the direct effect of Article 48 [*39*] EC see Case 167/73 *Commission v France* [1974] ECR 359, [1974] 2 CMLR 216; Article 52[*43*] EC, see Case 2/74 *Reyners v Belgian State* [1974] ECR 631, [1974] 2 CMLR 305; Article 59 [*49*] EC, see Case 33/74 *Van Binsbergen v Bestuur van de Bedrijfsvereniging voor de Metaalnijverheid* [1974] ECR 1299, [1975] 1 CMLR 298.

12 Some uncertainty has been created by the *Bosman* judgment. This reaffirmed the *Walrave & Koch* line of reasoning. One of the actions, however, was brought by the player directly against the club - i.e. it was a pure application of horizontal direct effect - and the Court made no attempt to distinguish this case

Case 36/74 Walrave & Koch v Association Union Cycliste Internationale [1974] ECR 1405, [1975] 1 CMLR 320

In medium-distance cycling events each competitor has a pacemaker who goes ahead on a motorcycle. The Association Union Cycliste Internationale, the international body that regulated the sport, introduced a ruling that, as from 1973, the pacemaker must be of the same nationality as the competitor. This was challenged by two Dutch pacemakers, who claimed it breached Articles 48 and 59 EC.

14. The main question in respect of all the Articles referred to is whether the rules of an international sporting federation can be regarded as incompatible with the Treaty.

15. It has been alleged that the prohibitions in these Articles refer only to restrictions which have their origin in acts of an authority and not to those resulting from legal acts of persons or associations who do not come under public law.

16. Articles 7, 48, 59 have in common the prohibition, in their respective spheres of application, of any discrimination on grounds of nationality.

17. Prohibition of such discrimination does not only apply to the action of public authorities but extends likewise to rules of any other nature aimed at regulating in a collective manner gainful employment and the provision of services.

18. The abolition as between Member States of obstacles to freedom of movement for persons and to freedom to provide services, which are fundamental objectives of the Community contained in Article 3(c) of the Treaty, would be compromised if the abolition of barriers of national origin could be neutralized by obstacles resulting from the exercise of their legal autonomy by associations or organizations which do not come under public law.

Secondly, identical principles apply to all three freedoms with regard to market access. The Court has therefore stated that the provisions must be interpreted identically in respect of entry and residence in the territory of Member States of persons covered by

---

from the others, Case C-415/93 *Union Royale Belge des Sociétés de Football Association ASBL v Bosman; Royal Club Liègeois SA v Bosman; Union des Associations Européennes de Football v Bosman* [1995] ECR I- 4921.

Community law. In *Roux*[13] it was held that a residence permit could not be denied by the Belgian State to a French waitress merely because it was unclear whether she was a worker or self-employed. The immigration aspects of services and establishment are touched upon further below but are dealt with primarily in the chapter on free movement of persons.[14]

Restrictions upon market access extend beyond restrictions on immigration, however. A person is excluded from a market just as effectively by a restriction being placed upon their pursuing a particular occupation, such as their being required to belong to a particular body or have a particular piece of paper, as by their being prevented from entering the country. The Court has therefore made clear that the provisions should be also interpreted identically in respect of market access. In *Commission v Italy*[15] the Italians recognised qualifications necessary for entering the profession of health auxiliary when those qualifications had been obtained abroad, if those qualifications had been obtained by an Italian national. The Court considered this to breach Articles 48 [*39*], 52 [*43*] and 59 [*49*] EC, as all these provisions required that access to activities for the employed and self-employed for Community nationals be on the same conditions as for a State's own nationals.

More recently, in *Commission v France*, in a judgment concerning discriminatory French restrictions on who could register vessels to fly the French flag, the Court considers that Articles 48 [*39*] and 52 EC [*43*] include the right to remain and reside in the Member State following the period of employment or business activities in question.[16]

---

13 Case C-363/89 *Roux v Belgian State* [1991] ECR I-273, [1993] 1 CMLR 3. See also Case 48/75 *Procureur du Roi v Royer* [1976] ECR 497, [1976] 2 CMLR 619.

14 See p. 101 ff.

15 Case C-58/90 *Commission v Italy* [1991] ECR I-4193. See also Case 168/85 *Commission v Italy* [1986] ECR 2945.

16 Case C-334/94 *Commission v France* [1996] ECR I-1307. For identical reasoning see Case C-151/96 *Commission v Ireland*, Judgment of 12 June 1997; Case C-62/96 *Commission v Greece*, Judgment of 27 November 1997.

Thirdly, identical principles applied as to a Member State may deny entry to another Member State's nationals. Article 66 [*55*] EC provides that the restrictions which may be applied in relation to establishment may also be applied in relation to Article 59 [*49*] EC, the general provision on services.

Article 66 [*55*] EC. The provisions of Articles 55 to 58 shall apply to the matters covered by this Chapter [the Chapter on Services].

Article 56 [*46*] EC gives the same grounds as Article 48(3) [*39(3)*] EC on which entry may be barred - namely public policy, public security or public health - and it is assumed the reasoning applies to each.[17] In addition, Member States may impose restrictions on freedom of establishment and freedom to provide services in relation to those activities which are connected, even occasionally, with the exercise of official authority.[18]

Article 55 [*45*] EC. The provisions of this Chapter shall not apply, so far as any given Member State is concerned, to activities which in that State are connected, even occasionally, with the exercise of official authority.

Case 2/74 Reyners v Belgium [1974] ECR 631, [1974] 2 CMLR 305[19]

Reyners was resident in Belgium and had completed his legal education there. He was, however, a Dutch national, and, under the Belgian Code Judiciaire, only Belgian nationals could practice the profession of 'avocat'. Reyners was refused a dispensation and challenged the requirement, claiming it breached Article 52

---

17 See p. 446 ff.

18 The equivalent provision for workers is Article 48(4) [*39(4)*] EC, although slightly different principles apply. See p. 441.

19 See also Case C-42/92 *Thijdienst v Controledienst voor de Verzekeringen* [1993] ECR I-4047 where insurance auditors were also found not to fall within this exception.

[*43*] EC. It was argued, however, that there were such close links between the lawyers and the judiciary that Article 55 [*45*] EC applied.

43. Having regard to the fundamental character of freedom of establishment and the rule on equal treatment with nationals in the system of the Treaty, the exceptions allowed by the first paragraph of Article 55 cannot be given a scope which would exceed the objective for which this exemption clause was inserted.

44. The first paragraph of Article 55 must enable Member States to exclude non-nationals from taking up functions involving the exercise of official authority which are connected with one of the activities of self-employed persons provided for in Article 52.

45. This need is fully satisfied when the exclusion of nationals is limited to those activities which, taken on their own, constitute a direct and specific connection with the exercise of official authority.

46. An extension of the exception allowed by Article 55 to a whole profession would be possible only in cases where such activities were linked with that profession in such a way that freedom of establishment would result in imposing on the Member State concerned the obligation to allow the exercise, even occasionally, by non-nationals of functions appertaining to official authority.

47. This extension is on the other hand not possible when, within the framework of an independent profession, the activities connected with the exercise of official authority are separable from the professional activity in question taken as a whole.

.....

51. Professional activities involving contacts, even regular and organic, with the courts, including even compulsory cooperation in their functioning, do not constitute, as such, connection with the exercise of official authority.

52. The most typical activities of the profession of avocat, in particular, such as consultation and legal assistance and also representation and the defence of parties in court, even when the intervention or assistance of the avocat is compulsory or is a legal monopoly, cannot be considered as connected with the exercise of official authority.

53. The exercise of these activities leaves the discretion of judicial authority and the free exercise of judicial power intact.

54. It is therefore right to reply to the question raised that the exception to freedom of establishment provided for by the first paragraph of Article 55 must be restricted to those of the activities referred to in Article 52 which in themselves involve a direct and specific connection with the exercise of official authority.

55. In any case it is not possible to give this description, in the context of a profession such as that of avocat, to activities such as consultation and legal assistance or the representation and defence of parties in court, even if the performance of these activities is compulsory or there is a legal monopoly in respect of it.

There are features of trade in services, however, which militate in favour of a more nuanced approach. The first is that the service sector is, by tradition, more heavily regulated than the goods sector.[20] This arises in part out of tradition. It also arises because the offeror of many services will often have a considerably greater knowledge of the service provided than the consumer. Whilst there are many services where this is not the case and many goods where this is the case, Van Empel has noted that this structural disadvantage for the consumer appears to be more prevalent in the services sector.[21]

Secondly, services are regulated in a different manner from goods. In particular, Bhagwati has observed that whilst the user of goods is protected by regulation applied to the good, the non-storability of the service has resulted in the user of services often being protected by regulation which applies to the provider of the service rather than the service itself.[22] Hindley has also observed that in service industries products are less standardised and are more likely to be custom made to individual clients. Consequently, the modes of regulating of goods through sampling and testing cannot be applied in the same manner to services. It is common in the field of services, therefore, for market externalities to be protected through regulation of the provider of services as well as regulation of the provision of the service itself.[23]

---

20 Bhagwati, J. 'Services' 207, 209 in Finger, M. & Olechowski, A. *The Uruguay Round - A Handbook on the Multilateral Trade Negotiations* (1987, World Bank, Washington DC); Hindley, B. & Smith, A. 'Comparative Advantage and Services' (1984) 7 *World Economy* 369, 377 *et seq.*

21 Van Empel, M. 'The Visible Hand in Invisible Trade' (1990/2) *LIEI* 23, 30-31; Nicholaides, P. 'Economic Aspects of Services: Implications for a GATT Agreement' (1989) 23 *JWTL* 125, 126-127.

22 Ibid., 209.

23 Hindley, B. 'Service Sector Protection: Considerations for Developing Countries' (1987) 2 *World Bank Economic Review* 205, 209; Vickers, J. 'Government Regulation Policy' (1991) 7 *Oxford Review of Economic Policy* 13.

Finally, and perhaps most importantly, as almost anything can be transactionalised, many economic activities are also social activities. The extent of the EC provisions on services could therefore amount to the 'economisation' of the social sphere, and have, potentially, considerable disruptive consequences. This can happen in two ways. First, individuals may challenge regimes which have, for years, worked on a system of social consensus. Based on accommodation, such regimes will not provide any one clear external objective and may indeed appear self-contradictory. They are therefore particularly vulnerable to attack on the grounds that they are not proportionate, 'rational' or have a clear public interest.[24] The second divisive feature of the services provisions is that as they encompass only economic activity, they reward the 'haves' but not the 'have-nots'. Thus, if a Member State restricts a particular medical service, the service provisions may be able invoked by those who can afford to have the service performed privately abroad.[25] They are of little value to those dependent on the national system of public health care. The freedom of the first patient merely widens the gulf in social provision between him and the second patient.

II. Freedom of Establishment

i. The Meaning of Establishment

Establishment is described in Article 52(2) [*43(2)*] EC as the taking up and pursuit of activities as self-employed, a description which was repeated in 1961 by the General Programme for the Abolition of Restriction on Freedom of Establishment.[26] In principle, measures which

---

24 Case C-275/92 *Her Majesty's Customs and Excise v Schindler* [1994] ECR I-1039, [1995] 1 CMLR 4.

25 *R v Human Fertilisation and Embryology Authority ex parte Blood* (CA) (1997) 147 NLJ Rep 253.

26 OJ Special Edition, Second Series, IX, 7. This programme was enacted pursuant to Article 54 [*44*] EC which required the Council to draw up such a programme by 1962.

discriminated on grounds of nationality in a manner which hindered the activities of the self-employed were to be eliminated. Professor Everling put it more eloquently when he stated that 'the right to freedom of establishment means the privilege to start and conduct non-wage earning activities. These activities include any independent activity aimed at the production of income.'[27] Within an EC context these descriptions are insufficient. Freedom of establishment has, first, a *geographical requirement* in that there must be some locational arbitrage in the sense of entry onto the market of another Member State.

Case 205/84 Commission v Germany [1986] ECR 3755, [1987] 2 CMLR 69

The Commission brought an action against German restrictions which required that persons offering insurance services on the German market be established in Germany and receive prior authorisation from the administrative authorities. The Court had, first of all, to consider the remit of the case.

21. In that respect, it must be acknowledged that an insurance undertaking of another Member State which maintains a permanent presence in the Member State in question comes within the scope of the provisions of the Treaty on the right of establishment, even if that presence does not take the form of a branch or agency, but consists merely of an office managed by the undertaking's own staff or by a person who is independent but authorized to act on a permanent basis for the undertaking, as would be the case with an agency. In the light of the aforementioned definition contained in the first paragraph of Article 60, such an insurance undertaking cannot therefore avail itself of Articles 59 and 60 with regard to its activities in the Member State in question.

22. Similarly, as the Court held in its judgment of 3 December 1974 (Case 33/74 *Van Binsbergen v Bedrijfsvereniging Metaalnijverheid* (1974) ECR 1299) a Member State cannot be denied the right to take measures to prevent the exercise by a person providing services whose activity is entirely or principally directed towards its territory of the freedom guaranteed by Article 59 for the purpose of avoiding the professional rules of conduct which would be applicable to him if he were established within that state. Such a situation may be subject to judicial control under the provisions of the chapter relating to the right of establishment and not of that on the provision of services.

---

[27] Everling, U. *The Right of Establishment in the Common Market* (1964, Commerce Clearing House, Chicago) 46.

The geographical requirement necessary to trigger Article 52 [*43*] EC is therefore not presence in another Member State but the direction of activities, principally or exclusively, towards the territory of that Member State. The geographical requirement is, *per se*, not sufficient to trigger Article 52 [*43*] EC. There is also a *temporal requirement* in that there must be, in addition, a *permanence* about the activity.

Case C-55/94 Gebhard v Consiglio dell'ordine degli avvocati e procuratori di Milano [1995] ECR I-4165, [1996] 1 CMLR 603.

Gebhard was a lawyer who practised both in Stuttgart, Germany, and in Milan, Italy, He resided in Milan, Italy. Disciplinary proceedings were instituted by the Milanese Bar Council against him for using the title 'avvocato' without authorisation. Gebhard argued that this was a breach of Article 59 [*49*] EC, the provision on services. The Bar Council argued that the matter fell instead within Article 52 [*43*] EC, which imposed less rigorous constraints on national regulatory regimes. Gebhard spent about 70% of his time working in Italy and 30% working in Germany and had been dividing his time in this manner for a number of years.

22. The provisions of the Chapter on services are subordinate to those of the Chapter on the right of establishment in so far, first, as the wording of the first paragraph of Article 59 assumes that the provider and the recipient of the service concerned are 'established' in two different Member States and, second, as the first paragraph of Article 60 specifies that the provisions relating to services apply only if those relating to the right of establishment do not apply. It is therefore necessary to consider the scope of the concept of 'establishment'.

23. The right of establishment, provided for in Articles 52 to 58 of the Treaty, is granted both to legal persons within the meaning of Article 58 and to natural persons who are nationals of a Member State of the Community. Subject to the exceptions and conditions laid down, it allows all types of self-employed activity to be taken up and pursued on the territory of any other Member State, undertakings to be formed and operated, and agencies, branches or subsidiaries to be set up.

24. It follows that a person may be established, within the meaning of the Treaty, in more than one Member State - in particular, in the case of companies, through the setting-up of agencies, branches or subsidiaries (Article 52) and, as the Court has held, in the case of members of the professions, by establishing a second professional base (see Case

107/83 *Ordre des avocats au barreau de Paris v Klopp* [1984] ECR 2971, paragraph 19).

25. The concept of establishment within the meaning of the Treaty is therefore a very broad one, allowing a Community national to participate, on a stable and continuous basis, in the economic life of a Member State other than his State of origin and to profit therefrom, so contributing to economic and social interpenetration within the community in the sphere of activities as self-employed persons (see, to this effect, Case 2/74 *Reyners v Belgium* [1974] ECR 631, paragraph 21).

26. In contrast, where the provider of services moves to another Member State, the provisions of the Chapter on services, in particular the third paragraph of Article 60, envisage that he is to pursue his activity there on a temporary basis.

27. As the Advocate General has pointed out, the temporary nature of the activities in question has to be determined in the light, not only of the duration of the provision of the service, but also of its regularity, periodicity or continuity. The fact that the provision of services is temporary does not mean that the provider of services within the meaning of the Treaty may not equip himself with some form of infrastructure in the host Member State (including an office, chambers or consulting rooms) in so far as such infrastructure is necessary for the purposes of performing the services in question.

28. However, that situation is to be distinguished from that of Mr Gebhard who, as a national of a Member State, pursues a professional activity on a stable and continuous basis in another Member State where he holds himself out from an established professional base to, amongst others, nationals of that State. Such a national comes under the provisions of the Chapter relating to the right of establishment and not those of the Chapter relating to services.

ii. The Taking Up of Economic Activities and the Pursuit of Economic Activities in Another Member State Compared

The Court of Justice has insisted that the right to establish includes, both the right for the self-employed to *take up activities* and the right to *pursue these activities*.[28] Whilst a distinction has never been explicitly drawn between the two by the Court, it is still useful to separate them.

---

28 Case 197/84 *Steinhauser v City of Biarritz* [1985] ECR 1819, [1986] 1 CMLR 53.

In the context of the single market, the right to take up activities is central to *entry* to the market of another Member State. It covers both *primary establishment* and *secondary establishment*. The former is where a trader either relocates its central place of business to another Member State or a person, for the first time, sets up a business in another Member State. Secondary establishment is the right to set up branches, agencies or subsidiaries in another Member State. It does not involve relocation of the primary establishment but, on the contrary, requires that the central place of business remain in the home State.

Pursuit of economic activity concerns activities of the trader carried out once the trader had set up on the market of the host State. Restrictions on pursuit of economic activity would, therefore, concern matters such as the health and safety regulations, fiscal provisions, planning requirements or access to credit.

The reason for the drawing of this distinction is that the question of discrimination is largely irrelevant to the question of market entry and the taking up of activities in another Member State. The non-discrimination principle is insufficient to ensure market access, for the noxious features of any measure restricting market access are its restrictive rather than its discriminatory effects. A good example is where the *home State* (not the host State) prevents its own nationals from leaving its territory to establish in another Member State. In such a circumstance, there is no discrimination on grounds of nationality but the measure is as antithetical to the working of the single market as a measure from the host State prohibiting the establishment of nationals of the home State within the former's territory. There is thus a particularly strong case for non-discriminatory restrictions on the right to take up activities falling within Article 52 [*43*] EC.

The position is different with regard to the pursuit of economic activities carried out by the trader established in another Member State. Once set up, a trader is primarily concerned about protecting its competitive position within the host State vis-à-vis that State's own nationals. For that reason it will be eager to ensure that it is treated in an equal manner to competitors, both in the opportunities made available to it and the costs imposed on it.

If Article 52 [*43*] EC is extended to cover non-discriminatory restrictions on the pursuit of economic activity, however, a considerable constraint is imposed on Member State regulatory capacities. In essence, it would result in any regulation of a foreign national or foreign company which had a permanent presence in a Member State being declared illegal unless that State could show that the measure pursued a public interest in a proportionate manner. Measures as diverse as general labour, environmental, consumer, health and safety legislation would all fall within Article 52 [*43*] EC.

Qualifications present a special case as they affect both the taking up and the pursuit of an economic activity. Where qualifications are necessary for entry into a profession, certain activities cannot be taken up without possession of those qualifications. The possession of qualifications or a title will also in many circumstances strengthen pursuit of economic activity and the trader's position in the marketplace by demonstrating recognition of a particular expertise. A further characteristic of qualifications is that they can equally be obtained in any of the Member States and so, like product characteristics, the expertise recognised by the qualifications moves with the trader. A doctor trained in the United Kingdom possesses the same expertise whether working in France or Britain. A restriction on the use of qualifications or titles by the host State amounts to double regulation in the same manner that the regulation of product characteristics by the importing Member State. There therefore seems to be a case for non-discriminatory restrictions on the use of qualifications or titles falling within Article 52 [*43*] EC.

iii. The Taking Up of Economic Activities in Another Member State

Article 52 [*43*] EC was initially perceived to be an application to the field of establishment of the principle in Article 6 [*12*] EC that there should be no discrimination against EC nationals on grounds of nationality. Article 52(2) [*43(2)*] EC, indeed, explicitly states that the freedom of establishment shall include the right to take up and pursue activities on the same conditions as a Member State lays down for its own nationals. In *Reyners* a Belgian requirement that one have Belgian nationality to practice as an advocate was therefore condemned as a breach of Article 52 [*43*] EC on the grounds that it discriminated against other EC nationals.[29] The judgment occurred in the period prior to *Cassis de Dijon* where it was widely assumed that the market freedoms contained in the Treaty only acted to prohibit discrimination.[30] Whilst the non-discrimination principle can be used to secure market access where access has been precluded through the imposition of a nationality or some other discriminatory requirement,[31] its limitations became apparent in a number of cases concerning secondary establishment.

Case 107/83 Ordre des Avocats au Barreau de Paris v Klopp [1984] ECR 2971

Klopp was a German lawyer who practised law in Dusseldorf. He applied to register with the Paris Bar Council in order to practice at the Paris Bar. His application was refused under a requirement, which applied both to French and non-French lawyers, prohibiting somebody from practising at the Paris Bar unless their principal office was in Paris and any other offices they worked from were in the environs of Paris.

17. It should be emphasized that under the second paragraph of Article 52 freedom of establishment includes access to and the pursuit of the activities of self-employed persons 'under the conditions laid down for its own nationals by the law of the country where such establishment is effected'. It follows from that provision and its context that in the absence of specific Community rules in the matter each Member State is free to regulate the exercise of the legal profession in its territory.

18. Nevertheless that rule does not mean that the legislation of a Member State may require a lawyer to have only one establishment throughout the Community territory. Such a restrictive interpretation would mean that a lawyer once established in a particular Member State would be able to enjoy the freedom of the treaty to establish himself in another Member State only at the price of abandoning the establishment he already had.

19. That freedom of establishment is not confined to the right to create a single establishment within the Community is confirmed by the very words of Article 52 of the

---

29 Case 2/74 *Reyners v Belgian State* [1974] ECR 631, [1974] 2 CMLR 305.

30 For a traditional '1970's' view of the ambit of the market freedoms see Parry & Hardy, *EEC Law* (1st Edition, 1973, Sweet & Maxwell, London) Chapters 21, 23 and 35. More particularly on establishment see Sundberg-Weitman, B. *Discrimination on Grounds of Nationality* (1977, North Holland Publishing Company, Amsterdam) 183-184.

31 Case 38/87 *Commission v Greece* [1988] ECR 4415.

Treaty, according to which the progressive abolition of the restrictions on freedom of establishment applies to restrictions on the setting up of agencies, branches or subsidiaries by nationals of any member state established in the territory of another Member State. That rule must be regarded as a specific statement of a general principle, applicable equally to the liberal professions, according to which the right of establishment includes freedom to set up and maintain, subject to observance of the professional rules of conduct, more than one place of work within the community.

20. In view of the special nature of the legal profession, however, the second Member State must have the right, in the interests of the due administration of justice, to require that lawyers enrolled at a bar in its territory should practise in such a way as to maintain sufficient contact with their clients and the judicial authorities and abide by the rules of the profession. Nevertheless such requirements must not prevent the nationals of other Member States from exercising properly the right of establishment guaranteed them by the treaty.

21. In that respect it must be pointed out that modern methods of transport and telecommunications facilitate proper contact with clients and the judicial authorities. Similarly, the existence of a second set of chambers in another Member State does not prevent the application of the rules of ethics in the host member state.

22. The question must therefore be answered to the effect that even in the absence of any directive coordinating national provisions governing access to and the exercise of the legal profession, Article 52 *et seq.* of the EEC Treaty prevent the competent authorities of a Member State from denying, on the basis of the national legislation and the rules of professional conduct which are in force in that State, to a national of another Member State the right to enter and to exercise the legal profession solely on the ground that he maintains chambers simultaneously in another Member State.

The reasoning in *Klopp* bears a strong resemblance to that in *Cassis de Dijon.* An assertion of local regulatory autonomy is tempered by the requirement that the host State allow nationals of other Member States entry to its market. This is, in turn, tempered by the development of a parallel 'mandatory requirements' doctrine that non-discriminatory restrictions falling within Article 52 [*43*] EC will be lawful if the measure is necessary to protect a legitimate interest, and does so in a manner which is not unnecessarily restrictive of trade. That said, it is difficult to envisage a situation where restrictions on secondary establishment can be justified. The Court noted in *Klopp* that modern telecommunications make access to a professional unproblematic even when, physically, they are very far away. In *Commission v France*[32] the French Government tried to justify a similar prohibition on secondary establishment in the case of doctors and dentists on the grounds that patients will often wish to have access to the same doctor. The Court was equally dismissive of such a justification, stating that even in general practice recent developments resulted in practitioners belonging to group practices. A patient could thus never ensure access to a particular practitioner.

Marenco has forcefully argued that the single-practice rule in both *Klopp* and *Commission v France* was, in reality, an example of material discrimination. For such a rule means that other Member State nationals who do not wish to give up their practice in their home State are entirely excluded from the host State. These measures impact disproportionately upon foreigners and these judgments do not therefore extend the reach of Article 52 [*43*] EC beyond being a prohibition on discrimination on grounds of nationality.[33]

Case 143/87 Stanton v INASTI [1988] ECR 3877, [1989] 3 CMLR 761[34]

Stanton, a British national, was employed in the United Kingdom. Wolf, a German national, and Dorchain, a Belgian national, were employed in Germany. All three were also directors of a Belgian company, NV Microtherm Europe. Under Belgian law company directors were categorised as self-employed. They were therefore required to pay social security contributions unless they were also employed in Belgium. The Belgian court asked whether such a regime breached the prohibition on discrimination in Article 7 EEC (now Article 6 [*12*] EC) or Article 52 [*43*] EC.

8. Article 7 [now Article 6] of the Treaty forbids any discrimination on grounds of nationality within the scope of application of the Treaty.

---

32 Case 96/85 *Commission v France* [1986] ECR 1475, [1986] 3 CMLR 57. Similar analysis can also be found in Case C-351/90 *Commission v Luxembourg* [1992] ECR I-3945, [1992] 3 CMLR 124.

33 Marenco, G. 'The Notion of Restriction on the Freedom of Establishment and Provision of Services in the case-law of the Court' (1991) 11 *YBEL* 111, 121.

34 See also Joined Cases 154 & 155/87 *Wolf* [1998] ECR 3897; Case C-53/95 *INASTI v Kammler* [1996] ECR I-703.

9. It appears, however, from the documents before the Court that the national legislation which gave rise to the main proceedings is applicable without distinction to all self-employed persons working in Belgium and does not discriminate according to the nationality of those persons. Although it is true that self-employed persons whose principal occupation is employment in a Member State other than Belgium are thereby placed at a disadvantage, nothing has been submitted to the Court to show that the persons disadvantaged are exclusively or mainly foreign nationals. Nor, therefore can the national legislation at issue be considered to result in indirect discrimination on grounds of nationality. Consequently, Article 7 of the Treaty may be dismissed from consideration.

10. The first paragraph of Article 52 of the Treaty requires the abolition of all restrictions on the freedom of establishment of nationals of a Member State in the territory of another Member State. It is settled law that is a directly applicable rule of Community law. Member States were therefore under the obligation to observe that rule even though, in the absence of Community legislation on social security for self-employed persons, they retained legislative jurisdiction in this field.

11. As the Court has held (in particular in the judgment of 12 July 1984 in Case 107/83 *Ordre des Avocats v Klopp* (1984) ECR 2971, and the judgment of 28 January 1986 in Case 270/83 *Commission v France* (1986) ECR 273), freedom of establishment is not confined to the right to create a single establishment within the Community, but entails the right to set up and maintain, subject to observance of the relevant professional rules of conduct, more than one place of work within the Community.

12. That is equally true in respect of a person who is employed in one Member State and wishes, in addition, to work in another Member State in a self-employed capacity.

13. The provisions of the Treaty relating to the free movement of persons are thus intended to facilitate the pursuit by Community citizens of occupational activities of all kinds throughout the community, and preclude national legislation which might place Community citizens at a disadvantage when they wish to extend their activities beyond the territory of a single Member State.

14. The legislation of a Member State which exempts persons whose principal occupation is employment in that Member State from the obligation to pay contributions to the scheme for self-employed persons but withholds such exemption from persons whose principal occupation is employment in another Member State has the effect of placing at a disadvantage the pursuit of occupational activities outside the territory of that Member State. Articles 48 and 52 of the Treaty therefore preclude such legislation.

The circumstances of *Stanton* were interesting because of the position of Dorchain, the Belgian. As a Belgian national it was impossible to assert that his right to establish in Belgium was being affected, as that would have been a purely internal situation which fell outside the scope of EC law.[35] The only manner in which rights could have been infringed under EC law was that the Belgian regime discouraged his *leaving* Belgium to pursue work or establish himself elsewhere in the Community. The corollary of this is that, unlike in goods, a parallel regime exists both for restrictions imposed by the host State and those imposed by the home State.[36]

The question of restrictions on exit from one Member State to another has proved to be particularly problematic for companies. Whilst the connecting factor for a natural person entitling them to exercise EC economic freedoms is nationality of a Member State, the connecting factor for legal persons is their formation in accordance with the law of the Member State.

Article 58 [*48*] EC. Companies or firms formed in accordance with the law of a Member State and having their registered office, central administration or principal place of business within the Community shall, for the purposes of this Chapter, be treated in the same way as natural persons who are nationals of Member States.

Member States often put conditions on companies if they are to retain their legal personality within that State. These include their headquarters or central administration being required to remain in that Member State. Companies are thus placed in a Catch 22 position. If they attempt to move their central place of administration to another Member State, they lose the legal personality which entitles them to exercise the right of establishment in the first place.

Case 81/87 R v HM Treasury ex parte Daily Mail [1988] ECR 5483, [1989] 3 CMLR 713

Under British law if a company's central management was located in Britain it was subject to British corporation tax. Such companies could not transfer their

---

35 See p 431.

36 Case C-370/90 *R v IAT & Surinder Singh, ex parte Secretary of State for the Home Department* [1992] ECR I-4265, [1992] 3 CMLR 373.

central management from Britain, and still retain their legal personality, without first obtaining the consent of the Treasury. The Daily Mail wished to transfer its central management to the Netherlands in order that it might sell off some of its shares without being subject to British capital gains tax. After negotiations with the Treasury broke down, it brought an action claiming that the British regime breached Article 52 [*43*] EC.

15. ... The Court must first point out, as it has done on numerous occasions, that freedom of establishment constitutes one of the fundamental principles of the community and that the provisions of the Treaty guaranteeing that freedom have been directly applicable since the end of the transitional period. Those provisions secure the right of establishment in another Member State not merely for Community nationals but also for the companies referred to in Article 58.

16. Even though those provisions are directed mainly to ensuring that foreign nationals and companies are treated in the host Member State in the same way as nationals of that State, they also prohibit the Member State of origin from hindering the establishment in another Member State of one of its nationals or of a company incorporated under its legislation which comes within the definition contained in Article 58. As the Commission rightly observed, the rights guaranteed by Articles 52 *et seq.* would be rendered meaningless if the Member State of origin could prohibit undertakings from leaving in order to establish themselves in another Member State. In regard to natural persons, the right to leave their territory for that purpose is expressly provided for in Directive 73/148, which is the subject of the second question referred to the Court.

17. In the case of a company, the right of establishment is generally exercised by the setting-up of agencies, branches or subsidiaries, as is expressly provided for in the second sentence of the first paragraph of Article 52. Indeed, that is the form of establishment in which the applicant engaged in this case by opening an investment management office in the Netherlands. A company may also exercise its right of establishment by taking part in the incorporation of a company in another Member State, and in that regard Article 221 of the Treaty ensures that it will receive the same treatment as nationals of that Member State as regards participation in the capital of the new company.

18. The provision of United Kingdom law at issue in the main proceedings imposes no restriction on transactions such as those described above. Nor does it stand in the way of a partial or total transfer of the activities of a company incorporated in the United Kingdom to a company newly incorporated in another Member State, if necessary after winding-up and, consequently, the settlement of the tax position of the United Kingdom company. It requires Treasury consent only where such a company seeks to transfer its central management and control out of the United Kingdom while maintaining its legal personality and its status as a United Kingdom company.

19. In that regard it should be borne in mind that, unlike natural persons, companies are creatures of the law and, in the present state of Community law, creatures of national law. They exist only by virtue of the varying national legislation which determines their incorporation and functioning.

20. As the Commission has emphasized, the legislation of the Member States varies widely in regard to both the factor providing a connection to the national territory required for the incorporation of a company and the question whether a company incorporated under the legislation of a Member State may subsequently modify that connecting factor. Certain States require that not merely the registered office but also the real head office, that is to say the central administration of the company, should be situated on their territory, and the removal of the central administration from that territory thus presupposes the winding-up of the company with all the consequences that winding-up entails in company law and tax law. The legislation of other states permits companies to transfer their central administration to a foreign country but certain of them, such as the United Kingdom, make that right subject to certain restrictions, and the legal consequences of a transfer, particularly in regard to taxation, vary from one Member State to another.

21. The Treaty has taken account of that variety in national legislation. In defining, in Article 58, the companies which enjoy the right of establishment, the Treaty places on the same footing, as connecting factors, the registered office, central administration and principal place of business of a company. Moreover, Article 220 of the Treaty provides for the conclusion, so far as is necessary, of agreements between the Member States with a view to securing inter alia the retention of legal personality in the event of transfer of the registered office of companies from one country to another. No convention in this area has yet come into force.

22. It should be added that none of the Directives on the coordination of company law adopted under Article 54(3)(g) of the Treaty deal with the differences at issue here.

23. It must therefore be held that the Treaty regards the differences in national legislation concerning the required connecting factor and the question whether - and if so how - the registered office or real head office of a company incorporated under national law may be transferred from one Member State to another as problems which are not resolved by the rules concerning the right of establishment but must be dealt with by future legislation or conventions.

24. Under those circumstances, Articles 52 and 58 of the Treaty cannot be interpreted as conferring on companies incorporated under the law of a Member State a right to transfer their central management and control and their central administration to another Member State while retaining their status as companies incorporated under the legislation of the first Member State.

Daily Mail does not prevent a company established in one Member State setting up of agencies, branches or subsidiaries in another. It merely prevents the transfer of the central place of administration. Wyatt and Dashwood observe that this is perfectly reasonable where the law of incorporation in the home State does not recognise the entity created i.e. where the company is not considered to exist if its central place of administration is not in that State. In such circumstances to hold a company could transfer its central administration would amount to a reshaping of that State's company law, as it would be allowing companies without their administrative headquarters in that State to retain legal personality. They consider the position to be less justifiable where the host State still recognises the company as having legal personality, as was the case here. In the United Kingdom, however, it is perfectly possible for companies registered there not to have their central place of administration. In certain instances, for fiscal reasons, consent from the authorities was required. No significant reshaping of British company law was required, and it could therefore be argued that the measure should have been found to violate Article 52 [*43*] EC.[37]

The judgment must also be seen in its fiscal context. A considerable number of Member States use the criterion of central place of administration to determine whether an undertaking is subject to their national corporation tax. If companies were permitted to shift their headquarters around the Community, this would provide clear incentives for them to locate their administration in that State with the lowest corporation tax. These fiscal incentives would in the normal run of events be the only incentive for such behaviour, as companies can still establish a commercial presence of any size in another Member State through setting up a branch, subsidiary or agency. There was therefore a danger of the 'Delaware effect'[38] developing, namely that Member States would strive to lower their taxes relative to each other to entice such relocation, if *Daily Mail* had been decided the other way.

---

37 Wyatt, D. & Dashwood, A. *European Community Law* (1993, 3rd Edition, Sweet & Maxwell, London) 300-302.

38 The 'Delaware effect' is named after a so-called race to the bottom in state company laws in the United States which was believed to have been initiated by the state of Delaware in the 1960's. Cary, W. 'Federalism and Corporate Law: Reflections Upon Delaware' (1974) 83 *Yale Law Journal* 663.

iv. The Pursuit of Economic Activity in Another Member State

a. Non-Discrimination and the Pursuit of Economic Activity

Article 52 [*43*] EC requires that EC nationals be not discriminated against in their pursuit of economic activity in another Member State.

Case 197/84 Steinhauser v City of Biarritz [1985] ECR 1819, [1986] 1 CMLR 53

Steinhauser was a German artist who lived in Biarritz. He applied to rent a *crampotte*, a fisherman's shed, from the local authority but was refused on the grounds that he was not a French national. In its reference the national court noted that the general question of the letting of a premises by a public authority was at issue here not rules relating to the taking up of a specific activity.

15. In that regard, it must also be borne in mind that, in the context of the abolition of restrictions on freedom of establishment, the General Programme adopted by the Council on 18 December 1961 provides ... useful guidance for the implementation of the relevant provisions of the Treaty. The Programme provides (in Section A of Title III: 'restrictions') for the abolition of provisions and practices which, in respect of foreign nationals, exclude, limit or impose conditions on the power to exercise rights normally attaching to the activity of a self-employed person. Those rights include, in particular, the power: (a) to enter into contracts for work, business or agricultural tenancies, and contracts of employment, and to enjoy all rights arising under such contracts; (b) to submit tenders for or to act directly as a party or as a subcontractor in contracts with the State or with any other legal person governed by public law; (c) to obtain licences or authorizations issued by the state or by any other legal person governed by public law; and (d) to acquire, use or dispose of movable or immovable property or rights therein.

16. It follows from the foregoing that any practice or rule adopted by a local authority of a Member State which discriminates against nationals of other Member States falls within the prohibition laid down by Article 52 of the Treaty. Moreover, it must be emphasized that freedom of establishment, as provided for by that Article, includes the right not only to take up activities as a self-employed person but also to pursue them in the broad sense of the term. The renting of premises for business purposes furthers the pursuit of an occupation and therefore falls within the scope of Article 52 of the EEC Treaty.

A measure will breach Article 52 [*43*] EC in the case of natural persons if it discriminates on grounds of nationality.[39] In the case of companies the Court has found the equivalent to be the place of registered office.[40] There is one important difference between registered office and nationality, however.

Marenco, G. 'The Notion of Restriction on the Freedom of Establishment and Provision of Services in the Case-law of the Court' (1991) 11 *Yearbook of European Law* 111, 113-114

However there can never be more than a partial equivalence of the nationality condition and that of the company's registered office on a national territory. The former indeed uses a purely formal criterion, with no concrete or substantial content, to exclude equality of treatment. Thus it cannot be justified on economic grounds, which is where freedom of establishment operates. By contrast, the registered office as criterion of the connection of a company with a State is simultaneously a concrete situation which might justify a difference in treatment. Thus it cannot be equated purely and simply with nationality.

This emerges in Case 270/83 *Commission v France* [[1986] ECR 273], which dealt with a French tax provision that denied tax credits in respect of dividends on shares in French companies held by branches or agencies of companies, the registered office of which was in another Member State. The Court, having found that this provision led to a difference in treatment between French companies and those in other Member States, took into consideration the French Government's arguments that this difference in treatment was in the circumstances justified by objective differences in the situations of the two types of company. While in the end finding in favour of the Commission, the Court observed, in refuting the French Government's arguments, that '.... the possibility cannot altogether be excluded that a distinction based on the location of the registered office of a company or the place of residence of a natural person may, under certain circumstances be justified in an area such as tax law...' The registered office is thus compared first with the nationality of physical persons and then with their residence. This double comparison reveals that the registered office condition plays a role at once formal and substantial.

---

39 One small exception to the general prohibition on discrimination was introduced by a Protocol to the TEU which allows Denmark to maintain its existing legislation prohibiting non-nationals from acquiring second homes in Denmark.

40 Case 270/83 *Commission v France* [1986] ECR 273, [1987] 1 CMLR 401.

Article 52 [*43*] EC operates to prohibit both overt and covert discrimination. A measure will not be classed as discriminatory if it operates against individual foreign traders, but only if it operates against foreign traders disproportionately as a group. In *Commission v Italy*[41] the Commission brought an action against an Italian requirement that public authorities in certain areas, notably taxation, health, agriculture and urban property, had to purchase data-processing systems from companies in which the Italian Government had a majority shareholding. In principle, this could equally well be companies registered in other Member States, yet the Court noted that the measure essentially favoured Italian companies as there was not a single foreign data-processing company the majority of whose shares were in Italian public ownership. Because of the multiplicity of factors, such as nationality of employees or shareholders, central place of administration, fiscal residence, which link a company with any Member State the issue of indirect discrimination has arisen most frequently in the case of legal persons. In *Factortame*[42] a requirement that the owners and operators of a shipping vessel be resident in the United Kingdom was considered to be discriminatory on the grounds that it was easier for British nationals to comply with this requirement. Similarly in *Commerzbank*[43] a tax exemption which was only granted to companies fiscally resident in the United Kingdom was considered to be discriminatory as very few companies not registered in the United Kingdom would be fiscally resident there.

As important as the criteria used to identify the existence of discrimination is the reach of activities covered by the principle. In principle, it is only where the trader is treated unequally in pursuit of its economic activity that Article 52 [*43*] EC applies. This limitation has been stretched, however, so that measures which have only an indirect effect on the pursuit of economic activity will fall within Article 52 [*43*]

---

41 Case C-3/88 *Commission v Italy* [1989] ECR 4035, [1991] 2 CMLR 115.

42 Case C-221/89 *R v Secretary of State ex parte Factortame* [1991] ECR I-3905, [1991] 3 CMLR 589. See also Case C-279/89 *Commission v United Kingdom* [1992] ECR I-5785.

43 Case C-330/91 *R v IRC ex parte Commerzbank* [1993] ECR I-4017.

EC if they are discriminatory.[44] In *Commission v Italy*[45] the Court was asked to consider the Italian policy of only making social housing and reduced rate mortgages available to Italian nationals. The Court recognised that housing policy could not be classed as some specific occupational rule, but reasoned that the purpose of Article 52 [*43*] EC was to ensure equality of treatment for the self-employed. If complete equality of competition was to be assured, any facilities which might alleviate the financial burden upon the self-employed had to be available equally.

It is a wide test indeed to recast the test so that anything placing another Member State national at a competitive disadvantage falls foul of Article 52 [*43*] EC. The most wideranging application of the non-discrimination principle was *Halliburton*.[46] The German subsidiary of Halliburton, a US parent company, wished to sell its assets in the Netherlands to the Dutch subsidiary. Under Dutch law such a sale would normally be exempt from tax on the grounds that it was part of an internal company reorganisation. This exemption did not apply in this instance because the vendor, the German subsidiary, was not incorporated in the Netherlands. The unusual feature of this case was that the tax was levied on the purchaser, the Dutch subsidiary. This seemed to be an internal matter unconnected with Community law, as it primarily concerned Dutch treatment of a Dutch company. The Court considered, however, that this resulted in discrimination against the German subsidiary under Article 52 [*43*] EC. For the tax on the sale to render the position of the vendor less favourable as the terms of sale for potential purchasers were not so favourable. Such reasoning was particularly stretched in this case as the sale was not an arms-length market transaction but a company reorganisation and it is difficult to believe that the tax featured heavily in the German subsidiary's decision to buy.

Such an embracing interpretation of the non-discrimination principle raises the question of whether the principle can be used to

---

44 Case C-122/96 *Saldanha et al. v Hiros Holding*, Judgment of 2 October 1997.

45 Case 63/86 *Commission v Italy* [1988] ECR 29, [1989] 2 CMLR 601. See also Case 305/87 *Commission v Greece* [1989] ECR 1461, [1991] 1 CMLR 611.

46 Case C-1/93 *Halliburton Services BV v Staatssecretaris van Financien* [1994] ECR I-1137, [1994] 3 CMLR 377.

require a Member State to grant all the social benefits to the self-employed which it grants to its own nationals. Such an interpretation would repair the anomaly presented by Regulation 1612/68/EEC, which grants considerable benefits to workers but not to the self-employed.[47] In *Commission v Italy*[48] we have seen the provision was used to give equal access to public housing, and similar arguments could no doubt be developed in fields such as public education for the trader or his family. The notion of competitive disadvantage does not fully cure the problem. The fundamentality of individual social rights is undermined if they are perceived merely as an adjunct to competitive position. Even at a practical level this manifests itself in a number of ways. With many public benefits, free access to museums for children sticks as an example, the benefit may, in financial terms, be simply too small for it to be plausibly argued that denial to them affects the trader's competitive position. Secondly, there are many benefits which have no immediate financial value. These fall outside Article 52 [*43*] EC. A prime example is equal access to education.[49] Another example is the right of workers in some instance to reside in a Member State after retirement. Whilst the self-employed are now granted equivalent rights,[50] such rights would have been excluded under the competitive disadvantage test.

b. Non-Discriminatory Restrictions on the Pursuit of Economic Activity in Another Member State

Article 52 [*43*] EC has not been traditionally extended to cover non-discriminatory restrictions on the pursuit of economic activity in another Member State. In *Fearon* the Court considered an Irish residence requirement allowing for compulsory acquisition of land where a person owning the land or, in the case of companies, the company directors had not been resident for more than a year within three miles of that land.[51]

---

47 OJ Special Edition, 1968(II), 475. See Chapter 9.

48 Case C-3/88 *Commission v Italy* [1989] ECR 4035, [1991] 2 CMLR 115.

49 Such discrimination may contravene Article 127 [*150*] EC. See pp. 472-475.

50 Directive 90/365/EEC, OJ 1990 L 180/28.

51 Case 182/83 *Fearon v Irish Land Commission* [1984] ECR 3677, [1985] 2 CMLR 228.

This was held to fall outside Article 52 [*43*] EC on the grounds that the measure did not discriminate against other Community nationals. It might be argued that the decision in *Fearon* was so soon after the decision in *Klopp* that the Court had not had time to consider whether non-discriminatory restrictions on the pursuit of economic activity should fall within Article 52 [*43*] EC. The Court has had an opportunity to reconsider the matter in a number of subsequent decisions.[52]

Case 292/86 Gullung v Conseil de l'Ordre des Avocats [1988] ECR 111, [1998] 2 CMLR 57

Gullung was a French and German national who applied to register as a conseil juridique at the Bar in Mulhouse, France. The local Bar Council refused him registration on grounds relating to his character. Gullung then set up an office in Mulhouse, upon which the local Bar Council ordered its members not to have anything to do with him. Gullung claimed that the requirement of registration contravened Article 52 [*43*] EC.

28. In order to reply to the question defined in that manner it is necessary to emphasize that under the second paragraph of Article 52 of the EEC Treaty freedom of establishment includes the right to take up and pursue activities as self-employed persons 'under the conditions laid down for its own nationals by the law of the country where such establishment is effected'. It follows from that provision, as the Court stated in its judgment of 12 July 1984 in Case 107/83 *Ordre des avocats au barreau de Paris v Klopp* (1984) ECR 2971, that in the absence of specific Community rules in the matter each Member State is, in principle, free to regulate the exercise of the legal profession in its territory.

29. It should be added that the requirement that lawyers be registered at a bar laid down by certain Member States must be regarded as lawful in relation to Community law provided, however, that such registration is open to nationals of all Member States without discrimination. The requirement seeks to ensure the observance of moral and ethical principles and the disciplinary control of the activity of lawyers and thus pursues an objective worthy of protection.

30. It follows from the foregoing that the Member States whose legislation lays down the requirement that any person wishing to establish himself in their territory as a lawyer

---

52 See also Case 221/85 *Commission v Belgium* [1987] ECR 719, [1988] 1 CMLR 620; Case 196/86 *Conradi, Hereth et soc.Metro v Direction de la Concurrence et des Prix* [1987] ECR 4469.

within the meaning of their national legislation must be registered at a bar may prescribe the same requirement for lawyers who come from other Member States and who rely on the right of establishment laid down in the EEC Treaty in order to benefit from the same status.

It has been argued earlier that there are dangers with overextending the economic freedoms.[53] This appears to have been avoided in the case of Article 52 [*43*] EC. Yet there are two reasons for thinking that the position is not as settled as it once was. The first stems from the close link between services and establishment. As all non-discriminatory restrictions on the provision of services now, formally at least, fall within Article 59 [*49*] EC,[54] it is to be expected that similar pressures will develop for Article 52 [*43*] EC to be interpreted likewise. The second is that the Court's language on non-discriminatory restrictions is becoming wider and more general in nature, suggesting that it might take such a step. In *Gebhard* it therefore stated:

> '**37.** It follows, however, from the Court's case-law that national measures liable to hinder or make less attractive the exercise of fundamental freedoms guaranteed by the treaty must fulfil four conditions: they must be applied in a non-discriminatory manner; they must be justified by imperative requirements in the general interest; they must be suitable for securing the attainment of the objective which they pursue; and they must not go beyond what is necessary in order to attain it.'[55]

Notwithstanding this, in its last decision the Court has refused to extend Article 52 [*43*] EC to cover non-discriminatory restrictions on the pursuit of economic activity.

---

53 See p. 289-291.

54 See p. 406 ff.

55 Case C-55/94 *Gebhard v Consiglio dell'ordine degli avvocati e procuratori di Milano* [1995] ECR I-4165

Case C-70/95 Sodemare SA *et al.* v Regione Lombardia, Judgment of 17 June 1997

Sodemare, a Luxembourg company, set up a capital company governed by Italian law, named Anni Azzurri Holding, which ran a number of companies which provided sheltered accommodation for elderly residents. In 1993 it was refused approval to enter into contracts with the public authorities which would have allowed it to be reimbursed for some of the health care services it provided. The reason for this was that under Lombard law such contracts were only available to non-profitmaking bodies. Sodemare challenged this law claiming it affected its ability to run its business.

32. In that regard, it must be stated that, as Community law stands at present, a Member State may, in the exercise of the powers it retains to organize its social security system, consider that a social welfare system of the kind at issue in this case necessarily implies, with a view to attaining its objectives, that the admission of private operators to that system as providers of social welfare services is to be made subject to the condition that they are non-profit-making.

33. Moreover, the fact that it is impossible for profit-making companies automatically to participate in the running of a statutory social welfare system of a Member State by concluding a contract which entitles them to be reimbursed by the public authorities for the costs of providing social welfare services of a health-care nature is not liable to place profit-making companies from other Member States in a less favourable factual or legal situation than profit-making companies in the Member State in which they are established.

34. In view of the foregoing, the non-profit condition cannot be regarded as contrary to Articles 52 and 58 of the Treaty.

c. Restrictions on the Use of Diplomas and Qualifications

Qualifications restrict both the taking up and the pursuit of economic activity. Moreover, as the acquisition of qualifications or diplomas can be perfectly well regulated in the State of origin, non-recognition of these qualifications constitutes a 'double burden' in a similar manner to product characteristics in the case of goods.[56]

Case C-340/89 Vlassopoulou v Ministerium für Justiz Bundes-und Europaangelegenheiten Baden-Württemberg [1991] ECR I-2357, [1993] 2 CMLR 221

Vlassopoulou, a Greek national, was admitted to the Greek Bar in 1982 and completed her doctorate at the University of Tubingen, Germany in that year. From 1983 until 1988 she worked with a German law firm in Mannheim. In 1988 she applied to become a *Rechtsanwalt*, a German lawyer, but was refused on the grounds that she did not have the necessary background in that she needed to have studied law at a German university for two years, completed the First State exams and undergone a period of training. The national court asked whether it was compatible with Article 52 [*43*] EC for no account to have been taken of her Greek qualifications or her experience in Germany.

14. Moreover, it is also clear from the judgment in Case 71/76 *Thieffry v Conseil de l'Ordre des avocats à la Cour de Paris* [1977] ECR 765, at paragraph 16, that, in so far as Community law makes no special provision, the objectives of the Treaty, and in particular freedom of establishment, may be achieved by measures enacted by the Member States, which, under Article 5 of the Treaty, must take 'all appropriate measures, whether general or particular, to ensure fulfilment of the obligations arising out of this Treaty or resulting from action taken by the institutions of the Community' and abstain from 'any measure which could jeopardize the attainment of the objectives of this Treaty'.

15. It must be stated in this regard that, even if applied without any discrimination on the basis of nationality, national requirements concerning qualifications may have the effect of hindering nationals of the other Member States in the exercise of their right of establishment guaranteed to them by Article 52 of the EEC Treaty. That could be the case if the national rules in question took no account of the knowledge and qualifications already acquired by the person concerned in another Member State.

16. Consequently, a Member State which receives a request to admit a person to a profession to which access, under national law, depends upon the possession of a

---

56 Similar reasoning has since been adopted in Case C-104/91 *Aguirre Borrell* [1992] ECR I-3003; Case C-319/92 *Salomone Haim* [1994] ECR I-425, [1994] 2 CMLR 169; Case C-55/94 *Gebhard v Consiglio dell'ordine degli avvocati e procuratori di Milano* [1995] ECR I-4165; Case C-164/94 *Aranitis v Land Berlin* [1996] ECR I-135.

diploma or a professional qualification must take into consideration the diplomas, certificates and other evidence of qualifications which the person concerned has acquired in order to exercise the same profession in another Member State by making a comparison between the specialized knowledge and abilities certified by those diplomas and the knowledge and qualifications required by the national rules.

17. That examination procedure must enable the authorities of the host Member State to assure themselves, on an objective basis, that the foreign diploma certifies that its holder has knowledge and qualifications which are, if not identical, at least equivalent to those certified by the national diploma. That assessment of the equivalence of the foreign diploma must be carried out exclusively in the light of the level of knowledge and qualifications which its holder can be assumed to possess in the light of that diploma, having regard to the nature and duration of the studies and practical training to which the diploma relates (see the judgment in Case 222/86 *Unectef v Heylens* [(1987) ECR 4097] paragraph 13).

18. In the course of that examination, a Member State may, however, take into consideration objective differences relating to both the legal framework of the profession in question in the Member State of origin and to its field of activity. In the case of the profession of lawyer, a Member State may therefore carry out a comparative examination of diplomas, taking account of the differences identified between the national legal systems concerned.

19. If that comparative examination of diplomas results in the finding that the knowledge and qualifications certified by the foreign diploma correspond to those required by the national provisions, the Member State must recognize that diploma as fulfilling the requirements laid down by its national provisions. If, on the other hand, the comparison reveals that the knowledge and qualifications certified by the foreign diploma and those required by the national provisions correspond only partially, the host Member State is entitled to require the person concerned to show that he has acquired the knowledge and qualifications which are lacking.

20. In this regard, the competent national authorities must assess whether the knowledge acquired in the host Member State, either during a course of study or by way of practical experience, is sufficient in order to prove possession of the knowledge which is lacking.

21. If completion of a period of preparation or training for entry into the profession is required by the rules applying in the host Member State, those national authorities must determine whether professional experience acquired in the Member State of origin or in the host Member State may be regarded as satisfying that requirement in full or in part.

22. Finally, it must be pointed out that the examination made to determine whether the knowledge and qualifications certified by the foreign diploma and those required by the legislation of the host Member State correspond must be carried out by the national authorities in accordance with a procedure which is in conformity with the requirements of Community law concerning the effective protection of the fundamental rights conferred by the Treaty on Community subjects. It follows that any decision taken must be capable of being made the subject of judicial proceedings in which its legality under Community law can be reviewed and that the person concerned must be able to ascertain the reasons for the decision taken in this regard (see the judgment in Case 222/86 *Unectef v Heylens*, cited above, paragraph 17).

Vlassopoulou concerned access to a profession and thus the taking up of an activity rather than its pursuit. It could therefore be seen merely as an extension of the *Klopp* line of reasoning, which outlaws restrictions on access to the market. The difficulty with such an approach would have been that, as a diploma or professional qualification may also facilitate the pursuit of an activity, the extent to which Member States could regulate professional qualification would depend for what purpose the qualification was to be used. This danger was met by *Kraus.*[57] Kraus was a German who had completed an LLM at Edinburgh University. He challenged a German requirement that a person needed authorisation from their *Land* before being able to use higher education titles acquired abroad. The Court noted that qualifications were necessary both for access to a profession and to facilitate, more generally, the exercise of economic activity. It considered that any conditions on the use of a title which hindered or made more difficult the exercise of the economic freedoms fell within Article 52 [*43*] EC. The Court refused to draw a distinction between those titles necessary for access to a profession and other titles. It did note, however that Member States could impose non-discriminatory restrictions on the use of titles to prevent fraud. An administrative authorisation, for these purposes, was compatible with Community law provided it was accessible, susceptible to judicial review, reasons were given for any refusal to approve a title, the administrative costs charged were not excessive and any sanctions imposed for the use of the title without authorisation were not disproportionately heavy.

In many ways, Article 52 [*43*] EC's bark was greater than its bite. The question as to when a migrant's home State qualifications are judged to be equivalent to those of the host State is left vague in *Vlassopolou.*

---

57 Case C-19/92 *Kraus v Land Baden-Württemberg* [1993] ECR I-1663.

Furthermore, the duty of mutual recognition only applied in those areas where an EC national already had equivalent qualifications and did not cover those situations where the migrant had some expertise but maybe not the expertise required by the host State. It has, to some extent, been superseded by legislative developments.

Article 57(1) [*47(1)*] EC. In order to make it easier for persons to take up and pursue activities as self-employed persons, the Council shall, acting in accordance with the procedure referred to in Article 189b [*251*], issue directives for the mutual recognition of diplomas, certificates and other evidence of formal qualifications.

Initially the EC pursued a 'harmonisation' or 'co-ordination' sectoral approach.[58] It was necessary to obtain agreement amongst all the Member States on the minimum standard of education or training and usually two Directives would be enacted - one dealing with the general level of education/training and the other listing the qualifications and diplomas awarded in the Member States which satisfied the conditions for recognition. The Council and the Commission took the view that the recognition of professional qualifications necessarily involved an investigation into the *training* curricula of the Member States thus mutual recognition hinged on the harmonisation of training curricula. Such an approach makes deep inroads into the independence of national educational policy in relation to training curricula and while a number of Directives were enacted particularly in the medical professions the approach was slow, piecemeal and not a great success. In 1974 the Council adopted a Resolution on the mutual recognition of formal qualifications expressing the hope that future work in the area of mutual recognition would be based upon flexible and qualitative criteria with the Directives resorting as little as possible to prescriptive detailed training requirements.[59]

---

58 An early example of this approach can be found in relation to general practitioners. On recognition see Directive 75/362/EEC, OJ 1975 L 167/1. On training see Directive 75/363/EEC, OJ 1975 L 167/14.

59 OJ 1974 C 98/1. See Zilioli, C. 'The Recognition of Diplomas and its Impact on Education Policies', in De Witte, B. (ed) *European Community Law of Education* (1989, Nomos, Baden-Baden).

The EC has moved from the sectoral approach to adopting general recognition Directives - the *Cassis de Dijon* approach. Because of the slow progress made in the development of sectoral mutual recognition Directives, an agreement was reached at the Fontainbleau Summit of June 1984 to adopting a general horizontal approach. Directive 89/48/EEC established a general system for the recognition of higher education diplomas.[60] It applies to those diplomas which show that the holder has successfully completed a post-secondary course of at least three years' duration and that the holder has the professional qualifications required for the taking up or pursuit of a regulated profession in the holder's home Member State.[61] The central requirement is contained in Article 3:

Article 3. Where, in a host Member State, the taking up or pursuit of a regulated profession is subject to possession of a diploma, the competent authority may not, on the grounds of inadequate qualifications, refuse to authorize a national of a Member State to take up or pursue that profession on the same conditions as apply to its own nationals:

(a) if the applicant holds the diploma required in another Member State for the taking up or pursuit of the profession in question in its territory, such diploma having been awarded in a Member State; or

(b) if the applicant has pursued the profession in question full-time for two years during the previous ten years in another Member State which does not regulate that profession, ... and possesses evidence of one or more formal qualifications:

---

60 Directive 89/48/EEC establishing a general system for the recognition of higher education diplomas awarded on completion of professional education and training of at least three years' duration, OJ 1989 L 19/16.

61 Ibid., Article 1(a). Article 52 [*43*] EC continues to apply to professions unregulated by the host State cf. Case C-164/94 *Aranitis v Land of Berlin* [1996] ECR I-135. Here the Land of Berlin had refused to recognise the Greek diploma awarded on the completion of a higher-education geology course as equivalent to a German diploma awarded on completion of a comparable course and consequently to authorise the applicant to use the title attaching to the German diploma. The Court ruled that since there were no laws, regulations or administrative provisions in Germany regulating access to the profession of geologist the profession could not be regarded as a 'regulated profession' within the meaning of Directive 89/48/EEC.

- which have been awarded by a competent authority in a Member State, designated in accordance with the laws, regulations or administrative provisions of such State,
- which show that the holder has successfully completed a post-secondary course of at least three years' duration, or of an equivalent duration part-time, at a university or establishment of higher education or another establishment of similar level of a Member State and, where appropriate, that he has successfully completed the professional training required in addition to the post-secondary course and
- which have prepared the holder for the pursuit of his profession.

The duty to allow the migrant to practice in these circumstances is accompanied by a duty to allow him to use the professional title used in that Member State.[62] These duties are not absolute, however. They can be rebutted where the host State has evidence that the individual does not possess the qualification or experience required. In *Van de Bijl*[63] the Court had to give an interpretation of Article 3 of Directive 64/427/EEC[64] on the activities of the self-employed in the manufacturing and processing industries. This required Member States, where taking up of an activity was dependent upon acquisition of a certain knowledge, to accept, as evidence of that knowledge, three years consecutive activity in another Member State. In the Netherlands a licence was required to be a painter. Van de Bijl, a Dutch painter, obtained a certificate from the British authorities indicating that he had worked as a painter in the United Kingdom for four years and five months. The Dutch authorities knew that Van de Bijl had been in the Netherlands for eight months in the middle of this period, and so refused to let him practice his business. The Court considered that whilst a host State was normally bound to believe the information contained in a certificate issued by the home State, there were two circumstances when this would not be the case. The first was when there were objective factors which might lead them to doubt the information. In which case they could ask for additional information. The second was that Member States were not obliged to overlook matters which happened on their

---

62 Ibid., Article 7.

63 Case 130/88 *Van de Bijl v Staatssecretaris van Economische Zaken* [1989] ECR 3089.

64 OJ, English Special Edition 1963-64, 11.

own territory which might lead them to doubt the information contained in that certificate.

A separate regime also applies if the duration of the person's training and education is at least one year less than that required in the host State.

Article 4(1). Notwithstanding Article 3, the host Member State may also require the applicant:

(a) to provide evidence of professional experience, where the duration of the education and training adduced in support of his application, as laid down in Article 3 (a) and (b), is at least one year less than that required in the host Member State. In this event, the period of professional experience required:
- may not exceed twice the shortfall in duration of education and training where the shortfall relates to post-secondary studies and/or to a period of probationary practice carried out under the control of a supervising professional person and ending with an examination;
- may not exceed the shortfall where the shortfall relates to professional practice acquired with the assistance of a qualified member of the profession.

.....

When applying these provisions, account must be taken of the professional experience referred to in Article 3 (b).

At all events, the professional experience required may not exceed four years;

(b) to complete an adaptation period not exceeding three years or take an aptitude test:
- where the matters covered by the education and training he has received as laid down in Article 3 (a) and (b), differ substantially from those covered by the diploma required in the host Member State; or
- where, in the case referred to in Article 3 (a), the profession regulated in the host Member State comprises one or more regulated professional activities which are not in the profession regulated in the Member State from which the applicant originates or comes and that difference corresponds to specific education and training required in the host Member State and covers matters which differ substantially from those covered by the diploma adduced by the applicant; or
- where, in the case referred to in Article 3 (b), the profession regulated in the host Member State comprises one or more regulated professional activities which are not in the profession pursued by the applicant in the Member State from which he originates or comes, and that difference corresponds to specific education and training required in the host Member State and covers matters which differ substantially from those covered by the evidence of formal qualifications adduced by the applicant.

Should the host Member State make use of this possibility, it must give the applicant the right to choose between an adaptation period and an aptitude test. By way of derogation from this principle, for professions whose practice requires precise knowledge of national law and in respect of which the provision of advice and/or assistance concerning national law is an essential and constant aspect of the professional activity, the host Member State may stipulate either an adaptation period or an aptitude test. ...

2. However, the host Member State may not apply the provisions of paragraph 1 (a) and (b) cumulatively.

Directive 92/51/EEC has extended the approach set out in Directive 89/48/EEC more generally to those diplomas which only required one year's post-secondary training.[65] The general approach has come under criticism on two fronts.

The first concerns its treatment of qualifications obtained outside the EU. Whilst Member States are free to recognise as equivalent to their own qualifications obtained in third countries, this will not bind other Member States. In *Tawil-Albertini* [66] a French national obtained dental qualifications in the Lebanon. These qualifications were recognised by the Belgian authorities as equivalent to a Belgian qualification. He was also authorised to practice in the United Kingdom and Ireland. The French authorities refused Tawil-Albertini permission to practice as a dentist in France. He argued that since his qualification had been recognised as equivalent to Belgian qualifications this should be sufficient to bring his qualification within the Council Directive on the mutual recognition of dental qualifications even though the Directive did not include any qualifications obtained outside the EC.[67] The Court pointed out that the Directive was based on the guarantees of specific minimum criteria. The co-ordination of training in non-Member States could only be achieved by agreements with individual States but this would not bring such qualifications within the scope of EC Directive and

65 Directive 92/51/EEC on a second general system for the recognition of professional education and training to supplement Directive 89/48/EEC, OJ 1992 L 209/25, as amended by Directive 95/43/EC, OJ 1995 L 184/21.

66 Case C-154/93 *Tawil-Albertini v Ministre des Affairs Sociales* [1994] ECR I-451, [1995] 1 CMLR 612.

67 Directive 78/686/EEC, OJ 1978 L 233/1.

bind the other Member States which did not recognise foreign qualifications.

Although a Recommendation attached to the General Recognition Directive obliges the Member States to take cognisance of qualifications obtained by *EC nationals* in third States,[68] there are fears that the EC approach may lead to further discrimination against non-EC nationals wanting to work and move between the Member States.

Szyszczak, E. 'Race Discrimination: The Limits of Market Equality?' in Hepple, B. and Szyszczak, E. (eds.) *Discrimination: The Limits of Law* (1993, Mansell, London) 127-129

... indirect discrimination may occur as a result of the operation of the Internal Market. Freedom of movement is an illusory right to a non-Community national. Equally, discrimination at the national level may lead to black and ethnic minorities having difficulty in obtaining the transportable Euro-skills.

.....

Overt Racism

A third fear of the consequences of the Internal Market is that by promoting a common European identity, even further alienation of black and ethnic minority groups will occur, fuelled by the lack of legal protection in national and Community law, the indirect discrimination consequences of the Internal Market and the growth of right-wing fascist groups in Europe. Even Mrs Thatcher, not the greatest supporter of the Internal Market, alluded to this in her famous speech at Bruges in 1988:

> From our perspective today, surely what strikes us most is our common experience. For instance the story of how Europeans colonised and (yes, without an apology) civilised much of the world, is an extraordinary tale of talent, skill and courage.

The fostering of a common European identity may prevent the acceptance of different 'non-European' forms of religion, languages, cultural ideas and education. Sivandan has warned: 'We are moving from an ethnocentric racism to a Eurocentric racism, from the different racisms of the member states to a common, market racism.'

Issues have already arisen in Europe over multi-racial schooling and the wearing of traditional clothes at school and at work. These are indicative of some of the

---

68 Recommendation 89/49/EEC, OJ 1989 L 19/24.

features of alienation already experienced. With cutbacks in public expenditure it is felt that even fewer resources will be available to finance projects relating to the education of black and ethnic minorities and that more attention will be paid to the teaching of European languages, history, politics and culture.

The second concern was that there were still regulated professions which fell outside the ambit of the regime. To that end the Commission has proposed a Directive whereby in any Member State where the pursuit of an activity is subject to possession of general, commercial or professional knowledge, that State will accept as evidence of such knowledge the fact that the migrant has pursued the activity in question in another Member State for a number of years. The length of time varies according to the activity in question.[69]

III. The Provision and Receipt of Services

i. Restrictions Imposed on the Provision of Services by the Importing State

a. The Prohibition on the Imposition of Discriminatory Restrictions

Article 59 [*49*] EC prohibits all discrimination against a provider of services on grounds of nationality or place of establishment. A law reserving the provision of certain services to a Member State's own nationals will, therefore, contravene Article 59 [*49*] EC.[70] As with Article 52 [*43*] EC, Article 59 [*49*] EC prohibits not only formal discrimination but also covertly discriminatory measures which act

---

69 OJ 1996, C 115/16.

70 e.g. Case C-375/92 *Commission v Spain* [1994] ECR I-923, [1994] 3 CMLR 500.

essentially in favour of domestic providers of services.[71] Whilst the non-discrimination principle has traditionally focused on the nationality or place of establishment of the *service provider*, there have been recent suggestions that discrimination between services provided from or to other Member States, on the one hand, and purely domestic services, on the other, might breach Article 59 [*49*] EC. In *Corsica Ferries, France*[72] the French Government installed a tax on passengers who arrived in Corsica from other Member State ports but did not impose a tax on those who arrived from other French ports. The Court considered that, in principle, there was an infringement of the freedom to provide services if a measure discriminated between the provision of services purely within a national context and between services provided between one Member State and the other. In *Corsica Ferries, Italia*[73], however, the Court appeared to retract by suggesting that discrimination between the services provided was insufficient, there needed to be discrimination between the providers of services for there to be an infringement of Article 59 [*49*] EC. In that instance operators were required to use the local piloting services at the port of Genoa. For operators who were engaged in cabotage, that is to say a journey between two Italian ports, a 30% discount was offered in the tariffs. The Court did not consider this distinction to be sufficient to infringe Article 59 [*49*] EC. It noted rather that as only ships flying the Italian flag could engage in cabotage, there existed a discrimination against foreign operators.

If the types of discrimination outlawed by Article 59 [*49*] EC are more multifarious, the reach of the principle is more problematic in this area. Nicolaides has noted:

'The major problem in capturing the meaning of services is that, in contrast to goods, which simply, are, services are judged, evaluated or defined by their results, outcome or effects. When procuring a service one actually defines the expected results or effects and, thus, one cannot be certain of the quality of the service until after it has been performed.

---

71 Joined Cases 62 & 63/81 *Seco* [1982] ECR 223; Case C-3/88 *Commission v Italy* [1989] ECR 4035, [1991] 2 CMLR 115.

72 Case C-49/89 *Corsica Ferries, France v Direction Générale des Douanes Français* [1989] ECR 4441

73 Case C-18/93 *Corsica Ferries, Italia v Corpo dei piloti del porto di Genova* [1994] ECR I-1783.

To put it more precisely, one does not transact in services as such. One merely procures the inputs which are expected to produce a service.'[74]

This separation of inputs and outcomes poses considerable problems for determining when services are competing, and are, therefore, comparable. Let us take the example of a financial adviser. If I hire a financial adviser, the expected outcome of the service is that he or she helps me make money. There might be doubt in my mind whether I want a high annual income or would prefer an investment that achieves faster growth but, in principle, from the consumer viewpoint most financial packages are economically substitutable. The inputs required to achieve this service, are from a supply side not substitutable at all. The example above would cover all the forms of investment which exist. Each of which may need to be regulated in a different manner. It is too simplistic to argue that all are competing, and should be subject to a level playing field.

Case C-275/92 Her Majesty's Customs and Excise v Schindler Brothers [1994] ECR I-1039, [1995] 1 CMLR 4

In the United Kingdom, with the exception of certain small-scale lotteries, lotteries were prohibited unless prior authorisation had been received from the British authorities. It was also illegal to advertise any such lottery. The Schindler Brothers promoted and sold tickets for lotteries organised by the South German Länder (regional authorities). They sent advertisements and application forms for the lottery through the post from the Netherlands to Britain inviting British nationals to take part in these lotteries. These were intercepted and confiscated by the British authorities. Schindler argued that the general ban on lotteries was discriminatory.

48. It is common ground that a prohibition such as that laid down in the United Kingdom legislation, which applies to the operation of large-scale lotteries and in particular to the advertising and distribution of tickets for such lotteries, applies irrespective of the nationality of the lottery operator or his agents and whatever the Member State or States in which the operator or his agents are established. It does not therefore discriminate on

---

[74] Nicolaides, P. 'The Problems of Regulation in Traded Services: The Implications for Reciprocal Liberalization' (1989) 44 *Aussenwirtschaft* 29, 32.

the basis of the nationality of the economic agents concerned or of the Member State in which they are established.

49. The Commission and the defendants in the main proceedings argue, however, that legislation such as the United Kingdom lotteries legislation is in fact discriminatory. They submit that, although such legislation prohibits large lotteries in the United Kingdom in an apparently non-discriminatory manner, it permits the simultaneous operation by the same person of several small lotteries, which is equivalent to one large lottery and further the operation of games of chance which are comparable in nature and scale to large lotteries, such as football pools or 'bingo'.

50. It is true that the prohibition in question in the main proceedings does not apply to all types of lottery, small-scale lotteries not conducted for private gain being permitted in the national territory and the prohibition being set in the more general context of the national legislation on gambling which permits certain forms of gambling similar to lotteries, such as football pools or 'bingo'.

51. However, even though the amounts at stake in the games so permitted in the United Kingdom may be comparable to those in large-scale lotteries and even though those games involve a significant element of chance they differ in their object, rules and methods of organization from those large-scale lotteries which were established in member states other than the United Kingdom before the enactment of the National Lottery etc. Act 1993. They are therefore not in a comparable situation to the lotteries prohibited by the United Kingdom legislation and, contrary to the arguments of the commission and the defendants in the main proceedings, cannot be assimilated to them.

52. In those circumstances legislation such as the United Kingdom legislation cannot be considered to be discriminatory.

b. Non-Discriminatory Restrictions on who can be Providers of Services

From as early as 1974 the Court began to move away from an approach using purely the language of non-discrimination. In *Van Binsbergen* the Court stated that an indistinctly applicable requirement that a service provider reside in the national territory was illegal as it would 'deprive

Article 59 [*49*] EC of all useful effect'.[75] The extension of Article 59 [*49*] EC to non-discriminatory restrictions on who can provide services was mostly clearly articulated in the *German Insurance* judgment.

Case 205/84 Commission v Germany [1986] ECR 3755, [1987] 2 CMLR 66[76]

26. ... the principal aim of that paragraph [Article 60(3) EC] is to enable the provider of the service to pursue his activities in the Member State where the service is given without suffering discrimination in favour of the nationals of the State. However, it does not follow from that paragraph that all national legislation applicable to nationals of that State and usually applied to the permanent activities of undertakings established therein may be similarly applied in its entirety to the temporary activities of undertakings which are established in other Member States.

27. The Court has nevertheless accepted, in particular in its judgments of 18 January 1979 (Joined Cases 110 and 111/78 *Ministère Public and another v Van Wesemael and others*(1979) ECR 35) and 17 December 1981 (Case 279/80 *Webb*, cited above [(1981) ECR 3305]), that regard being had to the particular nature of certain services, specific requirements imposed on the provider of the services cannot be considered to be incompatible with the Treaty where they have as their purpose the application of rules governing such activities. However, the freedom to provide services, as one of the fundamental principles of the Treaty, may be restricted only by provisions which are justified by the general good and which are applied to all persons or undertakings operating within the territory of the State in which the service is provided in so far as that interest is not safeguarded by the provisions to which the provider of a service is subject in the Member State of his establishment. In addition, such requirements must be objectively justified by the need to ensure that professional rules of conduct are complied with and that the interests which such rules are designed to safeguard are protected.

28. It must be stated that the requirements in question in these proceedings, namely that an insurer who is established in another Member State, authorized by the supervisory authority of that State and subject to the supervision of that authority, must have a permanent establishment within the territory of the State in which the service is provided and that he must obtain a separate authorization from the supervisory authority of that

---

[75] Case 33/74 *Van Binsbergen v Bestuur van de Bedrijsvereniging voor de Metaalnijverheid* [1974] ECR 1310, [1975] 1 CMLR 298. Similar reasoning can also be found in Case 39/75 *Coenen* [1975] ECR 1547, [1976] 1 CMLR 30.

[76] For the facts see p. 364.

State, constitute restrictions on the freedom to provide services inasmuch as they increase the cost of such services in the State in which they are provided, in particular where the insurer conducts business in that State only occasionally.

29. It follows that those requirements may be regarded as compatible with Articles 59 and 60 of the EEC Treaty only if it is established that in the field of activity concerned there are imperative reasons relating to the public interest which justify restrictions on the freedom to provide services, that the public interest is not already protected by the rules of the State of establishment and that the same result cannot be obtained by less restrictive rules.

(a) The existence of an interest justifying certain restrictions on the freedom to provide insurance services.

30. As the German Government and the parties intervening in its support have maintained, without being contradicted by the Commission or the United Kingdom and Netherlands Governments, the insurance sector is a particularly sensitive area from the point of view of the protection of the consumer both as a policy-holder and as an insured person. This is so in particular because of the specific nature of the service provided by the insurer, which is linked to future events, the occurrence of which, or at least the timing of which, is uncertain at the time when the contract is concluded. An insured person who does not obtain payment under a policy following an event giving rise to a claim may find himself in a very precarious position. Similarly, it is as a rule very difficult for a person seeking insurance to judge whether the likely future development of the insurer's financial position and the terms of the contract, usually imposed by the insurer, offer him sufficient guarantees that he will receive payment under the policy if a claimable event occurs.

31. It must also be borne in mind, as the German Government has pointed out, that in certain fields insurance has become a mass phenomenon. Contracts are concluded by such enormous numbers of policy-holders that the protection of the interests of insured persons and injured third parties affects virtually the whole population.

32. Those special characteristics, which are peculiar to the insurance sector, have led all the Member States to introduce legislation making insurance undertakings subject to mandatory rules both as regards their financial position and the conditions of insurance which they apply, and to permanent supervision to ensure that those rules are complied with.

33. It therefore appears that in the field in question there are imperative reasons relating to the public interest which may justify restrictions on the freedom to provide services, provided, however, that the rules of the state of establishment are not adequate in order to achieve the necessary level of protection and that the requirements of the State in which the service is provided do not exceed what is necessary in that respect.

.....

(b) The question of whether the public interest is already protected by the rules of the State of establishment.

42. The Commission does not dispute that the State in which the service is provided is entitled to exercise a certain control over insurance undertakings which provide services within its territory. At the hearing it even accepted that it was permissible to provide for certain measures of supervision of the undertaking concerned to be applied prior to its conducting any business in the context of the provision of services. It nevertheless maintained that such supervision should take a form less restrictive than that of authorization. It did not however explain how such a system might work.

43. The German Government and the Governments intervening in its support maintain that the necessary supervision can be carried out only by means of an authorization procedure which makes it possible to investigate the undertaking before it commences its activities, to monitor those activities continuously and to withdraw the authorization in the event of serious and repeated infringements.

44. In that respect it should be noted that in all the Member States the supervision of insurance undertakings is organized in the form of an authorization procedure and that the necessity of such a procedure is recognized in the two first coordination Directives as regards the activities to which they refer. In each of those Directives article 6 thereof provides that each Member State must make the taking-up of the business of insurance in its territory subject to an official authorization. An undertaking which sets up branches and agencies in Member States other than that in which its head office is situated must therefore obtain an authorization from the supervisory authority of each of those States.

45. It must also be observed that the proposal for a second Directive provides for the retention of that system. The undertaking must obtain an official authorization from each Member State in which it wishes to conduct business in the context of the provision of services. Although, according to that proposal, the authorization must be obtained from the supervisory authority of the State of establishment, that authority must first consult the authority of the state in which the service is to be provided and send it all the relevant papers. The proposal also envisages permanent cooperation between the two supervisory authorities, thus making it possible, in particular, for the authority of the state of establishment to take all appropriate measures, which may extend to withdrawal of the authorization, to put an end to the infringements which have been notified to it by the supervisory authority of the state in which the service is provided.

46. In those circumstances the German government's argument to the effect that only the requirement of an authorization can provide an effective means of ensuring the supervision which, having regard to the foregoing considerations, is justified on grounds relating to the protection of the consumer both as a policy-holder and as an insured person, must be accepted. Since a system such as that proposed in the draft for a second directive, which entrusts the operation of the authorization procedure to the Member State in which the undertaking is established, working in close cooperation with the State in which the service is provided, can be set up only by legislation, it must also be acknowledged that, in the present state of Community law, it is for the state in which the service is provided to grant and withdraw that authorization.

47. It should however be emphasized that the authorization must be granted on request to any undertaking established in another Member State which meets the conditions laid down by the legislation of the State in which the service is provided, that those conditions may not duplicate equivalent statutory conditions which have already been satisfied in the State in which the undertaking is established and that the supervisory authority of the state in which the service is provided must take into account supervision and verifications which have already been carried out in the Member State of establishment. According to the German Government, which has not been contradicted on that point by the Commission, the German authorization procedure conforms fully to those requirements.

48. It is still necessary to consider whether the requirement of authorization which, under the insurance supervision law, applies to any insurance business other than transport insurance, is justified in all its applications. In that respect it has been pointed out, in particular by the United Kingdom Government, that the free movement of services is of importance principally for commercial insurance and that with regard to that particular type of insurance the grounds relating to the protection of policy-holders relied on by the German Government and the Governments intervening in its support do not apply.

49. It follows from the foregoing that the requirement of authorization may be maintained only in so far as it is justified on the grounds relating to the protection of policy-holders and insured persons relied upon by the German Government. It must also be recognized that those grounds are not equally important in every sector of insurance and that there may be cases where, because of the nature of the risk insured and of the party seeking insurance, there is no need to protect the latter by the application of the mandatory rules of his national law.

.....

52. If the requirement of an authorization constitutes a restriction on the freedom to provide services, the requirement of a permanent establishment is the very negation of that freedom. It has the result of depriving Article 59 of the Treaty of all effectiveness, a provision whose very purpose is to abolish restrictions on the freedom to provide services of persons who are not established in the State in which the service is to be provided (see in particular the judgment of 3 December 1974, *cited above*, and the judgments of 26 November 1975 in Case 39/75 *Coenen v Sociaal-Economische Raad* (1975) ECR 1547, and 10 February 1982 in Case 76/81 *Transporoute v Minister for Public Works* (1982) ECR 417). If such a requirement is to be accepted, it must be shown that it constitutes a condition which is indispensable for attaining the objective pursued.

53. In that respect, the German Government points out in particular that the requirement of an establishment in the State in which the service is provided makes it possible for the supervisory authority of that state to carry out verifications *in situ* and to monitor continuously the activities carried on by the authorized insurer and that, without that requirement, the authority would be unable to perform its task.

54. The Court has already stressed in its decisions, most recently in its judgment of 3 February 1983 (Case 29/82 *Van Luipen* (1983) ECR 151), that considerations of an administrative nature cannot justify derogation by a Member State from the rules of Community law. That principle applies with even greater force where the derogation in question amounts to preventing the exercise of one of the fundamental freedoms guaranteed by the Treaty. In this instance it is therefore not sufficient that the presence on the undertaking's premises of all the documents needed for supervision by the authorities of the State in which the service is provided may make it easier for those authorities to perform their task. It must also be shown that those authorities cannot, even under an authorization procedure, carry out their supervisory tasks effectively unless the undertaking has in the aforesaid State a permanent establishment at which all the necessary documents are kept.

55. That has not been shown to be the case. As has been stated above, Community law on insurance does not, as it stands at present, prohibit the State in which the service is provided from requiring that the assets representing the technical reserves covering business conducted on its territory be localized in that State. In that case the presence of such assets may be verified *in situ*, even if the undertaking does not have any permanent establishment in the State. As regards the other conditions for the conduct of business which are subject to supervision, it appears to the Court that such supervision may be effected on the basis of copies of balance sheets, accounts and commercial documents, including the conditions of insurance and schemes of operation, sent from the State of establishment and duly certified by the authorities of that Member State. It is possible under an authorization procedure to subject the undertaking to such conditions of supervision by means of a provision in the certificate of authorization and to ensure compliance with those conditions, if necessary by withdrawing that certificate.

56. It has therefore not been established that the considerations acknowledged above concerning the protection of policy-holders and insured persons make the establishment of the insurer in the territory of the State in which the service is provided an indispensable requirement.

The principle of home State control and its sister, that of mutual recognition, are allocated the same structural role in the field of services they have been given in the field of goods. The predominant responsibility for regulation of the provision of services lies with the home State. This creates a presumption that regulation of services by the host State is an unnecessary restriction on trade which can only be rebutted through that Member State demonstrating that the regulation serves the public interest in a manner which does not duplicate the regulation of the Member State of establishment.

White Paper from the Commission to the European Council (Milan, 28-29 June 1985) COM (85) 310 final, Brussels, 14 June 1985

101. The liberalisation of financial services, linked to that of capital movements, will represent a major step towards Community financial integration.

102. The accent is now put increasingly on the free circulation of 'financial products', made ever easier by developments of technology. Some comparison can be made between the approach followed by the Commission after the 'Cassis de Dijon' judgments with regard to industrial and agricultural products and what now has to be done for insurance policies, home-ownership savings contracts, consumer credit, participation in collective investment schemes, etc. The Commission considers that it should be possible to facilitate the exchange of such 'financial products' at a Community level, using a minimal coordination of rules (especially on such matters as authorisation, financial supervision and reorganisation, winding up etc) as the basis for mutual recognition of Member States of what each does to safeguard the interests of the public.

103. Such harmonisation, particularly as regards the supervision of ongoing activities, should be guided by the principle of 'home country control'. This means attributing the primary task of supervising the financial institution to the competent authorities of its Member State of origin, to which would have to be communicated all information necessary for supervision. The authorities of the Member State which is the destination of the service, whilst not deprived of all power, would have a complementary role. There would have to be a minimum harmonisation of surveillance standards, though the need to reach agreements on this must not be allowed further to delay the necessary and overdue decisions.

Once the focus of Article 59 [*49*] EC extended to cover not merely measures characterised by *discriminatory effects* but also those which had *restrictive effects* on trade, the question also arose whether Article 59 [*49*] EC covered all measures which had restrictive effects on trade or only certain types of measure.

Marenco, G, 'The Notion of Restriction on the Freedom of Establishment and Provision of Services in the Case-law of the Court' (1991) 11 *Yearbook of European Law* 111, 128

The concept of restriction which counts in the area of establishment is often contrasted with that applicable to the freedom to provide services. It is argued that whilst the first is founded on the notion of non-discrimination, the second is wider and covers any unjustified obstacle to the provision of services. In the matter of services, then, the unlawfulness of a national measure would according to this opinion, be independent of any inequality of treatment and depend on the absence of a legitimate reason, or on some disproportion between the restriction and the reason.

The following examination of the case-law will demonstrate that, despite recent language used by the Court, any variance between the two freedoms operates not so much in terms of the criterion needed to establish the unlawfulness of a restriction, but rather at the application of this criterion to factual situations, which are by definition, different. In the case of establishment, the person or company which invokes the Treaty rule wants to put down roots in another Member State; whereas where services are provided the rule relied upon by those who wish occasionally to carry on economic activity for a client established in another Member State.

It should be emphasized right from the start that in order to assess the existence of discrimination in the area of freedom to provide services, the relevant comparison is not between national and non-national providers, but between those providers who are established and those who are not established. In dealing with the free provision of services the Treaty is concerned with ensuring freedom of cross-border transactions, regardless of the nationality of those involved; they may even be nationals of the State whose measure is called in question. In other words, the Treaty protects economic transactions originating from another Member State. In this, services are comparable to goods.

Clear examples of restrictions on who can provide services would include authorisation procedures or conditions such as membership of professional bodies, residence or establishment requirements or requirements of no prior conviction before one could provide services in another Member State.

A number of rationales may be put forward for distinguishing between regulating access to an activity, e.g. who can provide a service and regulating the conditions of exercise of an activity. Marenco bases the distinction upon the non-discrimination principle. A person lawfully providing services in another Member State by having to meet further criteria in the host State is placed with an additional barrier that does not have to be met by persons established in that State, as the latter only have to meet the criteria of that State and no other State.

A similar rationale is that of double regulation.[77] This rationale focuses not so much on the discriminatory effects of any regulation by the host State but rather on its being unnecessary and therefore unduly restrictive. Any provider of a service can be regulated, at a first step, in the home State. A person offering legal services from Britain, for example, can be regulated in Britain to ensure that person has the necessary expertise. Any ban by the French, for example, on that person offering their services in France would be double regulation. It would also prevent someone recognised as a provider of services within one part of the Community from offering that service to other parts of the Community.

With the provision of many services, the showing of a film for example, consumption and provision are simultaneous. Double regulation is impossible in such circumstances as the first point at which the service 'emerges' is in the host State. It is not therefore possible for the State of the service provider to have had an earlier opportunity to regulate that service. As there is no double regulation in these instances, it is argued, they should fall outside Article 59 [*49*] EC.

A final rationale is that restrictions on who can provide services regulate access to activity. They are therefore unlike conditions regulating the exercise of that activity, as they have the effect of preventing rather than merely hindering someone practising that activity.[78] This is clearly incompatible with the notion of free provision of services within a common market as provider of services lawfully providing a service in one part of the Community should be able to provide that service to anywhere else within the Community. Restrictions on the provision of services, *per se*, are not caught by this rationale, as the trader operating from another Member State can still provide the service to the host State, he must simply observe the

---

77 Such language is used most clearly in Case C-222/95 *Parodi v Banque Albert de Bary*, Judgment of 9 July 1997, where the Court talks of the restrictive effects of banks having to obtain fresh authorisations in the host State to provide services there.

78 See Advocate-General Gulmann in Case C-275/92 *Her Majesty's Customs and Excise v Schindler Brothers* [1994] ECR I-1039, paragraph 56.

modalities of regulation of the host State. Whilst this might hinder the flow of the services, crucially, it will not prevent the trader trading with that other Member State.

c. Non-Discriminatory Restrictions on the Conditions of Exercise of an Activity

In a series of judgments concerning restrictions upon who can provide services, the Court indicated that the ambit of Article 59 [*49*] EC might extend beyond non-discriminatory restrictions upon who can provide a service by suggesting that measures fell within Article 59 [*49*] EC if they were liable to prohibit or otherwise impede the activities of a provider of services established in another Member State who lawfully provides similar services in the latter.[79] Hatzopoulos has observed that by suggesting any measure which potentially restricts the flow of services falls within Article 59 [*49*] EC such a test is the functional equivalent of the *Dassonville* formula.[80] In *Gouda*[81] attention was turned for the first time to a non-discriminatory restriction on what services may be provided rather than upon who may provide the service.

Case C-288/89 Gouda v Commissariat voor de Media [1991] ECR I-4007

In the Netherlands the *Mediawet* imposed a number of restrictions on advertising by cable network operators, which was intended exclusively for the Dutch public. The advertisement had to be produced by a person separate from the suppliers of the programme and the advertising revenue received by the operator must all

---

79 Case C-154/89 *Commission v France* [1991] ECR I-659; Case C-180/89 *Commission v Italy* [1991] ECR I-709; Case C-198/89 *Commission v Greece* [1991] ECR I-727; Case C-76/90 *Säger v Dennemeyer* [1991] ECR I-4221.

80 Hatzopoulos, V. Note on *Schindler* (1995) 32 *CMLRev* 841, 847. See also Art, J-Y. 'Legislative Lacunae, the Court of Justice and the Freedom to Provide Services' in O'Keeffe, D. & Curtin, D. (eds.) *Constitutional Adjudication in European and National Law* (1992, Butterworth, London)

81 See also the sister case of Case C-353/89 *Commission v Netherlands* [1991] ECR I-4069.

be used for the production of the programmes. A number of conditions were also imposed on the advertisements themselves, in particular they had to be recognisable as advertisements and thus separated from other programmes, they must occupy no more than 5% of air time, and they must not be broadcast on Sunday.

10. ... the Court has consistently held (see, most recently, the judgments in Case C-154/89 *Commission v France* [1991] ECR I-659, paragraph 12, Case C-180/89 *Commission v Italy* [1991] ECR I-709, paragraph 15, and Case C-198/89 *Commission v Greece* [1991] ECR I-727, paragraph 16) that Article 59 of the Treaty entails, in the first place, the abolition of any discrimination against a person providing services on account of his nationality or the fact that he is established in a Member State other than the one in which the service is provided.

11. As the Court held in its judgment in Case 352/85 *Bond van Adverteerders* [1988] ECR 2085, at paragraphs 32 and 33, national rules which are not applicable to services without discrimination as regards their origin are compatible with Community law only if they can be brought within the scope of an express exemption, such as that contained in Article 56 of the Treaty. It also appears from that judgment (paragraph 34) that economic aims cannot constitute grounds of public policy within the meaning of Article 56 of the Treaty.

12. In the absence of harmonization of the rules applicable to services, or even of a system of equivalence, restrictions on the freedom guaranteed by the Treaty in this field may arise in the second place as a result of the application of national rules which affect any person established in the national territory to persons providing services established in the territory of another Member State *who already have to satisfy the requirements of that State's legislation* [authors' italics].

13. As the Court has consistently held (see, most recently, the judgments in *Commission v France*, cited above, paragraph 15; *Commission v Italy*, cited above, paragraph 18; and *Commission v Greece*, cited above, paragraph 18), such restrictions come within the scope of Article 59 if the application of the national legislation to foreign persons providing services is not justified by overriding reasons relating to the public interest or if the requirements embodied in that legislation are already satisfied by the rules imposed on those persons in the Member State in which they are established.

14. In this respect, the overriding reasons relating to the public interest which the Court has already recognized include professional rules intended to protect recipients of the service (Joined Cases 110/78 and 111/78 *Van Wesemael* [1979] ECR 35, paragraph 28); protection of intellectual property (Case 62/79 *Coditel* [1980] ECR 881); the protection of workers (Case 279/80 *Webb* [1981] ECR 3305, paragraph 19; Joined Cases 62/81 and 63/81 *Seco v Evi* [1982] ECR 223, paragraph 14; Case C-113/89 *Rush Portuguesa* [1990] ECR I-1417, paragraph 18); consumer protection (Case 220/83 *Commission v*

France [1986] ECR 3663, paragraph 20; Case 252/83 *Commission v Denmark* [1986] ECR 3713, paragraph 20; Case 205/84 *Commission v Germany* [1986] ECR 3755, paragraph 30; Case 206/84 *Commission v Ireland* [1986] ECR 3817, paragraph 20; *Commission v Italy*, cited above, paragraph 20; and *Commission v Greece*, cited above, paragraph 21), the conservation of the national historic and artistic heritage (*Commission v Italy*, cited above, paragraph 20); turning to account the archaeological, historical and artistic heritage of a country and the widest possible dissemination of knowledge of the artistic and cultural heritage of a country (*Commission v France*, cited above, paragraph 17, and *Commission v Greece*, cited above, paragraph 21).

15. Lastly, as the Court has consistently held, the application of national provisions to providers of services established in other Member States must be such as to guarantee the achievement of the intended aim and must not go beyond that which is necessary in order to achieve that objective. In other words, it must not be possible to obtain the same result by less restrictive rules (see, most recently, Case C-154/89 *Commission v France*, cited above, paragraphs 14 and 15; Case C-180/89 *Commission v Italy*, cited above, paragraphs 17 and 18; Case C-198/89 *Commission v Greece*, cited above, paragraphs 18 and 19).

16. It is in the light of those principles that it should be examined whether a provision such as article 66(1)(b) of the Mediawet, which, according to the national court, is not discriminatory, contains restrictions on freedom to provide services and, if so, whether those restrictions may be justified.

The existence of restrictions on the freedom to provide services.

17. It must be noted at the outset that conditions such as those imposed by the second sentence of article 66(1)(b) of the Mediawet contain a two-fold restriction on freedom to provide services. First, they prevent operators of cable networks established in a Member State from transmitting radio or television programmes supplied by broadcasters established in other Member States which do not satisfy those conditions. Secondly, they restrict the opportunities afforded to those broadcasting bodies to include in their programmes, for the benefit in particular of advertisers established in the State in which the programmes are received, advertising intended specifically for the public in that State.

The Dutch Government argued that these restrictions were necessary to maintain cultural pluralism. The Court replied, first, that cultural arguments could never be used to justify restrictions being placed on the structure of foreign broadcasters. Secondly, the Court noted that the restrictions on the advertisements only applied to those advertisements intended exclusively for the Dutch public and not to other advertisements. From this it concluded that the purpose of the restrictions was not to promote cultural policy but to protect the STER, the Dutch body in charge of arranging advertisements with Dutch broadcasters, from increased competition. The restrictions were therefore illegal.

The Court pursued this line of reasoning in *Van der Elst.*[82] Van der Elst, a Belgian national, was fined FF 121,520 for using four Moroccans to carry out a one month job demolishing and recovering materials from the Chateau Lanson in Reims, France. All the Moroccans had work permits for Belgium but only tourist visas for France. The Court considered that the French requirement of a work permit for the Moroccans increased Van der Elst's costs, and therefore hindered his ability to provide services within Article 59 [*49*] EC. The Court considered, moreover, that such a requirement could not be justified where the third country nationals were lawfully resident in another Member State and did not seek access to the labour market in the host State.

The Court has therefore reached a parallel position in services to that it reached in goods prior to *Keck*. The same uncertainties arise - the predominance of private interests over collective ones; the role of the judge vis-à-vis the legislature; excessive intrusion into the domestic domain and disruption of finely balanced systems of social accommodation.

Case C-398/95 Syndesmos ton en Elladi Touristikon kai Taxidiotikon Grafeion (SETTG) v Ypourgos Ergasias [1997] ECR I-3091

In Greece licenced tour guides could only retain their licence if they entered into employment relations with travel agencies. They were prohibited from freelancing. This rule had been adopted to resolve a long-running dispute between travel agencies and tour guides.

9. The first question which needs to be examined, therefore, is whether rules of the kind at issue in the main proceedings may, in the circumstances referred to in Article 59, affect the right of self-employed tourist guides from another Member State freely to provide services.

---

82 Case C-43/93 *Van der Elst v Office des Migrations Internationaux* [1994] ECR I-3803.

.....

12. The mere fact that tourist guides from another Member State do not need such a licence when they accompany a group of tourists to Greece does not mean that they cannot have an interest in acquiring the said diploma, in order to secure a higher qualification, and thus obtaining the licence to pursue the profession in that State. In those circumstances, the rules in question apply to them.

13. It follows that such rules may affect the right of self-employed tourist guides from another Member State freely to provide services where they are licenced to pursue the profession in the first State and offer their services in connection with the operation of tourist programmes organized in that State by tourist or travel agencies, wherever those agencies are established within the Community.

14. The next point to consider is whether rules of the kind at issue in the main proceedings constitute a barrier to the freedom of self-employed tourist guides from other Member States to provide services.

15. It is common ground that such rules apply without distinction to all licenced tourist guides.

16. However, Article 59 of the Treaty requires not only the elimination of all discrimination against a person providing services on the ground of his nationality but also the abolition of any restriction, even if it applies without distinction to nationals providing services and to those of other Member States, when it is liable to prohibit or otherwise impede the activities of a provider of services established in another Member State where he lawfully provides similar services (Case C-76/90 *Säger* [1991] ECR I-4221, paragraph 12).

17. It should be noted that such rules, in mandatorily characterizing as an employment relationship, for the purposes of national law, a relationship involving the provision of services by a tourist guide in connection with the operation of tourist programmes in the State concerned, deprive a tourist guide from another Member State of the possibility of working in the first Member State as a self-employed person.

18. Such rules therefore constitute a barrier to the freedom of tourist guides from other Member States to provide services of that kind as self-employed persons.

......

20. In its second question, the national court asks whether a barrier of that kind can be justified by reasons relating to the general interest in maintaining industrial peace in the sensitive area of the supply of tourist services, in respect of which the Greek State, as a country for which tourism is important, has a reasonable and justifiable interest in intervening by regulation.

21. The Court has consistently held that, as a fundamental principle of the Treaty, the freedom to provide services may be limited only by rules which are justified by overriding reasons relating to the general interest and which apply to all persons or undertakings pursuing an activity in the State of destination. In particular, the restrictions must be suitable for securing the attainment of the objective which they pursue and they must not go beyond what is necessary in order to attain it (*Säger*, cited above, paragraph 15; Case C-288/89 *Gouda and Others* [1991] ECR I-407, paragraphs 13 to 15; Case C-19/92 *Kraus* [1993] ECR I-1663, paragraph 32, and Case C-55/94 *Gebhard* [1995] ECR I-4165, paragraph 37).

22. With regard to the question whether maintaining industrial peace may constitute an overriding reason relating to the general interest which justifies the rules at issue in the main proceedings, it is apparent from the order for reference that those rules were adopted in order to settle long-standing disputes between tourist guides and travel and tourist agencies and thereby prevent any adverse effects on tourism, and consequently on the country's economy. In that regard, the Greek Government itself pointed out at the hearing that the rules at issue were adopted in order to ensure the proper functioning of the national economy.

23. However, maintaining industrial peace as a means of bringing a collective labour dispute to an end and thereby preventing any adverse effects on an economic sector, and consequently on the economy of the State, must be regarded as an economic aim which cannot constitute a reason relating to the general interest that justifies a restriction of a fundamental freedom guaranteed by the Treaty (see *Gouda and Others*, cited above, paragraph 11).

24. Furthermore, as the Advocate General has pointed out in point 66 of his Opinion, none of the parties which have submitted observations in these proceedings has contended that, in order to maintain industrial peace, it was necessary to impose on tourist guides from other Member States restrictions on working as self-employed persons in connection with the operation of tourist programmes organized in Greece by travel and tourist agencies.

Tension has manifested itself through the plethora of public interests found to justify restrictions on the provision of services.[83] Constraints have also begun to emerge in particularly problematic cases on the scope of Article 59 [*49*] EC itself. The first is a softening of the proportionality principle.

---

83 Case C-288/89 *Gouda v Commissariat voor de Media* [1991] ECR I-4007, paragraph 14.

Case C-275/92 Her Majesty's Customs and Excise v Schindler [1994] ECR I-1039, [1995] 1 CMLR 4[84]

39. The essence of the national court's fifth question is whether national legislation which, like the United Kingdom legislation on lotteries, prohibits, subject to specified exceptions, the holding of lotteries in a Member State constitutes an obstacle to the freedom to provide services.

.....

43. According to the case-law of the Court (see the judgment in Case C-76/90 *Säger v Dennemeyer* [1991] ECR I-4221, at paragraph 12) national legislation may fall within the ambit of Article 59 of the Treaty, even if it is applicable without distinction, when it is liable to prohibit or otherwise impede the activities of a provider of services established in another Member State where he lawfully provides similar services.

44. It is sufficient to note that this is the case with national legislation such as the United Kingdom legislation on lotteries which wholly precludes lottery operators from other Member States from promoting their lotteries and selling their tickets, whether directly or through independent agents, in the Member State which enacted that legislation.

45. Accordingly, the reply to the fifth question should be that national legislation which, like the United Kingdom legislation on lotteries, prohibits, subject to specified exceptions, the holding of lotteries in a Member State is an obstacle to the freedom to provide services.

The sixth question

46. The national court's sixth question raises the issue whether the Treaty provisions relating to the freedom to provide services preclude legislation such as the United Kingdom lotteries legislation, where there are concerns of social policy and of the prevention of fraud to justify it.

.....

57. According to the information provided by the referring court, the United Kingdom legislation, before its amendment by the 1993 Act establishing the National Lottery, pursued the following objectives: to prevent crime and to ensure that gamblers would be treated honestly; to avoid stimulating demand in the gambling sector which has damaging social consequences when taken to excess; and to ensure that lotteries could not be operated for personal and commercial profit but solely for charitable, sporting or cultural purposes.

---

84 For the facts see p. 396.

58. Those considerations, which must be taken together, concern the protection of the recipients of the service and, more generally, of consumers as well as the maintenance of order in society. The Court has already held that those objectives figure among those which can justify restrictions on freedom to provide services (see the judgments in Joined Cases 110 and 111/78 *Ministère Public v van Wesemael* (1979) ECR 35, at paragraph 28; Case 220/83 *Commission v France* [1986] ECR 3663, at paragraph 20; Case 15/78 *Société Générale Alsacienne de Banque v Koestler* [1978] ECR 1971, at paragraph 5).

59. Given the peculiar nature of lotteries, which has been stressed by many Member States, those considerations are such as to justify restrictions, as regards Article 59 of the Treaty, which may go so far as to prohibit lotteries in a Member State.

60. First of all, it is not possible to disregard the moral, religious or cultural aspects of lotteries, like other types of gambling, in all the Member States. The general tendency of the Member States is to restrict, or even prohibit, the practice of gambling and to prevent it from being a source of private profit. Secondly, lotteries involve a high risk of crime or fraud, given the size of the amounts which can be staked and of the winnings which they can hold out to the players, particularly when they are operated on a large scale. Thirdly, they are an incitement to spend which may have damaging individual and social consequences. A final ground which is not without relevance, although it cannot in itself be regarded as an objective justification, is that lotteries may make a significant contribution to the financing of benevolent or public interest activities such as social works, charitable works, sport or culture.

61. Those particular factors justify national authorities having a sufficient degree of latitude to determine what is required to protect the players and, more generally, in the light of the specific social and cultural features of each Member State, to maintain order in society, as regards the manner in which lotteries are operated, the size of the stakes, and the allocation of the profits they yield. In those circumstances, it is for them to assess not only whether it is necessary to restrict the activities of lotteries but also whether they should be prohibited, provided that those restrictions are not discriminatory.

62. When a Member State prohibits in its territory the operation of large-scale lotteries and in particular the advertising and distribution of tickets for that type of lottery, the prohibition on the importation of materials intended to enable nationals of that member state to participate in such lotteries organized in another Member State cannot be regarded as a measure involving an unjustified interference with the freedom to provide services. Such a prohibition on import is a necessary part of the protection which that Member State seeks to secure in its territory in relation to lotteries.

The considerable margin of latitude given here makes it difficult to see what form of restriction on lotteries, other than a discriminatory one, would actually be considered illegal.[85] Elsewhere the Court has used the standard formulation for the proportionality principles, but has given the national court a free hand in how it uses it. In *De Agostini* Swedish restrictions preventing advertising from being directed at children under the age of twelve or from making misleading claims was challenged as being incompatible with Article 59 [*49*] EC.[86] The Court considered that such restrictions fell within Article 59 [*49*] EC but would be lawful if they were necessary to protect the consumer or prevent unfair trading. It was entirely for the national court to decide whether this was the case.

Both in *Schindler* and in *Gouda* the Court only found the legislation to fall within Article 59 [*49*] EC because it applied to persons lawfully providing services in another Member State. This latter proviso has been seen by some as placing an additional limit on the ambit of Article 59 [*49*] EC.

Roth, W-H. Note on *Säger* (1993) 30 CMLRev 145, 152-153

One feature in defining 'restriction' under Article 59 EEC comes close to the language used in the so-called 'Cassis-de-Dijon' adjudication. The Court restricts the application of Article 59 to indiscriminately applied regulations in a case where the services are provided by a person who *lawfully* provides similar services in the State of establishment. The Court has never explained what purpose the 'lawfulness' criterion is meant to serve. Indeed, some commentators have argued that it serves no function at all, amounting to sheer rhetoric. It is suggested that the criterion is important for two reasons. First, the criterion of 'lawful' activities in the State of origin directly relates to the idea of a single market in which goods and services are traded in the State of origin can be traded everywhere. Goods and services shall - as a matter of principle - undergo only one set of regulations - the law of the State where the goods or services are provided. Second, in a case where the service or good produced does not conform with the law of the State of origin, the specific burden on the interstate movement of goods/interstate provision of services by double regulation is not present. Moreover, in such a case it is likely that the

---

85 This is reminiscent of the approach taken by the Court in the field of free movement of goods prior to *Keck*. See Chalmers, D. 'Free Movement of Goods within the European Community: An Unhealthy Addiction to Scotch Whisky?' (1993) 42 *ICLQ* 269, 290-294; Ross, M. 'Article 59 and the marketing of financial services' (1995) 20 *ELRev* 507, 512.

86 Joined Cases C-34/95, C-35/95 & C-36/95 *Konsumentombudsmannen v De Agostini (Svenska) Förlag et al.*, Judgment of 9 July 1997.

good/service is produced not for the market of the State of establishment, but for the market of the State where the service is to be provided or the good to be imported. Under these circumstances, it seems justified to allow the Member States of destination to apply their regulations indiscriminately without any further need to justify them by the public interest.

There is, potentially, a third constraint. It has already been noted that services require both an input and an output, a final outcome. In economic terms restrictions on inputs, such as what labour or materials may be used, can be as restrictive as restrictions on the final service provided, as, at the very least, they increase the cost of the service and therefore make it less attractive to potential recipients of that service. Such restrictions, however, in that they do not determine the nature of the final service provided are only indirect restrictions, as they only restrict the provision of the service through their influence on the price mechanism. Both *Gouda* and *Schindler* concerned direct restrictions on output, on the service provided, restrictions on advertising and a ban on lotteries respectively. They did not address the question of non-discriminatory indirect restrictions on services.

In *Van der Elst* this matter was considered briefly by the Court. The French Government argued that it was necessary to require work permits from the Moroccans working for M. Van der Elst in order to ensure that they were not being exploited and that French labour law was not being flouted. The Court dismissed this argument but said that nothing in Article 59 [*49*] EC precluded Member States from extending their minimum wage legislation, to foreign providers of services, thus suggesting that indirect restrictions fell outside Article 59 [*49*] EC.[87]

It would also appear that the Court is less likely to find a breach of Article 59 [*49*] EC where a particular activity is restricted but other methods of providing a similar service can be adopted. In *Perfili*[88] an Italian provision was challenged which only allowed representatives of litigants to bring a civil claim in criminal proceedings where they had been appointed by a special power of attorney and not where they had been appointed by a general power of attorney. This obviously increased

87 Case C-43/93 *Van der Elst v Office des Migrations Internationaux* [1994] ECR I-3803.

88 Case C-177/94 *Perfili* [1996] ECR I-161.

costs for the litigant as it required the drawing up of an additional document for the action. It also restricted the provision of a service in that it stopped a particular form of transaction taking place. The Court found no breach of Article 59 [*49*] EC, however, noting that nothing restricted the ability of a litigant to appoint a legal representative for actions of this kind.

ii. Restrictions on the Receipt of Services

The service economy is dependent not just upon movement by the provider of the service, but also movement by the consumer of the service. No mention is made of this in Article 59 [*49*] EC, so the Court has had to rely upon judicial creativity.

Joined Cases 286/82 & 26/83 Luisi and Carbone v Ministero del Tesero [1984] ECR 377, [1985] 3 CMLR 52

Mrs Luisi and Mr. Carbone were both fined for taking more Italian lira out of the country than was permitted. Mrs Luisi argued that this had been to pay for tourism and medical treatment in France and Germany. Mr Carbone had used the money to finance a three month trip to Germany. They argued that these restrictions infringed the then Article 106 EEC which required Member States to authorise any payment connected, *inter alia*, with the movement of services. In these instances, however, it was the recipient not the provider of the service who had moved.

10. By virtue of Article 59 of the Treaty, restrictions on freedom to provide such services are to be abolished in respect of nationals of Member States who are established in a Member State other than that of the person for whom the service is intended. In order to enable services to be provided, the person providing the service may go to the Member State where the person for whom it is provided is established or else the latter may go to the State in which the person providing the service is established. Whilst the former case is expressly mentioned in the third paragraph of Article 60, which permits the person providing the service to pursue his activity temporarily in the Member State where the service is provided, the latter case is the necessary corollary thereof, which fulfils the objective of liberalizing all gainful activity not covered by the free movement of goods, persons and capital.

11. For the implementation of those provisions, Title II of the General Programme for the Abolition of Restrictions on Freedom to Provide Services (Official Journal, English

Special Edition, second series ix, p. 3), which was drawn up by the Council pursuant to Article 63 of the Treaty on 18 December 1961, envisages *inter alia* the repeal of provisions laid down by law, regulation or administrative action which in any Member State govern, for economic purposes, the entry, exit and residence of nationals of Member States, where such provisions are not justified on grounds of public policy, public security or public health and are liable to hinder the provision of services by such persons.

12. According to Article 1 thereof, Council Directive 64/221/EEC of 25 February 1964 on the coordination of special measures concerning the movement and residence of foreign nationals which are justified on grounds of public policy, public security or public health (Official Journal, English Special Edition 1963-1964, p.117) applies *inter alia* to any national of a Member State who travels to another Member State 'as a recipient of services'. Council Directive 73/148/EEC of 21 May 1973 on the abolition of restrictions on movement and residence within the Community for nationals of Member States with regard to establishment and the provision of services (Official Journal 1973, L 172, p. 14) grants both the provider and the recipient of a service a right of residence co-terminous with the period during which the service is provided.

.....

16. It follows that the freedom to provide services includes the freedom, for the recipients of services to go to another Member State in order to receive a service there, without being obstructed by restrictions even in relation to payments, and that tourists, persons receiving medical treatment and persons travelling for the purpose of education or business are to be regarded as recipients of services.

The non-discrimination principle is a parasitic principle in that it only applies insofar as the activity in question falls within the scope of the EC Treaty. In *Cowan* the Court had to consider whether the principle only outlawed discrimination suffered in receipt of a particular service or whether it extended more widely to cover any social benefits.

Case 186/87 Cowan v Trésor Public [1989] ECR 195, [1990] 2 CMLR 613

Cowan was a British national who, upon a visit to Paris, was robbed in the Metro. He applied for compensation to the French Criminal Injuries Board but was refused on the grounds that he was neither a French national nor a national of a country which had a reciprocal agreement with France. He claimed a breach of the then Article 7 EEC (now Article 6 [*12*] EC).

14. Under Article 7 of the Treaty the prohibition of discrimination applies 'within the scope of application of this Treaty' and 'without prejudice to any special provisions contained therein'. This latter expression refers particularly to other provisions of the Treaty in which the application of the general principle set out in that Article is given concrete form in respect of specific situations. Examples of that are the provisions concerning free movement of workers, the right of establishment and the freedom to provide services.

15. On that last point, in its judgment of 31 January 1984 in Joined Cases 286/82 and 26/83 *Luisi and Carbone v Ministero del Tesoro* (1984) ECR 377, the Court held that the freedom to provide services includes the freedom for the recipients of services to go to another Member State in order to receive a service there, without being obstructed by restrictions, and that tourists, among others, must be regarded as recipients of services.

16. At the hearing the French Government submitted that as Community law now stands a recipient of services may not rely on the prohibition of discrimination to the extent that the national law at issue does not create any barrier to freedom of movement. A provision such as that at issue in the main proceedings, it says, imposes no restrictions in that respect. Furthermore, it concerns a right which is a manifestation of the principle of national solidarity. Such a right presupposes a closer bond with the State than that of a recipient of services, and for that reason it may be restricted to persons who are either nationals of that State or foreign nationals resident on the territory of that State.

17. That reasoning cannot be accepted. When Community law guarantees a natural person the freedom to go to another Member State the protection of that person from harm in the Member State in question, on the same basis as that of nationals and persons residing there, is a corollary of that freedom of movement. It follows that the prohibition of discrimination is applicable to recipients of services within the meaning of the Treaty as regards protection against the risk of assault and the right to obtain financial compensation provided for by national law when that risk materializes. The fact that the compensation at issue is financed by the public treasury cannot alter the rules regarding the protection of the rights guaranteed by the Treaty.

18. The French Government also submitted that compensation such as that at issue in the main proceedings is not subject to the prohibition of discrimination because it falls within the law of criminal procedure, which is not included within the scope of the Treaty.

19. Although in principle criminal legislation and the rules of criminal procedure, among which the national provision in issue is to be found, are matters for which the Member States are responsible, the Court has consistently held (see *inter alia* the judgment of 11 November 1981 in Case 203/80 *Casati* (1981) ECR 2595) that Community law sets certain limits to their power. Such legislative provisions may not discriminate against persons to whom Community law gives the right to equal treatment or restrict the fundamental freedoms guaranteed by Community law.

Cowan is an example of where the Court's enthusiasm for a particular result allowed the development of some particularly sloppy reasoning. The point that the corollary of the right to go to another Member State is the right to be protected against harm on the same conditions as nationals of that State was not at issue. Cowan was not seeking protection against possible harm threatened but compensation for harm suffered. Secondly, the Court does not establish sufficiently clearly the nature of the link between the receipt of service and the operation of non-discrimination principle. Put another way, is movement into another Member State sufficient to require that Member State to accord the recipient of the service the same benefits as its own nationals? If so, would it require a Member State to extend not just the same social rights but also the same civil and political rights, such as the right to vote, to the traveller?[89] If that were the case *Cowan* establishes an incipient form of European citizenship, as it requires Member States to extend the same benefits of allegiance granted to their own nationals to other Community nationals. Yet it is very one-sided form of citizenship, as citizenship not only confers rights upon the individual but often demands duties - jury service and conscription being two examples - from the individual towards the State.

iii. Restrictions on the Provision of Services Imposed by the State of Establishment

There is no equivalent to Article 34 [*29*] EC in the case of services. This is something of an anomaly, as there is no reason why the export of services cannot be restricted in a similar manner to that of goods. The expansion of Article 59 [*49*] EC to cover restrictions imposed by the host State has been a hesitant and recent process.

The case law on restrictions on the receipt of services can be seen as the first step in this direction. The focus on the recipient of the service who was not a national of the Member State in which the service

---

89 For a critical analysis of this see Green, N., Hartley, T. & Usher, J. *The Legal Foundations of the Single European Market* (1991, OUP, Oxford) 143-144.

was provided obscured the fact that the restriction being challenged was that of the State in which the provider of the service was established.

A further step was taken in *Corsica Ferries, France*.[90] As the discriminatory tax on ferry arrivals from other Member States attached to the service itself rather than the provider it could be seen as discriminating not only against those who wished to run ferry services into Corsica but also those who wished to run them out of Corsica, thus implying that Article 59 [*49*] EC also bound the exporting State.[91]

Explicit recognition that restrictions imposed by the host State fell within Article 59 [*49*] EC only occurred in *Corsica Ferries, Italia.*[92] The Court observed that the prohibition on discrimination contained in Article 59 [*49*] EC could be relied on by an undertaking against the State in which it is established, if the services were to be provided for persons established in another Member State. It was therefore possible in that instance for Italian nationals to challenge the piloting tariffs set up by the port of Genoa which discriminated against maritime services being carried out from or to other Member States.

From enjoying a less privileged position than exporters of goods, exporters of services have swiftly moved to a more exalted position with the *Alpine Investment* judgment holding that non-discriminatory restrictions imposed by the host State upon the movement of services fall within Article 59 [*49*] EC.

Case C-384/93 Alpine Investments v Minister van Financiën [1995] ECR I-1141.

Alpine Investments, a Dutch company, was an 'introducing broker'. That it is to say it took orders from clients in respect of transactions in the commodities futures markets which it passed on to brokers dealing in such markets. Under Dutch law it was required to have a licence not just for carrying out such

---

90 Case C-49/89 *Corsica Ferries, France v Direction Générale des Douanes Français* [1989] ECR I-4441.

91 Marenco, G. 'The Notion of Restriction on the Freedom of Establishment and Provision of Services in the Case-law of the Court' (1991) 11 *YBEL* 111, 144.

92 Case C-18/93 *Corsica Ferries, Italia v Corpo dei piloti del porto di Genova* [1994] ECR I-1783. See also Case C-379/92 *Peralta* [1994] ECR I-3453; Case C-381/93 *Commission v France* [1994] ECR I-5145.

transactions on the Dutch market, but, crucially, also if it wanted to carry out transactions on other markets. In January 1992 the Dutch Minister of Finance gave it a licence to act on behalf of the brokers Rodman & Renshaw Inc. on condition it did not engage in any 'cold calling', that is to say approaching prospective clients either by telephone or by writing unless the latter had agreed to be approached in such a manner. Alpine Investments challenged this decision on the grounds that the restriction on cold calling infringed Article 59 [*49*] EC.

26. First, it must be determined whether the prohibition against telephoning potential clients in another Member State without their prior consent can constitute a restriction on freedom to provide services. The national court draws the Court's attention to the fact that providers established in the Member States where the potential recipients reside are not necessarily subject to the same prohibition or in any event not on the same terms.

27. A prohibition such as that at issue in the main proceedings does not constitute a restriction on freedom to provide services within the meaning of Article 59 solely by virtue of the fact that other Member States apply less strict rules to providers of similar services established in their territory (see the judgment in Case C-379/92 *Peralta* [1994] ECR I-3453, paragraph 48).

28. However, such a prohibition deprives the operators concerned of a rapid and direct technique for marketing and for contacting potential clients in other Member States. It can therefore constitute a restriction on the freedom to provide cross-border services.

29. Secondly, it must be considered whether that conclusion may be affected by the fact that the prohibition at issue is imposed by the Member State in which the provider is established and not by the Member State in which the potential recipient is established.

30. The first paragraph of Article 59 of the Treaty prohibits restrictions on the freedom to provide services within the Community in general. Consequently, that provision covers not only the restrictions laid down by the State of destination but also those laid down by the State of origin. As the Court has frequently held, the right freely to provide services may be relied upon by an undertaking as against the State in which it is established if the services are provided for persons established in another Member State (see Case C-18/93 *Corsica Ferries Italia v Corpo dei Piloti del Porto di Genova* [1994] ECR I-1783, paragraph 30; *Peralta*, cited above, paragraph 40, and Case C-381/93 *Commission v France* [1994] ECR I-5145, paragraph 14).

31. It follows that the prohibition of cold calling does not fall outside the scope of Article 59 of the Treaty simply because it is imposed by the State in which the provider of services is established.

32. Finally, certain arguments adduced by the Netherlands Government and the United Kingdom must be considered.

33. They submit that the prohibition at issue falls outside the scope of Article 59 of the Treaty because it is a generally applicable measure, it is not discriminatory and neither its object nor its effect is to put the national market at an advantage over providers of services from other Member States. Since it affects only the way in which the services are offered, it is analogous to the non-discriminatory measures governing selling arrangements which, according to the decision in Joined Case C-267 and 268/91 *Keck and Mithouard* [1993] ECR I-6097, paragraph 16, do not fall within the scope of Article 30 of the Treaty.

34. Those arguments cannot be accepted.

35. Although a prohibition such as the one at issue in the main proceedings is general and non-discriminatory and neither its object nor its effect is to put the national market at an advantage over providers of services from other Member States, it can none the less, as has been held above (see paragraph 28), constitute a restriction on the freedom to provide cross-border services.

36. Such a prohibition is not analogous to the legislation concerning selling arrangements held in *Keck* and *Mithouard* to fall outside the scope of Article 30 of the Treaty.

37. According to that judgment, the application to products from other Member States of national provisions restricting or prohibiting, within the Member State of importation, certain selling arrangements is not such as to hinder trade between Member States so long, as first, those provisions apply to all relevant traders operating within the national territory and, secondly, they affect in the same manner, in law and in fact, the marketing of domestic products and of those from other Member States. The reason is that the application of such provisions is not such as to prevent access by the latter to the market of the Member State of importation or to impede such access more than it impedes access by domestic products.

38. A prohibition such as that at issue is imposed by the Member State in which the provider of the services is established and affects not only offers made by him to addressees who are established in that State or move there in order to receive services but also offers made to potential recipients in another Member State. It therefore *directly affects access to the market in services in the other Member States* [authors' italics] and is thus capable of hindering intra-Community trade in services.

The Court found that maintaining the good reputation of the financial sector was an interest which could legitimate a Member State imposing restrictions on the movement of services. It noted in this instance that cold calling to other Member States could only be regulated effectively by the Dutch authorities. It also noted that cold calling often caught people unawares in a position where they were unable to ascertain the risk inherent in the transaction. Since the commodities futures market was extremely risky, it was necessary for purchasers to be protected from aggressive selling techniques. The measure was therefore not 'inappropriate' to securing the integrity of the Dutch financial markets, and consequently did not contravene Article 59 [*49*] EC.

Commentators have noted that the case was unusual in that the Dutch law had extraterritorial effects in that it restricted traders providing the service not just to the Dutch market but also to any other market.[93] It is certainly true that the Court concentrated on the cross-border nature of the restriction and emphasised that it was a direct restriction on the flow of services between Member States. Yet the suggestion that non-discriminatory restrictions on export can fall within Article 59 [*49*] EC is tantamount to an abandonment of the principle of home State control. For implicit in the latter was the notion that the home State could regulate its own domestic products and services on condition that it did not discriminate against exports. There is more justification for such an abandonment in respect of services than of goods. It has already been pointed out that as a service is a form of transaction, it does not crystallise until the moment of commercialisation, which will often happen for the first time in the importing Member State. The concept of double regulatory burden is simply inappropriate in the case of many services.

The dilemmas posed by judicial encroachment upon the autonomy of other institutions which emerged in Article 30 [*28*] EC are likely to re-emerge with added force if courts are allowed to review non-discriminatory restrictions imposed by the State of establishment. In *Alpine Investments* the Dutch ban on cold calling was upheld. Many questions are therefore left unanswered. Will the Court apply the proportionality in the traditional manner by requiring that the measure be the less restrictive of trade necessary to secure its objectives, or will it apply in a softer manner as in *Schindler*? Equally intriguingly, the Court found the measure to be a direct restriction on access to other

---

93 Ross M. 'Article 59 and the marketing of financial services' (1995) 20 *ELRev* 507, 513; Hatzopoulos V. Note on *Schindler* (1995) 32 *CMLRev* 841, 854-855.

markets. This holds out the possibility that there may be other forms of restrictions which are only considered to restrict access indirectly, and as such may fall outside Article 59 [*49*] EC.

Further Reading

Art, J-Y. 'Legislative Lacunae, the Court of Justice and the Freedom to Provide Services' in O'Keefe, D. & Curtin, D. (eds.) *Constitutional Adjudication in European and National Law* (1992, Butterworth, London)
Bradley, C. '1992: The Case of Financial Services' (1991) 12 *Northwestern Journal of International Law and Business* 124
Charny, J. 'Competition among Jurisdictions in Formulating Corporate Law Rules: An American Perspective on the "Race to the Bottom" in the EC' (1991) 32 *Harvard International Law Journal* 423
Edward, D. 'Establishment and Services: An Analysis of the Insurance Cases' (1987) 12 *European Law Review* 231
Fernandez Martín, J-M. & O' Leary, S. 'Judicial Exceptions to the Free Provision of Services' (1995) 1 *European Law Journal* 308
Roth, W-H. 'The European Economic Community's Law on Services: Harmonisation' (1988) 25 *Common Market Law Review* 35
Van Empel, M. 'The Visible Hand in Invisible Trade' (1990/2) *Legal Issues of European Integration* 23

9. Free Movement of Labour

I. Introduction

Initially the right to free movement of persons within the common market was focused upon the free movement of labour. By 1968 a sophisticated notion of labour mobility was in place - based in part on the relative success of the Benelux model of free movement.[1] In EC law the right to move to work or seek work is contained in Article 48 [*39*] EC

Article 48(1) [*39(1)*]EC. Freedom of movement for workers shall be secured within the Community by the end of the transitional period at the latest.

II. The Concept of the Worker

Article 48[*39*] EC creates both vertical and horizontal direct effect.[2] In *Unger*[3] the Court ruled that the terms 'worker' and 'activity' as an

1 The immigration rights in relation to free movement of workers were supplemented with rights to protect the accumulation and transfer of social security rights between Member States through the use of Article 51 [*42*] EC and secondary legislation, most notably Regulation 1408/71/EEC. For an analysis of the problems relating to social security and the operation of the Internal Market see Laske, C. 'The Impact of the Single European Market on Social Protection for Migrant Workers' (1993) 30 *CMLRev* 515.

2 Case 167/73 *Commission v France* [1974] ECR 359; Case 36/74 *Walrave & Koch v AUCI* [1974] ECR 1405 [1975] 1 CMLR 320; Case 13/76 *Donà v Mantero* [1976] ECR 1333 [1976] 2 CMLR 578; Case C-415/93 *Union Royal Belge des Sociétés de Football Association ASBL v Bosman* [1995] ECR I-4921, [1996] 1 CMLR 603.

3 Case 75/63 *Hoekstra (née Unger) v Bestuur der Bedrijfsvereniging voor Detailhandel en Ambachten* [1964] ECR 177, [1964] CMLR 319.

employed person must have an EC law meaning. If that were not the case, the EC rules on freedom of movement for workers would be frustrated, as the meaning of those terms could be fixed and modified unilaterally and national laws would then be able to exclude certain categories of persons from the benefit of the free movement provisions. In subsequent cases the Court has provided a more concrete definition of the concept of a 'worker' in EC law. An underlying theme of the case law in this area - and in relation to labour law issues[4] is that, by virtue of Article 2[*2*] EC, the EC Treaty covers 'economic activities' 'throughout the Community' and that the Community, in order to promote a harmonious (and henceforth, balanced) development of those activities has as its task to establish a Single Market.[5]

Case 53/81 Levin v Staatssecretaris van Justitie [1982] ECR 1035, (1982) 2 CMLR 454

Levin, a British national, applied for a permit to reside in the Netherlands. The permit was refused on the ground that she was not engaged in a gainful occupation in the Netherlands and therefore could not be described as a 'favoured EEC citizen' within the meaning of the Dutch legislation. She appealed, claiming that she had, in the meantime, commenced activity as an employed person in the Netherlands as a part-time chambermaid and that, in any event, she and her husband had property and income more than sufficient to support themselves, even without undertaking the employment.

16. It follows that the concepts of 'worker' and 'activity as an employed person' must be interpreted as meaning that the rules relating to freedom of movement for workers also concern persons who pursue or wish to pursue minimum guaranteed remuneration in the sector under consideration. In this regard no distinction may be made between those who wish to make do with their income from such an activity and those who supplement that from the employment of a member of their family who accompanies them.

---

4 See Nielsen, R. and Szyszczak, E. *The Social Dimension of the European Union* (1997, 3rd Edition, Handelshojskolens Forlag, Copenhagen).

5 See, for example, Case 13/76 *Donà v Maria Matero* [1976] ECR 1333 where the Court ruled that '... the pursuit of an activity as an employed person or the provision of services for remuneration must be regarded as an economic activity within the meaning of Article 2 of the Treaty'.

A person need not be economically self-sufficient to be a worker.

Case 139/85 Kempf v Staatssecretaris van Justitie [1986] ECR 1741, [1987] 1 CMLR 764

Kempf, a German national, worked in the Netherlands as a part-time music teacher, giving 12 lessons a week. He received social assistance out of public funds to supplement this income. He applied for a residence permit but this was refused on the ground, *inter alia*, that he was not a favoured EC citizen according to Nethcrlands law because he had recourse to public funds in the Netherlands and was manifestly unable to meet his needs out of the income from his employment. The Raad van Staat asked whether the fact that a national claims financial assistance payable out of the public funds to supplement his income excluded him from the benefits of Article 48 [*39*] EC.

9. As regards, first, the criterion of effective and genuine work as opposed to marginal and ancillary activities not covered by the relevant Community rules, the Netherlands government expressed doubts [as] to whether the work of a teacher who gives 12 lessons a week may be regarded as constituting in itself effective and genuine work within the terms of the judgment in *Levin.*

.....

12. There is, however, no need to consider that question since the Raad van Staat, in the grounds of the judgment making the reference, expressly found that Mr Kempf's work was not on such a small scale as to be purely a marginal and ancillary activity. According to the division of jurisdiction between national courts and the Court of Justice in connection with references for preliminary ruling, it is for the national courts to establish and evaluate the facts of the case. The question submitted for a preliminary ruling must therefore be examined in the light of the assessment made by the Raad van Staat.

13. The Court has consistently held that freedom of movement for workers forms one of the foundations of the Community. The provisions laying down that fundamental freedom and, more particularly, the terms 'worker' and 'activity as an employed person' defining the sphere of application of those freedoms must be given a broad interpretation in that regard, movement for workers must be interpreted strictly.

14. It follows that the rules on this topic must be interpreted as meaning that a person in effective and genuine part-time employment cannot be excluded from their sphere of application merely because the remuneration he derives from it is below the level of the minimum means of subsistence and he seeks to supplement it by other lawful means of subsistence. In that regard it is irrelevant whether those supplement means of subsistence are derived from property or from the employment of a member of his family, as was the case of *Levin*, or whether, as in this instance, they are obtained from financial assistance drawn from the public funds of the Member State in which he resides, provided that the effective and genuine nature of this work is established.

Case 66/85 Lawrie-Blum v Land Baden-Württemberg [1986] ECR 2121, [1987] 3 CMLR 389

The question arose as to whether a trainee teacher was a 'worker' within the meaning of Article 48[*39*] EC.

17. [The concept of 'worker'] must be definition in accordance with objective criteria which distinguish the employment relationship by reference to the rights and duties of the persons concerned. The essential feature of an employment relationship, however, is that for a certain period of time a person performs services for and under the direction of another person in return for which he received remuneration.

18. In the present case, it is clear that during the entire period of preparatory service the trainee teacher is under the direction and supervision of the school to which he is assigned. It is the school that determines the services to be performed by him and his working hours and it is the school's instructions that he must carry out and its rules that he must observe. During a substantial part of the preparatory service he is required to give lessons to the school's pupils and thus provides a service of some economic value to the school. The amounts which he receives may be regarded as remuneration for the services provided and for the duties involved in completing the period of preparatory service. Consequently, the three criteria for the existence of an employment relationship are fulfilled in this case.

.....

21. The fact that trainee teachers give lessons for only a few hours a week and are paid remuneration below the starting salary of a qualified teacher does not prevent them from being regarded as workers. In [*Levin*], the Court held that the expressions 'worker' and 'activity as an employed person' must be understood as including persons who, because they are not employed full-time, received pay lower than that for full-time employment, provided that the activities performed are effective and genuine. The latter requirement is not called into question in this case.

Case 344/87 Bettray v Staatssecretaris van Justitie [1989] ECR 1621, [1991] 1 CMLR 459

Bettray, a German national, entered the Netherlands and applied for a residence permit. Because of his drug addiction, Bettray was employed under the system set up by the Social Employment Law, which was intended to provide work for the purpose of maintaining, restoring or improving the capacity for work of persons who, for an indefinite period, were unable, because of circumstances related to their situation, to work under normal conditions. Local authorities were set up, with financial support from the State, undertakings or work associations, the sole purpose of which was to provide the persons involved with an opportunity to engage in paid work. Bettray submitted an application for a residence permit giving as the reason for his stay 'work as an employed person'.

17. However, work under the Social Employment Law cannot be regarded as an effective and genuine economic activity if it constitutes merely a means of rehabilitation or reintegration for the persons concerned and the purpose of the paid employment, which is adapted to the physical and mental possibilities of each person, is to enable those persons sooner or later to recover their capacity to take up ordinary employment or to lead as normal as possible a life.

18. It also appears from the order for reference that persons employed under the Social Employment Law are not selected on the basis of their capacity to perform a certain activity; on the contrary, it is the activities which are chosen in the light of the capabilities of the persons who are going to perform them in order to maintain, re-establish or develop their capacity for work. Finally, the activities involved are pursued in the framework of undertakings or work associations created solely for that purpose by local authorities. The Court seems to be looking at the reason or purpose for undertaking work in adopting its restrictive approach. But arguably retraining and reintegrating workers into the workforce, irrespective of their nationality, is part of the needs of the smooth functioning of an internal market.

The jurisprudence of the Court shows that in order for an activity to be described as *economic* it must be performed for remuneration. From the Court's ruling in *Lawrie-Blum* decisive importance does not attach to the *sector* in which the activity is performed or even the *legal provisions* under which it takes place. From the ruling in *Steymann*[6] the element of remuneration, in the sense of economic consideration, does not presuppose the existence of a profit-making motive or the acceptance of commercial risks. Here, unwaged work, carried out by a member of a religious community was regarded as an *economic activity* within the meaning of the EC Treaty.

---

6 Case 196/87 *Steymann v Staatssecretaris van Justitie* [1988] ECR 6159.

For the last few decades Europe has seen high levels of unemployment. As a market correcting device one would expect the principle of free movement to allow individuals to travel within the EU to seek work and optimise their employment opportunities. The Member States have been reluctant to encourage this where the burden of unemployment will fall upon their social security budgets. This fact is seen in the qualification found in all the rights of residence directives that the person claiming the right of residence must have sickness insurance and sufficient resources to avoid becoming a burden on the social assistance system of the host State. Article 48 [*39*] EC protects the right of a migrant to enter a Member State and look for work. The United Kingdom government sought to argue that this right was conditional on the person finding work within a certain period of time. It was argued that this period should be three months since that was the period provided for in relation to receipt of social security in the host State and the minutes of a Council meeting when Directive 68/360/EEC,[7] on the abolition of restrictions on movement and residence for workers of Member States and their families, was adopted also recorded that this was the period intended by the Council. The Court, however, held that this declaration was of no legal significance, leaving the exercise of the right flexible.[8] However the Court has ruled that if a potential migrant worker has not found work after the three month period and cannot provide evidence that he/she is continuing to seek employment and that he/she has genuine chances of being engaged, he/she can be required to leave the territory of the host Member State.

In *Tsiotras*[9] the Court ruled that the length of the period of unemployment would justify a decision by a Member State to deport. Here the Court held that a Greek national has no right of residence in the territory of another Member State when, at the time of Greece's adhesion to the Community, the individual concerned was unemployed in that Member State after having been employed there for several years, and continued to be unemployed after such adhesion, it being objectively

---

7 OJ Spec Ed 1968 (II) 485.

8 Case C-292/89 *Antonissen v Secretary of State For Home Affairs* [1991] ECR I-745, [1991] 2 CMLR 373.

9 Case C-171/91 *Tsiotras v Landeshauptstadt Stuttgart* [1993] ECR I-2925.

impossible for him to find work. The question of how Article 8a [*18*] EC affects these rulings has to be addressed directly by the Court.

III. Reverse Discrimination

The Court of Justice has refused to extend the substantive rights relating to the free movement of workers and the principle of non-discrimination to situations which are considered to be purely internal to a Member State. In other words, a person must trigger the free movement provisions by crossing an immigration frontier to another Member State before he or she can rely upon EC law.[10]

Case 175/78 Saunders [1979] ECR 1129, [1979] 2 CMLR 216

Saunders, a British national was found guilty to a charge of theft. She was bound over in return for an undertaking to return to Northern Ireland and not to return to England or Wales for three years. She broke the undertaking and the question arose as to whether the restriction on internal free movement within a Member State was compatible with EC law.

10. Although the rights conferred upon workers by Article 48 may lead the Member States to amend their legislation, where necessary, even with respect to their own nationals, this provision does not however aim to restrict the power of the Member States to lay down restrictions, within their own territory, on the freedom of movement of all persons subject to their jurisdiction in implementation of domestic criminal law.

11. The provisions of the Treaty on freedom of movement for workers cannot therefore be applied to situations which are wholly internal to a Member State, in other words, where there is no factor connecting them to any of the situations envisaged by Community law.

12. The application by an authority or court of a Member State to a worker who is a national of that same state of measures which deprive or restrict the freedom of movement of that worker within the territory of that state as a penal measure provided for by national law by reason of acts committed within the territory of that state is a wholly

---

[10] See Case C-370/90 *R v IAT Surinder Singh ex parte Secretary of State for The Home Department* [1992] ECR I-4265, [1992] 3 CMLR 358.

domestic situation which falls outside the scope of the rules contained in the Treaty on freedom of movement for workers.

Case 180/83 Moser v Land Baden-Württemberg [1984] ECR 2539, [1984] 3 CMLR 720

Moser, a German national, was not allowed to undertake the post-graduate training necessary to secure entry to the teaching profession. The regional authorities based their refusal on the ground that there was insufficient certainty as to Moser's loyalty to the German Constitution. Moser was a member of the German Communist Party and had, for a long time and quite openly, been active in the party's affairs.

14. [It] must be pointed out that, as the Court held in [*Saunders*], [Article 48] aims, in implementation of the general principle laid down in Article 7, to abolish in the legislation of the Member States provisions regarding employment, remuneration and other conditions of work and employment by virtue of which a worker who is a national of another Member State is subject to more severe treatment or is placed in an unfavourable situation in law or in fact as compared with the situation of a national in the same circumstances.

15. It follows that the provisions of the Treaty concerning the free movement of workers and particularly Article 48 cannot be applied to situations [where] there is no factor connecting them to any of the situations envisaged by Community Law.

16. [The case concerns] a German national who has always lived and maintained his residence in the Federal Republic of Germany and who contests the refusal by the German authorities to allow him access, under the legislation of that State, to a particular kind of vocational training.

17. In order to establish a connection with the Community provisions, Mr Moser claimed in the observations which he submitted to the court that the application to him of the German legislation in question, by making it impossible for him to complete his training as a teacher, entails the result that he is precluded from applying for teaching posts in schools in the other Member States.

18. That argument cannot be upheld. A purely hypothetical prospect of employment in another Member State does not establish a sufficient connection with Community law to justify the application of Article 48 of the Treaty.

19. It follows that there is no factor connecting a personal situation of the kind referred to by the national court with the provisions of Community law on the free movement of workers.

IV. Beyond Discrimination: Towards A Market Integration Approach

The Court has moved towards applying a market integration analysis to Article 48 [*39*] EC by ruling that non-discriminatory national measures which hinder free movement of workers or freedom of establishment must be struck down unless they aim to protect a mandatory requirement, justified in the public interest, which cannot be accomplished by less restrictive measures, and take account of measures to protect such rights in the migrant's home State.[11]

Case C-415/93 Union Royal Belge des Sociétés de Football Association ASBL v Bosman [1995] ECR I-4921, [1996] 1 CMLR 645

UEFA/FIFA regulations governed the transfer of football players. A footballer was not free to work his contract out and then go on to the market and conclude a new contract with a new football club without the buying club paying a transfer fee. The UEFA/FIFA rules also restricted the number of foreign players who could play in a league football team in pan-European competitions. Bosman, a Belgian challenged these rules as being contrary to Article 48 [*39*] EC.[12] The Court ruled that the transfer fee requirement affected the planning of football clubs and restricted the employment opportunities of footballers.

94. ... the provisions of the Treaty relating to freedom of movement for persons are intended to facilitate the pursuit by Community citizens of occupational activities of all kinds throughout the Community, and preclude measures which might place Community citizens at a disadvantage when they wish to pursue an economic activity in the territory of another Member State (see Case 143/87 *Stanton v INASTI* [1988] ECR 3877 and Case C-370/90 *R v Immigration Appeal Tribunal ex parte Surinder Singh* [1992] ECR I-4265)

.....

96. Provisions which preclude or deter a national of a Member State from leaving his country of origin in order to exercise his right to freedom of movement therefore

---

11 See Weatherill, S. (1996) 33 *CMLRev* 991.

12 See also Case C-117/91 *Bosman v Commission* [1991] ECR I-4837.

constitute an obstacle to that freedom even if they apply without regard to the nationality of the workers concerned..

97. The Court has also stated in Case 81/87 *R v HM Treasury and Commissioners of Inland Revenue ex parte Daily Mail and General Trust plc [1988] ECR 5483* that even though the Treaty provisions relating to freedom of establishment are directed mainly to ensuring that foreign nationals and companies are treated in the host Member State in the same way as nationals of that State, they also prohibit the Member State of origin from hindering the establishment in another Member State of one of its nationals or of a company incorporated under its legislation which comes within the definition contained in Article 58. The rights guaranteed by Article 52 *et seq.* of the Treaty would be rendered meaningless if the Member State of origin could prohibit undertakings from leaving in order to establish themselves in another Member State. The same considerations apply, in relation to Article 48 of the Treaty, with regard to rules which impede the freedom of movement of nationals of one Member State wishing to engage in gainful employment in another Member State.

98. It is true that the transfer rules in issue in the main proceedings apply also to transfers of players between clubs belonging to different national associations within the same Member State and that similar rules govern transfers between clubs belonging to the same national association...

100. Since they provide that a professional footballer may not pursue his activity with a new club established in another Member State unless it has paid his former club a transfer fee agreed upon between the two clubs or determined in accordance with the regulations of the sporting associations, the said rules constitute an obstacle to freedom of movement for workers.

.....

104. Consequently the transfer rules constitute an obstacle to freedom of movement for workers prohibited in principle by Article 48 of the Treaty. It could only be otherwise if those rules pursued a legitimate aim compatible with the Treaty and were justified by pressing reasons of public interest. But even if that were so, application of those rules would still have to be such as to ensure achievement of the aim in question and not go beyond what is necessary for that purpose.

The *Bosman* ruling is part of a trend - described as a 'global approach' by Daniele[13] - of applying the same reasoning across the whole

---

[13] Daniele, L. 'Non-Discriminatory Restrictions to the Free Movement of Persons' (1997) 22 *ELRev* 191.

area of free movement of persons.[14] Caution is expressed by Daniele in this approach. A migrant worker can often not be equated with a service provider in terms of attachment to a Member State's labour market and issues on cultural/social integration since a service provider is viewed with less permanence in the logic of EC law and there are strong reasons why one Member State should take overall responsibility for the regulation of the service provider. Equally making comparisons with the case law on the free movement of goods may also provide insights into the limitations of the market integration approach. Daniele, for example, makes the point that the Court has been reluctant to apply a market integration approach to Article 34 [*29*] EC. In relation to workers, the Court has gone further in *Bosman* than it was prepared to go in relation to the free movement of goods. Equally, the underlying approach of Bosman - which is mirrored in the approach of the Court towards Article 30 [*28*] EC is, perhaps, an undue reliance upon the mandatory requirements doctrine. This can lead to uncertainty and to a case by case approach. The following extract explores the relationship between developments in the areas of free movement of goods and persons.

Johnson, E. & O'Keeffe, D. 'From Discrimination To Obstacles To Free Movement: Recent Developments Concerning the Free Movement of Workers 1989-1994' (1994) 31 *Common Market Law Review* 1313, 1329-130

Following the Court's judgment in *Keck*, the first question which arises is whether there are any conceivable consequences of *Keck* for the free movement of workers. The second, is whether there is an analogy possible between product regulations and the status of workers. It is too early to tell whether the *Keck* case law will carry over to this area. It should not be forgotten that *Keck* is a direct response to criticism of an over-expansive interpretation of Article 30, while no such criticism appears at present as regards the Court's Article 48 case law.

However, what might an application of *Keck* to Article 48 entail? It might mean that in certain areas, the Court would be willing to leave to Member States competence for measures affecting the regulation of national life, which were not specifically aimed against migrant workers, were indistinctly applicable, and did not discriminate against migrants in law or fact. If so, many cases of reverse discrimination could disappear...

---

14 See Case C-19/92 *Kraus* [1993] ECR I-1663; Case C-275/92 *Schindler* [1994] ECR I-1039.

However it appears difficult to imagine that the Court would abandon its traditional stewardship of migrants' rights, even partially. The citizenship provisions of the EC Treaty confirm the Court's case law giving a constitutional character to the free movement of persons, which certainly distinguishes them from goods. On balance, and in a purely speculative vein, we have difficulty in seeing the Court renouncing its centralist role in relation to Article 48.

V. Social Advantages

Article 48 [39] EC bans discrimination against the migrant worker.

Article 48(2) [*39(2)*] **EC.** Such freedom of movement shall entail the abolition of any discrimination based on nationality between workers of the Member States as regards employment, remuneration and other conditions of work and employment.

The protection against discrimination was extended by Regulation 1612/68/EEC.[15] An EC worker should not suffer any discrimination in the labour market. Article 3 of the Regulation outlaws measures which discriminate against EC nationals in the taking up of employment. Article 4 prohibits Member States from reserving quotas for their own nationals and prohibits the limiting of applications for and offers of employment. Article 5 requires foreign nationals to be granted the same assistance from employment offices as a State's own nationals. Article 6 states the engagement of another Member State national shall not depend on any criteria which are discriminatory on grounds of nationality. By virtue of Articles 8 and 9 EC migrant workers are also to be given the same trade union and housing rights as a State's own nationals. The most wide ranging protection, however, is contained in Article 7.[16]

---

15 OJ Spec Ed. 1968 (II) 475.

16 See O'Keeffe, D. 'Equal Rights For Migrants: the Concept of Social Advantages in Article 7(2), Regulation 1612/68' (1985) 5 *YBEL* 93; Peers, S. '"Social Advantages" and Discrimination in Employment: Case Law Confirmed and Clarified' (1997) 22 *ELRev* 157.

Article 7(1). A worker who is a national of a Member State may not, in the territory of another Member State, be treated differently from national workers by reason of his nationality in respect of any conditions of employment and work, in particular as regards remuneration, dismissal, and should he become unemployed, reinstatement or re-employment.

2. He shall enjoy the same social and tax advantages as national workers.
3. He shall also, by virtue of the same right and under the same conditions as national workers, have access to training in vocational schools and retraining centres.

The Court has given the term 'social advantage' a wide meaning, covering advantages such as subsidised transport granted to workers and their families outside of the contract of employment[17] and advantages such as childbirth loans granted on a discretionary basis.[18] In many respects these provisions have developed a notion of 'economic citizenship' rights way beyond the notion of general citizenship rights discussed in Chapter Two. The Court defined 'social advantages' in *Ministère Public v Even*[19] as benefits:

> ... which, whether or not linked to a contract of employment, are generally granted to national workers primarily because of their objective status as workers or by virtue of the mere fact of their residence in the national territory and the extension of which to workers who are not nationals of other Member States therefore seems suitable to facilitate their mobility within the Community.

In *de Vos*[20] the Court refused to bring employer contributions to social insurance schemes for employees fulfilling military service requirements within the scope of a 'social advantage'. Here the employer was under a duty to pay contributions for a German employee fulfilling

---

17 Case 32/75 *Fiorini v SNCF* [1975] ECR 1085, [1976] 1 CMLR 573.

18 Case 65/81 *Reina v Landeskreditbank Baden-Wurttemburg* [1982] ECR 33; Case C-237/94 *O'Flynn v Adjudication Officer* [1996] ECR I-2617.

19 Case 207/78 *Ministère Public v Even* [1979] ECR 2019.

20 Case C-315/94 *De Vos v Stadt Bielefeld* [1996] ECR I-1417.

military service in Germany but not where the military service was carried out by a Member State national in another Member State. The Court ruled that the contributions were not made by virtue of either a contractual or statutory obligation but were regarded as an advantage granted by the State as partial compensation for the obligation to fulfil military service. Secondly, the advantage was essentially linked to the performance of military service which was not accorded to national workers because of their objective status as workers or by virtue of their residence on the national territory and thus did not have the essential characteristics of social advantages as characterised by the Court in *Even*.

More recently the Commission brought an Article 169 [*226*] EC action against Belgium[21] concerning first, Belgium's policy of granting 'tideover' allowances between education and employment only to persons who had completed their secondary education in Belgium. It argued that this discriminated indirectly against the children of migrant workers from other Member States and was contrary to Article 7(2) of Regulation 1612/68. Secondly the Commission argued that the Belgian system for encouraging the hiring of the young unemployed was in breach of Article 3(1) of the Regulation, since the only unemployed who qualified for this programme were those in receipt of the 'tideover' allowance. The latter provision prohibits discrimination against foreign nationals in the offering of employment. On the first complaint the Court found that the conditions attached to the 'tideover' allowance were a form of indirect discrimination, akin to a condition of prior residence which could be more easily fulfilled by Belgian nationals. On the second complaint, the Court found that the measures were a form of unemployment insurance and not access to employment measures. It was therefore possible to deny these measures to young unemployed nationals of another Member State since such persons must be classified as 'workers' before they could participate in the Community system for co-ordinating unemployment benefits.

---

21 Case C-278/94 *Commission v Belgium* [1996] ECR I-4307.

While the Court has also refused to extend the benefits of Article 7(2) to the child of a migrant worker who is a job-seeker[22] it has allowed a migrant worker who is involuntarily unemployed and legitimately resident in the host State to undertake vocational training relying upon the principle of non-discrimination contained in Article 7(2). However, where a migrant worker voluntarily gives up work to undertake further vocational training there must be a link between the previous employment and the studies in order for the non-discrimination principle of Article 7(2) to apply.[23] In subsequent cases, however, the Court has granted a the status of 'worker' to persons engaged on short-term or flexible basis, leaving it for the national court to judge whether the work is effective and genuine.[24] By granting such a wide definition to Article 7(2) the Court has, in effect, facilitated the development of a set of social citizenship rights for migrant workers and their families.

VI. Immigration Rights of Family Members

In terms of migration policy a novel feature of the EC regime is to guarantee the rights of family members to join the migrant worker in the host State. The Community - and the Court - declined from an early

---

22 Case 316/85 *Centre Public de l'Aide Sociale de Courcelles v Lebon* [1987] ECR 2811.

23 Case 39/86 *Lair v University of Hannover* [1988] ECR 3161.

24 See Case C-357/89 *Raulin v Netherlands Ministry of Education and Science* [1992] ECR I-1027.

stage to develop a notion of 'guestworkers' for EC migrants.[25] The rights are set out in Regulation 1612/68.

Article 10 (1). The following shall, irrespective of their nationality, have the right to install themselves with a worker who is a national of one Member State and who is employed in the territory of another Member State:
(a) his spouse and their descendants who are under the age of 21 years or are dependants;
(b) dependant relatives in the ascending line of the worker and his spouse.

2. Member States shall facilitate the admission of any member of the family not coming within the provisions of paragraph 1 if dependent on the worker referred to above or living under his roof in the country whence he comes.
3. For the purposes of paragraphs 1 and 2, the worker must have available for his family housing considered as normal for national workers in the region where he is employed; this provision, however must not give rise to discrimination between national workers and workers from the other Member States.

In *Commission v Germany*[26] the Court ruled that the requirement of adequate housing outlined in Article 10(3) only applied to the first entry of the migrant's family and could not be used as an excuse later to deny the renewal of resident permits.

Article 11 of Regulation 1612/68/EEC grants the spouse and the children mentioned in Article 10 the right to take up an activity as an employed person in a Member State. Article 12 provides for the right to equal access for the children of a resident worker to the state's educational courses. The Court has used Article 7(2) of Regulation

---

25 The negation of EC migrants - and their families - as 'guest workers' is seen also in the enactment of Regulation 1251/70/EEC, OJ Spec Ed. 1970, L 142/44, which allows the migrant worker and her family to remain in the host State after her economic activity has ceased. Whilst in retirement the principle of equal treatment continues - even to members of the family after the migrant worker has died: Case 32/75 *Fiorini* [1975] ECR 1085, [1976] 1 CMLR 573. The Court has confirmed the right to reside in the host State after pursuing an economic activity Case C-334/94 *Commission* v *France* [1996] ECR I-1307; C-151/96 *Commission v Ireland*, Judgment of 12 June 1997; Case C-62/96 *Commission v Greece,* Judgment of 27 November 1997.

26 Case 249/86 *Commission v Germany* [1989] ECR 1263, [1990] 3 CMLR 540.

1612/68/EEC to develop social rights for the migrant worker's family.[27] But the Court has not been persuaded to expand the categories of family members in Article 10 of Regulation 1612/68/EEC who may take advantage of such rights.[28] The Commission has proposed an increase in the class of family members with rights to join a worker as well as increasing the rights that such family members should enjoy.[29] The Court has applied the principle of reverse discrimination to the rights of family members. In *Uecker*[30] a Norwegian national and a Russian national who were married to German nationals living and working in Germany unsuccessfully challenged discrimination in their terms and conditions of employment as being contrary to Article 48(2) [*39(2)*] EC and Articles 7(1) and 11 of Regulation 1612/68. The Court ruled that the cross-frontier element triggering Community law into play was not present in this situation.

VII. Exceptions to the Right to Free Movement

i. Public Service

It is estimated that some 25 million EU nationals work in the public service of employment. In the EC Treaty the Member States are allowed to exclude employment in the public service from the free movement provisions. For some years the Commission has been conducting a systematic campaign to open up four priority areas of the public service to workers from other EU states: State education, civilian research,

---

27 *Cf.* The restricted ruling of Case 76/72 *Michel S v Fonds National* [1973] ECR 457, with Case 32/75 *Fiorini v SNCF* [1975] ECR 1085, [1978] 1 CMLR 573; Case 63/76 *Inziirillo v CAFAL* [1976] ECR 2057, [1978] 3 CMLR 596.

28 Case 316/85 *Centre public d'aide sociale de Courcelles v Lebon* [1987] ECR 2811 [1989] 1 CMLR 337.

29 See COM (88) 815; COM (90) 108; COM (95) 134; COM (95) 348.

30 Joined Cases C-64 & C-65/96 *Land Nordrhein-Westfalen v Uecker & Jacquet*, [1997] ECR I-3171.

operational public health services and public bodies responsible for administering commercial services.[31]

Article 48 (4) [*39(4)*] EC. The provisions of this Article shall not apply to employment in the public service.

Sotgiu v Deutsche Bundespost[32] emphasised that the definition of the public service must be an EC law concept but it was some time before a clear understanding of the concept emerged in EC law.

Case 149/79 Commission v Belgium [1982] ECR 1845, [1982] 3 CMLR 539

Belgian nationality was a condition of entry for posts with Belgian local authorities and public undertakings regardless of the nature of the duties to be performed. Such posts involved those of unskilled railway workers, hospital nurses and night-watchmen. Belgium argued that when the EEC Treaty was drafted there was no EC concept of the objectives and scope of public authorities and that the Member States wished the conditions of entry to public office to remain within their control.

10. That provision [Article 48(4)] removes from the ambit of Article 48(1) to (3) a series of posts which involve direct or indirect participation in the exercise of powers conferred by public law and duties designed to safeguard the general interests of the State or of other public authorities. Such posts in fact presume on the part of those occupying them the existence of a special relationship of allegiance to the State and reciprocity of rights and duties which form the foundation of the bond of nationality.

11. The scope of the derogation made by Article 48(4) to the principles of freedom of movement and equality of treatment laid down in the first three paragraphs of the article should therefore be determined on the basis of the aim pursued by that Article. However, determining the sphere of application of Article 48(4) raises special difficulties since in the various Member States authorities acting under powers conferred by public law have assumed responsibilities of an economic and social nature or are involved in activities which are not identifiable with the functions which are typical of the public service yet which by their nature still come under the sphere of application of the Treaty. In these circumstances the effect of extending the exception contained in Article 48(4) to posts which, whilst coming under the States or other organizations governed by public law, still

---

31 OJ 1988 C 72/2.

32 Case 152/73 *Sotgiu v Deutsche Bundespost* [1974] ECR 153.

do not involve any association with tasks belonging to the public service properly so called, would be to remove a considerable number of posts from the ambit of the principles set out in the Treaty and to create inequalities between Member States according to the different ways in which the State and certain sectors of economic life are organised.

The EC law test to be applied is that there must be an exercise of power conferred by public law involving the safeguarding of the general interests of the State.[33] The Court ruled that it did not have sufficient information to identify which of the posts fell outside of Article 48(4) [*39(4)*] EC. It invited the Commission and Belgium to resolve the dispute in the light of its ruling. This proved impossible and the case was referred back to the Court which ruled that with the exception of a limited number of posts none of the disputed posts satisfied its criteria for the application of Article 48(4) [*39(4)*] EC.[34] The Belgian government, supported by the intervening governments of France, Germany and the United Kingdom argued that the wording of Article 48(4) [*39(4)*] EC implied an 'institutional concept'. These views were soundly criticised by Advocate General Mancini in subsequent infringement action against France involving nationality requirements for nursing posts in public hospitals.

Case 307/84 Commission v France [1986] ECR 1725, [1987] 3 CMLR 555

Advocate General Mancini

The decisions to which I have referred gave rise to severe criticism from academic lawyers and, what is more important, they have not been 'taken in' by numerous governments. Such resistance is not surprising if it is borne in mind how deep-rooted is the conviction that the public service is an area in which the State should exercise full sovereignty and how wide-spread is the tendency, in times of high unemployment, to see

---

33 Compare O'Keeffe, D. 'Judicial Interpretation of the Public Service Exception to the Free Movement of Workers' in Curtin, D. & O'Keeffe, D. (eds.) *Constitutional Adjudication in European Community and National Law* (1992, Butterworths, Ireland) with Handoll, J. 'Article 48(4) EEC and Non-National Access to Public Employment' (1988) 13 *ELRev* 223. See also Case 66/85 *Lawrie-Blum v Land Baden Württemberg* [1986] ECR 2121, [1987] 3 CMLR 389.

34 Case 149/79 *Commission v Belgium (No.2)* [1982] ECR 1845.

the public service as a convenient reservoir of posts. Such resistance is a matter for concern and should be tackled head-on before cases similar to the present one multiply.

.....

In short, in order to be made inaccessible to nationals of another State, it is not sufficient for the duties inherent in the post at issue to be directed specifically towards public objectives which influence the conduct and action of private individuals. Those who occupy the post must don full battle dress: in non-metaphorical terms, the duties must involve acts of will which affect private individuals by requiring their obedience or, in the event of disobedience, by compelling them to comply. To make a list ... is practically impossible; but certainly the first examples which come to mind are posts relating to policing, defence of the State, the administration of justice and assessments to tax.

... It is a fact that an extremist disciple of Hegel might truly think that access to posts like the ones at issue here should be denied to foreigners. But anyone who does not regard the State as 'the march of God in the world' must of necessity take the contrary view.

Despite the clarification from the Court of Justice discrimination in many *public sector* positions still continues. The Commission drew up an Action Plan for the elimination of restrictions on the grounds of nationality in access to posts in the public sector of employment,[35] although in reality this does nothing more than codify the Court's case law. O'Keeffe[36] argues that such a view is based upon a very traditional notion of loyalty to the State, finding its parallel in the denial to foreigners of political rights. It is now quite difficult to square such notions with the ideas of Citizenship of the Union contained in Article 8 [*17*] EC.

---

35 OJ C 1988 72/2. A series of infringement actions have followed see: Case C-473/93 *Commission v Luxembourg* [1996] ECR I-3207; Case C-173/94 *Commission v Belgium* [1996] ECR I-3265; Case C-290/94 *Commission v Greece* [1996] ECR I-3285.

36 O'Keeffe, D. 'Judicial Interpretation of the Public Service Exception to the Free Movement of Workers' in Curtin, D. & O'Keeffe, D. (eds.) *Constitutional Adjudication in European Community and National Law* (1992, Butterworths, Ireland).

ii. Other Limitations

Member States may still control entry to their territories. Until the area of freedom, security and justice enters into force, Member States still, as a matter of EC law, have the right to require that EC workers and their families produce a valid identity card or passport before allowing entry to their territory.[37] As proof of the right of residence Member States must issue a residence permit to all workers and family members entitled to reside with them.[38] This residence permit must be valid throughout the territory of the Member State which issued it and should, in principle, be valid for at least 5 years from the date of issue and be automatically renewable.[39] The one exception to this is where a worker is employed for more than three months but less than a year. In such circumstances the length of the permit can be limited to the length of employment.[40] This residence permit only has a declaratory effect, however.

Case 48/75 Royer [1976] ECR 497, [1976] 2 CMLR 619

Royer, a French national, had been convicted and sentenced to imprisonment for procuring in France. Royer's wife, also a French national, ran a cafe and dance hall in Belgium. Royer had joined her but failed to comply with the administrative formalities of entry on the Belgian population register. He was apprehended by the police and committed to prison. Before his release Royer was served with a ministerial decree of expulsion on the ground, *inter alia*, that he had no permit to establish himself in Belgium.

Articles 5-9 of Council Directive 64/221/EEC provide a set of procedural rights which may be invoked.

---

37 Directive 68/360/EEC, OJ Special Edition, 1968 (II) 485, Article 3(1). This has been foregone by States party to the Schengen Convention. See p. 105.

38 Ibid., Article 4(2). This duty does not extend to frontier workers, seasonal workers or those pursuing work which is not expected to last for more than three months, Ibid., Article 8.

39 Ibid., Article 6(1).

40 Ibid., Article 6(3).

Article 48 provides that freedom of movement of workers shall be secured within the Community. Paragraph (3) of that Article provides that it shall entail the right to enter the territory of Member States, to move freely there for the purpose of employment and to remain there after the end of this employment ...

Article 1 of Regulation No 1612/68 provides that any national of a Member State shall, irrespective of his place of residence, have 'the right to take up activity as an employed person and to pursue such activity within the territory of another Member State' and Article 10 of the same regulation extends the 'right to install themselves' to the members of the family of such a national.

Article 4 of Directive No 68/360 provides that 'Member States shall grant the right of residence in their territory' to the persons referred to and further states that as 'proof' of this right an individual residence permit shall be issued ...

These provisions show that the legislative authorities of the Community were aware that, while not creating new rights in favour of persons protected by Community law, the regulation and directives concerned determined the scope of detailed rules for the exercise of rights conferred directly by the Treaty.

It is therefore evident that the exception concerning the safeguard of public policy, public security and public health contained in Articles 48(3) and 56(1) of the Treaty must be regarded not as a condition precedent to the acquisition of the right of entry and residence but as providing the possibility, in the individual cases where there is sufficient justification, of imposing restrictions on the exercise of a right derived directly from the Treaty ...

It must therefore be concluded that this right is acquired independently of the issue of a residence permit by the competent authority of a Member State.

The grant of this permit is therefore to be regarded not as a measure giving rise to rights but as a measure by a Member State serving to prove the individual position of a national of another Member State with regard to provisions of Community law ...

The logical consequence of the foregoing is that the mere failure by a national of a Member State to complete the legal formalities concerning access, movement and residence of aliens does not justify a decision ordering expulsion.

Member States may restrict free movement on grounds of public policy, public security and public health. In the case of workers this is set out in Article 48(3) [39(3)] EC. Similar principles apply to the self-employed; providers and recipients of services and to the movement of persons more generally.[41]

---

[41] See Articles 56 [*46*] & 66 [*55*] EC; Directive 90/364/EEC, OJ 1990 L 180/26, Article 2(2).

Article 48(3) [39(3)] EC. [Freedom of movement for workers] shall entail the right, subject to limitations justified on grounds of public policy, public security or public health;

(a) to accept offers of employment actually made;

(b) to move freely within the territory of Member States for this purpose;

(c) to stay in a Member State for the purpose of employment in accordance with the provisions governing the employment of nationals of that state laid down by law, regulation or administrative action;

(d) to remain in the territory of a Member State after having been employed in that state, subject to conditions which shall be embodied in implementing regulations to be drawn up by the Commission.

The exceptions have been fleshed out in Directive 64/221/EEC.[42] The Directive applies only to movement of natural persons and to movement of companies of the employed; the self-employed and to *recipients* of services.[43]

a. Measures Taken to Protect Public Health

Article 4(1) of Directive 64/221 states that Member States may only refuse entry to the territory or issue a first residence permit if the migrant has one of the diseases listed in the Annex. Article 4(2) states, moreover, that diseases or disabilities occurring after the first residence permit has been issued shall not justify expulsion from the territory or refusal to renew the permit. This list has not been amended since 1964 and has posed problems for some Member States wishing to check for diseases, such as AIDS, which have emerged since then.[44]

42 [1963-4] OJ Spec. Ed. 117.

43 The Court has ruled that Member States must respect the fundamental rights of the person when invoking these Treaty derogations, Case 36/75 *Rutili v Minister for the Interior* [1975] ECR 1219, [1976] 1 CMLR 140. *Cf.* Hall, S. 'The ECHR and the Public Policy Exceptions to the Free Movement of Workers Under the EEC Treaty' (1991) 16 *ELRev* 466.

44 Pais Macedo van Overbeek, J. 'Aids/HIV Infection and the Free Movement of Workers within the European Economic Community' (1990) 27 *CMLRev* 791.

b. Measures Taken to Protect Public Policy and Security

These two headings are tended to merge into one general heading which is that of public policy. The standard of review was set out in *Adoui.*

Joined Cases 115 & 116/81 Adoui v Belgian State and City of Liège and Cornuaille v Belgian State [1982] ECR 1665, [1982] 3 CMLR 631

The plaintiffs, who were French nationals, were refused residence permits by the Belgian authorities on the ground that their conduct was considered to be contrary to public policy because they were waitresses in a bar which was suspected of acting as a brothel.

7. The reservations contained in Articles 48 and 56 of the EEC Treaty permit Member States to adopt, with respect to the nationals of other Member States and on the grounds specified in those provisions, in particular grounds justified by the requirements of public policy, measures which they cannot apply to their own nationals, inasmuch as they have no authority to expel the latter from the national territory or to deny them access thereto. Although that difference of treatment, which bears upon the nature of the measures must therefore be allowed, it must nevertheless be stressed that, in a Member State, the authority empowered to adopt such measures must not base the exercise of its powers on assessments of certain conduct which would have the effect of applying an arbitrary distinction to the detriment of nationals of other Member States.

8. It should be noted in that regard that reliance by a national authority upon the concept of public policy presupposes, as the Court held [in *Bouchereau*], the existence of a 'genuine and sufficiently serious threat affecting one of the fundamental interests of society'. Although Community law does not impose upon the Member States a uniform scale of values as regards the assessment of conduct which may be considered as contrary to public policy, it should nevertheless be stated that conduct may not be considered as being of sufficiently serious nature to justify restrictions on the admission to or residence within the territory of a Member State of a national of another Member State does not adopt with respect to the same conduct on the part of its own nationals repressive measure or other genuine and effective measures intended to combat such conduct.

Whilst many criminal acts may therefore justify deportation, Article 3(2) of Directive 64/221 states that previous convictions shall not in themselves justify grounds for deportation. In *Bouchereau*[45] the Court stated in relation to a French national working in Britain who had twice been convicted of drug offences that insofar as they illustrated a propensity to reoffend, they might be used as evidence of a present threat to public policy.

Decisions prohibiting entry can not be of unlimited duration. An EC migrant is entitled to have his/her situation re-examined if they consider that the circumstances which justified prohibiting him/her from entering the Member State have altered.[46] When a new application is made for entry or a residence permit, after a reasonable amount of time has elapsed since the preceding decision the migrant is entitled to a new decision which may be the subject of an appeal in accordance with the Directive.

In any case, by virtue of Article 3(1) of the Directive, any exclusionary measure must be based 'exclusively on the personal conduct of the individual'.

Case 67/74 Bonsignore v Oberstandtdirektor der Stadt Köln [1975] ECR 297, [1975] 1 CMLR 472

Bonsignore, an Italian national residing in Germany, accidentally caused the death of his brother by his careless handling of a firearm unlawfully in his possession. He was fined for an offence against the German firearm legislation and found guilty of causing death by negligence. The court imposed no punishment on this count, in view of the mental suffering caused to Bonsignore as a result of his carelessness. Following the convictions, the German Aliens Authority ordered Bonsignore to be deported. The local administrative court considered that the only possible justification for the deportation would be the reasons of a 'general preventive nature', namely the deterrent effect which the deportation of an alien found in possession of a firearm would have in immigrant circles.

6. With this in view, Article 3 of the Directive provides that measures adopted on grounds of public policy and for the maintenance of public security against the nationals

---

45 Case 30/77 *R v Bouchereau* [1977] ECR 1999, [1977] 2 CMLR 800.

46 Joined Cases C-65/95 & C-111/95 *R v Secretary of State for the Home Department ex parte Shingara and Radiom* [1997] ECR I-3343, [1997] 3 CMLR 703.

of Member States of the Community cannot be justified on grounds extraneous to the individual case, as is shown in particular by the requirement set out in Article 3(1) that only the 'personal conduct' of those affected by the measure is to be regarded as determinative.

As departures from the rules concerning the free movement of persons constitute exception which must be strictly construed, the concept of 'personal conduct' expresses the requirement that a deportation order may only be made for breaches of the peace and public security which might be committed by the individual affected.

7. The reply to the question referred should therefore be that Article 3(1) and (2) of Directive 64/221/EEC prevents the deportation of national court, on reasons of a 'general preventive nature'.

The concept of personal conduct has, however, been interpreted widely.

Case 41/74 Van Duyn v Home Office (No 2) [1974] ECR 1337, [1974] 1 CMLR 347

The Church of Scientology was considered by the United Kingdom government to be socially harmful. There was no legal power to prohibit the practice of Scientology, the government allowed the Church to function and did not place restrictions on United Kingdom nationals wishing to became members of the Church. However, the government considered that the Church was so objectionable that work permits for foreign nationals for work at a Scientology establishment would be refused. Van Duyn, a Dutch national, was offered employment of the Church. She claimed that she could not be excluded as the British Government's objections were not against her personally but against the organisation as whole.

17. It is necessary, first, to consider whether association with a body or an organisation can in itself constitute personal conduct within the meaning of Article 3 of Directive No 64/221. Although a person's past association cannot, in general, justify a decision refusing him the right to move freely within the Community, it is nevertheless the case that present association, which reflects participation in the activities of the body or of the organisation as well as identification with its aims or designs, may be considered a voluntary act of the person concerned and, consequently, as part of his personal conduct within the meaning of the provision cited.

In addition, any exclusion must, in principle, cover the whole national territory, and not merely part of it.

Case 36/75 Rutili v Minister for the Interior [1975] ECR 1219, [1976] 1 CMLR 140

The French Minister for the Interior granted Rutili, an Italian national, a residence permit attached to which was a prohibition on residence in specified regions of France.

46. Right of entry into the territory of Member States and right to say where and to move freely within it is defined in the Treaty by reference to the whole territory of these States and not by reference to its internal subdivisions.

47. The reservation contained in Article 48(3) concerning the protection of public policy has the same scope as the rights the exercise of which may, under that paragraph, be subject to limitations.

48. It follows that prohibitions on residence under the reservation inserted to this effect in Article 48(3) may be imposed only in respect of the whole of the national territory.

49. On the other hand, in the case of partial prohibitions on residence, limited to certain areas of the territory, persons covered by Community law must, under Article 7 of the Treaty and within the field of application of that provision, be treated on a footing of equality with the nationals of the Member State concerned.

50. It follows that a Member State cannot, in the case of an national of another Member State covered by the provisions of the Treaty, impose prohibitions on residence which are territorially limited except in circumstances where such prohibitions may be imposed on its own nationals.

51. The answer to the second question must, therefore, be that an appraisal as to whether measures designed to safeguard public policy are justified must have regard to all rules of Community law the object of which is, on the one hand, to limit the discretionary power of Member States in this respect and, on the other, to ensure that rights of persons subject thereunder to restrictive measures are protected.

52. These limitations and safeguards arise, in particular, from the duty imposed on Member States to base the measures adopted exclusively on the personal conduct of the individuals concerned, to refrain from adopting any measures in this respect which service ends unrelated to the requirement of public policy or which adversely affect the exercise of trade union rights and, finally, unless this is contrary to the interests of the security of the State involved, immediately to inform any person against whom a restrictive measure has been adapted of the grounds on which the decision taken is based to enable him to make effective use of legal remedies.

53. In particular, measures restricting the right of residence which are limited to part only of the national territory may not be imposed by a Member State on nationals of other Member States who are subject to the provisions of the Treaty except in the cases and circumstances in which such measures may be applied to nationals of the State concerned.

c. Procedural Safeguards

Directive 64/221 installs a number of procedural safeguards to protect persons subject to any measures taken under Article 48(3) [*39(3)*] EC. Article 7 of the Directive states that the person concerned must be officially notified of any decision to refuse the issue or renewal of a residence permit or to expel him from the territory. The period allowed for leaving the territory shall be stated in this notification. Save in cases of urgency, the period shall not be less than 15 days for persons who have not yet been issued a residence permit and not less than one month in all other cases. By virtue of Article 6 of the Directive, the person concerned must be informed of the grounds of public policy, public security or public health upon which the decision was taken unless this is contrary to the interests of State security. In *Adoui* the Court stated:

> It is clear from the purpose of the Directive that the notification of the grounds must be sufficiently detailed and precise to enable the person concerned to defend his interests. As regards the language to be used, it appears [that the plaintiffs] are of French nationality and that the decisions affecting them were drawn up in [French]. It is sufficient in any event if the notification is made in such a way as to enable the person concerned to comprehend the content and effect thereof.

The main procedural controls are set out in Articles 8 and 9 of the Directive. Article 8 provides that the migrant shall have the same rights of judicial review concerning any measure taken against him under

Article 48(3) [39(3)] EC as are available to nationals of that State in respect of acts of the administration.[47]

Article 9 sets out minimum procedural controls which must be adopted irrespective of how a Member State treats its own nationals.

Article 9(1). Where there is no right of appeal to a court of law, or where such appeal may be only in respect of the legal validity of the decision, or where the appeal cannot have suspensory effect, a decision refusing renewal of a residence permit or ordering the expulsion of the holder of a residence permit from the territory shall not be taken by the administrative authority, save in cases of urgency, until an opinion has been obtained from a competent authority of the host country before which the person concerned enjoys such rights of defence and of assistance or representation as the domestic law of that country provides for.

This authority shall not be the same as that empowered to take the decision refusing renewal of the residence permit or ordering expulsion.

2. Any decision refusing the issue of a first residence permit or ordering expulsion of the person concerned before the issue of the permit shall, where that person so requests, be referred for consideration to the authority whose prior opinion is required under paragraph 1. The person concerned shall then be entitled to submit his defence in person, except where this would be contrary to the interests of national security.

The distinction between the procedures in the first and second paragraphs is that the former applies to migrants who have already obtained their first residence permit, and allows them, in principle, to remain on the territory of the Member State pending an opinion of the competent authority. The second paragraph refers to migrants who have not yet obtained a first residence permit and does not grant them such a temporary stay of residence. The role of the competent authority was set out in more detail in *Gallagher*.

---

47 As Member States cannot expel their own national, the point of comparison is to be made with general rights of judicial review than the rights enjoyed by a State's own nationals to review decisions on their admission to a State's territory, Joined Cases C-65/95 & C-111/95 *R v Secretary of State for the Home Department ex parte Shingara and Radiom,* [1997] ECR I-3343.

Case C-175/94 R v Secretary of State for the Home Department ex parte Gallagher [1995] ECR I-4253, [1996] 1 CMLR 157

Gallagher was an Irish national who worked in England. In 1991 the Home Secretary issued an exclusion order against Gallagher under the Prevention of Terrorism (Temporary Provisions) Act 1989. Gallagher chose to leave England voluntarily but objected to the exclusion order and requested a personal interview with a person nominated by the Home Secretary. This interview took place in the British Embassy in Dublin but the interviewer did not reveal his identity or give any information on the grounds of exclusion. After reconsidering Gallagher's case the Home Secretary did not alter his decision. Gallagher instituted legal proceedings against the Home Secretary's acts arguing that contrary to Article 9 he had been excluded from the United Kingdom before he could make representations against the exclusion order or meet the person nominated by the Secretary of State. Gallagher also contended that the interviewer in Dublin was, by virtue of his manner of appointment, not competent to deliver the opinion required under Article 9.

16. It is settled law that the object of Article 9(1) of the directive is to ensure minimum procedural safeguards for persons affected by a decision refusing renewal of a residence permit or ordering the expulsion of the holder of a residence permit. That provision, which applies where there is no right of appeal to a court of law, or where such appeal may be only in respect of the legal validity of the decision, or where the appeal cannot have suspensory effect, envisages the intervention of a competent authority other than the authority empowered to take the decision. In proceedings before that competent authority the person concerned must enjoy such rights of defence and of assistance or representation as are provided for by the domestic law of that country (see, in particular, Joined Cases C-297/88 and C-197/89 *Dzodzi v Belgium* [1990] ECR I-3763, paragraph 62).

17. As the Court has already held, the purpose of the intervention of the competent authority referred to in Article 9(1) is to enable an exhaustive examination of all the facts and circumstances, including the expediency of the proposed measure, to be carried out before the decision is finally taken (Joined Cases 115/81 and 116/81 *Adoui and Cornuaille v Belgium* [1982] ECR 1665, paragraph 15, and Case 131/79 *R v Secretary of State for Home Affairs, ex parte Santillo* [1980] ECR 1585 paragraph 12). The Court has also ruled that, save in cases of urgency, the administrative authority may not take its decision until an opinion has been obtained from the competent authority (Case 98/79 *Pecastaing v Belgium* [1980] ECR 691, paragraph 17, and *Dzodzi,* paragraph 62).

.....

20. ... the distinction between Article 9(1) and Article 9(2) is precisely that, in situations covered by Article 9(1), the opinion must be obtained before the decision is taken, whereas in situations covered by Article 9(2) the opinion is obtained after the decision has been taken and only at the request of the person concerned if he has raised objections.

.....

22. ... Article 9(1) of Directive 64/221 must be interpreted as meaning that, save in cases of urgency, it prohibits the administrative authority from taking a decision ordering expulsion before a competent authority has given its opinion.

The sccond question

23. ... the Court is asked to rule whether Article 9(1) of the Directive precludes the competent authority referred to in that provision from being appointed by the same administrative authority as takes the decision ordering expulsion.

24. The Directive does not specify how the competent authority referred to in Article 9 is appointed. It does not require that that authority be a court or be composed of members of the judiciary. Nor does it require the members of the competent authority to be appointed for a specific period. The essential requirements are, first, that it be clearly established that the authority is to perform its duties in absolute independence and is not to be directly or indirectly subject, in the exercise of its duties, to any control by the authority empowered to take the measures provided for in the Directive and, second, that the authority follow a procedure enabling the person concerned, on the terms laid down by the directive, effectively to present his defence (*Dzodzi,* paragraph 65, and *Adoui and Cornuaille*, paragraph 16). It is for the national court to determine in each case whether those requirements have been met.

25. As regards the form of the opinion of the competent authority, the objectives of the system provided for by the directive require that the opinion be duly notified to the person concerned, but the Directive does not require the opinion to identify by the name the members of the authority or indicate their professional status (*Adoui and Cornuaille*, paragraph 18), since such identification is relevant only for the purpose of enabling the national court to determine whether the members of the authority are independent and impartial.

26. ... Article 9(1) of the Directive does not preclude the competent authority referred to in that provision from being appointed by the same administrative authority as takes the decision ordering expulsion, provided that the competent authority can perform its duties in absolute independence and is not subject to any control by the authority empowered to take the measures provided for in the Directive. It is for the national court to determine in each case whether those requirements have been met.

VIII. Third Country Nationals

Third country nationals derive few rights under EC law. Even the Court which normally interprets the free movement provisions liberally has found it difficult to ascribe EC competence to this area.[48] Yet third country nationals legally resident in the EC number, at a conservative estimate, some 10 million[49] and their status and treatment remains by and large within the competence of the Member States.[50] In relation to immigration control there is no equivalent of a common external border and Member States retain competence to administer their own immigration policies. While Article 6[*12*] EC provides protection against discrimination on the grounds of nationality the EC has limited competence to enact measures handling discrimination on the grounds of race, colour, ethnic origin. Yet arguably such issues may touch upon the functioning of the Internal Market, for example, Member States may allow firms to use and exploit non-EC labour thus creating a competitive advantage in the domestic labour or lack of protection against racial discrimination may be a disincentive to a person who would otherwise exercise the right to free movement.[51]

---

48 A number of immigration policy communications have been published in recent years: COM (79) 113; COM (85) 48; SEC (89) 924; SEC (90) 1813; SEC (91) 1855; COM (94) 23. The Commission has proposed a Convention on Migration OJ 1997 C 337/9.

49 COM (94) 23, Annex I, 22.

50 Note Article 2(3) of the Social Policy Agreement restricts any measures relating to the conditions of employment of third country nationals legally residing in Community territory to unanimity voting. See also Cases C-72 & 73/91 *Sloman Neptun* [1993] ECR I-887.

51 See further, Szyszczak, E. 'Race Discrimination: The Limits of Market Equality?' in Hepple, B. and Szyszczak, E. (eds.) *Race Discrimination: The Limits of Law* (1992, Mansell, London).

i. Existing Rights of Third Country Nationals Under EC Law

a. Non-EC Relatives of Migrant Workers

Under Regulation 1612/68/EEC non-EC relatives may derive rights under EC law. Such rights include the right to install themselves with the migrant worker in the host State, a conditional right to remain permanently in the host State, admission to the education system on the same conditions as the nationals of the host State, the right to work and access to social security benefits in the host State.[52]

Case 267/83 Diatta v Land Berlin [1985] ECR 567, [1986] 2 CMLR 164

Diatta, a Senegalese national, married a French national who had lived and worked in West Berlin for several years. After one year of marriage they separated and lived apart with the intention of divorcing. Diatta had obtained a temporary residence permit but when this expired her application for an extension was rejected on the ground that she was no longer a member of the family of a national of a Member State and that she no longer lived with her husband.

18. In providing that a member of a migrant worker's family has the right to install himself with the worker, Article 10 [does] not require that the member of the family in question must live permanently with the worker, but, as is clear from Article 10(3), only that the accommodation which the worker has available must be such as may be considered normal for the purpose of accommodating his family. A requirement that the family must live under the same roof permanently cannot be implied.

19. In addition such an interpretation corresponds to the spirit of Article 11 of the regulation, which gives the member of the family the right to take up any activity as an employed person throughout the territory of the Member State concerned, even though that activity is exercised at a place some distance away from the place where the migrant worker resides.

---

52 Joined Cases C-297/88 & C-197/89 *Dzodzi v Belgium* [1990] ECR 3763.

20. It must be added that the marital relationship cannot be regarded as dissolved so long as it has not been terminated by the competent authority. It is not dissolved merely because the spouses live separately, even where they intend to divorce at a later date.

21. As regards Article 11 of [Regulation] 1612/68, it is clear from the terms of that provision that it does not confer on the members of a migrant worker's family an independent right of residence, but solely a right to exercise any activity as employed persons throughout the territory of the state in question. Article 11 cannot therefore constitute the legal basis for a right of residence without reference to the conditions laid down in Article 10.

In limited circumstances these rights may be invoked by the relatives of an EC national against that national's own State.

Case C-370/90 R v IAT and Surinder Singh ex parte Secretary of State for the Home Department [1992] ECR I-4265, [1992] 3 CMLR 358

An Indian national had married a British national and both had worked in Germany for a number of years. They returned to the United Kingdom to set up a business but the marriage failed. A deportation order was served upon Mr Singh before the divorce procedure was complete. Mr Singh relied upon the fact that at the time of the deportation order he was the lawful spouse of a person who had exercised rights under Article 48 [*39*] EC and Article 52 [*43*] EC. The United Kingdom government argued that EC law did not come into play, that the matter was a situation internal to the United Kingdom. The Court ruled that the spouse of a person who had exercised the right to free movement must enjoy at least the same rights as would be granted under EC law if the spouse resided in another Member State.

19. A national of a Member State might be deterred from leaving his country of origin in order to pursue an activity as an employed or self-employed person as envisaged by the Treaty in the territory of another Member State if, on returning to the Member State of which he is a national in order to pursue an activity there as an employed or self-employed person, the conditions of his entry and residence were not at least equivalent to those which he would enjoy under the treaty or secondary law in the territory of another Member State.

20. He would in particular be deterred from so doing if his spouse and children were not also permitted to enter and reside in the territory of his Member State of origin under conditions at least equivalent to those granted them by Community law in the territory of another Member State.

The Court is silent on the position of Diatta and Surinder Singh when their marriages are formally dissolved. It is assumed that, the cloak of protection of EC law would fall away and that national law - tempered by the application of the European Convention on Fundamental Rights and Freedoms would apply. Recent cases have highlighted the limited protection the Court is willing to give to spouses who are in difficult marital situations unless they can show some economic reason/justification for moving away from the family home even where there are clear indications of domestic violence.[53] Hervey[54] argues that '... respect for the right to family life is not guaranteed where the enforcement or rights of family members in Community law depends upon a construction of the relevant provisions which reflects their *economic* function in preference to their social and human function'.

It is to be contrasted with the ruling of the European Court of Human Rights in *Berrehab*[55] where a Moroccan migrant in the Netherlands successfully argued that deportation after the breakdown of his marriage would deny him the right to see his child and would therefore be an infringement of the right to respect family life contained in Article 8 ECHR.[56]

b. International Agreements

Under agreements made between the EC and third states under Articles 228 [*300*] and 238 [*310*] EC the Member States may have to treat

---

53 Case C- 351/95 *Kadiman* [1995] ECR I- 2133; Hervey, T. 'Migrant Workers and Their Families in the European Union: the Pervasive Market Ideology of Community Law' in Shaw, J. & More, G. (eds.) *New Legal Dynamics of European Union* (1995, OUP, Oxford).

54 Hervey, T. 'A Gendered Perspective on the Right To Family Life in European Community Law' in Neuwahl, N. & Rosas, A. (eds.) *The European Union and Human Rights* (1995, Martinus Nijhoff, The Hague) 221, 229.

55 A/138 *Berrehab v The Netherlands* [1989] ECHR 322.

56 *Cf.* Cholewinski, R. 'Strasbourg's Hidden Agenda: The Protection of Second-Generation Migrants From Expulsion Under Article 8 of the European Convention on Human Rights' (1994) 3 *Netherlands Quarterly of Human Rights* 287.

nationals of the third States in a way which is compatible with EC law. The Court has ruled that such agreements may be the subject of a preliminary reference under Article 177 [*234*] EC and that certain provisions of the agreements may be capable of creating direct effects in the national courts.[57] This has resulted in a half-way house for some nationalities - they may enjoy economic rights to migration and other social advantages if they are exercising an economic activity but neither gain the full privileges of EU nationals - or suffer the same disadvantages as TCNs or their own nationals who are not exercising economic rights. Such persons have been called 'denizens'. Soysal[58] argues that these inroads into the simple division of rights-bearing citizens of nation States and rightless 'aliens' has been the product of two developments post World War II. First, the development of international interactions and secondly the inter-related growth of international human rights discourse.[59] However, as the case law reveals this new form of 'market denizenship', like the development of market citizenship discussed by Everson[60], is extremely limited. By November 1995 the EC had signed some twenty-four international agreements which granted rights to third-country nationals within the EC. The EEA agreement extends the *acquis comunautaire* to Norway, Iceland and Liechtenstein, Decisions 1/80 and 3/80 made by the EEC-Turkey Association Council grant rights of immigration and social security on Turkish workers[61] and rights are also given by the Maghreb Cooperation Agreements, the European Agreements with six Eastern European States, the partnership and Cooperation Agreements with five of the former Soviet Republics and the Lomé Convention with the ACP.

---

57 Case 12/86 *Demirel v Stadt Schwäbisch Gmünd* [1987] ECR 3719, (1989) 1 CMLR 421; Case C-192/89 *Sevince v Staatssecretaris van Justitie* [1990] ECR I-3461, (1992) 2 CMLR 57.

58 Soysal, Y. *Limits of Citizenship: Migrants and Post-National Membership in Europe* (1994, University of Chicago Press, London/Chicago).

59 *Cf.* Baubock, B. 'Citizenship and National Identities in the European Union', *Harvard Jean Monnet Chair Working Paper 4/97.*

60 Everson, M. 'The Legacy of the Market Citizen' in Shaw, J. and More, G. (eds.) *New Legal Dynamics of European Union* (1995, Clarendon Press, Oxford).

61 By 1994 there were some 2.7 million Turkish nationals resident in the EU, *Eurostat Yearbook* 1996, 84-85.

Although the Court has been willing to find that such Agreements may create direct effects it has rarely found that non-EC nationals can benefit from rights under the Agreements. Any rights are firmly tied to the exercise of economic activity and are a long way off the general rights of residence available to EU Citizens. For example, in *Sevince*[62] the application of a Turkish national living in the Netherlands for a new residence permit was rejected. He argued that Decisions adopted under the Association Agreement between Turkey and the EC implementing the provisions to freedom of movement created direct effects. Although the Court accepted that the provisions did create direct effects it concluded that since Sevince's residence permit had been revoked he was no longer in 'legal employment' and could not claim rights under the Agreement and implementing Decisions. Peers[63] has argued that this ruling of the Court was important in that it established that the legal system governing Turkish nationals' rights was subject to the same principles and legal system governing migrant EC nationals in other Member States - the first step in transforming Turks from 'aliens' into 'denizens'.[64]

In *Bozkurt*[65] the applicant worked for a Dutch company and paid Dutch tax as a long distance lorry driver between the Netherlands and the Middle East. He was granted a provisional Dutch residence permit which he claimed gave the right to remain in the Netherlands. Although the Court ruled that legal employment could be established and that such employment necessarily implies the recognition of a right of residence, however the Court went on to rule that Article 6(2) of Decision 1/80 did not give Bozkurt the right to remain in the Netherlands following an accident at work which rendered him permanently incapacitated for work.

---

62 Case 192/89 *Sevince v Staatssecretaris van Justitie* [1990] ECR I-3461.

63 Peers, S. 'Aliens, Workers or Humans? Judicial Activism and Turkish Nationals in the EU', Paper delivered at the Sociology of Law Symposium, Onti, Spain, September 1997.

64 See Rea, 'Social Citizenship and Ethnic Minorities in the European Union' in Martiniello, M. (ed.) *Migration, Citizenship and Etho-National Identities in the European Union* (1995, Avebury, Aldershot).

65 Case C-434/93 *Bozkurt v Staatssecretaris van Justite* [1995] ECR I-1475.

There are some positive decisions. For example in *Kus*[66] the Court held that while Decision 1/80 only expressly confers the right to work it must also encompass the right of residence. In *Kziber*[67] the defendant was the daughter of a Moroccan national who had retired in Belgium after having worked there. She argued that she was entitled to rely on Article 41(1) of the Cooperation Agreement concluded with Morocco in 1976 which provided for equal treatment in the field of social security for Moroccan workers employed in the Member States. The rights expressly mentioned in the Agreement include the aggregation of periods of insurance, employment and residence in different Member States, the right to family allowances for family members resident in the EC and the right to transfer pensions and other benefits to the state of origin. The Court ruled that social security in Article 41(1) of the Agreement must be understood by means of an analogy with the identical concept in Regulation 1408/71, the Regulation which coordinates and aggregates social security benefits for EC nationals. It therefore included unemployment benefits although they are not expressly mentioned in Article 41(1). The direct effect of Article 41 of the EEC-Morocco was used also in *Yousfi*[68] to counteract discrimination against the son of a Morrocon migrant worker who was denied a disability allowance after an accident at work.

In *Lopes de Veiga*[69] a Portuguese national successfully challenged a refusal of a residence permit by the Dutch authorities had been employed on a vessel flying the Dutch flag at the time of Portugal's accession to the EC but the Dutch authorities argued that the transitional rules relating to free movement of workers applied. The Court ruled that the purpose of such rules was to prevent the disruption of national labour markets at the time of Portugal's accession and since the applicant was already employed within a Member State the rules were not applicable.

---

66 Case C-237/91 *Kus v Landeshauptstadt Wiesbaden* [1992] ECR I-6781, [1993] 2 CMLR 887.

67 Case C-18/90 *Office National de l'Emploi v Kziber* [1991] ECR I-199.

68 Case C-58/93 *Yousfi v Belgian State* [1994] ECR I-1353.

69 Case C-9/88 [1989] *Lopes de Veiga* ECR I-2989, [1991] 1 CMLR 217.

In *Eroglu* [70] the daughter of a Turkish migrant worker joined him in Germany where she studied and then found work. Her application for a residence permit was rejected. Article 7 of Decision 1/80 allows members of the family who have been authorised to join the worker to a right to employment (subject to Community preference) after a three year period of legal residence and an unrestricted right to employment after legal residence of five years. In addition children of Turkish workers who have completed a course of vocational training in a Member State have a right of access to employment in that State irrespective of their length of their period of residence as long as one of their parents has been legally employed in that Member State for at least three years (Article 7(2)). The Court allowed the daughter to rely on this directly effective provision.[71]

IX. Education and Vocational Training

In addition to immigration rights and social rights to ensure the integration of migrant workers into the fabric of the host State the EC has developed an education policy designed to facilitate the free movement of persons as well as create EC competence in an area seen as a necessary adjunct - or flanking policy - to the Single Market. Jealous rivalry over sovereignty and competence has led to an uneven development of education as a distinct policy area. If we explore this development we see an incremental shift in emphasis from minimalist intervention on the part of the Community - and the Court - to facilitate the free movement of persons to seeing education as a policy of the Community in its own right and one with a necessary role to play in the development of a European labour market.

---

70 Case C-355/93 *Eroglu v Land Baden-Wurttemburg* [1994] ECR I-5113.

71 Five more decisions are currently pending before the Court concerning the interpretation of Decision 1/80: Case C-1/97 *Binder*; Case C-91/97 *Altiney*; Case C-329/97 *Akman*; Case C-329/97 *Ergat*; Case C-340/97 *Nazli*. The United Kingdom Divisional Court has referred a case of a self-employed Turkish national to the Court : *Savas*, not yet registered.

i. Legal Competence

Neither the original EEC Treaty nor the SEA mentioned EC competence in the field of education. Article 128 EEC empowered the Council of Ministers, acting by simple majority vote, to '... lay down general principles for implementing a common vocational training policy capable of contributing to the harmonious development both of the national economies and of the common market'. Decision 63/266/EEC[72] elaborated the general principles for an EC vocational training policy but there was little subsequent legislative activity. The term 'education' appears for the first time within EC competence as a result of the amendments made by the TEU 1992.

Article 3(p) [*3(p)*] EC. [For the purposes set out in Article 2 [*2*], the activities of the Community shall include, as provided by this Treaty and in accordance with the timetable set out therein:]
- a contribution to education and training of quality and to the flowering of the cultures of the Member States.

Article 126 (1) [*149(1)*] EC. The Community shall contribute to the development of quality education by encouraging cooperation between Member States and, if necessary, by supporting and supplementing their action, while fully respecting the responsibility of the Member States for the content of teaching and the organization of education systems and their cultural and linguistic diversity.

2. Community action shall be aimed at:
- developing the European dimension in education, particularly through the dissemination of the languages of the Member States;
- encouraging mobility of students and teachers, inter alia by encouraging the academic recognition of diplomas and periods of study;
- promoting cooperation between educational establishments;
- developing exchanges of information and experience on issues common to the education systems of the Member States;
- encouraging the development of youth exchanges and of exchanges of socio-educational instructors;
- encouraging the development of distance education.

---

72 OJ English Special Edition 1963/64, 25.

3. The Community and the Member States shall foster cooperation with third countries and the competent international organisations in the field of education, in particular the Council of Europe.

4. In order to contribute to the achievement of the objectives referred to in this Article, the Council:

- acting in accordance with the procedure referred to in Article 189b [*251*], after consulting the Economic and Social Committee and the Committee of the Regions, shall adopt incentive measures, excluding any harmonisation of the laws and regulations of the Member States;
- acting by a qualified majority on a proposal from the Commission, shall adopt recommendations.

Article 127(1) [*150(1)*] **EC.** The Community shall implement a vocational training policy which shall support and supplement the action of the Member States, while fully respecting the responsibility of the Member States for the content and origination of vocational training.

2. Community action shall aim to:

- facilitate adaptation to industrial changes, in particular through vocational training and retraining;
- improve initial and continuing vocational training in order to facilitate vocational integration and reintegration into the labour market;
- facilitate access to vocational training and encourage mobility of instructors and trainees and particularly young people;
- stimulate cooperation on training between educational or training establishments and firms;
- develop exchanges of information and experience on issues common to the training systems of the Member States.

3. The Community and the Member States shall foster cooperation with third countries and the competent international organisations in the sphere of vocational training.

4. The Council, acting in accordance with the procedure referred to in Article 189c [*251*] and after consulting the Economic and Social Committee, shall adopt measures to contribute to the achievement of the objectives referred to in this Article, excluding any harmonisation of the laws and regulations of the Member States.

There are, however, some constraints upon this competence since Article C [*3*] TEU states:

Article C [*3*] TEU. The Union shall be served by a single institutional framework which shall ensure the consistency and the continuity of the activities carried out in order to attain its objectives while respecting and building upon the 'acquis communautaire'.

Articles 126 [*149*] and 127 [*150*] EC are the successors to Article 128 EEC. Article C [*3*] TEU requires that Articles 126 [*149*] and 127 [*150*] EC must be interpreted and applied in such a way that Article 128 EEC is respected and built upon.

ii. Competence Prior to the TEU

Prior to the TEU, EC competence in the field of education can be discerned in three areas:

- Education issues were raised under Regulation 1612/68/EEC in relation to rights to facilitate the free movement of workers and for other members of their families who wished to study in another Member State.

- The EC had competence to enact legislation for the mutual recognition of educational and professional qualifications in order to facilitate the free movement of workers.

- Legislation was adopted to establish EC schemes in areas such as vocational training, foreign languages, educational exchanges and educational mobility (schemes such as Erasmus, Commett, Lingua) and to establish a European Training Foundation.

All three areas related to the facilitation of the free movement of labour.

a. Education Rights in Relation to the Free Movement of Persons

It was accepted that the Treaty rules alone would not be adequate to ensure the smooth working of the Common Market and therefore legislative powers were assigned to the Community. Where measures in the field of education would ensure the effectiveness of those powers the Community is entitled to enact measures even where no *express* power with regard to education policy has been conferred on the Community.[73] In *Casagrande*[74] the son of a Italian migrant worker in Germany was denied an educational grant which, under a statute of the Free State of Bavaria, was reserved to German nationals, stateless persons and aliens granted asylum. The Court stated:[75]

> **12.** ... although educational and training policy is not as such included in the spheres which the Treaty has entrusted to the Community institutions, it docs not follow that the exercise of powers transferred to the Community is in some way limited if it is of such a nature as to affect the measures taken in the execution of a policy such as that of education and training.

Two provisions of Regulation 1612/68/EEC have proved to be particularly central to the grant of educational rights. The first is Article 12:

> The children of a national of a Member State who is or has been employed in the territory of another Member State shall be admitted to that State's general educational, apprenticeship and vocational training courses under the same conditions as the nationals of that Statc, if such children are residing in its territory.
>
> Member States shall encourage all efforts to enable such children to attend these courses under the best possible conditions.

The Court also used Article 7(2) to cover finance for educational and maintenance costs. These were held to be a social advantage *of benefit to the migrant worker* even though applicable to the child. In

---

73 See Weiler J., 'The Transformation of Europe' (1991) 100 *Yale Law Journal* 2403, 2438 *et seq.*

74 Case 9/74 *Casagrande v Landeshauptstadt München* [1974] ECR 773, [1974] 2 CMLR 423.

75 Directive 77/486/EEC on the education of migrant workers' children OJ 1977 L 199/32. See also Commission Report on the Education of Migrants' Children in the European Union COM(94)80 final; Cullen, H. 'From Migrants To Citizens? EC Policy on Intercultural Education' (1996) 45 *ICLQ 109*.

Echternach and Moritz[76] the Court ruled that the child of a migrant worker retains the status of being a member of the worker's family even when the migrant worker has returned to the state of origin and even if the child temporarily interrupts his or her studies. In *Humbel*[77] the Court ruled that Article 12 only applied to children claiming rights in the host State. This case concerned the son of a French migrant worker in Luxembourg who wished to study in Belgium. Compare this ruling with:

Case C-308/89 Di Leo v Land Berlin [1990] ECR I-4185

Di Leo was an Italian national and the daughter of an Italian migrant worker employed in Germany. She enrolled to study medicine at the University of Sienna and applied for a grant. This was refused since a grant for attendance at an educational establishment abroad could only be awarded to Germans, stateless persons and foreigners granted asylum. Di Leo argued that the German policy was contrary to Article 12.

12. ... According to its actual wording, Article 12 is not confined to education or training within the host country. The condition of residence, laid down in Article 12 of Regulation 1612/68, is designed to restrict equal treatment as regards the advantages referred to in that Article solely to the children of Community workers who reside within their parents' host country. However, it does not mean that the right to equal treatment depends on the place in which the child concerned pursues his studies.

13. It must also be borne in mind that the aim of Regulation 1612/68, namely freedom of movement of workers, requires, for such freedom to be guaranteed in compliance with the principles of liberty and dignity, the best possible conditions for the integration of the Community worker's family in the society of the host country. If such integration is to be successful, it is essential for the child of a Community worker who resides with his family in the host Member State to have the opportunity to choose a course under the same conditions as a child of a national of that State.

Similarly in *Matteucci*[78] the Court held that Article 7(2) extended to cover grants which would enable an EC worker to pursue studies

---

76 Jointed Cases 389 & 390/87 *Echternach and Moritz v Netherlands Minister for Education* [1989] ECR 723, [1990] 2 CMLR 305.

77 Case 263/86 *Belgian State v Humbel* [1988] ECR 5365, [1989] 1 CMLR 393.

78 Case 235/87 *Matteucci v Communauté Français de Belgique* [1989] ECR 5589.

abroad if such grants were made available to its own nationals.[79] But the Court has not always provided such a generous interpretation of these provisions.

In *Brown*[80] a student had dual French/British nationality and had been domiciled in France for a number of years. He had worked for nine months for a firm in Scotland as training before commencing a university course at Cambridge. He was denied a maintenance grant and claimed that because he was a migrant worker he was entitled to such a grant on the same footing as British nationals under Article 6 [*12*] EC and Articles 7(2) and (3) of Regulation 1612/68/EEC. The Court ruled that he was a 'worker' within the meaning of Article 48 [*39*] EC but he was not entitled to a maintenance grant because his employment was merely ancillary to the course of study he wished to undertake, that is, he had become a worker exclusively as a result of his university place.

This case might be compared with *Lair*.[81] A French woman who had worked in Germany on a series of part-time contracts also applied for a maintenance grant to undertake a university course. The Court drew a distinction between a migrant worker who was involuntarily unemployed and legitimately resident in the host State and would be entitled to the same treatment as regards reinstatement or re-employment as national workers and a worker who gave up work in order to undertake further training in the host State. In the latter situation, a maintenance grant would only be available if there was some link between the studies and the previous work experience.

---

79 See also Case C-7/94 *Landesamt für Ausbidungs Förderung Nordrhein-Westfalen v Lubor Gaal* [1995] ECR I-1031, [1995] 3 CMLR 17 where the Court held that the definition of a child for the purposes of Article 12 is not subject to the same conditions of age or dependency as are the rights governed by Article 10(1) and 11 of the Regulation. Here the 'child' was over the age of twenty-one and was not dependent upon the migrant since his father had died and his sole means of support was an orphan's allowance.

80 Case 197/86 *Brown v Secretary of State For Scotland* [1988] ECR 3205, [1988] 3 CMLR 403.

81 Case 39/86 *Lair v University of Hannover* [1988] ECR 3161, [1989] 3 CMLR 545.

In *Bernini*[82] an Italian national who was employed for ten weeks as a paid trainee as part of her occupational training was not precluded from being classified as worker either by the fact that she received low wages or the fact that she only worked a small number of hours per week. However, the Court states that when assessing the genuine and effective nature of the services a national court may examine whether in all the circumstances the person concerned has completed a sufficient number of hours in order to familiarise themselves with the work. If the worker voluntarily left employment in order to take up a course of full-time study the status of worker would not be lost provided there was a link between the previous employment and the course of study.

This link between the studies and the previous occupational activity is again stressed in *Raulin.*[83] A French woman moved to the Netherlands and was engaged under a contract of employment classified as an 'on call' contract for sixty hours service as a waitress. After five months she began a full-time vocational course and applied to the Dutch authorities for a maintenance grant. This was refused on the grounds that she was not a Dutch national and that she did not hold a residence permit. Raulin argued that she was a worker within the meaning of Article 48 [*39*] EC and therefore entitled to equality of treatment with Dutch nationals. In applying the test of whether she was a worker under EC law, of looking to see if her work was 'genuine and effective', the Court ruled that there must be a consideration of all the occupational activities of the person in the *host* State but not of the activities engaged in elsewhere in the EC. The *duration* of the activities is an appropriate factor to be taken into account. This ruling is a significant concession to the Member States. White[84] argues that the ruling could be open to the objection that it raises national boundaries at a time when the completion of the internal market is based on the removal of national frontiers. It may be that the pattern of work undertaken in a number of Member States could establish the genuine and effective nature of the activities

---

82 Case C-3/90 *Bernini v Minister van Onderwijs en Wetenschappen* [1992] ECR I-1071.

83 Case 357/89 *Raulin v Netherlands Ministry of Education and Science* [1992] ECR 1027, [1994] 1 CMLR 227.

84 White, R. 'Free Movement of Workers and Social Security' (1992) 17 *ELRev* 522, 526.

whereas consideration of such activities in the host Member State might suggest much more marginal and ancillary activities.

Directive 93/96/EEC[85] granted the right of residence to students exercising the right to vocational training and to certain of their family members provided that they have adequate resources so as not to become a burden on the social security schemes of the Member States and are covered by sickness insurance. Prior to Directive 93/96 EEC coming into force, the Court in *Raulin* [86] ruled that the principle of non-discrimination deriving from Articles Article 6 [*12*] EC and 127 [*150*] EC granted the right of residence to an EC national who had been admitted to a vocational training course in another Member State for the duration of the course. The right was not contingent upon possession of a residence permit but a Member State could impose some conditions on the right to residence, to minimise public expenditure costs, such as maintenance costs or health insurance. But such conditions must not infringe the principle of equal access to vocational training.

b. EC Competence in the Field of Mutual Recognition of Professional Diplomas

A second area where there is the need for Community intervention in the field of education/vocational training is in the co-ordination of qualifications. Although most of the attention in this field has involved cases concerning the free movement of services/establishment the mutual recognition of qualifications is equally as important in the field of free movement of labour, particularly after the *Bosman* ruling.

85 OJ 1993 L 317/59.

86 Case 357/89 *Raulin v Netherlands Ministry of Education and Science* [1992] ECR 1027.

c. EC Competence With Regard to Education Regarded as Vocational Training

Article 127 [*150*] EC has been used as a teleological tool by the Court to extend rights under EC law by developing a notion of Community competence. This is seen in the following case where the applicant did not have a firm legal base upon which to invoke an EC law right but the Court was willing to extend EC competence into the area of education.

Case 293/83 Gravier v City of Liège [1985] ECR 593, [1985] 3 CMLR 1

Gravier, a French national, was a student at the Academie Royale des Beaux-Arts, Liège. She challenged the enrolment fee (minerval) levied on foreign students in Belgium. She contended that the discriminatory fee was contrary to Article 7 EEC [now Article 6 [*12*] EC] within the context of the establishment of a common vocational training policy under Article 128 EEC [now Article 127 [*150*] EC].

19. ... although educational organization and policy are not as such included in the spheres which the Treaty has entrusted to the Community institutions, access to and participation in courses of instruction and apprenticeship, in particular vocational training, are not unconnected with Community law.

20. Article 7 of Regulation No 1612/68 of the Council of 15 October 1968 on freedom of movement for workers within the Community (Official Journal English Special Edition 1968 (II), p. 475) provides that a worker who is a national of a Member State and who is employed in another Member State is to have access to training in vocational schools and retraining centres in that country by virtue of the same right and under the same conditions as national workers. Article 12 of the Regulation provides that the children of such workers are to be admitted to that State's general educational apprenticeship and vocational training courses under the same conditions as the nationals of that State.

21. With regard more particularly to vocational training, Article 128 of the Treaty provides that the Council is to lay down general principles for implementing common vocational training policy capable of contributing to the harmonious development both of the national economies and of the common market. The first principle established in Council Decision No 63/266/EEC of 2 April 196 laying down those general principles (Official Journal, English Special edition 1963-1964, p.25) states that the general principles must enable every person to receive adequate training, with due regard for freedom of choice of occupation, place of training, with due regard for freedom of choice of occupation, place of training and place of work.

22. The particular attention which the Community institutions have given to problems of access to vocational training and its improvement throughout the Community may be seen, moreover, in the 'general guidelines' which the Council laid down in 1971 for drawing up a Community programme on vocational training (Official Journal, English Special Edition, Second Series IX, p.50), in the Resolution of the Council and of the Ministers for Education meeting within the Council of 13 December 1976 concerning measures to be taken to improve the preparation of young people for work and to facilitate their transition from education to working life (OJ C 308/1) and the Council Resolution of 11 July 1983 concerning the vocational training policies in the European Community in the 1980s (OJ C 1983 193/2).

23. The common vocational training policy referred to in Article 128 of the Treaty is thus gradually being established. It constitutes, moreover, an indispensable element of the activities of the Community, whose objectives include *inter alia* the free movement of persons, the mobility of labour and the improvement of the living standards of workers.

24. Access to vocational training is in particular likely to promote free movement of persons throughout the Community, by enabling them to obtain a qualification in the Member State where they intend to work and by enabling them to complete their training and develop their particular talents in the Member State whose vocational training programmes include the special subject desired.

25. It follows ... that the conditions of access to vocational training fall within the scope of the Treaty.

26. ... the imposition on students who are nationals of other Member States, of a charge, a registration fee ... as a condition of access to vocational training, where the same fee is not imposed on students who are nationals of the host Member State, constitutes discrimination on grounds of nationality contrary to Article 7 of the Treaty.

The Court then went on to define vocational training:

30. ... any form of education which prepares for a qualification for a particular profession, trade or employment or which provides the necessary training and skills for such a profession, trade or employment as vocational training, whatever the age and the level of training of the pupils or students, and even if the training programme includes an element of general education.

In *Commission v Belgium*[87] the Court upheld the Commission's complaint that the measures introduced by Belgium to comply with the *Gravier* ruling which restricted only two per cent of 'outsiders' access to vocational training courses was incompatible with Article 6 [*12*] EC.[88]

Case 242/87 Commission v Council [1989] ECR 1425, [1991] 1 CMLR 478

This was an application for annulment under Article 173 [*230*] EC Decision 87/327/EEC adopting an EC action scheme for the mobility of university students (Erasmus). The Council, by unanimous vote had added Article 235 [*308*] EC to Article 128 EEC.

10. The Court has already noted, in its judgment of 13 February 1985 in Case 293/83 *Gravier v City of Liège* [1985] ECR 593, that the common vocational training policy referred to in Article 128 of the Treaty is gradually being established. The above mentioned Decision 63/266, which constitutes the point of departure for that process of gradual implementation, is based on the idea that the task of implementing the general principles of the common vocational training policy ... is one for the Member States and the Community institutions working in cooperation.

11. From an interpretation of Article 128 based on that conception it follows that the Council is entitled to adopt legal measures providing for Community action in the sphere of vocational training and imposing corresponding obligations of cooperation on the Member States. Such an interpretation is in accordance with the wording of Article 128 and also ensures the effectiveness of that provision.

.....

37. ... in as much as the contested decision concerns not only the sphere of vocational training but also that of scientific research, the Council did not have the power to adopt it pursuant to Article 128 alone and thus was bound, before the Single European Act entered into force, to base the decision on Article 235 as well. The Commission's first submission that the legal base chosen was unlawful must therefore be rejected.

---

87 Case 42/87 *Commission v Belgium* [1988] ECR 5445, [1989] 1 CMLR 457.

88 Further definitions of vocational training were given in Case 24/86 *Blaizot v University of Liège* [1988] ECR 379, [1989] 1 CMLR 57; Case 263/86 *Belgian State v Humbel* [1988] ECR 5365, [1989] 1 CMLR 393.

Case C-295/90 Parliament v Council [1992] ECR I-4193, [1992] 3 CMLR 281

The Parliament challenged Directive 90/366/EEC granting rights of residence to students on the grounds that the Council was wrong to alter its legal base from Article 7(2) EEC [now Article 6(2) [*12(2)*] EC] to Article 235 [*308*] EC.

15. As the Court pointed out in Case C-357/89 *Raulin v Minister van Onderwijs en Wetenschappen* [1992] ECR I-1027 ... the right to equal treatment in relation to the conditions of access to vocational training applies not only to requirements imposed by the educational establishment in question, such as registration fees, but also to any measure liable to hinder the exercise of that right. It is obvious that a student who is admitted to a course may be unable to follow it if he has no right to reside in the Member State where the course is being held. It follows that the principle of non-discrimination in relation to the conditions of access to vocational training which derive from Articles 7 and 128 EEC mean that a national of a Member State who has been admitted to a course of vocational training in another Member State enjoys the right to reside in the latter State for the duration of the course.

Further attention was paid to vocational training in the 1989 Community Charter on the Fundamental Social Rights of Workers:[89]

15. Every worker of the European Community must be able to have access to vocational training and to benefit therefrom throughout his working life. In the conditions governing access to such training there may be no discrimination on grounds of nationality.

The competent public authorities, undertakings or the two sides of industry, each within their own sphere of competence, should set up continuing and permanent training systems enabling every person to undergo retraining more especially through leave for training purposes, to improve his skills or to acquire new skills, particularly in the light of technical developments.

89 See also *Memorandum on the rationalisation and coordination of vocational training programmes at Community level,* COM (90) 334 final.

iii. Community Competence in the Field of Education after the TEU

Freedland, M. 'Vocational Training in EC Law and Policy' (1996) 25 *Industrial Law Journal* 110, 113

However, I think there was a gradual shift of balance towards the development of EC vocational training policy through educational institutions as a matter of educational policy, so that from the mid-1980s onwards we find a proliferation of EC vocational training programmes, such as the Erasmus programme, which really created a platform for EC intervention into the further and higher education systems of the Member States. This evolution towards a double-track approach to vocational training, with an education track as well as an employment policy track, was decisively confirmed by the 1992 Maastricht Treaty. On the one hand, on the employment policy front, Article 123 was amended to make it explicit that vocational training and retraining were the particular means by which the Social Fund was to facilitate adaptation to industrial changes and changes in production systems.

On the other hand, a complete new Treaty chapter was created entitled Education, Vocational Training and Youth. This conferred powers and imposed duties on the Community, which were quite distinct from those relating to the Social Fund, in respect of the development of education (Article 126) and vocational training (Article 127).

.....

The interest of Article 127 is not, however, in the enlargement of the overall competence of the Community in respect of vocational training, but in the way that it locates some of that competence in the field of education policy rather than employment policy.

Lenaerts, K. 'Education in European Community Law After 'Maastricht' (1994) 31 *Common Market Law Review* 7, 24-25

The Union Treaty has taken up both education and vocational training in the EC Treaty (in Articles 126 and 127 respectively) as two separate policy matters over which the Community exercises powers. The question of the relationship between them is of major importance, since the content of the Community powers which they delineate is not identical, and neither is the way in which those powers are exercised. The decision-making procedure with regard to education is so-called 'co-decision' (Article 189B EC), whereas that with regard to vocational training is 'cooperation' (Article 189C EC). The demarcation line between education and vocational training has been made more difficult to draw by the fact that the dynamic interpretation which the Court has given to the expression 'vocational training' in connection with Article 128 EEC has caused a great number of educational curricula to be regarded as vocational training. In the context of the *acquis communautaire* the terms 'education' and 'vocational training' are therefore no longer mutually exclusive, although not all forms of vocational training are provided in an educational context.

Now, all forms of education which were not classified as 'vocational training' and falling within Article 127 [*150*] EC will be covered by the new Article 126 [*149*] EC. This will include pre-school, primary education, general secondary education and university courses for people wishing to improve their general knowledge rather than prepare themselves for an occupation. Indeed it is arguable that Article 126 [*149*] EC has become the *lex generalis* with Article 127 [*150*] the *lex specialis*.[90] One issue is whether Article 235 [*308*] EC can still be used to give the EC competence in matters excluded from the scope of these Articles. Compare the following Resolution of the European Parliament:

Resolution A3-0139/92 of 15 May 1992 on education and training policy in the run-up to 1993, OJ 1992 C 150/366, 368, I.2

[The European Parliament] considers that the fields of action referred to in Arts. 126 and 127 are not exhaustive but are rather in the nature of examples, and that the new Treaty forms a solid basis, while respecting the areas of responsibility of the Member States and/or regions, for action in the areas referred to and in other areas in which action proves necessary, to bring about the necessary cohesion between measures to be taken in the field of education and training by the Community and in the political sphere by the Member States.

Lenaerts, K. 'Education in European Community Law After "Maastricht"' (1994) 31 *Common Market Law Review* 7

The new Articles 126 and 127 EC consolidate the *acquis communautaire* with regard to education and vocational-training policy by introducing a legally certain, constitutional basis for that policy and democratizing the relevant decision-making procedures. In

---

90 See Decision 94/819/EC OJ 1994 L 340/8 establishing an Action Programme for the Implementation of an EC Vocational Training Policy, (the 'Leonardo Decision').

addition, education has been taken out of its one-sided, economically-oriented perspective. The Community may henceforward contribute to 'the development of quality education' irrespective of the vocational aim of the education. This broader policy perspective with regard to education is supplemented in specific respects - here plainly from an economically-oriented viewpoint - by Community vocational training policy (which also relates to aspects of education which are not covered by the general Article 126).

Both provisions embody an expression of the principle of subsidiarity. In accordance therewith, the Community is to take action only 'if and so far as the objectives of the proposed action cannot be sufficiently achieved by the Member States and can therefore, by reason of the scale or effects of the proposed action, be better achieved by the Community'. The confirmation of the responsibility of the Member States (or their constituent entities) for the content of teaching, the organization of the education system (or the content and organization of vocational training) and the safeguarding of their cultural and linguistic identity boils down to the introduction of an irrebuttable presumption that they are better placed to deal with these policy matters. Community action is confined to aspects of educational and vocational-training policy which are manifestly cross-border and for which it would be difficult for each Member State to act efficiently on an individual basis. Thus, a Member State may not compel the others to exchange information cast in a particular form. The Community may simply impose such an obligation on all the Member States concurrently. Moreover, it alone is in a position to set up incentive mechanisms to entice all Member States to join in European cooperation. Where the initiative comes from one or more Member States, it does not have the same political credibility.

Some legal questions still await a clear answer. The demarcation between education and vocational training remains uncertain for some Community actions, even in the light of the principles discussed here. It is to be expected that the Court will first have to rule on a number of disputes dealing with the legal basis for measures, possibly initiated by the European Parliament, which is making a markedly greater contribution in the field of education,[91] before the demarcation line can become really clear. Also the demarcation between the Member States' protected powers and the Community's power to impose co-operation on the Member States will most probably take shape in the future case law of the Court, even if the Community decides not to impose cooperation so often, but rather to encourage it, support it and supplement it. That second issue was in fact already latent in the background to the *Erasmus* judgment, but the Court paid little heed to it because it did not hold the effect of the Community action on the Member States' educational policies to be substantial. After 'Maastricht', the Member States' powers with regard to education will in any event have to be taken *au serieux*.

---

91 *Cf.* Case C-70/88 *European Parliament v Council* [1990] ECR I-2041, [1992] 1 CMLR 91; Case C-295/90 *European Parliament v Council* [1992] ECR I-4193, [1992] 3 CMLR 281.

Lane, R. 'New Community Competences Under The Maastricht Treaty' (1993) 30 *Common Market Law Review* 939, 950-951

The Maastricht approach to vocational training, but particularly to education generally, is clearly a softly-softly approach. It is not surprising. Education is an area intimately bound to the social and public policy of each Member State. Hitherto inroads have been permitted only where there is a sufficient economic nexus to justify Community measures legitimately adopted under some other authority in the Treaty. Otherwise Community action has been considered to be beyond the reach even of Article 235. Its very recognition in the Treaty is therefore radically new and deeply controversial.

There are also practical and constitutional reasons to justify a softly-softly approach. Education is an area inevitably reserved to the regions of a federation. Whilst reference in the Maastricht Treaty to a federal Community, which might have safeguarded national sovereignty, was dropped, it is difficult to envisage how a more ambitious, or dirigiste, Community authority in the fields could co-exist with the principle of subsidiarity which is to be part of Community law. And since it falls within the exclusive competences of the lander, education is an area in which Community action could give rise to serious constitutional difficulties in Germany, which unlike the protection of fundamental rights, have yet to be confronted or resolved.

As a result, the Maastricht Treaty in the main seeks only minimal and complementary Community authority in the fields. National autonomy is meticulously safeguarded: even the very limited Community competences may be deployed only 'if necessary' and whilst fully respecting 'the responsibility of the member states', explicit tests related to but distinct from subsidiarity which extend the burden of justifying Community action beyond that generally required by Article 3b, whatever that may come to be. In the area of vocational training in its narrower, more generally accepted sense, a coherent Community-wide response may be appropriate, and this is reflected in the marginally wider powers to be assumed by the Community. It is less justified in the field of education generally. And once education is specifically recognised in the Treaty, it will be interesting to see whether the present Community law meaning of vocational training, embracing as it does so much of higher education survives.

Whatever education may come to mean, the legislative competence of the Community within the field is to be restricted to incentive measures and recommendations, and Community interest therefore limited to support and coordination of national activities and, at best, a catalyst by which the Member States might be persuaded to adopt a Community orientation - in short, what the Community does now. The new provisions will give Community policy legitimacy and direction, but even so they contain pregnant ambiguities. The 'European dimension of education' is not defined, and sounds like Orwellian Newspeak. It is difficult to quibble with the benefits of the one example cited - the teaching and dissemination of the languages of the Member States; but will that include various languages of the Member States - Scots Gaelic, Friesian, Basque, for example - which are not recognised by the Community? Will it include other languages not indigenous to the Member States but which are widely spoken in various small pockets of the Community? Is it not likely to inhibit the teaching of non-Community languages, knowledge of which national authorities may see as a priority? 'Incentive measures' may on their face appear innocuous, but experience in federations of financial support for education from the centre show that the regions with the constitutional competence can be subject to significant pressure to adopt a line they would not otherwise take. The novelty of and sensitivity attached to education will require a new deftness of touch from all Community institutions.

The Leonardo Decision[92] is regarded as a key instrument in the new EC policy towards education and vocational training. Article 3 [*3*] EC lays down a common framework of objectives for EC action. Freedland calls it 'a new constitution for EC vocational training policy in all but name'. Freedland argues that there is now a tendency to see vocational training policy as a matter of educational, rather than employment, policy. This is seen in the Leonardo Decision and also the Education White Paper.[93] He argues that important dimensions of the question, of the scope and purpose of vocational training are lost or down-played if employment policy is not given sufficient emphasis.

Freedland, M. 'Vocational Training in EC Law and Policy' (1996) 25 *Industrial Law Journal* 110, 118-119

... [this] ... leads on to a critique of the educational bias of current EC policy-making in the field of vocational training. At one level, it seems quite inappropriate to imply a criticism of the EC for concentrating on the educational dimension of vocational training. There is a respectable economic case for generally concentrating efforts and resources upon that aspect of vocational training arrangements and the educational objectives of the EC in the field of vocational training would generally be regarded as laudable and important. Moreover, one might say that it is legitimate for the EC in particular to concentrate upon that aspect if it is judged that there is greater scope for super-national development in the field of education policy than in the field of employment policy. Finally, one might think that the EC should be free to produce an educational programme and an education policy document for vocational training without having at the same time to make parallel pronouncements in the field of employment policy.

However, all that being admitted, one might nevertheless feel some concern if the pursuit of education policy for vocational training were at the expense of the development of employment policy with regard to vocational training, and in particular

---

92 Decision 94/819/EC establishing an action programme for the implementation of a European Community vocational training policy, OJ 1994 L 340/8.

93 EC Commission, *Teaching and Learning - Towards the Learning Society* (1996, OOPEC, Luxembourg).

if the need to face up to difficult choices in the field of employment policy was concealed behind a discourse which was easier and less controversial because it was developed in the field of educational policy. The effects of vocational training arrangements upon the structure of the labour market, and upon the existence and levels of labour standards, are much too important to be relegated to being the secondary outcomes of a primarily educational debate or policy-making process.

Moreover, there is real concern about what those secondary outcomes might be. That is to say, there is danger that an educational policy in favour of ever greater flexibility and adaptability in vocational training may be conducive to an over-ready endorsement of all forms and types of flexibility as a matter of employment policy. No doubt it is necessary to ensure that vocational training prepares people to be mobile and to expect a precarious and episodic employment experience. But there are worries about making a virtue of that necessity, and the discourse of education policy does tend to do precisely that.

Further Reading

Alexander, W. 'Free Movement of Non-EC Nationals: A Review of the Case Law of the Court of Justice' (1992) 3 *European Journal of International Law* 53

De Witte, B. (ed.) *European Law of Education* (1989, Nomos, Baden-Baden)

Evans, A. 'Third Country Nationals and the Treaty on European Union' (1994) 5 *European Journal of International Law* 199

Flynn, J. 'Vocational Training in Community Law and Practice' (1988) 8 *Yearbook of European Law* 59

Hennis, W. 'Access to Education in the European Communities' (1990) 3 *Leiden Journal of International Law* 35

Hervey, T. *EC Social Law* (1998, Longman, London)

Laslett, J. 'The Mutual Recognition of Diplomas, Certificates and Other Evidence of Formal Qualifications in the European Community' (1990/1) *Legal Issues of European Integration* 1

Lonbay, J. 'Education and the Law: The Community Context' (1989) 14 *European Law Review* 363

10. Social Policy

I. Legal Base/Political Will Problems

The issue of whether a social dimension was necessary for the operation of the Single Market has long been controversial. Social policy, as understood in EC law, is capable of a wide and varied definition and its boundaries are difficult to chart.[1] The provisions relating to social policy in the EC Treaty are geographically scattered and conceptually diffuse. As a result social policy could be said to embrace socio-economic rights such as the free movement of persons, provisions, human rights, citizenship rights, general principles such as the principle of non-discrimination in relation to nationality, rights to education, vocational training, public health, consumer protection as well as general programmes relating to poverty, social exclusion and racism. There is one area generically termed 'social policy', where a particular Chapter of the EEC Treaty 1957 identified a set of socio-economic rights based broadly upon labour market participation, with Article 117 EC stating that:

> Member States agree upon the need to promote improved working conditions and an improved standard of living for workers, so as to make possible their harmonisation while the improvement is being maintained.
>
> They believe that such a development will ensure not only from the functioning of the common market, which will favour the harmonisation of social systems, but also from the procedures provided for in this Treaty and from the approximation of provisions laid down by law, regulation or administrative action.

---

1 See Hervey, T. *European Social Law and Policy* (1998, Longman, Harlow); Majone, G. 'The European Community Between Social Policy and Social Regulation' (1993) 31 *JCMS* 153.

But the legal base for developing a set of substantive social policy rights was fragile, with Article 119 [*141*] EC providing the only firm legal obligation to provide equal pay for equal work. The EC was obliged to fall back upon Articles 100 [*94*], and 235 [*308*] EC to provide a legal base for the substantive provisions of EC social policy law. Both Articles required unanimity voting and had trigger mechanisms which justified their use.[2] Article 118 EC entitles the Commission to promote cooperation in the social field.

Article 118 EC. Without prejudice to the other provisions of this Treaty and in conformity with its general objectives, the Commission shall have the task of promoting close co-operation between Member States in the social field, particularly in matters relating to:

- employment;
- labour law and working conditions;
- basic and advanced vocational training;
- social security;
- prevention of occupational accidents and diseases;
- occupational hygiene; the right of association, and collective bargaining between employers and workers.

To this end, the Commission shall act in close contact with Member States by making studies, delivering opinions and arranging consultations both on problems arising at national level and on those of concern to international organisations.

Before delivering the opinions provided for in this Article, the Commission shall consult the Economic and Social Committee.

The Commission attempted to use Article 118 EC as the legal base for a Decision initiating a prior notification and consultation procedure on migration policy in respect of TCNs.

---

2 See the discussion of the development of Community social policy/labour law by Davies, P. 'The Emergence of European Labour Law' in McCarthy, W. (ed.) *Legal Intervention in Industrial Relations: Gains and Losses* (1992, Oxford, Blackwell); Sciarra, S. 'European Social Policy and Labour Law - Challenges and Perspectives', *Collected Courses of the Academy of European Law, Volume IV, Book 1,* (1995) 301-340; Addison, J. & Siebert, W. *Labour Markets in Europe* (1997, London, The Dryden Press); Nielsen, R. & Szyszczak, E. *The Social Dimension of the EU* (1997, 3rd ed., Handelshøjskolens Forlag, Copenhagen).

Joined Cases 281, 283-285, 287/85 Germany *et al.* v Commission [1987] ECR 3203

The Commission adopted Decision 85/381/EEC initiating a procedure for prior notification of, and consultation on, migration policies in respect of non-EC States. The Decision was based upon Article 118 EC with the Preamble referring to Council Resolutions of 1974 and 1976 and the fact that the harmonisation of legislation concerning foreigners had been advocated by the European Council in 1974 and 1984 and by a European Parliament Resolution in 1983. The legal base at that time allowed the Commission to promote cooperation in the social field. Five Member States lodged an application with the Court of Justice under Article 173 [*230*] EC to have the Decision declared void, as *inter alia*, the Commission lacked competence to adopt the Decision. The Court adopted two perspectives. It first rejected the view that migration policies fell entirely *outside* the scope of Article 118 EC.

14. ... whilst Article 118 of the EEC Treaty does not encroach upon the Member States' powers in the social field in so far as the latter is not covered by other provisions of the Treaty ... it nevertheless provides that those powers must be exercised in the framework of co-operation between Member States, which is to be organised by the Commission.

The second question was whether the Commission had the competence to adopt binding measures under Article 118(2) EC. The Court stipulated that where a Treaty Article conferred a specific task on the Commission, the power given to the Commission was regarded as a procedural power to establish the notification and consultation machinery leading towards the adoption of a common position on the part of the Member States. The Court accepted the Member States' contention that the Commission had exceeded its powers. The Commission had no power to determine the result to be achieved in the consultation process and it could not prevent the Member States from implementing measures which the Commission might consider to be contrary to EC policies and action. Furthermore, Article 1 of the Decision, in extending consultation to cover issues relating to the cultural integration of non-EC workers and their families exceeded the Commission's competence.[3]

---

[3] See the criticism by Simmonds, K. 'The concertation of Community migration policy' (1988) 25 *CMLRev* 177 where he argues that the reasoning of the Court 'denied perhaps the most important element of successful integration - the

An attempt was made to liberate social policy from the economic basis of the EEC Treaty 1957 by the *political* Declaration of the Heads of State or Government 1972 when it was emphasised:

> ... that vigorous action in the social sphere is ... just as important as achieving economic and monetary union.[4]

But the political commitment was weak. Despite an Action Programme linking participative democracy to the evolution of social policy very few substantive measures emerged. Many of the Commission's measures were reduced to 'soft law' or never saw the light of day.[5] The impetus for the development of social policy law has, by and large, been sustained by the interventions of the Court through a number of dramatic rulings under Article 177 [*234*] EC - the majority of the early rulings centred upon Article 119 [*141*] EC and its potential to create vertical and horizontal direct effect.

Case 43/75 Defrenne v Sabena [1976] ECR 455, [1976] 2 CMLR 98

Defrenne brought a series of test cases in the Belgian courts to test the direct effect of Article 119 [*141*] EC after intransigence on the part of the Member States to implement further national measures to secure the principle of equal pay. The question raised the issue of whether Article 119 [*141*] EC gave rise to direct effect in the national courts.

8. Article 119 pursues a double aim.

9. First, in the light of the different stages of the development of social legislation in the various Member States, the aim of Article 119 is to avoid a situation in which undertaking established in States which have actually implemented the principle of equal pay suffer

---

achievement of an inter-relationship between the two cultures in which the immigrant lives'. The Council has now passed a Resolution on the integration of resident third country nationals, OJ C 1996 80/2.

4 EC Bulletin 10-1972, para 6.

5 Nielsen, R. & Szyszczak, E. *The Social Dimension of the European Community* (1997 3rd ed, Handelshojskølens Forlag, Copenhagen), Ch. 1; Hepple, B. 'The Crisis in EEC Labour Law' (1987) 18 *ILJ* 129.

a competitive disadvantage in intra-Community competition as compared with undertakings established in States which have not yet eliminated discrimination against women workers as regards pay.

10. Secondly, this provisions forms part of the social objectives of the Community, which is not merely an economic union, but is at the same time intended, by common action, to ensure social progress and seek the constant improvement of the living and working conditions of their peoples, as is emphasised by the Preamble to the Treaty.

.....

12. This double aim, which is at once economic and social, shows that the principle of equal pay forms part of the foundations of the Community.

The impetus from this ruling led to a number of Directives on equal treatment, soft law measures, as well as the development of an infra-structure to look at equal opportunities within the Community.[6] The impact of direct effect was felt not only in strategic litigation, but, as Sciarra points out, it provoked the visibility of equal treatment and non-discrimination at the national level providing an impulse to the enforcement of effective sanctions and fertilized the ground of social policies.[7] It has also led to what Sciarra describes as a form of proceduralised law which takes advantage of the multiplicity of actors involved as well as the differentiated legal instruments to be adopted.[8]

The development of EC social policy law can be divided into a number of distinct phases:

- a period of neo-liberalism 1957-1972
- a period of social action 1972-1980
- a period of stagnation or crisis 1980-1986
- a period of optimism 1986 -1993.

---

6 See Nielsen, R. & Szyszczak, E. The Social Dimension of the European Union 1997, 3rd ed. Handelshøjskolens Forlag, Copenhagen).

7 Sciarra, S. 'European Social Policy and Labour Law - Challenges and Perspectives' in *Collected Courses of the Academy of European Law, Vol IV, Book I* (1995, Kluwer, Deventer) 301-340.

8 For a similar thesis see Bercusson, B. *European Labour Law* (1996, Butterworths, London).

It is now argued[9] that there is a fifth phase emerging after the publication of the Commission's White Paper, *European Social Policy - A Way Forward For The Union.*[10] There is now greater emphasis on involving the social partners in the decision-making process as well as a demonstrable shift away from previous efforts to *harmonise* social rights to a greater reliance upon subsidiarity, technocratic support, addressing macro-economic policy issues and the use of soft law. The Commission has chosen new priorities in the form of combating unemployment and social exclusion. These issues have found a site within the new provisions of Title XI of the Treaty of Amsterdam addressing the issues of social policy, education, vocational training and youth.

II. Development of Social Policy by the European Court of Justice

The intransigence on the part of the Member States to develop a coherent legislative policy in the social field has been tempered by the Court of Justice which has been instrumental in maintaining a role for social policy, utilising a number of legal devices.[11] It has used interpretative mechanisms as teleological tools to develop EC law. In *Defrenne v Sabena*[12] the Court stated:

> **10.** [Article 119 EC] forms part of the social objectives of the Community, which is not merely an economic union, but at the same time intended, by common action, to ensure social progress and seek the constant improvement of the living and working conditions [of the people of Europe].

---

9 See Campbell, E. & Cullen, H. 'The Future of Social Policy-Making in the European Union' in Craig, P. & Harlow, C. (eds.). *Law Making in the European Union* (1998, Round Hall Press, Sweet and Maxwell, Dublin).

10 COM (94) 333.

11 See Simitis, S. 'Dismantling or Strengthening Labour Law: The Case of the European Court of Justice' (1996) 2 *ELJ* 156; Szyszczak, E. Future Directions in European Union Social Policy Law' (1995) 24 *ILJ* 19, 31.

12 Case 43/75 *Defrenne* v *Sabena* [1976] ECR 455, [1976] 2 CMLR 98.

In *Zaera*[13] a civil servant challenged a Spanish law which prohibited him from holding a post in the public service at the same time as being in receipt of a retirement pension. The Court was asked to rule on whether Articles 2[*2*], 117, 118 EC prevented a Member State from introducing such rules.

10. Article 2 of the Treaty describes the task of the European Economic Community. The aims laid down in that provision are concerned with the existence and functioning of the Community; they are to be achieved through the establishment of the Common Market and the progressive approximation of the economic policies of the Member States, which are also aims whose implementation is the essential object of the Treaty.

11. With regard to the promotion of an accelerated raising of the standard of living, in particular, it should therefore be stated that this was one of the aims which inspired the creation of the European Economic Community and which, owing to its general terms and its systematic dependence on the establishment of the Common Market and progressive approximation of economic policies, cannot impose legal obligations on Member States or confer rights on individuals.

.....

14. The fact that the objectives of Social Policy laid down in Article 117 are in the nature of a programme does not mean that they are deprived of legal effect. They constitute an important aid, in particular for the interpretation of other provisions of the Treaty and of secondary legislation in the social field.

In *Sloman Neptun*[14] the Court of Justice went further in denying direct effect to Article 117 EC. The Court has also enhanced the role of 'soft law' as an interpretative mechanism. In *Grimaldi*[15] an Italian who migrated to France and then to Belgium where he worked *inter alia* as an underground miner asked for official recognition that he suffered from an occupational disease which had been listed in an Annex to a Commission Recommendation of 23 July 1962 on the adoption of a European schedule of occupational diseases. Belgium had not introduced

---

13 Case 126/86 *Zaera v Institution Nacionale de la Seguridad Social* [1987] ECR 3697.

14 Joined Cases C-72/91 & C-73/91 *Sloman Neptun Schiffahrts AG v Seebetriebsrat Bod Ziesemer der Sloman Schiffahrts* [1993] ECR I-887.

15 Case C-322/88 *Grimaldi v Fonds des Maladies Professionelles* [1987] ECR 4407, [1989] 1 CMLR 827.

All in all, the question is not whether a directive acquires horizontal direct effect or, to be more precise, effect with regard to third parties, as a result of a provision of international law: if a provision of international law actually takes effect as between individuals in the Community's legal system, that is on the basis of its own ambit. A directive can help to render a provision of international law more precise within the Community thereby removing a possible obstacle to the effect of that provision with regard to third parties (its lack of precision) within the Community and in a given sphere.

.....

Ultimately it is for the Member States to determine, on their own responsibility (sanctioned by international law), how to comply with their obligations under Treaties. In connection with European Convention, to which the Court attaches particular importance for the interpretation of the fundamental rights forming part of Community law, that would seem to imply that it is for the Court, by way of a uniform interpretation valid throughout the Community.

Case 24/86 Blaizot v University of Liège [1988] ECR 379, [1989] 1 CMLR 57

A challenge was made to the discriminatory fees charged by the Belgian authorities. The issue arose as to whether university education could be considered 'vocational training' thus bringing it within the scope of the equal treatment principle of Community law.

17. It should be added that Article 10 of the European Social Charter, to which most of the Member States are contracting parties, treats university education as a type of vocational training.

Case 222/84 Johnston v Chief Constable of the RUC [1986] ECR 1651, 3 CMLR 240

A challenge was made to the policy of the Chief Constable of the RUC not to allow female officers of the RUC to carry hand guns. It was argued that this policy was contrary to the Equal Treatment Directive 76/207/EEC but it was not possible to challenge the policy by judicial means in Northern Ireland. The Court elevated the principle of effective judicial protection into one of the general principles of Community law invoking the European Convention on Human Rights and the Joint Declaration of the respect for fundamental human rights issued by the Institutions in 1977 to confirm the significance of this right.

8. The requirement of judicial control stipulated by [Article 6 of Council Directive 76/207/EEC] reflects a general principle of law which underlies the constitutional traditions common to the Member States. That principle is also laid down in Articles 6 and 13 of the European Convention for the Protection of Human Rights and Fundamental Freedoms of 4 November 1950. As the European Parliament, Council and Commission recognised in their Joint Declaration of 5 April 1977 (OJ C 103/1) and as the Court has recognised in its decisions, the principles on which that Convention is based must be taken into consideration in Community law.

.....

38. It must also be borne in mind that, in determining the scope of any derogation from an individual right such as equal treatment of men and women provided for by the directive, the principle of proportionality, one of the general principles of law underlying the Community legal order, must be observed.

III. The Single European Act 1986

The stagnation of social policy law during the eighties focused academic and political debate on the urgency to create a 'social Europe' in the framework of the plans for an Internal Market. Yet surprisingly the 1985 Commission White Paper paid minimal attention to these issues. Discussions did take place as to whether a social dimension to the Internal Market was necessary but the final outcome was rather limited. A number of changes were made to the social policy law provisions of the Treaty by the SEA. Qualified majority voting was introduced for social policy areas involved in the working environment in relation to the health and safety of workers. Initially it was hoped that the Commission would take a wide view of the term 'working environment' especially as it was capable of a broad meaning within the Nordic tradition of labour law.[18]

Article 118a(1) EC. Member States shall pay particular attention to encouraging improvements, especially in the working environment, as regards the health and safety of workers, and shall set as their objective the harmonisation of conditions in this area, while maintaining the improvements made.

---

18 See Nielsen, R. & Szyszczak, E. *The Social Dimension of the European Community* (1991, Handelshøjskolens Forlag, Copenhagen) 24.

2. In order to help achieve the objective laid down in the first paragraph, the Council, [acting in accordance with the procedure referred to in Article 189c and after consulting the Economic and Social Committee, shall adopt by means of directives, minimum requirements for gradual implementation, having regard to the conditions and technical rules obtaining in each of the Member States.

Such directives shall avoid imposing administrative, financial and legal constraints in a way which would hold back the creation and development of small and medium-sized undertakings.

3. The provisions adopted pursuant to this Article shall not prevent any Member State from maintaining or introducing more stringent measures for the protection of working conditions compatible with this Treaty.

Article 118a EC has been used by the Commission in a cautious manner in the field of health and safety at work measures. A framework directive[19] has spawned a number of directives on specific risks and some tentative attempts have been made to cover conditions at work such as Directive 91/383/EEC[20] and Directive 92/85/EEC.[21] But one of the most controversial measures concerning aspects of working time[22] faced a challenge in the Court of Justice by the United Kingdom. Advocate General Léger delivered an Opinion in March 1996 where he gave a broad interpretation to Article 118a EC.

Case C-84/94 United Kingdom v Council [1996] ECR I-5755

The United Kingdom brought an action under Article 173 [*230*] EC for the annulment of the whole of Directive 93/104/EEC[23] concerning aspects of the organisation of working time[24] and alternatively for the annulment of Articles 4,

---

19 Directive 89/391/EEC, on the introduction of measures to encourage improvements in the safety and health of workers at work, OJ 1989 L 183/1.

20 Supplementing the measures to encourage improvements in the safety and health at work of workers with a fixed-duration employment relationship or a temporary employment relationship, Directive 91/383/EEC, OJ 1991 L 206/19.

21 On the introduction of measures to encourage improvements in the safety and health at work of pregnant workers and workers who have recently given birth or are breast-feeding, Directive 92/85/EEC, OJ 1992 L 348/1.

22 Directive 93/104/EC, OJ 1993 L 307/18.

23 OJ 1993 L 307/18.

24 OJ 1993 L 307/18.

5 (first and second sentences), 6(2) and 7 on the grounds of lack of competence, defective legal base, breach of the principle of proportionality, misuse of powers and infringement of essential procedural requirements.

Advocate General Léger

42. Confirmation of the view favouring a broad interpretation of [the concept of the working environment] may be found in the origin of Article 118a, namely in a proposal made by the Kingdom of Denmark at the Intergovernmental Conference on the Single Act. The concept of 'working environment' (arbejdsmilfo) in Danish law is a very broad one, covering the performance of work and conditions at the workplace, as well as technical equipment and the substances and materials used. ... The concept of the 'working environment' is not immutable, but reflects the social and technical evolution of society.

.....

44. Ultimately, the only limits on the definition of the concept of 'working environment' which I have proposed are to be found in the term *workers*, which it underlies. That rules out the possibility of using Article 118a as a basis for a measure whose subject-matter is the safety and health of the population *in general*, perhaps by reference to a risk which is not peculiar to workers.[[25]]

The Court

11. The applicant observes ... that, because Article 118a of the Treaty must be regarded as an exception to Article 100 - which, pursuant to Article 100a(2), is the Article that covers provisions 'relating to the rights and interests of employed persons' - it must be interpreted strictly.

12. As the Court pointed out in Opinion 2/91 of 19 March 1993 [1993] ECR I-1061, paragraph 17), Article 118a confers upon the Community internal legislative competence in the area of social policy. The existence of other provisions in the treaty does not have the effect of restricting the scope of Article 118a. Appearing as it does in the chapter of the Treaty which deals with 'Social Provisions', Article 118a relates only to measures concerning the protection of the health and safety of workers. It therefore constitutes a more specific rule than Articles 100 and 100a. That interpretation is confirmed by the actual wording of Article 100a(1) itself, which states that its provisions are to apply 'save where otherwise provided in this Treaty'. The applicant's argument cannot therefore be accepted.

---

[25] The possibility cannot be ruled out, however, that '... taking measures to protect the health and safety of workers at work also helps, in certain cases, to preserve the health and possibly the safety of persons residing with them', according to the wording of the eighth recital in the preamble to the framework directive.

.....

15. There is nothing in the wording of Article 118a to indicate that the concepts of 'working environment', 'safety' and 'health' as used in that provision should, in the absence of other indications, be interpreted restrictively, and not as embracing all factors, physical or otherwise, capable of affecting the health and safety of the worker in his working environment, including in particular certain aspects of the organization of working time. On the contrary, the words 'especially in the working environment' militate in favour of a broad interpretation of the powers which Article 118a confers upon the Council for the protection of the health and safety of workers. Moreover, such an interpretation of the words 'safety' and 'health' derives support in particular from the preamble to the Constitution of the World Health Organization to which all the member states belong. Health is there defined as a state of complete physical, mental and social well-being that does not consist only in the absence of illness or infirmity.

The case confirms the *lex specialis* of Article 118a EC and has opened the way for the development of more social policy measures to be developed without being subordinated to pure economic considerations. Whether this will lead to a more proactive approach and use of Article 118a EC remains to be seen since the use of macro-economic policy tools in the Treaty of Amsterdam may dilute the emphasis on 'social citizenship' rights.[26] The Commission regards the number of exclusions from the Working Time Directive to be unacceptable and has indicated that these will be tackled in a further Directive. Attempts to introduce a more ambitious role for collective bargaining in the social policy legislative process were watered down completely finding their expression in the rather vague clause of Article 118b EC.[27]

Article 118b EC. The Commission shall endeavour to develop the dialogue between management and labour at European level which could, if the two sides consider it desirable, lead to relations based on agreement.

---

26 *Cf.* Fitzpatrick, B. 'Straining the Definition of Health and Safety' (1997) 26 *ILJ* 115; Shaw, J. 'The Many Pasts and Futures of Citizenship' (1997) 22 *ELRev* 554.

27 See Nielsen, R. & Szyszczak, E. *The Social Dimension of the European Union* (1997, 3rd ed. Handelshøjskolens Forlag, Copenhagen) 33-34.

This vague measure was overtaken by the social dialogue in the Social Policy Agreement annexed to the EC Treaty by the TEU and now incorporated into the main body of EC law by the Treaty of Amsterdam.[28]

The new 'Internal Market' legal base of Article 100a [*95*] EC was problematic. The way forward of using qualified majority voting was thwarted by Article 100a(2) [*95(2)*] which seemed to consign labour law/labour market issues to an unanimous vote. There was controversy as to whether it is possible to use Article 100a(1) [*95(a)1*] EC as a legal base for social policy law. In particular how does one distinguish between labour market measures which have as their object the establishment and functioning of the Internal Market and measures whose primary object relates to the rights and interests of employed persons?[29] The role of the European Parliament under Article 189b [*251*] EC is also of interest - it may have prerogatives it wants to protect.

In 1989 eleven of the then twelve Member States (the United Kingdom abstained) signed the Community Charter of Fundamental Social Rights of Workers.[30] Although this did not change the legal base on which social policy law measures could be enacted the Commission drew up an Action Programme which revitalised social policy legislation for a brief time in the early 1990s[31] and provided a framework for future measures.

---

28 For a discussion of the social dialogue at the EC level see EC Commission, *Communication on the Development of the Social Dialogue at Community Level* COM (960) 448 final.

29 See Vogel-Polsky, E. 'What Future Is There For a Social Europe Following the Strasbourg Summit?' (1990) 19 *ILJ* 65.

30 COM (92) 562 final. The recognition of fundamental social rights is now recognised in the revised Preamble to the Treaty on European Union made by the Treaty of Amsterdam.

31 COM (89) 568 final.

IV. The Treaty on European Union

i. The Social Policy Protocol and Agreement

An attempt was made to introduce a new chapter on social policy into the EC Treaty at the Intergovernmental Conference held in Maastricht in 1991. The idea was to turn more areas of social policy legislation over to qualified majority voting with greater involvement of the European Parliament and the alternative use of Europe-wide collective agreements to replace Commission proposals for legislation. The United Kingdom held out against any further competence being granted to the EC in social policy matters. At the eleventh hour, when it was clear that the United Kingdom would not make any further concessions, the Heads of State or Government agreed to a Protocol annexed to the EC Treaty which allowed the eleven Member States to use a Social Policy Agreement (SPA) annexed to the Protocol when agreement could not be reached by the twelve Member States in the Council of Ministers. This was a novel and unusual way to handle the political impasse which had put a brake upon the development of social policy law in the past, but in so doing attracted much critical comment.[32] A wider legal base for social policy measures was created in Article 2(2) of the SPA allowing for qualified majority voting to take place. In addition a greater role for the social partners was created by allowing them to consider making a European-wide collective agreement to take the place of Community legislation.[33] In fact the 'opt-out' did not generate much legislation and turned out to be more of a 'mopping up' exercise to clear the backlog of proposals lying around since the 1980s rather than presenting a new dynamic to social policy thinking. At the time of writing only two proposals have passed through the new framework. The first was a Directive on Works Councils[34] - adopted after negotiations with the social partners quickly broke down. The second measure was a Directive on parental leave -

32 See Curtin, D. 'The Constitutional Structure of the Union: A Europe of Bits and Pieces' (1993) 30 *CMLRev* 17.

33 Article 4 SPA.

34 Directive 94/45/EC, OJ 1994 L 254/64.

negotiated as a Community wide agreement between the social partners but amended in its final form by the Council of Ministers and issued as a Directive.[35] On 15 December 1997 the Council adopted a Directive on a framework agreement on part-time work concluded by the pan European industrial and labour organisations, UNICE, CEEP and ETUC, and a Directive on the burden of proof in cases of discrimination based on sex.[36] A Directive on sexual harassment at work is also being discussed in the Council after the social partners decided not to pursue a collective agreement.

ii. New Social Policy Measures in the EC Treaty

As a result of the Social Policy Agreement the rump of social policy measures introduced by the TEU created a set of *ad hoc* measures. A new Part Two of the EC Treaty created the concept of 'Citizenship of the Union' (Article 8[*17*]). Part Three, Title VIII was renamed 'Social Policy, Education, Vocational Training and Youth'. Articles 117-122 EC remained the same with Article 123 [*146*] EC extending the scope of the Social Fund to facilitate the 'adaptation (of workers) to industrial changes and to changes in production systems, in particular through vocational training and re-training'. New Articles 126-127 [*149-150*] EC related to 'Education, Vocational Training and Youth' with Article 128 [*151*] EC a separate Title on Culture. In addition, there were some new 'mission statements', for example, in the Preamble to the TEU the High Contracting Parties indicate their determination:

> to promote economic and social progress for their peoples, within the context of the accomplishment of the internal market and of reinforced cohesion and environmental protection, and to implement policies ensuring that advances in economic integration are accompanied by parallel progress in other fields.

---

35 Directive 96/34/EC, OJ 1996 L 145/4.

36 Directive 97/80/EC, OJ 1998 L 14/6; Directive 97/81/EC, OJ 1998 L 14/9.

One of the aims of the Union outlined in Article B [*2*] TEU was:

> ... to promote economic and social progress which is balanced and sustainable, in particular through the creation of an area without internal frontiers, through the strengthening of economic and social cohesion and through the establishment of economic and monetary union. ...

iii. Economic and Social Cohesion

Articles 130a-e EC [*158-162*] were introduced by the SEA. Economic and social cohesion was identified by the Commission as one of the six priority areas in the completion of the Internal Market.[37] The Structural Funds (the European Regional Development Fund and the European Social Fund and the Guidance Section of FEOGA) and the European Investment Bank have been used to support economic and social cohesion. Cohesion is necessary to fulfil the principal objective of the EC Treaty: economic and monetary union. Thus the EC Treaty strengthened the importance of such cohesion in Article 3(j) [3*k*] and Article 2 [*2*] and provided a new Chapter XIV, Articles 130a-e [*158-162*]. The essential policy and its implementation remain the same: to promote overall harmonious development and to reduce disparities amongst the various regions of the EC through the structural funds and the application of the principle of additionality in the conduct and coordination of national economic policies. The EC Treaty provided the Council with the authority to adopt, after due consultation, necessary action outside the structural funds (Article 130b [*159*]) and to create Cohesion Fund to contribute to projects in the fields of environment and trans-European networks on transport infrastructure (Article 130d [*161*]).[38] Article 130b [*159*] also stipulates that the formulation and implementation of policies and activities of the Internal Market must take into account, and contribute to the achievement of, the policy objectives of economic and social cohesion.

---

37 *EC Commission, The Single Act: A New Frontier for Europe* COM (87) 100.

38 Regulation 1164/94/EC, OJ 1994 L 130/1.

Lane, R. 'New Community Competences Under The Maastricht Treaty' (1993) 30 *Common Market Law Review* 939, 962-963

The simple question then remains whether this will provide the yawning economic disparity within the Community with anything more than sticking plaster. Notwithstanding the doubling of expenditure under the structural funds, according to the Commission[39] support for economic and social cohesion will require commitment appropriations of ECU 11 thousand million by 1997. *That* will require not only significant reform of the compulsory component of the Community budget ... so as to free resources for non-compulsory expenditure, but also from the Member States the economic wherewithal and the political will to provide it. The Delors II package was welcomed, at least in some quarters, with great wailing and gnashing of teeth. Nevertheless, the European Council at Edinburgh agreed upon an average increase in resources for the Structural Funds of ECU 1.5 thousand million per year and a commitment to the Cohesion Fund of just over ECU 15 thousand million to the end of the year 1999. Whether this will be enough in the light of the fissures which appeared in the Exchange Rate mechanism in September 1992 and its more comprehensive collapse in August 1993, the unforeseen costs of German reunification and the Community contribution to the restructuring of Eastern Europe remains to be seen.

Shaw, J. 'Twin-Track Social Europe - The Inside Track' in O'Keeffe, D. & Twomey, P. (eds.) *Legal Issues of the Maastricht Treaty* (1994, London, Chancery) 295, 305

Economic and social cohesion

The Community's principal redistributive policies hide modestly behind a piece of 'Euro-jargon' - *economic and social cohesion.* This is the forgotten face of Community Social Policy, where the Member States have found it easier to reach a consensus than in respect of the harmonization programme which involves a more obvious invasion of national interests and national sovereignty and often requires the import of 'foreign' provisions into the domestic legal system. Social policy of this nature is also intended to be enabling and facilitative *vis à vis* its beneficiaries, rather than restrictive and regulatory, as social policy harmonization measures can sometimes be characterized. Thus although these policies do involve governmental intervention in the market place in order to mitigate some of the harsher effects of the free market, they are not treated with the same suspicion as policies based on harmonization by the Member States. It is conventional wisdom that some of the Member States who were sceptical of the ability of pure market-led growth alone to regenerate the fortunes of the western European economy were signed up to support the

---

39 From the Single Act to Maastricht and Beyond: The Means To Match Our Ambitions (the '*Delors II Package*') COM (92) 200.

internal market project on the promise of a reorientation of the Community's financial commitments in favour of the structural policies.

V. Social Policy after the Treaty of Amsterdam

The Treaty of Amsterdam inserts a new recital into the Preamble to the Treaty on European Union confirming the Member States' attachment to fundamental social rights as defined in the European Social Charter 1961 and the Community Charter of the Fundamental Social Rights of Workers 1989. A revised *Article 2 TEU* adds '*... and a high level of employment*' to the list of aims of the Union. An amended *Article 2 EC* now includes equality between men and women as one of the purposes of the Community and employment and social protection are moved from fourth place to second place in the list of purposes. Competitiveness has also joined convergence in *Article 2 EC*. The new indent to *Article 3 EC* sets up a co-ordinated employment strategy as an activity of the Community, the constituent elements of which are to be found in the new Title VIII to the amended Treaty. There is also a new legal base introduced in *Article 13* EC which reads:

> *Without prejudice to the other provisions of this Treaty and within the limits of the powers conferred by it upon the Community, the Council, acting unanimously on a proposal from the Commission and after consulting the European Parliament, may take appropriate action to combat discrimination based on sex, racial or ethnic origin, religion or belief, disability, age or sexual orientation.*

In addition there is a Declaration to the Final Act regarding persons with a disability in that it is agreed that in drawing up harmonisation measures under *Article 95 EC* the Institutions of the Community shall take account of the needs of persons with a disability. These measures are in some way a disappointment since, initially, it was hoped that a new general non-discrimination clause would be inserted into the Treaty fulfilling a role similar to that performed by Article 6 [*12*] EC banning discrimination on grounds of nationality. Given the uneven development of these forms of non-discrimination legislation across the EU it is likely that different bargaining strengths together with some indifference upon the part of some Member States will make the development of new forms of anti-discrimination legislation protracted, piecemeal and uneven.[40]

i. Integration of the Social Policy Agreement into the EC Treaty

The election of a new labour administration in the United Kingdom on 1 May 1997 allowed for the re-integration of social policy into the fold of EC competence. Articles 117-120 EC are re-written so as to integrate the Social Policy Agreement annexed to the EC Treaty by the Social Policy Protocol into the main body of the EC Treaty. Once the Treaty of Amsterdam is in force the principal legal base for social policy law relating to labour law issues will be *Article 137 EC*. *Article 137(2) EC* provides for the use of *qualified majority* voting in the Council using the codecision procedure in the following areas:

- improvement in particular of the working environment to protect workers' health and safety;
- working conditions;
- the information and consultation of workers;
- the integration of persons excluded from the labour market, without prejudice to the vocational training procedures in Article *150 EC*;
- equality between men and women with regard to labour market opportunities and treatment at work

Any Directives adopted must be aimed at imposing minimum requirements which are in tune with the Members States' conditions and technical rules and must avoid imposing administrative, financial and legal constraints in a way which would hold back the creation and development of small and medium-sized undertakings. Using the same

---

40 See Szyszczak, E. 'Building a European Constitutional Order: Prospects For a General Non-discrimination Standard' in Dashwood, A. & O'Leary, S. (eds.) *The Principle of Equal Treatment in EC Law* (1997, Sweet and Maxwell, London).

procedure the Council may also adopt measures designed to encourage cooperation between Member States through initiatives aimed at improving knowledge, developing exchanges of information and best practices promoting innovative approaches and evaluating experiences in order to combat social exclusion. Under the new *Article 137(3) EC* the Council, using a *unanimous* vote, may adopt Directives in the following areas:

- social security and social protection of workers;
- protection of workers where their employment contract is terminated;
- representation and collective defence of the interests of workers and employers, including co-determination;
- conditions of employment for third-country nationals legally residing in Community territory;
- financial contributions for promotion of employment and job-creation, without prejudice to the provisions relating to the Social Fund.

Article 137(6) EC excludes pay, the right of association, the right to strike and the right to impose lock-outs from the ambit of the new legal base. Despite this, for the first time since the inception of the Community there is now a firm legal base with clearly defined boundaries and procedures for introducing social policy law measures into Community competence. New *Articles 138 and 139 EC* confirm the importance of bolstering collective bargaining at the European level and repeat the provisions of Article 4 of the SPA allowing Community proposals to be implemented by means of collective agreements. At the Amsterdam Summit the British Prime Minister Blair gave the go ahead for the two proposals which had passed through the SPA, the Works Council Directive and the Parental Leave Directive to apply to the United Kingdom. The Commission re-issued the two Directives using Article 100 [*94*] EC as the legal base for the measures to apply to the fifteen Member States.[41] The two Directives were adopted without discussion at the Council meeting of 15 December 1997.[42] The Treaty of Amsterdam has used the re-integration of the SPA into the main body of the Treaty as the opportunity to consolidate the Court's case law by

41 COM (97) 387 final.

42 Directive 97/74/EC, OJ 1998 L 10/22; Directive 97/76/EC, OJ 1998 L 10/24.

introducing the concept of equal pay for work of equal value as well as equal work.

Article 141(1) EC. *Each Member State shall ensure that the principle of equal pay for male and female workers for equal work or work of equal value is applied.*

2. *For the purpose of this Article, 'pay' means the ordinary basic or minimum wage or salary and any other consideration, whether in cash or in kind, which the worker receives directly or indirectly, in respect of his employment, from his employer.*

Equal Pay without discrimination based on sex means:

(a) that pay for the same work at piece rates shall be calculated on the basis of the same unit of measurement.

(b) that pay for work at time rates shall be the same for the same job.

3. *The Council, acting in accordance with the procedure referred to in Article 251, and after consulting the Economic and Social Committee, shall adopt measures to ensure the application of the principle of equal opportunities and equal treatment of men and women in matters of employment and occupation, including the principle of equal pay for equal work or work of equal value.*

4. *With a view to ensuring full equality in practice between men and women in working life, the principle of equal treatment shall not prevent any Member State from maintaining or adopting measures providing for specific advantages in order to make it easier for the under-represented sex to pursue a vocational activity or to prevent or compensate for disadvantages in professional careers.*

Article 141(4) must be read with Article 2(4) of the Equal Treatment Directive[43] which allows Member States to take measures 'to promote equal opportunity for men and women, in particular by removing existing qualities ...' The Court of Justice has interpreted this provision in a restrictive way[44] in that any positive action measures must be of a specific rather than a general nature applying to areas where existing inequalities are shown to exist. In *Kalanke* the Court went further and stated that a tie-break rule which automatically gave

---

43 Directive 76/207/EEC, OJ 1976 L 39/40.

44 Case 312/86 *Commission v France* [1988] ECR 6315, [1989] 3 CMLR 359.

preference to the under-represented sex was incompatible with Article 2(4).

Case C-450/93 Kalanke v Freie Hansestadt Bremen [1995] ECR I-3051

A male candidate for a public sector post was turned down in favour of a female candidate when a 'soft' form of positive action scheme was applied. The Bremen Law on Equal Treatment for Men and Women in the Public Service 1990 applied a tie-break rule where two candidates were equally qualified for a post and there was an under-representation of one sex (less than fifty per cent) then the member of the under-represented sex should be appointed. Kalanke challenged the positive action measure as being contrary to Article 2(1) and 2(4) of the Equal Treatment Directive 76/207/EEC.

16. A national rule that, where men and women who are candidates for the same promotion are equally qualified, women are automatically to be given priority in sectors where they are under-represented, involves discrimination on grounds of sex.

.....

22. National rules which guarantee women absolute and unconditional priority for appointment or promotion go beyond promoting equal opportunities and overstep the limits of the exception in Article 2(4) of the Directive.

In response the Commission issued a Communication[45] proposing an amendment of Article 2(4) together with guidelines as to what forms of positive action were permissible.[46]

In *Marschall* Advocate General Jacobs drew upon the *Kalanke* judgment as authority to support the argument that positive action measures which sought to impose *equality of representation* rather than to promote *equality of opportunity* were contrary to the Equal Treatment Directive. The Advocate General took the view that the Court should not

---

45 COM (96) 88.

46 See Szyszczak, E. 'Positive Action After Kalanke' (1996) 59 *MLR* 876; Schiek, D. 'Positive Action in Community Law' (1996) 25 *ILJ* 239; Peters, A. 'The Many Meanings of Equality and Positive Action in Favour of Women Under EC Law - A Conceptual Analysis' (1996) 2 *ELJ* 177.

usurp the role of the legislature in tailoring policy and that it was the role of the legislature to review out of date social legislation - not the courts. He argued that:

32. It is axiomatic that there is no equal opportunity for men and women in an individual case if, where all else is equal, one is appointed or promoted in preference to the other solely by virtue of his or her sex.

The Court took a more nuanced approach.

Case C-409/95 Marschall v Land Nordrhein-Westfalen, Judgment of 11 November 1997

Marschall applied for a promotion at a comprehensive school in Germany. The District Authority informed him that it intended to appoint a female candidate to the position. Marschall lodged a complaint on the ground that both candidates were equally qualified but that the woman candidate had been appointed using a positive action measure contained in Paragraph 25(5) of the Law on Civil Servants of the Land 1981 which provided that where there were fewer women than men in the particular higher grade post in the career bracket, women are to be given priority for promotion in the event of equal suitability, competence and professional performance, unless reasons specific to an individual male candidate tilt the balance in his favour.

5. In providing that priority is to be given to the promotion of women 'unless reasons specific to an individual [male] candidate tilt the balance in his favour', the legislature deliberately chose, according to the *land*, a legally imprecise expression in order to ensure sufficient flexibility and, in particular, to allow the administration latitude to take into account any reasons which may be specific to individual candidates. Consequently, notwithstanding the rule of priority, the administration can always give preference to a male candidate on the basis of promotion criteria, traditional or otherwise.

.....

15. The *Land* observes ... that the priority accorded to female candidates is intended to counteract traditional promotion criteria without, however, replacing them. The Austrian Government considers that a national rule such as that in question is designed to correct discriminatory procedures in the selection of staff.

16. The Finnish, Swedish and Norwegian Governments add that the national rule in question promotes access by women to posts of responsibility and thus helps to restore balance to labour markets which, in their present state, are still broadly partitioned on the basis of gender in that they concentrate female labour in lower positions in the occupational hierarchy. According to the Finnish Government, past experience shows in particular that action limited to providing occupational training and guidance for women or to influence the sharing of occupational and family responsibilities is not sufficient to put an end to this partioning of labour markets.

17. Finally the *Land* and all those governments take the view that the provision in question does not guarantee absolute and unconditional priority for women and that it is therefore within the limits outlined by the Court in *Kalanke.*

.....

21. The Court observes that the purpose of the Directive, as is clear from Article 1(1), is to put into effect in the Member States the principle of equal treatment for men and women as regards, *inter alia*, access to employment, including promotion. Article 2(1) states that the principle of equal treatment means that 'there shall be no discrimination whatsoever on grounds of sex either directly or indirectly'.

22. According to Article 2(4), the Directive is to 'be without prejudice to measures to promote equal opportunity for men and women, in particular by removing existing inequalities which affect women's opportunities in the areas referred to in Article 1(1)'.

23. In paragraph 16 of its judgment in *Kalanke*, the Court held that a national rule which provides that, where equally qualified men and women are candidates for the same promotion in fields where there are fewer women than men at the level of the relevant post, women are automatically to be given priority, involves discrimination on grounds of sex.

24. However, unlike the provisions in question in *Kalanke*, the provision in question in this case contains a clause ('Öffnungsklausel', hereinafter 'saving clause') to the effect that women are not to be given priority in promotion if reasons specific to an individual male candidate tilt the balance in his favour.

25. It is therefore necessary to consider whether a national rule containing such a clause is designed to promote equality of opportunity between men and women within the meaning of Article 2(4) of the Directive.

26. Article 2(4) is specifically and exclusively designed to authorize measures which, although discriminatory in appearance, are in fact intended to eliminate or reduce actual instances of inequality which may exist in the reality of social life (Case 312/86 *Commission v France* [1988] ECR 6315, and *Kalanke*, paragraph 18.

ii. A New Title on Employment

A far-reaching change made by the Treaty of Amsterdam is the acceptance of Community responsibility for the co-ordination of macro-economic policy vis á vis national labour markets. *Article 125* EC charges the Member States *and the Community* with the task of working towards developing a coordinated strategy for employment, in particular for promoting a skilled, trained adaptable workforce and labour markets which are responsive to economic change which achieve the objectives set out in *Article 2 EC* and *Article 2 TEU. Article 126 (2) EC* makes the task of promoting employment[47] a matter of common concern - with the proviso that national practices related to the responsibilities of management and labour should be taken into account. The first paragraph of *Article 126 EC* makes clear the marriage between employment policies and economic policies.

Article 126(1) EC. *Member States, through their employment policies, shall contribute to the achievement of the objectives referred to in Article 125 in a way consistent with the broad guidelines of the economic policies of the Member States adopted pursuant to Article 99(2).*

2. Member States, having regard to national practices related to the responsibilities of management and labour, shall regard promoting employment as a matter of common concern and shall coordinate their action in this respect within the Council, in accordance with the provisions of Article 128.

With unemployment standing at an 'official' figure of 18 million the Heads of State or Government moved fast. An extraordinary European Council Meeting was held in Luxembourg on 20 - 21 November 1997 and an action plan on unemployment outlined.[48] By June 1998 the Member States are to draw up a national employment action

---

47 *Cf. Article 127 EC* where the objective of a 'high level of employment' is seen as a Community task - and an objective which must be taken into consideration in the formulation and implementation of Community policies and activities.

48 (1998) 288 *EIRR* 35.

plan based upon Union-wide employment guidelines, and present it to the Council. After assessment of each Member State recommendations will be made in order to achieve convergence on unemployment targets. What worked for EMU is deemed appropriate to deal with unemployment.

Employment will be placed firmly upon the Council agenda by virtue of *Article 128 EC.* Each year the European Council shall consider the employment situation in the Community and adopt conclusions on the basis of a joint annual report by the Council and the Commission. On the basis of these conclusions the Council, acting by a qualified majority on a proposal from the Commission, and after consulting the European Parliament, the Economic and Social Committee, the Committee of the Regions and the new Employment Committee, established under *Article 130 EC*, shall draw up guidelines which the Member States shall take into account in their employment policies. Such guidelines must be consistent with the broad economic guidelines adopted in the field of economic and monetary policy under *Article 99(2) EC.* The Member States are to be monitored by presenting an annual report to the Council and the Commission which will provide for review the principal measures taken by the Member State to implement the employment guidelines.

The most far-reaching measures, however, are to be found in *Article 128(4)* EC which allows the Council to act by qualified majority on a recommendation from the Commission, to make recommendations to a Member State on how to conduct its employment policy. After the examination process the Council and the Commission shall make a joint annual report to the European Council on the employment situation in the Community and on the implementation of the guidelines for employment.

Article 130 EC allows the Council to establish an Employment Committee (after consulting the European Parliament). The Committee will be composed of two representatives appointed by each Member State and the Commission. The role of this Committee seems to be purely advisory relating to the task of promoting coordination between Member States on employment and labour market policies.[49] The new

---

[49] *Article 130 EC* states that the Committee's tasks will be to monitor the employment situation and employment policies in the Member States and the Community and, without prejudice to the powers of COREPER, to formulate opinions at the request of either the Council or the Commission, *or on its own*

Employment Committee of Amsterdam was suggested by Sweden and is intended to be a counter-balance to the Economic and Financial Committee established by the TEU (Article 109c(2) [*114*]).

Employment policy was a bone of contention in relation to the incentive measures which implied expenditure[50] and a Declaration was inserted reiterating the principle of subsidiarity in the field of employment policy. The accentuation of employment as part of the EU's economic policy brings into play the role of ECOFIN - the Council of economic and finance ministers in guiding the economic policies of the Member States under the third stage of EMU.[51] The implications for employment policy concern the fact that ECOFIN will be responsible for the multilateral surveillance of the economic performance of the Member States and that ECOFIN can make policy recommendations to individual governments by qualified majority voting.

VI. The Future Direction of Social Policy

The consolidation of labour law and social policies in the Amsterdam Treaty, as well as developing new priorities and mission statements, serves to underline the fragmentary approach to social policy adopted by the Community. The tensions of the multi-layered decision-making process of EU social policy law have played an important contribution in

---

initiative, and to contribute to the Council meetings referred to in *Article 128 EC.*

50 Article 109r [*129*] EC. Extra funding for the new employment measures will be available through the European Investment Bank which has pledged ECU 10 billion, available for small businesses, new technology, new sectors and trans-European networks. The Council and the Parliament have agreed a new budget heading *(European Employment Initiative*) to which funds will be allocated to finance employment creation in small and medium-sized businesses. A total of ECU 450 million will be allocated to this heading over the next three years. For the Commission's position see EC Commission, *Modernising and Improving Social Policy in the European Union* COM (97) 102 final.

51 Article 103 [*99*] EC.

the development of the EU's fragmentary approach.[52] Grahl and Teague argue that the European social model (which they understand to be a specific combination of comprehensive welfare systems and strongly institutionalised and politicised forms of industrial relations) is in serious crisis as a result of general economic developments which have undermined the European social model's functionality. An important index as to whether influential political forces will be able to modernise the European social model will be the strength and progress of European integration.[53] Streeck has argued that social policy in an integrated Europe can only be understood if we disassociate ourselves from looking at social policy as part of a steadily evolving welfare state to analysing the function played by social policy in the political process of European integration.

Streeck, W. 'Neo-Voluntarism: A New European Social Policy Regime?' (1995) 1 *European Law Journal* 1, 31

... social policy in integrated Europe can be understood only if one dissociates oneself radically from the received image of a slowly but steadily evolving European federal welfare state. That image is responsible for the weaknesses of most previous analyses of the subject, which tended to interpret the results and non-results of Community, or now Union, social policy in terms of steps taken, or not yet taken, towards a supranational welfare state that was to perform basically the same function as its national predecessors, for integrated Europe as a whole, and that would gradually penetrate and absorb the national systems that had preceded it. Taking the end point for granted, the assumption that integration could lead only to replication of the familiar on a larger scale resulted in the typical discussions on the 'social dimension' of integrated Europe, which were essentially about the question of whether the glass was already half full or still half empty. The answer depended on individual points of view, the interests one felt sympathetic with, and how patient one was willing to be. Throughout, however, given that the Community's 'really existing' social policy seemed so little in comparison to what it was supposed to become, it was discussed much more in terms of what it was not, or not yet, rather than what it was - which largely explains the analytical shallowness and the normative-declaratory tone of most of the debate.

---

52 Leibfried, S. & Pierson, P. (eds.) *European Social Policy. Between Fragmentation and Integration* (1995, Brookings Institute, Washington DC).

53 Grahl, J. & Teague, P. 'Is the European Social Model Fragmenting?' (1997) 2 *New Political Economy* 405.

Overcoming this requires taking account of the basic institutional properties of European Union as we now know them, which in turn implies breaking once and for all with the teleological federalism that has informed most of the past debate. As soon as this is done, and indeed only then, the empirical realities of European integration begin to matter and make sense, and the historical defeat of the Social Action Programme of the 1970s and the Social Dimension Project of the 1980s can be taken seriously - instead of being treated by definition as no more than a contingent temporary delay in the functionally inevitable progress of European-federal welfare-state building. Once it is recognised that the political and economic regime that is developing in Western Europe, whatever it may be, is a new kind of animal that is altogether different from the national state, especially in its relation to the economy, the problem in analysing European social policy changes from how empty or full the glass is, to what kind of glass we are dealing with and what purposes it may serve.

A new development in the formulation of future social policy initiatives is the use of a consultative document in the form of a Green Paper, *European Social Policy:Options For The Future*[54] followed by a White Paper, *European Social Policy - A Way Forward For The Union.*[55] But the Commission's Medium Term Social Action Programme (1995-97)[56] in fact contains little innovation but is essentially a 'mopping up' exercise consolidating existing proposals which have been hanging around for a number of years. Spicker[57] makes the point that social policy has come to occupy an increasingly prominent role in the policy agenda of the EU. He argues that in the Commission's Green Paper, *European Policy Options For The Future*[58] social policy is no longer confined to looking at the implications of the Internal Market but is widened to include issues normally dealt with at the national level such as health care, employment and training, family structure, education, youth policy, racism, welfare of the elderly and rural development. While some

---

54 COM (93) 551.

55 COM (94) 333 final.

56 COM (95) 134 final.

57 Spicker, P. 'Concepts of Subsidiarity in the European Community' (1996) 5 *Current Politics and Economics in Europe* 163; 'Exclusion' (1997) 35 *JCMS* 133.

58 COM (93) 551.

commentators[59] see the subsequent White Paper as a step backwards since it recognised that the development of social policy might conflict with economic priorities, Spicker points out that the Green and White Papers do not question the legitimacy of EU intervention in these areas.

Szyszczak, E. 'Future Directions in European Union Social Policy Law' (1995) 24 *Industrial Law Journal* 19, 22

Reading the White Paper ... it is apparent that the underlying tension of *how* to regulate the labour market continues to restrict the Commission to an uneasy compromise between those who argue that excessively high labour standards result in costs which blunt the competitive edge of companies and those who believe that productivity is the key to competitiveness and that high labour standards have always formed an integral part of a competitive labour market. Thus proposals for expansion of labour standards are cautious. Detailed studies on the situation in Member States are being undertaken on protection against individual dismissal and the protection of the privacy of workers in particular with regard to the processing (including the collection and disclosure) of workers' data.

Sciarra, S. 'Social Values and the Multiple Sources of European Social Law' (1995) 1 *European Law Journal* 60, 73

A. The White Paper on Social Policy

This document is inspired by the idea of compatibility between economic competitiveness and social law; indeed the fear that the latter might stop developing and give way to irrational choices within the economic systems is put forward and is described as a deviation from the political order - based on full employment and the growth of welfare states - that has prevailed in Europe after the second world war. Anti-inflationary and price control measures are thought of as functional devices for the creation of employment; structural occupational policies are linked to investment policies; the expected outcome is that political interest should develop around the problem of poverty and weakness in the labour market, as occurred for environmental issues.

In this very broad frame of reference, groups and social institutions acquire a new relevance: changes in society are compared to those that occurred after the industrial revolution, and which influenced the state, as well as enterprises and the family. Particularly the latter may play an important part in redefining the border-lines of social

59 Kuper, B. 'The Green and White Papers of the European Union: The Apparent Goal of Reduced Social Benefits' (1994) 4 *Journal of European Social Policy* 129.

law: the changing structures of families, due among other reasons to the larger number of working women and to the increase in one-parent families, causes a different organisation of services and care...

Nevertheless, a connection must be developed among the Commission's official documents, which have been presented as the conclusion of an 'era' but also constitute a bridge towards future social policies. The White Paper on social policy has transferred the original proposals into concrete Community actions to be evaluated and possibly undertaken by the new Commission in 1995. Its political value can be determined by the choice of priorities indicated: the enactment of social norms, the guarantee of minimum standards in health and safety, the avoidance of social dumping, the recourse to social dialogue and to collective bargaining, optimal utilisation of training, in particular the adoption of specific programmes for young unemployed persons.

The Commission's White Paper must be read in the light of its White Paper on *Growth, Competitiveness, Employment* 1993.[60] This White Paper puts forward proposals for a medium-term strategy in the form of broad guidelines aimed at the coordination of national economic efforts. The dominant theme is 'pulling out' of the current recession in view of new growth by the use of monetary policies, investment policies in infrastructures, housing and environment. Many of the structural measures will have implications for social policy law - for example, greater flexibility in the regulatory framework of employment rights, efficient labour markets. Small and medium-sized enterprises are seen as central to this plan and to support them the EU must develop a strategy allowing them to be competitive, for example, by simplifying the administrative and legislative environment. Similarly the welfare system must address new forms of solidarity between those in paid work and those who are not, between rich and poor regions and intergenerational equity in a redistribution process. The White Paper thus envisages a restructuring of the macro-economic system with the launching of European information networks, trans-European transport and energy networks and the assessment of research.

---

60 (1993) EC Bulletin Supplement 6.

Sciarra, S. 'Social Values and the Multiple Sources of European Social Law' (1995) 1 *European Law Journal* 60, 76

Both Commission documents ... blend together, since they rely on the same economic and human resources and address the same objectives. They both stress the importance of decentralised economies, and are seen as the produce of market economy and growing competitiveness. This might appear in contrast with the assumption ... that a strong impulse must come from the centre, for the creation of European social law and for the control of national economic performances. We have seen how frail the edifice of social law is and how precarious the political equilibrium among Member States may become, when it comes to producing social norms. The principle of subsidiarity, which seems to co-exist with the notion of decentralised economies, does not automatically give rise to minimum standards in the social field; its positive effects still have to be demonstrated against the reluctance and the delays of governments.

In the labour lawyer's sub-conscious social dumping is a land mine, which could explode at any time. The therapy is laid out in the Commission's proposals, but the question is: Who will the therapist be?

Streeck, W. 'Neo-Voluntarism: A New European Social Policy Regime?' (1995) 1 *European Law Journal* 1, 32-38

II. The Institutional Framework of European Union

The future shape of European social policy will be circumscribed by six fundamental conditions that have, in one way or another, worked their way into the *de facto* constitution of post-Maastricht European Union.

A. From the Luxembourg compromise to the Union Treaty, the Member States of the Union have with surprising success defended their position as the masters of their Community.

.....

B. Due to the survival of the nation-state as the pivotal political entity in integrated Europe, *European social policy will for the foreseeable future be made in a two-tier polity,* consisting of a set of supranational and international institutions on the one hand, and a number of sovereign nation-states on the other. Rather than absorption of the latter into the former, the making of social policy, or any other policy in Europe will therefore increasingly involve complex 'nested games' proceeding simultaneously in the international and, at present, twelve national political arenas - resulting in *a patchwork of heterogeneous national policies constrained and modified by international rules and market interactions.*

.....

C. Economic governance through fragmented sovereignty and international relations is more suited to market-making by way of negative integration and efficiency-enhancing regulation than to institution-building and redistributive intervention, or 'market distortion'.

.....

D. The desire to preserve national sovereignty in an internationalised economy gives rise to a historical coalition between nationalism and neo-liberalism.

.....

E. The national fragmentation of democratic sovereignty within a competitive market and the continued dominance of the Member States in the political system of European Union reinforces notions of national interest, in stark contrast with older expectations of growing common European interests.

.....

F. Rather than moving towards a functionally integrated and territorially consolidated state, or state-like entity, the European Union is developing into a *collection of overlapping functionally specific arrangements for mutual coordination among varying sets of participating countries.*

Social policy is entering a new phase. There is a demonstrable shift away from efforts to *harmonise* social rights towards a greater reliance upon subsidiarity, technocratic support addressing macro-economic policy issues and the use of soft law.[61] From the Green and White Papers we see the Commission shifting the focus of social policy to concentrate upon goals rather than an individualisation of individual rights perspective. The two dominant goals being the reduction of unemployment and the elimination of social exclusion. The political agenda for the Amsterdam amendments was established and, to some extent, implemented before the IGC began its formal deliberations. The meeting of the European Council in Essen 1994 identified five areas to

61 See Campbell, E. & Cullen, H. 'The Future of Social Policy-Making in the European Union' in Craig, P. & Harlow, C. (eds.). *Law Making in the European Union* (1998, Round Hall Press, Sweet and Maxwell, Dublin).

tackle (un)employment.[62] The European Council asked the Commission to monitor employment trends and national policies and to report back to the European Council. The Commission in response encouraged the Member States to take account of the Essen objectives in their convergence programmes and made a number of proposals for Decisions in the employment field, approving projects relating to the Essen employment strategy. This trend is now seen in the attempts post-Amsterdam to co-ordinate EU (un)employment policies. But most of the changes made to social policy law in the Treaty of Amsterdam are cosmetic. What the new Treaty does is confirm the substantial shift that has taken place since the Essen European Council in 1994 linking the need for an 'adaptable workforce and labour markets responsive to economic change' as necessary adjuncts to Economic and Monetary Union which continues to dominate thinking in European integration. Post-Amsterdam the fragility of EU social policy law is even more evident. The effects of meeting the convergence criteria for the second stage of EMU are being felt - quite harshly- in some Member States in the form of high levels of unemployment. Equally the future is uncertain - with EMU in place what other structural mechanisms will take the place of exchange rate adjustments? High levels of unemployment and lower social costs may be the answer to economic and fiscal difficulties but they are not very palatable within the historically welfarist political arena. Feldstein,[63] has argued that the economic consequences of EMU are likely to be negative. He argues that imposing a single interest rate and an inflexible exchange rate on countries that are characterised by different economic shocks, inflexible wages, low labour mobility and separate national fiscal systems without significant cross-border cyclical transfers will raise the overall level of cyclical unemployment among the EMU members. Equally the emphasis upon common economic and social

---

62 These were (i) improving employment opportunities for the labour force by promoting investment in vocational training; (ii) increasing the employment intensiveness of growth; (iii) reducing non-wage labour costs extensively; (iv) improving the effectiveness of labour market policy; (v) improving measures to help groups which are particularly affected by unemployment.

63 Feldstein, M. 'The Political Economy of the European Economic and Monetary Union: Political Sources of an Economic Liability' (1997) 11 *Journal of Economic Perspectives* 23.

policies will reduce the scope for experimentation and competition that would otherwise lead to reductions in the current high levels of structural unemployment. Nielsen and Szyszczak[64] argue other factors beyond EMU may also influence the future direction of EU social policy, such as the changing industrial geography of the EU and the relocation of industry to Central and Eastern Europe.

Further Reading

Barnard, C. *EC Employment Law* (1995, Wiley Chancery, London)

Bercusson, B. 'The Collective Labour Law of the European Union' (1995) 1 *European Law Journal* 157

Burrows, N. & Mair, J. *European Social Law* (1996, Wiley, Chichester)

Fitzpatrick, B. 'Community Social Law After Maastricht' (1992) 21 *Industrial Law Journal* 199

Hervey, T. *European Social Law and Policy* (1998, Longman, Harlow)

Hervey, T. & O'Keeffe, D. (eds.) *Sex Equality Law in the European Union* (1996, Chichester, Wiley)

Jacobs, A. & Ziejen, H. European Labour Law and Social Policy (1993, Tilburg,Tilburg University Press)

Kenner, J. 'EC Labour Law: 'The Softly, Softly Approach' (1995) *International Journal of Comparative Labour Law and Industrial Relations* 307

Nielsen, R. & Szyszczak, E. *The Social Dimension of the European Union* (1997, 3rd ed, Handelshøjskolens Forlag, Copenhagen)

Streeck, W. 'From Market-Making to State Building? Reflections on the Political Economy of European Social Policy' in Leibfried, S. & Pierson, P. (eds.) *Prospects For Social Europe: The European Community's Social Dimension in Comparative Perspective* (1995, Brookings Institute, Washington DC)

---

64 Nielsen, R. & Szyszczak, E. *The Social Dimension of the European Union* (1997, 3rd ed, Handelshøjskolens Forlag, Copenhagen) Ch 1.

11. Boundaries and Enforcement of EC Competition Law

I. Introduction

One of the principal objectives of the EC Treaty set out in Article 3(g) [*3(g)*] EC is to maintain a system ensuring that competition in the common market is not distorted. There are a number of important EC Treaty Articles which pursue this objective. Article 90 [*86*] EC regulates the behaviour of public undertakings; Articles 91 [*repealed*] EC regulates dumping and Articles 92-94 [*87-89*] EC regulates State aids.

The two central provisions governing the behaviour of private individuals are Articles 85 [*81*] and 86 [*82*] EC.[1] Article 85 [*81*] EC concerns itself with cartels.

Article 85 [*81*] (1) EC. The following shall be prohibited as incompatible with the common market: all agreements between undertakings, decisions by associations of undertakings and concerted practices which may affect trade between Member States and which have as their object or effect the prevention, restriction or distortion of competition within the common market, and in particular those which:

(a) directly or indirectly fix purchase or selling prices or any other trading conditions;
(b) limit or control production, markets, technical development, or investment;
(c) share markets or sources of supply;
(d) apply dissimilar conditions to equivalent transactions with other trading parties, thereby placing them at a competitive disadvantage;
(e) make the conclusion of contracts subject to acceptance by the other parties of

1 These provisions only apply to the acts of undertakings which are taken on their own initiative. They will not apply where national legislation requires undertakings to carry out particular measures, Joined Cases C-359/95P & C-379/95P *Commission & France v Ladbroke Racing*, Judgment of 11 November 1997.

supplementary obligations which, by their nature or according to commercial usage, have no connection with the subject of such contracts.

2. Any agreements or decisions prohibited pursuant to this Article shall be automatically void.

3. The provisions of paragraph 1 may, however, be declared inapplicable in the case of:
- any agreement or category of agreements between undertakings;
- any decision or category of decisions by associations of undertakings;
- any concerted practice or category of concerted practices;

which contributes to improving the production or distribution of goods or to promoting technical or economic progress, while allowing consumers a fair share of the resulting benefit, and which does not:

(a) impose on undertakings concerned restrictions which are not indispensable to the attainment of these objectives;
(b) afford such undertakings the possibility of eliminating competition in respect of a substantial part of the products in question.

Article 86 [*82*] EC is more concerned with the abuse of economic power by monopolies and oligopolies.

Article 86 [*82*] EC. Any abuse by one or more undertakings of a dominant position within the common market or in a substantial part of it shall be prohibited as incompatible with the common market in so far as it may affect trade between Member States. Such abuse may, in particular, consist in:

(a) directly or indirectly imposing unfair purchase or selling prices or unfair trading conditions;
(b) limiting production, markets or technical development to the prejudice of consumers;
(c) applying dissimilar conditions to equivalent transactions with other trading parties, thereby placing them at a competitive disadvantage;
(d) making the conclusion of contracts subject to acceptance by the other parties of supplementary obligations which, by their nature or according to commercial usage, have no connection with the subject of such contracts.

Before examining the substantive rules, it is necessary to consider what is meant by competition. Competition is based upon two pillars, independence and rivalry. Law students applying for articles at a firm of solicitors are competing, as they cannot send joint applications and are therefore independent, and are rivals in that, as there are probably more applications than places, each will be seeking a place to the exclusion of someone else.

If that is competition, why should the EC seek to promote it? Overt competitiveness is rarely a quality we find attractive in others. Furthermore, a competitive society presupposes an individualistic society where each person looks after himself at the expense of others rather than collaborating with others in pursuit of the common good.

II. Ideologies Underpinning EC Competition Law

i. The Promotion of Efficiency

Whish, R. ***Competition Law*** **(1993, 3rd Edition, Butterworths, London) 1-3**

Under perfect competition economic resources are allocated between different goods and services in precisely the quantities which consumers wish (their desires being expressed by the price they are prepared to pay on the market). This is termed allocative efficiency. Apart from allocative efficiency many economists, and non-economists too, think that under perfect competition goods and services will be produced at the lowest cost possible, which means that as little of society's wealth is expended in the production process as necessary. This is termed productive efficiency. The combined effect of allocative and productive efficiency is that society's overall wealth is maximized.

Two further desirable effects follow from perfect competition. First the price at which a good or service is sold never rises above the marginal cost of production (cost for this purpose including a sufficient profit margin to have encouraged the producer to invest his capital in the industry in the first place, but no more)... Secondly, and this cannot be proved scientifically, in a competitive market producers will constantly innovate and develop new products as part of the continual battle of striving for consumers' business...

Allocative efficiency is achieved under perfect competition because the producer, assuming that he is acting rationally has a desire to maximize his profits, will expand his production for as long as it is privately profitable to do so. As long he can earn more by producing one extra unit of whatever he produces than it costs to make it, he will presumably do so. Only when the cost of a further unit (the 'marginal cost') exceeds the price he would obtain for it will he cease to expand production. Where competition is perfect, a producer will increase output to the point at which marginal cost and marginal revenue (the net addition to revenue of selling the last unit) coincide: a reduction in his output cannot affect the affect the market price and so there is no reason to limit it. This means that output is maintained at an optimal level and that consumers can obtain the amounts of goods they require at the price they are prepared to pay: resources are allocated according to their wishes.

Productive efficiency is achieved because a producer is unable to sell above cost (if he did his customers would desert him) and he will not of course sell below it (because then he would make no profit). If by chance a producer were to charge above cost, other competitors would move into the market in the hope of profitable activity. They would attempt to produce on a more efficient basis so that they could earn a greater profit. In the long-run the tendency of this will be to force producers to incur the lowest cost possible in order to earn any profit at all. Eventually the point will be reached where price and the average cost of producing goods necessarily coincide.

Even cursory reflection reveals that perfect competition exists only in models and not in social reality.

Sosnick, S, 'A Critique of Concepts of Workable Competition' (1958) 72 *Quarterly Journal of Economics* 380, 383-384

The point is that the set of market structure and market conduct attributes which define 'perfect competition' constitute individually and collectively neither a normative ideal nor a satisfactory basis for appraising actual market conditions.

What came to be called 'perfect competition' involves an effectively infinite number of relatively small buyers and sellers of a standardized product, each rationally seeking his maximum advantage, independently of other traders and free of public 'controls,' in a continuous market with 'complete' and costless knowledge, access, and mobility. The arguments against idealizing atomistic competition, perfect and imperfect, cover a variety of issues - non optimum conditions elsewhere, economies of scale, poor management, capital shortage, requisites and effects of exploration and of research and development, external economies and diseconomies, dispersion and individuality in traders and variety in outputs, immobile excess capacity, chronic distress, unfair tactics, depression-spreading, incorrect and inconsistent expectations, atoms blundering about a moving equilibrium. In addition, it is recognized that the extremes which define atomistic and otherwise-perfect competition tell us nothing about desirable gradations in even the few dimensions to which they refer; yet market characteristics are scaled, not either-or, so that the choices open to normative appraisal relate not to whether, but to how much there should be of concentration, bigness, heterogeneity, price flexibility etc.

The rejection of perfect competition as a model for market appraisal led to the development of the school of *workable competition.*[2] The basis of this school was that perfect competition was neither attainable nor desirable. There should merely be a sufficient intensity of competition. Aware that this was something of a vague goal, proponents of workable competition would set a series of criteria against which a market would be judged to assess whether it was competitive or not. These would be *conduct*, *structure* and *performance*. Conduct criteria relate to how firms behave, and are aimed predominantly at outlawing certain forms of conduct. The duties they impose on public authorities relate exclusively to their role as competition authorities. The criteria of structure and performance relate, however, predominantly to the market environment in which the firms operate, and therefore bear more directly on public authorities' more general regulatory powers.

Scherer, F. and Ross, D, *Industrial Market Structure and Market Performance* (1990, 3rd Edition, Houghton, New York) 53-54.

... the criteria of workability suggested by diverse writers can be divided into structural, conduct and performance categories.

Structural criteria:

- The number of traders should be at least as large as scale economies permit.
- There should be no artificial inhibitions on mobility and entry.
- There should be moderate and price-sensitive quality differentials in the products offered.

Conduct criteria:

- Some uncertainty should exist in the minds of rivals as to whether price initiatives will be followed.
- Firms should strive to attain their goals independently, without collusion.
- There should be no unfair, exclusionary, predatory, or coercive tactics.
- Inefficient suppliers and customers not be shielded permanently.

---

2 The founder of this school is taken to be Clark, J. 'Towards a Concept of Workable Competition' (1940) 30 *American Economic Review* 241. A useful summary is given in Sosnick, S. 'A Critique of Concepts of Workable Competition' (1958) 72 *Quarterly Journal of Economics* 380.

- Sales promotion should be informative, or at least not be misleading.
- There should be no persistent, harmful price discrimination.

Performance criteria

- Firm's production and distributions operations should be efficient and not wasteful of resources.
- Output levels and product quality (that is variety, durability, safety, reliability and so forth) should be responsive to consumer demands.
- Profits should be at levels just sufficient to reward investment, efficiency, and innovation.
- Prices should encourage rational choice, guide markets towards equilibrium and not intensify cyclical instability.
- Opportunities for introducing technically superior new products and processes should be exploited.
- Promotional expenses should not be excessive.
- Success should accrue to sellers who best serve consumer wants.

Critics have questioned whether the approach is as operational as its proponents suggest. Difficult quantitative judgments are required on many of the individual variables. How price sensitive must quality differentials be? When are promotional expenses excessive, and when are they not? How long must price discrimination persist before it is persistent? Furthermore, fulfilment of many of these criteria is difficult to measure. Finally, how should the workability of competition be evaluated if some but not all of the criteria are satisfied?

The strongest attack on the concept of workable competition came from the Chicago School. This School attacked workable competition, first, on the grounds that the elusive nature of the concept resulted in resort being had to vague notions such as 'fairness' or 'market structure' which did not accord with sound economics, and allowed too wide and ill-defined a discretion to competition authorities and courts. The second criticism of the Chicago School stemmed from its belief that markets freed from State intervention were generally self-correcting. They thus often corresponded to the economically most optimal solution available. The workable competition school with its formulaic emphasis on market structure and market performance was therefore criticised as being too interventionist and too formalistic, in that intervention would often take place, irrespective of the individual characteristics of the market in question.[3]

The Chicago School of thought, considered at one stage to be on the 'lunatic fringe' of writing in this field,[4] though subject to increasing criticism on both sides of the Atlantic, has probably been the most influential school of thought, internationally, in competition law. The salient tenets of the School are outlined below by one of its critics.[5]

Hovenkamp, H. 'Antitrust Policy after Chicago' (1986) 84 *Michigan Law Review* 213, 226-228

(1) Economic efficiency, the pursuit of which should be the exclusive goal of the antitrust law laws, consists of two relevant parts: allocative efficiency and productive efficiency. Occasionally practices that increase a firm's productive efficiency reduce the market's allocative efficiency. For example, construction of a large plant and acquisition of a large market share may increase a firm's productive efficiency by enabling it to achieve economies of scale; however, these actions may simultaneously reduce allocative efficiency by facilitating monopoly pricing. A properly defined antitrust policy will attempt to maximise *net* efficiency gains.
(2) Most markets are competitive, even if they contain a relatively small number of sellers. Furthermore, product differentiation tends to undermine competition far less than was formerly presumed. As a result, neither high market concentration nor product differentiation are the anti-competitive problems earlier oligopoly theorists believed them to be.

---

3 Easterbrook, F. 'Workable Antitrust Policy' (1986) 84 *Michigan Law Review* 1696.

4 Posner, R. 'The Chicago School of Antitrust Analysis' (1979) 127 *University of Pennsylvania Law Review* 925, 931.

5 Probably the most celebrated piece of legal writing of the Chicago School is Bork, R. *The Antitrust Paradox: A Policy at War with Itself* (1993, Reprint, Macmillan, New York). In addition to the article by Hovenkamp, other leading analyses of the School, both sympathetic and critical are Posner, R. 'The Chicago School of Antitrust Analysis' (1979) 127 *University of Pennsylvania Law Review* 925; Pitofsky, R. 'The Political Content of Antitrust' (1979) 127 *University of Pennsylvania Law Review* 1051; Schwarz, 'Justice' and Other Non-Economic Goals of Antitrust' (1979) 127 *University of Pennsylvania Law Review* 1076; Easterbrook, R. 'The Limits of Antitrust' (1984) 63 *Texas Law Review* 1; Fox, E. and Sullivan, L. 'Antitrust - Retrospective and Prospective: Where are We Coming From? Where are We Going?' (1987) 62 *New York University Law Review* 936.

(3) Monopoly, when it exists, tends to be self-correcting; that is the monopolist's higher profits generally attract new entry into the monopolist's market, with the result that the monopolist's position is quickly eroded. About the best that the judicial process can do is hasten the correction process.
(4) 'Natural' barriers to entry are more imagined than real. As a general rule investment will flow into any market where the rate of return is high. The one significant exception consists of barriers to entry that are not natural - that is, barriers that are created by government itself. In most markets, the government would be best off if it left entry and exit unregulated.
(5) Economies of scale are far more pervasive than economists once believed, largely because earlier economists looked only at intra-plant or production economies, and neglected economies of distribution. As a result, many more industries than were formerly thought may operate most economically only at fairly highly concentration levels.
(6) Business-firms are profit maximizers. That is, their managers generally make decisions that they anticipate will make the firm more profitable than any alternative decision. The model would not be undermined, however, if it should turn out that many firms are not profit maximizers, but are motivated by some alternative goal, such as revenue maximization, sales maximization, or 'satisficing'.[6] The integrity of the market efficiency model requires only that a few firms be profit-maximizers. In that case, the profits and market shares of these firms will grow at the expense of the other firms in the market.
(7) Antitrust enforcement should be designed in such a way as to penalize conduct precisely to the point that it is inefficient, but to tolerate or encourage it when it is efficient. ...
(8) The decision to make the neoclassical market efficiency model the exclusive guide for antitrust policy is nonpolitical.

---

6 The term 'satisficing' refers to a theory of firm behaviour that is contrary to the theory of profit maximisation adopted by the Chicago School today. A firm 'satisfices' when its management adopts a certain goal for profits, sales or market share and then tries to meet the goal but not necessarily to exceed it. The theory posits that initially the firm's management will not be inclined to set an extremely high goal, because if they later fail to achieve this goal they will appear to the stockholders to be failures. Furthermore, once the goal is established the stockholders will demand an even higher goal in the future, and that higher goal will be that more difficult to achieve. The theory of satisficing is part of a more general theory of the firm, which hypothesises that the owners of capital (stockholders) and the managers of capital may have different motives, and that this circumstance makes the firm less efficient than the Chicago School would have us believe.

The economic assumptions of the Chicago School are increasingly being contested.[7] Equally contested is the assumption that the concept of efficiency provides some clearly defined beacon towards which competition policy can be steered. Efficiency, it can be argued, should not be an end in itself, but should be an instrument to achieve other societal goals, such as freedom of choice or consumer welfare. In addition, Fox has observed that whilst there is a consensus that competition law should increase producer responsiveness to consumer wants, there is considerable disagreement as to the means that should be used to reach that end. She therefore sees efficiency as a very fickle lodestone.[8]

Fox notes that three models of efficiency can be put forward. The first concentrates on *output*. It considers anything to be inefficient which leads to an artificial restriction on output. Yet such a theory is too narrow, in that it fails to reflect producers' capacity to reduce costs or to innovate. It is artificial as output on a market can only be restricted where all actors on the market participate, as otherwise some actors will merely expand output to capture excess demand. The second model of efficiency relies upon business *autonomy*. It is based upon a presumption that business is more efficient which is only rebutted by the clearest evidence. Yet a linkage between autonomy and efficiency taken to its

---

7 The most recent criticism comes from the so-called 'post Chicagoan' school. This school's roots are based in theories of industrial organisation. It requires far more empirical analysis of the industrial structure and nuances of individual markets than the Chicago School would require. For the latter believe that most markets possess self-correcting features in the sense that if supra-competitive prices are charged new competitors will be attracted to the market. The post-Chicagoan school places more emphasis on barriers to entry, noting that most changes to market structure, such as mergers, are irreversible, and that the Chicagoan School understates the ability of firms to act strategically, in particular to attempt foreclosure, i.e. barring access to the market for new competitors. See in particular Riordan, M. & Salop, S. 'Evaluating Vertical Mergers: A Post Chicago Approach' (1995) 63 *Antitrust Law Journal* 513; Sullivan, L. 'Post-Chicago Economics: Economists, Lawyers, Judges, and Enforcement Officials in a Less Determinate Theoretical World' (1995) 63 *Antitrust Law Journal* 669.

8 Fox, E. 'The Modernization of Antitrust: A New Equilibrium' (1981) 66 *Cornell Law Review* 1140 esp., 1157 *et seq.*

extreme would rebut the need for competition law, as the purpose of the latter is to control individual behaviour.

Fox favours a third approach which views competition as a process which is likely to produce an environment based upon rivalry which is likely to produce efficient outcomes. For her such an approach allows efficiency to be viewed as merely one of the goals of competition policy. This in turn allows other values - something she claims has been the traditional role of competition policy - to be introduced to create a backdrop which reflects a number of social choices about economic behaviour. Yet even such a view is problematic. It is often difficult to determine if a particular market environment is competitive. Intense competition can exist even where there are only a few undertakings on the market in question.[9] The local market may have to be juxtaposed next to the global market. In order to compete globally a firm may have to be dominant locally. It would therefore be operating both on a global market which was highly competitive, and on a local market that was less competitive.[10] More generally, questions are left unanswered about the relative value of efficiency in such a system vis-à-vis other values.

ii. Competition Policy as an Instrument of Integration

Without competition law there is a danger that barriers to free movement erected by States dismantled by the economic freedoms and EC harmonisation could be rebuilt by private parties refusing to trade in each other's markets. Competition law has therefore also been used as an instrument of market integration.

---

9 Bork, R. *The Antitrust Paradox: A Policy at War with Itself* (1993, Reprint, Macmillan, New York) Chapter 8, especially 178-195.

10 Hay, G., Hilke, J. & Nelson, P. 'Geographic Market Definition in an International Context' (1990) *Fordham Corporate Law Institute* 51.

Joined Cases 56 & 58/64 Etablissements Consten SA & Grundig GmbH v Commission [1966] ECR 299, [1966] CMLR 418

Consten and Grundig concluded an excluded distribution agreement under which Consten would distribute Grundig's radios and televisions in France, and Grundig would attempt to ensure that none of its goods were supplied from Germany to France. The Commission considered such an agreement to breach Article 85 [*81*] EC, the provision on cartels. Consten and Grundig challenged this.

Finally, an agreement between producer and distributor which might tend to restore the national divisions in trade between Member States might be such as to frustrate the most fundamcntal objcct of thc Community. The Treaty, whose preamble and content aim at abolishing the barriers between States, and which in several provisions gives evidence of a stern attitude with regard to their reappearance, could not allow undertakings to reconstruct such barriers. Article 85(1) is designed to pursue this aim, even in the case of agreements between undertakings placed at different levels in the economic process.

Gerber, D. 'The Transformation of European Community Competition Law' (1994) 35 *Harvard International Law Journal* 97, 108-109

The Court's definition of its role in the competition law system was part of the broader process of defining its role within the Community, and here timing was a critical factor. The first significant competition cases came to the Court in the mid-1960s, just as General De Gaulle's resistance to Europeanization threatened to impede integration and destroy the Community. De Gaulle changed the 'constitution' of the Community by demanding a unanimity requirement for virtually all Council decisions, thus hobbling the Community's political organs. As a consequence, the Court was the only institution capable of maintaining the momentum of integration. Moreover, the crisis of confidence resulting from these events encouraged the Court to assert a bold leadership role.

The Court thus structured the competition law system to serve as a central tool for promoting integration. It articulated a broad conception of competition law as central to the process of integration, and its decisions in this area sought to make that conception viable and convincing.

The role that the European Court sculpted for itself in this competition law system centred on intellectual leadership. Rather than limiting itself to ruling on the facts of individual cases, the Court frequently enunciated broad principles and values. It looked to the future and aimed at guiding the Commission in its development of competition policy. As one commentator has suggested, the Court began to provide the Commission with 'windows of opportunity' in which the Court indicated its willingness to support particular lines of development of competition law doctrine.[[11]]

---

11 Goyder, D. *EEC Competition Law* (1988, OUP, Oxford) 413.

As one of the rationales for market integration is the creation of a more efficient economic environment, the goals of market integration and efficiency have often coalesced within EC competition policy. The need for market construction can be seen, however, as occasionally justifying greater intervention by competition authorities. This is particularly so in the case of *vertical restraints*. These are restraints made between operators operating at different levels on the market, such as a distributor and supplier, or franchiser and franchisee. They are distinct from *horizontal restraints* which are made between competitors operating at the same level on the market. Whilst horizontal restraints primarily affect *inter-brand* competition - i.e. competition between different products - vertical restraints affect predominantly *intra-brand* competition - i.e. competition between sellers of the same brand of product. In many circumstances, intra-brand competition is seen as being quite weak and it has therefore been argued that vertical restraints may even be pro-competitive.[12] From the point of view of market integration, however, vertical restraints are almost always an anathema as they contribute to market partitioning. They allow a supplier to ensure that only particular distributors sell the goods in one territory. With different distributors selling the goods across the EC, and without any competition between them, the difference in mark-ups is likely to result in different prices being charged across the EC.

The requirements of integration may be becoming a less central influence within EC competition law. As the single market reaches maturity, the emphasis is increasingly turning from market construction to market regulation. In addition, the Commission has, over time, developed a competition policy of its own through block exemptions issued under Article 85 [*81*](3) EC. As the number of these have increased, so they have created something akin to a mature and sophisticated competition policy, which has, in turn, reduced the need for the Court to intervene.[13] Finally, in the 1990s there has been a move towards a looser, less regulated internal market. This would also seem to require a less interventionist competition policy.

---

12 See pp. 612-615.

13 Gerber, D. 'The Transformation of European Community Competition Law' (1994) 35 *Harvard International Law Journal* 97, 124 *et seq.*

iii. EC Competition Policy as an Instrument for Controlling Economic Power

A traditional aim of all competition law has been not merely the promotion of economic efficiency, but also the control of economic power.[14] It was a particularly prevalent concern of the German ordoliberal school of thought, which contributed considerably to the inception of EC competition policy.[15] Whilst it has never been mentioned explicitly by the Court, the existence of Article 86 [*82*] EC, a provision to control the use of economic power, suggests that it is also an implicit assumption of EC competition policy.

Gerber, D. 'Constitutionalizing the Economy: German Neo-liberalism, Competition Law and the "New" Europe' (1994) 42 *American Journal of Comparative Law* 25, 36-37

But the ordoliberals expanded the lens of liberalism. For them, it was not sufficient to protect the individual from the power of government, because governments were not the only threats to individual freedom. Powerful economic institutions could also destroy or limit freedom, especially economic freedom. Having witnessed the use of private economic power during the Weimar period to destroy political and social institutions, the ordoliberals emphasised the need to protect individuals from misuses of such power. This meant that the state had to be strong enough to resist the influence of private power groups. In order for government officials to be in a position to create the structures of the new society, the government of which they were a part would have to be able to protect them against private influences.

The Weimar experience led ordoliberals to demand the dispersion of not only political power, but economic power as well. For most, this meant the elimination of monopolies. For others, such as Wilhelm Röpke, the concentration of economic resources was an evil unto itself; they sought an economy composed, to the extent possible, of small

---

14 On the relationship between American antitrust law and the dispersion of economic power see Fox, E. 'The Modernization of Antitrust: A New Equilibrium' (1981) 66 *Cornell Law Review* 1140, 1141 *et seq.*

15 On this Gerber, D. 'Constitutionalizing the Economy: German Neo-liberalism, Competition Law and the "New" Europe' (1994) 42 *American Journal of Comparative Law* 25, 69-74. The most celebrated ordoliberal work in the field of competition law is Böhm, F. *Wettbewerb und Monopolkampf* (1933, Heymans, Berlin).

and medium-sized firms. Both groups tended to view economic concentration with suspicion and sought to protect the existence and the economic freedom of small and medium-sized businesses.

Concern about economic power would lead competition authorities to intervene even where to do so might not result in the most efficient outcome. In EC law, concentration on the excessive accumulation of economic power has been achieved through analysis of the structure of a particular market.

Case 6/72 Europemballage Corp. & Continental Can Co. v Commission [1973] ECR 215, [1973] CMLR 199

Continental Can, an American manufacturer of metal packaging, engaged in a friendly takeover of TDV, a Dutch manufacturer. The Commission considered that this takeover breached Article 86 [*82*] EC as it substantially eliminated competition in the market for metal containers in the BENELUX and northern Germany. Continental Can challenged the Decision.

20. Article 86 (1) of the Treaty says 'any abuse by one or more undertakings of a dominant position within the common market or in a substantial part of it shall be prohibited as incompatible with the common market in so far as it may affect trade between Member States'. The question is whether the word 'abuse' in Article 86 refers only to practices of undertakings which may directly affect the market and are detrimental to production or sales, to purchasers or consumers, or whether this word refers also to changes in the structure of an undertaking, which lead to competition being seriously disturbed in a substantial part of the Common Market.

21. The distinction between measures which concern the structure of the undertaking and practices which affect the market cannot be decisive, for any structural measure may influence market conditions, if it increases the size and the economic power of the undertaking.

22. In order to answer this question, one has to go back to the spirit, general scheme and wording of Article 86, as well as to the system and objectives of the Treaty.

23. Article 86 is part of the Chapter devoted to the common rules on the Community's policy in the field of competition. This policy is based on Article 3(f) of the Treaty according to which the Community's activity shall include the institution of a system ensuring that competition in the Common Market is not distorted. The applicants' argument that this provision merely contains a general programme devoid of legal effect, ignores the fact that Article 3 considers the pursuit of the objectives which it lays down to be indispensable for the achievement of the Community's tasks. As regards in particular the aim mentioned in (f), the Treaty in several provisions contains more detailed regulations for the interpretation of which this aim is decisive.

24. But if Article 3(f) provides for the institution of a system ensuring that competition in the Common Market is not distorted, then it requires *a fortiori* that competition must not be eliminated. This requirement is so essential that without it numerous provisions of the Treaty would be pointless. Moreover, it corresponds to the precept of Article 2 of the Treaty according to which one of the tasks of the Community is 'to promote throughout the Community a harmonious development of economic activities'. Thus the restraints on competition which the Treaty allows under certain conditions because of the need to harmonize the various objectives of the Treaty, are limited by the requirements of Articles 2 and 3. Going beyond this limit involves the risk that the weakening of competition would conflict with the aims of the Common Market.

Competition law is a blunt instrument with which to control economic power. It might be that there are other instruments, such as the promotion of industrial democracy through the development of company or labour law, which might be more suitable. For it is not the market power of the enterprise, *per se*, which provokes concern but rather its accountability. It is therefore more important to ensure that there are appropriate checks and balances than merely to control a firm's markct powcr.

iv. EC Competition Policy and Market Externalities

The atomistic nature of competition law with its presumption of rivalry and independence can, if left unfettered, give rise to potential social costs. The most prominent are so-called market externalities. The price mechanism at the heart of competition policy is based upon motivations of private gain and private cost. The supplier supplies at the lowest private cost to itself. Similarly, the purchaser similarly buys those goods or services which are of most private utility. Yet the actions of both purchaser and supplier can have consequences for other parties of which an unregulated market would not take account. This could be damage to the environment in the form of pollution or it could be that my purchasing a good from one supplier will result in another supplier going out of business.[16]

A response might be that this is of only peripheral interest to competition lawyers. A regulatory framework can be developed to counter these costs. Within the limits of this superstructure, the competitive process can continue relatively unabashed. Increasingly, however, 'command and control' forms of regulation requiring operators to comply with legislation are being seen as problematic on the grounds that they are insufficiently sensitive to risk, full compliance is rare and enforcement costs can be considerable.[17] Attention has therefore shifted to other forms of regulation. The Fifth Action Plan on the Environment consequently recognised the utility of private Codes of Conduct or voluntary agreements between operators.[18] The difficulties such practices pose EC competition law are that, being based on coordination, they appear often to be anti-competitive. In the field of the environment, the Commission has, to some extent, acknowledged this, and has been prepared to give individual exemptions under Article 85 [*81*](3) EC to certain forms of agreement which benefit the environment.[19]

Even for environmental costs, such an arrangement is not entirely satisfactory. Exemption can only given to those practices which fall under Article 85 [*81*] EC. Furthermore, as it is an exemption which is being given, operators are required to undergo a long, costly and

---

16 Swann, D. *Competition and Consumer Protection* (1979, Harmondsworth, Penguin) 20.

17 On the shortcomings of the harmonisation process within the EC context see Dehousse, R., Joerges, C., Majone, G., Snyder, F. & Everson, M. *Europe after 1992 - New Regulatory Strategies* (EUI Working Paper No. 92/31, Florence, 1992) esp. 4-6.

18 Council Resolution on a Community Programme of policy and action in relation to the environment and sustainable development, OJ 1993 C 138/1, 29. See also EC Commission, *On Environmental Agreements* COM (96) 561.

19 Jacobs, R. 'EEC Competition Law and the Protection of the Environment' (1993/2) *LIEI* 37, 49-58; Vogelaar, F. 'Towards an Improved Integration of EC Environmental Policy and EC Competition Policy: An Interim Report' (1994). *Fordham Corporate Law Institute* 529; Chalmers, D. 'Environmental Protection and the Single Market: An Unsustainable Development. Does the EC Treaty need a Title on the Environment (1995/1) *LIEI* 65, 83-86.

uncertain wait whilst the arrangement is notified to and then considered by the Commission. Recently, however, the question has been considered whether social costs can be taken into account in the context of the Merger Regulation in the Nestlé/Perrier judgment.[20]

Case T-96/92 Comité d'Entreprise de la Société Générale des Grandes Sources & Others v Commission [1995] ECR II-1213

The Commission is required to appraise whether mergers (concentrations) are compatible with the common market under Article 2 of Regulation 4064/89, the Merger Regulation. In 1992 Nestlé notified the Commission that one of its subsidiaries, Demilac, was going to take over Perrier, the bottled water producer. Following the giving of a number of undertakings, the Commission approved the takeover. A number of trade unions representing Perrier employees wished to challenge the Commission decision, as they alleged Nestlé proposed to dismiss 740 of the workforce. The Court had to consider whether these organisations had standing under the Regulation. It considered that the time limits for judicial review had expired but stated:

28. For that purpose it must be noted to begin with that in the scheme of Regulation 4064/89, the primacy given to the establishment of a system of free competition may in certain cases be reconciled, in the context of the assessment of whether a concentration is compatible with the common market, with the taking into consideration of the social effects of that operation if they are liable to affect adversely the social objectives referred to in Article 2 of the Treaty. The Commission may therefore have to ascertain whether the concentration is liable to have consequences, even if only indirectly, for the position of the employees in the undertakings in question, such as to affect the level or conditions of employment in the Community or a substantial part of it.

29. Article 2(1)(b) of Regulation 4064/89 requires the Commission to draw up an economic balance for the concentration in question, which may, in some circumstances, entail considerations of a social nature, as is confirmed by the thirteenth recital in the Preamble to the Regulation, which states that 'the Commission must place its appraisal within the general framework of the achievement of the fundamental objectives referred to in Article 2 of the Treaty, including that of strengthening the Community's economic and social cohesion, referred to in Article 130a'. In that legal context, the express provision in Article 18(4) of the Regulation, giving specific expression to the principle

---

20 See also the parallel judgment given on the same day of Case T-12/93 *Comité d'Entreprise de la Société Anonyme Vittel & Others v Commission* [1995] ECR II-1247.

stated in the nineteenth recital that the representatives of the employees of the undertakings concerned are entitled, upon application, to be heard, manifests an intention to ensure that the collective interests of those employees are taken into consideration in the administrative procedure.

30. In those circumstances, the Court considers that, in the scheme of Regulation No 4064/89, the position of the employees of the undertakings which are the subject of the concentration may in certain cases be taken into consideration by the Commission when adopting its decision. That is why the Regulation makes individual mention of the recognized representatives of the employees of those undertakings, who constitute a closed category clearly defined at the time of adoption of the decision, by expressly and specifically giving them the right to submit their observations in the administrative procedure. Those organizations, who are responsible for upholding the collective interests of the employees they represent, have a relevant interest with respect to the social considerations which may in appropriate cases be taken into account by the Commission in the context of its appraisal of whether the concentration is lawful from the point of view of Community law.

III. The Remit of EC Competition Law

i. The Internal Dimension

Competition policy is an area of mixed competence. EC competition law and national competition law co-exist alongside each other, each in its own sphere of competence. This intrudes time and again upon the development of EC competition law, as Member States resist its extension for fear of their own regimes being diminished. In each area of EC competition law the point at which something becomes a matter of EC jurisdiction varies. Yet all take a common starting point. This delimitation point is not territorial. Anti-competitive practices taking place exclusively within the territory of one Member State can fall within the remit of EC competition law.[21] The ambit of EC competition law is defined rather by reference to the ambit of the single market.[22]

---

21 Case 322/81 *Michelin v Commission* [1983] ECR 3461, [1985] 1 CMLR 282.

22 Faull, J. 'Effect on Trade between Member States and Community - Member State Jurisdiction' (1989) *Fordham Corporate Law Institute* 485.

Case T-70/89 BBC v Commission [1991] ECR II 535[23]

The BBC owned the copyright to the listings of its programmes. It allowed newspapers to publish daily listings and weekly 'highlights' but prosecuted anyone who published weekly listings. These could therefore only be obtained in its magazine the 'Radio Times'. Magill wished to publish weekly listings for the island of Ireland and, when prevented from doing so, complained to the Commission. The Commission found there was a breach of Article 86 [*82*] EC.

64. ... Community law covers any agreement or any practice which is capable of constituting a threat to freedom of trade between Member States in a manner which might harm the attainment of the objectives of a single market between the Member States, in particular by partitioning the national markets or by affecting the structure of competition within the common market (judgment of the Court of Justice of 31 May 1979 in Case 22/78 *Hugin v Commission* [1979] ECR 1869, paragraph 17; see also the judgment of 6 March 1974 in Joined Cases 6 and 7/73 *Commercial Solvents v Commission* [1974] ECR 223, paragraph 32; the judgment of 13 February 1979 in Case 85/76 *Hoffmann-LaRoche v Commission* [1979] ECR 461, paragraph 125; and the judgment of 14 February 1978 in Case 27/76 *United Brands v Commission* [1978] ECR 207, paragraph 201). It is enough, in order for Article 86 to be applicable, that the abusive conduct should be capable of affecting trade between Member States. It is therefore not necessary to find that there is a real and present effect on inter-state trade (see, inter alia, the judgment of the Court of Justice of 9 November 1983 in Case 322/81, *Michelin v Commission* [1983] ECR 3461, paragraph 104, and its judgment of 23 April 1991 in Case C-41/90, *Höfner and Elser v Macrotron*, [1991] ECR I-1979, paragraph 32).

65. In the present case, the Court finds that the applicant's conduct modified the structure of competition on the market for television guides in Ireland and Northern Ireland and thus affected potential trade flows between Ireland and the United Kingdom. The applicant's refusal to authorize interested third parties to publish its weekly listings had decisive repercussions on the structure of competition in the field of television magazines in the territory of Ireland and Northern Ireland. Through its licensing policy which prevented, *inter alia*, Magill from publishing a general television magazine to be marketed in both Ireland and Northern Ireland, the applicant not only eliminated a competing undertaking from the market for television guides but also excluded any potential competition from that market, thus in effect maintaining the partitioning of the markets represented by Ireland and Northern Ireland respectively. The conduct in question was therefore undeniably capable of affecting trade between Member States.

---

23 For an example of similar reasoning in relation to Article 85 [*81*] EC see Case T-77/92 *Parker Pen v Commission* [1994] ECR II 549.

There is a logic to using the single market as a basis for Community jurisdiction in the field of competition. Ehlermann has noted that competition policy is both an essential element and an engine of the single market.[24] The single market both provides increased scope for competition and cannot be sustained without trade and competition between private parties. Linking EC competition policy to market integration results, however, in all the fuzzy edges of the latter infecting the former. Use of the requirement that a practice be capable of affecting trade as a touchstone for determining the reach of EC competition policy is unhelpful, as it is so wide as to prevent any meaningful delimitation.[25] Further requirements have therefore been added, in that the anti-competitive practice must have a *significant* effect on inter-State trade[26] or affect a substantial part of the common market before EC competence is triggered.[27] All these have been criticised for adopting an over-expansive view of EC jurisdiction which both stretches the EC's administrative capacities and stultifies local choice.[28] Certainly, they are relative concepts whose focus will have to reflect the balance between the need for market integration and the desire for local regulatory autonomy.[29] This balance might not merely vary in time but also, as shall be seen, manifests itself in different ways according to whether it is market power or restrictive practices which are being regulated.[30]

---

24 Ehlermann, C-D. 'The Contribution of EC Competition Policy to the Single Market' (1992) 29 *CMLRev* 257, 265.

25 Wesseling, W. 'The Commission Notice on Decentralisation and EC Antitrust Law' (1997) 2 *ECLR* 94, 96.

26 The *de minimis* test, requiring that there be a significant effect on trade before Article 85 [*81*] EC is triggered, was first developed in Case 5/69 *Volk v Vervaecke* [1969] ECR 295, [1969] CMLR 273. It has traditionally been treated quite separately from the question of whether patterns of trade are affected between Member States. The two were merged in Case T-77/92 *Parker Pen v Commission* [1994] ECR II 549, [1995] 5 CMLR 435.

27 This is required for Article 86 [*82*] EC to be triggered.

28 Wesseling, W. 'Subsidiarity in Community Antitrust Law: Setting the Right Agenda' (1997) 22 *ELRev* 35.

29 For discussion of this in another context see Wils, W. 'The Search for the Rule in Article 30 EEC: Much Ado about Nothing?' (1993) 18 *ELRev* 475, 478.

30 The precise balance is examined in each Chapter.

ii. The External Dimension

The question of the reach of EC competition law has not only an internal but also an external dimension. If the increased transnational nature and globalisation of economic activity was arguably one of the factors which led to the need for an EC competence in competition policy, that very same globalisation has a corresponding dysfunctional effect on the competence of the EC competition authorities. On the one hand, transnational activities can be of such a scale that it transcends the Community - the activities of some of the software or broadcasting multinationals are a case in point. On the other, problems might arise not from the scale of the activity but simply from its taking place partly in the EC and partly in a third country.

In principal, a parallel logic could be applied. For example, two Japanese undertakings based in Tokyo who have 80% of the EC market between them can partition the EC market through an agreement made in Tokyo as effectively as two British companies could in London. The test for extraterritorial jurisdiction could therefore be identical to that used for internal jurisdiction. If any practice affects inter-State trade, wherever its origins, it falls within EC jurisdiction. The first problem with such an approach is that because it is so wideranging, just as some limit has been put on the test in the case of the internal division of powers, so some limit must be imposed in the case of the EC's extraterritorial jurisdiction. The second problem is the acceptance by the international community of such a test. When the 'effects' doctrine was adopted by the United States after the Second World War, it met with considerable opposition from States who considered that particular practices, having been committed within their territory, fell within their exclusive jurisdiction.[31]

---

31 Lange, D. & Sandage, J. 'The *Wood Pulp* Decision and Its Implications for the Scope of EC Competition Law' (1989) 26 *CMLRev* 136, 140-142; Roth, P. 'Reasonable Extraterritoriality: Correcting the "Balance of Interests"' (1992) 41 *ICLQ* 245, 246-252.

Joined Cases 89, 104, 116-117, 125-129/85 Ålström *et al.* v Commission (Woodpulp) [1988] ECR 3359, [1988] 4 CMLR 901.

The Commission fined 41 wood pulp producers, all of whom had their offices either in Finland, Switzerland, Canada or the United States, alleging that they had been engaged in a price fixing cartel. According to the Commission this cartel affected two thirds of wood pulp shipments to the Community and 60% of the wood pulp consumed within the Community. The applicants challenged the Decision on the grounds that the Commission lacked jurisdiction, as they all had their offices outside the Community and any alleged agreement would have been made outside the Community.

Advocate General Darmon

It is on the basis of those considerations and of the criteria of international law that it is necessary to define the characteristics of an effect whose location justifies the assertion of prescriptive jurisdiction over undertakings established outside the Community.

According to some writers, such effects should correspond to those which are covered where the interference with competition is the result of conduct within the territory of the State which claims jurisdiction. ... However, as I have pointed out, it is unclear whether the concept of effect provided for in Article 85 of the EEC Treaty in order to establish the existence of an infringement of the competition rules is identical to that required by Community law, and accepted by international law, in order to determine whether there is jurisdiction over undertakings established outside the Community.

According to the substantive provisions of Community law, the restriction of competition must be 'perceptible' ... or 'appreciable'. The adverse affect on competition may be either direct or indirect and objectively or reasonably foreseeable. Those are the characteristics of the effect envisaged as a constituent element of interference with freedom of competition within the Community.

In my view, not all of those characteristics have to be adopted if the effect is taken as the criterion of extraterritorial jurisdiction. The most important reservation in that regard concerns indirect effect ... I would remind the Court that Mayras AG suggested, in his Opinion in the DYESTUFFS cases, the adoption of the criterion of the direct and immediate, reasonably foreseeable and substantial effect ([1972] ECR 619 at 694). I agree with that solution and, for the reasons which he sets forth, I would adopt his analysis which is as follows:

'Surely the Commission would be disarmed if, faced with a concerted practice, the initiative for which was taken and the responsibility for which was assumed exclusively by undertakings outside the Common Market, it was deprived of the power to take any decision against them? This would also mean giving up a way of defending the Common Market and one necessary for bringing about the major objectives of the European Economic Community.'

The Court

12. It should be noted that the main sources of supply of wood pulp are outside the Community, in Canada, the United States, Sweden and Finland and that the market therefore has global dimensions. Where wood pulp producers established in those countries sell directly to purchasers established in the Community and engage in price competition in order to win orders from those customers, that constitutes competition within the common market.

13. It follows that where those producers concert on the prices to be charged to their customers in the Community and put that concentration into effect by selling at prices which are actually coordinated, they are taking part in concentration which has the object and effect of restricting competition within the common market within the meaning of Article 85 of the Treaty.

14. Accordingly, it must be concluded that by applying the competition rules in the Treaty in the circumstances of this case to undertakings whose registered offices are situated outside the Community, the Commission has not made an incorrect assessment of the territorial scope of Article 85.

15. The applicants have submitted that the decision is incompatible with public international law on the grounds that the application of the competition rules in this case was founded exclusively on the economic repercussions within the common market of conduct restricting competition which was adopted outside the Community.

16. It should be observed that an infringement of Article 85, such as the conclusion of an agreement which has had the effect of restricting competition within the common market, consists of conduct made up of two elements, the formation of the agreement, decision or concerted practice and the implementation thereof. If the applicability of prohibitions laid down under competition law were made to depend on the place where the agreement, decision or concerted practice was formed, the result would obviously be to give undertakings an easy means of evading those prohibitions. The decisive factor is therefore the place where it is implemented.

17. The producers in this case implemented their pricing agreement within the common market. It is immaterial in that respect whether or not they had recourse to subsidiaries, agents, sub-agents, or branches within the Community in order to make their contacts with purchasers within the Community.

18. Accordingly the Community's jurisdiction to apply its competition rules to such conduct is covered by the territoriality principle as universally recognized in public international law.

The Court dressed its argument up in the territoriality principle, which is widely accepted as a head of jurisdiction in public international law.[32] The traditional application of this principle allows States jurisdiction over persons within their own territory. Under it a parent located outside the European Union is responsible for the acts of any subsidiary, agent, sub-agent or branch located within the Union.[33] Yet the Court suggests a wider basis for jurisdiction by focusing on the concept of 'implementation', irrespective of whether the undertaking had recourse to agents within the EC. The determinative factor is whether some essential constituent element of the alleged illicit practice took place in the EC.[34] This has been seen by some as potentially so wide-ranging as to introduce the effects doctrine into EC law through the back door.[35] Yet if that is so, it was strange that the Court did not simply follow the Advocate General's Opinion. One suggestion by Lange and Sandage is that jurisdiction will only be found to exist if the undertaking concerned is directly involved in a transaction with an undertaking situated in the European Union.[36] Certainly in such cases this will be easier to illustrate than that the practice has been 'implemented' within the Union.

Be that as it may, EC competition law finds itself between a rock and a hard place. The pressures placed on it by globalisation and the increasing number of pan-global players push for an expansive interpretation of the EC's jurisdiction. International comity pushes for a narrow one. One response to this might be more agreements along the lines of the Cooperation Agreement between the EC and United States.[37]

---

32 Akehurst, M. 'Jurisdiction in International Law' (1975) 46 *BYIL* 145.

33 This is sometimes known as the 'economic entity' test, and was established in Case 48/69 *ICI v Commission* [1972] ECR 619, [1972] CMLR 557.

34 Lange, D. & Sandage, J. supra n.29, 158-159; Christoforou, T. & Rockwell, D. 'European Economic Community Law: The Territorial Scope of Application of EEC Antitrust law - the Wood Pulp Judgment' (1989) 30 *Harvard International Law Journal* 195.

35 Mann, F. 'The Public International Law of Restrictive Practices in the European Court of Justice' (1989) 38 *ICLQ* 375; Roth, P. supra n.31, 262.

36 Lange, D. & Sandage, J. supra n.31, 161.

37 Decision of 10 April 1995 on the Agreement between the European Communities and the Government of the United States regarding application of competition law, OJ 1995, L 95/45. See Torremans, P. 'Extraterritorial

This requires not just that one party notify the other if the activities of its enforcement authorities affect important interests of the latter. It also requires each to consider enforcement activities on the other's behalf. Yet such a scheme is only possible where there is some convergence between systems of competition law. One is left otherwise with a regime where officials would be taking enforcement activities against measures which if implemented locally would be considered entirely lawful.

IV. The Enforcement of Competition Law

i. The Division of Responsibilities between the Commission and the National Courts

The Commission has exclusive responsibility for the orientation of competition policy.[38] It therefore has exclusive competence to grant either individual or block exemptions under Article 85 [*81*](3) EC. In addition, wide-ranging powers are granted to it by Regulation 17/62 to enforce EC competition law.[39] Under the Regulation the Commission has both investigative powers and quasi-judicial powers which enable it both to order practices in breach of the EC competition rules to be annulled and to impose severe penalties for breach of those rules. The possession of such an extensive set of powers has been criticised as unfair on the grounds that the Commission acts both as prosecutor and judge.[40] The Commission is subject to the scrutiny of the CFI, to whom any parties subject to a Commission Decision can go.

---

application of EC and US Competition Law' (1996) 21 *ELRev* 280.

38 Case C-234/89 *Delimitis v Henninger Brau AG* [1991] ECR I-935, [1992] 5 CMLR 210.

39 OJ Spec. Ed. 1962, 204/62, 87. Regulation 17/62 does not apply to transport and agriculture, where separate albeit similar regimes apply.

40 Van Bael, I.'The Antitrust Settlement of the EC Commission' (1986) 23 *CMLRev* 61; Brent, R. 'The Binding of Leviathan? - The Changing Role of the European Commission in Competition Cases' (1995) 44 *ICLQ* 255.

The direct effect of Articles 85 [*81*] and 86 [*82*] EC has provided another route for enforcing EC competition law, namely through national courts.[41] There has traditionally been a reluctance on the part of the latter to apply EC competition rules.[42] This resulted over the years in a considerable overstretching of the Commission's resources.[43] The general push towards legislative and administrative decentralisation in the 1990's resulted in the Commission issuing a Notice stating that it would concentrate on those practices which had a political, economic or legal significance for the Community.

Notice on Co-operation between National Courts and the Commission in Applying Articles 85 and 86 EEC Treaty[44]

13. As the administrative authority responsible for the Community's competition policy, the Commission must serve the Community's general interest. The administrative resources at the Commission's disposal are necessarily limited and cannot be used to deal with all the cases brought to its attention. The Commission is therefore obliged, in general, to take all organizational measures necessary for the performance of its task and, in particular to establish priorities.

14. The Commission intends, in implementing its decision-making powers to concentrate on notifications, complaints and own-initiative proceedings having particular political, economic or legal significance for the Community. Where these features are absent in a particular case, notifications will normally be dealt with by means of comfort letter and complaints should, as a rule, be handled by national court or authorities.

---

41 Case 127/73 *BRT v SABAM* [1974] ECR 51, [1974] 2 CMLR 177. National courts cannot grant exemptions, but can apply Commission exemptions made under Article 85(3) [81(3)], Case 31/80 *L'Oréal v Commission* [1980] ECR 3775, [1981] 2 CMLR 235.

42 Temple Lang, J. 'EEC Antitrust Law-Compliance and Enforcement' (1981) 18 *CMLRev* 335. On practice across the Member States Behrens, T . (ed.) *EEC Competition Rules in National Courts, Part One* (1992, Nomos, Baden-Baden) & Behrens, T. (ed.) *EEC Competition Rules in National Courts, Part Two* (1994, Nomos, Baden-Baden).

43 In 1996 the Commission registered 670 new cases for Articles 85 [*81*] and 86 [*82*] EC. EC Commission, *Twenty Sixth Report on Competition* Policy (1997, OOPEC, Luxembourg) 341.

44 OJ 1993 C 39/6. See also Riley, A. 'More Radicalism Please: The Notice on Cooperation between National Courts and the Commission in applying Articles 85 and 86 of the EEC Treaty' (1993) 3 *ECLR* 91.

15. The Commission considers there is not normally a sufficient Community interest in examining a case when the plaintiff is able to secure adequate protection of his rights before national courts. In these circumstances the complaint will normally be filed.

16. In this respect the Commission would like to make it clear that the application of Community competition law by the national courts has considerable advantages for individuals and companies:
- the Commission cannot award compensation for loss suffered as a result of an infringement of Article 85 or Article 86. Such claims may be brought only before national courts. Companies are more likely to avoid infringement of the Community competition rules if they risk having to pay damages or interest in such an event,
- national courts can usually adopt interim measures and order the ending of infringements more quickly than the Commission is able to do,
- before national courts it is possible to combine a claim under Community law with a claim under national law. This is not possible in a procedure before the Commission,
- in some Member States, the courts have the power to award legal costs to the successful applicant. This is never possible in the administrative procedure before the Commission.

Shaw, J. 'Decentralization and Law Enforcement in EC Competition Law' (1995) 15 *Legal Studies* 128, 128-129

These policy statements signalled at the very least a significant shift in the emphasis of the enforcement of EC competition rules. Although it has been established for some time that individuals harmed by breaches of the competition rules may themselves seek redress before the national courts, relying upon the direct effect of the key provisions of the Treaty, and although there does exist as substantial jurisprudence on these matters in some member states, the general thrust of competition law enforcement has remained centred around the Commission. This is not in itself surprising as the Commission is not only endowed with considerable powers of investigation and enforcement under Regulation 17 which go well beyond those of any national court, but it is also the body which has, over the years, set the essential tone and basic content of competition policy and has determined - subject to judicial review by the Court of Justice and, lately by the Court of First Instance - the interpretation to be placed on the scope, meaning and effect of arts 85 and 86 EC. Third parties have commonly sought redress by complaining to the Commission under art 3(2)(b) of regulation 17; this has been the cheapest and often the most effective way for the victim of abusive conduct such as predatory pricing or a refusal to supply, or of anti-competitive conduct such as the operation of a territorially based distribution network excluding parallel imports, to obtain legal protection. Many but not all complainants have been economically more vulnerable than the firms complained about; in fact complaining to the Commission has become part of a culture of corporate strategies which seek to make use of legal rules such as arts 85 and 86 EC. Now, it would appear that national courts - described in 1984 as 'a great untapped resource in the application of the competition rules'[45] - are to play a much more active role, sharing explicitly in the enforcement of competition rules in the interests of an effective division of tasks. The availability of national remedies has become, for the first time, an express variable in the equation determining whether or not the Commission will intervene.

The practice has now been legitimised by the CFI.

Case T-114/92 Bureau Européen des médias de l' industrie musicale (BEMIM) v Commission [1995] ECR II-147

The applicant complained to the Commission in 1986 that SACEM, an organisation which manages copyright in musical works in France, was only allowing music to be played in French discos under conditions which breached Article 86 [*81*] EC. In 1992, following an investigation, the Commission rejected the applicant's complaint, stating, *inter alia*, that there was insufficient Community interest in its pursuing the matter, as the practices all occurred on the territory of one Member State.

80. It is clear from the principles developed by this Court in its judgment in *Automec II* that the Commission is entitled to reject a complaint when it considers that the case does not display a sufficient Community interest to justify further investigation of the case (paragraph 85). In that case, the Court of First Instance made it clear that, in order to assess the Community interest in further investigation of a case, the Commission must take account of the circumstances of the case and in particular the matters of fact and law to which its attention is drawn in the complaint submitted to it. It must, in particular, balance the significance of the alleged infringement as regards the functioning of the common market, the probability of its being able to establish the existence of the infringement and the extent of the investigative measures required for it to perform, under the best possible conditions, its task of making sure that Articles 85 and 86 are complied with (paragraph 86). The fact that a national court or national competition authority is already dealing with a case concerning the compatibility of an agreement or practice with Article 85 or 86 of the Treaty is a factor which the Commission may take into account in evaluating the extent to which a case displays a Community interest.

---

45 Forrester, I. & Norall, C. 'The Laicization of Community Law: Self-help and the Rule of Reason: How Competition Law is and could be applied' (1984) 21 *CMLRev* 11, 45.

81. It is true, as the applicant points out, that in *Automec II* the Commission rejected the complaint for lack of a Community interest without undertaking investigative measures. The court considers, however, that the Commission may take a decision to shelve a complaint for lack of a sufficient Community interest not only before commencing an investigation of the case but also after taking investigative measures, if that course seems appropriate to it at that stage of the procedure. To conclude otherwise would be tantamount to placing the Commission under an obligation, once it had taken investigative measures following the submission of an application under Article 3(2) of Regulation no 17, to adopt a decision as to whether or not either Article 85 or Article 86 of the Treaty, or both, had been infringed. Such an interpretation would not only be contrary to the very wording of Article 3(1) of Regulation no 17, according to which the Commission 'may' adopt a decision concerning the existence of the alleged infringement, but would also conflict with the settled case-law of the Court of Justice and Court of First Instance cited in paragraph 62 above according to which a complainant has no right to obtain from the Commission a decision within the meaning of Article 189 of the Treaty.

82. It is apparent, in the present case, from paragraphs 6 and 8 of the contested decision that the Commission concluded, after its examination, that there was no sufficient Community interest in further investigation of the case, since the centre of gravity of the infringement was in France and similar cases were pending before several French courts and the French Conseil de la Concurrence.

83. As regards the essentially national effect of the practices criticized, namely the allegedly excessive and discriminatory rate of royalties charged by SACEM and SACEM's alleged refusal to allow French discothèques to use only the foreign repertoire, the Court considers that the fact that a course of conduct or a practice is liable to affect trade between Member States, within the meaning of Article 86 of the Treaty, does not in itself prevent the effects of that conduct from being confined essentially to the territory of a single Member State. In the present case, it is apparent from the documents before the Court that only French discothèques have been the victims of SACEM's allegedly abusive conduct and that the effects of the practices criticized, in so far as they were such as to affect trade between Member States, made themselves felt only in frontier areas. In any event, the Court finds that the applicant, which expressly stated in its complaint that SACEM's practices have created 'discrimination, in particular involving discothèques on each side of the border between France and another Member State (Belgium, Luxembourg, Germany and Italy)', has produced no evidence to show that the Commission made any factual error in taking the view that 'the centre of gravity of the alleged infringement is in France'.

84. Furthermore, the Court observes that it is common ground that several French courts, in proceedings between SACEM and certain of the applicant's members, and the French Conseil de la concurrence, have been asked to decide whether the practices criticized in the complaint are compatible with Articles 85 and 86 of the Treaty.

85. It is therefore necessary to consider whether, in the present case, the Commission, on the basis of that factual information, has committed a manifest error of appraisal regarding the Community interest in further investigation of the case.

86. The Court considers that where the effects of the infringements alleged in a complaint are essentially confined to the territory of one Member State and where proceedings have been brought before the courts and competent administrative authorities of that Member State by the complainant - or members of it, in cases such as the present one where the complainant is an association of undertakings - against the body against which the complaint was made, the Commission is entitled to reject the complaint through lack of any sufficient Community interest in further investigation of the case, provided however that the rights of the complainant or of its members can be adequately safeguarded, in particular by the national courts (*Automec II*, paragraphs 89 to 96).

87. The applicant considers that, because the French courts do not have the necessary powers to undertake an investigation of such great scope, the referral of the matter to the national courts was not justifiable in this case.

88. The Court considers, first, that the fact that the national court might encounter difficulties in interpreting Article 85 or 86 of the Treaty is not, in view of the possibilities available under Article 177 of the Treaty, a factor which the Commission is required to take into account in appraising the Community interest in further investigation of a case. Furthermore, that provision of the treaty is designed in particular to ensure uniform application of the Treaty by providing that national courts against whose decisions there is no judicial remedy under national law are required to refer a question to the Court of Justice for a preliminary ruling where a question is raised before them concerning the interpretation of provisions of the Treaty. The Court considers, on the other hand, that the rights of a complainant could not be regarded as sufficiently protected before the national court if that court were not reasonably able, in view of the complexity of the case, to gather the factual information necessary in order to determine whether the practices criticized in the complaint constituted an infringement of the said Treaty provisions.

The Commission has sought to elaborate upon this division in a draft Notice published in 1996.[46] It considered three factors should be particularly taken into account:

---

46 Preliminary Draft Commission Notice on Cooperation between national competition authorities and the Commission in handling cases falling within the scope of Articles 85 or Article 86 of the EC Treaty, OJ 1996 C 262/7.

- If the practice had mainly national effects, it should be dealt with by national authorities. This would be the case if the effects of a practice occurred mainly within the territory of a Member State;

- The Commission should deal with those practices which national authorities were unable to deal with. This would necessarily be those cases where the Commission had exclusive competence, namely the granting or withdrawal of an exemption under Article 85(3) EC;

- The Commission should be able to intervene in cases, whatever their size, of particular significance to the Community. These will be cases which raise new points of law or where important interests of firms from other Member States are involved.

The draft Notice suggests a further decentralisation of the enforcement of EC competition. The following piece, in referring to the 1993 Notice, suggests that national courts should not be seen as a panacea.

Shaw, J. 'Decentralization and Law Enforcement in EC Competition Law' (1995) 15 *Legal Studies* 128, 136-137.

It [the Notice] does not mention two further advantages, namely the ability of a court to make a binding order, where failure to comply will attract severe consequences such as contempt of court, and the flexibility given to the litigants who control their own proceedings and who may settle before a final decision if that proves more attractive. Significantly also, the Notice does not allude to the many disadvantages for undertakings in taking proceedings in the national court such as the fact that significant costs will accrue without any advance guarantee of recovery, whereas making a complaint to the Commission can be almost entirely costless for the complainant. In addition, there may be difficulties in obtaining evidence where it is located in more than one jurisdiction, and consequently severe difficulties of proof, for example, where it is contended that there is a concerted practice in operation. Other procedural obstacles may include rules on discovery and difficulties in framing an appropriate cause of action which not only satisfies the requirements of competition law, but also fits with the procedural framework of national law.

ii. Enforcement by the Commission

a. The Investigative Powers of the Commission

Undertakings are not under a duty to notify to the Commission practices which might be anti-competitive, but there are considerable incentives to do so. Undertakings can only obtain an exemption under Article 85 [*81*] (3) EC if the agreement is notified to the Commission,[47] and they cannot be fined for participation in any illegal agreement during the period of notification.[48] There are disincentives, however. The time taken by the Commission to consider the agreement may be lengthy, resulting in a period of corresponding commercial uncertainty. In addition, insofar as EC competition law prohibits certain practices taking place which may be advantageous to the parties involved, there are incentives for them to try to evade the system.[49]

The Commission has therefore been granted investigative powers by the EC Treaty.

Article 89 [*85*] (1) EC. Without prejudice to Article 88 [*84*], the Commission shall, as soon as it takes up its duties, ensure the application of the principles laid down in Articles 85 [*81*] and 86 [*82*]. On application by a Member State or on its own initiative, and in co-operation with the competent authorities in the Member States, who shall give it their assistance, the Commission shall investigate cases of suspected infringement of these principles. If it finds that there has been an infringement, it shall propose appropriate measures to bring it to an end.

2. If the infringement is not brought to an end, the Commission shall record such infringement of the principles in a reasoned decision. The Commission may publish its decision and authorise Member States to take the measures, the conditions and details of which it shall determine, needed to remedy the situation.

---

47 Regulation 17/62, Article 4(1).

48 Regulation 17/62, Article 15(5). The Commission can tell the parties to discontinue the agreement, whilst it considers it. Should they continue, they are subject to fines, Article 15(6).

49 Brown, A 'Notification of Agreements to the EC Commission: Whether to Submit to a Flawed System' (1992) 17 *ELRev* 323.

These powers are expanded upon in Regulation 17/62. The Commission may begin an investigation either on its own initiative or upon an application by a Member State or a third party claiming a legitimate interest.[50] The Commission is under a duty to consider any complaint made, since failure to do so may expose it to an action under Article 175 [*232*] EC.[51] If it initiates proceedings it must grant a hearing to persons who have a sufficient interest.[52] The CFI has, however, recognised that the Commission has limited resources and may prioritise the cases it investigates.

Case T-24/90 Automec Srl v Commission [1992] ECR II-2223, [1992] 5 CMLR 431.

Automec lodged a complaint with the Commission that BMW had terminated its dealership arrangement in breach of Article 85 [*81*](1) EC. The Commission refused to grant an order compelling BMW to resume supply arguing that the matter had been dealt with in the Italian courts and that there was not enough EC interest to involve the EC Commission. Automec appealed to the CFI against this decision.

75. ... it is clear from the case law of the Court of Justice ... that the rights conferred upon complainants by Regulations 17 and 99/63 do not include a right to obtain a decision, within the meaning of Article 189 EEC, as to the existence or otherwise of the alleged infringement. It follows that the Commission cannot be required to give a ruling in that connection unless the subject-matter of the complaint is within its exclusive remit, such as the withdrawal of an exemption granted pursuant to Article 85(3) EEC.

76. As the Commission has no obligation to rule on the existence or otherwise of an infringement it cannot be compelled to conduct an investigation, because this could have no purpose other than to seek evidence of the existence or otherwise of an infringement the existence of which it is not required to establish...

77. In this connection it should be observed that, for an institution performing a public-service task, the power to take all the organizational measures necessary for the fulfilment of that task, including settling priorities in the framework laid down by law, where those

---

50 Regulation 17/62, Article 3(1).

51 Case 210/81 *Demo-Studio Schmidt v Commission* [1983] ECR 3045, [1984] 1 CMLR 63.

52 Regulation 17/62, Article 19(2).

priorities have not been settled by the legislature, is an inherent part of the work of the administration. This must apply particularly where an authority has been given a supervisory and regulatory function as general and extensive as that assigned to the Commission in the field of competition. Therefore the fact that the Commission allocates different degrees of priority to the matters referred to it in the field of competition is compatible with its obligations under Community law.

The first procedure open to the Commission under Regulation 17 is to request information from the undertakings involved.

Article 11(1). In carrying out the duties assigned to it by Article 89 and by provisions adopted under Article 87 of the Treaty, the Commission may obtain all necessary information from the Governments and competent authorities of the Member States and from undertakings and associations of undertakings.

2. When sending a request for information to an undertaking or association of undertakings, the Commission shall at the same time forward a copy of the request to the competent authority of the Member State in whose territory the seat of the undertaking or association of undertakings is situated.

3. In its request the Commission shall state the legal basis and the purpose of the request and also the penalties provided for in Article 15(1)(b) for supplying incorrect information.

4. The owners of the undertakings or their representatives and, in the case of legal persons, companies or firms, or of associations having no legal personality, the persons authorised to represent them by law or by their constitution shall supply the information requested.

5. Where an undertaking or association of undertakings does not supply the information requested within the time limit fixed by the Commission, or supplies incomplete information, the Commission shall by decision require the information to be supplied. The decision shall specify what information is required, fix an appropriate time limit within which it is to be supplied and indicate the penalties provided for in Article 15(1)(b) and Article 16(1)(c) and the right to have the decision reviewed by the Court of Justice.

6. The Commission shall at the same time forward a copy of its decision to the competent authority of the Member State in whose territory the seat of the undertaking or association of undertakings is situated.

There are both procedural and substantive limits on the information which the Commission can require undertakings to supply. It will be clear from Article 11(5) that the Commission can only require the firm to supply information once the firm has refused an informal request by it for the information.[53] The Commission can, furthermore, only ask for information which is related to the investigation. It cannot therefore go on general 'fishing' expeditions.[54] The undertaking is, furthermore, not obliged to supply any information which might compromise its rights of defence.

Joined Cases 374/87 & 27/88 Orkem & Solvay v Commission [1989] ECR 3283; [1991] 4 CMLR 502

The applicants sought to annul a Decision taken by the Commission after an inquiry into the existence of agreements or concerted practices in the thermoplastics industry.

14. It must be stated, with respect to the Commission's right to require the disclosure of the documents in connection with a request for information that Articles 11 and 14 of Regulation No 17 establish two entirely independent procedures. The fact that an investigation under Article 14 has already taken place cannot in any way diminish the powers of investigation available to the Commission under Article 11. No consideration of a procedural nature inherent in Regulation No 17 thus prevents the Commission from requiring, for the purposes of a request for information, the disclosure of documents of which it was unable to take a copy or extract when carrying out a previous investigation.

15. With regard to the necessity of the information requested, it must be borne in mind that Regulation No 17 confers on the Commission wide powers to make investigations and to obtain information by providing in the eight recital in its preamble that the Commission must be empowered throughout the Common Market, to require such information to be supplied and to undertake such investigations as are necessary to bring to light infringements of Articles 85 and 86 of the Treaty. As the Court held in its judgment of 18 May 1982 in Case 155/79 AM&S Europe Limited v Commission [1982] ECR 1575, it is for the Commission to decide, for the purposes of an investigation under Article 14, whether particular information is necessary to enable it to bring to light an infringement of the competition rules. Even if it already has evidence, or indeed proof of

53 The Commission can fine firms between 100 and 5,000 ECU which refuse, negligently or intentionally, either to supply the information or supply incorrect or misleading information, Regulation 17/62, Article 15(1).

54 Case T-39/90 *Samenwerkende v Commission* [1991] ECR II-1497.

the existence of an infringement, the Commission may legitimately take the view that it is necessary to request further information to better define the scope of the infringement, to determine its duration or to identify the circle of undertakings involved.

.....

18. The applicant claims, essentially, that the Commission used the contested decision to compel it to incriminate itself by confessing to an infringement of the competition rules and to inform against other undertakings. By doing so, the Commission has, in its view, infringed the general principle that no one may be compelled to give evidence against himself, which forms part of Community law in so far as it is principle upheld by the laws of the Member States, by the European Convention For The Protection of Human Rights and Fundamental Freedoms of 4 November 1950 ... and by the International Covenant on Civil and Political Rights of 19 December 1966 ... It has thus, in the applicant's view, infringed the rights of the defence.

19. In considering whether that submission is well-founded, it should be recalled that, as the Court held in its judgment in Case 136/79 National Panasonic ... the aim of the power as given to the Commission by Regulation No 17 is to enable it to carry out its duty under the EEC Treaty of ensuring that the rules on competition are applied in the Common Market. The function of those rules, as is apparent from the fourth recital in the Preamble to the Treaty, Article 3(f) and Articles 85 and 86, is to prevent competition from being distorted to the detriment of the public interest, individual undertakings and consumers. The exercise of powers given to the Commission by Regulation No 17 contributes to the maintenance of the system of competition intended by the Treaty which undertakings have an absolute duty to comply with.

.....

28. In the absence of any right to remain silent expressly embodied in Regulation No 17, it is appropriate to consider whether and to what extent the general principles of Community Law, of which fundamental rights form an integral part and in the light of which all Community legislation must be interpreted, require, as the applicant claims, recognition of the right not to supply information capable of being used in order to establish against the person supplying it, the existence of an infringement of the competition rules.

29. In general, the laws of the Member States grant the right not to give evidence against oneself only to a natural person charged with an offence in criminal proceedings. A comparative analysis of national law does not therefore indicate the existence of such a principle, common to the laws of the Member States, which may be relied upon by legal persons in relation to infringements in the economic sphere, in particular infringements of competition law.

30. As far as Article 6 of the European Convention is concerned, although it may be relied upon by an undertaking subject to an investigation relating to competition law, it must be observed that neither the wording of that Article nor the decisions of the European Court of Human Rights indicate that it upholds the right not to give evidence against oneself.

31. Article 14 of the International Covenant, which upholds, in addition to the presumption of innocence, the right (in paragraph 3(g)) not to give evidence against oneself or to confess to guilt, relates only to persons accused of a criminal offence in court proceedings and thus has no bearing on investigations in the field of competition law.

32. It is necessary, however, to consider whether certain limitations on the Commission's powers of investigation are implied by the need to safeguard the rights of the defence which the Court has held to be a fundamental principle of the Community legal order (Judgment of 9 November 1983 in Case 322/82 Michelin v Commission (1983) ECR 3461, paragraph 7).

33. In that connection, the Court observed recently, in its judgment of 21 September 1989 in Joined Cases 46/87 and 227/88 Hoechst v Commission (1989) ECR 2859, paragraph 15, that whilst it is true that the rights of defence must be observed in the administrative procedures which may lead to the imposition of penalties, it is necessary to prevent those rights from being irremediably impaired during preliminary inquiry procedures which may be decisive in providing evidence of the unlawful nature of the conduct engaged in by undertakings and for which they may be liable. Consequently, although certain rights of the defence relate only to contentious proceedings which follow the delivery of the statement of objections, other rights must be respected even during the preliminary inquiry.

34. Accordingly, whilst the Commission is entitled, in order to preserve the useful effect of Article 11(2) and (5) of Regulation No 17, to compel an undertaking to provide all necessary information concerning such facts as may be known to it and to disclose to it, if necessary, such documents relating thereto as are in its possession, even if the latter may be used to establish, against it or another undertaking, the existence of anti-competitive conduct, it may not, by means of a decision calling for information, undermine the rights of defence of the undertaking concerned.

35. Thus, the Commission may not compel an undertaking to provide it with answers which might involve an admission on its part of the existence of an infringement which is incumbent upon the Commission to prove.

The second option open to the Commission under Regulation 17 is to carry out an investigation.

Article 14(1). In carrying out the duties assigned to it by Article 89 and by provisions adopted under Article 87 of the Treaty, the Commission may undertake all necessary investigations into undertakings and associations of undertakings. To this end the officials authorised by the Commission are empowered:

(a) to examine the books and other business records;
(b) to take copies of or extracts from the books and business records;
(c) to ask for oral explanations on the spot;
(d) to enter any premises, land and means of transport of undertakings.

In carrying out these investigations the Commission can request assistance from the national authorities in carrying out these investigations.[55] It can also levy fines if incomplete records are produced during the investigation.[56] There are two forms of investigation. The first under Article 14(2) is the voluntary investigations. Commission officials must produce a written authorisation which specifies the subject-matter and purpose of the investigation and indicates the penalties which can be incurred if incomplete records are produced. Such investigations cannot be carried out without the undertaking. Increasingly common are the mandatory investigations of Article 14(3).[57]

Article 14(3). Undertakings and associations of undertakings shall submit to investigations ordered by decision of the Commission. The decision shall specify the subject-matter and purpose of the investigation, appoint the date on which it is to begin and indicate the penalties provided for in Article 15(1)(c) and Article 16(1)(d) and the right to have the decision reviewed by the Court of Justice.

This provision is the basis for the famous 'dawn raids' where the Commission turns up on the doorstep of an undertaking. Undertakings cannot refuse to submit to such an investigation.[58] The Article 14

55 Regulation 17/62, Article 14(5) & (6).

56 Ibid., Article 15(1) (c).

57 There is a procedural difference between Article 14(3) investigations and Article 14(2). The former requires the adoption of a formal decision by the Commission before it can be carried out. See Kerse, C. *EC Antitrust Procedure* (1994, 3rd Edition, Sweet & Maxwell, London) 113.

58 Regulation 17/62, Article 16(1)(d).

investigation is a more brutal procedure than the Article 11 request for information. It does not require the same prior notice or that the Commission has sought to gain access with an undertaking's cooperation before it carry out an Article 14(3) investigation.

Case 136/79 National Panasonic (UK) v Commission [1980] ECR 2033, [1980] 3 CMLR 169

The Commission adopted a Decision to investigate National Pansonic which provided that notification of the Decision would be by the personal handing over of the Decision to a representative of the firm immediately before the investigation was to begin. The investigation took place without waiting for the arrival of the firm's solicitor and several notes and documents were taken away at the end of the investigation.

8.The applicant maintains first of all that the contested decision is unlawful because it does not comply with the spirit and letter of the provisions of Article 14(3) of Regulation No 17 of the Council. To this end it maintains that on a proper construction those provisions provide for a two-stage procedure which permits the Commission to adopt a Decision requiring an undertaking to submit to an investigation only after attempting to carry out that investigation on the basis of a written authorisation to its own officials. This interpretation is confirmed, according to the applicant, by Article 11 of the same Regulation which is similar in structure and provides for a two-stage procedure and by Article 13(1) which makes a distinction between an investigation carried out by the Commission informally and that ordered by Decision.

9. These arguments do not appear to be well-founded. In order to enable the Commission to accomplish its task of ensuring that the rules of competition in the Common Market are complied with, the eighth recital of the Preamble to Regulation 17 provides that it 'must ... be empowered, throughout the common market, to require such information to be supplied and to undertake such investigations as are necessary to bring to light any agreement, decision or concerted practice prohibited by Article 85(1) or any abuse of a dominant position prohibited by Article 86'. For this purpose, that Regulation provides for separate procedures, which shows that the exercise of the powers given to the Commission with regard to information and investigations is not subject to the same conditions.

Article 14 investigations are subject to certain procedural constraints.

Joined Cases 46/87 & 227/88 Hoechst AG v Commission [1989] ECR 2859, [1991] 4 CMLR 410

Hoechst refused to submit to a dawn raid by Commission officials. The Commission obtained access to the firm's premises by a search warrant obtained under national law and Hoechst was fined for non-compliance with an Article 14(3) Decision. Hoechst argued that such searches could only be carried out with advance warning and that the Commission's procedures were incompatible with the right to respect for private life guaranteed under Article 8(1) of the European Convention on Human Rights and Freedoms.

12. It should be noted, before the nature and scope of the Commission's powers of investigation under Article 14 of Regulation 17 are examined, that Article cannot be interpreted in such a way as to give rise to results which are incompatible with the general principles of Community law and in particular with fundamental rights.

.....

26. Both the purpose of Regulation 17 and the list of powers conferred on Commission officials by Article 14 thereof show that the scope of investigations may be very wide. In that regard, the right to enter any premises ... is of particular importance inasmuch as it is intended to permit the Commission to obtain evidence of infringements of the competition rules in the places in which such evidence is normally to be found, that is to say, on the business premises of undertakings.

27. That right of access would serve no useful purpose if the Commission officials could do no more than ask for documents or files which they could identify in advance. On the contrary, such a right implies the power to search for various items of information which are not already known or fully identified. Without such a power, it would be impossible for the Commission to obtain the information necessary to carry out the investigation if the undertakings concerned refused to co-operate or adopted an obstructive attitude.

28. Although Article 14 of Regulation 17 thus confers wide powers of investigation on the Commission, the exercise of those powers is subject to conditions serving to ensure that the rights of undertakings concerned are respected.

.....

30. It should also be pointed out that the conditions for the exercise of the Commission's investigative powers vary according to the procedure which the Commission has chosen, the attitude of the undertakings concerned and the intervention of the national authorities.

31. Article 14 of Regulation No 17 deals in the first place with investigations carried out with the cooperation of the undertakings concerned, either voluntarily, where there is a written authorization, or by virtue of an obligation arising under a decision ordering an investigation. In the latter case, which is the situation here, the Commission's officials have, *inter alia*, the power to have shown to them the documents they request, to enter such premises as they choose, and to have shown to them the contents of any piece of furniture which they indicate. On the other hand, they may not obtain access to premises or furniture by force or oblige the staff of the undertaking to give them such access, or carry out searches without the permission of the management of the undertaking.

32. The situation is completely different if the undertakings concerned oppose the Commission's investigation. In that case, the Commission's officials may, on the basis of Article 14(6) and without the cooperation of the undertakings, search for any information necessary for the investigation with the assistance of the national authorities, which are required to afford them the assistance necessary for the performance of their duties. Although such assistance is required only if the undertaking expresses its opposition, it may also be requested as a precautionary measure, in order to overcome any opposition on the part of the undertaking.

33. It follows from Article 14(6) that it is for each Member State to determine the conditions under which the national authorities will afford assistance to the Commission's officials. In that regard, the Member States are required to ensure that the Commission's action is effective, while respecting the general principles set out above. It follows that, within those limits, the appropriate procedural rules designed to ensure respect for undertakings' rights are those laid down by national law.

34. Consequently, if the Commission intends, with the assistance of the national authorities, to carry out an investigation other than with the cooperation of the undertakings concerned, it is required to respect the relevant procedural guarantees laid down by national law.

35. The Commission must make sure that the competent body under national law has all that it needs to exercise its own supervisory powers. It should be pointed out that body, whether judicial or otherwise, cannot in this respect substitute its own assessment of the need for the investigations ordered for that of the Commission, the lawfulness of whose assessments of fact and law is subject only to review by the Court of Justice. On the other hand, it is within the powers of the national body, after satisfying itself that the decision ordering the investigation is authentic, to consider whether the measures of constraint envisaged are arbitrary or excessive having regard to the subject-matter of the investigation and to ensure that the rules of national law are complied with in the application of those measures.

36. In the light of the foregoing, it must be held that the measures which the contested decision ordering the investigation permitted the Commission's officials to take did not exceed their powers under Article 14 of Regulation No 17. Article 1 of that decision merely requires the applicant 'to permit officials authorized by the Commission to enter its premises during normal office hours, to produce for inspection and to permit copies to be made of business documents related to the subject-matter of the enquiry which are requested by the said officials and to provide immediately any explanations which those officials may seek'.

b. The Rights of Defence of the Parties

The right to protection against self-incrimination and the procedural constraints placed upon the Commission's powers of investigation form but part of the rights of defence which constrain the Commission's behaviour in this area. There are other constraints which apply, whichever procedure the Commission uses. One is that the Commission is not allowed access to legally privileged documents.

Case 155/79 AM and S Europe Ltd. v Commission [1982] ECR 1575, [1982] 2 CMLR 264

AM & S Europe Ltd. refused to disclose documents during a Commission investigation, arguing that they were protected by the legal professional privilege rules found in all Member States which prevent confidential communications between lawyer and client being disclosed.

18. However, the above rules do not exclude the possibility of recognising, subject to certain conditions, that certain business records are of a confidential nature. Community law, which derives from not only the economic but also the legal interpenetration of the Member States, must take into account the principles and concepts common to the laws of those states concerning the observance of confidentiality, in particular, as regards certain communications between lawyer and client. That confidentiality serves the requirements, the importance of which is recognised in all the Member States, that any person must be able, without constraint, to consult a lawyer whose profession entails the giving of independent legal advice to all those in need of it.

19. As far as the protection of written communications between lawyer and client are concerned, it is apparent from the legal systems of the Member States that, although the principle of such protection is generally recognised, its scope and the criteria for applying it vary.

.....

21. Apart from these differences, however, there are to be found in the national laws of the Member States common criteria inasmuch as those laws protect, in similar circumstances, the confidentiality of written communications between lawyer and client provided that, on the one hand, such communications are made for the purposes and in the interests of the client's rights of defence, and on the other hand, they emanate from independent lawyers, that is to say, lawyers who are not bound to the client by a relationship of employment.

22. Viewed in that context Regulation No 17 must be interpreted as protecting, in its turn, the confidentiality of written communications between lawyer and client subject to those two conditions, and thus incorporating such elements of that protection as are common to the laws of the Member States.

The definition of legal privilege in *AM & S* was narrower than most national jurisdictions, where either all lawyer-client correspondence or all correspondence issued in connection with the defence is protected. The result was that often crucial correspondence, such as correspondence with in-house lawyers is not protected.[59]

Commission investigations pose another threat to undertakings. Third parties have a right to be heard by the Commission if they can demonstrate a sufficient interest.[60] There is a danger therefore that an investigation might result in perfectly legitimate business secrets being divulged to competitors. In *AKZO Chemie* the Court accepted that there was a requirement on the part of the Commission to protect business secrets.[61] This raises the question of what should be considered to be a business secret.

Case T-30/89A Hilti AG v Commission [1990] ECR II-163, [1990] 4 CMLR 602.

Hilti brought an action to annul a decision of the EC Commission finding an infringement of Article 86 [*82*] EC. Two undertakings, Bauco (UK) Ltd. and

59 Christoforou, T. 'Protection of Legal Privilege in EEC Competition Law: The Imperfections of a Case' (1985) *Fordham International Law Journal* 1.

60 Regulation 17, Article 19(2).

61 Case 53/85 *AKZO Chemie BV v Commission* [1986] ECR 1965, [1987] 1 CMLR 231. Such a duty is also contained in Regulation 17/62, Article 20. See Joshua, J. 'Balancing the Public Interests: Confidentiality, Trade Secrets and Disclosure of Evidence in EC Competition Procedures' (1994) 2 *ECLR* 68.

Profix Distribution Ltd. requested leave to intervene in the case. Hilti asked for certain documents to be treated as confidential on the grounds of business secrecy.

15. [The]... category of documents for which confidential treatment is requested is composed of two documents, excerpts from which have been incorporated in the defence. According to the applicant, those documents report on legal advice which was received by it and which itself was covered by legal professional privilege. The applicant submits that a report of such advice is by its very nature confidential and should not be disclosed to the interveners.

16. An examination of the aforesaid documents shows that they are, essentially, notes internal to the undertaking reporting the content of advice received from independent, and thus external, legal advisers.

17. Such legal advice would be covered by the principle of the protection of confidentiality laid down by the Court of Justice if it had been received from independent legal advisers by way of written communication.

18. In this case it appears that legal advice was reported on in internal notes distributed within the undertaking so that it might be the subject of consideration by managerial staff. In such a case, and although the aforesaid legal advice was not received by way of correspondence, it must be held that the principle of the protection of written communications between lawyer and client must, in view of its purpose, be regarded as extending also to the internal notes which are confined to reporting the text or the content of those communications. It follows that the request for confidential treatment made by the applicant must be allowed in so far as it refers to those documents.

19. The third category referred to contains a large number of documents, or excerpts from documents, and of various items of information. The applicant submits in this respect that in the normal course of events the disclosure of such information to a competitor would be prohibited by Article 85(1) of the EEC Treaty. The applicant submits that, since business secrets are afforded, by virtue of Article 20 of Regulation No 17/62, confidential treatment in administrative proceedings before the Commission, all such items of information and documents should be afforded confidential treatment also vis a vis the interveners. According to the applicant, it follows from the nature of the information and documents for which confidential treatment is claimed that the applicant has an interest in ensuring that they are not disclosed to third parties who are competitors. Disclosure to the intervenors would, therefore damage that interest, albeit that the applicant is not in a position a priori, to attribute a financial value to that damage.

20. The Court has examined in minute detail each of the documents or excerpts from documents falling within the third category described in the request for confidential treatment. That examination shows that a large number of those documents or excerpts from documents do qualify by reason of their nature, as 'secret or confidential documents' within the meaning of Article 93(4) of the Rules of Procedure. The same examination, carried out in the light of the criteria set out above ... discloses sufficient grounds for holding that the application of the aforementioned provision is also justified as regards the majority of the documents and excerpts from documents in question.

.....

23. As regards the applicant's request that the Court make it clear to the interveners that the documents in the case are made available to them for the purposes of the proceedings in this case, it should be observed that the rules governing the procedure before the court do not contain any provision on which such a direction could be based. The request must therefore be rejected.

The duty not to divulge business secrets does not just apply to the Commission. In *Spanish Banks* it was extended to national authorities who come into contact with business secrets as a result of assisting Commission investigations.[62] The Court noted that the Commission needed to pass information on to these authorities either to inform Member States of its investigations or to enhance the provision of information to itself by comparing the submissions given by the undertaking with any information which the national authorities may have. Whilst such information may be used as circumstantial evidence to justify separate proceedings, the information was not to be used for a purpose for which it had not been provided. The national authorities could not therefore use it as the basis for instigating a preliminary investigation procedure or to justify a decision based on either national or EC competition law.

Once the latter have seen the information, however, they cannot be expected to forget it. In *Samenwerkende* the Court therefore stated that if the Commission proposed to hand information over to national authorities, it had to inform the undertaking concerned in order that the latter could seek to contest the decision and show that its secrets would not be adequately protected.[63]

---

62 Case C-67/91 *Dirección General de la Defensa de la Competencia v Asociación Española de Banca Privada & Others* [1992] ECR I-4785.

63 Case C-36/92P *Samenwerkende Elecktriciteits-produktiebedrijven NV v Commission* [1994] ECR I-1911.

In addition to question of privilege and protection of business secrets, a third point of contention that has arisen during investigations is the right of the defendant to have access to its file. This right extends both to documents on which the Commission bases its decision ('inculpatory documents') and to documents which might be useful for the defence of the undertaking ('exculpatory documents').

Case T-30/91 Solvay v Commission [1995] ECR II-1772

The Commission carried out an investigation into a market sharing cartel between the two main soda ash producers, Solvay and ICI. The firms expressed concerns about the disclosure of business secrets. The EC Commission confirmed that documents to support its allegations had been sent to both firms but stated that secret or confidential matters which did not relate directly to the suspected infringement had been deleted. At the hearing Solvay declined to take part and subsequently complained that ICI had used certain documents in its defence which Solvay had not been given by the Commission. After having been fined by the Commission, Solvay challenged the Decision, claiming, *inter alia*, that its rights of defence had been violated as it had neither had access to the documents which incriminated it nor to certain documents which served to exonerate it. The CFI first of all considered the question of the alleged incriminatory documents.

58. However, even if the use of the documents in question were to be characterized as unlawful on the grounds that it infringed the applicant's rights of defence, such a procedural defect could, in the present case, only result in those documents being excluded as evidence. Far from leading to the annulment of the entire decision, that exclusion would be relevant only in so far as the objection made by the Commission in relation thereto could be proved only by reference to those documents (judgment of the Court of Justice in Case 107/82 *AEG v Commission* [1983] ECR 3151, paragraphs 24 to 30). That question therefore falls within the scope of other pleas in law concerning the correctness of the Commission's factual assessments. Consequently, the first part of the plea must be rejected in any event.

The CFI then considered the exculpatory documents.

59. As regards the question of access to the documents marked 'v' and other documents which may have been of use in the applicant's defence, the Court observes at the outset that the purpose of providing access to the file in competition cases is to enable the addressees of statements of objections to examine evidence in the Commission's file so that they are in a position effectively to express their views on the conclusions reached by the Commission in its statement of objections on the basis of that evidence. Access to the file is thus one of the procedural safeguards intended to protect the rights of the defence (judgments of the Court of First Instance in Joined Cases T-10/92 to T-12/92 and T-15/92 *Cimenteries CBR and Others v Commission* [1992] ECR II-2667, paragraph 38, and Case T-65/89 *BPB Industries and British Gypsum v Commission* [1993] ECR II-389, paragraph 30). Respect for the rights of the defence in all proceedings in which sanctions may be imposed is a fundamental principle of Community law which must be respected in all circumstances, even if the proceedings in question are administrative proceedings. The proper observance of that general principle requires that the undertaking concerned be afforded the opportunity during the administrative procedure to make known its views on the truth and relevance of the facts, charges and circumstances relied on by the Commission (judgment of the Court of Justice in Case 85/76 *Hoffman-La Roche v Commission* [1979] ECR 461, paragraphs 9 and 11).

60. The Court considers that an infringement of the rights of the defence must therefore be examined in relation to the specific circumstances of each particular case, since it depends essentially on the objections raised by the Commission in order to prove the infringement which the undertaking concerned is alleged to have committed. In order to determine whether the plea in question, considered in its two parts, is well founded, it is therefore necessary to examine the burden of the substantive objections raised by the Commission in the statement of objections and in the contested decision.

In a Notice adopted early in 1997 the Commission sought to standardise administrative practice on access to the file.[64] In principle, parties are to have access to all documents unless these are 'non-communicable'. Non-communicable documents fall into three categories. These are Commission internal documents; information for which confidentiality has been requested and which enables the supplier of the information to be identified, and business secrets. In certain circumstances access can be had to the latter category:

Where business secrets provide evidence of an infringement or tend to exonerate a firm, the Commission must reconcile the interest in the protection of sensitive information, the public interest in having the infringement of the competition rules terminated, and the rights of defence. This calls for an assessment of

(i) the relevance of the information to determining whether or not an infringement has been committed;

---

64 Commission Notice on the internal rules of procedure for processing requests for access to the file, OJ 1997 C 23/3.

(ii) its probative value;
(iii) whether it is indispensable;
(iv) the degree of sensitivity involved (to what extent would disclosure of the information harm the interests of the firm?);
(v) the seriousness of the infringement.

Each document must be assessed individually to determine whether the need to disclose it is greater than the harm which might result from disclosure.[65]

Arguably the most important right of defence is the right to a hearing. This is provided for by Regulation 17.

Article 19(1). Before taking decisions as provided for in Articles 2,3,6,7,8,15 and 16, the Commission shall give the undertakings or associations of undertakings concerned the opportunity of being heard on the matters to which the Commission has taken objection.

The procedure for the conduct of these hearings is contained in Regulation 99/63.[66] The Commission must first set out a statement of objections so that the parties have sufficient opportunity to prepare their case.[67] A hearing is then arranged.[68] Parties under investigation are to make known their views in writing before the hearing.[69] In addition, third parties with a sufficient interest are to be given the opportunity to put forward their views.[70]

c. The Decision-Making Powers of the Commission

The Commission has the power to safeguard the effectiveness of any eventual decision through issuing interim measures to secure the

65 Ibid., 4.
66 OJ Spec. Ed. 1963, 2268/63, 47
67 Ibid., Article 2. Case 17/74 *Transocean Marine Paint v Commission* [1974] ECR 1963, [1974] 2 CMLR 453.
68 Ibid., Article 8.
69 Ibid., Article 3.
70 Ibid., Article 7.

termination of anti-competitive practices. Interim measures can only be taken if the matter is urgent and there is a risk of serious and irreparable damage. They must be temporary, conservatory and proportionate.[71]

There are two formal ways in which the Commission can find a practice lawful. The first is through granting an *exemption* under Article 85 [*81*](3) EC to those practices which come within Article 85 [*81*](1) EC. This must be issued for a specific period and conditions may be attached.[72] The other is through granting a negative clearance. This is a Commission statement that the practice does not breach Article 85 [*81*] or 86 [*82*] EC. Such a statement is not a formal decision and, as such, avoids the time-consuming procedures involved. Safeguards to protect third parties' interests have been put in place. The clearance must be published,[73] and interested third parties must be given an opportunity to submit their observations.[74] From the parties' perspective, the advantage of a negative clearance is the speed with which it can be issued. Its disadvantage is its lack of legal certainty, as it is unclear to what extent it binds a national court.

The Commission has two options if it finds the practice to breach EC competition law. It can, first, require the practice to be terminated.[75] This power also allows it to negotiate with undertakings, so that it can insist upon compliance with certain conditions before it will allow a practice to continue. Secondly, where parties intentionally or negligently breach Article 85 [*81*] or 86 [*82*] EC, the Commission can fine the undertakings.[76] The fines imposed can be large, amounting to 10% of global annual turnover.[77] Yet this limit will be rarely approached as the

---

71 Case 792/79R *Camera Care v Commission* [1980] ECR 19, [1980] 1 CMLR 334. See Temple Lang, J. 'The Powers of the Commission to Order Interim Measures in Competition Cases' (1981) 18 *CMLRev* 48; Antunes, L-M. 'Interim Measures under EC Competition Law - Recent Developments' (1993) 13 *YBEL* 83.

72 Regulation 17/62, Article 8.

73 Ibid., Article 21.

74 Ibid., Article 19(3).

75 Ibid., Article 3(1).

76 Ibid., Article 15(2).

77 Ibid., Article 15(2). Case 246/86 *Belasco v Commission* [1989] ECR 2117, [1991] 4 CMLR 96. The largest fine imposed was 248 million ECU, Decision 94/815/EC, OJ 1994 L 343/1. See Furse, M. 'Article 15(2) of Regulation 17:

Commission is bound by the principle of proportionality, so must levy a fine which is commensurate with the severity of the abuse.[78] The test of proportionality is an opaque one which will rarely give an undertaking an idea of the size of any likely fine. The Commission has recently sought to add transparency to this area through standardising practice.

Guidelines on the method of setting fines imposed pursuant to Article 15(2) of Regulation 17[79]

1. Basic Amount

The basic amount will be determined according to the gravity and duration of the infringement, which are the only criteria referred to in Article 15 (2) of Regulation No 17.

A. *Gravity*

In assessing the gravity of the infringement, account must be taken of its nature, its actual impact on the market, where this can be measured, and the size of the relevant geographic market.

Infringements will thus be put into one of three categories: minor infringements, serious infringements and very serious infringements.

- *minor infringements:*

  These might be trade restrictions, usually of a vertical nature, but with a limited market impact and affecting only a substantial but relatively limited part of the Community market.

  Likely fines: ECU 1000 to ECU 1 million.

- *serious infringements:*

  These wi!l more often than not be horizontal or vertical restrictions of the same type as above, but more rigorously applied, with a wider market impact, and with effects in extensive areas of the common market. There might also be

---

Fines and the Commission's Discretion' (1995) 2 *ECLR* 110. More generally see Wils, W. 'EC Competition Fines: To Deter or Not to Deter' (1995) 15 *YBEL* 17.

78 Joined Cases 100-103/80 *Musique Diffusion Française v Commission* [1983] ECR 1825, [1983] 3 CMLR 221.

79 OJ 1998 C 9/3.

abuse of a dominant position (refusals to supply, discrimination, exclusion, loyalty discounts made by dominant firms in order to shut competitors out of the market, etc.).

Likely fines: ECU 1 million to ECU 20 million.

- *very serious infringements:*

These will generally be horizontal restrictions such as price cartels and market-sharing quotas, or other practices which jeopardize the proper functioning of the single market, such as the partitioning of national markets and clear-cut abuse of a dominant position by undertakings holding a virtual monopoly.

Likely fines: above ECU 20 million

Within each of these categories, and in particular as far as serious and very serious infringements are concerned, the proposed scale of fines will make it possible to apply differential treatment to undertakings according to the nature of the infringement committed.

It will also be necessary to take account of the effective economic capacity of offenders to cause significant damage to other operators, in particular consumers, and to set the fine at a level which ensures that it has a sufficiently deterrent effect.

Generally speaking, account may also be taken of the fact that large undertakings usually have legal and economic knowledge and infrastructures which enable them more easily to recognise that their conduct constitutes an infringement and be aware of the consequences stemming from it under competition law.

Where an infringement involves several undertakings (e.g. cartels), it might be necessary in some cases to apply weightings to the amounts determined within each of the three categories in order to take account of the specific weight and, therefore, the real impact of the offending conduct of each undertaking on competition, particularly where there is considerable disparity between the sizes of the undertakings committing infringements of the same type.

Thus, the principle of equal punishment for the same conduct may, if the circumstances so warrant, lead to different fines being imposed on the undertakings concerned without this differentiation being governed by arithmetic calculation.

B. *Duration*

A distinction should be made between the following:

- infringements of short duration (in general, less than one year): no increase in amount,
- infringements of medium duration (in general, one to five years): increase of up to 50% in the amount determined for gravity,
- infringements of long duration (in general, more than five years): increase of up to 10% per year in the amount determined for gravity.

This approach will therefore point to a possible increase in the amount of the fine.

Generally speaking, the increase in the fine for long-term infringements represents a considerable strengthening of the previous practice with a view to imposing effective sanctions on restrictions which have had a harmful impact on consumers over a long period. Moreover, this new approach is consistent with the expected effect of the notice of 18 July 1996 on the non-imposition or reduction of fines in cartel cases. The risk of having to pay a much larger fine, proportionate to the duration of the infringement, will necessarily increase the incentive to denounce it or to co-operate with the Commission.

The basic amount will result from the addition of the two amounts established in accordance with the above:

x gravity + y duration = basic amount

2. Aggravating Circumstances

The basic amount will be increased where there are aggravating circumstances such as:

- repeated infringement of the same type by the same undertaking(s),
- refusal to co-operate with or attempts to obstruct the Commission in carrying out its investigations,
- role of leader in, or instigator of the infringement,
- retaliatory measures against other undertakings with a view to enforcing practices which constitute an infringement,
- need to increase the penalty in order to exceed the amount of gains improperly made as a result of the infringement when it is objectively possible to estimate that amount,
- other.

3. Attenuating Circumstances

the basic amount will be reduced where there are attenuating circumstances such as:
- an exclusively passive or 'follow-my-leader' role in the infringement,
- non-implementation in practice of the offending agreements or practices,
- termination of the infringement as soon as the Commission intervenes (in particular when it carries out checks),
- existence of reasonable doubt on the part of the undertaking as to whether the restrictive conduct does indeed constitute an infringement,
- infringements committed as a result of negligence or unintentionally,
- effective co-operation by the undertaking in the proceedings, outside the scope of the Notice of 18 July 1996 on the non-imposition or reduction of fines in cartel cases,
- other.

The Commission has recently began to use this power to fine to create incentives for participants to a cartel to 'whistle-blow' on that cartel.[80] An undertaking will obtain a 75% to 100% reduction in its fine if it does all the following:

- informs the Commission about a secret cartel before the Commission has undertaken an investigation, ordered by decision, of the undertakings, provided that the Commission already does not have sufficient information to establish the existence of the alleged cartel;
- be the first to adduce decisive evidence of the cartel's existence;
- put an end to its involvement in the illegal activity no later than the time at which it discloses the cartel;
- provide the Commission with all the relevant information and all the documents and evidence available to it regarding the cartel and maintain continuous and complete cooperation throughout the investigation;
- have not compelled another undertaking to take part in the cartel and not acted as an instigator or played a determining role in the illegal activity.

There is a sliding scale so that an undertaking benefits from a 50-75% reduction if it meets these conditions once the Commission has begun an investigation. Lesser reductions are available for cooperation. At the bottom end of the scale the Notice provides little incentives for undertakings to 'whistle blow'. It is intended, however, to create a climate of mistrust between cartel participants where none can ever know if the other is carrying out the cartel in 'good faith'.

The Commission has been so overwhelmed by case work that it has looked to a number of informal ways in which to handle the number of notifications made to it under Regulation 17. The usual way a notification is handled is by an informal 'comfort letter' stating that the

---

80 OJ 1996, C 207/4. See Hornby, S. & Hunter, J. 'New Incentives for "Whistle Blowing": will the EC Commission's Notice Bear Fruit?' (1997) 1 *ECLR* 38; Wils, W. 'The Commission Notice on the Non-Imposition or Reduction of Fines in Cartel Cases: A Legal and Economic Analysis' (1997) 22 *ELRev* 125.

Commission is willing to 'close the file'. Such letters are administrative letters. Whilst their essential content is now published, the procedural safeguards for third parties do not exist which exist elsewhere.[81] Nor do they prevent the Commission from reopening the file should it think that circumstances so require.[82] Equally importantly, whilst national courts can take account of comfort letters, they are not required to do so.[83] Weatherill and Beaumont have observed that this creates particular problems where a comfort letter states that a measure is exempted by Article 85 [*81*](3) EC. The national court might look to the comfort letter to find a measure to be within Article 85 [*81*](1) EC but is prevented from exempting it under Article 85 [*81*](3) EC.[84]

The other practice which has developed is resort to the 'opposition procedure'. In a number of areas a practice will be granted exemption if it is notified to the Commission and the Commission does not oppose it within six months, either because of its own volition or because of a request from a Member State.[85] The key to the opposition procedure is the automatic manner in which an exemption is granted in the absence of opposition. The advantage of the procedure is once again the time and administrative inconvenience it saves. Yet, like the comfort letter, they have also been criticised for their lack of transparency and shortcutting of procedural safeguards. In particular, it is unclear what legal effect non-opposition by the Commission has. No formal decision has been taken which can be challenged by third parties, nor has any

---

81 Korah, V. 'Comfort Letters - Reflections on the Perfume Cases' (1981) 6 *ELRev* 14; Waelbroeck, D. 'New Forms of Settlement of Antitrust Cases and Procedural Safeguards: Is Regulation 17 Falling into Abeyance? (1986) 11 *ELRev* 268; Stevens, D. 'The 'Comfort Letter': Old Problems, New Developments' (1994) 2 *ECLR* 81.

82 Joined Cases 253/78 & 1-3/79 *Procureur de la République v Guerlain* [1980] ECR 2327, [1981] 2 CMLR 99.

83 Joined Cases 253/78, 1-3/79 *Procureur de la République v Giry & Guerlain SA* [1980] ECR 2327, [1981] 2 CMLR 99.

84 Weatherill, S. & Beaumont, P. *EC Law - The Essential Guide to the Legal Workings of the European Community* (1995, 2nd Edition, Penguin, Harmondsworth) 778

85 The opposition procedure is used within the context of the block exemptions, five of which use it. See p. 618.

formal exemption been granted which would protect the parties in national courts.[86]

iii. Enforcement in the National Courts

National courts can, like the Commission, declare practices which breach Articles 85 [*81*] and 86 [*82*] EC to be void.[87] In addition, they have a number of options available to them which are not available to the Commission. They can award compensation for loss to third parties who may be able to combine a claim under national law with a claim under EC law.[88] Interim measures can sometimes be adopted faster by national courts, and, finally, parties can recover their legal costs which is not possible in administrative procedures before the Commission.

The difficulties of a dual regime of administration are those of dysfunction. This can happen, first, through national courts applying Articles 85 [*81*] or 86 [*82*] EC in a different manner from the Commission. As with any area of joint competence, the Court has ruled that adjustment difficulties are to be modulated through the duty of cooperation contained in Article 5 [*10*] EC. Within this framework national courts are free to contact the Commission for advice or information and the Commission is bound to assist them.[89]

Particular problems occur, first, where a cartel falls within the scope of Article 85 [*81*](1) EC but might potentially benefit from an exemption under Article 85 [*81*](3) EC. The national court cannot itself give the exemption - this is the prerogative of the Commission - yet if it

---

86 Venit, J. 'The Commission's Opposition Procedure - Between the Scylla of Ultra Vires and the Charybis of Perfume: Legal Consequences and Tactical Considerations' (1985) 22 *CMLRev* 167.

87 Case 56/65 *La Technique Minière v Maschinenbau Ulm* [1966] ECR 235, [1966] 1 CMLR 357.

88 It was suggested by Advocate General Van Gerven in Case C-128/92 *Banks v British Coal Corporation* [1994] ECR I-1209 that a *Francovich*-style claim for compensation may be available against private parties who breach either Article 85 [*81*] or 86 [*82*] EC.

89 Case C-234/89 *Stergios Delimitis v Henninger Bräu* [1991] ECR I-935, [1992] 5 CMLR 210.

were to hold the practice illegal, that might thwart the Commission's power to exempt. The 1993 Notice, although not binding upon national courts, suggested the practice which should be adopted.

Notice on Co-operation between National Courts and the Commission in Applying Articles 85 and 86 EEC Treaty[90]

28. The national court must first examine whether the procedural conditions necessary for securing exemption are fulfilled, notably whether the agreement, decision or concerted practice has been duly notified in accordance with Article 4(1) of Regulation No 17. Where no such notification has been made, and subject to Article 4(2) of Regulation No 17, exemption under Article 85(3) is ruled out, so that the national court may decide, pursuant to Article 85(2), that the agreement, decision or concerted practice is void.

29. Where the agreement, decision or concerted practice has been duly notified to the Commission, the national court will assess the likelihood of an exemption being granted in the case in question in the light of the relevant criteria developed by the case law of the Court of Justice and the Court of First Instance and by previous regulations and decisions of the Commission.

30. Where the national court has in this way ascertained that the agreement, decision or concerted at issue cannot be the subject of an individual exemption, it will take the measures necessary to comply with the requirements of Article 85(1) and (2). On the other hand, if it takes the view that individual exemption is possible, the national court should suspend the proceedings while awaiting the Commission's decision. If the national court does suspend the proceedings, it nevertheless remains free, according to the rules of the applicable national law, to adopt any interim measures it deems necessary.

The other problem which has arisen is one of information and expertise. National courts will not deal with cases involving EC competition law on the same regular basis as the Commission. They will often not have the resources or knowledge available to the Commission. The 1993 Notice observes that cooperation between the Commission and national courts within the framework of Article 5 [*10*] EC is particularly important in this regard.

---

[90] OJ 1993 C 39/6.

Notice on Co-operation between National Courts and the Commission in Applying Articles 85 and 86 EEC Treaty[91]

34. The Commission considers that such cooperation is essential in order to guarantee the strict, effective and consistent application of Community competition law. In addition, more effective participation by the national courts in the day-to-day application of competition law gives the Commission more time to perform its administrative task, namely to steer competition policy in the Community.

35. In the light of these considerations, the Commission intends to work towards closer cooperation with national courts in the following manner.

36. The Commission conducts its policy so as to give the parties concerned useful pointers to the application of competition rules. To this end, it will continue its policy in relation to block exemption regulations and general notices. These general texts, the case-law of the Court of Justice and the Court of First Instance, the decisions previously taken by the Commission and the annual reports on competition policy are all elements of secondary legislation or explanations which may assist national courts in examining individual cases.

37. If these general pointers are insufficient, national courts may, within the limits of their national procedural law, ask the Commission and in particular its Directorate-General for Competition for the following information.

First they may ask for information of a procedural nature to enable them to discover whether a certain case is pending before the Commission, whether a case has been the subject of a notification, whether the Commission has officially initiated a procedure or whether it has already taken a position through an official decision or through a comfort letter sent by its services. If necessary, national courts may also ask the Commission to give an opinion as to how much time is likely to be required for granting or refusing individual exemption for notified agreements or practices, so as to be able to determine the conditions for any decision to suspend proceedings or whether interim measures need to be adopted. The Commission, for its part, will endeavour to give priority to cases which are the subject of national proceedings suspended in this way, in particular when the outcome of a civil dispute depends on them.

38. Next, national courts may consult the Commission on points of law. Where the application of Article 85(1) and Article 86 causes them particular difficulties, national courts may consult the Commission on its customary practice in relation to the Community law at issue. As far as Articles 85 and 86 are concerned, these difficulties relate in particular to the conditions for applying these Articles as regards the effect on trade between Member States and as regards the extent to which the restriction of competition resulting from the practices specified in these provisions is appreciable. In

---

[91] OJ 1993 C 39/6.

its replies, the Commission does not consider the merits of the case. In addition, where they have doubts as to whether a contested agreement, decision or concerted practice is eligible for an individual exemption, they may ask the Commission to provide them with an interim opinion. If the Commission says that the case in question is unlikely to qualify for an exemption, national courts will be able to waive a stay of proceedings and rule on the validity of the agreement, decision or concerted practice.

39. The answers given by the Commission are not binding on the courts which have requested them. In its replies the Commission makes it clear that its view is not definitive and that the right for the national court to refer to the Court of Justice, pursuant to Article 177, is not affected. Nevertheless, the Commission considers that it gives them useful guidance for resolving disputes.

40. Lastly, national courts can obtain information from the Commission regarding factual data: statistics, market studies and economic analyses. The Commission will endeavour to communicate these data, within the limits laid down in the following paragraph, or will indicate the source from which they can be obtained.

41. It is in the interests of the proper administration of justice that the Commission should answer requests for legal and factual information in the shortest possible time. Nevertheless, the Commission cannot accede to such requests unless several conditions are met. First, the requisite data must actually be at its disposal. Secondly, the Commission may communicate this data only so far as permitted by the general principle of sound administrative practice.

Further Reading

Ehlermann, C-D. 'Reflections on a European Cartel Office' (1995) 32 *CMLRev* 471

Fox, E. 'The Modernisation of Antitrust: A New Equilibrium' (1981) 66 *Cornell Law Review* 1140

Harding, C. *European Community Investigations and Sanctions* (1993, Leicester University Press, Leicester)

Kerse, C. *EC Antitrust Procedure* (1994, 3rd Edition, Sweet & Maxwell, London)

----- 'The Complainant in Competition Cases: A Progress Report' (1997) 34 *Common Market Law Review* 213

McGowan, L. & Wilks, S. 'The first supranational policy in the European Union: competition policy' (1995) 28 *European Journal of Political Research* 141

Ortiz-Blanco, L. *EC Competition Procedure* (1996, Clarendon Press, Oxford)

Shaw, J. 'Competition Complainants: A Comprehensive System of Remedies' (1993) 18 *ELRev* 427

Sullivan, L. 'Post-Chicago Economics: Economists, Lawyers, Judges, and Enforcement Officials in a Less Determinate Theoretical World' (1995) 63 *Antitrust Law Journal* 669

Vesterdorf, B. 'Complaints concerning infringements of competition law within the context of European Community law' (1994) 31 *CMLRev* 77

Waelbroeck, D. 'New Forms of Settlement of Antitrust Cases and Procedural Safeguards: Is Regulation 17 Falling into Abeyance' (1986) 11 *ELRev* 268

Wesseling, R. 'Subsidiarity in Community Antitrust Law: Setting the Right Agenda' (1997) 22 *European Law Review* 35

Whish, R. 'The Enforcement of EC Competition Law in the Domestic Courts by Member States' in Lonbay, J. (ed.) *Frontiers of Competition Law* (Wiley, Chancery, London, 1994)

Wils, W. 'The Commission Notice on the Non-Imposition or Reduction of Fines in Cartel Cases: A Legal and Economic Analysis' (1997) 22 *European Law Review* 125

12. Cartels

I. Introduction

Cartels exist where undertakings substitute collusion and cooperation for this rivalry. It is the function of Article 85 [*81*] EC to regulate cartels and preserve the atomistic features within EC competition law. It can only apply, therefore, to situations which involve more than one undertaking.

In this regard the notion of an undertaking has been widely interpreted. The Commission has taken the view that any body engaged in commercial activities constitutes an undertaking.[1] For these purposes an individual can be an undertaking. A cartel between two natural persons can fall within Article 85 [*81*] EC.[2] Nor is it necessary that the body be profit-making. Providing it is engaged in commercial activity, it falls within Article 85 [*81*] EC.[3]

The requirement that there be more than one undertaking poses particular problems for parent-subsidiary relations. A subsidiary is distinguished from a branch as it enjoys separate legal personality from its parent. If all parent-subsidiary relations were to be governed by

---

1 *Re Polypropylene Cartel*, OJ 1986 L 230/1.

2 *RAI v UNITEL*, OJ 1978 L 157/39, [1978] 3 CMLR 306.

3 *Re Distribution of Package Tours During the 1990 World Cup*, OJ 1992, L 326/31. Bodies managing compulsory social security schemes have been excluded from the rigour of the competition provisions. The basis for this is the principle of solidarity which requires a compulsory system managed by a single body. If membership of any scheme is voluntary, therefore, it will be covered by the competition provisions. Joined Cases C-159/91 *Poucet v Assurances Generales de France & Caisse Mutuelle Régionale de Languedoc-Rousillon*, C-160/91 *Pistre v Caisse Autonome Nationale de Compensation de l'Assurance Vieillesse des Artisans* [1993] ECR I-637; Case C-244/94 *Fédération Française des Sociétés d'Assurance v Ministère de l'Agriculture et de la Pêche* [1995] ECR I-4013.

Article 85 [*81*] EC, however, not only would artificial distinctions be created as parent companies will often exercise an identical degree of control over both subsidiaries and branches but Article 85 [*81*] EC would be transformed into a tool for limiting and preventing the development of corporate groups - a task for which it is not well suited. The orthodox position therefore is that what is axiomatic is not whether undertakings enjoy separate legal personality, but whether they enjoy economic independence from one another.[4] Only if this is the case will the matter fall within Article 85 [*81*] EC. This will depend both upon the formal powers of control a parent enjoys over a subsidiary and the extent to which it exercises those powers.[5] The position was muddied in *Bodson*, which concerned a series of concessions to run funeral services which were distributed by a parent among subsidiaries.[6] There, the Court suggested that parent-subsidiary collusion would only fall outside Article 85 [*81*] EC if it concerned merely the internal allocation of tasks. This suggested that Article 85 [*81*] EC might be used to develop an intra-enterprise conspiracy doctrine which would control internal group developments. This doctrine has not been developed since *Bodson*, however.

II. The Requirement of Collusion or Coordination

Three forms of collusion or coordination are found Article 85(1) [*81(1)*] EC - *agreements between undertakings*, *decisions by associations of undertakings* and *concerted practices*.

The distinguishing feature of an agreement is the expression of a joint intention. It is unnecessary that the intention be acted upon.

---

4 Case 48/69 *ICI v Commission* [1972] ECR 619, [1972] CMLR 557; Case 22/71 *Béguelin Import v GL Import Export* [1971] ECR 949, [1972] CMLR 81; Joined Cases T-68/89 & T-77-78/89 *Società Italiana Vetro v Commission* [1992] ECR II-1403, [1992] 5 CMLR 302.

5 Case 107/82 *AEG-Telefunken v Commission* [1983] ECR 3151, [1984] 3 CMLR 325.

6 Case 30/87 *Bodson v Pompes Funèbres* [1988] ECR 2479, [1989] 4 CMLR 984.

Executory contracts are therefore as much caught by the provision as executed ones. Joint intention has been interpreted to cover any continuous relationship which provides a framework for commercial relations. Unilateral acts taken within the parameters of this framework have also been held to fall within Article 85 [*81*] EC.[7]

The consequence of this wide definition has been to marginalise the second category of cooperation, decisions by trade associations. Such associations are normally founded upon an agreement, and thus even where the decision is taken by an association, it is treated as an agreement between undertakings.[8]

The most contentious form of cooperation falling within Article 85 [*81*] EC, however, is that of the concerted practice. This is a form of coordination, conscious parallelism, which is not dependent upon any evidence of joint intention. This concept has a wider embrace than exists elsewhere. In US law, for example, section 1 of the Sherman Act 1890 permits such parallelism as it only sanctions conduct which involves some element of conspiracy.[9] The differences between an agreement and a concerted practice are illustrated by the following judgment.

Case T-7/89 SA Hercules Chemicals v Commission (Polypropylene Cartel) [1991] ECR II-1711, [1992] 4 CMLR 84

In 1986 the Commission found that 15 manufacturers of the plastic, polypropylene, accounting for 64% of Community turnover, had engaged in a cartel between 1977 and 1983. The cartel took two forms. The first consisted of a series of non-binding, oral agreements about the target (minimum) prices at which the good should be sold within the Community. The second consisted of a series of meetings where information which would normally have been regarded as confidential was exchanged between the undertakings.[10]

---

7 A requirement imposed unilaterally by a supplier on distributors with whom it had a long-term relationship was found to fall within Article 85 [*81*] EC, Case C-277/87 *Sandoz v Commission* [1990] ECR I-45.

8 Case 246/86 *Belasco v Commission* [1989] ECR 2117, [1991] 4 CMLR 96.

9 *Theatre Enterprises v Paramount Film Distributing Corporation* 346 US 537 (1954).

10 This was one of a series of judgments. The Advocate General's Opinion was given in Case T-1/89 *Rhône-Poulenc v Commission* [1991] ECR II-867. The matter was deal with at greatest length by the Court in *Hercules*. See also

Judge Vesterdorf (acting as Advocate General)

... Is it sufficient [to constitute a concerted practice], as the Commission believes, that there is proof of concertation, that is to say, is the coordination or the exchange of information sufficient? Or, in other words, does the concertation *constitute in itself* a concerted practice?

... There is little support to be found for assuming that such an interpretation of the concept of 'concerted practice' is correct. That interpretation might perhaps be desirable from the point of view of legal policy but it is difficult to reconcile with the ordinary meaning of the words of the provision; nor is it corroborated by the history of the provision. I therefore consider that such an interpretation should be rejected.

We have to ask ourselves, however, what is it that happens when undertakings have entered into concertation? Why is the concertation something so crucial that, in the view of the Court of Justice, it follows from Article 85 that 'any direct or indirect contact between such operators, the object or effect whereof is ... to influence the conduct on the market of an actual or potential competitor' is categorically prohibited, as it stated in the more recent *Sugar*[[11]] and *Züchner*[[12]] cases ... In my view, the reason is that such undertakings will then necessarily, and normally unavoidably, act on the market in the light of the knowledge and on the basis of discussions which have taken place in connection with the concertation...

... it is therefore necessary, in my view, for action to be taken [for there to be a concerted practice] with the knowledge and awareness that results from the concertation.

The Court

256. ... in order for there to be agreement within the meaning of Article 85(1) of the EEC Treaty it is sufficient if the undertakings in question have expressed their joint intention to conduct themselves on the market in a specific way ... this Court holds that the Commission was entitled to treat the common intentions existing between the applicant and other polypropylene producers, which the Commission has proved to the requisite legal standard and which related to target prices for the period from July to December 1979 and sale volume targets for the years 1979 and 1980, as agreements within the meaning of Article 85(1) EEC.

Cases T-2/89 *Petrofina v Commission* [1991] ECR II-1087; T-3/89 *Atochem v Commission* [1991] ECR II-1177; T-4/89 *BASF v Commission* [1991] ECR II-1523; T-6/89 *ANIC v Commission* [1991] ECR II-1623; T-8/89 *DSM v Commission* [1991] ECR II-1833.

11 Joined Cases 40-48, 50, 54-56, 111, 113, & 114/73 *Suiker Unie v Commission* [1975] ECR 1663, [1976] 1 CMLR 295.

12 Case 172/80 *Züchner v Bayerische Vereinsbank AG* [1981] ECR 2021, [1982] 1 CMLR 313.

257. Furthermore, having established to the requisite legal standard that the effects of the price initiatives continued to last until November 1983, the Commission was fully entitled to take the view that the infringement continued until at least November 1983. It is indeed clear from the case law of the Court of Justice that Article 85 is also applicable to agreements which are no longer in force but which continue to produce their effects after they have formally ceased to be in force (Case 243/83 *Binon & Cie SA v Agence et Messagerie de la Presse SA* [1985] ECR 2015).

258. For a definition of the concept of concerted practice, reference must be made to the case law of the Court of Justice, which shows that the criteria of co-ordination and co-operation previously laid down by the Court must be understood in the light of the concept inherent in the competition provisions of the EEC Treaty according to which each economic operator must determine independently the policy which he intends to adopt on the Common Market. Although this requirement of independence does not deprive economic operators of the right to adapt themselves intelligently to the existing and anticipated conduct of their competitors, it does however strictly preclude any direct or indirect contact between such operators, the object or effect whereof is either to influence the conduct on the market of an actual or potential competitor or to disclose to such a competitor the course of conduct which they themselves have decided to adopt or contemplate adopting on the market: Joined Cases 40-48, 50, 54-56, 111, 113 & 114/73 *Suiker Unie v Commission* [1975] ECR 1663, paragraphs 173 and 174.

259. In the present case, the applicant participated in meetings having as their purpose the fixing of price and sale volume targets during which information was exchanged between competitors about the prices they wished to see charged on the market, about the prices they intended to charge, about their profitability thresholds, about the sale volume restrictions they judged to be necessary, about their sales figures or about the identity of their customers. Through its participation in those meetings, it took part together with its competitors, in concerted action the purpose of which was to influence their conduct on the market and to disclose to each other the course of conduct which each of the producers itself contemplated adopting on the market.

260. Thus, not only did the applicant pursue the aim of eliminating in advance uncertainty about the future conduct of its competitors but also, in determining the policy which it intended to follow on the market, it could not fail to take account, directly or indirectly, of the information obtained during the course of those meetings. Similarly, in determining the policy which they intended to follow, its competitors were bound to take into account, directly or indirectly, the information disclosed to them by the applicant about the course of conduct which the applicant itself had decided upon or which it contemplated adopting on the market.

261. The Commission was accordingly justified, in the alternative, having regard to their purpose, in categorising the regular meetings of polypropylene producers in which the applicant participated between the beginning of 1979 and August 1983 and its participation in fixing sale volume targets for the years 1979 to 1982 as concerted practices within the meaning of Article 85(1) EEC.

A view was taken prior to *Polypropylene*[13] that an essential element of a concerted practice was some form of parallel conduct in the market in question. This view was rejected by the Court, which considered an exchange of information to be sufficient. This prompted further questions, however. What exchanges of information constituted a concerted practice for the purposes of Article 85 [*81*] EC? Conversely could a concerted practice be found to exist in the absence of direct evidence of contacts between the undertakings concerned?

Joined Cases C-89, 104, 114, 116-117, 125-129/85 Ahlström *et al.* v Commission (Woodpulp Cartel) [1993] ECR I-1307, [1993] 4 CMLR 407[14]

In 1984 the Commission found that many of the main manufacturers of woodpulp had engaged in a price cartel. Part of the basis for its finding was that on the wood pulp market all manufacturers made an announcement on the price of their pulp a few days before each quarter began. The Commission considered that these announcements were sufficient to constitute a concerted practice under Article 85 [*81*] EC as they allowed other undertakings to adjust their price accordingly.

63. According to the Court's judgment in *Suiker Unie*,[[15]] a concerted practice refers to a form of co-ordination between undertakings which, without having been taken to the stage where an agreement properly so-called has been concluded, knowingly substitutes for the risks of competition practical co-operation between them. In the same judgment, the Court added that the criteria of co-ordination and co-operation must be understood in the light of the concept inherent in the provisions of the Treaty relating to competition that each economic operator must determine independently the policy which he intends to adopt on the Common Market.

---

13 For a discussion of the literature see the Opinion of Judge Vesterdorf in Case T-1/89 *Rhône-Poulenc v Commission* [1991] ECR II-867, 935-939.

14 Antunes, L. 'Agreements and Concerted Practices under EEC Competition Law: Is the Distinction Relevant?' (1991) 11 *YBEL* 57; Van Gerven, G. & Varona, E. 'The Wood Pulp Case and the Future of Concerted Practices' (1994) 31 *CMLRev* 575; Stevens, D. 'Covert Collusion and Conscious Parallelism in Oligopolistic Markets' (1995) 15 *YBEL* 47.

15 Joined Cases 40-48, 50, 54-56, 111, 113, & 114/73 *Suiker Unie v Commission* [1975] ECR 1663, [1976] 1 CMLR 295.

64. In this case, the communications arise from the price announcements made to users. They constitute in themselves market behaviour which does not lessen each undertaking's uncertainty as to the future attitude of its competitors. At the time when each undertaking engages in such behaviour, it cannot be sure of the future conduct of the others.

65. Accordingly, the system of quarterly price announcements on the pulp market is not to be regarded as constituting in itself an infringement of Article 85(1) EEC.

.....

70. Since the Commission has no documents which directly establish the existence of concertation between the producers concerned, it is necessary to ascertain whether the system of quarterly price announcements, the simultaneity or near-simultaneity of the price announcements and the parallelism of price announcements as found during the period from 1975 to 1981 constitute a firm, precise and consistent body of evidence of prior concertation.

71. In determining the probative value of those different factors, it must be noted that parallel conduct cannot be regarded as furnishing proof of concertation unless concertation constitutes the only plausible explanation for such conduct. It is necessary to bear in mind that, although Article 85 EEC prohibits any form of collusion which distorts competition, it does not deprive economic operators of the right to adapt themselves intelligently to the existing and anticipated conduct of their competitors (see *Suiker Unie*, cited above, paragraph 174).

Korah has criticised the idea that market conduct, *per se*, can provide sufficient evidence for a finding of a concerted practice.[16] She notes that a characteristic of oligopolistic markets is that they have only a few sellers, who will frequently respond to each other and parallel each other's conduct without there being any active collusion on the part of the firms. Unilateral action by one, such as a price cut, is, thus, likely to be counterproductive, because as that supplier represents a principal source of competition to other actors on the market, they will merely react by matching the price cut.[17] It will frequently be impossible to differentiate this conduct from collusion. Evidence for this is provided

---

16 Korah, V. *An Introductory Guide to EC Competition Law and Practice* (1997, 6th Edition, Hart Publishing, Oxford) 48-50.

17 Sweezy, P. 'Demand under Conditions of Oligopoly' (1937) 47 *Journal of Political Economy* 568.

by the *Woodpulp* judgment itself where the Court had to bring in its own analysts to reach a finding on this point.

Such an objection is based on behavioural analysis. The presumption behind this is that undertakings, in the absence of collusion, have simply done nothing wrong, and should not therefore be punished. This view is problematic. Both parallel conduct and genuine collusion lead to the same end result, an absence of price competition. In those circumstances it might be that the *structure* of the market rather than the behaviour of the undertaking justifies a more interventionist policy if competition is to be maintained. This conclusion is reinforced by the reason for limited numbers of suppliers on certain markets often being the high entry costs to those markets.[18]

III. The Community Dimension: The Practice Must Have a Significant Effect on Inter-State Trade

A practice will only fall within Article 85 [*81*] EC if it has a Community dimension. As has already been noted, the notion of a Community dimension was initially constructed so widely that it lost any effective demarcatory function.[19] Any measure having an influence on the pattern of trade between Member States, be it direct or indirect, actual or potential, was stated to fall within Article 85 [*81*] EC.[20] The position was exacerbated by the ruling in *Windsurfing International*[21] that it was unnecessary for the anti-competitive clause to affect trade between Member States, it is sufficient if the agreement as a whole affects trade between Member States.

The *de minimis* doctrine has been far more important in delimiting Article 85 [*81*] EC. In *Völk v Vervaecke*[22] the Court held that

---

18 See also Whish, R. & Sufrin, B. 'Oligopolistic Markets and EC Competition Law' (1992) 12 *YBEL* 59, 62-65.

19 See pp. 536-538.

20 Case 56/65 *Société Technique Minière v Maschinenbau Ulm* [1966] ECR 234, [1966] CMLR 357.

21 Case 193/83 *Windsurfing International v Commission* [1986] ECR 611, [1986] 3 CMLR 489.

22 Case 5/69 *Völk v Vervaecke* [1969] ECR 295, [1969] CMLR 273.

an agreement would not fall within the ambit of Article 85(1) [*81(1)*] EC if its effects on inter-State trade were not significant.

Commission Notice on Agreements of Minor Importance which do not fall under the EEC Treaty[23]

9. The Commission holds the view that agreements between undertakings engaged in the production or distribution of goods or in the provision of services do not fall under the prohibition in Article 85(1) if the aggregate market share held by all of the participating undertakings do not exceed, on any of the relevant markets:

(a) the 5% threshold, where the agreement is made between undertakings operating at the same level of production or marketing ('horizontal' agreement);

(b) the 10% threshold, where the agreement is made between undertakings operating at different economic levels ('vertical' agreement).

In the case of a mixed horizontal/vertical agreement or where it is difficult to classify the agreement as either horizontal or vertical, the 5% threshold is applicable.

10. The Commission also holds the view that the said agreements do not fall under the prohibition of Article 85(1) if the market shares given at point 9 are exceeded by no more than one tenth during two successive financial years.

11. With regard to:

(a) horizontal agreements which have as their object
- to fix prices or to limit production or sales, or
- to share markets or sources of supply,

(b) vertical agreements which have as their object

- to fix resale prices, or
- to confer territorial protection on the participating undertakings or third undertakings,

the applicability of Article 85(1) cannot be ruled out even where the aggregate market shares held by all of the participating undertakings remain below the thresholds mentioned in points 9 and 10.

The Commission considers, however, that in the first instance it is for the authorities and courts of the Member States to take action on any agreements envisaged above in (a) and (b). Accordingly, it will only intervene in such cases when it considers

---

[23] OJ 1997 C 372/13.

that the interest of the Community so demands, and in particular if the agreements impair the proper functioning of the internal market.

.....

18. [The above] shall not apply where in a relevant market competition is restricted by the cumulative effects of parallel networks of similar agreements established by several manufacturers or dealers.

The Notice is a guideline which, by its own terms, is only to apply generally. With regard to earlier Notices, the CFI has therefore suggested that even if a practice exceeds the thresholds, this will not necessarily mean that it is caught by Article 85 [*81*] EC.[24] Even within the Notice there are problems of demarcation. Agreements, for example, rarely confer absolute territorial protection on participating undertakings, but degrees of territorial protection. It is not clear from the Notice how severe the territorial protection conferred must be before the thresholds are inapplicable. There appear two circumstances, moreover, in which the Notice is inapplicable.

The first is where the market is extremely fragmented. In *Musique Diffusion Française*[25] it therefore found that an exclusive distribution on hi-fi stereos had a significant effect on trade between Member States, notwithstanding the fact that the producers accounted for only 3.38% of the French market and 3.18% of the British market. The reason was the market position of the parties. Despite their low market share, they were still the largest producers of hi-fis on the market in question.

Secondly, the Notice is inapplicable where the agreement is part of a network of agreements which have a wider effect upon the market.

---

24 Case T-9/93 *Schöller v Commission* [1995] ECR II-1611; Case T-77/94 *VGB v Commission*, [1997] ECR II-759.

25 Joined Cases 100-103/80 *Musique Diffusion Française v Commission* [1983] ECR 1825, [1983] 3 CMLR 221.

Case C-234/89 Stergios Delimitis v Henninger Bräu [1991] ECR I-935, [1992] 5 CMLR 210

Stergios Delimitis rented a café in Frankfurt from the German brewery, Henninger Bräu. The agreement was a 'tied-house' agreement where the tenant was required to purchase a minimum amount of beer produced by Henninger Bräu and not to purchase beer or soft drinks from other undertakings established in Germany. Such agreements were extremely common and covered about 60% of the cafés and bars which sold beer in Germany. The tenant terminated the agreement on grounds of ill-health. Henninger Bräu claimed it was owed money as a penalty for the tenant's failing to comply with the minimum purchasing requirement. The national court asked whether an agreement could fall within Article 85 [*81*] EC where, although it did not have a significant effect on inter-State trade, it formed part of a bundle of agreements which did have a significant effect on inter-State trade.

14. In its judgment in Case 23/67 *Brasserie de Haecht v Wilkin* [1967] ECR 407, the Court held that the effects of such an agreement had to be assessed in the context in which they occur and where they might combine with others to have a cumulative effect on competition. It also follows from that judgment that the cumulative effect of several similar agreements constitutes one factor amongst others in ascertaining whether, by way of a possible alteration of competition, trade between Member States is capable of being affected.

15. Consequently, in the present case it is necessary to analyse the effects of a beer supply agreement, taken together with other contracts of the same type, on the opportunities of national competitors or those from other Member States, to gain access to the market for beer consumption or to increase their market share and, accordingly, the effects on the range of products offered to consumers.

16. In making that analysis, the relevant market must first be determined. The relevant market is primarily defined on the basis of the nature of the economic activity in question.

.....

18. Secondly, the relevant market is delimited from a geographical point of view. It should be noted that most beer supply agreements are still entered into at a national level. It follows that, in applying the Community competition rules, account is to be taken of the national market for beer distribution in premises for the sale and consumption of drinks.

.....

23. If an examination of all similar contracts entered into on the relevant market and the other factors relevant to the economic and legal context in which the contract must be examined shows that those agreements do not have the cumulative effect of denying access to that market to new national and foreign competitors, the individual agreements comprising the bundle of agreements cannot be held to restrict competition within the meaning of Article 85(1) of the Treaty. They do not, therefore, fall under the prohibition laid down in that provision.

24. If, on the other hand, such examination reveals that it is difficult to gain access to the relevant market, it is necessary to assess the extent to which the agreements entered into by the brewery in question contribute to the cumulative effect produced in that respect by the totality of the similar contracts found on that market. Under the Community rules on competition, responsibility for such an effect of closing off the market must be attributed to the breweries which make an appreciable contribution thereto. Beer supply agreements entered into by breweries whose contribution to the cumulative effect is insignificant do not therefore fall under the prohibition under Article 85(1).

25. In order to assess the extent of the contribution of the beer supply agreements entered into by a brewery to the cumulative sealing-off effect mentioned above, the market position of the contracting parties must be taken into consideration. That position is not determined solely by the market share held by the brewery and any group to which it may belong, but also by the number of outlets tied to it or to its group, in relation to the total number of premises for the sale and consumption of drinks found in the relevant market.

26. The contribution of the individual contracts entered into by a brewery to the sealing-off of that market also depends on their duration. If the duration is manifestly excessive in relation to the average duration of beer supply agreements generally entered into on the relevant market, the individual contract falls under the prohibition under Article 85(1). A brewery with a relatively small market share which ties its sales outlets for many years may make as significant a contribution to a sealing-off of the market as a brewery in a relatively strong market position which regularly releases sales outlets at shorter intervals.

27. The reply to be given ... is therefore that a beer supply agreement is prohibited by Article 85(1) of the EEC Treaty, if two cumulative conditions are met. The first is that, having regard to the economic and legal context of the agreement at issue, it is difficult for competitors who could enter the market or increase their market share to gain access to the national market for the distribution of beer in premises for the sale and consumption of drinks. The fact that, in that market, the agreement in issue is one of a number of similar agreements having a cumulative effect on competition constitutes only one factor amongst others in assessing whether access to that market is indeed difficult. The second condition is that the agreement in question must make a significant contribution to the sealing-off effect brought about by the totality of those agreements in their economic and legal context. The extent of the contribution made by the individual agreement depends on the position of the contracting parties in the relevant market and on the duration of the agreement.

Delimitis has been repeatedly applied, so that relatively small agreements which form part of a network of agreements fall within Article 85 [*81*] EC if their cumulative effect is to partition off a market.[26] The network is, however, a fuzzy concept which brings with it its own difficulties, in particular, when will an agreement be sufficiently integrated into a patchwork of other agreements to form part of a network of agreements?

In *VGB* a Dutch cooperative society of flower growers, VBA, required all plants grown by its members to be sold through its premises.[27] In addition, it charged a 'user fee' for non-members who sold flowers on its premises. As only batches of a certain size were sold on VBA's premises, small dealers were, in practice, excluded. To remedy this VBA sold flowers to a series of wholesale centres, which imposed no restrictions on the number of flowers which could be bought. The agreements between the VBA and the wholesalers were extremely restrictive agreements under which all bar one of the wholesalers agreed to purchase their flowers exclusively from VBA. Nobody denied that VBA's general trade rules were sufficiently insignificant not to affect trade. The wholesale agreements were, in quantitative terms, a lot less significant. It was argued, however, that the latter should be seen as part of the general VBA regime. The CFI rejected this. It found there was no direct link between the wholesale agreements and the other business of the VBA. The two were to all intents and purposes separate. On that basis it considered the wholesale agreements too insignificant to fall within Article 85 [*81*] EC.

---

26 Case T-7/93 *Langnese-Iglo v Commission* [1995] ECR II-1533; Case T-9/93 *Schöller Lebensmittel v Commission* [1995] ECR II-1611.

27 Case T-77/94 *VGB et al. v Commission*, [1997] ECR II-759.

IV. The Cartel Must Have the Object or Effect of Preventing, Restricting or Distorting Competition

i. Restrictions on Conduct and Restrictions Upon Competition

Initial writing compared the requirement in Article 85 [*81*] EC that the agreement or practice have the object or effect of preventing, restricting or distorting competition to the doctrine of *Wettbewerbsbeschränkung* (restriction on competition) in German competition law.[28] Under the *Gegenstandstheorie* in German law, restrictions on competition were equated with restrictions on freedom of decision. In this manner many contracts, purely through limiting autonomy, were considered to be anti-competitive. This was criticised on the grounds that it would catch many insignificant agreements, whilst failing to regulate equally anti-competitive informal cartels.[29] Joliet also suggested that it did not fit in with a literal analysis of Article 85 [*81*] EC which also catches concerted practices:[30]

> The competition which Article 85 of the Rome Treaty seeks to protect is the same as the competition with which the policy of the [United States] Sherman Act is concerned: it is competition at large as the regulating factor of the free market and it is not necessarily synonymous with the freedom of action of the individual traders. Restraints, actual or intended, prohibited by Article 85(1) are only those which are so substantial as to affect market conditions.[31]

---

28 For a description of the literature see Joliet, R. *The Rule of Reason in Antitrust Law: American, German and Common Market Laws in Perspective* (1967, Martijnus Nijhoff, The Hague) 12-13 and 119-123.

29 Ibid., 123.

30 Ibid., 124-125.

31 Ibid., 129-130.

Case 23/67 Brasserie de Haecht v Wilkin *et al.* [1967] ECR 407, [1968] CMLR 26

The Belgian brewery, Brasserie de Haecht, loaned Oscar Wilkin BF 98,710 in 1963 on condition that the latter's café purchased beer exclusively from it. It discovered in 1966 that Wilkin had breached the exclusive purchase agreement and sought to recover its loan. Wilkin argued in his defence that the restriction on whom he could purchase his beer from contravened Article 85 [*81*] EC, and therefore the contract was void.

Furthermore, by basing its application to agreements, decisions or practices not only on their subject-matter but also on their effects in relation to competition, Article 85(1) implies that regard must be had to such effects in the context in which they occur, that is to say, in the economic and legal context of such agreements, decisions or practices and where they might combine with others to have a cumulative effect on competition. In fact, it would be pointless to consider an agreement, decision or practice by reason of its effects if those effects were to be taken distinct from the market in which they are seen to operate and could only be examined apart from the body of effects, whether convergent or not, surrounding their implementation. Thus in order to examine whether it is caught by Article 85(1) an agreement cannot be examined in isolation from the above context, that is, from the factual or legal circumstances causing it to prevent, restrict or distort competition.

Following it is clear that only some restrictions on conduct will be considered to be restrictions on competition. Subsequent developments have resulted in a spectrum being created. At one end exist certain forms of restriction which can almost never be justified. In these instances the Court focuses almost exclusively on the agreement itself and less on the market context. At the other end of the spectrum exist types of collusion whose anti-competitive effects are more ambiguous. In these instances, the Court focuses much more on the background context.

ii. The *Per Se* Rule

Certain forms of agreement are considered to be so distortive of competition that they, *per se*, breach Article 85(1) EC. The first form of agreement which fall into this agreement are those explicitly mentioned in Article 85(1) EC.[32]

Case 27/87 Erauw-Jacquery Sprl v La Hesbignonne Société Co-opérative [1988] ECR 1919, [1988] 4 CMLR 576

Erauw-Jacquery bred plant seeds. It gave La Hesbignonne an exclusive licence to sell certain of its varieties of plant seed in Belgium. The contract both imposed an obligation on La Hesbignonne not to export seeds or sell them to other distributors on the Belgian market and required it not to sell the seeds at a price below that fixed by Erauw-Jacquery.

12. Secondly, the national court seeks to establish whether a provision of that same agreement which obliges the grower to comply with minimum prices fixed by the other party falls within the prohibition set out in Article 85(1) of the EEC Treaty.

.....

15. In this connection it must be pointed out that Article 85(1) of the Treaty expressly mentions as being incompatible with the common market agreements which 'directly or indirectly fix purchase or selling prices or any other trading conditions'. According to the judgment of the national court the plaintiff in the main proceedings concluded with other growers agreements identical to the contested agreement, as a result of which those agreements have the same effects as a price system fixed by a horizontal agreement. In such circumstances the object and effect of such a provision is to restrict competition within the common market.

The second form of agreement always found to breach Article 85(1) [*81(1)*] EC is one which confers absolute territorial protection on one of the parties. The noxious elements of such an agreement are that by partitioning the single market, it prevents market integration.

---

32 These are agreements which directly or indirectly fix purchase or selling prices or any other trading conditions; limit or control production, markets, technical development, or investment; share markets or sources of supply; apply dissimilar conditions to equivalent transactions with other trading parties, thereby placing them at a competitive disadvantage; make the conclusion of contracts subject to acceptance by the other parties of supplementary obligations which, by their nature or according to commercial usage, have no connection with the subject of such contracts.

Joined Cases 56 & 58/64 Etablissements Consten SA & Grundig GmbH v Commission [1966] ECR 299, [1966] CMLR 418

In 1957 Grundig, the German producer of radios and televisions, made an exclusive distribution agreement with Consten, a French producer under which it was agreed that Consten would enjoy exclusive rights to sell Grundig's products in France. Consten duly registered Grundig's products under its trademark, GINT. In 1961 UNEF bought Grundig products from suppliers in Germany and then resold them in France. Consten brought an action claiming unfair competition and breach of its trademark. UNEF applied to the Commission claiming that the exclusive distribution agreement breached Article 85 [*81*] EC.

It thus remains to consider whether the contested decision was right in founding the prohibition of the disputed agreement under Article 85(1) on the restriction on competition created by the agreement in the sphere of the distribution of Grundig products alone. The infringement which was found to exist by the contested decision results from the absolute territorial protection created by the said contract in favour of Consten on the basis of French law. The applicants thus wished to eliminate any possibility of competition at the wholesale level in Grundig products in the territory specified in the contract essentially by two methods.

First, Grundig undertook not to deliver even indirectly to third parties products intended for the area covered by the contract. The restrictive nature of that undertaking is obvious if it is considered in the light of the prohibition on exporting which was imposed not only on Consten but also on all the other sole concessionaires of Grundig, as well as the German wholesalers. Secondly, the registration in France by Consten of the GINT trade mark, which Grundig affixes to all its products, is intended to increase the protection inherent in the disputed agreement, against the risk of parallel imports into France of Grundig products, by adding the protection deriving from the law on industrial property rights. Thus no third party could import Grundig products from other Member States of the Community for resale in France without running serious risks.

.....

The situation as ascertained above results in the isolation of the French market and makes it possible to charge for the products in question prices which are sheltered from all effective competition. In addition, the more producers succeed in their efforts to render their own makes of product individually distinct in the eyes of the consumer, the more the effectiveness of competition between producers tends to diminish. Because of the considerable impact of distribution costs on the aggregate cost price, it seems important that competition between dealers should also be stimulated. The efforts of the dealer are stimulated by competition between distributors of products of the same make. Since the agreement thus aims at isolating the French market for Grundig products and maintaining artificially, for products of a very well-known brand, separate national markets within the Community, it is therefore such as to distort competition in the Common Market.

It was therefore proper for the contested decision to hold that the agreement constitutes an infringement of Article 85(1). No further considerations, whether of economic data (price differences between France and Germany, representative character of the type of appliance considered, level of overheads borne by Consten) or of the corrections of the criteria upon which the Commission relied in its comparisons between the situations of the French and German markets, and no possible favourable effects of the agreement in other respects, can in any way lead, in the face of above-mentioned restrictions, to a different solution under Article 85(1).

Korah, V. 'EEC Competition Policy-Legal Form or Economic Efficiency' (1986) 39 *Current Legal Problems* 85, 87 & 93-94

A dealer will not pay for pre-sale services, such as providing sound-proof booths where customers can listen to hi-fi equipment or records, keeping stock readily available and paying skilled staff to demonstrate the equipment and advise customers in pleasant surroundings, if the latter could make their selection on his premises but buy the equipment at a discount shop round the corner or by mail. If the brand owner pays for the investment himself, he will have to check how the money is spent and monitoring may be costly. Moreover, he may be less familiar with local markets and less able than the dealer to decide how much investment, and what kinds, pay. It is not always practicable to charge consumers directly for many pre-sales services. One possibility is to give the dealer an incentive to develop the brand in one area and to protect him from free riders through exclusivity, no-poaching or location clauses confining other dealers to specified premises, or re-sale price maintenance. Such protection does restrict one dealer in a branded product from competing with other dealers of the same brand, but without it that brand might not be available at all, in which case no realistic possibility of competition is constrained by such protection...

.....

At a second glance, however, the free rider argument [in *Consten and Grundig*] was strong. Consten had to develop a French market for apparatus made in the country of its former enemy. It could not expect substantial turnover until quotas were eventually abrogated in 1962. It had to establish a trade network, organise stockholding, advisory and repair services. When quotas were abolished in 1962, parallel traders began to import the apparatus by persuading German wholesalers to break their contracts, and within nine months UNEF, one of the parallel importers, was selling 10 per cent. of the Grundig apparatus being sold in France, Grundig having some 17 per cent. of the market there for similar apparatus.

Neither Commission nor Court enquired whether Consten would have established the market so effectively, or at all, without absolute territorial protection from parallel imports, nor whether UNEF and other importers would have been so successful if it had not. If the answer to both questions was negative, then even absolute territorial protection would have been necessary for the development of any competition in France for Grundig products at that time. Indeed, it would have helped to integrate the market. The analysis of Court and Commission, limited to the terms of the transactions and ignoring their effect on the market, may have led to the wrong result.

The arguments, as to possible efficiency losses, are more pressing now than when the *Consten* judgment was issued. In the 1960's, the Community was far more concerned with establishing the common market and allowing the penetration of national markets than in the 1990's, where with many national markets having been entered, focus should be turned to the *regulation* rather than the establishment of the single market. The issue of market integration is, therefore, possibly a less pressing one. With the onset of subsidiarity and the development of a looser, less homogenous Community, the institutional arguments also pushes away from market integration insofar as they support a competition policy run increasingly by national courts and authorities. Yet, at the moment, the Court continues to insist that a restraint resulting in absolute territorial protection will automatically breach Article 85(1) [*81(1)*] EC. [33]

---

33 Recent examples of where the principle of absolute territorial protection resulted in an automatic breach of Article 85(1) [*81(1)*] EC are Joined Cases C-89/85, C-104/85, C-114/85, C-116/85, C-117/85 and C-125/85 to C-129/85 *Ahlström Osakeyhtioe and Others v Commission* [1993] ECR I-1307, [1993] 4 CMLR 207; Case T-66/92 *Herlitz v Commission* [1994] ECR II-531; Case T-38/92 *All Weather Sport BENELUX v Commission* [1994] ECR II-211, [1995] 4 CMLR 43; Case T-43/92 *Dunlop Slazenger International v Commission* [1994] ECR II-441, [1995] 5 CMLR 458; Case T-77/92 *Parker Pen v Commission* [1994] ECR II-549, [1995] 5 CMLR 435; Case T-102/92 *Viho Europe v Commission* [1995] ECR II-17; Case C-70/93 *BMW V ALD Autoleasing* [1995] ECR I-3439.

iii. Anti-Competitive Restraints necessary to support Pro-Competitive Agreements

There are circumstances where business ventures might not go ahead if restrictions are not included in the agreement granting one or other of the parties protection from competition. Such agreements can often be pro-competitive rather than anti-competitive. This is particularly likely to be the case where the parties are not already in competition. Perceived *ex ante*, there is no competition actually being restrained. It is only *ex post* that it is possible to talk of restraints on competition.[34]

In the United States this problem is accommodated through the doctrine of *ancillary restraints*.[35] If an agreement promotes a wider lawful purpose, restraints on competition ancillary to that agreement and without which the agreement would not have come into effect will not be deemed to breach the Sherman Act.

The Merger Regulation refers to ancillary 'restrictions directly related and necessary to the concentration',[36] and one finds similar style language in some of the Commission's Decisions taken under Article 85(3) [*81(3)*] EC.[37] Care must be taken with adoption of this term in that it might suggest inappropriate American analogies. Nevertheless the Court has indicated in a couple of judgments that where enterprises would not enter an agreement but for the addition of certain restrictive provisions, it is prepared to take a more lenient view of those provisions than might otherwise be the case. Whish has characterised this reasoning as the development of a generic set of restrictions which will be

---

34 Korah, V. *An Introductory Guide to EC Competition Law and Practice* (1997, 6th Edition, Hart Publishing, Oxford) 171-172.

35 This was first developed by Judge Taft in *US v Addyston Pipe & Steel*, 85 Fed. 271 (6th Cir. 1898).

36 Regulation 4064/89/EEC, on the control of concentrations between undertakings, OJ 1989 L 395/1, as amended by Regulation 1310/97/EC, OJ 1997 L 180/1, Article 8(2). See in this respect Commission Decision 94/449/EC (iv/m.308- Kali & Salz/MDK/Treuhand) OJ 1994 L 186/38.

37 Recent examples include Commission Decision 94/986/EC (iv/34.252 - Phillips-Osram), OJ 1994 L 378/37; Commission Decision 94/771/EC (iv/34.410 - Olivetti Digital) OJ 1994 L 309/24; Commission Decision 94/579/EC (iv/34.857- BT-MCI) OJ 1994 L 223/36.

permitted when appended to certain forms of pro-competitive arrangement, of which a transfer of an undertaking is one and a franchise is another.[38]

The first such agreement is one which increases the number of manufacturers on the market. In *Remia*[39] Nutricia sold Remia, a company which manufactured sauces and margarine, back to its original owner. Nutricia was itself a food manufacturer. By freeing Remia from Nutricia's shackles, the agreement thus increased the number of manufacturers on the market. The sale contained a 'no-competition' provision that Nutricia would not sell or produce sauce in the Netherlands for 10 years. The Court noted that the sale increased, in the long-term, the number of manufacturers on the Dutch market. It also considered that but for the 'no competition' clause the agreement would not have taken effect as the purchaser would have had to carry the risk of competition from the vendor who had intimate knowledge of the undertaking. In such circumstances a 'no-competition' clause would not breach Article 85(1) [*81(1)*] EC but:

> such clauses must be necessary to the transfer of the undertaking concerned and their duration and scope must be strictly limited to that purpose.

Despite the language of the judgment, the facts of Remia suggest that what is central is not that restriction be necessary for the conclusion of the agreement but that it not be excessively restrictive of competition. The ten year 'no-competition' provision formed part of the agreement. Without it there would have been no sale. The Court considered, however, that its length was excessive, and that consequently it should be reduced to four years.

The second form of permissible ancillary restraint are franchises.

---

38 Whish, R. *Competition Law* (1993, 3rd Edition, Butterworths, London) 210.

39 Case 42/84 *Remia v Commission* [1985] ECR 2545, [1987] 1 CMLR 1.

Case 161/84 Pronuptia v Schillgalis [1986] ECR 353, [1986] 1 CMLR 414

Schillgalis entered into a franchise agreement with Pronuptia under which it agreed to set up a shop to sell the latter's wedding dresses. Pronuptia was to provide Schillgalis with commercial assistance in advertising the product, establishing and stocking the shop, and training the staff. Schillgalis was required not to open other shops in Germany, to purchase at least 80% of the goods it sold from Pronuptia, to equip the shop in 'the image of Pronuptia', not to grant the 'Pronuptia' trademark to third parties, not to open another shop for at least a year after the expiry of the agreement, and to pay royalties of 10% of all sales to Pronuptia. A dispute broke out about the payment of royalties.

15. In a system of distribution franchises of that kind an undertaking which has established itself as a distributor on a given market and thus developed certain business methods grants independent traders, for a fee, the right to establish themselves in other markets using its business name and the business methods which have made it successful. Rather than a method of distribution, it is a way for an undertaking to derive financial benefit from its expertise without investing its own capital. Moreover, the system gives traders who do not have the necessary experience access to methods which they could not have learned without considerable effort and allows them to benefit from the reputation of the franchiser's business name. Franchise agreements for the distribution of goods differ in that regard from dealerships or contracts which incorporate approved retailers into a selective distribution system, which do not involve the use of a single business name, the application of uniform business methods or the payment of royalties in return for the benefits granted. Such a system, which allows the franchiser to profit from his success, does not in itself interfere with competition. In order for the system to work two conditions must be met.

16. First, the franchiser must be able to communicate his know-how to the franchisees and provide them with the necessary assistance in order to enable them to apply his methods, without running the risk that know-how and assistance might benefit competitors, even indirectly. It follows that provisions which are essential in order to avoid that risk do not constitute restrictions on competition for the purposes of Article 85(1). That is also true of a clause prohibiting the franchisee, during the period of validity of the contract and for a reasonable period after its expiry, from opening a shop of the same or a similar nature in an area where he may compete with a member of the network. The same may be said of the franchisee's obligation not to transfer his shop to another party without the prior approval of the franchiser; that provision is intended to prevent competitors from indirectly benefiting from the know-how and assistance provided.

17. Secondly, the franchiser must be able to take the measures necessary for maintaining the identity and reputation of the network bearing his business name or symbol. It follows that provisions which establish the means of control necessary for that purpose do not constitute restrictions on competition for the purposes of Article 85(1).

18. The same is true of the franchisee's obligation to apply the business methods developed by the franchiser and to use the know-how provided.

19. That is also the case with regard to the franchisee's obligation to sell the goods covered by the contract only in premises laid out and decorated according to the franchiser's instructions, which is intended to ensure uniform presentation in conformity with certain requirements. The same requirements apply to the location of the shop, the choice of which is also likely to affect the network's reputation. It is thus understandable that the franchisee cannot transfer his shop to another location without the franchiser's approval.

20. The prohibition of the assignment by the franchisee of his rights and obligations under the contract without the franchiser's approval protects the latter's right freely to choose the franchisees, on whose business qualifications the establishment and maintenance of the network's reputation depend.

21. By means of the control exerted by the franchiser on the selection of goods offered by the franchisee, the public is able to obtain goods of the same quality from each franchisee. It may in certain cases - for instance, the distribution of fashion articles - be impractical to lay down objective quality specifications. Because of the large number of franchisees it may also be too expensive to ensure that such specifications are observed. In such circumstances a provision requiring the franchisee to sell only products supplied by the franchiser or by suppliers selected by him may be considered necessary for the protection of the network' s reputation. Such a provision may not however have the effect of preventing the franchisee from obtaining those products from other franchisees.

22. Finally, since advertising helps to define the image of the network's name or symbol in the eyes of the public, a provision requiring the franchisee to obtain the franchiser's approval for all advertising is also essential for the maintenance of the network's identity, so long as that provision concerns only the nature of the advertising.

23. It must be emphasized on the other hand that, far from being necessary for the protection of the know-how provided or the maintenance of the network's identity and reputation, certain provisions restrict competition between the members of the network. That is true of provisions which share markets between the franchiser and franchisees or between franchisees or prevent franchisees from engaging in price competition with each other.

24. In that regard, the attention of the national court should be drawn to the provision which obliges the franchisee to sell goods covered by the contract only in the premises specified therein. That provision prohibits the franchisee from opening a second shop. Its real effect becomes clear if it is examined in conjunction with the franchiser's undertaking to ensure that the franchisee has the exclusive use of his business name or symbol in a given territory. In order to comply with that undertaking the franchiser must not only refrain from establishing himself within that territory but also require other franchisees to give an undertaking not to open a second shop outside their own territory. A combination of provisions of that kind results in a sharing of markets between the franchiser and the franchisees or between franchisees and thus restricts competition within the network. As is clear from the judgment of 13 July 1966 (Joined Cases 56 and 58/64 *Consten and Grundig v Commission* [1966] ECR 299), a restriction of that kind constitutes a limitation of competition for the purposes of Article 85(1) if it concerns a business name or symbol which is already well-known. It is of course possible that a prospective franchisee would not take the risk of becoming part of the chain, investing his own money, paying a relatively high entry fee and undertaking to pay a substantial annual royalty, unless he could hope, thanks to a degree of protection against competition on the part of the franchiser and other franchisees, that his business would be profitable. That consideration, however, is relevant only to an examination of the agreement in the light of the conditions laid down in Article 85(3).

25. Although provisions which impair the franchisee's freedom to determine his own prices are restrictive of competition, that is not the case where the franchiser simply provides franchisees with price guidelines, so long as there is no concerted practice between the franchiser and the franchisees or between the franchisees themselves for the actual application of such prices. It is for the national court to determine whether that is indeed the case.

In *Remia* the Court considered it possible for a provision preventing competition between two competitors to be lawful. In *Pronuptia* the opposite conclusion was reached in relation to a provision preventing competition between franchisees. It is doubtful therefore whether the clauses in *Pronuptia* were any more restrictive of competition than the four year 'no competition' clause provided for in *Remia*. Whilst the franchiser was in a position to eliminate all intra-brand price competition between franchisees by completing a series of agreements with them all, this freedom was limited by competition from other brands. The most probable explanation for this distinction is rather the prevention of market partitioning. Whilst price constraints may have had a minimal effect on the wedding dress market overall, they would have limited the possibilities for movements of Pronuptia goods. The result would have been possible considerable differences in price for the same goods in the different Member States - a feature perceived to be at odds with the notion of a single market.

iv. Penetration of New Markets by Existing Suppliers

It is clearly in the EC interest for undertakings to enter new markets within the EC. Without such an exploration process a single market would not be possible. Such a process carries increased risk for an undertaking. The demand for any of its products will be uncertain. Distributors may be unwilling to bear part of the risk for marketing a new product, and may have to be paid a premium to do so. In these circumstances, rents offered by exclusive distribution rights act to lower the risks for the distributor and as a form of additional payment for the risks involved. In those circumstances the Court will examine not merely the agreement but also its legal and economic context, in particular the position of the undertaking on the market, whether the agreement is part of a network of agreements and how severely the restraint distorts competition.

Case 56/65 Société Technique Minière v Maschinenbau Ulm [1966] ECR 235, [1966] CMLR 357

Machinenbau Ulm, a German producer of grading machines, concluded an agreement, whereby Société Technique Minière was to be its exclusive distributor in France for a two year period. Following a contractual dispute the latter claimed that the agreement was void on the grounds that it contravened Article 85 [*81*] EC.

... for the agreement at issue to be caught by the prohibition contained in Article 85(1) it must have as its 'object or effect the prevention, restriction or distortion of competition within the Common Market'.

The fact that these are not cumulative but alternative requirements, indicated by the conjunction 'or', leads first to the need to consider the precise purpose of the agreement, in the economic context in which it is to be applied. This interference with competition referred to in Article 85(1) must result from all or some of the clauses of the agreement itself.

Where, however, an analysis of the said clauses does not reveal the effect on competition to be sufficiently deleterious, the consequences of the agreement should then be considered and for it to be caught by the prohibition it is then necessary to find that those factors are present which show that competition has in fact been prevented or restricted or distorted to an appreciable extent. The competition in question must be understood within the actual context in which it would occur in the absence of the agreement in dispute. *In particular it may be doubted whether there is an interference with competition if the said agreement seems really necessary for the penetration of a new area by an undertaking* [authors' italics]. Therefore, in order to decide whether an agreement containing a clause 'granting an exclusive right of sale' is to be considered as prohibited by reason of its object or of its effect, it is appropriate to take into account in particular the nature and quantity, limited or otherwise, of the products covered by the agreement, the position and importance of the grantor and the concessionaire on the market for the products concerned, the isolated nature of the disputed agreement or, alternatively, its position in a series of agreements, the severity of the clauses intended to protect the exclusive dealership or, alternatively, the opportunities allowed for other commercial competitors in the same products by way of parallel re-exportation and importation.

There is an overlap between this category and that of ancillary restraints. Any agreement allowing an undertaking to enter a new market is likely to be pro-competitive in nature as it increases the number of competitors on that market. In recent years the Court has therefore moved towards a generic style of reasoning similar to the doctrine of ancillary restraints whereby agreements which allow undertakings to enter a market for the first time will not be considered to breach Article 85(1) [*81(1)*] EC unless they contain excessively restrictive restraints or partition the single market.

Case 27/87 Erauw-Jacquery Sprl v La Hesbignonne Société Co-opérative [1988] ECR 1919, [1988] 4 CMLR 576[40]

9. The Commission and the breeder maintain that the provision prohibiting the sale and exportation of E2 basic seed, which is placed at the disposal of the growers only for the purposes of propagation, is not contrary to Article 85(1) of the Treaty. Such a provision falls within the ambit of the plant breeder's rights.

10. In this respect, it must be pointed out that, as the Court acknowledged in its judgment of 8 June 1982 (in Case 258/78 *Nungesser v Commission* [1982] ECR 2015), the development of the basic lines may involve considerable financial commitment. Consequently, a person who has made considerable efforts to develop varieties of basic seed which may be the subject-matter of plant breeders' rights must be allowed to protect himself against any improper handling of those varieties of seed. To that end, the breeder must be entitled to restrict propagation to the growers which he has selected as licensees.

---

40 For the facts see p. 593

To that extent, the provision prohibiting the licensee from selling and exporting basic seed falls outside the prohibition contained in Article 85(1).

v. Agreements with Ambiguous Competitive Effects

There are instances where not merely the competitive effects of the arrangement in hand but also of that class of arrangement, generally, are considered to be ambiguous. This question has arisen principally in the context of distribution agreements, where there is considerable controversy as to whether they are anti-competitive at all. In particular the effects of the restraint are likely to be dependent less upon the contents of the agreement than on the nature of the market in question and the position of the parties on that market. The Court has therefore, in these circumstances, tended to engage in a balancing act where it weighs the pro-competitive effects of the agreement against its anti-competitive effects. In so doing, it focuses as much, if not more, on the market context as on the provisions of the agreement itself.

Case 31/80 L'Oréal v De Nieuwe AMCK [1980] ECR 3775, [1981] 2 CMLR 235

L'Oréal set up a distribution network where its 'Kerastase' hair care products could only be sold by approved 'hairdressing consultants'. It claimed that it gave its distributors technical assistance, and each distributor agreed to abide by certain rules in selling the product. Each distributor also gave an undertaking not to sell the products to any other distributor other than approved hairdressing consultants. De Nieuwe was not on the network but was selling Kerastase. L'Oréal brought an action on the grounds that De Nieuwe could only have obtained the products through someone else breaching a contract and that this constituted an unfair trading practice under Belgian law. De Nieuwe argued that the distribution agreement breached Article 85 [*81*] EC.

15. As the Court observed in its judgment of 25 October 1977 (Case 26/76 *Metro v Commission* [1977] ECR 1875), selective distribution systems constitute an aspect of competition which accords with Article 85(1) provided that re-sellers are chosen on the basis of objective criteria of a qualitative nature relating to the technical qualifications of the re-seller and his staff and the suitability of his trading premises and that such conditions are laid down uniformly for all potential re-sellers and are not applied in a discriminatory fashion.

16. In order to determine the exact nature of such 'qualitative' criteria for the selection of re-sellers, it is also necessary to consider whether the characteristics of the product in question necessitate a selective distribution system in order to preserve its quality and ensure its proper use, and whether those objectives are not already satisfied by national rules governing admission to the re-sale trade or the conditions of sale of the product in question. Finally, inquiry should be made as to whether the criteria laid down do not go beyond what is necessary. In that regard it should be recalled that in Case 26/76, *Metro v Commission cited above*, the Court considered that the obligation to participate in the setting up of a distribution system, commitments relating to the achievement of turnovers and obligations relating to minimum supply and to stocks exceeded the requirements of a selective distribution system based on qualitative requirements.

17. When admission to a selective distribution network is made subject to conditions which go beyond simple objective selection of a qualitative nature and, in particular, when it is based on quantitative criteria, the distribution system falls in principle within the prohibition in Article 85(1), provided that, as the Court observed in its judgment of 30 June 1966 (*Société Technique Minière v Maschinenbau Ulm Gmbh*, Case 56/65, [1966] ECR 235), the agreement fulfils certain conditions depending less on its legal nature than on its effects first on 'trade between Member States' and secondly on 'competition'.

18. To decide, on the one hand, whether an agreement may affect trade between Member States it is necessary to decide on the basis of a set of objective factors of law or of fact and in particular with regard to the consequences of the agreement in question on the possibilities of parallel importation whether it is possible to foresee with a sufficient degree of probability that the agreement in question may have an influence, direct or indirect, actual or potential, on the pattern of trade between Member States.

19. On the other hand, in order to decide whether an agreement is to be considered as prohibited by reason of the distortion of competition which is its object or its effect, it is necessary to consider the competition within the actual context in which it would occur in the absence of the agreement in dispute. To that end, it is appropriate to take into account in particular the nature and quantity, limited or otherwise, of the products covered by the agreement, the position and the importance of the parties on the market for the products concerned, and the isolated nature of the disputed agreement or, alternatively, its position in a series of agreements. In that regard the Court stated in its judgment of 12 December 1967 (in Case 23/67 *Brasserie de Haecht* [1967] ECR 407) that, although not necessarily decisive, the existence of similar contracts is a circumstance which, together with others, is capable of constituting an economic and legal context within which the contract must be judged.

20. It is for the national court to decide, on the basis of all the relevant information, whether the agreement in fact satisfies the requirements necessary for it to fall under the prohibition laid down in Article 85(1).

Particular factors to be taken into account are the number of similar agreements existing on that market, and the extent to which those agreements have restricted the degree of competition on that market.[41] The heavy reliance on the economic context by this style of reasoning has been criticised as engendering an uncertainty which is not conducive to forward planning by business persons.[42] It might even be suggested, as it has in the US context, that it would be better for the law to set broad and relatively clear standards, albeit ones that might occasionally bring along results that are difficult to justify.[43]

vi. EC Competition Law and the Rule of Reason

The limited market analysis of some of the judgments of the Court has resulted in the accusation that Article 85(1) [*81(1)*] EC is being interpreted in a 'literal, almost mathematical, manner'.[44] Comparisons have therefore increasingly been sought with United States anti-trust law. Section 1 of the Sherman Act 1890, the US equivalent of Article 85(1) [*81(1)*] EC is equally delphic:

> Every contract, combination ..., or conspiracy, in restraint of trade or commerce ..., is declared to be illegal.

---

41 Case 75/84 *Metro v Commission (No.2)* [1986] ECR 3021, [1987] 1 CMLR 118.

42 Whish, R. & Sufrin, B. 'Article 85 and the Rule of Reason' (1987) 7 *YBEL* 1, 28-29.

43 Comanor, W. 'Vertical Price-Fixing, Vertical Market Restrictions and the New Antitrust Policy' (1985) 98 *Harvard Law Review* 983, 1001.

44 Forrester, I. & Norrall, C. 'The Laicization of Community Law: Self-Help and the Rule of Reason: How Competition Law Is and Could be Applied' (1984) 21 *CMLRev* 11, 12.

The US courts were faced with the dilemma of how to ensure that not all restrictions on conduct were considered to be restrictions on competition. The problem was particularly pressing, as US law contains no equivalent to Article 85(3) [*81(3)*] EC, whereby cartels could be found to be legal, notwithstanding their effects on competition. The solution was the development of the 'rule of reason'. According to Judge Brandeis in *Chicago Board of Trade*:[45]

> 'The true test of legality is whether the restraint imposed is such as merely regulates and perhaps thereby promotes competition or whether it is such as may suppress or even destroy competition. To determine that question the Court must ordinarily consider the facts peculiar to the business to which the restraint is applied; its conditions before and after the restraint was imposed; the nature of the restraint and its effect, actual or probable.'

Courts were required therefore to weigh up whether the agreement was pro- or anti-competitive as a whole.[46] This placed a heavy burden upon the courts with everything depending upon the individual circumstances of the case. Unsurprisingly, the courts resorted to a formalistic approach in respect of types of arrangements, such as price fixing or market sharing agreements, whose anti-competitive effects were most apparent. Such cartels were considered to breach the Sherman Act, as they were presumed to be always anti-competitive.[47] The implications for an arrangement which fell within the *per se* rule was that a less comprehensive analysis of the anti-competitive effects of the arrangement was required, as it was presumed that the arrangement would be anti-competitive. Schechter has therefore described how the development of the *per se* rule and the rule of reason has resulted in US courts being required to engage in varying degrees of analysis. If the agreement is of an ambiguous competitive nature, further analysis is

---

45 *Board of Trade of City of Chicago v U.S.*, 246 U.S. 231 (1918).

46 Whish, R. & Sufrin, B. 'Article 85 and the Rule of Reason' (1987) 7 *YBEL* 1, 4-8.

47 *Northern Pacific Railway v US*, 356 US 1 (1958). On the relationship between the *per se* rule and the rule of reason see Bork, R. 'The Rule of Reason and the Per Se Concept: Price Fixing and Market Division' (1965) 74 *Yale Law Journal* 775 & (1966) 75 *Yale Law Journal* 373.

necessary under the rule of reason. This analysis needs to be less wideranging the more direct the restraint on competition and the closer the relationship between the parties until one reaches the *per se* rule, where the form of the arrangement is sufficiently conclusive of an agreement's anti-competitive effects for no further analysis to be necessary.[48]

Simple reference to the development of a rule of reason is something of an empty point. Bork has stated:

> 'The rule of reason ... is simply a set of general categories that are given content by ideas about the proper goals of the law, economics, and the requirements of the judicial process.'[49]

The development of a rule of reason therefore leaves unanswered the more fundamental question of what goals should shape competition law and how a balance should be struck between them. Boiled down, it can be taken as meaning no more than that each case should be taken on its individual merits.

Notwithstanding its difficulties of application in the United States, considerable support has developed for the introduction of a rule of reason into EC competition law. First suggested by Joliet in 1967,[50] pressure for such a development was particularly prominent during the early 1980s.[51] The debate must be considered in both its institutional and substantive context.

---

48 Schechter, M. 'The Rule of Reason in European Competition Law' (1982/2) *LIEI* 1, 12-13.

49 Bork, R. *The Antitrust Paradox: A Policy At War with Itself* (1993, Free Press, New York) 21.

50 Joliet, R. *The Rule of Reason in Antitrust Law: American, German and Common Market Laws in Comparative Perspective* (1967, Martijnus Nijhoff, The Hague) 183-188.

51 Korah, V. 'The Rise and Fall of Provisional Validity - the Need for a Rule of Reason in EEC Antitrust' (1981) *Northwestern Journal of International Law and Business* 320; Kon, S. 'Article 85(3): A Case for Application by National Courts' (1982) 19 *CMLRev* 541; Schechter, M. 'The Rule of Reason in European Competition Law' (1982/2) *LIEI* 1; Forrester, I. & Norall, C. 'The Laicization of Community Law: Self-Help and the Rule of Reason: How Competition Law Is and Could be Applied' (1984) 21 *CMLRev* 11; Steindorff, E. 'Article 85 and the Rule of Reason' (1984) 21 *CMLRev* 639.

Forrester, I. & Norrall, C. 'The Laicization of Community Law: Self-Help and the Rule of Reason: How Competition Law Is and Could be Applied' (1984) 21 *Common Market Law Review* 11, 13-14 & 16-18

There are far too many cases notified to the Commission for it to be able to handle individually. The notification process has, from a functional point of view, come to be used as a law-making tool rather than as a mechanism for approving individual cases. To a large extent, the Commission selects those notifications as to which it is interested in stating, clarifying or developing the law and reacts with decisions. The backlog of unanswered notifications is large: 3,715 in December 1982. The number of exemptions is small: 31 in ten years. The files containing about 2,000 notifications during the same ten year period were closed, some because the agreements had expired, some because one or other group exemption was available, others following informal comments from the Commission. Clearly, notification does not work as a mechanism by which any party to an agreement caught by Article 85(1) can obtain an exemption under Article 85(3). ...

At least from a theoretical point of view, so long as exemption is legally necessary but unavailable in many if not most cases, the consequences appear to be rather serious. An agreement caught by paragraph (1) of Article 85 is void and unenforceable under paragraph (2) if it has not been exempted under paragraph (3). A system which purports to make so much depend on the issuance of exemptions which it is unable as a practical matter to deliver is open to rather harsh criticism. Far from creating legal uncertainty, it is a source of uncertainty.

The anomalies of the situation are evident to businessmen and their legal advisers, and certain practices have evolved by way of response to the problem. There has developed an alternative system of observance which is not without merit. Lawyers and businessmen may decide not to notify agreements, concluding instead that the agreements and underlying conduct are consistent with Article 85, even if this is in part for reasons which would traditionally have been thought to come under paragraph (3) rather than paragraph (1). ...

Another practice which is widespread - strikingly so when compared to, for example, the United States - is for businessmen simply to ignore the competition rules entirely. ...

It is submitted that the time is ripe for a number of changes. The characteristics of a mature, coherent and properly functioning system of competition law are that it permeates the consciousness of the economic and legal system, and is applied almost routinely by businessmen, lawyers and judges on their own responsibility. In such a system, the role of law enforcement officials like the Commission should be not to exercise a theoretically all-embracing but practically unworkable surveillance over an immense number of individual transactions and agreements, but rather to observe the scene as a whole, to formulate policy, and for the rest to concentrate necessarily limited resources on carefully selected targets where intervention is necessary and effective. National courts should genuinely be available for the resolution of competition law problems, whether raised by complainants or by others.

Among the steps which should be taken is a relaxing of the interpretation of paragraph (1) of Article 85 so as to broaden the number of cases where economic behaviour can be said to comply with Article 85 without having resort to the criteria or procedures of paragraph (3).

The question of expertise is a particular problem in the context of the rule of reason. For that rule calls for judicial analysis precisely in those cases where the competitive effects of an agreement are at their most ambiguous. Even one of the leading advocates of a rule of reason has therefore expressed doubts over whether national courts are capable of giving any more sophisticated analyses than the Commission.

Korah, V. 'EEC Competition Policy - Legal Form or Economic Efficiency' (1986) 39 *Current Legal Problems* 85, 103

The problem remains for national courts attempting to make economic analyses of complex markets, especially in cases that involve small amounts. Have commercial advocates and judges the expertise to organise such cases at reasonable cost and speed? Can the appropriate kinds of evidence be introduced to ordinary commercial courts or would they be excluded by rules such as that against hearsay evidence? Is nullity an appropriate remedy? Such questions were answered negatively by Stevens and Yamey 20 years ago in relation to the Restrictive Practices Court in the United Kingdom and that analysis was limited to the easier task of controlling agreements between competitors keeping up prices.[[52]]

A second institutional argument in favour of the rule of reason might be that even if the quality of decision-making might be lower in national courts, access to the latter is easier and the process less centralised and time-consuming. This is essentially a resources point. It can be addressed either by giving more resources to the Commission or, as has happened, through a system of structured devolution of tasks to national courts.[53] The rule of reason is an unsuitable instrument for such a division of duties, as it establishes no clear criteria along which such

---

52 *The Restrictive Practices Court: A Study of the Judicial Process and Economic Policy* (1965, Weidenfeld & Nicolson, London).

53 EC Commission, Notice on cooperation between national courts and the Commission in applying Articles 85 & 86 EC, OJ 1993 C 39/6.

a division should take place. Whish and Sufrin have suggested, indeed that a diminution of the role of the Commission carries risks, due to EC competition law's young and undeveloped nature. Without the Commission taking a proactive role, it will be difficult for unresolved areas of competition law to be mapped out.[54] A wide rule of reason at this stage in the Community's development might therefore result in a fragmentation and a stunting of the growth of EC competition law and policy.

A separate line of reasoning supporting a rule of reason relates not to the institutional context but to the substance of the law itself. Joliet considers that the conditions for exempting anti-competitive practices contained in Article 85(3) [*81(3)*] EC are unduly strict. A rule of reason would be a more sensitive and flexible vehicle through which to introduce the values which shape competition law.[55] Korah has, additionally, argued that a rule of reason would improve the quality of the Court's analysis resulting in a less formalistic and more flexible line of reasoning more in line with market realities.[56] If calls for a rule of reason were merely a call for sophisticated analysis by the Commission and the Court, few could disagree. But, as Whish and Sufrin observe, the use of the American terminology is unnecessary and also undesirable. It suggests the import into EC competition law of the values and doctrine present in US antitrust law. The history and context within which the two systems have evolved is different. There is a different institutional structure within the EC, so that neither the Court's nor the Commission's style of analysis fits easily within a framework structured around any form of rule of reason. The EC is not yet and may never be a fully evolved single market in the manner in which the American market is.[57]

---

54 Whish, R. & Sufrin, B. 'Article 85 and the Rule of Reason' (1987) 7 *YBEL* 1, 16-17.

55 Joliet, R. supra n.50, 115-116.

56 Korah, V. 'The Rise and Fall of Provisional Validity - The Need for a Rule of Reason in EEC Antitrust' (1981) *North Western Journal of International Law and Business* 320, 354-355; Korah, V. 'EEC Competition Policy - Legal Form or Economic Efficiency' (1986) 39 *Current Legal Problems* 85, 91-94.

57 Supra n.54, 12-20 & 35-36.

vii. Vertical Restraints

Vertical restraints take a number of forms. (EDAs) are agreements whereby a producer agrees to sell goods solely to one distributor within a given territory. They are predominantly concluded to compensate a distributor for adopting a risk, and are often executed to protect the distributor. *Selective distribution agreements* (SDAs), on the other hand, are agreements where only those distributors will be appointed for a particular territory who fulfil certain criteria. They are often used as a form of quality control in that the distribution of certain goods might require a certain expertise or a certain 'name'. *Exclusive purchasing agreements* (EPAs) are the converse of EDAs as they involve the distributor agreeing to certain goods exclusively from the supplier. The potential advantages of such agreements is that they can lead to improvements in distribution by enabling the supplier to plan his sales with greater certainty and to ensure that the distributor's needs are met on a regular basis. The final form are *franchise agreements*. The franchiser will usually supply the franchisee with its business name and format. In return for this the franchisee will pay the franchiser a royalty. In addition, the franchiser will often insist upon the imposition of uniform business methods, such as how the shop should be laid out, the nature of the advertising or from where goods are to be purchased. The potential advantages of such agreements are that because there is no capital outlay on its part, the franchiser can set up a distribution network faster. From the point of the view of the franchisee, it allows them to set up business more easily, as they can benefit from the franchiser's expertise and goodwill.

Many of these types of restraint have proved problematic for the Court and the Commission. The Court is thus genuinely ambivalent about the competitive effects of selective distribution agreements; it is prepared to permit franchises which contain some ancillary restraints but not others, and exclusive *distribution agreements if they facilitate market penetration.* The reason for this is that the effects of such restraints are highly ambiguous. They can facilitate market integration by reducing the risks of market entry and facilitating flows of information between manufacturers and distributers. Conversely, they can hinder market integration by restricting a distributor's freedom to supply competing goods or a manufacturer's freedom to supply different manufacturers.[58] Their effects on competition are also variable. For a period during the 1980's, there was a view that they were actually pro-competitive.[59]

Schechter, M. 'The Rule of Reason in European Competition Law' (1982/2) *Legal Issues of European Integration* 1, 17-19

The development of a proper analytical framework for assessing the competitive impact of vertical restraints requires a recognition of their pro-competitive and anti-competitive potential. The immediate effect of a vertical restriction is to reduce intra-brand competition - competition among the dealers of the same manufacturer. In most circumstances the loss of intra-brand competition is entirely irrelevant to competition in the market for like products, since supra-competitive profits will be whittled away by competition from other brands. If a manufacturer possesses market power, it rarely will pass the profits deriving from that power to its downstream dealers. Consequently, it is not surprising that vertical restrictions usually serve purposes other than the enrichment of dealers, and that those purposes are often pro-competitive. Vertical restraints can promote consumer welfare in a number of ways. They may be used to protect from free-riders those dealers that a manufacturer determines should engage in the marketing and servicing of its product. Vertical restraints also may be used to create marketing areas sufficiently large to capture economies of scale in distribution and marketing. Moreover, they may reduce transaction costs arising from the independent dealer/manufacturer relationship. Although the magnitude of such benefits may vary from market to market, the anti-competitive potential of vertical restraints is fairly remote.

Although vertical restraints restrict independent dealer action, they are capable of producing anti-competitive consequences in only one of two situations: (1) where they are used to facilitate horizontal collusion, tacit or express, among manufacturers or dealers, or (2) where they raise barriers to entry at the manufacturing level by foreclosing a substantial portion of the dealer market.

Vertical restraints may facilitate collusion among dealers of different manufacturers by limiting the total number of dealers in a market area or by limiting the independent pricing discretion of the area dealers. This result presupposes the existence of several conditions. There must be few enough dealers of the various manufacturers in the market to make collusion possible, or every manufacturer must impose a sufficiently rigid vertical restriction. Second, either the dealers must have the power to coerce the manufacturers into imposing vertical restraints, which requires barriers to entry at the

---

58 EC Commission, *Green Paper on Vertical Restraints in EC Competition Policy* COM (96) 721 final, paras 80-84.

59 See also Hawk, B. 'System Failure: Vertical Restraints and EC Competition Law' (1995) 32 *CMLRev* 973.

dealer level, or the manufacturers must be able somehow to share the benefits of the dealer collusion.

Vertical restraints might also be employed by manufacturers to facilitate tacit or express collusion at the manufacturing level. In the case of express collusion, vertical restraints may allow manufacturers better to monitor their rivals' prices to assure conformity to a pricing agreement or effect a territorial allocation. In the absence of an express agreement, vertical restraints may be imposed by oligopolistic manufacturers to effect tacit collusion by facilitating oligopolistic interdependence - 'the mutual recognition that adherence to a common non-competitive price is in the individual self-interest of all firms'.[60] As in the case of express collusion, the vertical restraints may allow manufacturers to better monitor the prices being charged by rivals. The restraint is used as a mechanism to facilitate non-competitive interdependent pricing, by curing the complicating factor of inadequate rival pricing information.

Finally, vertical restraints theoretically may be used by manufacturers to raise barriers to entry at the manufacturing level. Where the restraints necessitate multilevel entry, and it is more difficult than single level entry, existing market power may be enhanced. However, if either a manufacturer, or several manufacturers in an oligopolistic market, lack market power or control an insufficiently large share of the downstream dealer market, anti-competitive effects of this type are improbable.

In sum, the prospects of vertical restrictions generally producing anti-competitive effects are slight, and the prospects for an enhancement of competition are great. It should be axiomatic to say that every vertical restriction should be carefully examined before it is proscribed.

Many of the anti-competitive effects of vertical restraints dismissed by Schechter can take place in markets where there is either little inter-brand competition, barriers to entry or individual distributors or manufacturers enjoy considerable market power. The Commission has thus suggested that there will be markets where vertical restraints can have anti-competitive effects. Agreements with retailers can be used by manufacturers to reinforce price agreements between themselves. Exclusive distribution agreements can be used, through the tying up of retailers, to foreclose access to the market for other manufacturers. In oligopolistic markets exclusive distribution agreements can also be used to restrict inter-brand competition further by limiting the range of goods sold at the different outlets. In the Commission's view, analysis needed

---

60 Hay, G. 'Oligopoly, Shared Monopoly and Antitrust Law' (1982) 67 *Cornell Law Review* 439, 451.

to be focused, therefore, not on the form of the agreement but rather upon its actual market impact.[61]

This suggests a future regime which may be more fragmented in nature. Increasingly, what will be determinative is not whether the agreement is a franchise, a selective or an exclusive distribution agreement but the conditions which persist on the market at the time, and questions such the number of market participants and the scale of the barriers to market entry.

V. The Commission's Powers of Exemption under Article 85(3) [*81(3)*] EC

i. Individual Exemptions

Under Article 85(3) [*81(3)*] EC, the Commission can exempt any individual agreement falling within Article 85(1) [*81(1)*] EC, which satisfies four conditions:[62]

- the agreement must contribute to improving the production or distribution of goods or to promoting technical or economic progress;
- it must allow consumers a fair share of the resulting benefit;
- the agreement must not impose restrictions on the undertakings concerned which are not indispensable to the attainment of the objectives of the agreement;
- it must not afford the undertakings the possibility of eliminating competition in respect of a substantial part of the products in question.

---

61 EC Commission, *Green Paper on Vertical Restraints in EC Competition Policy* COM (96) 721 final, paras 57-64 & 85-86.

62 For a review of the Commission's exercise of its discretion to grant individual exemptions under Article 85(3) [*81(3)*] EC see Bellamy, C. & Child, G. *Common Market Law of Competition* (1993, 4th Edition, Sweet & Maxwell, London) paragraphs 3-017 - 3-051.

All four of the conditions must be satisfied before an exemption will be given. The first two conditions listed above are positive ones. An account below is given of how the Commission exercises its discretion in considering whether these conditions are satisfied.

Weatherill, S. & Beaumont, P. *EC Law: The Essential Guide to the Legal Workings of the European Community* (1995, 2nd Edition, Penguin, London) 705

... the agreement must contribute to improving the production or distribution of goods or to promoting technical or economic progress. This formula invites a general appraisal of the economic context of the arrangement. Although some Commission decisions single out one particular aspect, the formula may be summarized as the requirement of an *economic benefit*. In addition, however, the second condition, the *consumer benefit* criterion, insists that the deal shall yield a fair share of its benefits to the consumer. This is a plainly more broad aspiration than precisely measurable criterion, but at least the inclusion of this condition indicates a demand for a broader focus than the commercial interests of the parties themselves. It requires a steady trickle down of economic success as a pre-condition for exemption.

Equally importantly, it must be shown that these economic and consumer benefits could not have been produced by the competitive process.

***Re Bayer and Gist-Brocades NV*[63]**

Bayer and Gist Brocades, two producers of penicillin, entered a specialisation agreement whereby the former would only make an intermediate form of penicillin, and the latter would only make raw penicillin. They would also supply each other's penicillin needs. The agreement was found to be in breach of Article 85(1) [*81(1)*] EC but was exempted under Article 85(3) [*81(3)*] EC.

57.1. For the agreements to contribute to the improvement of production or distribution, or to promote technical and economic progress, they must objectively constitute an improvement on the situation that would otherwise exist. The fundamental principle in this respect, established at the time the common market was formed, lays down that fair and undistorted competition is the best guarantee of regular supply on the best terms. Thus the question of a contribution to economic progress within the meaning of Article

---

63 OJ 1976 L 30/13, [1976] 1 CMLR D98.

85(3) can only arise in those exceptional cases where the free play of competition is unable to produce the best result economically speaking.

The other two conditions are negative ones. The requirement that any restraint be indispensable to the objectives of the agreement is, in essence, a proportionality test, which requires some form of evaluation of the anti-competitive effects of a measure against its benefits. The final requirement is that the restraint must not prevent competition. In *Metro (No.1)*[64] the Court stated that the Commission's duty under Article 85(3) [*81(3)*] EC was to maintain 'workable competition'. The purpose of the final condition is therefore to ensure that while competition may be reduced by the practice, it should not be suppressed altogether. Whilst all the others involve balancing a number of considerations against each other, this is a far more absolute test. It suggests that no matter how great their other social benefits, the disruptive effects of some measures on competition are so great that they can never be exempted.

A wide measure of discretion is left to the Commission to determine whether these conditions are satisfied.

Joined Cases 56 & 58/64 Etablissements Consten SA & Grundig GmbH v Commission [1966] ECR 299, [1966] CMLR 418[65]

The undertakings are entitled to an appropriate examination by the Commission of their requests for Article 85(3) to be applied. For this purpose the Commission may not confine itself to requiring from undertakings proof of the fulfilment of the requirements for the grant of the exemption but must, as a matter of good administration, play its part, using the means available to it, in ascertaining the relevant facts and circumstances.

Furthermore, the exercise of the Commission's powers necessarily implies complex evaluations on economic matters. A judicial review of these evaluations must take account of their nature by confining itself to an examination of the relevance of the facts and of the legal consequences which the Commission deduces therefrom. This review must in the first place be carried out in respect of the reasons given for the decisions which must set out the facts and considerations on which the said evaluations are based.

---

64 Case 26/76 *Metro v Commission (No.1)* [1977] ECR 1875, [1978] 2 CMLR 1.

65 For the facts see p. 529.

It is rare that the Court will find that the Commission has erred in its discretion under Article 85(3) [*81(3)*] EC.[66] When juxtaposed next to the uncertainty surrounding the ambit of Article 85(1) [*81(1)*] EC, this strengthens the Commission's position as the fulcrum of EC competition policy. It will be a brave undertaking which does not notify the agreement to the Commission for negative clearance, given the unenforceability of the arrangement and the possible fines that might otherwise accrue if the Commission were to find an undertaking had taken part in an unnotified agreement which fell within Article 85(1) [*81(1)*] EC.[67]

ii. The Quasi-Legislative Framework of the Block Exemptions

Wideranging powers have been delegated to the Commission by the Council to exempt categories of agreement on the basis of the criteria set out in Article 85(3) [*81(3)*] EC. Block Exemptions have been developed for many of the common form of agreements. There are, therefore, Block Exemptions on, *inter alia*, specialisation agreements;[68] research and development agreements;[69] exclusive distribution

---

66 For such an example see Joined Cases 19 & 20/74 *Kali & Salz v Commission* [1975] ECR 499, [1975] 2 CMLR 154.

67 For a critical view see Van Bael, I. 'Insufficient Judicial Control of EC Competition Law Enforcement' (1992) *Fordham Corporate Law Institute* 733.

68 Regulation 417/85/EEC, OJ 1985 L 53/1, as amended by Regulation 151/93/EEC, OJ 1993 L 21/8 and Regulation 2236/97/EC, OJ 1997 L 306/12.

69 Regulation 418//85/EEC, OJ 1985 L 53/5 as amended by Regulation 151/93/EEC, OJ 1993 L 21/8 and Regulation 2236/97/EC, OJ 1997 L 306/12. See Korah, V. *R & D Joint Ventures and the EEC Competition Rules: Regulation 418/85* (1986, ESC, London); Venit, J. 'The Research and Development Block Exemption' (1985) 10 *ELRev* 151; White, E. 'Research and Development Joint Ventures under EEC Competition Law' (1985) *IIC* 663.

agreements;[70] exclusive purchasing agreements,[71] technology transfer agreements[72] and franchises.[73] The purpose of Block Exemptions is, in part, an attempt to reduce the administrative burden of EC competition law created by the requirement of notification. Unless otherwise specified,[74] undertakings are not obliged to notify agreements falling within the Block Exemption to the Commission. All Block Exemptions share certain common characteristics. They will, first of all, give a definition of the particular form of agreement, be it a research and development agreement, an exclusive distribution agreement or a franchise agreement. All agreements meeting the criteria set out in this definition fall, *prima facie,* within the scope of the Block Exemption. The exemptions then deal with three forms of restraints. The first are what is known in the jargon as *white-listed restraints*. These are restraints which fall within Article 85(1) [*81(1)*] EC but are given exemption by the Block Exemption. *Grey listed restraints* are those restraints which do not clearly fall within Article 85(1) [*81(1)*] EC, but which, for purposes of legal certainty are granted exemption by the Block Exemption. *Black listed restraints* are restraints whose inclusion in an agreement will take that agreement outside the ambit of a Block Exemption.

Whilst Block Exemptions are the products of earlier Commission experience and Court judgments, they are also acts of a general nature. They represent an attempt to introduce a more rule-based approach to EC competition law. Their general and detailed nature bring about a

---

70 Regulation 1983/83/EEC, OJ 1983 L 173/1 as last amended by Regulation 1582/97/EC, OJ 1997, L 214/27. See Korah, V. & Rothnie, W. *Exclusive Distribution and the EEC Competition Rules: Regulations 1983/83 and 1984/83* (1992, 2nd Edition, Sweet & Maxwell, London).

71 Regulation 1984/83/EEC, OJ 1983 L 173/5 as last amended by Regulation 1582/97, OJ 1997 L 214/27.

72 Regulation 240/96/EC, OJ 1996 L 31/2. See Korah, V. *Technology Transfer Agreements and EC Competition Rules* (1996, Clarendon, Oxford).

73 Regulation 4087/88/EEC, OJ 1988, L 359/46. See Korah, V. *Franchising and the EEC Competition Rules - Regulation 4087/88* (1989, ESC, London); Cockbourne, 'The New EEC Block Exemption Regulation on Franchising' (1989) 12 *Fordham International Law Journal* 242.

74 Regulation 417/85/EEC, Article 4; Regulation 418/85/EEC, Article 7; Regulation 240/96/EC, Article 4.

comprehensiveness and standardisation, which would not be possible merely through the exercise of Commission and Court discretion in individual cases. This standardisation offers the possibility to private actors to develop standard model contracts which will be presumed not to need notification. Block Exemptions thus move the content of EC competition law away from a strictly sectoral approach towards forming the beginnings of a more general European commercial law. They should not, however, be seen as trouble-free.

McBarnet, D. & Whelan, C. 'The Elusive Spirit of the Law: Formalism and the Struggle for Legal Control' (1991) 54 *Modern Law Review* 848, 849-851

Although the term formalism has been used in divergent ways, at its heart 'lies the concept of decision making according to *rule*',[75] rule implying here that the language of a rule's formulation - its literal mandate - be followed, even when this ill serves its purpose. ...

Creative compliance uses formalism to avoid legal control, whether a tax liability or some regulatory obstacle to raising finance, effecting a controversial takeover or securing other corporate, or management, objectives. The combination of specific rules and an emphasis on legal form and literalism can be used artificially, in a manipulative way to circumvent or undermine the purpose of regulation. Using this approach, transactions, relationships or legal forms are constructed in order to avoid the apparent bounds of specific legal rules. In this sense, the detailed rules contribute to the defeat of legal policy. ...

Creative compliance highlights the limits of formalism as a strategy of legal control. A formalistic approach, which relies upon a 'cookbook' or code of specific and rigid rules and emphasises the legal form of transactions, can fail to 'control' for a variety of reasons. Unless the rules promote the overall purpose of the law, compliance with them and insisting on their literal interpretation or enforcement will not achieve the declared objectives. The letter of the rule may not accord with the spirit in which the law was framed; a literal application of the rules may not produce the desired end, it may be counter-productive; there may be gaps, omissions or loopholes in the rules which undermine their effectiveness. The rules may be out of date and no longer relevant. There may be other problems too. The legal form of a transaction or a relationship may not reflect its legal or its economic or commercial substance. The totality of a transaction or relationship may not be reflected in any individual part. There may be a dynamic adaptation to escape rules. Formalistic regulation may increasingly drift from any relationship with the real world and any chance of effectively controlling it.

---

75 Schauer, F. 'Formalism' (1989) 97 *Yale Law Journal* 509, 510.

Further Reading

The literature in this area is enormous. Merely the principal works are listed below.

Bellamy, C. & Child, G. (edited by Rose, V.) *Common Market Law of Competition* (1993, 4th Edition, Sweet & Maxwell, London)(as amended by 1st Supplt, editor P. Roth, 1996, Sweet & Maxwell, London)
Goyder, D. *EEC Competition Law* (1992, 2nd Edition, Clarendon Press, Oxford)
Green, N. *Commercial Agreements and Competition Law: Practice and Procedure in the UK and EEC* (1992, 2nd Edition, Graham & Trotman, London)
Joliet, R. *The Rule of Reason in Antitrust Law - American, German and Common Market Laws in Comparative Perspective* (1967, Martijnus Nijhoff, The Hague)
Korah, V. *An Introductory Guide to EC Competition Law and Practice* (1997, 6th Edition, Hart Publishing, Oxford)
Van Bael, I. & Bellis, J-F. *Competition Law of the European Community* (1996, 3rd Edition, CCH, Bicester)
Whish, R. *Competition Law* (1993, 3rd Edition, Butterworths, London)

13. Abuse of Market Power

I. Introduction

The wave of competition laws enacted in Europe during the late 1940s and 1950s reflected a view of competition as a *process* of striving and rivalry. Cartels were perceived as particularly inimical to this process and were regulated in all those States which had competition laws[1] and by Article 85 [*81*] EC. Many economists take, however, a *structural* view of competition. Competition only exists where the number of undertakings selling an object is so large that no single undertaking can influence the market price of the product.[2] Scherer and Ross thus observe that in competitive markets 'price is a parameter to the competitive seller - it is determined by market forces and not subject to the individual seller's control'.[3] There are additional reasons for intervention in uncompetitive markets, as firms are less tightly constrained by the rigours of the competitive process in these markets.

This latter view initially enjoyed only limited influence in national competition laws. Monopolies were regulated in only a few countries, notably Belgium and Germany. There was a feeling that there might be a relationship between size and efficiency, and many national markets were seen as being too small to support a number of firms.[4] Notwithstanding this, Article 86 [*82*] EC was introduced into the EC Treaty to regulate those situations where a firm(s) enjoyed significant market power.

---

1. For an interesting comparative study see Thorelli, H. 'Antitrust in Europe: National Policies after 1945' (1959) 26 *University of Chicago Law Review* 222.
2. Scherer, F. & Ross, D. *Industrial Structure and Market Performance* (1990, 3rd Edition, Houghton, New York) 15-18.
3. Ibid., 16.
4. Supra n.1, 233.

The process of gauging whether or not an undertaking enjoys market dominance is dependent upon prior identification of the relevant market. The material aspect of the market, its subject-matter, must first be defined. This is called the *relevant product market.* In addition, the territorial aspect, the area over which the market extends, must be established. This is called the *relevant geographical market.*

II. The Product Market

Product markets are defined by reference both to demand and to supply.

i. Demand Side Substitutability

Case 27/76 United Brands v Commission [1978] ECR 207, [1978] 1 CMLR 429

United Brands sold 'Chiquita' and 'Fyffes' bananas within the European Community. It held the largest share of both the world and Community banana markets. The Commission considered that United Brands had a dominant position on the banana market in a number of Member States and had breached Article 86 [*82*] EC in a number of ways. It forbade distributors from reselling bananas which were still green, it charged different prices in different parts of the Community, and it had refused to supply a Danish firm, Olesen, with bananas. United Brands claimed that one of the reasons that the Commission's decision was erroneous was that the banana market was not a separate market and that instead the Commission should have considered the market for fresh fruit as a whole.

12. As far as the product market is concerned it is first of all necessary to ascertain whether, as the applicant maintains, bananas are an integral part of the fresh fruit market, because they are reasonably interchangeable by consumers with other kinds of fresh fruit such as apples, oranges, grapes, peaches, strawberries, etc. Or whether the relevant market consists solely of the banana market which includes both branded bananas and unlabelled bananas and is a market sufficiently homogeneous and distinct from the market of other fresh fruit.

.....

22. For the banana to be regarded as forming a market which is sufficiently differentiated from other fruit markets it must be possible for it to be singled out by such special features distinguishing it from other fruits that it is only to a limited extent interchangeable with them and is only exposed to their competition in a way that is hardly perceptible.

23. The ripening of bananas takes place the whole year round without any season having to be taken into account.

24. Throughout the year production exceeds demand and can satisfy it at any time.

25. Owing to this particular feature the banana is a privileged fruit and its production and marketing can be adapted to the seasonal fluctuations of other fresh fruit which are known and can be computed.

26. There is no unavoidable seasonal substitution since the consumer can obtain this fruit all the year round.

27. Since the banana is a fruit which is always available in sufficient quantities the question whether it can be replaced by other fruits must be determined over the whole of the year for the purpose of ascertaining the degree of competition between it and other fresh fruit.

28. The studies of the banana market on the Court's file show that on the latter market there is no significant long term cross-elasticity any more than - as has been mentioned - there is any seasonal substitutability in general between the banana and all the seasonal fruits, as this only exists between the banana and two fruits (peaches and table grapes) in one of the countries (West Germany) of the relevant geographic market.

29. As far as concerns the two fruits available throughout the year (oranges and apples) the first are not interchangeable and in the case of the second there is only a relative degree of substitutability.

30. This small degree of substitutability is accounted for by the specific features of the banana and all the factors which influence consumer choice.

31. The banana has certain characteristics, appearance, taste, softness, seedlessness, easy handling, a constant level of production which enable it to satisfy the constant needs of an important section of the population consisting of the very young, the old and the sick.

32. As far as prices are concerned two FAO studies show that the banana is only affected by the prices - falling prices - of other fruits (and only of peaches and table grapes) during the summer months and mainly in July and then by an amount not exceeding 20%.

33. Although it cannot be denied that during these months and some weeks at the end of the year this product is exposed to competition from other fruits, the flexible way in which the volume of imports and their marketing on the relevant geographic market is adjusted means that the conditions of competition are extremely limited and that its price adapts without any serious difficulties to this situation where supplies of fruit are plentiful.

34. It follows from all these considerations that a very large number of consumers having a constant need for bananas are not noticeably or even appreciably enticed away from the consumption of this product by the arrival of other fresh fruit on the market and that even the personal peak periods only affect it for a limited period of time and to a very limited extent from the point of view of substitutability.

35. Consequently the banana market is a market which is sufficiently distinct from the other fresh fruit markets.

In a recent Notice the Commission suggested that substitutability, or, as it is often called, cross-elasticity of demand, will exist if customers would switch to readily available substitutes if the undertaking imposed a small but permanent price increase.[5] It will thus use marketing studies and take account of evidence of substitutability in the past. Such a test is a hypothetical and artificial one. Habit and the cost of searching for substitutes suggest that consumers do not switch their purchases even in competitive markets.The markets examined under Article 86 [82] EC are more problematic still, as they usually contain few suppliers and have a high degree of price inelasticity.

Demand substitutability has also proved difficult for the Court to review. It is a far cry from the textual analysis normally engaged in by courts. It is unsurprising, therefore, that the Court's findings have been subjected to considerable criticism on account of the paucity of their economic analysis.

---

5 EC Commission, *Notice on the Definition of the relevant market for the purposes of Community Competition law*, OJ 1997 C 372/5, para 17.

Baden Fuller, C.' Article 86 EEC: Economic Analysis of the Existence of a Dominant Position' (1979) 4 *European Law Review* 423, 425-426

In *UBC*, the Court failed to note an important distinction in the market, because they ignored the time dimension. ..., the Court noted that for the banana to be regarded as forming part of a market which is sufficiently differentiated from other fruit markets, it must be possible for it to be singled out by such special features distinguishing it from other fruits that it is only a to limited extent interchangeable with them. Now, the Court noted that during the summer months, but not the winter months, the price of other fruits was competitive with bananas, in the sense that a change in their price influenced the quantities sold (and, hence, the price) of bananas. Because bananas cannot be stored, it seems obvious that there were two markets defined by the seasons. In winter, bananas had few substitutes, but in summer, had substitutes. In winter, the relevant market was bananas, in summer, surely it was bananas and other fruit; but the Court did not see this distinction because it failed to grasp the importance of the time dimension.

In *UBC* (para.31), the Court also noted that the banana has certain characteristics which enable it to satisfy the constant needs of the very young, the old and the sick; and that, for this group, bananas may not have any close substitutes. If this is so, then the Court could have defined the relevant market as being only those bananas sold to these groups of people. In this case, other fruits would not be substitutes, even in summer. Any definition of the market should not preclude a market analysis which extends beyond the relevant market.

The risks of undue formalism were highlighted by the *Hugin* judgment.[6]

Case 22/78 Hugin v Commission [1979] ECR 1869, [1979] 3 CMLR 345

Hugin, a British supplier of cash registers refused to supply spare parts for its registers to Liptons, a competitor. In finding such behaviour to be abusive under Article 86 [*82*] EC the Commission considered the relevant market to be the market for spare parts for Hugin's machines needed by independent repairers. Hugin claimed that the appropriate market was the market for cash registers in general, a market in which it did not hold a dominant position.

5. To resolve the dispute it is necessary, first, to determine the relevant market. In this respect account must be taken of the fact that the conduct alleged against Hugin consists

---

6 Korah, V. 'The Concept of a Dominant Position within the Meaning of Article 86' (1980) 17 *CMLRev* 395, 402-403.

in the refusal to supply spare parts to Liptons and, generally, to any independent undertaking outside its distribution network. The question is, therefore, whether the supply of spare parts constitutes a specific market or whether it forms part of a wider market. To answer that question it is necessary to determine the category of clients who require such parts.

6. In this respect it is established, on the one hand, that cash registers are of such a technical nature that the user cannot fit the spare parts into the machine but requires the services of a specialized technician and, on the other, that the value of the spare parts is of little significance in relation to the cost of maintenance and repairs. That being the case, users of cash registers do not operate on the market as purchasers of spare parts, however they have their machines maintained and repaired. Whether they avail themselves of Hugin's after-sales service or whether they rely on independent undertakings engaged in maintenance and repair work, their spare part requirements are not manifested directly and independently on the market. While there certainly exists amongst users a market for maintenance and repairs which is distinct from the market in new cash registers, it is essentially a market for the provision of services and not for the sale of a product such as spare parts, the refusal to supply which forms the subject-matter of the Commission's decision.

7. On the other hand, there exists a separate market for Hugin spare parts at another level, namely that of independent undertakings which specialize in the maintenance and repair of cash registers, in the reconditioning of used machines and in the sale of used machines and the renting out of machines. The role of those undertakings on the market is that of businesses which require spare parts for their various activities. They need such parts in order to provide services for cash register users in the form of maintenance and repairs and for the reconditioning of used machines intended for re-sale or renting out. Finally, they require spare parts for the maintenance and repair of new or used machines belonging to them which are rented out to their clients. It is, moreover, established that there is a specific demand for Hugin spare parts, since those parts are not interchangeable with spare parts for cash registers of other makes.

8. Consequently the market thus constituted by Hugin spare parts required by independent undertakings must be regarded as the relevant market for the purposes of the application of Article 86 of the facts of the case. It is in fact the market on which the alleged abuse was committed.

Baden Fuller C., 'Article 86 EEC: Economic Analysis of the Existence of a Dominant Position' (1979) 4 *European Law Review* 423, 426-427

In *Hugin* (para.8), the Court defined the relevant market as Hugin spare parts required by independent undertakings.

... the Court defined the relevant market without discussing the existence of possible substitutes on the demand side for independent undertakings. This is not a minor point.

Consider those independent undertakings in the business of repairing, maintaining or refurbishing (but not renting or leasing) cash registers for independent customers. They often dealt in more than one brand of machine. Their engineers could, and did, repair more than one brand. In this respect, substitutes did exist on the demand side from the point of view of independent undertakings. The Court never discussed whether this substitution was easy, that is, whether the cross-elasticity was high or low. Hugin, in refusing to Liptons, apparently forced the latter to turn to servicing other machines. Liptons had said this shift was costly. The Commission in its Decision (paras. 27 and 28) did not show a proper analysis of this cost. Moreover, it did not even give figures on sales, costs or profits for Lipton's servicing business for outside customers separated from its other activities such as renting and leasing. Without such an analysis, it is not clear that the shift was so costly or difficult that it is reasonable to consider each brand of spare parts as forming a separate market. To me, the only sensible definitions of the relevant market are those which make specific reference to the owners of the machines. I believe the Court should have defined the market as: 'Spare Parts required by those who are owners of Hugin machines.'

Baden Fuller suggests a market definition which is, if anything, narrower than that chosen by the Court of Justice. As if to illustrate the problematic nature of market definition, others have suggested that a broader definition would have been more appropriate. Fox has noted that, at the time, in US law a company's own brand would almost certainly never be a market. She provides *Hugins* as an example. If Hugins made its spare parts too expensive, the effect would be that its cash registers would become unattractive to purchase in the first place. The relevant product market would therefore be cash registers as a whole, a market on which Hugins did not enjoy a monopoly.[7]

7 Fox, E. 'Monopolization and Dominance in the United States and the European Community: Efficiency, Opportunity and Fairness' (1986) *Notre Dame Law Review* 981, 1003. This position has now been overturned so that an 'aftermarket' in a firm's own brand can constitute a market. The reason is that firms get 'locked in' to a brand, so that competition from other brands is more apparent than real, *Eastman Kodak Co. v Image Technical Services Inc.* 199 L.Ed.2d 265 (1992). Hovenkamp, H. 'Market Power in Aftermarkets: Antitrust Policy and the Kodak Case' (1993) 40 *UCLA LRev* 1447.

ii. Supply Side Substitutability

Demand side substitutability examines the actual competition encountered by a product. A firm is constrained in its market behaviour not just by actual competition but also by potential behaviour. It will not engage in a practice which will have the effect of drawing a number of fresh competitors irreversibly into the market. The concept of potential competition is an amorphous one, as anybody is a potential competition. The Court instead turns to supply side competition. It will consider as part of the market all suppliers who arc able to switch production to the relevant products and market them in the short term without incurring significant additional costs.

Case 6/72 Continental Can v Commission [1973] ECR 215, [1973] CMLR 199

Continental Can, an American manufacturer of metal packaging, engaged, through its subsidiary Europemballage, in a friendly take-over of TDV, a Dutch manufacturer. The Commission considered that Continental Can, through another of its subsidiaries SLW, already had a dominant position on the market in metal containers for packaging fish and meat and on the market for metal closures for glass containers. Continental Can argued that these were not markets in their own right, as all producers of packaging could easily switch over from one form of packaging to another.

33. In this context recitals Nos 5 to 7 of the second part of the decision deal in turn with a 'market for light containers for canned meat products', a 'market for light containers for canned seafood', and a 'market for metal closures for the food packing industry, other than crown corks', all allegedly dominated by SLW and in which the disputed merger threatens to eliminate competition. The decision does not, however, give any details of how these three markets differ from each other, and must therefore be considered separately. Similarly, nothing is said about how these three markets differ from the general market for light metal containers, namely the market for metal containers for fruit and vegetables, condensed milk, olive oil, fruit juices and chemico-technical products. In order to be regarded as constituting a distinct market, the products in question must be individualized, not only by the mere fact that they are used for packing certain products, but by particular characteristics of production which make them specifically suitable for this purpose. Consequently, a dominant position on the market for light metal containers for meat and fish cannot be decisive, as long as it has not been proved that competitors from other sectors of the market for light metal containers are not in a position to enter this market, by a simple adaptation, with sufficient strength to create a serious counterweight.

Supply side substitutability, and correspondingly the size of the market, will be determined by the extent to which there are barriers to entry to the market.[8] One form of barrier which is uncontested is foreclosure. This occurs where existing firms on the market through a series of predatory activities, such as tying in customers or predatory pricing, seek to prevent newcomers entering the market. The second form of barrier to entry is far more contested. This concerns structural barriers to entry which stem from the nature of the market itself.

Geroski, P. & Jacquemin, A. 'Industrial change, barriers to mobility and European industrial policy' (1985) 1 *Economic Policy* 170, 182-183

In his pioneering study, Bain identified three sources of structural entry barriers: product differentiation, absolute cost advantages, and scale economies.[[9]] Product differentiation poses difficulties for entrants because prior purchases of the incumbent's brand are sunk investments by consumers. When product characteristics cannot be easily evaluated by inspection, and differ in unusual and complex ways, the opportunity cost to a consumer of trying a new brand with uncertain attributes may be high. Absolute cost advantages arise whenever the entrant has a higher unit cost curve than the incumbent, as, for example, when the incumbent enjoys superior access to technology, location or factor markets. Scale economies restrict the number of firms that can profitably compete in a market, forcing entrants to choose between operation at sub-optimal scale and a cost disadvantage relative to incumbents or operation at optimal scale facing a depressed market price.

By now we have accumulated a fair bit of evidence on the height of these three entry barriers. In most cases, scale economies do not seem to pose a substantial entry barrier... What does seem to be true is that the capital requirements of building large plants may pose substantial difficulties for entrants, the absolute cost disadvantage arising largely from unequal access to capital markets. Considerable evidence exists in the UK

---

8 This has recently been criticised on the grounds that examining potential competition confuses the problem of market definition with that of how much market power is enjoyed by an undertaking, Crowther, P. 'Product Market Definition in E.C. Competition Law: The Compatibility of Legal and Economic Approaches' (1996) *JBL* 177.

9 Bain, J. *Barriers to New Competition* (1956, Harvard University Press, Cambridge, Mass).

to suggest that the important distinction here may not be entrant versus incumbent so much as unquoted versus quoted firms. In part, the problem arises from the concentration of financial power, as personal savings are increasingly managed by life assurance firms, pension funds, and building societies. 'The vast funds put at the disposal of ... institutional intermediaries, by being placed preferentially in large quoted companies, have contributed to financial pressures which have encouraged the formation of large industrial groups'.[10] Whereas large quoted companies can raise capital through new issues, unquoted firms generally finance their expansion through retained earnings and short term credit. These financial problems often severely restrict new firm formation. Other absolute cost advantages - control of scarce resources, limited access to new technology, etc. - can be important in particular cases, but it is hard to generalize. Product differentiation advantages are certainly the most controversial to identify in practice, although many industrial economists suspect that they are the most important of all. Although again it is hard to generalize, space packing, product proliferation, the inflation of styling costs, differential access to retailing networks and advertising have all been documented as causes of barriers in particular cases.

Whilst there is a wealth of material documenting the existence of particular types of entry barriers, there are few evaluations of the overall height of barriers in particular sectors, much less for economies as a whole. Nevertheless, our reading of this material suggests that, in general, barriers can be appreciable.

Bork, R. *The Antitrust Paradox: A Policy at War with Itself* (1978, Macmillan, New York) 310-311

We may begin by asking what a barrier to entry is. There appears to be no precise definition, and in current usages a 'barrier' often seems to be anything that makes the entry of new firms into an industry more difficult. It is at once apparent that an ambiguity lies in the concept, and it is this ambiguity that causes the trouble. When existing firms are efficient and possess valuable plants, equipment, knowledge, skill and reputation, potential entrants will find it correspondingly more difficult to enter the industry, since they must acquire those things. It is harder to enter the steel industry than the business of retailing shoes or pizzas, and it is harder to enter either of these fields than to become a suburban handyman. But these difficulties are natural; they inhere in the nature of the tasks to be performed. There can be no objection to barriers of this sort. Their existence means only that when market power is achieved by means other than efficiency, entry will not dissipate the objectionable power instantaneously, and law may therefore have a role to play. If entry were instantaneous, market forces would break up cartels before a typist in the Antitrust Division could rap out a form complaint. Antitrust is valuable because in some cases it can achieve results more rapidly than can market forces. We need not suffer losses while waiting for the market to erode cartels and monopolistic mergers.

---

10 Prais, S. *The Evolution of Giant Firms in the UK* (1976, Cambridge University Press, Cambridge).

> The question for antitrust is whether there exist artificial entry barriers. These may be barriers that are not forms of superior efficiency and which yet prevent the forces of the market-entry or growth of smaller firms already within the industry - from operating to erode market positions not based on efficiency. Care must be taken to distinguish between forms of efficiency and artificial barriers. Otherwise the law will find itself- indeed, it has found itself - attacking efficiency in the name of market freedom. Joe Bain, whose work has done much to popularize the concept, lists among entry barriers such things as economies of scale, capital requirements, and product differentiation. There may be disagreement about two of these barriers, but it is clear that at least one of them, economies of scale, is a form of efficiency. Uncritical adapters of Bain's work have not sufficiently enquired whether the others may not also be efficiencies.

It is questionable whether Bork is addressing the same issue as Geroski and Jacquemin. Many structural barriers may be signs of an efficient industry, yet, even in such markets, barriers to entry will be considerable because of the high start up costs and the element of risk involved. In considering the existence and degree of market power, it is irrelevant whether the barriers to entry which protect and consolidate that power are 'artificial' or not. Bork can only therefore be suggesting that such markets need no special regulation on the grounds that they are competitive. Such an argument is premised on a view which perceives the exclusive function of competition as being to maximise efficiency gains. A view of competition policy which holds it to embrace wider social objectives would be forced to take such barriers to entry seriously.

III. The Geographical Market

Establishment of the geographical market is important not only as a preliminary to establishing whether an undertaking enjoys a dominant position, but also to determine EC competence. For Article 86 [82] EC to be triggered, it must be shown that, at the very least, the market encompasses a substantial part of the common market. This is not simply a territorial test.

Joined Cases 40-48, 50, 54-56, 111, 113 & 114/73 Suiker Unie v Commission [1975] ECR 1663, [1976] 1 CMLR 295

In 1973 the Commission adopted a Decision declaring a market partitioning cartel between sixteen of the principal Community sugar producers to be illegal. In addition it considered that certain producers had breached Article 86 [82] EC by forcing their distributors not to resell sugar in a manner which might undermine the cartel. Among these was Raffinerie Tirlemontoise, a Belgian producer, who, the Commission considered, occupied a dominant position on the Belgo-Luxembourg sugar market.

For the purpose of determining whether a specific territory is large enough to amount to 'a substantial part of the Common Market' within the meaning of Article 86 of the Treaty the pattern and volume of the production and consumption of the said product as well as the habits and economic opportunities of vendors and purchasers must be considered.

So far as sugar in particular is concerned it is advisable to take into consideration in addition to the high freight rates in relation to the price of the product and the habits of the processing industries and consumers the fact that Community rules have consolidated most of the special features of the former national markets.

From 1968-69 to 1971-72 Belgian production and total Community production increased respectively from 530,000 to 770,000 metric tons and from 6,800,000 to 8,100,000 metric tons...

During these marketing years Belgian consumption was approximately 350,000 metric tons whereas Community consumption increased from 5,900,000 to 6,500,000 metric tons...

If the other criteria mentioned above are taken into account these market shares are sufficiently large for the area covered by Belgium and Luxembourg to be considered, so far as sugar is concerned, as a substantial part of the Common Market in this product.

The test for establishing the geographical market is laid out below.

Case 27/76 United Brands v Commission [1978] ECR 207, [1978] 1 CMLR 429

The Commission considered that the relevant geographical market was the German, Danish, Irish, Dutch and BLEU (Belgian-Luxembourg Economic Union) markets. It excluded the other States of the European Community on the grounds that both France and the United Kingdom had preferential import arrangements for bananas produced in their former colonies and Italy operated a national system of import quotas on bananas. These features, in particular, distinguished these markets from the rest of the Community. The Court upheld the Commission's evaluation on the basis of the following reasoning.

10. In order to determine whether UBC has a dominant position on the banana market it is necessary to define this market both from the standpoint of the product and from the geographic point of view.

11. The opportunities for competition under Article 86 of the Treaty must be considered having regard to the particular features of the product in question and with reference to a clearly defined geographic area in which it is marketed and where the conditions of competition are sufficiently homogeneous for the effect of the economic power of the undertaking concerned to be able to be evaluated.

When will the Commission consider that economic conditions in an area are sufficiently homogenous for that area to be treated as a market in its own right? In its 1997 Notice the Commission suggests that it will look at the distribution of market shares between competitors in different markets and at price differences.[11] Differences in market share or price will give a preliminary indication as to whether markets are separate or not. The Commission will then check this against demand characteristics, such as local preferences, local patterns of purchases and local product differentation. This is to verify whether companies in different areas could constitute a real alternative source of supply for customers. Finally, the Commission may examine supply factors. In particular, it will consider whether there are regulatory reasons or difficulties with access to distribution which may prevent undertakings in other areas relocating onto the market.

IV. Establishing Market Power

A firm will only be bound by Article 86 [*82*] EC if it enjoys a dominant position on the relevant market.This creates a paradox. The wider the

---

11 EC Commission, *Notice on the definition of the relevant market for the purposes of Community Competition law*, OJ 1997 C 372/9, paras 28-31.

geographical market is drawn, the easier it will be to establish EC competence. Yet the wider the market is drawn, the harder it is to establish market dominance.

Market dominance can occur, first, through an undertaking being granted a legally protected monopoly.[12] A firm can also enjoy a dominant position on a market where it reaches, through its own endeavours, a position of sufficient market strength. Economists view this as existing when the undertaking can unilaterally influence the price for the respective commodity on the relevant market.[13]

Case 27/76 United Brands v Commission [1978] ECR 207, [1978] 1 CMLR 429[14]

63. Article 86 is an application of the general objective of the activities of the Community laid down by Article 3(f) of the Treaty: the institution of a system ensuring that competition in the common market is not distorted.

64. This Article prohibits any abuse by an undertaking of a dominant position in a substantial part of the common market in so far as it may affect trade between Member States.

65. The dominant position referred to in this Article relates to a position of economic strength enjoyed by an undertaking which enables it to prevent effective competition being maintained on the relevant market by giving it the power to behave to an appreciable extent independently of its competitors, customers and ultimately of its consumers.

66. In general a dominant position derives from a combination of several factors which, taken separately, are not necessarily determinative.

67. In order to find out whether UBC is an undertaking in a dominant position on the relevant market it is necessary first of all to examine its structure and then the situation on the said market as far as competition is concerned.

---

12 e.g. Case 226/84 *British Leyland v Commission* [1986] ECR 3263, [1987] 1 CMLR 185.

13 For an excellent discussion see Landes, W. & Posner, R. 'Market Power in Antitrust Cases' (1981) 94 *Harvard Law Review* 937.

14 For the facts see p. 623.

68. In doing so it may be advisable to take account if need be of the facts put forward as acts amounting to abuses without necessarily having to acknowledge that they are abuses.

Paragraph 1. The Structure of UBC

69. It is advisable to examine in turn UBC's resources for and methods of producing, packaging, transporting, selling and displaying its product.

70. UBC is an undertaking vertically integrated to a high degree.

71. This integration is evident at each of the stages from the plantation to the loading on wagons or lorries in the ports of delivery and after those stages, as far as ripening and sale prices are concerned, UBC even extends its control to ripener/distributors and wholesalers by setting up a complete network of agents.

The Court then went on to find that UBC's internal structure reflected considerable market strength in a number of ways. It had its own production, and insofar as that production did not meet its needs, it could easily obtain supplies from independent suppliers. It had its own system of factories, transport, plant and material which enabled it to package and transport the goods independently. It had a system of quality control which enabled it to establish a brand image. Finally, at the selling stage it had a regular number of customers which in turn enabled it to consolidate its economic strength.

Paragraph 2. The Situation with regard to Competition

98. ... account must only be taken of its (UBC's) operations on the relevant market.
.....

107. A trader can only be in a dominant position on the market for a product if he has succeeded in winning a large part of this market.

108. Without going into a discussion about percentages, which when fixed are bound to be to some extent approximations, it can be considered to be an established fact that UBC's share of the relevant market is always more than 40% and nearly 45%.

109. This percentage does not however permit the conclusion that UBC automatically controls the market.

110. It must be determined having regard to the strength and number of the competitors.

111. It is necessary first of all to establish that on the whole of the relevant market the said percentage represents *grosso modo* a share several times greater than that of its competitor Castle and Cooke which is the best placed of all the competitors, the others coming far behind.

112. This fact together with the others to which attention has already been drawn may be regarded as a factor which affords evidence of UBC's preponderant strength.

113. However an undertaking does not have to have eliminated all opportunity for competition in order to be in a dominant position.

114. In this case there was in fact a very lively competitive struggle on several occasions in 1973 as Castle and Cooke had mounted a large-scale advertising and promotion campaign with price rebates on the Danish and German markets.

115. At the same time Alba cut prices and offered promotional material.

116. Recently the competition of the Villeman et Tas firm on the Netherlands market has been so lively that prices have dropped below those on the German market which are traditionally the lowest.

117. It must however be recorded that in spite of their exertions these firms have not succeeded in increasing their market share appreciable on the national markets where they launched their attacks.

118. It must be noted that these periods of competition limited in time and space did not cover the whole of the relevant market.

119. Even if the local attacks of some competitors can be described as 'fierce' it can only be placed on record that UBC held out against them successfully either by adapting its prices for the time being (in the Netherlands in answer to the challenge from Villeman et Tas) or by bringing indirect pressure to bear on the intermediaries.

120. Furthermore if UBC's position on each of the national markets concerned is considered it emerges that, except in Ireland, it sells direct and also, as far as concerns Germany, indirectly through Scipio, almost twice as many bananas as the best placed competitor and that there is no appreciable fall in its sales figures even when new competitors appear on these markets.

121. UBC's economic strength has thus enabled it to adopt a flexible overall strategy directed against new competitors establishing themselves on the whole of the relevant market.

122. The particular barriers to competitors entering the market are the exceptionally large capital investments required for the creation and running of banana plantations, the need to increase sources of supply in order to avoid the effects of fruit diseases and bad weather (hurricanes, floods), the introduction of an essential system of logistics which the distribution of a very perishable product makes necessary, economies of scale from which newcomers to the market cannot derive any immediate benefit and the actual cost of entry made up *inter alia* of all the general expenses incurred in penetrating the market such as the setting up of an adequate commercial network, the mounting of very large-scale advertising campaigns, all those financial risks, the costs of which are irrecoverable if the attempt fails.

123. Thus, although, as UBC has pointed out, it is true that competitors are able to use the same methods of production and distribution as the applicant, they come up against almost insuperable practical and financial obstacles.

124. That is another factor peculiar to a dominant position.

125. However UBC takes into account the losses which its banana division made from 1971 to 1976 - whereas during this period its competitors made profits - for the purpose of inferring that, since dominance is in essence the power to fix prices, making losses is inconsistent with the existence of a dominant position.

126. An undertaking's economic strength is not measured by its profitability; a reduced profit margin or even losses for a time are not incompatible with a dominant position, just as large profits may be compatible with a situation where there is effective competition.

127. The fact that UBC's profitability is for a time moderate or non-existent must be considered in the light of the whole of its operations.

128. The finding that, whatever losses UBC may make, the customers continue to buy more goods from UBC which is the dearest vendor, is more significant and this fact is a particular feature of the dominant position and its verification is determinative in this case.

129. The cumulative effect of all the advantages enjoyed by UBC thus ensures that is has a dominant position on the relevant market.

The difficulty with establishing market power is, as Landes and Posner have put it, that the fact of market power must be distinguished from the amount of market power.[15] There may be times where a firm will be able to increase its price above that which is competitive, yet intervention is unnecessary as this represents no more than a blip in what

---

15 Supra n.13, 939.

is usually a competitive market. For an undertaking to have sufficient market power to justify intervention, it must be shown that it has had that power over a sufficient period of time.[16]

Baden Fuller, C. 'Article 86 EEC: Economic Analysis of the Existence of a Dominant Position' (1979) 4 *European Law Review* 423, 436-437

Economists have noted that few monopolies other than those prescribed by law have lasted more than decade or two, as even without anti-monopoly laws, the process of competition is very powerful. But those applying the EEC Treaty may have (rightly or wrongly) shorter time horizons. Marshall[[17]] distinguished the short time period from the long period. In the short period, productive capacity is fixed - in the long period it is variable. As was said earlier, firms may have some power in the very short run - but such power does not define monopoly. Monopoly is the power to raise prices without entry taking place in time. Relevant indicators which might be useful in defining the time period are the time required to build, and the life of a new plant of minimum efficient scale, the rate of technical change in the industry, and ease with which customers can switch from one supplier to another. Clearly, when time required to build a plant is long, as with, say, aluminium smelting, then competition is a slower process than when the time period is short, as with, say, garment fabrication.

V. Collective Dominance

A distinction has so far been drawn between those markets where no individual undertaking can influence the price and those where it can. In the real world, of course, such a stark dichotomy does not always exist. Instead, there is the intermediate position of the oligopolistic market. Oligopolistic markets are those on which there are only a few suppliers. They therefore cover a multitude of situations. Whish notes that 'some are at the end of the continuum at which markets are competitive while

---

16 This is the view of the Commission. Brittan, L. 'The Law and Policy of Merger Control in the EEC' (1990) 15 *ELRev* 351, 354.

17 A. Marshall's treatment of time, e.g. that in *Principles of Economics* (Macmillan 1930), and his path-breaking distinction between the short run and the long run, is considered to be path-breaking by economists - most economics treatises and textbooks acknowledge this debt.

in others one of the oligopolists may be close to a position of market dominance'.[18] Advocates of a particular regime for regulating oligopolies argue that the distinctive feature of oligopolies is the level of interdependence on such markets.[19] A critic of the theory of oligopolistic interdependence explains its salient features below.

Posner, R. 'Oligopoly and the Antitrust Laws: A Suggested Approach' (1969) 21 *Stanford Law Review* 1562, 1563-1564

In a market of many sellers the individual seller is too small for his decisions on pricing and output to affect the market price. He can sell all that he can produce at the market price, and nothing above it. He can shade the price without fear of retaliation because the resulting expansion of his output at the expense of his rivals will divert an imperceptible amount of business from each...

In contrast in a market where sellers are few, a price reduction that produces a substantial expansion in the output of one will result in so substantial a contraction in the output of the others that they will quickly respond to the reduction. If, for example, there are three sellers of equal size in the market, a 20 per cent expansion of the output of one will cause the output of each of the others to fall ... by 10 per cent, a contraction the victims can hardly overlook. Anticipating a prompt reaction by his rivals that will quickly nullify his gains, the seller in a concentrated market will be less likely to initiate a price reduction than his counterpart in the atomized market. Oligopolies are thus 'interdependent' in their pricing. They base their pricing decisions in part on anticipated reaction to them. The result is a tendency to avoid rigorous price competition.

It was argued by some in the United States that it was difficult and unnecessary to look for conscious concertation in an oligopolistic market. The reason was that parallelism would occur naturally not because of concertation but as a natural response on the part of each supplier towards its market environment. To prohibit such parallelism would be to prohibit each supplier from taking account of the behaviour

---

18 Whish, R. *Competition Law* (1993, 3rd Edition, Butterworths, London) 467.

19 The starting point for further reading on oligopolistic interdependence is Chamberlin, E. *The Theory of Monopolistic Competition: a reorientation of the theory of value* (1966, 8th Edition, Harvard University Press, Cambridge, Mass.).

of its competitors. The solution to this was to prevent the development of new oligopolies.[20]

This theory has come under attack on a number of counts. First, a limited number of suppliers can be the sign of an efficient market. The minimum efficient scale for a particular market may mean that a supplier must be of a certain size and have a certain market share before it can benefit from the economies of scale which will allow it to produce the product at the optimal price. Secondly, the nature of oligopolistic markets, where there are a few large suppliers rather than one dominant one, will often indicate that the barriers to entry may be lower than for monopolistic markets. In both these circumstances it would seem inadvisable for Article 86 [82] EC to be used to break up the market - in the first case because the market is an efficient one and in the second because the firms have limited market power. More fundamentally, however, the very existence of interdependence has been questioned.

Whish, R. *Competition Law* (1993, 3rd Edition, Butterworths, London) 469-470

The theory of interdependence has attracted criticism. Four particular problems with it have been pointed out. The first is that the theory overstates the interdependence of oligopolists. Even in a symmetrical three-firm oligopoly one firm might be able to steal a march on its rivals by cutting its price if, for example, there would be a delay before the others discovered what it had done...

A second problem is that the theory of oligopoly presents too simplistic a picture of industrial market structures. In a symmetrical oligopoly where producers produce identical goods at the same costs interdependence may be strong, but in reality market conditions are more complex. The oligopolists themselves will almost inevitably have different cost levels; they may be producing differentiated goods and will usually command at least some consumer loyalty; and their market shares will often not be equal. Furthermore there may be a fringe of smaller sellers which exert some competitive pressure upon the oligopolists and other firms not operating on the market may be capable of entering it if and when it becomes clear that supra-competitive profits are available...

---

20 e.g. Turner, D. 'The Definition of Agreement under the Sherman Act: Conscious Parallelism and Refusals to Deal' (1962) 75 *Harvard Law Review* 655; Turner, D. 'The Scope of Antitrust and Other Economic Regulatory Policies' (1969) 82 *Harvard Law Review* 1207.

A third problem with the theory of interdependence is that it fails to explain why in some oligopolistic markets competition is intense. Firms quite clearly do compete with one another in some oligopolies. Such competition may take various forms. Open price competition may be limited, although price wars do break out periodically in some oligopolistic markets, for example between supermarkets or petrol companies. Where open price competition is restricted, this does not mean that secret price cutting does not occur (for example, where an oligopolist negotiates discounts or rebates off list prices with individual customers) ... Non-price competition may be particularly strong in oligopolistic markets. This may manifest itself in various ways: offering better quality products and after-sales service; striving for a lead in technical innovation and research and development (sometimes described as the 'grass roots' of competition in oligopoly); and by making large investments in advertising to improve brand image...

A fourth objection to the theory of oligopolistic interdependence is that it does not explain satisfactorily its central proposition, which is that oligopolists can earn supra-competitive profits without actually colluding. The interdependence theory says they cannot increase prices unilaterally because they will lose custom to their rivals and yet, to earn supra-competitive profits, prices must have been increased from time to time: how could this have been achieved without collusion?

Notwithstanding these reservations, the theory of interdependence was adopted by the Commission in 1986.[21]

Sixteenth Report of the EC Commission on Competition Policy (1986, OOPEC, Luxembourg).

331. The two essential features of shared dominance are:
(i) the fact that a small number of enterprises account for most of the turnover in the market in question without any single enterprise having a dominant position;
(ii) the high degree of interdependence among the decisions of the enterprises.

One of the aims of competition policy is to ensure that certain types of behaviour by the enterprises concerned do not preclude a sufficient level of competition in such markets. In the case of a tight oligopoly, the reduction in the intensity of competition does not necessarily lead to the appearance of tacit collusion. Tacit collusion may, however, arise from the fact that members of the oligopoly become aware of their interdependence and of the probably unfavourable consequences of adopting a competitive attitude...

---

21 The influence of the theory of interdependence within EC law and other jurisdictions is discussed in Winckler, A. & Hansen, M. 'Collective Dominance under the EC Merger Control Regulation' (1993) 30 *CMLRev* 787, 788-798.

333. Abuse of shared dominant positions may have many unfavourable consequences for the economy as a whole, including the final consumer (e.g. higher prices, a slowdown of technological progress, imposition of unfair terms of trade).

Although Article 86 may be applied in order to punish such conduct, it should be the aim of competition policy to prevent situations arising which form a hotbed for tacit collusive behaviour...

The question of the appropriateness of Article 86 [*82*] EC for regulating markets on which firms had a shared dominant position was first considered by the Court of First Instance in the *Italian Flat Glass* judgment.

Joined Cases T-68, 77 & 78/89 *Società Italiana Vetro v Commission* ('Italian Flat Glass') [1992] ECR II-1403, [1992] 5 CMLR 302

The market for flat glass has high start up costs, as it costs about 100 million ECU to set up a production line. In Italy three undertakings accounted for 80% of the production on that market. In 1986 the Commission found that these undertakings had established a system of cooperation whereby, *inter alia*, they required suppliers of their glass to sell the glass at similar prices and under similar terms and imposed quotas on how much automotive glass suppliers could individually sell. The Commission did not consider any one to be individually dominant, but that they were dominant collectively, and that such conduct breached Article 86 [*82*] EC.

357. The Court notes that the very words of the first paragraph of Article 86(1) provide that 'one or more undertakings' may abuse a dominant position. It has consistently been held, as indeed all the parties acknowledge, that the concept of agreement or concerted practice between undertakings does not cover agreements or concerted practices among undertakings belonging to the same group if the undertakings form an economic unit (see, for example, the judgment in Case 15/74 *Centrafarm v Sterling Drug* [1978] ECR 1147, paragraph 41). It follows that when Article 85 refers to agreements or concerted practices between 'undertakings', it is referring to relations between two or more economic entities which are capable of competing with one another.

358. The Court considers that there is no legal or economic reason to suppose that the term 'undertaking' in Article 86 has a different meaning from the one given to it in the context of Article 85. There is nothing, in principle, to prevent two or more independent economic entities from being, on a specific market, united by such economic links that, by virtue of that fact, together they hold a dominant position *vis-à-vis* the other operators on the same market. This could be the case, for example, where two or more independent undertakings jointly have, through agreements or licences, a technological lead affording them the power to behave to an appreciable extent independently of their competitors, their customers and ultimately of their consumers (judgment of the Court in Case 85/76 *Hoffmann-La Roche v Commission* [1979] ECR 461, paragraphs 38 and 48).

359. The Court finds support for that interpretation in the wording of Article 8 of Council Regulation (EEC) No 4056/86 laying down detailed rules for the application of Articles 85 and 86 of the Treaty to maritime transport. Article 8(2) provides that the conduct of a liner conference benefiting from an exemption from a prohibition laid down by Article 85(1) of the Treaty may have effects which are incompatible with Article 86 EEC. A request by a conference to be exempted from the prohibition laid down by Article 85(1) necessarily presupposes an agreement between two or more independent economic undertakings.

360. However, it should be pointed out that for the purposes of establishing an infringement of Article 86 of the Treaty, it is not sufficient, as the Commission's agent claimed at the hearing, to 'recycle' the facts constituting an infringement of Article 85, deducing from them the finding that the parties to an agreement or to an unlawful practice jointly hold a substantial share of the market, that by virtue of that fact alone they hold a collective dominant position. and that their unlawful behaviour constitutes an abuse of that collective dominant position. Amongst other considerations, a finding of a dominant position, which is in any case not in itself a matter of reproach, presupposes that the market in question has been defined (judgment of the Court of Justice in Case 6/72 *Continental Can v Commission* [1973] E.C.R. 215, paragraph 32; Case 322/81 *Michelin v Commission* [1983] E.C.R. 3461, paragraph 57). The Court must therefore examine, first, by the analysis of the market made in the decision and, secondly, the circumstances relied on in support of the finding of a collective dominant position...

Collective dominance is accepted by the CFI on a much narrower basis than that suggested by the Commission. Whilst the Commission considered the structure of the market to be determinative, the Court indicates that it should be based on the nature of the economic links between the parties.

The Court of Justice adopted the CFI's position in *Almelo*.[22] The Court had to consider the legality of an exclusive purchasing requirement imposed upon local distributors by a regional distributor of electricity within the Netherlands. There existed four regional

---

22 Case C-393/92 *Municipality of Almelo v NV Energiebedrijf Ijsselmij* [1994] ECR I-1477. See also Joined Cases C-140-142/94 *Dip Spa v Comune di Bassano del Grappa* [1995] ECR I-3257.

distributors within the Netherlands. The Court considered that collective dominance would only be found

> if they were linked in such a way that they adopt the same conduct on the market.

The need for there to be formal links between undertakings for collective dominance to be found has resulted in a remodelling, within the EC context, of the theory of oligopolistic interdependence. Economic interdependence will be insufficient for undertakings to fall within Article 86 [*82*] EC, there must be formal interdependence. Such a narrow reading of collective dominance undoubtedly avoids many of the criticisms of the interdependence theory. It has, however, resulted in the concept of collective dominance applying only rarely with the result that no special provision is made for many markets on which there are only a few suppliers and which are correspondingly opaque.

VI. Establishing An Abuse

Dominance, or collective dominance, of a market is not illegal *per se.* It is only those activities carried out by an undertaking enjoying such a position which are abusive in nature which are illegal. An understanding of the 'abuse' concept requires some appreciation of its historical context. At the time of the Treaty of Rome one of the few States to control monopolistic behaviour was Germany whose 1957 Competition Law also referred to the notion of abusive behaviour by undertakings enjoying a position of dominance. It has *been* argued that the debate surrounding the inception of German competition law shaped the structure of EC competition law, and in particular Article 86 [*82*] EC.[23]

---

[23] Gerber, D. 'Law and the Abuse of Economic Power in Europe' (1987) 62 *Tulane Law Review* 57, 86.

Gerber, D. 'Law and the Abuse of Economic Power in Europê' (1987) 62 *Tulane Law Review* 57, 69-70

The original draft of the GWB [the German Competition Law], the so-called Josten draft, was based on the ideas of the 'Ordo-Liberal School' of economists...

One of the central components of the Ordo-Liberal program was the idea that where competition was weak or non-existent, the state should require enterprises to conduct themselves *as if* there were essentially perfect competition. This concept of 'as-if' competition rested on the assumption that economic science could determine with reasonable accuracy whether conduct was consistent with conditions defined as 'competitive.' This notion of 'as-if' competition was closely associated with the concept of 'performance competition' or 'competition on the merits'. The Ordo-Liberals assumed that in enforcing the standard of 'as-if' competition the state would be assuring that success in the market place was the result of better performance rather than of the use of economic power.

There are a number of problems with the 'as-if' test. Pursuit of the illusory ideal of perfect competition will result in a considerable amount of second-guessing by competition authorities and courts. The danger of excessive regulatory intervention and formalism this may provoke may actually result in competition being stifled. Commentators have therefore chosen to focus on other concepts.

The first is that of *exploitative abuse*. Exploitative abuses involve the obtaining of benefits by the undertaking which would not have been available to it if there had been effective competition. The most obvious example is manipulation of the price mechanism, such as charging excessive prices, as this is a practice only open to undertakings in a dominant position. There is little controversy over such forms of abuse being illegal.

More controversial are *anti-competitive abuses*. The undertaking is not, in this instance dependent upon the lack of effective competition and its dominant position to carry out such practices. Examples are a merger or a refusal to supply someone. These activities are still considered to be anti-competitive, however, despite others being able to engage in them, either because they weaken market structure or because they do not appear to be an appropriate form of competition.[24]

i. Exploitative Abuses

a. Excessive Prices

As the ability to adjust price irrespective of market conditions is a sign of market dominance, any pricing practice will always only be an exploitative abuse.

Case 27/76 United Brands v Commission [1978] ECR 207, [1978] 1 CMLR 429

The Commission found that United Brands sold its bananas in Ireland at a far lower price than in other parts of the Community, with there being an 80% differential between the price of those bananas sold in Ireland and those in Belgium. It considered that this illustrated that United Brands was charging excessive prices for its bananas elsewhere in the Community.

248. The imposition by an undertaking in a dominant position directly or indirectly of unfair purchase or selling prices is an abuse to which exception can be taken under Article 86 of the Treaty.

249. It is advisable therefore to ascertain whether the dominant undertaking has made use of the opportunities arising out of its dominant position in such a way as to reap trading benefits which it would not have reaped if there had been normal and sufficiently effective competition.

---

[24] On the distinction between these two forms of abuse see Temple Lang, J. 'Monopolisation and the definition of "Abuse" of a Dominant Position under Article 86 EEC Treaty' (1979) 16 *CMLRev* 345; Whish, R. supra n.18, 270-271; Bellamy, C. & Child, G. *Common Market Law of Competition* (1993, 4th Edition, Sweet & Maxwell) 617-619.

250. In this case charging a price which is excessive because it has no reasonable relation to the economic value of the product supplied would be such an abuse.

251. This excess could, *inter alia*, be determined objectively if it were possible for it to be calculated by making a comparison between the selling price of the product in question and its cost of production, which would disclose the amount of the profit margin; however the Commission has not done this since it has not analysed UBC's costs structure.

252. The questions therefore to be determined are whether the difference between the costs actually incurred and the price actually charged is excessive, and, if the answer to this question is in the affirmative, whether a price has been imposed which is either unfair in itself or when compared to competing products.

The Court then found that the Commission had not proved excessive pricing by UBC. Excessive pricing is implicit in Article 86(2)(a) [*82(2)(a)*] EC which states that abusive behaviour may consist in directly or indirectly imposing unfair purchase or selling prices or unfair trading conditions. Linked to this abuse is the one, contained in Article 86(2)(b) [*82(2)(b)*] EC, of limiting production, markets or technical development to the detriment of consumers. For a restriction on output will frequently lead to a rise in the price of the product.

b. Discriminatory Pricing

In *United Brands* the Court had to consider another pricing practice, price discrimination.[25]

---

[25] There is some reference in Article 86(2)(c) [*82(2)(c)*] EC to price discrimination which states that an abuse may consist in applying dissimilar conditions to equivalent transactions with other trading parties, thereby placing them at a competitive disadvantage. Price discrimination is, in one sense, a wider concept as it applies not merely to sales to other traders but also sales to consumers.

Case 27/76 United Brands v Commission [1978] ECR 207, [1978] 1 CMLR 429

The Commission also found that United Brands were charging their customers differing prices for Chiquita bananas in different Member States within the Community. The Court found that the price differential was often between 30 and 50% for the same bananas, and this differential could not be justified on the basis of transport costs, as it was the purchasers who were responsible for transport within the Community.

226. This policy of discriminatory prices has been applied by UBC since 1971 to customers of Germany, the Netherlands and the BLEU and was extended at the beginning of 1973 to customers in Denmark and in November 1973 to customers in Ireland.

227. Although the responsibility for establishing the single banana market does not lie with the applicant, it can only endeavour to take 'what the market can bear' provided that it complies with the rules for the regulation and coordination of the market laid down by the Treaty.

228. Once it can be grasped that differences in transport costs, taxation, customs duties, the wages of the labour force, the conditions of marketing, the differences in the parity of currencies, the density of competition may eventually culminate in different retail selling price levels according to the Member States, then it follows those differences are factors which UBC only has to take into account to a limited extent since it sells a product which is always the same and at the same place to ripener/distributors who - alone - bear the risks of the consumers' market.

229. The interplay of supply and demand should, owing to its nature, only be applied to each stage where it is really manifest.

230. The mechanisms of the market are adversely affected if the price is calculated by leaving out one stage of the market and taking into account the law of supply and demand as between the vendor and the ultimate consumer and not as between the vendor (UBC) and the purchaser (the ripener/distributors).

231. Thus, by reason of its dominant position UBC, fed with information by its local representatives, was in fact able to impose its selling price on the intermediate purchaser...

232. These discriminatory prices, which varied according to the circumstances of the Member States, were just so many obstacles to the free movement of goods and their effect was intensified by the clause forbidding the resale of bananas while still green and by reducing the deliveries of the quantities ordered.

233. A rigid partitioning of national markets was thus created at price levels, which were artificially different, placing certain distributor/ripeners at a competitive disadvantage, since compared with what it should have been competition had thereby been distorted.

234. Consequently the policy of differing prices enabling UBC to apply dissimilar conditions to equivalent transactions with other trading parties, thereby placing them at a competitive disadvantage, was an abuse of a dominant position.

It is not only price discrimination between different geographical markets which is outlawed. In *Hoffmann La Roche*[26] the Court found that Hoffmann La Roche's practice of giving fidelity rebates (i.e lower prices) to existing customers of its vitamins was price discrimination as it applied dissimilar conditions to equivalent transactions in that the price purchasers paid varied according to whether they obtained their supplies exclusively from Hoffmann La Roche or from a number of sources.

The first rationale given for outlawing price discrimination was that it tampered with the interplay of supply and demand. This implies that price discrimination results in a restriction in output in one part of the territory and a consequent unnecessary raising of prices. Bork notes that price discrimination can often occur not where the producer is attempting to restrict output, but where he is trying to expand it.

Bork, R. *The Antitrust Paradox: A Policy At War with Itself* (1978, Free Press, New York) 397-398

We tend to discuss the theory as though the seller were instituting discrimination between two classes of customers he already serves, but discrimination may be a way of adding an entire category of customers he would not otherwise approach because the lower price would have spoiled his existing market. It is possible, also, that there are situations in which a product or service would not be produced at all without discrimination...

Finally, since we are comparing the results of a policy of permissiveness with an alternative of legally required non-discrimination, it may be useful to suggest that the short-run and long-run effects of a rule prohibiting discrimination will not invariable be identical. If the seller has some costs that he cannot discontinue at once, he may find it profitable, when freedom to discriminate is initially denied, to charge in both markets a single compromise price. This may give him the greatest net revenues over his temporary

---

26 Case 85/76 *Hoffmann-La Roche v Commission* [1979] ECR 461, [1979] 3 CMLR 211.

unalterable costs. But over time the seller may fail to replace equipment, facilities and personnel, thereby rearranging his cost structure so that he is finally able to sell in the higher-priced market alone. He will then abandon the lower-priced market and make a greater return on investment. The long-run effect of prohibiting discrimination will have been to decrease output. These considerations, some of them admittedly minor, taken together appear to increase the likelihood that two-market discrimination will have an output-expanding effect.

If the better guess is that two-price systems usually increase output over legally compelled uniform pricing, the general policy of antitrust should prefer such discrimination to non-discrimination. If, as seems probable, the relative output effects of two-market discrimination and non-discrimination are at worst indeterminate, there is no affirmative case for legal interference with the seller's choice.

The second reason given for outlawing price discrimination is that it partitions the single market. This has also come under attack.

Bishop, W. 'Price Discrimination under Article 86: Political Economy in the European Court' (1981) 44 *Modern Law Review* 282, 289-290

... the essential characteristic required for a common market is not the existence of identical input prices in each region, any more than it is the existence of identical factor endowments in each region. Rather what is required is the absence of barriers to import and export among regions. Import prices for competing firms will inevitably differ sharply between Member States owing to different wage rates, different soil and growing conditions, different mineral resources, different transport costs, different taxes and much else. The fact that one firm must pay more for some input in Germany than its competitor in England is no more a violation of the single market principle than is the existence of greater sunshine in Sicily a violation because it makes growing oranges cheaper there than in Denmark.

c. Predatory Pricing

Predation is behaviour by an undertaking which does not, in the short term, increase a firm's profits but does increase its market share. Predatory pricing is thus selling at excessively low prices with a view to either weakening or forcing one's competitors out of business or with a view to preventing new undertakings entering the market. Commentators point to two features which suggest that predatory pricing is a rare phenomenon.[27] The first is that in any price war, the absolute loss suffered by the predator will always be greater than the victim. This is because the predator will have to sell a greater number of products at below cost to increase market share. The second is that predators will only forego the lost profits in the short-term, if they consider these can be more than offset by the probability of higher profits in the long-term. Such a situation will normally exist only in markets with high barriers to entry.

Case C-62/86 Akzo Chemie BV v Commission [1991] ECR I-3359, [1993] 5 CMLR 215

Akzo, a Dutch undertaking, produced peroxides, some of which could be used in the flour industry and others of which could be used in the plastics industry. ECS, a British company, traditionally produced peroxides for the flour market. Upon its entering the market for plastics AKZO retaliated by dropping the price of the peroxides it supplied on the flour market below that of average total cost (i.e the total cost of production divided by the number of products sold).

70. ... Article 86 prohibits a dominant undertaking from eliminating a competitor and thereby strengthening its position by using methods other than those which come within the scope of competition on the basis of quality. From that point of view, however, not all competition by means of price can be regarded as legitimate.

71. Prices below average variable costs (that is to say, those which vary depending on the quantities produced) by means of which a dominant undertaking seeks to eliminate a competitor must be regarded as abusive. A dominant undertaking has no interest in applying such prices except that of eliminating competitors so as to enable it subsequently to raise its prices by taking advantage of its monopolistic position, since each sale generates a loss, namely the total amount of the fixed costs (that is to say, those which remain constant regardless of the quantities produced) and, at least, part of the variable costs relating to the unit produced.

72. Moreover, prices below average total costs, that is to say, fixed costs plus variable costs, but above average variable costs, must be regarded as abusive if they are

---

[27] e.g. Brodley, J. & Hay, G. 'Predatory Pricing: Competing Economic Theories and the Evolution of Legal Standards' (1981) 66 *Cornell Law Review* 738, 744-745; Smith, P. 'The Wolf in Wolf's Clothing: The Problem with Predatory Pricing' (1989) 14 *ELRev* 209, 212.

determined as part of a plan for eliminating a competitor. Such prices can drive from the market undertakings which are perhaps as efficient as the dominant undertaking but which, because of their smaller financial resources, are incapable of withstanding the competition waged against them.

The costs-based approach to predatory pricing adopted by the Court[28] has been criticised for ignoring the inter-temporal aspect of predatory pricing. Ordover and Willig have argued that the central issue of predation is that the predator expects to recoup its profit sacrifice in future profits.[29] The extent to which the present sacrifice falls below current costs is largely irrelevant. The central question is whether it falls below hypothetical future profits, as it is that which will determine whether an undertaking is attempting to increase market share. This line of argument is extremely persuasive, yet it highlights the problematic nature of predatory pricing. Calculation of hypothetical future profits is no science. Assumptions about risk and new market entrants have to be made which are often no more than educated guesswork. Arguments of legal certainty therefore suggest that it might be more appropriate to have a blunt but relatively clear test, albeit one that will throw up occasional injustices.

---

28 In this it appears to have followed the Areeda-Turner model which has been so influential in the United States, Areeda, P. & Turner, D. 'Predatory Pricing and Related Practices under Section 2 of the Sherman Act' (1975) 88 *Harvard Law Review* 697. There are some differences. Areeda and Turner consider that a price above marginal cost is always lawful. Prices below marginal cost are generally considered to be predatory except in conditions of strong demand (i.e. where there is room for expansion in the market). For an excellent discussion of the literature generated see Brodley, J. & Hay, G. 'Predatory Pricing: Competing Economic Theories and the Evolution of Legal Standards' (1981) 66 *Cornell Law Review* 738. For further literature see also Smith, P. supra n.27, 211 n.13.

29 Ordover, J. & Willig, R. 'An Economic Definition of Predation: Pricing and Product Innovation' (1982) 91 *Yale Law Journal* 8. For criticism and a reply see Sidak, J. 'Debunking Predatory Innovation' (1983) 83 *Columbia Law Review* 1121; Ordover, J. Willig, R. & Sykes, A. 'Predatory Systems Rivalry: A Reply' (1983) 83 *Columbia Law Review* 1150.

d. Tying In

The last form of practice listed in Article 86 [*82*] EC is that of tying-in. This makes, in the words of Article 86(2)(d) [*82(2)(d)*] EC, the conclusion of contracts subject to acceptance by other parties of supplementary obligations which, by their nature or according to commercial usage, have no connection with the subject of the initial contract. In *Hilti*[30] the CFI thus found that Hilti's requiring purchasers of its nail cartridges to buy nails with them constituted abusive behaviour. Tying in is seen as exploitative 'because it imposes on the buyer an obligation to buy something he may not want and gives the seller a benefit which he might not have obtained in a competitive market'.[31]

ii. Anti-Competitive Practices

US anti-trust regulation has focused on attempts by the monopolist to garner or strengthen market power by excluding potential or actual competitors from competing on the market place.[32] It therefore concentrates on primary-line injury - behaviour which adversely affects competing undertakings - and makes a distinction between legitimate and illegitimate attempts to consolidate and enhance this power. In the case of the European Community, Joliet in his seminal work on monopolization noted that all the abuses listed in Article 86 [*82*] EC - imposition of unfair purchase or selling prices; limiting output; applying

---

30 Case T-30/89 *Hilti v Commission* [1991] ECR II-1439. This was confirmed on appeal see Case C-53/92P *Hilti v Commission* [1994] ECR I-667. For another example of tying in see Case 85/76 *Hoffmann-La Roche v Commission* [1979] ECR 461, [1979] 3 CMLR 211.

31 Temple Lang, J. n.24, 346.

32 The starting point for the 'market power' theory is *Standard Oil of N.J v United States*, 221 U.S.1 (1911). For withering criticism of this judgment see Bork, R. *The Antitrust Paradox: A Policy at War with Itself* (1978, Macmillan, New York) 33-41.

dissimilar conditions to equivalent transactions with other trading parties and making the conclusion of contracts subject to acceptance of supplementary obligations which have no connection with the subject of such contracts - are examples of what is called secondary-line injury - injury which, first and foremost, affects suppliers, consumers and purchasers.[33] The feature of all secondary line injury is that it can only be inflicted by exploitative abuses of market power, as it involves practices a monopolist could not engage in for any period of time in the face of effective competition, as consumers or suppliers would simply switch their economic activities elsewhere. From this Joliet concluded that Article 86 [*82*] EC could not be extended to primary-line practices which were aimed at competitors, and were anti-competitive rather than exploitative in nature.[34]

The alternative view was put by Mestmäcker who considered that Article 86 [*82*] EC should be read in the light of the other provisions of the Treaty whose general aim was to ensure the maintenance of a system of undistorted competition. Competition, in his view, could only be maintained if competitors were protected, and a degree of workable competition preserved. Article 86 [*82*] EC should therefore be extended to anti-competitive practices.[35] The Court had to decide between these opposing views in *Continental Can.*

Case 6/72 Continental Can v Commission [1973] ECR 215, [1973] CMLR 199[36]

19. The applicants maintain that the Commission by its decision, based on an erroneous interpretation of Article 86 of the EEC Treaty, is trying to introduce a control of mergers of undertakings, thus exceeding its powers. Such an attempt runs contrary to the intention of the authors of the Treaty, which is clearly seen not only from a literal interpretation of

---

33 Joliet, R. *Monopolization and Abuse of Dominant Position* (1970, Martijnus Nijhoff, The Hague) 247. For further analysis on primary-line and secondary-line injury see Whish, R. supra n.18, 508-510.

34 Ibid., 247-252.

35 Mestmäcker, 'Die Beurteilung von Unternehmungszusammenschlüssen nach Article 86 des Vertrages über die Europäische Wirtschaftsgemeinschaft' in *Festschift für Walter Hallstein* (1966, Frankfurt).

36 For the facts see p. 629.

Article 86, but also from a comparison of the EEC Treaty and the national legal provisions of the Member States. The examples given in Article 86 of abuse of a dominant position confirm this conclusion, for they show that the Treaty refers only to practices which have effects on the market and are to the detriment of consumers or trade partners. Further, Article 86 reveals that the use of economic power linked with a dominant position can be regarded as an abuse of this position only if it constitutes the means through which the abuse is effected. But structural measures of undertakings - such as strengthening a dominant position by way of merger - do not amount to abuse of this position within the meaning of Article 86 of the Treaty. The decision contested is, therefore, said to be void as lacking the required legal basis...

21. The distinction between measures which concern the structure of the undertaking and practices which affect the market cannot be decisive, for any structural measure may influence market conditions, if it increases the size and the economic power of the undertaking.

22. In order to answer this question, one has to go back to the spirit, general scheme and wording of Article 86, as well as to the system and objectives of the Treaty...

23. Article 86 is part of the Chapter devoted to the common rules on the Community's policy in the field of competition. This policy is based on Article 3(f) of the Treaty according to which the Community's activity shall include the institution of a system ensuring that competition in the Common Market is not distorted. The applicants' argument that this provision merely contains a general programme devoid of legal effect, ignores the fact that Article 3 considers the pursuit of the objectives which it lays down to be indispensable for the achievement of the Community's tasks. As regards in particular the aim mentioned in (f), the Treaty in several provisions contains more detailed regulations for the interpretation of which this aim is decisive.

24. But if Article 3(f) provides for the institution of a system ensuring that competition in the Common Market is not distorted, then it requires *a fortiori* that competition must not be eliminated. This requirement is so essential that without it numerous provisions of the Treaty would be pointless. Moreover, it corresponds to the precept of Article 2 of the Treaty according to which one of the tasks of the Community is 'to promote throughout the Community a harmonious development of economic activities'. Thus the restraints on competition which the Treaty allows under certain conditions because of the need to harmonize the various objectives of the Treaty, are limited by the requirements of Articles 2 and 3. Going beyond this limit involves the risk that the weakening of competition would conflict with the aims of the common market.

25. With a view to safeguarding the principles and attaining the objectives set out in Articles 2 and 3 of the Treaty, Articles 85 to 90 have laid down general rules applicable to undertakings. Article 85 concerns agreements between undertakings, decisions of associations of undertakings and concerted practices, while Article 86 concerns unilateral activity of one or more undertakings. Articles 85 and 86 seek to achieve the same aim on different levels, viz the maintenance of effective competition within the Common Market. The restraint of competition which is prohibited if it is the result of behaviour falling under Article 85, cannot become permissible by the fact that such behaviour succeeds under the influence of a dominant undertaking and results in the merger of the undertakings concerned. In the absence of explicit provisions one cannot assume that the Treaty, which prohibits in Article 85 certain decisions of ordinary associations of undertakings restricting competition without eliminating it, permits in Article 86 that undertakings, after merging into an organic unity, should reach such a dominant position that any serious chance of competition is practically rendered impossible. Such a diverse legal treatment would make a breach in the entire competition law which could jeopardize the proper functioning of the Common Market. If, in order to avoid the prohibitions in Article 85, it sufficed to establish such close connections between the undertakings that they escaped the prohibition of Article 85 without coming within the scope of that of Article 86, then, in contradiction to the basic principles of the Common Market, the partitioning of a substantial part of this market would be allowed. The endeavour of the authors of the Treaty to maintain in the market real or potential competition even in cases in which restraints on competition are permitted, was explicitly laid down in Article 85(3)(b) of the Treaty. Article 86 does not contain the same explicit provisions, but this can be explained by the fact that the system fixed there for dominant positions, unlike Article 85(3), does not recognize any exemption from the prohibition. With such a system the obligation to observe the basic objectives of the Treaty, in particular that of Article 3(f), results from the obligatory force of these objectives. In any case Articles 85 and 86 cannot be interpreted in such a way that they contradict each other, because they serve to achieve the same aim.

26. It is in the light of these considerations that the condition imposed by Article 86 is to be interpreted whereby in order to come within the prohibition a dominant position must have been abused. The provision states a certain number of abusive practices which it prohibits. The list merely gives examples, not an exhaustive enumeration of the sort of abuses of a dominant position prohibited by the Treaty. As may further be seen from letters (c) and (d) of Article 86(2), the provision is not only aimed at practices which may cause damage to consumers directly, but also at those which are detrimental to them through their impact on an effective competition structure, such as is mentioned in Article 3(f) of the Treaty. Abuse may therefore occur if an undertaking in a dominant position strengthens such position in such a way that the degree of dominance reached substantially fetters competition, i.e. that only undertakings remain in the market whose behaviour depends on the dominant one.

27. Such being the meaning and the scope of Article 86 of the EEC Treaty, the question of the link of causality raised by the applicants which in their opinion has to question exist between the dominant position and its abuse, is of no consequence, for the strengthening of the position of an undertaking may be an abuse and prohibited under Article 86 of the Treaty, regardless of the means and procedure by which it is achieved, if it has the effects mentioned above.

The extension of Article 86 [*82*] EC to maintaining workable competition has a number of consequences.

Vogelenzang, P. 'Abuse of a Dominant Position in Article 86: The Problem of Causality and some Applications' (1976) 13 *Common Market Law Review* 61, 64-66

The freedom to compete of one company must be balanced against the interest other companies have not to be hurt. The balancing must be done against the background of what is needed for *workable competition.* Workable competition means the structure and behaviour needed to make the market function properly, perceived from the traditional criteria of factor-allocation and need-satisfaction. Such additional balancing has as its ultimate purpose the ideal of 'workable competition', and therefore is only to apply where the interests of several individual market participants are at stake. It would not be right to also require a balance between the freedom to compete of a particular firm on the one hand and the proper functioning of competitive processes on the other; doing so would bypass our goal, since the latter has to prevail anyhow. If there is damage to competitive processes, there is no additional requirement that damage be undue; in the hierarchy of values involved here, with workable competition as the supreme value any damage to workable competition is undue, whereas damage caused by one market participant to another may only be considered undue after an evaluation in the light of that supreme value

We need a normative element: that only *undue* infliction of damage is to be prohibited...

... We may say that market behaviour can never be abusive when such behaviour is actually necessary for a proper functioning of the market, and thus forms a necessary element of workable competition. Only if this necessity is lacking, the damage to other market participants becomes undue.

We can now extend our formula for abuse to: 'market behaviour damaging competitive processes, or unduly damaging consumers or other market participants.'

Anti-competitive abuses have to be divided into *structural abuses* and *behavioural abuses*. Structural abuses are practices which damage market structures and are abusive *per se.* They can never be justified. Behavioural abuses are practices which principally damage other competitors' interests rather than the intensity of competition and may in certain circumstances be justified.

iii. Structural Abuses

Mergers - *Continental Can* established that mergers involving a dominant undertaking which substantially fetter effective competition constitute abusive behaviour. These will be discussed in greater detail later on in this Chapter.

Acquisition of Technology - In *Tetra Pak*[37] the Court considered that acquisition by Tetra Pak, the container producer, of an exclusive licence which protect new techniques in the sterilisation milk cartons constituted an abuse not because of the acquisition, *per se*, but because it lead to competition being weakened on the relevant market. The facts of *Tetra Pak* were unusual, however, as Tetra Pak had a 90% share of the market at the time of the acquisition. It is likely that only in rare circumstances of considerable market dominance will acquisition of technology sufficiently weaken competition to constitute an abuse.

iv. Behavioural Abuses

a. Refusal to Supply and Related Practices

The first form of practice found to be a behavioural abuse was a refusal to supply goods to a customer without good reason. In *Commercial Solvents*[38] an Italian subsidiary of Commercial Solvents, an American corporation, refused to supply Zoja, an Italian company, with aminobutanol which was used as raw material for the drug ethambutol. The Court found that this refusal to supply was abusive behaviour as by threatening to put Zoja out of business it had the effect of eliminating competition.

---

37 Case T-51/89 *Tetra Pak v Commission* [1990] ECR II-309, [1991] 4 CMLR 334.

38 Joined Cases 6-7/73 *Commercial Solvents and Others v Commission* [1974] ECR 223, [1974] 1 CMLR 309.

Over the years the refusal to supply concept has been extended in a number of ways. First, it has been extended to cover practices such as a refusal to license out intellectual property rights.[39] Secondly, both the Commission and the Court have reasoned by analogy to find other forms of behavioural abuse. Where a firm in a dominant position on one market carries out activities in another market downstream, the effect is similar to that of a refusal to supply, as it prevents other firms from supplying services to that company which is, by definition, likely to be one of their largest customers.

Case 311/84 Centre Belge d'Etudes de Marché Télémarketing v CLT [1985] ECR 3261, [1986] 2 CMLR 558

The Belgian company, Information Publicité, was responsible for all advertising on the Belgian television channel, RTL. It gave Centre Belge exclusive rights to carry out telemarketing operations for RTL for 12 months. At the end of this period Information Publicité informed all advertisers that all advertising would now be done exclusively through it. The Belgian court asked whether such a reservation of activities to itself breached Article 86 [*82*] EC.

25. In order to answer the national court's second question, reference must first be made to the aforesaid judgment of 6 March 1974 [Joined Cases 6 and 7/73 *Commercial Solvents and Others v Commission* (1974) ECR 223), in which the Court held that an undertaking which holds a dominant position on a market in raw materials and which, with the object of reserving those materials for its own production of derivatives, refuses to supply a customer who also produces those derivatives, with the possibility of eliminating all competition from that customer, is abusing its dominant position within the meaning of Article 86.

26. That ruling also applies to the case of an undertaking holding a dominant position on the market in a service which is indispensable for the activities of another undertaking on another market. If, as the national court has already held in its order for reference, telemarketing activities constitute a separate market from that of the chosen advertising medium, although closely associated with it, and if those activities mainly consist in making available to advertisers the telephone lines and team of telephonists of the

---

39 Case T-69/89 *RTE v Commission* [1991] ECR II-485; Case T-70/89 *BBC v Commission* [1991] ECR II-535; Case T-76/89 *ITP v Commission* [1991] ECR II-575. These cases were confirmed on appeal see Joined Cases C-241 & 242/91P *RTE & ITP v Commission* [1995] ECR I 743, [1995] 4 CMLR 718.

telemarketing undertaking, to subject the sale of broadcasting time to the condition that the telephone lines of an advertising agent belonging to the same group as the television station should be used amounts in practice to a refusal to supply the services of that station to any other telemarketing undertaking. If, further, that refusal is not justified by technical or commercial requirements relating to the nature of the television, but is intended to reserve to the agent any telemarketing operation broadcast by the said station, with the possibility of eliminating all competition from another undertaking, such conduct amounts to an abuse prohibited by Article 86, provided that the other conditions of that Article are satisfied.

b. The 'Essential Facilities' Doctrine

The essential facilities doctrine emerged from the United States. It requires undertakings in a dominant position who control facilities which cannot be duplicated and access to which is essential for competitors to grant access to those facilities where feasible. By enjoining undertakings to engage in positive acts, the doctrine is highly constraining. The rationale for the doctrine is that, in such circumstances, the undertakings 'continued exercise of market power is not attributable to the firm's own efforts but to the externalities that make it impossible for rivals to duplicate the facilities'.[40] Whilst it has not yet been considered by Court, it has, arguably, been adopted by the Commission.[41]

---

40 Venit, J. & Kallaugher, J. 'Essential Facilities: A Comparative Law Approach' (1994) *Fordham Corporate Law Institute* 315, 321.

41 Temple Lang, J. 'Defining Legitimate Competition: Companies' Duties to Supply Competitors and Access to Essential Facilities' (1994) 18 *Fordham International Law Journal* 437; Furse, M. 'The "Essential Facilities" Doctrine in Community Law' (1995) 8 *ECLR* 469; Cowan, T. 'The Essential Facilities Doctrine in EC Competition Law: Towards a "Matrix Structure"' (1995) *Fordham Corporate Law Institute* 521; Ridyard, D. 'Essential Facilities and the Obligation to Supply Competitors under UK and EC Competition Law' (1996) 8 *ECLR* 438.

Commission Decision 94/19 EC (*iv/34.689 - Sea Containers - Stena Sealink - interim measures*)[42]

Stena Sealink was the port authority for Holyhead and therefore had a dominant position in the market for provision of port facilities for passenger and car ferries between the United Kingdom and Ireland. It also ran car ferry services from Holyhead in Wales to Ireland. Sea Containers, a competitor, wished to operate sea cat service between Holyhead and Dublin. For a variety of reasons Stena Sealink refused it port facilities at Holyhead. Sea Containers sought interim measures from the Commission, pending a final decision, allowing it to use Holyhead. Sea Containers were subsequently offered facilities. The Commission did consider, however, whether an abuse had been committed.

66. An undertaking which occupies a dominant position in the provision of an essential facility and itself uses that facility (i.e. a facility or infrastructure, without access to which competitors cannot provide services to their customers), and which refuses other companies access to that facility without objective justification or grants access to competitors only on terms less favourable than those which it gives its own services, infringes Article 86 if the other conditions of that Article are met. An undertaking in a dominant position may not discriminate in favour of its own activities in a related market. The owner of an essential facility which uses its power in one market in order to protect or strengthen its position in another related market, in particular, by refusing to grant access to a competitor, or by granting access on less favourable terms than those of its own services, and thus imposing a competitive disadvantage on its competitor, infringes Article 86.

The doctrine is controversial on two fronts. The first criticism is that it is an inappropriate introduction of American law into EC law.[43] In the United States the doctrine is tightly construed and only applies where the undertaking has considerable power in downstream markets. It normally applies therefore where the dominant undertaking is trying to foreclose competitors in those markets. There was no evidence of such downstream market presence in *Stena Sealink.* Secondly, the doctrine has been heavily criticised in the US as providing too crude an analysis of the social costs of forcing an undertaking to share its assets

---

42 OJ 1994 L 15/8. See also *Re Access to Facilities of port of Rødby*, OJ 1994 L 55/52.

43 Venit, J. & Kallaugher, J. 'Essential Facilities: A Comparative Law Approach' (1994) *Fordham Corporate Law Institute* 315.

with its rivals.[44] In some cases there may be a justification for this. In others where the undertaking has had to undertake considerable risks or development costs to obtaining the essential facility, the doctrine merely acts as an obstacle to innovation and risk-taking.

c. The Defence of Objective Justification

An undertaking occupying a dominant position can lawfully engage in many activities which harm its competitors' interests. Thus, expansion of output or selling better quality products at lower prices will never be considered abusive even though a competitor may be so severely affected that he may be put out of business. Distinguishing such activities from anti-competitive behavioural abuses is difficult, as many of these abuses do not immediately harm the consumer.

The Court has therefore stated that anti-competitive behavioural 'abuses' will not breach Article 86 [*82*] EC if there is an objective justification for them. There is one exception to this defence of objective justification. It is an abuse for a monopolist to prevent or put pressure on its distributors not to import or export goods to or from another Member State.[45] This is an anti-competitive rather than an exploitative practice as it can be carried out by any supplier. It is a breach of Article 86 [*82*] EC, however, as it serves not just to restrict competition but also prevents market integration. As the latter is an overriding goal of EC competition law, such a practice can never be objectively justified.

The defence of objective justification is particularly uncertain, however, as the next case illustrates.

---

44 See, in particular, Areeda, D. 'Essential Facilities: An Epithet in Need of Limiting Principles' (1989) 58 *Antitrust Law Journal* 845.

45 e.g. Case 226/84 *British Leyland v Commission* [1986] ECR 3623, [1987] 1 CMLR 185; Case T-30/89 *Hilti v Commission* [1991] ECR II-1439, [1992] 4 CMLR 16.

Case 77/77 BP v Commission [1978] ECR 1513, [1978] 3 CMLR 174

The Commission found that BP had breached Article 86 [*82*] EC by refusing to continue to supply ABG, a Dutch customer with crude oil. The Court disagreed.

24. It is common ground that on 21 November 1972 BP terminated the agreement which had been in existence since 1968 with ABG and thus put an end to its commercial relationship with that company as regards its supply of motor spirit...

28. It emerges from the contested decision that the fact that BP in November 1972 terminated its commercial relations with ABG was connected with the regrouping of BP's operational activities which was made necessary by the nationalization of a large part of that company's interests in the production sector and by the participation of the producer countries in its extracting activities and is thus explained by considerations which have nothing to do with its relations with ABG.

29. It therefore follows that at the time of the crisis and even from November 1972, ABG's position in relation to BP was no longer, as regards the supply of motor spirit, that of a contractual customer but that of an occasional customer.

30. The principle laid down by the contested decision that reductions in supplies ought to have been carried out on the basis of a reference period fixed in the year before the crisis, although it may be explicable in cases in which a continued supply relationship has been maintained, during that period, between seller and purchaser, cannot be applied when the supplier ceased during the course of that same period to carry on such relations with its customer, regard being had in particular to the fact that the plans of any undertaking are normally based on reasonable forecasts.

31. Moreover, the advances in petrol against crude oil agreed to by BP in pursuance of the processing agreement, as they occur within the context of an agreement whose purpose was solely the refining of crude oil supplied by ABG and not the supplying of ABG with motor spirit, cannot serve as a valid argument to compare ABG's position in this case in relation to BP with that of a traditional customer of BP during the above-mentioned reference period.

32. For all these reasons, since ABG's position in relation to BP had been, for several months before the crisis occurred, that of an occasional customer, BP cannot be accused of having applied to it during the crisis less favourable treatment than that which it reserved for its traditional customers.

Monopolists are placed in an invidious position if not even the Commission and the Court can agree upon when it is justifiable to refuse to supply goods. Given the potential liability, undertakings' likely response is simply not to engage in these practices even where they are justifiable. Such constraints place them peculiarly in a worse position than undertakings operating in a competitive market.

This criticism must be tempered by realisation that it is necessary to regulate both behavioural and structural abuses if workable competition is to be preserved. It would be self-defeating to regulate only structural abuses, as market structures would eventually be weakened through other firms being pushed out of the market through behavioural abuses. Regulating for a competitive *environment* is always likely to be an imprecise art. For it is impossible to pinpoint the moment at which an undertaking stops legitimately interacting with the competitive environment and starts unduly interfering with it. A cost of seeking to preserve workable competition is that the instruments used will be perceived to be blunt and may create individual cases of injustice.

VII. Mergers

i. The Political Economy of Mergers

The concept of a merger is a wideranging one. The name suggests the establishment of a union between two firms. This can either be established on an amicable basis or through a hostile takeover. There are also a number of forms of merger. The *horizontal merger* is one which takes place between competitors operating at the same level on the commercial cycle. The converse of this is the *vertical merger* which takes place between undertakings which operate on different levels - such as production and distribution - of the commercial cycle. Finally, there are *conglomerate mergers* which join together undertakings who do not operate on the same product or geographical market.

The first form of efficiency claimed for mergers is that of a reduction in production and transaction costs. These can arise from economies of scale. Certain industries require a minimum size to run efficiently. Mergers help attain that size. These can also arise from 'scope economies'. In certain cases producing two products separately may be more costly than producing them together. To the extent that mergers facilitate co-production they enable savings to be made.

The second perceived benefit of mergers is that they improve the quality of management. In principle, inefficiently managed undertakings should be the ones which result in the most apparent gains from a take-over.[46] Mergers therefore act to displace poor management, and as a knock-on effect, provide an incentive for good management elsewhere.

There is also a link between EC merger policy and an EC *industrial policy*. It is argued that to be able to compete on the world market with the large Japanese and American transnationals, European firms should be allowed to merge to attain a comparable size.[47]

Jacquemin has observed that realisation of many of these benefits is often problematic.[48] The first set of benefits are dependent upon realisation of internal efficiencies which might not arise because of difficulties arising out of the merger such as poor communications, clash of corporate cultures, poor industrial relations, insufficient coordination or flexibility. The second argument that mergers improve managerial efficiencies assumes that the stock market is an accurate gauge of a company's performance. Even if this were the case, take-overs may still take place of competitive firms, in particular where larger companies want to dispose of a smaller more efficient competitor or to engage in asset stripping. It might also be asked whether this pursuit of efficiency is desirable from a wider social perspective. What it represents is a

---

46 Inefficient managers in this context are those who do not maximise the return for the owner of the undertaking. Mergers offer an alternative to the owners of such an undertaking by offering them a potentially higher return than they would get from the existing management.

47 Paradoxically, this argument shares all the weaknesses of the structural approach's objections to mergers in that it makes a correlation between size and efficiency, which can often be ill-placed. Neumann, M. 'Industrial Policy and Competition Policy' (1990) 34 *European Economic Review* 562, 565-566.

48 Jacquemin, A. 'Horizontal Concentration and European Merger Policy' (1990) 34 *European Economic Review* 539, 540 *et seq.* The starting point for the celebrated cost-benefit approach to mergers is Williamson, O. 'Economies as an antitrust defence: The welfare tradeoffs' (1968) 58 *American Economic Review* 18. See also Demsetz, H. 'Two systems of belief about monopoly' in Goldschmid, D., Mann, H. & Weston, J. *Industrial Concentration: The New Learning* (1974, Little Brown, Boston).

maximisation of the shareholder's returns. By seeking to achieve economic rationalisation and avoidance of duplication, mergers can in many circumstances lead to redundancies and closure of plants. At least in the short-term this can clearly have considerable adverse consequences not only for the merged firms' workforce but also for the surrounding economy and region.

Particular problems have arisen in relation to vertical mergers. Such mergers can result in the development of further anti-competitive practices in a number of ways. The downstream part of the industry may choose to purchase supplies from its related upstream division, notwithstanding that cheaper supplies may be available from other upstream suppliers, thus depriving these suppliers of potentially very important markets. Conversely, the upstream division may not supply competitors of its downstream division with parts or may only supply them at a higher price. There is, finally, a danger of increased price collusion in markets where there are vertically integrated undertakings. For the downstream part of the industry, as a potential purchaser, will have access to price information which it can then pass on to the upstream part of the industry.[49]

Empirical studies have therefore shown that many of the expected gains from mergers simply do not materialise with surveys suggesting that only a limited number of companies recover the capital invested.[50] The illusory nature of many of the benefits of mergers has focused attention on the economic costs of mergers which are principally the increased market power and the diminution in the number of actors on the market which result from a merger.

Jacquemin, A. & George, K. 'Dominant Firms and Mergers' (1992) 102 *The Economic Journal* 148, 148-149

The structural approach ... presumes that there is, in general, a positive link between intense competition and increases in social welfare: competition and competitive market structures should thus be defended, because the benefits from competition will outweigh

---

49 On these dangers see Riordan, M. & Salop, S. 'Evaluating Vertical Mergers: A Post-Chicago Approach' (1995) 63 *Antitrust Law Journal* 513.

50 For a survey of the surveys see Jacquemin, A. supra n.48, 541-542.

any benefits from increased firm size. Thus, the structural approach to the control of market power implies that large firms should be controlled by preserving or creating a competitive market environment, and the structural approach to mergers is to prohibit any mergers that would create or consolidate an undesirably concentrated market structure. In other words, the philosophy behind the structural approach to policy - which accepts the importance of the causal links between structure, conduct and performance, with a definite preference for competitive structures - is that, if we look after market structure, market conduct and performance will look after themselves...

... A structural approach must necessarily include a policy for merger control as well as a policy towards existing large firms, since to maintain competitive market structures it must be possible to prevent mergers and also to break up existing firms.

A structural approach meets all the problems encountered, however, by the school of workable competition. Fewer firms on a market is not necessarily symptomatic of a less efficient market. Concentration can often be in line with minimum efficient scales or, even where economies of scale do not pose a problem, of an efficient market, as the absence of new entrants can be a sign that the firm is operating efficiently. If the structural approach suggests there is a need for a merger policy, its limitations also suggest that policy will be an imprecise art.

ii. The Need for an EC Merger Regulation

Mergers fall within the remit of both Article 85 [*81*] and Article 86 [*82*] EC. We have already considered their position under Article 86 [*82*] EC in *Continental Can.*[51] Fourteen years later the question arose as to the compatibility of mergers with Article 85 [*81*] EC. In *BAT*[52] the Commission gave negative clearance to the sale of a 30% shareholding in Rothmans, a cigarette manufacturer, by Rembrandt, its owner, to Philip Morris, another cigarette manufacturer. This decision was challenged by two competitors. The Court considered that while

---

51 Case 6/72 *Continental Can v Commission* [1973] ECR 215, [1973] CMLR 215.

52 Joined Cases 142 & 156/84 *BAT & Reynolds v Commission* [1987] ECR 4487, [1988] 4 CMLR 24.

acquisition of an interest in another company did not fall within Article 85(1) [*81(1)*] EC, *per se*, it would if it could be used as an instrument for influencing the conduct of the two companies or for distorting competition. Whilst the Court considered this was not the case here, it considered it would be the case if either the investment resulted in one company having legal or *de facto* control over the other, the agreement provided for commercial cooperation between the companies or it created a structure which was likely to be used for that purpose. Practice has shown there to be a number of both substantive and institutional problems, however, in Articles 85 and 86 EC to mergers.

- In respect of Article 85 [*81*] EC, it was unclear whether it would apply to takeovers which resulted in one company having total control over the other rather than merely *de facto* control. It was also unclear whether it applied to hostile takeovers, as in such circumstances the requirement of agreement or concertation in Article 85 [*81*] EC was lacking.

- In the case of Article 86 [82] EC, it only applied to those undertakings which were dominant position prior to the merger, it could not apply to those undertakings which acquired a dominant position *through* the merger. Article 86 [82] EC provides no possibility for taking account of regional, social or technological arguments. The concept of abuse in Article 86 [*82*] EC also fails to provide any criteria against which the benefits and costs of mergers can be evaluated.

- The system for clearance in Regulation 17 is essentially an *ex post facto* one, namely the particular practice is presented as a *fait accompli* before the Commission. If the Commission considers it to be illegal, it insists that it be undone. This works for most forms of anti-competitive practice. It does not work well for mergers, as if it is often to unravel a merger and refloat the undertaking that had been subject to a bid.

From as early as 1973 the Commission proposed that there should therefore be a Merger Regulation.[53] The Merger Regulation, Regulation 4064/89 EEC[54], was not however adopted until the end of 1989. There was considerable debate both as to what elements of merger

---

53 OJ 1973 C 92/1.

54 OJ 1989 L 395/1, as amended by Regulation 1310/97/EC, OJ 1997 L 180/1.

control should fall within Community competence and what principles should guide Community merger policy. Few would argue that the Regulation is perfect but it represents the least unacceptable solution to the greatest number.[55] It should be assessed within this context and on the basis of whether it improves on the previous regime and not against some idealised model.

iii. The Material Scope of the Merger Regulation

Article 1(1) states that the Regulation is applied to *concentrations* which have a *Community dimension*. Concentrations are defined in Article 3.

Article 3(1). A concentration shall be deemed to arise where :
(a) two or more previously independent undertakings merge, or
(b) - one or more persons already controlling at least one undertaking,
or
- one or more undertakings acquire, whether by purchase of securities or assets, by contract or by any other means, direct or indirect control of the whole or parts of one or more other undertakings.

2. The creation of a joint venture performing on a lasting basis all the functions of an autonomous economic entity shall constitute a concentration within the meaning of paragraph 1(b).

3. For the purposes of this Regulation, control shall be constituted by rights, contracts or any other means which, either separately or jointly and having regard to the considerations of fact or law involved, confer the possibility of exercising decisive influence on an undertaking, in particular by :
(a) ownership or the right to use all or part of the assets of an undertaking;
(b) rights or contracts which confer decisive influence on the composition, voting or decisions of the organs of an undertaking.

---

55 For a brief summary of the background to the Regulation see Venit, J. 'The "Merger" Control Regulation: Europe Comes of Age ... or Caliban's Dinner' (1990) 27 *CMLRev* 7, 7-11.

The first scenario in which a concentration will be found to exist is where there is a *complete merger*.[56] This will occur when two independent undertakings amalgamate and cease to exist as different legal entities or where one undertaking is absorbed by the other and loses its legal identity. It can also occur where the two undertakings retain their legal identities, but create a 'common economic management' which leads to a *de facto* amalgamation of the undertakings into a common economic unit with a single management.[57]

The second scenario in which a concentration will be found to exist is where one or more undertakings acquire *control* of another.[58] Control will be found to exist where one undertaking exercises decisive influence over another. This can be established through legal control, where one undertaking has 50% or more of another's shares. It can also be established upon a *de facto* basis through acquisition of a minority holding, the acquisition of assets, or the development of contractual provisions which result in one undertaking being economically dependent upon the other.[59] In *Arjomari-Prioux/Wiggins Teape Appleton*, for example, the Commission found that a concentration had taken place despite Arjomari's acquiring only 39% of the shares. The reason was that no other shareholder held more than 4% of the shares. The dispersed ownership of the other shares thus resulted in Arjomari having a decisive influence.[60]

A concentration will also exist where two or more undertakings acquire joint control of an undertaking. This will be the case where these parties can block the taking of any important strategic decisions. Examples are where two parent companies share equally the voting

---

56 Supra n.54, Article 3(1)(a).

57 Commission Notice on the notion of a concentration under Regulation 4064/89, OJ 1994 C 385/5, paras 6 & 7.

58 Supra n.54, Article 3(1)(b).

59 Supra n.55, para.8. For an early piece on the manner in which control can be acquired see Siragusa, M. & Subiotto, R. 'The EEC Merger Control Regulation: The Commission's Evolving Case Law' (1991) 28 *CMLRev* 877, 886-895.

60 IV/M/025 *Arjomari Prioux/Wiggins Teape*, OJ 1990 C 321/16, [1991] 4 CMLR 854. See also Commission Notice on the notion of a concentration under Regulation 4064/89, OJ 1994 C 385/5, paras 13-17.

rights to a joint venture or where even though one does not have equal voting rights to the other, it has the right to veto strategic decisions.[61]

The third scenario in which a concentration will exist is where two or more undertakings create a 'full function' joint venture. This is a separate legal structure which performs 'on a lasting basis all the functions of an autonomous economic entity'.[62] Joint ventures constitute coordination between two or more or more undertakings and would normally fall within Article 85 [*81*] EC. The reason 'full function' joint ventures are treated differently is that the creation of an autonomous permanent new body can enhance the competitive process.

Hawk, B. and Huser, H. 'A Bright Line Shareholding Test to End the Nightmare under the EEC Merger Regulation' (1993) 30 *Common Market Law Review* 1155, 1158-1161[63]

First, a joint venture can never eliminate competition more than a full merger or acquisition between the same parties and, instead often presents a significantly lower risk of competitive harm. Full mergers and acquisition of sole control totally and permanently eliminate all actual or potential competition between the parties. ... In comparison, joint ventures (especially limited duration and/or partial function ventures) often create lower risks of competitive harm than full mergers and acquisitions (or classic cartels) because (i) joint ventures may preserve some degree of competition (e.g. independent pricing discretion) between the parents in the joint venture's market (when their operations are not fully merged); and (ii) joint ventures may be more likely to break up at some later date (when the parents' operations are not permanently merged), which would either maintain or reintroduce both parents as independent competitors (or independent suppliers/purchasers) in the joint venture's market(s)...

Second, virtually all joint ventures, including limited duration and/or partial function joint ventures, will (like full mergers and acquisitions) involve some degree of functional integration of economic resources (the principal source of economic efficiencies). The only exception is in rare situations where a joint venture (or other minority shareholding) 'form' is adopted by the parties, but the economic substance of their transaction is nothing more than a classic cartel arrangement - that is, a mere 'sham'.

The types and magnitude of economic integration created by a (non-sham) joint venture often equal those created by a full merger or acquisition between the same parties. They include realization of scale or scope economies, risk allocation, facilitation

61 Ibid., paras18-45.

62 Supra n.54, Article 3(2).

63 See also Brodley, W. 'Joint Ventures and Antitrust Policy' (1982) 95 *Harvard Law Review* 1521, much of whose style of analysis is adopted by this article.

of new product development or geographic entry, and synergies resulting from combining complementary operations. Indeed, in some situations where full mergers and acquisitions are not feasible (say for legal, political or other reasons), joint ventures may provide greater opportunities for economic integration given that they are the only means to realize competitive benefits.

The point of concern for the regulatory authorities is not therefore the joint venture's effect upon the price mechanism but rather that it will result in a concentration of market power. The question is how to tell, however, when a joint venture falls within the Merger Regulation rather than Article 85 [*81*] EC.

Commission Notice on the Distinction between Concentrative and Cooperative Operations under Regulation 4064/89[64]

13. Essentially this [a full function joint venture] means that the joint venture must operate on a market, performing the functions normally carried out by other undertakings operating on the same market. In order to do so the joint venture must have sufficient financial and other resources including finance, staff, and assets (tangible and intangible) in order to operate a business activity on a lasting basis. In respect of intellectual property rights it is sufficient that these rights are licensed to the joint venture for its duration. Joint ventures which satisfy this requirement are commonly described as 'full-function' joint ventures.

14. A joint venture is not full-function venture if it only takes over one specific function within the parent companies' business activities without access to the market. This is the case, for example, for joint ventures limited to R & D or production. Such joint ventures are auxiliary to their parent companies' business activities. This is also the case where a joint venture is essentially limited to the distribution or sales of its parent companies' products and, therefore, acts principally as a sales agency. However, the fact that a joint venture makes use of the distribution network or outlet of one or more of its parent companies, normally will not disqualify it as 'full-function' as long as the parent companies are acting only as agents of the joint venture.

15. The strong presence of the parent companies in upstream or downstream markets is a factor to be taken into consideration in assessing the full-function character of a joint venture where this presence leads to substantial sales or purchases between the parent companies and the joint venture. The fact that the joint venture relies almost entirely on

---

64 OJ 1994 C 385/1.

sales to its parent companies or purchases from them only for an initial start-up period may be necessary in order to establish the joint venture on a market. It will normally not exceed a time period of three years, depending on the specific conditions of the market in question.

Where sales from the joint venture to the parent companies are intended to be made on a lasting basis the essential question is whether regardless of these sales the joint venture is geared to play an active role on the market. In this respect the relative proportion of these sales compared with the total production of the joint venture is an important factor. Another factor is that sales to the parent companies are made on the basis of normal commercial conditions.

In relation to purchases made by the joint venture from its parent companies, the full-function character of the joint venture is questionable in particular where little value is added to the products or services concerned at the level of the joint venture itself. In such a situation, the joint venture may be closer to a joint sales agency. However, in contrast to this situation where a joint venture is active in a trade market and performs the normal functions of a trading company in such a market, it normally will not be an auxiliary sales agency but a full-function joint venture. A trade market is characterised by the existence of companies which specialise in the selling and distribution of products without being vertically integrated in addition to those which may be integrated, and where different sources of supply are available for the products in question. In addition, many trade markets may require operators to invest in specific facilities such as outlets, stockholding, warehouses, depots, transport fleets and sales personnel. In order to constitute a full-function joint venture in a trading market, it must have the necessary facilities and be likely to obtain a substantial proportion of its supplies not only from its parent companies but also from other competing sources.

16. Furthermore, the joint venture must be intended to operate on a lasting basis. The fact that the parent companies commit to the joint venture the resources described above normally demonstrates that this is the case. In addition, agreements setting up a joint venture often provide for certain contingencies, for example, the failure of the joint venture or fundamental disagreement as between the parent companies. This may be achieved by the incorporation of provisions for the eventual dissolution of the joint venture itself or the possibility for one or more parent companies to withdraw from the joint venture. This kind of provision does not prevent the joint venture from being considered as operating on a lasting basis. The same is normally true where the agreement specifies a period for the duration of the joint venture where this period is sufficiently long in order to bring about a lasting change in the structure of the undertaking concerned, or where the agreement provides for the possible continuation of the joint venture beyond this period. By contrast, the joint venture will not be considered to operate on a lasting basis where it is established for a short finite duration. This would be the case, for example, where a joint venture is established in order to construct a specific project such a as power plant, but it will not be involved in the operation of the plant once its construction has been completed.

The autonomy of a joint venture will often be a matter of degree. An enquiry based upon 'complex, fact-intensive substantive anti-trust criteria'[65] will often be necessary to establish whether the joint venture is genuinely autonomous. Hawk and Huser have noted that this creates a 'cart before the horse' dilemma, as the Commission and the parties are often forced to complete much of the assessments upon the merits at the time of determining jurisdiction.[66]

There is a second problem. Prior to the 1997 amendment of the Merger Regulation 'full function' joint ventures would fall outside the scope of the Regulation if they were no more than a shell through which cartelisation develops. This can take a number of forms. First, a parent might be an actual or potential competitor. If it is involved in a cooperative joint venture there is a danger of coordination and reduced competition. Secondly, there is a risk of vertical foreclosure. Parents in related or downmarket markets are provided with incentives to collaborate with the joint venture. Thirdly, there is the risk of spillover collusion. The joint venture might act as a medium for collaboration between the parents which allows for collusion in other areas.[67]

Joint ventures which were 'cooperative in nature' and led to coordination upon the part of the undertakings setting up the joint venture or between the joint venture and one or both of the undertakings were thus dealt with by Article 85 [*81*] EC rather than the Merger Regulation. This distinction was much criticised as it led to transactions with almost identical economic effects being treated very differently.[68] These difficulties were acknowledged by the Commission in its Green Paper on Review of the Merger Regulation.[69] All 'full function' joint ventures were brought within the Merger Regulation and treated

---

65 Hawk, B. & Huser, H. 'A Bright Line Shareholding Test to End the Nightmare under the EEC Merger Regulation' (1993) 30 *CMLRev* 1155, 1162; Sibree, W. 'EEC Merger Control and Joint Ventures' (1992) 17 *ELRev* 91.

66 Ibid., 1164.

67 Jones, C. & Gonzalez-Diaz, F. (ed. Overbury, C.) *The EEC Merger Regulation* (1992, Sweet & Maxwell, London) 51-52.

68 e.g. Jones, C., van der Woude, C. & Pathak, A. Competition Law Checklist (1992) 18 *ELRev* 28-29.

69 EC Commission, *Green Paper on Review of the Merger Regulation*, COM (96) 19 final.

identically in procedural terms. To deal with the possibility of joint ventures acting as a vehicle for cartelisation, the Regulation proposes a different standard of review for joint ventures which have as their object or effect the coordination of competitive behaviour between undertakings.

Article 2(4). To the extent that the creation of a joint venture constituting a concentration pursuant to Article 3 has as its object or effect the coordination of the competitive behaviour of undertakings that remain independent, such coordination shall be appraised in accordance with the criteria of Article 85(1) and (3) of the Treaty, with a view to establishing whether or not the operation is compatible with the common market.

In making this appraisal, the Commission shall take into account in particular:- whether two or more parent companies retain to a significant extent activities in the same market as the joint venture or in a market which is downstream or upstream from that of the joint venture or in a neighbouring market closely related to this market, whether the coordination which is the direct consequence of the creation of the joint venture affords the undertakings concerned the possibility of eliminating competition in respect of a substantial part of the products or services in question.

The concentrative/cooperative dichotomy which was so criticised has therefore been retained, albeit only as a standard of review. The criticisms that were made in the past thus still remain - namely that virtually identical transactions will be treated differently and that the application of Article 85 [*81*] EC to any full function joint venture will ignore the benefits of functional integration that it brings and thus deter many desirable forms of cooperation.

iv. The Community Dimension to the Merger Regulation

The Merger Regulation only regulates those concentrations with a Community dimension.

Article 1(2). For the purposes of this Regulation, a concentration has a Community dimension where:
(a) the combined aggregate worldwide turnover of all the undertakings concerned is more than ECU 5,000 million; and

(b) the aggregate Community-wide turnover of each of at least two of the undertakings concerned is more than ECU 250 million, unless each of the undertakings concerned achieves more than two-thirds of its aggregate Community-wide turnover within one and the same Member State.

The 'Dutch clause' allows the Commission to review concentrations which do not meet these criteria, where asked to do so by a Member State.

Article 22(3). If the Commission finds at the request of a Member State or at the joint request of two or more Member States, that a concentration as defined in Article 3 that has no Community dimension within the meaning of Article 1 creates or strengthens a dominant position as a result of which effective competition would be significantly impeded within the territory of the Member State or States making the joint request it may, insofar as that concentration affects trade adopt the decisions provided for in Article 8(2) and subparagraph, (3) and (4).[70]

.....

5. Pursuant to paragraph 3 the Commission shall take only the measures strictly necessary to maintain or restore effective competition within the territory of the Member State or States at the request of which it intervenes.

Notwithstanding the Dutch clause, these thresholds were subject to considerable debate. It was considered that they would result in relatively few mergers being considered by the Commission, and only 40 to 50 mergers would be notified to the Commission each year.[71] This forecast has proved to be an underestimate with 125 cases being decided by the Commission in 1996.[72]

The Commission has still expressed dissatisfaction with the high levels of the thresholds. In its Green Paper it noted that only 293 companies had a world-wide turnover in excess of ECU 2.5 billion and

---

70 Article 8 gives the Commission powers of appraisal under the Regulation.

71 Venit, J. 'The "Merger" Control Regulation: Europe Comes of Age ... or Caliban's Dinner' (1990) 27 *CMLRev* 7, n.15.

72 EC Commission, *Twenty Sixth Report on Competition Policy* (1997, OOPEC, Luxembourg) para 127.

would thus come under Community control in a concentration involving companies of equal size. In some sectors such as textiles, printing and publishing or hotels and catering, not even the largest companies in the sector met the thresholds. In others very few companies did. The high thresholds had led in the Commission's view to concentrations with significant cross-border thresholds being subject to a variety of national merger laws and to multiple filings having to be made with the various national authorities. The Member States and industry were receptive to the last point, and the thresholds have been altered for concentrations which involve undertakings from at least three Member States.

Article 1(3). For the purposes of this Regulation, a concentration that does not meet the thresholds laid down in paragraph 2 has a Community dimension where:
(a) the combined aggregate worldwide turnover of all the undertakings concerned is more than ECU 2,500 million;
(b) in each of at least three Member States, the combined aggregate turnover of all the undertakings concerned is more than ECU 100 million;
(c) in each of at least three Member States included for the purpose of point (b), the aggregate turnover of each of at least two of the undertakings concerned is more than ECU 25 million; and
(d) the aggregate Community-wide turnover of each of at least two of the undertakings concerned is more than ECU 100 million;
unless each of the undertakings concerned achieves more than two-thirds of its aggregate Community-wide turnover within one and the same Member State.

The main boast of the Regulation is that it provides a 'one-stop shop'. Whereas previously mergers would be reviewed for their compatibility with both national and EC merger law, the Merger Regulation required that such mergers should only be considered by the Commission.

Article 21(1). Subject to review by the Court of Justice, the Commission shall have sole jurisdiction to take the decisions provided for in this Regulation.

2. No Member State shall apply its national legislation on competition to any consideration that has a Community dimension.

This seemingly clear cut division between national and EC competence has been undermined by a couple of exceptions which allow for mergers to be reviewed by national authorities, notwithstanding that the former pass the Community thresholds. The most salient is the 'German clause' - so-called because it was insisted upon by the German authorities.

Article 9(1). The Commission may, by means of a decision notified without delay to the undertakings concerned and the competent authorities of the other Member States, refer a notified concentration to the competent authorities of the Member State concerned in the following circumstances.

2. Within three weeks of the date of receipt of the copy of the notification a Member State may inform the Commission, which shall inform the undertakings concerned that:
(a) a concentration threatens to create or to strengthen a dominant position as a result of which effective competition would be significantly impeded on a market, within that Member State, which presents all the characteristics of a distinct market, or
(b) a concentration affects competition on a market within that Member State, which presents all the characteristics of a distinct market and which does not constitute a substantial part of the common market.

3. If the Commission considers that, having regard to the market for the products or services in question and the geographical reference market within the meaning of paragraph 7, there is such a distinct market and that such a threat exists, either:
(a) it shall itself deal with the case in order to maintain or restore effective competition on the market concerned; or
(b) it shall refer the whole or part of the case to the competent authorities of the Member State concerned with a view to the application of that State's national competition law.

In cases where a Member State informs the Commission that a concentration affects competition in a distinct market within its territory that does not form a substantial part of the common market, the Commission shall refer the whole or part of the case relating to the distinct market concerned, if it considers that such a distinct market is affected.

Whilst the German clause provides for a 'distinct national market' exception to the Community thresholds, it prevents dysfunction through establishing a system of administrative cooperation whereby the Commission is still the first port of call for all mergers of a certain dimension. The position is less clear in respect of the second exception.

Article 21(3). Notwithstanding paragraphs 1 and 2, Member States may take appropriate measures to protect legitimate interests other than those taken into consideration by this Regulation and compatible with the general principles and other provisions of Community law.

Public security, plurality of the media and prudential rules shall be regarded as legitimate interests within the meaning of the first paragraph.

Any other public interest must be communicated to the Commission by the Member State concerned and shall be recognised by the Commission after an assessment of its compatibility with the general principles and other provisions of Community law before the measures referred to above may be taken. The Commission shall inform the Member State concerned within one month of that communication.

v. Substantive Appraisal of the Merger

Once a concentration with a Community dimension is established, it can be substantively appraised.

Article 2(1). Concentrations within the scope of this Regulation shall be appraised in accordance with the following provisions with a view to establishing whether or not they are compatible with the common market.
In making this appraisal, the Commission shall take into account:
(a) the need to maintain and develop effective competition within the common market in view of, among other things, the structure of all the markets concerned and the actual or potential competition from undertakings located either within or outwith the Community;
(b) the market position of the undertakings concerned and their economic and financial power, the alternatives available to suppliers and users, their access to supplies or markets, any legal or other barriers to entry, supply and demand trends for the relevant goods and services, the interests of the intermediate and ultimate consumers, and the development of technical and economic progress provided that it is to consumers' advantage and does not form an obstacle to competition.

2. A concentration which does not create or strengthen a dominant position as a result of which effective competition would be significantly impeded in the common market or in a substantial part of it shall be declared compatible with the common market.

3. A concentration which creates or strengthens a dominant position as a result of which effective competition would be significantly impeded in the common market or in a substantial part of it shall be declared incompatible with the common market.

The standard of review in Article 2 is not dissimilar to that in Article 86 [*82*] EC. The relevant product and geographical markets must be identified in the same manner. Whilst a concentration need only acquire a dominant position to fall within the Regulation rather than already occupy one, as is the case with Article 86 [*82*] EC, reference is made to the notion of market dominance in both. Similar language is also used to that found in *Continental Can*[73] as to when a merger is incompatible with the common market. Whereas Continental Can therefore suggests that there will be a breach of Article 86 [*82*] EC wherever a merger 'substantially fetters competition', there is a breach of Article 2 wherever a concentration creates or strengthens a dominant position which'significantly impedes competition'. In this respect joint dominance can be established under the Merger Regulation in the same manner as under Article 86 [*82*] EC.[74]

By the end of 1997, eight concentrations had been found to be incompatible with the common market. Analysis of all concentrations is located very much in the particularities of the organisation of the market in question. *ATR/De Havilland*, the first concentration to be declared incompatible with the common market, is, however, representative of the general style of analysis used.

Case IV/M053 Aérospatiale-Alenia/de Havilland[75]

Aérospatiale and Alenia controlled ATR, the world's largest supplier of turbo-prop regional aircraft. They proposed to takeover de Havilland, their largest competitor. The Commission found the relevant product market to be aircraft with 20 to 79 seats, with three sub-markets - that for aircraft with between 20 and 39 seats, that for aircraft with 40-59 seats and that for aircraft with 60-79 seats. The relevant geographical market was the world market. The Commission then considered whether the concentration was incompatible with the common market.

---

73 Case 6/72 *Continental Can v Commission* [1973] ECR 215, [1973] CMLR 199.

74 IV/M190 *Nestlé/Perrier* [1993] 4 CMLR M17. For analysis see Winckler, A. & Hansen, M. 'Collective Dominance under the EC Merger Control Regulation' (1993) 30 *CMLRev* 787.

75 OJ 1991 L 334/42.

A. Effect on ATR's position

27. The proposed concentration would significantly strengthen ATR's position on the commuter markets, for the following reasons in particular:
- high combined market share on the 40 to 59-seat market, and of the overall commuter market
- elimination of de Havilland as a competitor
- coverage of the whole range of commuter aircraft
- considerable extension of the customer base.

(a) Increase in Market Share

28. The proposed concentration would lead to an increase in market shares for ATR in the world market for commuters between 40 to 59 seats from 46 % to 63 %. The nearest competitor (Fokker) would have 22 %...

29. ATR would increase its share of the overall worldwide commuter market of 20 to 70 seats from around 30 % to around 50 %. The nearest competitor (SAAB) would only have around 19 %. On the basis of this the new entity would have half the overall world market and more than two and a half times the share of its nearest competitor.

30. The combined market share may further increase after the concentration. The higher market share could give ATR more flexibility to compete on price (including financing) than its smaller competitors. ATR would be able to react with more flexibility to initiatives of competitors in the market place.

Following a concentration between ATR and de Havilland, the competitors would be faced with the combined strength of two large companies. This would mean that where an airline was considering placing a new order, the competitors would be in competition with the combined product range of ATR and de Havilland. The sales strategy of the formerly separate companies would now be concerted. The combination could enable the new entity ATR/de Havilland to be more flexible in setting its price than its competitors where a sale is contestable, because of their absolute size advantage in terms of sales base. Furthermore, unlike the competitors, the combined entity would have all the advantages of a family of commuters to offer. This may give rise to the ability, *inter alia*, of offering favourable conditions for a specific type of aircraft in mixed deals.

(b) Elimination of de Havilland as a Competitor

31. In terms of aircraft sold, de Havilland is the most successful competitor of ATR. In the relevant product market of 40 to 59 seats, Fokker has a higher market share than de Havilland, but Fokker at the end of 1990 had a backlog of only 27 orders for the Fokker 50 whilst de Havilland had a backlog of 72 orders for the Dash 8-300 (second only to ATR with 103 orders for the ATR 42). Furthermore, de Havilland has plans to develop a new aircraft - the Dash 8-400 - to compete in the top segment (60 seats and over). If the concentration goes ahead, therefore, de Havilland would be eliminated as a potential competitor from this segment where ATR has a market share of 76%.

(c) Coverage of the Whole Range of Commuter Aircraft

32. The new entity ATR/de Havilland would be the only commuter manufacturer present in all the various commuter markets as defined above.

In practice the advantages of having complete coverage of the market are only present where airlines have or intend to have a fleet consisting of aircraft in different product markets. According to figures supplied by Fokker, over half of the aircraft sold in the markets of 40 seats and above for example are operated in fleets where there are also aircraft of around 30 seats. It appears therefore that at least having a more complete coverage of the market is significant.

(d) Broadening of Customer Base

33. ATR would significantly broaden its customer base after the concentration. On the basis of deliveries to date, the parties state that ATR has currently delivered commuters to 44 customers worldwide and de Havilland has delivered commuters to 36 other customers, giving a combination of 80 customers in all. This compares with, for example, Saab which has 27 operating airline customers, and Fokker which has around 20 airline customers operating the Fokker 50. This figure of 80 customers does not take into account however the substantial backlog of orders not yet delivered of both companies placed by yet other customers. It is likely therefore that the customer base would be higher in the foreseeable future. This is already reflected in the market share figures.The customer base is an important element of market power for aircraft manufacturers since there is at least to some extent a lock-in effect for customers once their initial choice of aircraft is made.

Once a customer has made a commitment to a particular manufacturer, then there is usually a cost consideration in placing orders with another manufacturer. Customers indicate that there are relatively high costs arising from different technology used leading to training costs for maintenance and for pilots, and to different spare part requirements...

B. Assessment of the Strength of the Remaining Competition

34. In order to be able to assess whether the new combined entity would be able to act independently of its competitors, in view of its strengthened position, it is necessary to assess the current and expected future strength of the remaining competitors.

The Commission examined the strength and market share of existing competitors.

Overall Evaluation of the Remaining Competition

42. It follows from the above that effective competition for the combined entity would only be maintained in the market of 20 to 39-seat commuters, although even here the ability of the competitors to compete with the combined entity would lessen to a certain extent given the overall advantages to ATR/de Havilland arising form a broad sales base and coverage of all the markets. In the markets for commuters of 40 seats and over, apart from the limited competition from the Saab 2000, it is questionable whether the other existing competitors could provide effective competition in the medium to long term.

C. Assessment of the Customers

43. In order to be able to assess whether the new combined entity would be able to act independently of customers, in view of its strong position and the relative weakness of the competitors, the position of customers in the commuter markets must be examined...

.....

48. From the customers' replies to the Commission's enquiry, it seems that most established airlines found it difficult to assess the impact of the proposed concentration on the general conditions of competition based on the information available to them. Half of the respondents stated that there would be not a direct impact on their company since they already have a commitment to a particular commuter manufacturer and have thus no plans, nor even a realistic possibility, to switch to another manufacturer. Some of these airlines have already placed their orders to fulfil their medium-term demand and others anticipate no further orders.

25 % of the airlines which replied nonetheless expressed concern about the reduction of choice and elimination of competition which they perceived to be a direct result of the concentration.

It appears therefore that for most established airlines a direct negative effect from the proposed concentration would only appear over time. The impact would be immediate for airlines which will come on to the market in the future, in particular following deregulation in the Community.

49. Even if in general terms customers would want to switch to a significant extent to the competitors of ATR/de Havilland, there is only a limited possibility given that the existing capacity of each competitor on average is estimated to be capable only of an increase of some 15 to 20 % in one to two years. This amounts to under 10 % of the overall current worldwide commuter production capacity.

.....

D. Summary of Effect of the Proposed Concentration on the Commuter Markets

51.The combined entity ATR/de Havilland will obtain a very strong position in the world and Community commuter markets of 40 seats and over, and in the overall world and Community commuter market, as a result of the proposed concentration. The competitors in these markets are relatively weak. The bargaining ability of the customers is limited. The combination of these factors leads to the conclusion that the new entity could act to a significant extent independently of its competitors and customers, and would thus have a dominant position on the commuter markets as defined.

.....

E. Potential Entry into the Market

53. In general terms, a concentration which leads to the creation of a dominant position may however be compatible with the common market within the meaning of Article2(2) of the Merger Regulation if there exists strong evidence that this position is only temporary and would be quickly eroded because of high probability of strong market entry. With such market entry the dominant position is not likely to significantly impede effective competition within the meaning of Article 2(3) of the Merger Regulation. In order to assess whether the dominant position of ATR/de Havilland is likely to significantly impede effective competition therefore, it is necessary to assess the likelihood of new entry into the market.

54. Any theoretical attractiveness of entry into the commuter market by a new player must be put into perspective taking into account the forecast demand and the time and cost considerations to enter the market.

55. Even for a company currently active in a related industry not already present on the commuter market - in practice this would seem to be limited to large jet aircraft manufacturers - it would be very expensive to develop a new commuter from scratch. According to the study submitted by the parties, there are high sunk initial costs of entering the regional aircraft market and delays in designing, testing and gaining regulatory approval to sell the aircraft. ... The magnitude of the initial sunk development costs of the aircraft constitutes a significant risk associated with commitment to a particular aircraft. If the manufacturer errs in design, these initial costs are not recoverable.

56. It follows from the above that a new entrant into the market would face high risk. Furthermore, given the time necessary to develop a new aircraft and the foreseeable development of the market as described above, a new manufacturer may come too late into the market to catch the expected period of relatively high demand. Any new market entry at this stage could only come when the market would have declined from current levels and have stabilized. It is therefore doubtful whether a break-even level of sales could be achieved by a new entrant since even existing competitors are not yet at break-even point in their product cycles.

.....

63. It follows that there is no realistic significant potential competition in the commuter markets in the foreseeable future.

.....

F. Other General Considerations

65. The parties argue that one of their objectives in acquiring de Havilland is to reduce costs. The potential cost savings arising from the concentration which have been identified amount to only some ECU 5 million per year. According to the estimates of the parties' economic consultants, these cost savings to the combined entity would arise from rationalizing parts procurement, marketing and product support.

Without prejudice as to whether such considerations are relevant for assessment under Article 2 of the Merger Regulation, such cost savings would have a negligible impact on the overall operation of ATR/de Havilland, amounting to around 0.5 % of the combined turnover. The parties have identified (although not quantified) cost savings which could be made by better management of certain aspects of de Havilland's internal operation. These cost savings would not arise as a consequence of the concentration *per se*, but are cost savings which could be achieved by de Havilland's existing owner or by any other potential acquirer.

.....

69. ... the Commission does not consider that the proposed concentration would contribute to the development of technical and economic progress within the meaning of Article 2(1)(b) of the Merger Regulation. Even if there was such progress, this would not be to the consumers' advantage.

The consumers will be faced with a dominant position which combines the most popular aircraft families on the market. Choice will be significantly reduced. There is a high risk that in the foreseeable future, the dominant position of ATR/de Havilland would be translated into a monopoly.

Both British Aerospace and Fokker, the two principal competitors in the markets of 40 seats and above, have stated that the concentration would seriously jeopardize the survival of the ATP and Fokker 50 aircraft. These two competitors expect that the proposed concentration would lead to ATR/de Havilland pursuing a strategy of initially lowering prices so as to eliminate the competitors at least in the key markets of 40 seats and above.

Neither Fokker nor British Aerospace consider it possible for them to withstand such a price war. Consequently, both would leave the markets. In evaluating these statements, it is noted that such conduct could be rational since the proposed concentration would mean that ATR/de Havilland would exceed the threshold of market shares which would make such a pricing policy likely given that it would be the optimal profit-maximizing strategy.

Having established a monopoly, ATR/de Havilland would be able to increase prices without any competitive check.

70. With this perspective, the proposed concentration would become even more harmful to the customers over time as the dominant position translates to a monopoly. Higher prices for commuters have a proportionally large impact on regional airlines since the price of an aircraft accounts for some 30 to 40 % of their total operating costs.

71. The proposed concentration would also lead to adverse effects in the adjacent 100-seat jet market. The British Aerospace BAE 146 jet is produced in the same factory as the ATP commuter so that fixed costs are spread over the two aircraft. A similar interdependency exists between the Fokker F100 jet and the Fokker 50 commuter. Removal of the commuter product lines of both companies would therefore weaken their competitiveness in the 100-seat jet market where they are already facing strong competition from the Boeing 737.

E. Conclusion

72. For the reasons outlined above, it is considered that the proposed concentration would lead to a situation whereby the combined entity ATR/de Havilland could act to a significant extent independently of its competitors and customers on the world markets as defined for commuters of 40 to 59 seats and 60 seats and over. The proposed concentration therefore creates a dominant position on the world markets. Furthermore, according to the above analysis, this dominant position is not merely temporary and will therefore significantly impede effective competition.

It is considered that such a dominant position is also created even if the relevant product market is the overall 20 to 70-seat market.

.....

The *ATR/de Havilland* Decision suggests three considerations are likely to be salient in any appraisal by the Commission. The first is the extent to which effective competition is maintained in the relevant market. The second is the extent to which the concentration results in an accumulation of market power. The third is the extent to which the concentration contributes to technological progress and to which it advances consumers' interests. Jenny has suggested that in *ATR/de Havilland* the Commission concentrated excessively on the first two considerations to the detriment of the third. He noted that cost savings would result from the concentration through carriers only having to deal with one producer for all their needs. The concentration would also lead to efficiency gains through providing a more integrated service in supplying new parts or servicing plans and benefiting from an integrated marketing strategy.

Jenny, F. 'EEC Merger Control: Economies as an Antitrust Defense or an Antitrust Attack?' (1992) *Fordham Corporate Law Institute* 591, 602-603

One of the reasons for which the Commission assigns so little value to the productive efficiency gains from the ATR/de Havilland merger could be ... that the Merger Regulation is exclusively concerned with consumer surplus. The Commission possibly feels that any productive efficiency gain from a merger giving the merging firms a competitive advantage over their competitors would enable them to increase their market power, with the result that they would increase prices and reduce output so that consumer surplus would automatically decrease.

Yet it can easily be shown that even in the worst case scenario, assuming that the market for commuter aircrafts is perfectly competitive before the merger and that ATR/de Havilland holds a complete monopoly after the merger, it is possible that the consumer surplus will increase so that, contrary to what the Commission declares, the merger is not necessarily harmful to consumers.

On the one hand, the overall cost to airlines which need both large and small commuter planes may decrease as a result of the merger ... The reason is that for these airlines, the increase in the price of planes from the competitive level before the merger to the level maximising the monopoly profits of ATR/de Havilland once these firms have merged will not necessarily match the decrease in the cost of dealing with several manufacturers. In such a case, the consumer surplus of these airlines will increase simultaneously with the profits of the merged firms.

On the other hand, the cost of aircraft for airlines which need only one type of commuter plane is likely to increase as a consequence of the acquisition of monopoly power by ATR/de Havilland (at least for the uncommitted airlines).

Thus, the overall effect of the ATR/de Havilland merger on the consumer surplus of all airlines cannot be assessed solely on the basis which the Commission presented in its decision because it depends on a host of other variable such as the price elasticity of demand for commuter planes, the importance of the costs incurred by airlines with large diversified fleets of dealing with several suppliers, the proportion of planes bought by these airlines in the overall sales of commuter aircrafts etc.

There are arguably other factors, unrelated to efficiency gains, which the Commission must take into account in making its appraisal. The French, in particular, insisted that merger policy should not be devoted merely to securing a more competitive environment but should also take account of other concerns such as economic and social cohesion.[76] The relevant Commissioner at the time, Sir Leon Brittan saw this provision as having little significance, observing that competition would bring about economic and social cohesion.[77] Commission policy in this respect was confused with some statements suggesting account must be taken of these wider considerations in appraisal of a concentration, and others suggesting the opposite.[78]

The Court of First Instance has now had an opportunity to consider this in *Nestlé/Perrier.*[79] A French trade union brought an action challenging the Commission authorising the take-over of Perrier by Demilac, a subsidiary of Nestle, and the sale of Volvic, a Perrier subsidiary, to a competitor, the BSN group. The Court considered that whilst primacy was given in the Merger Regulation to the need for effective competition, the Commission may take into account the social effects of the concentration where these were liable to affect adversely the objectives contained in Article 2 EC. It followed from this that, whilst it lost on the point it was challenging, the trade union was granted *locus standi* to challenge the decision. Given the width of the objectives in Article 2 EC, this allows the Commission to take into account any social, environmental or regional effects of the concentration. This should not, however, be seen as a *carte blanche* for the Commission to develop an industrial policy based around the Merger Regulation. The

---

76 This was taken into account in Recital 13 of the Regulation which states 'the Commission must place its appraisal within the general framework of the achievement of the fundamental objectives referred to in Article 2 of the Treaty, including that of strengthening the Community's economic and social cohesion, referred to in Article130a; On the background to the adoption of this recital see Langeheine, B. 'Substantive Review under the EEC Merger Regulation' (1990) *Fordham Corporate Law Institute* 481, 497-499.

77 Brittan, L. 'The Law and Policy of Merger Control in the EEC' (1990) 15 *ELRev* 351, 353.

78 See the contrasting views expressed in the Commission's Interpretative statement on Article 2(1) in *EC Bulletin Supplement 2/90,* 23 and its statement in EC Commission, *Nineteenth Report of the Commission on Competition Policy* (1990, OOPEC, Luxembourg) paragraph 16.

79 Case T-96/92 *Comité Central d'Entreprise de la Société Générale des Grandes Sources v Commission* [1995] ECR II-1213.

primary purpose of the Regulation is still the protection of competition, and any social effects of a concentration will still be evaluated against the backdrop of an ethos in favour of competition.

vi. Enforcement and Mergers

The Merger Regulation is subject to EC primary legislation, in particular Articles 85 and 86 EC. This creates two problems. The first is the uncertainty engendered by the co-existence of two autonomous regimes. The second is that if the Treaty Articles take precedence over the Merger Regulation, it is not immediately clear how the Regulation can remedy the defective nature of the former provisions.

Article 22(1). This Regulation alone shall apply to concentrations as defined in Article 3, ...

2. Regulation No. 17 ... shall not apply to concentrations as defined in Article 3.

Whish, R. *Competition Law* (1993, 3rd Edition, Butterworths, London) 725-726

Two issues must be considered: first, the effect that Article 22 has on the Commission; secondly, the direct effect of Articles 85 and 86 in national courts.
(A) THE COMMISSION. Clearly the Commission has lost its powers under the general implementations regulations to oppose mergers under Articles 85 and 86. However, this leaves it with the general powers contained in Article 89 of the Treaty to investigate suspected infringements of Articles 85 and 86 and to authorize Member States to take measures to remedy the situation. It could therefore investigate a merger that falls below the Community dimension threshold. Although it would have no power to block the merger, the undertakings would face the trouble and expense of having to cooperate with the investigation. The Commission said at the time of the adoption of the Regulation that it would rarely take this step, but the theoretical possibility of such an investigation remains.[[80]]

---

80 [1990] 4 CMLR 314.

(B) NATIONAL COURTS. The second issue raised by Article 22 is whether the disapplication of the implementing regulations can have taken away the direct effect of Articles 85 and 86. If the answer to this question is that Articles 85 and 86 remain directly effective, then the possibility exists that an undertaking that objects to a merger, for example a target company resisting a bid or a third party complainant, could bring an action in a domestic court. This would be a serious breach of the one-stop principle as it would mean that mergers below the Community dimension threshold, in respect of which the Commission has no powers under the Regulation, could nonetheless be challenged under Articles 85 and 86.

A large number of the Commission's powers under the Merger Regulation are identical to, and subject to the same constraints as those contained under Regulation 17.

- Its investigative powers are identical. It can request information,[81] carry out its own investigations[82] or request the competent national authorities to carry out investigations.[83]

- It can also impose fines[84] or periodic penalty payments.[85] The fines which may be imposed for non-notification or for supplying false or incomplete information and the periodic penalty payments are larger than those under Regulation 17.[86]

- There is identical provision for hearings[87] and liaison with national authorities.[88]

- A duty of confidentiality is imposed upon the Commission.[89] It is safe to assume that the Commission is constrained by the same general principles of law, in

---

81 Supra n.54, Article 11.

82 Ibid., Article 13.

83 Ibid., Article 12.

84 Ibid., Article 14.

85 Ibid., Article 15.

86 The maximum fine that may be imposed for non-cooperation under the Merger Regulation is ECU 50,000. Ibid., 14. The maximum periodic penalty payments are ECU 25,000 per day for each day where an undertaking refuses to submit to an investigation or to supply information, Ibid., 15(1) and ECU 100,000 for each day it refuses to comply with a Commission decision, Ibid., 15(2).

87 Ibid., Article 18. See also Articles 11-17 of Commission Regulation 3384/94/EC, OJ 1994 L 377/1.

88 Ibid., Article 19.

89 Ibid., Article 17.

particular those respecting the rights of the defence, as is the case for Regulation 17.[90] The rights of intervention for third parties is more limited. There is no formal procedure providing for complaints from third parties. Whilst the Commission is required to give a hearing to any third party who shows sufficient interest, these parties do not have a right to know the final details of any settlement reached between the Commission and the parties to the concentration.[91]

There are, however, important differences. The most salient is the duty of prior notification to the Commission.[92] This enables the Commission to appraise a concentration before it becomes too late to unravel. Concentrations cannot therefore be put into effect either before they have been notified.[93]

Article 4(1). Concentrations with a Community dimension defined in this Regulation shall be notified to the Commission not more than one week after the conclusion of the agreement, or the announcement of the public bid, or the acquisition of a controlling interest. That week shall begin when the first of those events occurs.

2. A concentration which consists of a merger within the meaning of Article 3(1)(a) or in the acquisition of joint control within the meaning of Article 3(1)(b) shall be notified jointly by the parties to the merger or by those acquiring joint control as the case may be. In all other cases, the notification shall be effected by the person or undertaking acquiring control of the whole or parts of one or more undertakings.

3. Where the Commission finds that a notified concentration falls within the scope of this regulation, it shall publish the fact of the notification, at the same time indicating the names of the parties, the nature of the concentration and the economic sectors involved.

---

90 An identical power is given to the Court to review the Commission's decisions. Ibid., Article 16.

91 Case T-290/94 *Kaysersberg v Commission*, Judgment of 27 November 1997.

92 A special Merger Task Force has been set up within the Commission specifically to deal with concentrations.

93 Ibid., Article 7(1). The Commission also has a discretion to continue the suspension following a preliminary investigation, Ibid., Article 7(2). The Commission may derogate from these provisions in order to prevent serious damage either to one of the undertakings concerned or to a third party, Ibid., Article 7(4).

The Commission shall take account of the legitimate interest of undertakings in the protection of their business secrets.[94]

There is a two phase procedure following notification. In the first phase the Commission engages in a preliminary examination of the concentration.[95] It shall not oppose the concentration if, during that examination, it finds that either the concentration does not fall within the scope of the Regulation[96] or that there are no serious doubts about the concentration's compatibility with the common market.[97] If either of these scenarios are met, the parties can go ahead with the concentration. It is not uncommon for the Commission to enter into negotiations with the parties during this stage, and it is lawful for the parties to propose modifications so that the Commission will give them a green light at this stage.[98]

It is only if the Commission finds that serious doubts are raised about the concentration's compatibility with the common market that it 'initiates proceedings' and moves to the second phase.[99] This involves a more detailed appraisal of the concentration which must be closed by a decision.[100] This decision may declare the concentration compatible with the common market. In this respect qualified approval may be given in that the Commission may require certain conditions to be met.[101] Alternatively, the concentration may be declared incompatible with the common market.[102] If, notwithstanding this, a concentration has already been implemented, the Commission may require separation or dissolution of the concentration.[103]

---

94 See also Commission Regulation 3384/94, supra n.87, Articles 1-5 for implementation of Article 4.

95 Supra n.54, Article 6.

96 Ibid., Article 6(1)(a).

97 Ibid., Article 6(1)(b).

98 Case T-290/94 *Kaysersberg v Commission*, Judgment of 27 November 1997.

99 Supra n.54, Article 6(1)(c).

100 Ibid., Article 8(1).

101 Ibid., Article 8(2). Such modifications must be communicated to the Commission within three months, Regulation 3384/94, supra n.87, Article 18.

102 Ibid., Article 8(3).

103 Ibid., Article 8(4).

As a *quid pro quo* for the duty of prior notification imposed upon undertakings a system of tough *time limits* is introduced. The preliminary examination should be concluded within a month of notification.[104] Where proceedings are initiated, a decision should in principle be taken within four months of initiation of proceedings.[105] This deadline may be exceptionally extended, where, due to the behaviour of the undertakings, the Commission has either had to request information or launch an investigation.[106] The sanction for the Commission failing to observe these time limits is severe, as the concentration shall be deemed to be compatible with the common market.[107]

As these time limits are relatively short, concentrations were not to be put into effect until either a preliminary investigation had been carried out which revealed that either the concentration was not incompatible with the common market; a final decision had been taken or the time limits had expired.[108] It was still felt that this led in some circumstances to unnecessary delay. The Commission can therefore grant on request a derogation which would allow the concentration to be put into effect notwithstanding that its compatibility with the common market is still being considered. In deciding whether to grant a derogation the Commission must consider the impact upon other undertakings concerned and may attach conditions.[109]

Further Reading

There is once again a wealth of literature on the subject. Only the main works are listed here.

---

[104] Ibid., Article 10(1).

[105] Ibid., Article 10(3).

[106] Ibid., Article 10(4).

[107] Ibid., Article 10(6). For more details on how these time limits are calculated see Regulation 3384/94 supra n.87, Articles 6-10.

[108] Ibid., Article 7.

[109] Ibid., Article 7(4).

Bain, J. *Barriers to New Competition* (1956, Harvard, Cambridge, Mass.)
Bos, P., Stuyck, J. & Wytinck, P. *Concentration Control in the EEC* (1992, Graham & Trotman, London)
Demsetz, H. *Efficiency, Competition and Policy* (1989, OUP)
Downes, T. & Ellison, J. *The Legal Control of Mergers in the European Communities* (1991, Blackstone, London)
Fairburn, J. & Kay, J. (eds.) *Mergers and Merger Policy* (1989, OUP)
Fine, F. *Mergers and Joint Ventures: the law and policy of the EEC* (1994, 2nd Edition, Graham & Trotman, London)
Frazer, T. *Monopoly, Competition and the Law* (1992, Wheatsheaf, Sussex)
Joliet, R. *Monopolisation and Abuse of Dominant Position* (1970, Martijnus Nijhoff, The Hague)
Jones, C. & Gonzalez Diaz, E. *The EEC Merger Regulation* (1992, Sweet & Maxwell, London)
Portwood, T. *Mergers under EEC Competition Law* (1994, Athlone Press, London)

14. Taxation

I. Introduction

The manner in which EC law has developed in the field of taxation provides a microcosm for many of the tensions within the integration process. With the establishment of the customs union, it concentrated on those most direct barriers to trade, customs duties and charges having equivalent effect. With the completion of the customs union, the difficulties posed by Member States' systems indirect taxation became more apparent. Differences in the manner in which indirect taxation was assessed and the rates at which it was assessed distorted competition within the single market by placing differing fiscal burdens upon undertakings and obstructed free movement of goods through the tax adjustments which had to be made at borders. More recently the EC has focused on the barriers to investment created by differing regimes of direct taxation, as differing levels of corporate taxation or the risk of double taxation has influenced investment decisions.

While the demands of the single market make a strong case for a high level of judicial intervention and fiscal harmonisation, national governments are keen to retain their fiscal autonomy. It is the power to tax which provides much of the financial resources which allows them to govern. The acquisition of fiscal powers by authorities and the corresponding submission to fiscal obligations by citizens have also been central to the building of the nation-state.[1] Tax-raising powers therefore have a symbolic resonance for Member States which extends beyond the simple revenue they provide. As Community activity has expanded, it has pressed ever more closely against this countervailing force. The result has been that, as the Community has moved away from the

---

1 Bourdieu, P. 'Rethinking the State: Genesis and Structure of the Bureaucratic Field' (1994) 12 *Sociological Theory* 1, 7.

certainties of the customs union, the legislation has become every more patchwork and the case law ever less certain.

II. The Customs Union

i. The Prohibition on Customs Duties and Charges Having Equivalent Effect (CEE)

One of the legal foundations of the Community is the customs union. Article 9(1) [*23(1)*] EC states:

> The Community shall be based upon a customs union which shall cover all trade in goods and which shall involve the prohibition between Member States of customs duties on imports and exports and of all charges having equivalent effect, and the adoption of a common customs tariff in their relations with third countries.

The customs union is one of the success stories of the European Community. It was due, initially, to be in place by 1 January 1970.[2] The Council adopted a decision, however, bringing forward the date to 1 July 1968.[3] The consequences of the entry into force of the customs union were twofold. The first was the establishment of the common external tariff, setting up a common regime on customs duties for goods from third States entering the Community.[4] The other was that customs duties and charges having equivalent effect on both imports[5] and exports[6] were to be abolished by that date. Movement of goods within the customs union was to be regulated by Article 12 [*24*] EC from that date onwards.

---

2 Article 7(1) EC [*repealed*].
3 Decision 66/532 EEC, OJ 1966, 2971.
4 Regulation 950/68 EEC, OJ 1968 L 172/1.
5 Article 13 EC [*repealed*].
6 Article 16 EC [*repealed*].

Article 12 [*24*] EC. Member States shall refrain from introducing between themselves any new customs duties on imports or exports or any charges having equivalent effect...

The provision is directly effective.[7] The corollary of this is that Member States are under a duty to repay any taxes levied in breach of this Article unless they can prove that the trader has passed on the tax to the customer. Even where the trader has been able to pass the tax on to the customer, damages may still be claimed if the trader can show that the resulting increase in price led to a reduction in sales.[8]

The provision applies not just to goods produced within the Community but to all goods from third States which have entered the Community,[9] provided that they have complied with any administrative frontiers and any customs duties or CEE have been paid.[10] The purpose of the provision is to eliminate customs frontiers within the Community.[11] These include not merely frontiers between Member States but also fiscal frontiers to free movement of goods within Member States.

---

7 Case 26/62 *Van Gend en Loos v Nederlandse Administratie der Belastingen* [1963] ECR 1, [1963] CMLR 105.

8 It is for the national court to determine to what extent a tax may have been passed onto customers and whether this resulted in a reduction in sales, Joined Cases C-192/95-C-218/95 *Société Comateb et al. v Directeur Général des Douanes* [1997] ECR I-165.

9 Article 9(2) [*23(2)*] EC. Third country goods in free circulation also benefit from the protection of Article 95 [*90*] EC, Case 193/85 *Cooperative Cofrutta v Amministrazione delle Finanze dello Stato* [1987] ECR 2085.

10 Article 10(1) [*24(1)*] EC.

11 The provision therefore applies equally to customs duties and CEEs levied both upon imports and upon exports. See most recently Case C-426/92 *Federal Republic of Germany v Deutsches Milch-Kontor GmbH* [1994] ECR I-2757, [1996] 1 CMLR 415; Case C-130/93 *Lamaire NV v Nationale Dienst voor Afzet van Land* [1994] ECR I-3215, [1995] 3 CMLR 534.

Joined Cases C-363/93 & C-407-11/93 Lancry SA v Direction Générale des Douanes [1994] ECR I-3957, [1994] 1 CMLR 473

By virtue of Article 227(2) [*299(2)*] EC the free movement of goods provisions apply to the French overseas territories. These territories had in place a system of 'dock dues' which were levied on all goods entering them. Lancry marketed flour in Martinique which was imported from mainland France, on which he had to pay a tax of 20%. The question was referred whether a tax of this kind, which applied not to movement between Member States but to movement within a Member State was caught by the customs union provisions.

25. ... the Court has consistently held that the justification for the prohibition of customs duties and charges having equivalent effect is based on the fact that any pecuniary charges imposed on goods by reason of the fact that they cross a frontier constitutes an obstacle to the movement of such goods (see, in particular, the judgment in Joined Cases 2/69 & 3/69 *Diamantarbeiders v Brachfeld* [1969] ECR 211, point 14).

26. In the *Legros* judgment, (Case C-163/90 *Administration des Douanes et Droits Indirects v Legros* [1992] ECR I-4625) the Court noted (at paragraph 16) that a charge levied at a regional frontier by reason of the fact that goods are brought into one region of a Member State undermines the unity of the Community customs territory and constitutes an obstacle to the free movement of goods at least as serious as a charge levied at a national frontier on products entering a Member State as a whole.

27. The unity of the community customs territory is undermined by the establishment of a regional customs frontier just the same, whether the products on which a charge is levied by reason of the fact that they cross a frontier are domestic products or come from other Member States.

28. Furthermore, the obstacle to the free movement of goods created by the imposition on domestic products of a charge levied by reason of their crossing that frontier is no less serious than that created by the collection of a charge of the same kind on products from another Member State.

29. Since the very principle of a customs union covers all trade in goods, as provided for by Article 9 of the Treaty, it requires the free movement of goods generally, as opposed to inter-State trade alone, to be ensured within the union. Although Article 9 *et seq.* makes express reference only to trade between Member States, that is because it was assumed that there were no charges exhibiting the features of a customs duty in existence within the Member States. Since the absence of such charges is an essential precondition for the attainment of a customs union covering all trade in goods, it follows that they are likewise prohibited by Article 9 *et seq*.

30. Secondly, the situation does not appear to be of a kind where all the components are wholly confined to one Member State. As the French Government has correctly pointed out, the levying of charges exhibiting the features of dock dues could be classified as a purely internal situation only if the dues were levied exclusively on products from the same Member State. It is not disputed that dock dues apply to all products entering the overseas department concerned, irrespective of their origin. It would accordingly be inconsistent to hold, on the one hand, that dock dues constitute charges having equivalent effect in so far as they are levied on goods from other Member States and to concede, on the other, that those dues do not constitute charges having equivalent effect where they are levied on goods from metropolitan France.

Whilst it is relatively easy to identify customs frontiers which took the form of customs duties, the notion of a charge having equivalent effect is more open-ended and has been interpreted widely.

Joined Cases 2 & 3/69 Sociaal Fonds voor de Diamantarbeiders v S A Ch Brachfeld & Sons *et al.* [1969] ECR 211, [1969] CMLR 335

In Belgium traders were required to pay tax of 0.33% on imports of unworked diamonds to the Sociaal Fonds voor de Diamantarbeiders, a social fund set up to offer assistance to those Belgians who had worked in the diamond industry. The Sociaal Fonds brought an action against 200 importers for failure to pay this tax, who, in turn, claimed that the tax breached Article 12 [*25*] EC.

5/6. According to Article 9, the Community shall be based upon a customs union founded upon the prohibition between Member States of customs duties and of 'all charges having equivalent effect', and the adoption of a common customs tariff in their relations with third countries. Article 12 prohibits the introduction of 'new customs duties on imports ... or any charges having equivalent effect'.

7/10. The position of these Articles at the beginning of that part of the Treaty reserved for the 'Foundations of the Community', Article 9 being the first provision appearing at the very beginning of the Title dealing with the 'Free movement of goods' and Article 12 heading the section on the 'elimination of customs duties between Member States', is sufficient to show the fundamental role of the prohibitions laid down therein. The importance of these prohibitions is such that, in order to prevent their circumvention by means of various customs and fiscal measures, the Treaty was intended to prevent any possible failure in their implementation. Article 17 therefore specifies that the prohibitions in Article 9 shall also apply to customs duties of a fiscal nature. Article 95, which appears both in that part of the Treaty which deals with the 'policy of the Community' and in the Chapter on 'Tax Provisions', is intended to fill in any breaches which a fiscal measure might open in the prohibitions laid down, by prohibiting the imposition on imported products of internal taxation in excess of that imposed on domestic products.

11/14. In prohibiting the imposition of customs duties, the Treaty does not distinguish between goods according to whether or not they enter into competition with the products of the importing country. Thus, the purpose of the abolition of customs barriers is not merely to eliminate their protective nature, as the Treaty sought on the contrary to give general scope and effect to the rule on the elimination of customs duties and charges having equivalent effect in order to ensure the free movement of goods. It follows from the system as a whole and from the general and absolute nature of the prohibition of any customs duty applicable to goods moving between Member States that customs duties are prohibited independently of any consideration of the purpose for which they were introduced and the destination of the revenue obtained therefrom. The justification for this prohibition is based on the fact that any pecuniary charge - however small - imposed on goods by reason of the fact that they cross a frontier constitutes an obstacle to the movement of such goods.

15/18. The extension of the prohibition of customs duties to charges having equivalent effect is intended to supplement the prohibition against obstacles to trade created by such duties by increasing its efficiency. The use of these two complementary concepts thus tends, in trade between Member States, to avoid the imposition of any pecuniary charge on goods circulating within the Community by virtue of the fact that they cross a national frontier. Thus, in order to ascribe to a charge an effect equivalent to a customs duty, it is important to consider this effect in the light of the objectives of the Treaty, in the Parts, Titles and Chapters in which Articles 9 and 12 are to be found, particularly in relation to the free movement of goods. Consequently, any pecuniary charge, however small and whatever its designation and mode of application, which is imposed unilaterally on domestic or foreign goods by reason of the fact that they cross a frontier, and which is not a customs duty in the strict sense, constitutes a charge having equivalent effect within the meaning of Articles 9 and 12 of the Treaty, even if it is not imposed for the benefit of the State, is not discriminatory or protective in effect or if the product on which the charge is imposed is not in competition with any domestic product.

The remit of Article 12 [*25*] EC is still limited by its dealing only with border-measures rather than obstacles which flow more generally from a Member State's fiscal regulation of its economy. Within these confines the Court has defined CEEs quite aggressively. As the Court considers the purpose of Article 12 [*25*] EC to be to promote free movement of goods rather than to prohibit protectionism, it is irrelevant whether similar measures are imposed on domestic industry.[12] Similarly, as it is the effects of the tax which are pernicious, it is irrelevant how the tax is characterised. The Court has also held on a number of occasions that Member States cannot rely on Article 36 [*30*] EC to justify a CEE, as the latter can never effectively protect the objectives listed in that provision.[13] Adoption of such an absolutist approach has not been without its problems. For the question arises of who should pay for the various controls on cross-border trade, such as customs controls or health inspections, which are justified in the public interest. In answering this question the Court has relaxed the rigour of Article 12 [*25*] EC in a number of circumstances.

ii. Limits on the Prohibition on CEEs

a. Charges for Services Rendered

A charge levied at the border will not be considered to be a CEE if it is considered to be no more than remuneration for a service provided by the State, which was provided at the request of the trader.

In *Commission v Belgium*[14] the Court considered a system of 'storage charges' levied by the Belgian and Luxembourgeois authorities on imports that were stored at customs warehouses. Imports would be placed in these warehouses in two circumstances. The first was where the trader had not decided what customs procedure to be used - whether the goods were for transit, reexportation, the host State or were temporary imports which were therefore free from internal duties. Goods could be kept in these warehouses for up to 15 days whilst a decision was being made. The second circumstance was that goods

---

[12] Case 87/75 *Bresciani v Amministrazione Italiana delle Finanze* [1976] ECR 129, [1976] 2 CMLR 62.

[13] Case 7/68 *Commission v Italy* [1968] ECR 428, [1969] CMLR 1; Cases 2 & 3/69 *Sociaal Fonds voor de Diamantarbeiders v S A Ch Brachfeld & Sons et al* [1969] ECR 211, [1969] CMLR 335.

[14] Case 132/82 *Commission v Belgium* [1983] ECR 1049, [1983] 3 CMLR 600.

could pass through customs formalities at these warehouses rather than at the border or on the trader's premises.

The Court considered the first set of charges to be lawful, as the goods could only be stored in the warehouse at the request of the trader. A service was therefore clearly rendered to the trader with the charges representing the remuneration. It considered, however, the charges imposed for completing customs formalities at the warehouse to be a CEE and therefore contrary to Article 12 [*25*] EC. It noted that completion of customs formalities was compulsory and was done in the public, and not the trader's, interest. There could be no question of levying charges in such circumstances

The reason for distinguishing between CEE and charges paid by a trader in return for services rendered is quite persuasive. In the latter context the State is shedding its role as administrator and merely acting as a market operator. It should be free to act in the same manner as private operators, and correspondingly be able to charge for its services. An inequality of bargaining power can arise, however, where the State has a monopoly over the provision of important frontier services. In such circumstances, the freedom a trader has to accept a service might be illusory, as the Member State has considerable leverage through its power to admit or refuse goods entry on to its territory. There are two ways in which the trader is protected in this respect. The first relates to the adequacy of the benefit. The benefit provided by the State authorities to the trader must be direct and specific rather than general in nature.[15] The second is that the Court will not infer that a service has been rendered where it considers the service is being done in the public interest rather than in the interest of the trader, and the trader has little genuine choice in the matter.[16]

---

15 Case 24/68 *Commission v Italy* [1969] ECR 193, [1971] CMLR 611; Case 63/74 *Cadsky SpA v Instituto Nazionale per il Commercio Estero* [1975] ECR 281, [1975] 2 CMLR 246.

16 This has been reiterated in a whole series of cases. Case 87/75 *Bresciani v Amministrazione Italiana delle Finanze* [1976] ECR 129, [1976] 2 CMLR 62; Case 132/82 *Commission v Belgium* [1983] ECR 1049, [1983] 3 CMLR 600; Case 314/82 *Commission v Belgium* [1984] ECR 1543, [1985] 3 CMLR 134; Case 340/87 *Commission v Italy* [1989] ECR 1483, [1991] 1 CMLR 437; Case C-119/92 *Commission v Italy* [1994] ECR I-393, [1994] 3 CMLR 774.

b. Charges Levied for Tasks Carried Out Pursuant to Community Law

The second set of circumstances where a Court will not infer a CEE is where a Member State is required to carry out some task either by Community law[17] or by international law[18]. It is allowed to charge traders for the execution of this task.[19]

Case 46/76 Bauhuis v Netherlands [1977] ECR 5

Under Directive 64/432/EEC Member States were under a duty to inspect cattle and pigs destined for export in order to check that they carried no contagious diseases. The Netherlands levied a fee for these inspections. Bauhuis, a Dutch cattle dealer, brought an action for the restitution of the fees that he had paid, claiming that the levy breached Article 12 [*25*] EC.

27. ... This organization by the exporting State has been made obligatory in the Directive so that inspections at the frontier organized unilaterally by the importing Member State become unnecessary or are at least reduced to an occasional check that the veterinary and public health measures which are required to be taken in the exporting Member State have been complied with.

28. These measures are laid down unilaterally by each Member State but have been made obligatory and uniform in the case of all the products in question whichever the exporting Member State or the Member State of destination may be.

29. On the other hand they are not prescribed by each Member State in order to protect some interest of its own but by the Council in the general interest of the Community.

---

17 See also Case 1/83 *IFG v Freistaat Bayern* [1984] ECR 349, [1985] 1 CMLR 453; Case 18/87 *Commission v Germany* [1988] ECR 5427, [1990] 1 CMLR 561.

18 Case 89/76 *Commission v Netherlands* [1977] ECR 1355, [1978] 3 CMLR 630.

19 See Barents, R. 'Charges of Equivalent Effect to Customs Duties' (1978) 15 *CMLRev* 415.

30. They cannot therefore be regarded as unilateral measures which hinder trade but rather as operations intended to promote the free movement of goods, in particular by rendering ineffective the obstacles to this free movement which might be created by the measures for veterinary and public health inspections adopted pursuant to Article 36.

31. In these circumstances fees charged for veterinary and public health inspections, which are prescribed by a Community provision, which are uniform and are required to be carried out before despatch within the exporting country do not constitute charges having an effect equivalent to customs duties on exports, provided that they do not exceed the actual cost of the inspection for which they were charged.

32. The reasons for the prohibition of any obstacle to intra-Community trade, whether such obstacle takes the form of charges having an effect equivalent to customs duties or of measures having an effect equivalent to quantitative restrictions, do not apply to this case.

33. Moreover, as far as the question whether it is lawful to demand a fee is concerned, a distinction must be made between the inspections prescribed by the Directive and those occasional inspections which, according to its provisions, only Member States are permitted to carry out at the frontier, because the former are obligatory and of general application so that they affect all the goods concerned, whereas the fees charged for the latter, which are only carried out in a random manner, are only borne by the goods which are inspected.

34. It is a question moreover of the compensation, justified on economic and financial grounds, for an obligation imposed by Community law on all the Member States equally.

The judgment only applies to those tasks required by EC law and not to those tasks permitted or authorised by EC law. The Court was, moreover, no doubt influenced by the fact that many Member States require traders to bear the costs of veterinary inspections of livestock destined for the home market. To have exempted livestock for export would have smacked of forcing States to pick up some of the traders' production costs.

There must, however, be grave reservations about the reasoning of the judgment. Whilst the judgment relies upon the Directive's facilitating free movement of livestock as a justification for national imposition of charges, the Directive is silent about the levying of charges. These do nothing to facilitate free movement at all. Indeed in

Ramel[20] the Court struck down a Community provision which authorised France to levy a charge on Italian wine on the grounds that it infringed the principle of free movement of goods. The Directive could not therefore lawfully have authorised Member States to levy inspection fees.

Elsewhere the Court has stated that Member States must normally bear the costs of tasks carried out in the public interest.[21] There is good reason for this statement. Free movement of goods is considered to be a fundamental right. Yet the fundamentality of that right is undermined, if its exercise is contingent upon payment of a sum of money.

c. All Levies Must Be Commensurate

Charged levied either for services rendered or pursuant to tasks required by either Community or international law will only be lawful if they are proportionate. For this to be the case there must be a direct link between the cost of the operation performed and the fee charged.[22]

Case C-209/89 Commission v Italy [1991] ECR-I 1575, [1993] 1 CMLR 155.

In Italy firms were required to pay a system of charges where customs formalities were completed outside normal customs office hours or if they were completed outside the customs area. The fees were charged at an hourly rate but the Commission alleged they were disproportionate for two reasons. First, in calculating the amount, any fraction of an hour incurred was rounded up to the full hour. Secondly, where customs formalities were carried out simultaneously on batches belonging to several undertakings, each undertaking was required to pay the full amount, irrespective of the fact that other batches had also been done

---

20 Joined Cases 80 & 81/77 *Ramel v Receveur des Douanes* [1978] ECR 927.

21 e.g. Case 314/82 *Commission v Belgium* [1984] ECR 1543, [1985] 3 CMLR 134.

22 See also Case C-16/94 *Dubois et fils et al. v Garanor Exploitation SA* [1995] ECR I-2421.

during that time. The one exception to this was where a single batch belonging to several undertakings was examined. In such circumstances each undertaking was only responsible for a proportionate fraction of the fee. In its defence the Italian Government noted that the fees levied only covered a third of the cost of running the service.

10. ... In its judgment in Case C-111/89 *Bakker Hillegom* [1990] ECR I-1735, at paragraph 12, the Court pointed out that the condition [that the amount charged does not exceed the cost of the operations] was satisfied only where there was a direct link between the amount of the fee and the cost of the actual inspection in respect of which the fee was charged. The Court added (in the same judgment, at paragraph 13) that such a link was present where the amount of the fee was calculated on the basis of the duration of the inspection, the number of persons required, the cost of materials, overheads or any other similar factors.

11. Furthermore, in its aforesaid judgment in *Bakker*, at paragraph 13, the Court stated that the details it had given as to the factors which may be taken into account in calculating the amount of the fee did not preclude a fixed-rate assessment of inspection costs, such as, for example, a fixed hourly rate.

12. So far as concerns the contested Italian rules, it should be noted at once that it is common ground that in the circumstances a service is rendered to undertakings, and secondly that, having regard to the above mentioned case-law, the principle of a fixed-rate assessment of the charge cannot be called in question.

13. As regards the Italian authorities' method of calculating the rate, however, it should be noted that the rules at issue, which impose on each undertaking individually, where services are rendered simultaneously to several traders, the whole of the fixed-rate charge corresponding to an hour's work, even where the inspection takes considerably less time, are liable to entail, in certain circumstances, payment of an amount in excess of the actual cost of the operation in question, as that concept has been defined by the Court in the aforesaid case-law. The method of calculation applied in Italy may lead, for example, to five traders each being required to pay the charge per hour for a total of thirty minutes' work.

14. It follows therefore from the figures which the Italian Government has itself put forward in relation to the hourly rate and the cost of inspection that, in certain cases, the total payment demanded from the undertakings concerned may exceed, at times by a considerable amount, the total cost which, according to the Italian Government, the service provided entails for the State's finances.

15. Even on the assumption that the Italian Government is correct in stating that the hourly rate charged represents on average only one third of the cost of the service provided, the amount of the charges payable by traders exceeds, as the Advocate General has pointed out in paragraph 14 of his Opinion, the cost of the inspection in all cases in which the service is rendered simultaneously to more than three undertakings.

16. In those circumstances, the Italian rules at issue lead, in certain cases, to the imposition of an amount disproportionate to the service rendered to traders, in that it entails the levying of as many charges as there are undertakings involved and the charge payable by them exceeds, therefore, the actual cost of the inspections.

17. As for the argument put forward by the Italian Government that it would be impracticable to divide the charge payable in proportion to the time employed in carrying out an operation for the benefit of several undertakings, and impossible to demand payment of that charge from a single undertaking, it is sufficient to recall that, as the Court has consistently held, a Member State may not plead difficulties of a practical nature in order to justify a failure to comply with the obligations laid down by Community law.

III. Article 95 [*90*] EC and Indirect Taxation

i. Introduction

Indirect taxation is taxation which can be shifted by the taxpayer onto someone else.[23] Thus taxes which are personal in nature, such as taxes on individuals or corporations, are considered to be direct taxation, whilst taxes on goods are considered normally to be indirect taxation, as the good can always be transferred to someone else. Article 95 [*90*] EC seeks to ensure that indirect taxes are not used to place imports at a competitive disadvantage to domestic products.

> '[The aim of Article 95 EC] is to ensure free movement of goods between the Member States in normal conditions of competition by the elimination of all forms of protection which result from the application of internal taxation which discriminates against products from other Member States. As the Commission has correctly stated, Article 95 must guarantee the complete neutrality of internal taxation as regards competition between domestic products and imported products.'[24]

---

23 Farmer, P. & Lyal, R. *EC Tax Law* (1994, Clarendon, Oxford) 3.

24 Case 168/78 *Commission v France* [1980] ECR 347, [1981] 2 CMLR 631.

The requirement of fiscal neutrality has had to be balanced against the autonomy Member States are recognised to have in this field.

> '... It must be emphasized in this regard that Article 95 of the Treaty does not provide a basis for censuring the excessiveness of the level of taxation which the Member States might adopt for particular products in the light of considerations of social policy... As Community law stands at present, the Member States are at liberty to subject products such as cars to a system of tax which increases progressively in amount according to an objective criterion, such as cylinder capacity, provided that the system of taxation is free from any discriminatory or protective effect.'[25]

These tensions are difficult to reconcile. For it is impossible to insist on fiscal neutrality without compromising fiscal autonomy, and vice versa.

Easson, A. 'Fiscal Discrimination: New Perspectives on Article 95 of the EEC Treaty' (1981) 18 *Common Market Law Review* 521

Tax rules are by their very nature discriminatory. To tax one product and to exempt another, or to tax the one more heavily than the other, is to discriminate between them. To tax a class of products according to one criterion - for example, volume - produces one result, to tax those products according to some other criterion - for example, value - produces another. The former system may be said to discriminate in favour of those products whose value is high in proportion to volume, the latter system discriminates against those same products. There is no such thing as a truly 'neutral' tax system. Fiscal policy is thus a matter of choices - which types of discrimination best accord with economic and social needs?

---

25 Case C-132/88 *Commission v Greece* [1990] ECR I-1567, [1991] 3 CMLR 1. See also Case 112/84 *Humblot v Directeur des Services Fiscaux* [1985] ECR 1367, [1986] 2 CMLR 338; Case 200/85 *Commission v Italy* [1986] ECR 3953, [1988] 1 CMLR 97.

ii. The Reach of Article 95 [*90*] EC

Article 95 [*90*] EC applies only to taxes on goods and on their use. The most clear-cut example of this in the case law involves its sister provision, Article 96 [*91*] EC. This allows Member States to repay any internal taxation on goods which are exported from that Member State. In *Commission v Italy*[26] the Court agreed with the Commission that Italy was not permitted to repay stamp duties, mortgage duties and taxes on licences and concessions imposed on Italian exporters of motor cars, as these were taxes imposed upon the producer rather than upon particular products. The distinction between taxes on producers and taxes on products has been blurred, however, by the Court ruling that any tax which has an immediate effect upon the cost of a product falls within the remit of Article 95 [*90*] EC. A German road haulage tax was therefore found to fall within Article 95 [*90*] EC.[27] Clearly all taxes insofar as they affect production costs affect the price product. The key element would appear to be the *proximity* of the relationship between the tax and the price of the product - a matter which has been left completely opaque in the case law.

The second feature of Article 95 [*90*] EC is that although, on its face, it only applies to imports, it has been extended to apply equally to exports. In *Larsen*[28] Denmark imposed a charge on all precious metals to cover the costs of supervising the quality of metals on the Danish market. Larsen, an exporter of gold, claimed that payment of this charge discriminated against him for, as his goods were intended for export, he did not derive any benefit from the supervision. The Court stated that as the aim of Article 95 [*90*] EC was to ensure that internal taxation was neutral as between products, it should apply equally to exports. In this case, however, it considered there to be no discrimination as the charge was applied equally on goods intended for the domestic market.

---

26 Case 45/64 *Commission v Italy* [1965] ECR 857, [1966] CMLR 97.

27 Case 20/76 *Schöttle v Finanzamt Freudenstadt* [1977] ECR 247, [1977] 2 CMLR 98.

28 Case 142/77 *Statens Kontrol v Larsen* [1978] ECR 1543, [1979] 2 CMLR 680.

Article 95 [*90*] EC does not extend, by contrast, to prohibit taxes which place domestic products at a competitive disadvantage to imports. In *Peureux*[29] France exempted certain imported ethyl from a tax imposed on domestic production. The Court held that Article 95 [*90*] EC is insufficiently broad to prevent a Member State imposing taxes upon its domestic production in excess of those imposed upon imports. This was a standard application of the principle of reverse discrimination, namely that a Member State is free to allow imports to enjoy a privileged position vis-à-vis domestic products.

The most difficult problem concerning the remit of Article 95[*90*] EC is its relationship with Article 12 [*25*] EC. The two provisions are mutually exclusive.

> '**12/13.**.... One and the same scheme of taxation cannot, under the system of the Treaty, belong simultaneously to both the categories mentioned, having regard to the fact that the charges referred to in Article 13(2) must be purely and simply abolished whilst, for the purpose of applying internal taxation, Article 95 provides solely for the elimination of any form of discrimination, direct or indirect, in the treatment of the domestic products of the Member States and of products originating in other Member States.'[30]

Article 95 [*90*] EC has been characterised as applying to those systems of taxation which 'constitute internal dues applied systematically and in accordance with the same criteria to domestic products',[31] whilst Article 12 [*25*] EC covers those taxes which only apply by reason of a good crossing a frontier. In reality, this dichotomy between frontier taxes and internal taxes has proved to be just a little too neat, and the Court has had to elaborate upon the distinction in a number of circumstances.

The first is that of the 'exotic import', a good which is not produced domestically but is only imported. These goods may have to pay a variety of consumption or value added taxes upon entry into a

---

29 Case 86/78 *Peureux v Directeur des Services Fiscaux de la Haute-Saône* [1979] ECR 897, [1980] 3 CMLR 337.

30 Case 94/74 *IGAV v ENCC* [1975] ECR 699, [1976] 2 CMLR 37.

31 See Case C-345/93 *Fazenda Publica v Tadeu* [1995] ECR I-479, [1996] 2 CMLR 45.

Member State. As no equivalent domestic production exists, it would appear to be impossible to claim that the tax formed part of an internal system of taxation which applied both to imports and domestic products. Yet if this were to be so, 'exotic imports' would enjoy a privileged status as Member States would be effectively precluded from imposing any form of indirect taxation upon them.

The matter first came up for consideration in *Cofrutta.*[32] The Italian Government levied a consumer tax upon bananas. Banana production in Italy was minimal, accounting in 1985 for 120 tonnes out a total 375,500 tonnes consumed. Cofrutta, an Italian cooperative, had to pay this tax on a batch of Colombian bananas which had been imported via the BENELUX. It claimed the tax was a disguised CEE. The tax, however, formed part of a fiscal regime which consisted of 19 such taxes, some of which were levied upon 'exotic products' such as coffee and cocoa, the rest of which were not. The Court stated that the absence of domestic production did not result, in itself, in a tax applied on imports being a CEE. The crucial determinant was whether the tax formed part of a general system of internal dues. This would be the case, as it was here, if the tax formed part of a common fiscal regime which levied charges on categories of products irrespective of their origin.

For a tax regime to be considered to be based on objective criteria it will need to be shown that it applies to a sufficient range of products. In *Commission v Denmark*,[33] therefore, the Court considered that levies for health inspections on groundnuts and Brazil nuts did not fall within Article 95 [*90*] EC, as it applied to insufficient products for it to be said that the tax had been determined according to general and objective criteria.

Conversely, there are circumstances where taxes levied both on imports and domestic products may still fall under Article 12 [*25*] EC.

The first example of this is where the manner in which the domestic tax is levied is so discriminatory that the tax on imports and the tax on domestic products are not considered to form part of the same

---

32 Case 193/85 *Cooperativa Co-frutta v Amministrazione delle Finanze dello Stato* [1987] ECR 2085.

33 Case 158/82 *Commission v Denmark* [1983] ECR 3573, [1984] 2 CMLR 658.

system. In *Commission v Belgium*[34] the Court considered a system of charges which were levied for health inspections on rabbits, poultry and game. The same basic law provided the legal basis both for the charges imposed upon domestic products and those imposed upon imports. The Court considered, however, that there were two features which prevented the levies on imports being considered to be part of the same system of taxation as the levies upon domestic products. The first was that whilst the levies on domestic products were paid directly to the relevant veterinary organisations, the levies on imports went straight into the State Budget and therefore only indirectly covered the costs of the inspections. Secondly, the criteria used to assess the amount of tax paid were different. In the case of domestic products it was a fixed sum according to the animal inspected. For imports the sum was calculated on the basis of the weight of the animal.[35]

The other circumstance where a tax on both imports and domestic products will be considered to be a CEE is where even if the tax is levied upon both at the same rate, the proceeds of the tax are used to benefit domestic production exclusively. The presumption behind the above analysis is that the use of the proceeds to benefit domestic products has resulted in their effectively not being taxed. The Court has stated that such a tax will be a CEE in only two circumstances. The first is where domestic production is reimbursed the full amount.[36] The second is where domestic producers are not reimbursed the full amount directly but the advantages flowing to them from the proceeds of the tax offset the burden borne by the domestic product. If the proceeds only partly offset the fiscal burden, the matter falls under Article 95 [*90*] EC.[37] If, on the other hand, they fully offset the fiscal burden imposed

---

34 Case 314/82 *Commission v Belgium* [1984] ECR 1543, [1985] 3 CMLR 134.

35 Similar imports and domestic products being placed in different fiscal categories will normally result in the tax being classed as a CEE. Case C-45/94 *Camera de Comercio, Industria y Navigacion, Ceuta v Municipality of Ceuta* [1995] ECR I-4385.

36 Joined Cases C-149-150/91 *Sanders Addour SNC v Directeur des Services Fiscaux des Pyrenées Atlantiques* [1992] ECR I-3899.

37 See Joined Cases C-78-83/90 *Compagnie Commerciale de l'Ouest v Receveur Principal des douanes de la Pallice Port* [1992] ECR I-1847, [1994] 2 CMLR 425; Case C-17/91 *Lornoy en Zonen* [1992] ECR I-6523; Case C-114/91 *Criminal Proceedings v Claeys* [1992] ECR I-6559; Joined Cases C-144 & C-

upon domestic products or provide a benefit to domestic producers which is financially equivalent, they fall within Article 12[*25*] EC. The distinction has implications for the amount of tax that the authorities will have to repay. If the measure falls within Article 12[*25*] EC, the tax is illegal, *per se*, and, in principle, the full amount must be repaid. If it falls within Article 95[*90*] EC, the tax is not itself illegal, but must be simply reduced proportionately to eliminate the discrimination.[38]

iii. Article 95(1) [*90(1)*] EC: Imports Must Not be Levied Taxes in Excess of Those Imposed upon Similar Domestic Products

Article 95 [*90*] EC is divided into two paragraphs. The first paragraph, Article 95(1) [*90(1)*] EC, states:

> No Member State shall impose, direct or indirectly, on the products of other Member States any internal taxation of any kind in excess that imposed directly or indirectly on similar domestic products.[39]

Article 95(1) [*90(1)*] EC's remit is limited by the comparator for imports being that of *similar* domestic products.

Case 243/84 John Walker v Minister for Skatter [1986] ECR 875, [1987] 2 CMLR 278

Denmark levied duties upon fruit wine with an alcohol content of less than 20% on the basis of volume. Fruit wine with a higher alcoholic content, grape wines with an alcoholic content of more than 23% and grain-based spirits were taxed according to the alcoholic content of the drink. John Walker imported scotch whisky, which had an alcoholic content of 40%. John Walker claimed that fruit

---

145/91 *Demoor en Zonen v Belgian State* [1992] ECR I-6613; Case C-266/91 *Cellulose Beira Industrial SA (CELBI) v Fazenda Publica* [1993] ECR I-4337.

38 Case C-347/95 *Fazenda Pública v UCAL*, Judgment of 17 September 1997.

39 Article 95(1) [*90(1)*] EC is directly effective. Case 57/65 *Lütticke v Hauptzollamt Saarlouis* [1966] ECR 205.

wine and whisky were similar drinks. Denmark was therefore in breach of Article 95(1) [*90(1)*] EC, as on a volume basis, because of their respective alcoholic contents, the fiscal burden was greater for whisky than for fruit wine.

11. In order to determine whether products are similar within the terms of the prohibition laid down in the first paragraph of Article 95 it is necessary to consider, as the Court stated in its judgment of 17 February 1976 in Case 45/75 *Rewe v Hauptzollamt Landau* [1976] ECR 181, whether they have similar characteristics and meet the same needs from the point of view of consumers. The Court endorsed a broad interpretation of the concept of similarity in its judgments of 27 February 1980 in Case 168/78 *Commission v France* [1980] ECR 347 and 15 July 1982 in Case 216/81 *Cogis v Amministrazione delle Finanze dello Stato* [1982] ECR 2701 and assessed the similarity of the products not according to whether they were strictly identical, but according to whether their use was similar and comparable. Consequently, in order to determine whether products are similar it is necessary first to consider certain objective characteristics of both categories of beverages, such as their origin, the method of manufacture and their organoleptic properties, in particular taste and alcohol content, and secondly to consider whether or not both categories of beverages are capable of meeting the same needs from the point of view of consumers.

12. It should be noted that the two categories of beverages exhibit manifestly different characteristics. Fruit wine of the liqueur type is a fruit-based product obtained by natural fermentation, whereas scotch whisky is a cereal-based product obtained by distillation. The organoleptic properties of the two products are also different. As the Court held in *Rewe supra*, the fact that the same raw material, for example alcohol, is to be found in the two products is not sufficient reason to apply the prohibition contained in the first paragraph of Article 95. For the products to be regarded as similar that raw material must also be present in more or less equal proportions in both products. In that regard, it must be pointed out that the alcoholic strength of scotch whisky is 40% by volume, whereas the alcoholic strength of fruit wine of the liqueur type, to which the Danish tax legislation applies, does not exceed 20% by volume.

13. The contention that scotch whisky may be consumed in the same way as fruit wine of the liqueur type, as an aperitif diluted with water or with fruit juice, even if it were established, would not be sufficient to render scotch whisky similar to fruit wine of the liqueur type, whose intrinsic characteristics are fundamentally different.

The requirement that a domestic good be similar to a domestic product, both from the viewpoint of consumer demand (the 'subjective' part of the test) and in terms of their characteristics and methods of manufacture (the 'objective' part of the test), is very restrictive. There is good reason for such a narrow interpretation. By restricting a Member

State from taxing *any* import in excess of a similar *domestic* good, Article 95(1) [*90(1)*]EC places considerable constraints on a Member State's power to tax. In *Bobie*,[40] in order to aid small brewers, Germany taxed German beer at a varying rate according to the output of the brewery. As this was impracticable in the case of imported beer, a standard rate was imposed which was equivalent to the average rate imposed on German beer. The system placed imported beer at a competitive advantage vis-à-vis the large domestic brewers but at a disadvantage vis-à-vis the small brewers. The Court held that a fiscal system, breached Article 95(1) [*90(1)*] EC, if imports were taxed more highly, albeit only in certain cases, more heavily than any domestic product. If an importer can find one similar domestic product which has a lower tax burden, the importer will therefore be able to claim a breach of Article 95(1) [*90(1)*] EC.

The rigour of the provision is further increased by the Court's insistence that attention must be focused upon the effect of the tax on imports and domestic products. Thus, in *Dansk Denkavit*[41] it stated:

> '... with a view to ensuring the correct application of that provision [Article 95(1) EC], a comparison must be made of the tax burden imposed on those products, by taking into consideration, at each stage of production or marketing, the rate of the tax, its basis of assessment and the detailed rules for its collection.'

The most wideranging example of the Court's attempts to ensure that imports are not taxed in excess of similar domestic products is *Schul*.

Case 15/81 Schul [1982] ECR 1409, [1982] 3 CMLR 229

Schul, a Dutch company, imported a second-hand boat into the Netherlands from France on behalf of a Dutch individual. The Dutch authorities duly claimed a turnover tax of 18% of the value of the boat. Schul objected on the grounds that the boat had already been subject to turnover tax in France for which no

---

40 Case 127/75 *Bobie* [1976] ECR 1079.

41 Case 42/83 *Dansk Denkavit v Ministeriet for Skatter* [1984] ECR 2649.

remission had been possible. The Dutch authorities requiring a turnover tax, it alleged, thus amounted to a form of double taxation which discriminated against imports.

31. It may be observed that at the present stage of Community law the Member States are free, by virtue of Article 95, to charge the same amount on the importation of products as the value-added tax which they charge on similar domestic products. Nevertheless, this compensation is justified only in so far as the imported products are not already burdened with value-added tax in the Member State of exportation since otherwise the tax on importation would in fact be an additional charge burdening imported products more heavily than similar domestic products.

32. That view derives in the first place from the terms of Article 95 of the Treaty which prohibits not only the direct but also the indirect imposition of internal taxation on products from other Member States in excess of that on similar domestic products. That prohibition would not be complied with if imported products could be subject to the value-added tax applicable to similar domestic products without account being taken of the proportion of value-added tax with which those products are still burdened at the time of their importation.

33. Such an interpretation accords with the need to take account of the objectives of the Treaty which are laid down in Articles 2 and 3 among which appears, in the first place, the establishment of a common market. The concept of a common market as defined by the Court in a consistent line of decisions involves the elimination of all obstacles to intra-Community trade in order to merge the national markets into a single market bringing about conditions as close as possible to those of a genuine internal market. It is important that not only commerce as such but also private persons who happen to be conducting an economic transaction across national frontiers should be able to enjoy the benefits of that market.

34. Consequently, it is necessary also to take into account the value-added tax levied in the Member State of exportation for the purpose of determining the compatibility with the requirements of Article 95 of a charge to value-added tax on products from another Member State supplied by private persons where the supply of similar products within the territory of the Member State of importation is not so liable. Accordingly, in so far as such an imported product supplied by a private person may not lawfully benefit from a remission of tax on exportation and so remains burdened upon importation with part of the value-added tax paid in the Member State of exportation the amount of value-added tax payable on importation must be reduced by the residual part of the value-added tax of the Member State of exportation which is still contained in the value of the product when it is imported. The amount of this reduction may not, however, be greater than the amount of value-added tax actually paid in the Member State of exportation.

35. The Member States which have taken part in these proceedings have objected to this interpretation on the ground that the value-added tax paid in the Member State of exportation is difficult to check since both the rate of the tax and its basis of assessment may have varied in the course of time.

36. In that regard it should be pointed out that it is for the person who seeks exemption from or a reduction in the value-added tax normally levied on importation to establish that he satisfies the conditions for such exemption or reduction. Accordingly it is open to the Member State of importation to require such an importer to provide the necessary documentary proof that the value-added tax was levied in the Member State of exportation and still burdens the product on importation.

37. Further, the Member States maintained that the establishment of a system ensuring the complete neutrality of internal taxation with regard to intra-Community trade could take place only by strict application of the principle of taxation in the Member State of destination and that would mean full remission of tax on all products at the time of exportation. It is for the political institutions of the Community to adopt such a solution since it involves a political choice.

38. Nevertheless although the establishment of a system of complete neutrality in the field of competition involving full remission of tax on exportation is indeed a matter for the Community legislature, so long as such a system is not established Article 95 of the Treaty prevents an importing Member State from applying its system of value-added tax to imported products in a manner contrary to the principles embodied in that Article.

39. Finally, it is also necessary to dismiss the objections based on possible difficulties of a technical and administrative nature which may result from taking into account the value-added tax of the Member State of exportation and those based on the need to prevent fraudulent circumventions and distortions in competition within the Community. The first category of objections must be dismissed since it is for the individual who seeks to claim the benefit of exemption from or reduction in value-added tax on importation to provide proof that the conditions are satisfied. The second category of objections is irrelevant since the levying of the differential amount of value-added tax removes any incentive to deflect trade.

An importing Member State is thus required to deduct the residual amount of VAT of the exporting Member State still present in the value of the good from the amount of tax it charges. At the time this judgment appeared to have little relevance, as many exporters reclaimed tax from the exporting State upon exporting the good. Very rarely was there therefore any residual tax left in a good by the time it entered the importing State. Conceptually, however, the judgment was quite radical.[42]

Barents, R. 'Recent Case Law on the Prohibition of Fiscal Discrimination under Article 95' (1986) 23 *Common Market Law Review* 641, 656-657

... To apply this provision [Article 95 EC] to the problem of double taxation, which in legal terms means the result of a disparity between differing national tax legislation, required that this provision had to be interpreted as a prohibition of material discrimination. Interpreted in the 'classical' manner as a prohibition of formal discrimination Article 95 would be useless. To take the example of the Schul case, from the point of view of the Dutch tax authorities it could be said that the imported second hand boat had been treated in the same manner as a nationally sold second hand boat, as the final result in both cases was that the consumer paid Dutch VAT, be it at a different stage. Accordingly, seen from the point of view of the importing Member State both cases were treated equally and no discrimination was present ... However, if account is taken of the fact that the imported boat had already been subjected to VAT in the exporting Member State, both cases can no longer be considered as equal, with the result that equal treatment by the importing Member State constitutes material discrimination, which can only be eliminated by deduction of the residual part of the VAT actually paid in the exporting Member State. Although the text of Article 95 does not prevent such an interpretation, it must nevertheless be realized that, as a result of this interpretation, this provision is now also applicable to disparities between national tax legislations, a domain in which Article 95 was not intended to be used.

The second observation is of a more hypothetical nature. One may interpret the *Schul* doctrine as relating only to a specific VAT problem, not yet solved by the Community legislator. It is however also possible to interpret this doctrine as an expression of the principle that once a product has been subjected to VAT, it enters - from a fiscal point of view - unrestricted circulation in the common market. This would imply that, once the harmonization of taxes is complete, the common market should embody a prohibition of double taxation. An indication in this sense is given by the definition the Court gave in the *Schul I* case of the concept of a common market.

The full implications of the judgment cannot be understood without a description of the *origin principle* and the *destination principle*. The former requires that tax on a good be paid in the State of production. The latter reflects international practice by requiring tax to be paid in the State of consumption. *Schul* suggests that in a single

---

42 See Case 47/84 *Schul* [1985] ECR 1491, [1986] 1 CMLR 559 for a more detailed description of how these calculations are made.

market, the appropriate place for taxation is in the State of 'origin' rather than in the State of destination. For it required the Dutch authorities to take cognizance of the French taxation. It therefore implied that whilst it will not review the actions of the country of origin, it will require the State of destination, that of importation, to take account of the actions of the State of origin and adjust its tax accordingly.

This duty of recognition has considerable implications for the harmonisation process. It means that if bases and rates of indirect taxes are harmonised, there will be free movement of goods. As a State has to give credit for any residual tax on an import, the effect of harmonisation will be that the amount of residual tax for which it will have to give credit will be identical to the amount of tax it would otherwise have levied, if the rates of taxation in all Member States are identical,. There will thus be no reason for a State to levy taxes on imports, as the amount it can raise will be zero. The product need only therefore be taxed once, in the country of origin. Once that happens, it has the right from a fiscal point of view to unrestricted circulation in the single market, and not to be subjected to taxation again.

iv. Article 95(2) [*90(2)*] EC: Internal Taxation Must Not Protect Domestic Production from Competing Imports

The remit of Article 95(2) [*90(2)*] EC is wider than that of Article 95 [*90(1)*] EC. It states:

> Furthermore, no Member State shall impose on the products of other Member States any internal taxation of such a nature as to afford indirect protection to other products.[43]

Protection has been extended to all imports which are *competing* against domestic products. The obligation contained in Article 95(2) [*90(2)*] EC is less constraining than in Article 95(1) [*90(1)*] EC in that

---

43 The provision is directly effective, Case 27/67 *Firma Finkfrucht v München-Landsbergerstrasse* [1968] ECR 223, [1968] CMLR 228.

it merely requires that the taxation imposed upon imports does not protect domestic products.

Case 168/78 Commission v France [1980] ECR 347, [1981] 2 CMLR 631

France subjected all spirits to a 'purchase tax' which was calculated on the alcoholic content in the drink. In addition, all spirits were also subjected to a 'manufacturing tax'. This was also assessed on the basis of alcoholic content, but the rates varied. For genevas and other cereal-based spirits the rate charged was FF 2,110 per hectolitre of alcohol. For wine-based and fruit-based spirits, such as vermouth or brandy, the rate was lower, being FF 710 per hectolitre of alcohol. The Commission brought an Article 169 [*226*] EC action claiming that the 'manufacturing tax' violated Article 95 [*90*] EC. The French Government claimed that the two types of spirits were not competing. In particular, it noted that they appeared, for customs purposes, in different tax headings; cereals-based spirits tasted very different from other spirits, and that fruit-based and wine-based spirits were often drunk as an aperitif, whilst cereal-based ones were not.

39. ... The Court deems it unnecessary for the purposes of solving this dispute to give a ruling on the question whether or not the spirituous beverages concerned are wholly or partly similar products within the meaning of the first paragraph of Article 95 when it is impossible reasonably to contest that without exception they are in at least partial competition with the domestic products to which the application refers and that it is impossible to deny the protective nature of the French tax system within the second paragraph of Article 95.

40. In fact, as indicated above, spirits obtained from cereals, including genevas, have, as products obtained from distillation, sufficient characteristics in common with other spirits to constitute at least in certain circumstances an alternative choice for consumers. Because of their characteristics, spirits obtained from cereals and genevas may be consumed in very varied circumstances and at the same time compete with beverages described as 'aperitifs' and 'digestives' according to French tax practice whilst, moreover, serving purposes which do not come within either of those two categories.

41. As the competitive and substitution relationships between the beverages in question are such, the protective nature of the tax system criticized by the Commission is clear. A characteristic of that system is in fact that an essential part of domestic production, in other words spirits obtained from wine and fruit, come within the most favourable tax category whereas at least two types of product, almost all of which are imported from other Member States, are subject to higher taxation under the 'manufacturing tax'. The fact that another domestic product, aniseed spirits, is similarly placed at a disadvantage does not rule out the protective nature of the system as regards the treatment for tax purposes of spirits obtained from wine and fruit or the existence of at least partial competition between those spirits and the imported products in question. As for the fact that the market share of whisky has increased in spite of the tax disadvantage which it suffers, this fact does not prove that there is no protective effect.

42. It is necessary to state in conclusion from the foregoing that the tax system applied in the French Republic under the provisions of the Code Général des Impots is incompatible with the requirements laid down in Article 95 of the Treaty as regards taxation on the one hand on genevas and other alcoholic beverages obtained from the distillation of cereals and, on the other, on spirits obtained from wine and fruit.

For there to be a breach of Article 95(2) [*90(2)*] EC it is insufficient for any one import to claim that a fiscal provision has placed it at a competitive disadvantage vis-à-vis any single domestic product. The system was only found to be illegal because it benefited an 'essential part of domestic production'. A corollary to domestic products being placed in the lower bands is that if it is predominantly imports which are to be found in the higher tax brackets a measure is also likely be declared illegal.

In *Humblot*[44] an action was brought against a French car tax based on the horse power of the engine. This tax went up at a fairly even rate until 16 CV horsepower. Cars rated at above 16 CV had to pay, however, a special tax which was levied at a single lump sum. In 1984 this was FF 8,856, which was more than five times the highest rate paid by owners of cars with 16 CV or less. Humblot owned a Mercedes car rated at 36 CV. He sought to obtain a refund for the difference between the lump sum he had to pay and the highest rate paid on the differential tax. The Court noted that Article 95 [*90*] EC allowed Member States to set up taxes which increased progressively based on objective criteria such as power rating. It considered that the tax still breached Article 95(2) [*90(2)*] EC. For all the cars produced in France had a horsepower rating of 16 CV or less and thus fell in the lower tax bracket. It was only imported cars which were subjected to the special tax and placed at a competitive disadvantage by that tax.

---

44 Case 112/84 *Humblot v Directeur des Services Fiscaux* [1985] ECR 1367, [1986] 2 CMLR 338.

Barents has suggested, therefore, that a fiscal criterion which differentiates between products so as to apply exclusively or in the majority of cases to imports is, *per se,* illegal under Article 95(2) [*90(2)*] EC.[45] It is clear that if the tax regime is arranged in such a way that, definitionally, only imports can fall into the highest bracket, then it will be illegal. A Danish tax placing grape wines in the highest fiscal category was therefore illegal,[46] as was a Danish shipping tax for which the chargeable event was importation itself.[47] Yet where the tax does not use criteria which inevitably place imports at a disadvantage, there are still circumstances where a tax will be lawful even though it is predominantly imports which are taxed more heavily.

a. The Margin of Appreciation Case Law

Case 356/85 Commission v Belgium [1987] ECR 3299, [1988] 3 CMLR 277

Belgium is one of the Community's most celebrated beer-producers. It does not produce any wine, however. The VAT levied on wine was at 25% of the value of the drink, whilst the VAT levied upon beer was at 19%. The Commission brought an action claiming that this breached Article 95(2) [*90(2)*] EC.

14. In its judgment of 27 February 1980 Case 168/78 *Commission v France* [1980] ECR 347 the Court held that whilst the criterion indicated in the first paragraph of Article 95 consists in the comparison of tax burdens whether in terms of the rate, the mode of assessment or other detailed rules for their application, in view of the difficulty of making sufficiently precise comparisons between the products in question the second paragraph of that Article is based upon a more general criterion, namely the protective nature of the system of internal taxation.

15. It follows that any assessment of the compatibility of a given tax with the second paragraph of Article 95 must take account of the impact of that tax on the competitive relationship between the products concerned. The essential question is therefore whether or not the tax is of such a kind as to have the effect, on the market in question, of reducing

---

45 Barents, R. 'Recent Case Law on the Prohibition of Fiscal Discrimination under Article 95' (1986) 23 *CMLRev* 641, 646 *et seq*.

46 Case 106/84 *Commission v Denmark* [1986] ECR 833. Grapes cannot be grown on a significant commercial basis in Denmark!

47 Case C-90/94 *Haahr Petroleum v Åbenrå Havn*, Judgment of 17 July 1997.

potential consumption of imported products to the advantage of competing domestic products.

16. Consequently, in considering to what extent a protective effect actually exists, the difference between the respective selling prices of beer and wine competing with beer cannot be disregarded. The Belgian Government has stated that the price of a litre of beer, including tax, is on average BF 29.75, whereas the corresponding price of a litre of ordinary wine is around BF 125, four times the price of beer, giving a difference in price per litre of BF 95.25. In the Belgian Government's view it follows that even if a single rate were applied to both products, the price difference between the two would continue to be substantial; the reduction in that difference would be so insignificant that it could not influence consumer preference.

17. In response to that argument the Commission drew attention to the fact that in two Belgian establishments named by it the wine most commonly consumed is sold at BF 61 per litre, including tax. The Belgian Government did not challenge that figure but stated that, according to the information given to it by one of those establishments, the sale of wines priced at less than BF 80, which include wines sold in five-litre plastic containers and cooking wines, account for only about 15.6% of total wine sales. According to the Belgian Government, it is more appropriate to compare such wines with table beer which is sold for as little as BF 17 per litre.

18. In view of those observations, it must be concluded that the Commission has not shown that the difference between the respective prices for comparable qualities of beer and wine is so small that the difference of 6% between the VAT rates applied to the two products is capable of influencing consumer behaviour. The Commission has thus not shown that that difference gives rise to any protective effect favouring beer intended for domestic consumption.

19. Nor do the statistics produced by the Commission comparing trends in beer and wine consumption indicate the existence of any protective effect. The Commission stated that beer consumption in Belgium reached a peak in 1973 and has been on the decline since then. By contrast, wine consumption has tripled during the last 20 years; however, from 1980 onwards, the growth in wine consumption slowed down and it levelled off in 1982 and 1983.

20. Whilst those figures show the general trends in the consumption of the products in question, they do not show with any certainty that there is any causal connexion between the patterns of consumption described and the introduction in 1977 of a higher rate of VAT for wine. Consequently, the Commission cannot successfully rely upon them to support its view that the progressive increase in wine consumption was slowed down and finally brought to a halt precisely because of the introduction of a higher rate of VAT for wine. Moreover, that view does not appear to be borne out by the fact, pointed out by the Belgian government and not contested by the Commission, that between 1978 and 1983 the rate of VAT applicable to beer was increased on three occasions without there being in the medium term any restrictive effect on the consumption of beer to the advantage of wine.

21. It follows that the Commission has not established that the tax system in question actually has a protective effect. Accordingly, the application must be dismissed.

On Barents' analysis, as all imports fell into the higher bracket, this is the sort of case where one would expect the measure to be *per se* illegal. The Court suggests, however, that the competitive relationship between goods will also be a relevant factor in assessing whether there is a breach of Article 95(1) [*90(1)*] EC.[48] A spectrum is thus drawn. The stronger the competitive relationship is between goods, the smaller the differential will need to be for there to be a breach of Article 95(2) [*90(2)*] EC. A very strict test is thus taken for similar products, but a much weaker one for products in partial competition. In the latter scenario it appears there can be quite a considerable differential in treatment before there is a breach of Article 95(2) [*90(2)*]EC. The difficulty with this is that it is hard to predicate with any certainty how much leeway is given to Member States in their tax regimes by a tailoring off in the competitive relationship.

b. The Fiscal System Pursues Legitimate Policy Objectives

A fiscal regime which appears to place domestic production at a competitive advantage may be considered not to breach Article 95 [*90*] EC if it is seen as promoting an objective regarded as legitimate under EC law, be it environment, social or regional.

Case 46/80 Vinal SpA v Orbat SpA [1981] ECR 77, [1981] 3 CMLR 524

In Italy tax was levied on alcohol that was fermented at the rate of 1,000 Italian lira per hectolitre, whilst alcohol which was produced industrially was taxed at the rate of 12,000 Italian lira per hectolitre. Orbat concluded a contract with

---

48 This has now been reaffirmed in Joined Cases C-367-377/93 *Roders BV et al. v Inspecteur der Invoerrechten Accijnzen* [1995] ECR I-2229.

Vinal to supply the latter 10 litres of industrially produced alcohol from France. Orbat refused to reimburse Vinal the tax levied upon the alcohol, claiming that it breached Article 95 [*90*] EC. No synthetically produced alcohol was manufactured in Italy.

11. ... [The Italian Government] recalls that in a number of judgments the Court has recognized that the Member States may lay down differing tax arrangements, even for identical products, on the basis of objective criteria such as the conditions of production and the raw materials used (judgment of 22 June 1976 in Case 127/75 *Bobie* [1976] ECR 1079; judgment of 10 October 1978 in Case 148/77 *Hansen* [1978] ECR 1787; judgment of 8 January 1980 in Case 21/79 *Commission v Italy* [1980] ECR 1). According to the Court, such arrangements are compatible with the Treaty if they are laid down on the basis of objective factors and are not discriminatory or protective in their nature.

12. The arrangements challenged before the national court meet these requirements. In fact the different taxation of synthetic alcohol and of alcohol produced by fermentation in Italy is the result of an economic policy decision to favour the manufacture of alcohol from agricultural products and, correspondingly, to restrain the processing into alcohol of ethylene, a derivative of petroleum, in order to reserve that raw material for other more important economic uses. It accordingly constitutes a legitimate choice of economic policy to which effect is given by fiscal means. The implementation of that policy does not lead to any discrimination since although it results in discouraging imports of synthetic alcohol into Italy, it also has the consequence of hampering the development in Italy itself of production of alcohol from ethylene, that production being technically perfectly possible.

13. As the Court has stated on many occasions, particularly in the judgments cited by the Italian Government, in its present stage of development Community law does not restrict the freedom of each Member State to lay down tax arrangements which differentiate between certain products on the basis of objective criteria, such as the nature of the raw materials used or the production processes employed. Such differentiation is compatible with Community law if it pursues economic policy objectives which are themselves compatible with the requirements of the Treaty and its secondary law and if the detailed rules are such as to avoid any form of discrimination, direct or indirect, in regard to imports from other Member States or any form of protection of competing domestic products.

14. Differential taxation such as that which exists in Italy for denatured synthetic alcohol on the one hand and denatured alcohol obtained by fermentation on the other satisfies these requirements. It appears in fact that that system of taxation pursues an objective of legitimate industrial policy in that it is such as to promote the distillation of agricultural products as against the manufacture of alcohol from petroleum derivatives. That choice does not conflict with the rules of Community law or the requirements of a policy decided within the framework of the Community.

15. The detailed provisions of the legislation at issue before the national court cannot be considered as discriminatory since, on the one hand, it is not disputed that imports from other Member States of alcohol obtained by fermentation qualify for the same tax treatment as Italian alcohol produced by fermentation and, on the other hand, although the rate of tax prescribed for synthetic alcohol results in restraining the importation of synthetic alcohol originating in other Member States, it has an equivalent economic effect in the national territory in that it also hampers the establishment of profitable production of the same product by Italian industry.

The question of justification in *Vinal* is not seen as an exception to Article 95 [*90*] EC but is linked directly to the question of the existence of discrimination. Traditionally, the non-discrimination principle has been used to protect comparative advantage. In determining which cases should be treated in a similar manner the Court has considered whether the goods are competing. A measure promoting regional objectives would, therefore, seem to be discriminatory through its protecting local industry. If the non-discrimination principle were to be interpreted in a manner to take other considerations - such as protection of the environment, or social or regional objectives - into account, the comparators would not necessarily be those goods which were competing but in the case of protection of the environment, for example, those goods that were similar from an environmental viewpoint. This seems quite desirable in many instances. A road tax which imposes a toll on the distance goods have travelled might well impose a heavier burden upon imports but it could sensibly be argued that there was no discrimination as the carriage of the imports posed a more serious threat to the environment than transport of goods from nearby regions.[49]

Whilst this style of reasoning can often be beneficial, the objectives which are being used as a source of interpretation must be closely scrutinised. In *Vinal* they were industrial policy ones. In essence, the aims were therefore economic, and indeed the system had been so

49 For similar reasoning in relation to Article 30[*28*] EC see Case C-2/90 *Commission v Belgium* [1992] ECR I-4431, [1993] 1 CMLR 365.

effective that there was no Italian industrial produced alcohol. Such analysis is out of keeping with the Court's analysis elsewhere where it has been held that trade restrictions cannot be imposed for economic ends.[50] The prime reason for this is that trade-instruments are not generally perceived to be an effective and transparent mechanism of income distribution.[51] Whilst *Vinal* is certainly a good authority for Member States being able to tax goods in a manner which pursues legitimate objectives even where the fiscal regime adversely hits imports, it is doubtful how good an authority it is for Member States being able to use internal taxation as an instrument of industrial policy to protect certain types of good.

c. The Fiscal Regime Does Not 'Favour' Domestic Production

In recent years the Court has moved towards suggesting that there is a third set of circumstances where a fiscal regime will be held to be compatible with Article 95(2) [*90(2)*] EC, notwithstanding that only imports fall in the highest band. This is where the Court considers that the tax regime has not been aligned in a manner that it substantially protects domestic production.

Case C-113/94 Jacquier v Directeur-Général des Impots [1995] ECR I-4203

Under a French tax regime cars were to be taxed on the basis of their cylinder capacity multiplied by a coefficient. The coefficient was 1.2 for all cars in the bands up to 17-18 CV, and 1.5 thereafter. Mme Jacquier owned a Mercedes with a fiscal horsepower of 40 CV. She challenged the tax claiming it was discriminatory as no French cars had a horsepower of more than 18 CV.

---

50 Case 72/83 *Campus Oil v Minister for Energy* [1984] ECR 2727, [1984] 3 CMLR 544.

51 Petersmann, E-U. 'Strengthening the Domestic Legal Framework of the GATT Multilateral Trade System: Possibilities and Problems of Making GATT Rules Effective in Domestic Legal Systems' 33, 41-51 in Petersmann, E-U. & Hilf, M. *The New GATT Round of Multilateral Trade Negotiations: Legal and Economic Problems* (1991, 2nd Edition, Kluwer, Deventer).

20. ... it must be ascertained whether a system of progression as described by the national court is free from any discriminatory or protective effect.

21. A system of taxation cannot be regarded as discriminatory solely because only imported products, in particular those from other Member States, come within the most heavily taxed category (Case 140/79 *Chemial Farmaceutici v DAF* [1981] ECR 1, paragraph 18, and Case C-132/88 *Commission v Greece* [1990] ECR I-1567, paragraph 18).

22. To determine whether the increase in the progression coefficient of the differential tax above the 18 CV threshold has a discriminatory or protective effect, it must be examined whether that increase may deter consumers from purchasing vehicles with a fiscal horsepower of over 18 CV, which are all of foreign manufacture, to the benefit of vehicles of domestic manufacture.

23. If the increase in the coefficient for vehicles with a fiscal horsepower of over 18 CV does indeed deter some consumers from buying such vehicles, those consumers will choose a model in the tax band immediately below, the 17-18 CV band, or even, as the Advocate General notes in point 27 of his opinion, a model in the 15-16 CV band.

24. The 15-16 CV and 17-18 CV tax bands, however, include both imported vehicles and vehicles of domestic manufacture. In the 17-18 CV band, it is apparent from the documents in the case that the vehicles are nearly all of foreign manufacture and that domestic manufacturers have a market share of only about 5% of total car sales in that band. In the 15-16 CV band, while the majority of vehicles sold are indeed of domestic manufacture, firstly, consumers do nevertheless have a wide choice of imported vehicles in that band, and secondly, as appears from paragraph 6 of this judgment, the progression coefficients for the 15-16 CV and the 17-18 CV bands are the same, in round figures, so that consumers who are looking for a vehicle from the top of the range will not thereby be induced to purchase a vehicle in the 15-16 CV band.

25. In a system such as that at issue in the present case, therefore, it does not appear that the increase in the progression coefficient can have the effect of favouring the sale of vehicles of domestic manufacture.

Central to the Court's reasoning in *Jacquier* was that the tax differential would probably have led a purchaser to buy another imported car, as it was they that formed the majority of products which fell into the nearest low-tax band. A lenient view has therefore also been taken of regimes where domestic production is minimal. In *Commission v*

Greece[52] there was a similar tax regime to that in *Jacquier* which jumped up suddenly at 1,800 cc. No cars with a cylinder capacity of more than 1,600 cc were produced in Greece. The Court held that the tax regime would have induced a purchaser to buy a car with a cylinder capacity between 1,600 cc and 1,800 cc, all of which were imported. There was therefore no breach of Article 95(2) [*90(2)*]EC.

These judgments can be criticised, as the fiscal regimes in question were disproportionate insofar as they impacted particularly severely upon imports.[53] The leniency with which the Court viewed these regimes has also engendered further uncertainty about the ambit of Article 95(2) [*90(2)*] EC. The facts bear striking similarities to *Humblot*,[54] where the French car regime was held to be illegal. The determining factor, it would appear, will be the amount of domestic production in neighbouring tax brackets. How significant this need be, before there is a breach of Article 95(2) [*90(2)*] EC has as yet been unanswered.

d. Must the Fiscal Regime Have a Protective Intent to Breach Article 95 [*90*] EC?

We have seen that a number of variables - the competitive relationship between imports and domestic products, the objectives of the fiscal regime and possibly the size of the domestic industry - affect the interpretation of Article 95 [*90*]EC. The interaction between these variables is difficult to predict with the result that the case law in this area is characterised by great uncertainty.[55] Some authors have tried to bring the different variables together under an umbrella approach, whereby they suggest a fiscal regime will in principle only be illegal if it

---

52 Case C-132/88 *Commission v Greece* [1990] ECR I-1567, [1991] 3 CMLR 1.

53 Wyatt, D. & Dashwood, A. *European Community Law* (1994, 3rd Edition, Sweet and Maxwell, London) 193-194.

54 Case 112/84 *Humblot v Directeur des Services Fiscaux* [1985] ECR 1367, [1986] 2 CMLR 378.

55 Heidemann-Robinson, M. 'Indirect Taxation: Article 95(1) EC, Back to Front and Inside Out?' (1995) 1 *European Public Law* 439.

has protective *intent* rather than if it has protective effects. The initial exponent of this view was Professor Easson.[56] The most recent detailed support for such a thesis comes, however, from Danusso and Denton.

Danusso, M. & Denton, R. 'Does the European Court of Justice Look for a Protectionist Motive under Article 95?' (1990/1) *Legal Issues of European Integration* 67, 70-71

Primarily the Court looks to the intent underlying the national legislation. If the statute clearly on its face discriminates between domestic and foreign products then the Court will strike the statute down, since the measure intends to protect domestic production. Conversely, if the statute is not formally discriminatory and pursues a policy which does not discriminate between producers on the basis of nationality, then *ceteris paribus*, the statute will be upheld. However some factual circumstances will raise the presumption of protection. In this case the Court applies an additional series of tests:

- if the statute is formally non-discriminatory but operates so that *in fact* only the domestic product can qualify for the preferable treatment, or can never qualify for the worse treatment, then the Court will strike the statute down, since the statute is presumed to intend to protect domestic production;
- if the statute is formally non-discriminatory but operates in such a way that a significant amount of the foreign product is denied the preferable tax treatment then the Court will strike the statue down, since there is evidence of protection of domestic production.

In both cases, however, a statute may be upheld if the Member State offers a convincing explanation of why the purpose (and not necessarily the effect) of the statute is *not* protectionist.

The motive test is inherently problematic and even its founder, Easson, has stated that it cannot give a conclusive explanation of all the case law.[57] The primary difficulty is that the phrase 'legislative intent' is essentially rhetorical. Legislatures, being inanimate, can have no intention of their own. 'Legislative intent' has therefore to be derived from a number of external factors - many of which have been listed above - which are in themselves rarely conclusive one way or another.

---

56 Easson, A. 'Fiscal Discrimination: New Perspectives on Article 95 of the EEC Treaty' (1981) 18 *CMLRev* 521; Easson, A. 'Cheaper Wine or Dearer Beer' (1984) 9 *ELRev* 57.

57 Easson, A. *Taxation in the European Community* (1993, Athlone Press, London) 64.

Even on this basis the motive test fails to explain fully the Court's case law. There are plenty of examples where the fiscal regime seemed quite protectionist in its intent but where the Court considered it not to breach Article 95 [*90*] EC. The two most obvious are *Commission v Belgium* and *Vinal*, both of which are cited above. In both instances there was no domestic production of the more highly taxed product. In *Vinal*, in particular the Court recognised the tax to be an instrument of industrial policy, thereby acknowledging that its intent was to favour one industry over another, which contained no Italian producers. The judgment most destructive of the motive thesis is *Commission v Italy.*[58] In Italy diesel-powered cars over 2,000 cc were taxed at a rate of 38%, whilst cars below that were taxed at a rate of 20%. At the very instant that Italian industry was about to model a diesel-powered car of 2,500 cc, the threshold was changed to 2,500 cc. The circumstantial evidence therefore pointed very heavily to protectionist intent. The Court found that the system did not breach Article 95 [*90*] EC, as the change benefited not only the new Italian car but also a large number of imports.

IV. Harmonisation of Indirect Taxation

Judicial intervention, by itself, will not lead to the elimination of fiscal frontiers caused by differences in indirect taxation.[59] Guieu and Bonnet have observed that harmonisation of indirect taxation has needed to take a three-stage process to bring about completion of the single market. The first is the establishment of fiscal neutrality in the different systems of taxation used in intra-Community trade. The second is simplification of administrative procedures, and the third is harmonisation of tax rates leading to establishment of an internal market.[60]

---

58 Case 200/85 *Commission v Italy* [1986] ECR 3953, [1988] 1 CMLR 97.

59 See in this regard EC Commission, *Programme for the Simplification of value added tax procedures and formalities in intra-Community trade*, OJ 1981 C 244/4.

60 Guieu, P. & Bonnet, C. 'Completion of the Internal Market and Indirect Taxation' (1987) 25 *JCMS* 209.

i. Fiscal Neutrality and the Establishment of the Common System of Value Added Tax

Differences in the methods used to calculate the fiscal burden borne by goods can lead to competitive distortions arising. The most clear-cut example of this was the 'cascade' system of taxation which used to be applied in various Member States. A tax was levied, under this system, upon the product each time it changed hands. There was no uniformity as to when this was considered to take place. In some Member States no taxes were paid for transfers within integrated businesses. In others the tax was only paid up to the retail stage. With such a scheme it was very difficult to assess what fiscal burden goods were bearing, and thus whether there was any semblance of fiscal neutrality.[61] The cascade system was not merely opaque, but, by imposing a cost on transactions it also encouraged unnecessary vertical integration among enterprises. In 1967, a common system of value added tax was introduced to bring about a semblance of transparency and neutrality.[62]

Farmer, P. & Lyal, R. *EC Tax Law* (1994, Clarendon Press, Oxford) 85-86

The First Directive of 11 April 1967, in conjunction with the Second Directive of the same date, required Member States to introduce, no later than 1 January 1970, a common system of Value Added Tax to replace existing systems of turnover tax. Article 2 of the First Directive described the common system in the following terms:

'The principle of the common system of Value Added Tax involves the application to goods and services of a general tax on consumption exactly proportional to the price of the goods and services, whatever the number of transactions which take place in the production and distribution process before the stage at which the tax is charged.

On each transaction, Value Added Tax, calculated on the price of the goods or services at the rate applicable to such goods or services, shall be chargeable after

---

61 On the cascade tax see *The EEC Reports on Tax Harmonisation* (1963, IBFD, Amsterdam); Farmer, P. & Lyal, R. *EC Tax Law* (1994, Clarendon, Oxford) 4 *et seq.*

62 Directive 67/227/EEC, OJ 1967 Special Edition,14; Directive 67/228 EEC, OJ 1967 Special Edition,16.

deduction of the amount of Value Added Tax borne directly by the various cost components.

The common system of Value Added Tax shall be applied up to and including the retail trade stage.'

The above definition sets out the essential characteristics of a theoretical model to which the actual Community system aspires. According to that model, the tax applies at all commercial stages from production to retail and to all categories of goods and services. Although a tax on consumer expenditure, it is collected by traders, who add it to the selling price of their supplies. Multiple taxation is avoided by allowing traders, when calculating the tax due to the authorities, to deduct from the VAT which they collect from customers the VAT which they themselves have been charged by their suppliers. The effect of this mechanism is to ensure that, regardless of the number of commercial stages involved in the production and distribution process, the VAT burden on goods or services at any given moment is always equal to the VAT charged by the last supplier. Tax is definitively borne only by the final consumer, who, not being a trader, has no right of deduction.

VAT was chosen by the Community legislature because, in contrast to the cumulative multi-stage taxes which preceded it, it was less likely to 'distort conditions of competition or to hinder the free movement of goods and services within the common market'.[[63]] The tax was 'bound ... to result in neutrality in competition, in that within each country similar goods bear the same tax burden, whatever the length of the production and distribution chain, and that in international trade the amount of the tax burden borne by goods is known so that an exact equalization of that amount may be ensured'.[[64]]

The EC VAT regime was consolidated and developed in the Sixth VAT Directive, Directive 77/388/EEC.[65] A detailed analysis of this Directive would take up the better part of a tax course. It is the purpose here only to give the broadest outline. The basic principle is established in Article 2:

The following shall be subject to Value Added Tax:
1. the supply of goods or services effected for consideration within the territory of the country by a taxable person acting as such;
2. the importation of goods.[66]

---

63 2nd recital in the preamble to the 1st Directive.

64 Ibid., 8th recital.

65 OJ 1977 L 145/1.

66 This only includes imports from third States, Directive 91/680/EC, OJ 1991 L 376/1, Article 7.

This description warrants a few brief comments. The supply of goods and services are only subject to VAT if affected by a *taxable person*. This is any person who independently carries out economic activity.[67] Public authorities[68] and persons working under a contract of employment[69] are exempted from this category. The system is, furthermore, based on the 'territoriality principle'. A Member State is to tax only those supplies and imports which are made on its territory. Within this overall structure, the system is subject to a series of exemptions.

The first category are those which fall under the transitional arrangements. These allow Member States to exempt from tax a large number of activities which are set out in Annex F of the Directive.[70] In principle, this exemption was only to apply for five years but it is subject to automatic extension. Importantly, however, the exemption only allows Member States to retain exemptions which are already in force. Once something is taxed, a Member State cannot therefore lift the tax burden.

The second category consists of activities whose exemption is not subject to any transitional arrangements. These include, on the one hand, activities such as postal services, broadcasting, health, education, social welfare, sport and cultural and religious activities whose social merit is considered to justify exemption.[71] There are other exemptions for activities, such as banking, insurance, real estate and gambling, where the rationale is less clear.[72] In respect of this second category, Member States may conversely impose VAT during the transitional period.[73] Taxes cannot be imposed on these activities which were not already taxed at the beginning of the transitional period.

---

67 Supra n.65, Articles 4(1) and 4(2).

68 Ibid., Article 4(5).

69 Ibid., Article 4(4).

70 Ibid., Article 28(3)(b).

71 Ibid., Article 13(A).

72 Ibid., Article 13(B).

73 Ibid., Article 28(3)(a).

ii. VAT and the Internal Market

In principle, there need not be fiscal frontiers within the Community if the *origin principle* were adopted, namely that goods be taxed in the place of production rather than the place of consumption. As a good would only be taxed upon its entering the market for the first time in the Community, it would be free to circulate unencumbered from that point onwards. Whilst *Schul* provides a basis for the adoption of such a principle, the principle traditionally applied within the Community has been the 'destination' principle.[74] This leads more readily to fiscal frontiers, as goods crossing a border are, on thc onc hand, entitled to a remittance of the tax from the exporting State, but, on the other, are required to present themselves to be taxed by the regime of the importing Member State. From a national fiscal perspective the destination principle has a number of advantages.[75]

Terra, B. 'VAT in the EEC: The Place of Supply' (1989) 26 *Common Market Law Review* 449, 453-454

The destination principle means that goods which are moved across frontiers, are only taxed in the country of consumption; the tax on exported goods is refunded. Alternatively, the origin principle taxes goods where they are produced. Thus, exports are taxed and imports are exempt under the principle. The disadvantage of the origin principle is, that the tax burden on imported products and locally produced products is not necessarily the same, notably when the country of origin apples a different rate. Application of the destination principle generally leads to compensation in the form of a (sur)charge on imports not exceeding the internal tax on corresponding domestic products. Imported products cross the border tax-free since on exportation the tax was already borne by the article in the country of production and has been refunded. The advantage of the destination principle is that all products bear the same tax burden when finally sold to the consumer. The disadvantage is that border tax adjustments always seem necessary [either

---

74 Georgakoupolos, T. & Hitiris, T. 'On the Superiority of the Destination over the Origin Principle of Taxation for Intra-Union Trade' (1992) 102 *Economic Journal* 117.

75 See also Cnossen, A. 'Harmonisation of Indirect Taxes in the EEC' (1983) 4 *British Tax Review* 232; Bos, M. & Nelson, H. 'Indirect Taxation and the Completion of the Internal Market of the EC' (1988) 27 *JCMS* 27, 35-37.

by actual tax frontiers, or by a method of compensation as between the tax authorities involved]. ...

VAT, like most sales taxes, has little to do with ability to pay. It can hardly be used as a tool of redistribution of wealth. From this perspective, no arguments can be derived in favour of or against the destination or origin principle. The guiding principle to choose in favour of the country of destination is the so-called benefit principle.

The benefit principle

According to the benefit principle, the choice between consumption and production as the basis for taxation should depend on the nature of the goods and services provided by the public sector. Under this principle, an origin-based tax is only justifiable if public services were primarily supportive of productive activities. It can hardly be assumed that goods and services subject to a general indirect tax on consumption (like the VAT in Europe) in a given country are taxed primarily in relation with production, so that based on an origin principle goods and services may carry a tax burden upon exportation. If the consumers are primarily the beneficiaries of the government services which the VAT finances, they shall bear the full burden of these taxes in their own country. It is therefore suggested that taxes on consumption of private consumers should exclusively benefit the country in which the expenditure takes place, the country of destination.

The Commission sought to reconcile the difficulties the destination principle posed for the single market with those the origin principle posed for revenue collection by making the following proposals:

(a) tax should in principle be collected in the Member State of origin;
(b) a Community clearing mechanism would be introduced so that revenue would accrue actually to the Member State of destination;
(c) harmonisation of VAT. The proposed system was a two rate system where the standard rate would be between 14 and 20% and the reduced rate between 4 and 9%.[76]

The proposal met opposition on three fronts. They leant too much towards the origin principle; there were doubts about how effectively the clearing mechanism would work, and worries about

---

76 EC Commission, *Completion of the Internal Market and Approximation of Indirect Tax Rates and Harmonization of Indirect Tax Structure*, COM (87) 320 final.

whether these would provide sufficient guarantees against fraud.[77] The eventual compromise takes a number of different lines.

Harmonisation of Taxes:- Under a transitional regime which is to apply until 31 December 1998, Member States are required to apply a standard rate of not less than 15%.[78] The possibilities for complete harmonisation are reduced in a number of ways. First, Member States are allowed to apply a reduced rate of not less than 5% to a number of goods and activities.[79] Secondly, special regimes apply to antiques, agricultural outputs and gold.[80] Thirdly, Member States are allowed to retain existing exemptions.[81]

Allocation of Revenue:- The Sixth VAT Directive has been amended by Directive 91/680/EEC[82] and Directive 92/111/EEC[83] in order to reduce fiscal frontiers. This is a transitional regime, which was in principle to apply only until 31 December 1996, but has continued to run since.[84] This regime is extremely detailed and complex, but an outline is given below.

Farmer, P. & Lyal, R. *EC Tax Law* (1994, Clarendon Press, Oxford) 136-137

The purpose of the transitional arrangements is to remove tax frontiers within the Community while continuing to ensure that the majority of trade in goods is taxed in the country of consumption. The arrangements are basically as follows:

---

77 For discussion of the Commission's initial proposals see Bos, M. & Nelson, H. 'Indirect Taxation and the Completion of the Internal Market of the EC' (1988) 27 *JCMS* 27; Van der Zanden, J. & Terra, B. 'The Removal of Tax Barriers; White Paper from the Commission to the European Council/The Creation of an Internal Market; Follow Up to the White Paper' *LIEI* (1990/1) 137.

78 Directive 77/388/EEC, supra n.65, Article 12(3) as amended by Directive 96/95 EC, OJ 1996 L 338/89.

79 Ibid., Article 1(1)(b) and Annex H.

80 Ibid., Articles 1(1)(c), 1(1)(d) and 1(1)(e).

81 Ibid., Article 1(4).

82 OJ 1991 L 376/1.

83 OJ 1992 L 384/47.

84 There is, as yet, no Commission proposal to amend the Directive. It will continue automatically, in force until there is. Directive 77/388/EEC, supra n.65, Article 28l.

Since 1 January 1993 VAT has ceased to be charged on imports of goods from other Member States and has been imposed under Member States' internal systems. The arrangements embody two principles:

(a) Trade between taxable persons continues to be taxed in the country of consumption. Goods purchased by taxable persons from suppliers in other Member States continue to be relieved of tax (by exemption together with a refund of input tax) in the State of the supplier but are now taxed as an intra-Community acquisition in the state of the customer, who enters the acquisition on his internal VAT return. He is entitled to deduct VAT on his acquisitions on the same basis as VAT charged by his domestic suppliers.

(b) Tax frontiers for private individuals and non-taxable legal persons have, in principle, been superseded by taxation in the country of origin. However, that principle must be read subject to a series of special arrangements designed to prevent 'cross-border shopping'; in the case of purchases by non-taxable legal persons, the scope of those arrangements is such that they in fact largely supplant the rule.

Special Arrangements to Prevent Division of Trade

A major concern during the legislative process was that, in the absence of harmonized rates of tax, private individuals and non-taxable legal persons such as government departments and local authorities, all of whom must bear tax definitively on their purchases might be induced to purchase goods from other Member States applying lower rates of tax. Mail-order companies selling goods to private individuals might be induced to relocate to lower-tax Member States. Special arrangements were therefore made to ensure that the following important categories of sales to non-taxable persons remained taxable in the country of consumption:

(i) Distance sales to individuals: where a supplier arranges for his goods to be transported to another Member State to a customer who is a private individual, he is deemed to make a taxable supply in the state of the customer unless his total annual sales to individuals in that state fall below a certain threshold. Thus, for example, a mail-order firm with significant sales to other Member States must account for tax to the authorities in those states.

(ii) Non-taxable legal persons: where non-commercial bodies such as government departments and local authorities makes purchases of goods exceeding a certain threshold from suppliers in other Member States, they are obliged to account for tax on such intra-Community acquisitions in the same way as taxable persons.

(iii) New means of transport (certain boats, aircraft and land vehicles): irrespective of who the customer is, the sale of such goods is exempt with refund of tax in the country of the supplier and is taxable as an intra-Community acquisition in the state of arrival. Member States are obliged to lay down the detailed arrangements for collection of tax required by the extension of the acquisition mechanism to private individuals.

(iv) Goods subject to excise duty (mineral oils, alcohol and alcoholic beverages, and manufactured tobacco): the VAT arrangements mirror those for excise duty in Council Directive 92/12, which establishes the principle that excise duty is payable in the country of consumption unless the goods are acquired by private individuals for their own use and transported by them. Such goods therefore fall to be taxed in the country of consumption under the exemption/acquisition or distance sales mechanism, without the benefit of the de minimis provisions which restrict the application of those mechanisms in the case of normal goods.

Despite the elaborate nature of this regime, the destination principle continues to remain the predominant principle of taxation. The use of the term 'intra-Community acquisition' does not alter the fact that VAT will therefore continue to be charged on imports by the importing State. It may also be wondered how well the system protects against fraud. By allowing the 'origin' principle to be used by non-taxable persons, a mixed system of taxation has been created which provides incentives for traders in the importing State to pass themselves off as 'non-taxable' persons or to get 'non-taxable' persons, such as private individuals, to carry out tasks for them. Such fraud can only be prevented by a system of transnational cooperation between tax authorities which allows the authorities to check the *bona fides* of different people reliably and quickly.[85]

iii. Excise Duties

Excise duties are a form of indirect taxation levied upon particular goods, such as petrol, alcohol or tobacco. They are levied normally in addition to other taxes. They can be levied either upon the consumption or upon the production of the good, and the tax can be either *ad valorem*, like with VAT, or be a fixed amount. In the context of the single market they pose the same problems as VAT, namely that the imposition of different rates by Member States can lead to distortions of competition, and, insofar as the destination principle is applied, lead to border-tax adjustments which restrict the free movement of goods.

The basic regime is set out in Directive 92/12/EEC.[86] Member States retain the right to levy indirect taxes, but with the exception of

---

85 Regulation 218/92/EEC on administrative cooperation in the field of indirect taxation, OJ 1992 L 24/1.

86 OJ 1992 L 76/1.

indirect taxes on mineral oils, alcohol and manufactured tobacco, these taxes must not give rise to border-tax adjustments.[87] In practice, this means that, in the absence of harmonisation, the origin principle applies to all forms of indirect taxes, other than VAT and taxes on the three categories of products listed above. This greatly reduces their efficacy, for if Member States raise excise duties upon a particular product traders and consumers will simply purchase the product from a State with a lower rate of duty.

The destination principle normally applies to excise levies raised in respect of mineral oils, alcohol and manufactured tobacco.[88] The principal exception to this are goods purchased by private individuals for their own use, in which case the origin principle applies.[89] To benefit from this, however, the individuals must transport the goods themselves. In practice, this has been shown to be a considerable lacuna. The guide levels for private use are very generous indeed,[90] and have proved to be very difficult to enforce as it is difficult to ascertain the final destination of particular goods.

Limited harmonisation has also occurred in respect of the rates of duty imposed upon these products. In each case this has taken the form of a minimum rate being set, and in the case of mineral oils and

87 Ibid., Article 3.

88 Ibid., Article 7.

89 Ibid., Article 8.

90 One would need to be a chain-smoking alcoholic to use up fully the guidelines on tobacco and alcohol! In one trip, one is allowed to take back 800 cigarettes, 400 cigarillos, 200 cigars, 1 kilogram of smoking tobacco, ten litres of spirits, twenty litres of 'intermediate products', ninety litres of wine and one hundred and ten litres of beer. Ibid., Article 9(2). The absurdity of these guidelines is illustrated by the fact that an average family car would struggle to contain all this.

alcohol, a fiscal structure.[91] These minimum rates, however, do no more than set the barest of floors, as they are relatively low.[92]

V. Direct Taxation

EC law has moved increasingly into the field of direct taxation.[93] There is some EC legislation in the corporate field.[94] The Merger Directive of 1990 sought to abolish the imposition of tax in connection with mergers, divisions, transfers of assets or exchanges of shares between companies.[95] The Parent-Subsidiary Directive, which was also passed in 1990, regulates the conditions under which Member States could tax dividends passed from a subsidiary to its parent.[96]

---

91 Directive 92/79 on the approximation of taxes on cigarettes, OJ 1992 L 316/8; Directive 92/80 on the approximation of taxes on manufactured tobacco other than cigarettes, OJ 1992 L 316/10; Directive 92/81 on the harmonisation of structures of duty on mineral oils, OJ 1992 L 316/12; Directive 92/82, on the approximation of rates of excise duties on mineral oil, OJ 1992 L 312/16; Directive 92/83 on the harmonisation of structures of excise duties on alcohol and alcoholic beverages, OJ 1992 L 312/21; Directive 92/84 on the approximation of rates of excise duty on alcoholic beverages, OJ 1992 L 316/29.

92 The minimum rate for beer is merely ECU 0.748 per hectolitre per degree Plato.

93 Most recently a Code of Conduct on Business Taxation has been agreed within the Council which seeks to prevent regulatory competition between the different fiscal jurisdictions, Resolution of the Council on a Code of Conduct for Business Taxation, 2053rd Council Meeting - EOCFIN, *12671/97*.

94 Radaelli, C. 'Corporate direct taxation in European Union: explaining the policy process' (1995) 15 *Journal of Public Policy* 153; Radaelli, C. 'Fiscal Federalism as a catalyst for policy development? In search of a framework for European direct tax harmonisation' (1996) 3 JEPP 402.

95 Directive 90/434/EEC, OJ 1990 L 225/1. Most Member States had traditionally extended tax relief to these operations within a national context. To prevent trans-national operations being placed at a competitive disadvantage, the Directive extended this to cross-border operations.

96 Directive 90/435/EEC, OJ 1990 L 225/6.

The greatest intrusion on national autonomy in this field has come, however, from the Court of Justice.[97] Any fiscal regime which discriminated against foreigners on account of their nationality potentially breaches Articles 48 [*39*], 52 [*43*] and 59 [*49*] EC. In *Commission v France*[98] the Court stated that any regime which discriminated between residents and non-residents could also breach these provisions on the grounds that as most non-residents were foreigners, a residence requirement constituted a form of indirect discrimination. Such a holding flew in the face of established international practice.

Wattel, P. 'The EC Court's Attempts to Reconcile the Treaty Freedoms with International Tax Law' (1996) 33 *Common Market Law Review* 223, 223-224

One of the basic principles of international tax law is the distinction between taxation based on residence (unlimited tax lability: worldwide taxation) and source taxation (limited tax liability). Worldwide (unlimited; total income) taxation is applied to resident taxpayers, the idea being that all persons resident in a certain State, benefiting from the economic, social, cultural and physical infrastructure of that State and usually deriving most of their income in that State, should contribute according to their ability to pay. Therefore, their worldwide income and their personal circumstances should be taken into account. Source taxation, on the other hand, is applied to non-residents, the idea being that the country in which income is earned should have a fair share of that income, wherever the beneficiary may reside. Taxation based on residence therefore focuses on the person of the taxpayer, especially on his ability to pay, whereas source taxation

97 There is now a wealth of literature on this see Wouters, J. 'The case law of the Court of Justice on Direct Taxes: Variation upon a theme' (1994) 1 *Maastricht Journal of European & Comparative Law* 179; Wouters, J.'Fiscal Barriers to Companies' Cross-Border Establishment in the Case-Law of the Court of Justice' (1994) 14 *YBEL* 73; Farmer, P. 'Article 48 EC and the Taxation of Frontier Workers' (1995) 20 *ELRev* 310; Keeling, E. & Shipwright, A. 'Some Taxing Problems Concerning Non-Discrimination and the EC Treaty' (1995) 20 *ELRev* 580; Vanistendael, F. 'The Consequences of Schumacker and Wielockx: Two Steps Forward in the Tax Procession of Echternach' (1996) 33 *CMLRev* 255.

98 Case 270/83 *Commission v France* [1986] ECR 273, [1987] 1 CMLR 401. See also Case C-330/91 *R v Inland Revenue Commissioners ex parte Commerzbank* [1993] ECR I-4017.

focuses on the fact that income was earned within a certain territory, irrespective of the person of the beneficiary. Unlike the home State, the source State is not in a position to determine the personal circumstances and ability to pay of the taxpayer since he does not live there.

The Court has partly retracted from its position in *Commission v France*. It has allowed Member States to differentiate between residents and certain non-residents. To do this it has had to draw a distinction between different categories of non-resident.

Case C-279/93 Finanzamt Köln-Altstadt v Schumacker [1995] ECR I-225, [1996] 2 CMLR 450

The German authorities taxed persons permanently resident in Germany on all their income, wherever it was earned. Others were only taxed on the income they earned in Germany. The latter suffered a number of disadvantages under the German tax regime compared to residents. They did not qualify for the same range of family allowances (a so-called 'splitting tariff'). They were unable to deduct social expenses, such as unemployment benefits from their tax burden and they did not have the same procedures available to them to claim reimbursement of overpaid tax. Schumacker was a Belgian who worked in Germany whilst continuing to live in Belgium. His wife was unemployed. He claimed the family allowance available to German residents and sought to have the corresponding amount reimbursed. The German authorities refused.

28. However, national rules of that kind, under which a distinction is drawn on the basis of residence in that non-residents are denied certain benefits which are, conversely, granted to persons residing within national territory, are liable to operate mainly to the detriment of nationals of other Member States. Non-residents are in the majority of cases foreigners.

29. In those circumstances, tax benefits granted only to residents of a Member State may constitute indirect discrimination by reason of nationality.

30. It is also settled law that discrimination can arise only through the application of different rules to comparable situations or the application of the same rule to different situations.

31. In relation to direct taxes, the situations of residents and of non-residents are not, as a rule, comparable.

32. Income received in the territory of a Member State by a non-resident is in most cases only a part of his total income, which is concentrated at his place of residence. Moreover, a non-resident's personal ability to pay tax, determined by reference to his aggregate income and his personal and family circumstances, is more easy to assess at the place where his personal and financial interests are centred. In general, that is the place where he has his usual abode. Accordingly, international tax law, and in particular the Model Double Taxation Treaty of the Organization for Economic Cooperation and Development (OECD), recognizes that in principle the overall taxation of taxpayers, taking account of their personal and family circumstances, is a matter for the State of residence.

33. The situation of a resident is different in so far as the major part of his income is normally concentrated in the State of residence. Moreover, that State generally has available all the information needed to assess the taxpayer's overall ability to pay, taking account of his personal and family circumstances.

34. Consequently, the fact that a Member State does not grant to a non-resident certain tax benefits which it grants to a resident is not, as a rule, discriminatory since those two categories of taxpayer are not in a comparable situation.

....

36. The position is different, however, in a case such as this one where the non-resident receives no significant income in the State of his residence and obtains the major part of his taxable income from an activity performed in the State of employment, with the result that the State of his residence is not in a position to grant him the benefits resulting from the taking into account of his personal and family circumstances.

37. There is no objective difference between the situations of such a non-resident and a resident engaged in comparable employment, such as to justify different treatment as regards the taking into account for taxation purposes of the taxpayer's personal and family circumstances.

38. In the case of a non-resident who receives the major part of his income and almost all his family income in a Member State other than that of his residence, discrimination arises from the fact that his personal and family circumstances are taken into account neither in the State of residence nor in the State of employment.

39. The further question arises whether there is any justification for such discrimination.

40. The view has been advanced, by those Member States which have submitted observations, that discriminatory treatment ... was justified by the need for consistent application of tax regimes to non-residents. That justification, based on the need for cohesion of the tax system, was upheld by the Court in Case C-204/90 *Bachmann v Belgium* [1992] ECR I-249, paragraph 28). According to those Member States, there is a link between the taking into account of personal and family circumstances and the right to tax worldwide income. Since the taking into account of those circumstances is a matter for the Member State of residence, which is alone entitled to tax worldwide income, they contend that the State on whose territory the non-resident works does not have to take account of his personal and family circumstances since otherwise the personal and family circumstances of the non-resident would be taken into account twice and he would enjoy the corresponding tax benefits in both States.

41. That argument cannot be upheld. In a situation such as that in the main proceedings, the State of residence cannot take account of the taxpayer's personal and family circumstances because the tax payable there is insufficient to enable it to do so. Where that is the case, the Community principle of equal treatment requires that, in the state of employment, the personal and family circumstances of a foreign non-resident be taken into account in the same way as those of resident nationals and that the same tax benefits should be granted to him.

42. The distinction at issue in the main proceedings is thus in no way justified by the need to ensure the cohesion of the applicable tax system.

43. At the hearing, the Finanzamt argued that administrative difficulties prevent the State of employment from ascertaining the income which non-residents working in its territory receive in their State of residence.

44. That argument likewise cannot be upheld.

45. Council Directive 77/799/EEC of 19 December 1977 concerning mutual assistance by the competent authorities of the Member States in the field of direct taxation (OJ 1977 L 336, 15) provides for ways of obtaining information comparable to those existing between tax authorities at national level. There is thus no administrative obstacle to account being taken in the State of employment of a non-resident's personal and family circumstances.

46. More particularly, it must be pointed out that the Federal Republic of Germany grants frontier workers resident in the Netherlands and working in Germany the tax benefits resulting from the taking into account of their personal and family circumstances, including the 'splitting tariff'. Provided that they receive at least 90% of their income in Germany, those Community nationals are treated in the same way as German nationals under the German law of 21 October 1980 implementing the Additional Protocol of 13 March 1980 to the Double Taxation Treaty between the Federal Republic of Germany and the Kingdom of the Netherlands of 16 June 1959.

The Court then found that the German tax provisions also discriminated procedurally against non-residents.

58. It follows that Article 48 of the Treaty requires equal treatment at procedural level for non-resident Community nationals and resident nationals. Refusal to grant non-resident community nationals the benefit of annual adjustment procedures which are available to resident nationals constitutes unjustified discrimination.

In insisting that Member States treat identically residents and non-residents who earn almost all their income in that State, the Court has, as Vanistendael observes, created a new rule in international tax law.[99] Whereas previously States applied source taxation to non-residents, focusing on the income earned within the territory rather than the person earning that income, they will be unable to do that for those non-residents earning all or almost all their income in that State.[100] They will instead have to focus on the person, as someone who should benefit from the social infrastructure that the State has to offer and should therefore be allowed the appropriate fiscal benefits.

The flip side of this is the creation of further ambiguities and uncertainties. What percentage of his income must a non-resident be earning in a Member State to be protected?[101] Also, there is no general right for a Member State to tax non-residents more highly than residents. In Asscher, therefore, a Dutch law which applied a higher rate of income tax to non-residents was declared unlawful.[102] Likewise, in *Commission v Luxembourg* a requirement that individuals would not be repaid excess tax unless they were permanently resident in Luxembourg or had been employed there for a minimum of 9 months in the last year was also considered illegal on the grounds that it was discriminatory.[103] Non-residents, who earn only a fraction of their income in the host State, have only been distinguished from residents on two grounds. The first is the example of Schumacker where the State will not have available all

---

99 Vanistendael, F. 'The Consequences of Schumacker and Wielockx: Two Steps Forward in the Tax Process of Echternach' (1996) 33 *CMLRev* 255, 256.

100 See also Case C-80/94 *Wielockx v Inspecteur der Belastingen* [1995] ECR I-2493, [1995] 3 CMLR 85

101 Wattel, P. 'The EC Court's Attempts to Reconcile the Treaty Freedoms with International Tax Law' (1996) 33 *CMLRev* 223, 235-237.

102 Case C-107/94 *Asscher v Staatssecretaris van Financiën* [1996] ECR I-3089, [1996] 3 CMLR 61.

103 Case C-151/94 *Commission v Luxembourg* [1995] ECR I-3685.

the information necessary to carry out an accurate assessment. The other relates to the territoriality principle. This requires that, in principle, taxes should be paid in the territory where the activities are carried out. An individual should not therefore be able to claim tax advantages for activities carried out in another Member State.[104] Both these circumstances relate to the calculation of the grant of allowances or fiscal benefits. It appears that only in these limited circumstances will differential treatment be allowed.

Even if a measure is found to discriminate indirectly against other EC nationals, that will not be the end of the matter. It may still be lawful if the Court find some 'objective justification' for the practice.

Case C-204/90 Bachmann v Belgian State [1992] ECR I-249, [1993] 1 CMLR 785

Bachmann was a German working in Belgium. He challenged a refusal by the Belgian authorities to allow him to deduct tax from payments into a German life insurance. The authorities only allowed contributions to be deducted if they were made into a Belgian scheme. The Court noted that such a scheme discriminated against foreigners, as they were the most likely to take out a life insurance scheme abroad. The Belgian authorities claimed the distinction was necessary for the cohesion of their tax order. As, in Belgium, payments made out of any scheme were taxed and the Belgian authorities had insufficient means of checking whether companies located outside Belgium were complying with this requirement.

21. As regards the need to preserve the cohesion of the tax system, the Court held, in its judgment delivered today in Case C-300/90 *Commission v Belgium* [1992] ECR I-305 that there exists under the Belgian rules a connection between the deductibility of contributions and the liability to tax of sums payable by the insurers under pension and life assurance contracts. According to Article 32a of the CIR, cited above, pensions, annuities, capital sums or surrender values under life assurance contracts are exempt from tax where there has been no deduction of contributions under Article 54.

22. It follows that in such a tax system the loss of revenue resulting from the deduction of life assurance contributions from total taxable income - which includes pensions and insurance payable in the event of death - is offset by the taxation of pensions, annuities

---

104 Case C-250/95 *Futura Participations SA and Singer v Administration des Contributions*, Judgment of 15 May 1997.

or capital sums payable by the insurers. Where such contributions have not been deducted, those sums are exempt from tax.

23. The cohesion of such a tax system, the formulation of which is a matter for each Member State, therefore presupposes that, in the event of a State being obliged to allow the deduction of life assurance contributions paid in another Member State, it should be able to tax sums payable by insurers.

24. An undertaking by an insurer to pay such tax cannot constitute an adequate safeguard. If the undertaking were not honoured, it would be necessary to enforce it in the Member State in which the insurer is established, and quite apart from the problems encountered by a State in discovering the existence and amount of the payments made by insurers established in another State, there remains the possibility that the recovery of the tax might then be prevented on the grounds of public policy.

25. It would certainly be possible in principle for such an undertaking to be accompanied by the deposit by the insurer of a guarantee, but this would involve the insurer in additional expense which would have to be passed on in the insurance premiums, with the result that the insured, who may moreover be subjected to double taxation on the sums payable under the contracts, would cease to have any interest in maintaining them.

26. It is true that bilateral conventions exist between certain Member States, allowing the deduction for tax purposes of contributions paid in a Contracting State other than that in which the advantage is granted, and recognizing the power of a single State to tax sums payable by insurers under the contracts concluded with them. However, such a solution is possible only by means of such conventions or by the adoption by the Council of the necessary coordination or harmonization measures.

27. It follows that, as Community law stands at present, it is not possible to ensure the cohesion of such a tax system by means of measures which are less restrictive than those at issue in the main proceedings, and that the consequences of any other measure ensuring the recovery by the State concerned of the tax due under its legislation on sums payable by insurers pursuant to the contracts concluded with them would ultimately be similar to those resulting from the non-deductibility of contributions.

Member States will not be able to plead cohesion of their tax order as a defence where they have a double taxation agreement in the issue in question with the migrant's State of residence. In Wielockx the Dutch authorities refused to grant tax reductions on the pension contributions of a physiotherapist who resided in Belgium but worked in the Netherlands. The facts were similar to Bachmann except that the Court had forgone their rights to tax Wielockx' pension contributions by virtue of the double taxation agreement between them and Belgium which stated that pension contributions were to be taxed in the State of residence.[105]

In *Futura* Luxembourg allowed losses to be carried forward and set against tax.[106] The losses had to be calculated in accordance with national accounting laws. The Court found that such a condition was discriminatory within the meaning of Article 52 [*43*] EC as it required undertakings established in one Member State to have different accounting rules for branches set up in another. The discrimination was justified in the Court's view, as in the absence of harmonisation, it would be impossible for the Luxembourg authorities to assess the amount which could be set off against tax.

Further Reading

Barents, R. 'Charges of Equivalent Effect to Customs Duties' (1978) 15 *Common Market Law Review* 415

Bos, M. & Nelson, H. 'Indirect Taxation and the Completion of the Internal Market' (1988) 27 *Journal of Common Market Studies* 27

Easson, A. *Taxation in the European Community* (1993, Athlone Press, London)

Guieu, P. & Bonnet, C. 'Completion of the Internal Market and Indirect Taxation' (1987) 25 *Journal of Common Market Studies* 209

Keeling, E. & Shipwright, A. 'Some Taxing Problems Concerning Non-Discrimination and the EC Treaty' (1995) 20 *European Law Review* 580

Schwarze, J. 'The Member States' discretionary powers under the tax provisions of the EEC Treaty' in Schwarze, J. (ed.) *Discretionary Powers of Member States in the field of Economic Policy and their Limits* (1988, Nomos, Baden Baden)

Smith, S. 'Excise Duties and the Internal Market' (1988) 27 *Journal of Common Market Studies* 147

---

105 Case C-80/94 *Wielockx v Inspecteur der Belastingen* [1995] ECR I-2493, [1995] 3 CMLR 85.

106 Case C-250/95 *Futura Participations SA and Singer v Administration des Contributions*, Judgment of 15 May 1997.

Terra, B & Kajus, J. *A Guide to the European VAT Directives* (1993, IBFD, Amsterdam)
Tiley, J. 'The Law of Taxation in a European Environment' (1992) 51 *Cambridge Law Journal* 451
Van der Zanden, J. & Terra, B. 'The Removal of Tax Barriers: White Paper from the Commission to the European Council/The Creation of an Internal Market: Follow Up to the White Paper' (1990/1) *Legal Issues of European Integration* 137
Vanistendael, F. 'The Limits to the New Community Tax Order' (1994) 31 *Common Market Law Review* 293
----- 'The Consequences of Schumacker and Wielockx: Two Steps Forward in the Tax Procession of Echternach' (1996) 33 *Common Market Law Review* 255
Wouters, J. 'The case law of the Court of Justice on Direct Taxes: Variation upon a theme' (1994) 1 *Maastricht Journal of European & Comparative Law* 179
----- 'Fiscal Barriers to Companies' Cross-Border Establishment in the Case-Law of the Court of Justice' (1994) 14 *Yearbook of European Law* 73

Index